BOTTOM LINE YEAR BOOK 2003

BY THE EDITORS OF

Bottom Line
PERSONAL

www.BottomLineSecrets.com

Contents

8 • TAX TRAPS AND OPPORTUNITIES

9 • SMART INVESTMENT STRATEGIES

10 • CONSUMER KNOW-HOW

PART THREE: YOUR FINANCIAL FUTURE

17 • YOUR PERSONAL BEST

PART FIVE: YOUR LIFE

18 • BUSINESS AND CAREER SAVVY

19 • EDUCATION SMARTS

20 • SAFE AND SOUND

1

Health Confidential

Medical Red Flags: Seven Symptoms Never to Ignore

Most of us know to see a doctor if we detect a suspicious lump or changes in a mole. If severe chest pain occurs, even a stoic will head to the nearest emergency room.

Other symptoms are easier to miss—or *dismiss*. But prompt diagnosis and treatment will safeguard your health...and possibly save your life—or that of a loved one.

Here are seven red flags that may signal a medical emergency...

ABDOMINAL DISTRESS

Persistent cramps, bloating, vomiting or a change in appetite or bowel habits can indicate a variety of problems.

Best-case scenario: Spastic colon...viral infection...lactose intolerance...or indigestion.

Worst-case scenario: An ulcer...tumor... ruptured appendix...ovarian cyst...intestinal obstruction...inflammatory bowel disease...or inflammation of the digestive tract, gallbladder or pancreas.

Seek emergency treatment: If you're vomiting and haven't moved your bowels or passed gas in 24 hours—or if you have sudden, acute abdominal pain accompanied by fever—you may require emergency surgery.

Note: If your condition is serious enough to warrant emergency treatment, it's probably best to avoid driving. Call 911 or ask someone to take you to the nearest hospital.

For milder discomfort, eliminate possible culprits, including aspirin, caffeine, alcohol, dairy products and artificial sweeteners. Try easing any symptoms with an over-the-counter (OTC) product, like Maalox or Pepto-Bismol.

See your doctor: If symptoms persist for one week, get a checkup.

Marie Savard, MD, internist, clinical associate professor, Thomas Jefferson University Hospital, Philadelphia, and author of *How to Save Your Own Life* (Warner Books). *www.drsavard.com.*

COUGH

A dry, nonproductive cough that lasts for more than two weeks requires medical attention.

Best-case scenario: Post-nasal drip...acid reflux...or continuing irritation from coughing.

Worst-case scenario: Infection...severe asthma...lung cancer...malignancy of the lymphatic system (lymphoma)...or congestive heart failure.

See your doctor: Get a physical exam and chest X ray within one week.

HEADACHE

The worst headache of your life—especially if accompanied by vomiting—should not be ignored.

Best-case scenario: Acute viral infection... or migraine.

Worst-case scenario: A leaking aneurysm ...infection of the lining covering the brain and spinal cord (bacterial meningitis) if accompanied by fever and stiff neck...or brain tumor.

Seek emergency treatment: You will need to undergo a CT scan or magnetic resonance imaging (MRI) scan to determine the cause. If it's an aneurysm, you may require emergency surgery. For bacterial meningitis, intravenous antibiotics should be given as soon as possible.

MENTAL CHANGES

Watch for confusion, memory lapses or odd or impaired thinking.

Best-case scenario: Mild depression... stress...low blood sugar...or a deficiency in vitamin B-12.

Worst-case scenario: Severe depression... brain tumor...encephalitis...or an adverse drug reaction. Many drug combinations can cause this reaction, but antihistamines and sedatives are particularly suspect.

Important: Discuss possible drug interactions with your doctor and pharmacist before taking any new medication.

Seek emergency treatment: If disorientation is sudden and acute, mental changes could reflect a serious problem with the central nervous system. Therefore, a prompt evaluation is critical.

See your doctor: For mild or gradual symptoms, get a checkup within 24 hours.

RECTAL BLEEDING

Be concerned if you pass a dark black or maroon stool...or see bright red blood on toilet paper or in the bowl.

Best-case scenario: Hemorrhoids or a tear in the lining of the anus (fissure) can cause bright red blood...iron supplements or Pepto-Bismol can cause black stool.

Worst-case scenario: Rectal cancer if blood is bright red...or colon cancer, bleeding ulcer or diverticulosis (outpouchings, or sacs, usually in the large intestine) if stool is black or maroon.

Seek emergency treatment: If stool is black or maroon and accompanied by dizziness or lightheadedness, you could be suffering from internal bleeding caused by a stomach ulcer or diverticulosis. Treatment includes blood transfusions and surgery.

See your doctor: For black stool not attributable to iron supplements or Pepto-Bismol, get evaluated as soon as possible. For bright red blood, get a checkup within two weeks. Don't assume hemorrhoids.

UNEXPLAINED WEIGHT LOSS

If you lose your appetite or drop more than 5% of your body weight, despite normal eating, something is wrong.

Best-case scenario: Mild depression... diabetes...overactive thyroid (hyperthyroidism) ...or intestinal parasites.

Worst-case scenario: Severe depression... cancer...hepatitis or other liver disease...tuberculosis...or chronic inflammation of the intestinal wall (Crohn's disease).

See your doctor: Get a complete physical, including a thorough blood workup, within two weeks.

VISION DISTURBANCES

Don't shrug it off if you experience blurred or cloudy vision, wavy lines, redness, intense pain or itching in the eye.

Best-case scenario: Allergies...diabetes... pink eye (conjunctivitis)...or outdated corrective lenses.

Worst-case scenario: Retinal tear or detachment...glaucoma...inflammation of the muscular lining of the eye (uveitis)...or foreign matter in the eye.

See your doctor: Have a checkup from an ophthalmologist within 24 hours.

Keys to Living to 100

Thomas T. Perls, MD, coauthor with Margery Silver, EdD, of *Living to 100: Lessons in Living to Your Maximum Potential at Any Age* (Basic Books).

The number of centenarians is exploding —there are now 61,000 Americans age 100 or older, compared with 37,000 just 10 years ago. The number of centenarians is expected to grow to between 800,000 and four million by 2050.

Fact: Persons age 100 or older are surprisingly healthy.

A recent study sought the common factors associated with extreme longevity.

Factors you can't control…

•**Heredity.** Persons who have long-lived relatives have an above-average likelihood of enjoying long, healthy lives themselves.

•**Being female.** Eighty-five percent of centenarians are women. (And women who give birth after age 40 are up to five times as likely to live to 100 as those who don't.)

Factors you can control…

•**Active lifestyle.** Many centenarians are active in their communities and enjoy practicing their skills (such as music, art and writing) and hobbies.

•**Healthful lifestyle.** Few centenarians are overweight. Most are physically active.

•**Human contact.** Centenarians enjoy people and stay engaged with friends and family.

•**Adaptability.** Centenarians adjust well to changing circumstances. Many have had difficult lives and suffered tragic losses, but know how to grieve and move on.

Vaccines for Adults

The "childhood" diseases can be more serious in adults than in children…and some adults may need booster shots.

Examples: Get tetanus and diphtheria shots every 10 years. If you did not have chicken pox during childhood, get a vaccination. Health-care workers and people with multiple sex partners should be vaccinated against hepatitis B. People at risk for pneumonia and similar respiratory diseases, such as seniors and those with heart disease or asthma, should be vaccinated against influenza and pneumococcal disease. Consult your doctor.

Raymond Strikas, MD, medical epidemiologist for the National Immunization Program, Centers for Disease Control and Prevention, Atlanta.

Are Cholesterol-Lowering Medications Safe?

Timothy McCall, MD, a Boston internist, the author of *Examining Your Doctor: A Patient's Guide to Avoiding Harmful Medical Care* (Citadel Press) and a commentator for the National Public Radio program *Marketplace.*

When the popular cholesterol-lowering medication *cerivastatin* (Baycol) was recently recalled after being linked to several deaths, millions of Americans who take the statins were left wondering whether their health was at risk. The Baycol users who died had suffered muscle inflammation (myositis)— a side effect that can progress to kidney failure and death.

Five statins remain on the market—*lovastatin* (Mevacor), *simvastatin* (Zocor), *pravastatin* (Pravachol), *atorvastatin* (Lipitor) and *fluvastatin* (Lescol). Each of these can cause myositis. Overall, however, the drugs appear to be fairly safe. *Here's what I suggest to lower your risk of problems:*

•**Try nondrug options before committing to medication.** Renowned cardiologist Dean Ornish, MD, has found that a comprehensive program of lifestyle change—including yoga, group psychotherapy, walking regularly and a low-fat vegetarian diet—can reverse the buildup of fatty deposits in coronary arteries. Interestingly, the control group in his experiments, some of whom took cholesterol-lowering drugs, had more symptoms and heart attacks than those who followed his program. Dr. Ornish's program isn't for everyone. But those who are willing to change their lifestyles may have a more powerful—and safer—alternative than drug therapy.

Other nondrug options that may help lower cholesterol include fiber supplements (Metamucil) and oat bran. Alcohol in moderation, low-dose aspirin therapy, black or green tea and antioxidants, such as vitamin E, may independently lower heart attack risk. Discuss dosages with your doctor.

● **Get monitored for side effects.** Most people who take statins don't observe any side effects, which has given some patients—and some doctors—a false sense of confidence. Blood tests for liver function are advised six weeks after starting statin therapy and every four to six months thereafter. Unfortunately, few doctors insist on these tests.

If you develop unexplained muscle soreness, weakness or fever, stop taking the drug and consult your doctor. If your urine turns brown, seek care immediately. This can be a sign of kidney failure.

● **Watch out for drug combinations.** One-third of the Baycol users who died were also taking *gemfibrozil* (Lopid), another cholesterol-lowering drug. Tragically, doctors were warned not to prescribe these drugs together.

In general, the more medications you take—especially if they're newer ones—the greater your risk for drug interactions. Baycol was introduced less than four years ago. Lipitor, currently the top-selling drug in the country, is also a relative newcomer.

My advice: Avoid new drugs for the first several years unless they offer significant advantages over older, time-tested drugs.

The Baycol recall reminds all of us of the fact that you cannot always count on physicians to do what they are supposed to do. Some don't bother to look up a medication to check for side effects, drug interactions and warnings before

prescribing it. Some are too busy and simply make mistakes. Whatever the cause, you can help avoid this kind of problem by reading the package insert for every drug you're prescribed. Request it from your pharmacist.

Although we often seem to forget it, *all* drugs have side effects. What matters is whether the potential benefits outweigh the risks. If a person is at high risk for heart disease—but hasn't had much success with diet, exercise and other nondrug approaches—a statin is clearly appropriate. In fact, the side effects of not taking the drug could be much worse.

Beyond Cholesterol: Six Threats to Your Heart Doctors Often Overlook

Michael Mogadam, MD, clinical assistant professor of medicine at Georgetown University in Washington, DC, and an internist and lipid specialist in private practice in Alexandria, VA. He is the author of *Every Heart Attack Is Preventable* (LifeLine Press).

Most doctors believe that elevated cholesterol is the primary cause of heart disease. But seven out of 10 heart attack victims have cholesterol levels in the "borderline" range of 180 to 240.

Clearly, cholesterol levels are important. High levels of LDL (bad) cholesterol or triglycerides and/or low levels of HDL (good) cholesterol are risk factors. So are smoking, obesity, hypertension, diabetes, etc. *But other risk factors are also important...*

CHLAMYDIA INFECTION

A common respiratory tract germ, *Chlamydia pneumoniae,* can migrate to the arteries and spark an infection that can damage the linings. *C. pneumoniae* is related to, but different from, the microorganism that causes the sexually transmitted disease commonly known as chlamydia.

More than half of adults with atherosclerosis (hardening of the arteries) are believed to be infected with *C. pneumoniae.* Only 5% of people with healthy arteries are infected.

Self-defense: Anyone with chronic sinusitis or bronchitis who has two or more risk factors for heart disease should have a blood test for *C. pneumoniae.*

Treatment typically includes a 14-day course of the oral antibiotic *arithromycin* (Zithromax), followed by one pill a week for three months.

DEPRESSED MOOD

Ten percent of American adults have a syndrome known as HAD—hostility, anger and depression. HAD increases the risk for coronary artery disease as much as high cholesterol or hypertension.

Self-defense: People who get frustrated easily...lose their temper...and often feel angry should discuss this with a physician.

Stress-reduction techniques, such as meditation, deep breathing and yoga, are helpful. In fact, a recent study at Duke University found that stress reduction can reduce the risk for coronary artery disease by 70%.

ELEVATED FIBRINOGEN

Fibrinogen is a blood protein involved in clotting. An elevated level (above 250 mg/dl) *triples* the risk for coronary artery disease.

Self-defense: People who eat a high-fat diet and have one or more risk factors for heart disease should receive a blood test to measure his/her fibrinogen level.

Eliminate fried foods, margarine and other foods that contain trans-fatty acids from your diet. These fats stimulate the liver to produce elevated fibrinogen.

Also helpful: Consuming fatty fish, such as tuna, mackerel and salmon, three or four times per week. The omega-3 fatty acids in fish lower fibrinogen and reduce the risk for blood clots. Taking an 81-mg aspirin tablet (one baby aspirin) along with 400 international units (IU) to 800 IU of vitamin E daily should also counteract elevated fibrinogen levels.

Important: If you have elevated fibrinogen and have suffered a heart attack or stroke or have peripheral-artery disease (poor blood circulation in the legs), your doctor may recommend the B vitamin niacin and/or a cholesterol-lowering drug, such as *pravastatin* (Pravachol).

HIGH HEMATOCRIT

Hematocrit is the percentage of your whole blood volume that is comprised of red blood cells. At the higher levels—48% to 51%—red blood cells make blood thicker and impair circulation. Elevated hematocrit can *triple* the risk for heart attack.

Self-defense: Anyone with a ruddy complexion...morning fatigue...or occasional dizziness or confusion should be tested. Your hematocrit level is routinely measured during blood tests—and when donating blood.

Your doctor will need to rule out conditions that increase levels of red blood cells, such as lung or bone marrow disorders.

If you're otherwise healthy: Donate one pint of blood every few weeks until your hematocrit level drops to 42% to 45%. Continue donating blood every 90 days to maintain a healthful level.

ELEVATED HOMOCYSTEINE

An abnormally high level of this blood protein can actually *double* the risk for heart attack and stroke.

An elevated homocysteine level damages artery linings and increases the risk for clots.

Self-defense: Anyone with a personal or family history of cardiovascular disease—or with one or more risk factors—should be tested for elevated homocysteine.

If your blood contains more than 9 micromoles per liter, ask your doctor about taking B-vitamin supplements. I recommend 1,000 micrograms (mcg) to 2,000 mcg each of folate and vitamin B-12 twice daily.

If your homocysteine level remains high after eight to 10 weeks, I recommend adding 50 mg to 100 mg of vitamin B-6 twice daily.

PLATELET ABNORMALITIES

In some people, blood platelets—cell-like structures that assist in clotting—function more than they should, increasing the risk for clots that can cause heart attack. Excessive platelet levels—above 250,000 per milliliter of blood—are also a threat.

Self-defense: People with one or more heart disease risk factors should receive a blood test to measure platelet levels.

If platelet levels are elevated, take one 81-mg aspirin tablet daily and one 325-mg aspirin every two weeks to boost the effectiveness of your daily low-dose aspirin.

The prescription drug *clopidogrel* (Plavix) also has antiplatelet effects. It is useful for people who are allergic to aspirin.

All men over age 35 and women over 45 should ask their doctors about taking a low-dose aspirin daily—even if they have no coronary risk factors. It may save their hearts—and their lives.

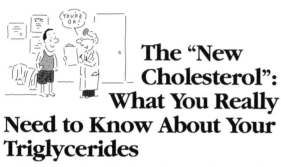

The "New Cholesterol": What You Really Need to Know About Your Triglycerides

Dennis Sprecher, MD, head of preventive cardiology, Cleveland Clinic, OH. He is the author of *What You Should Know About Triglycerides—The Missing Link in Heart Disease* (Avon).

Physicians pay very close attention to the blood levels of *LDL* (bad) and *HDL* (good) cholesterol as markers of heart disease risk.

Levels of triglycerides, however, have traditionally been viewed as a secondary issue—of concern only if levels of bad cholesterol were also too high.

But new evidence suggests that triglycerides play just as important a role in clogging the arteries as does cholesterol. Doctors should place more emphasis on bringing down elevated triglyceride levels. This is true even if cholesterol levels are normal.

Recent finding: Men with high triglyceride levels are twice as likely to develop coronary artery disease as men with low levels. Postmenopausal women with high triglycerides may be at even greater risk.

WHAT ARE TRIGLYCERIDES?

Triglycerides are the microscopic bundles of fat which circulate throughout your blood alongside other blood lipids such as bad cholesterol and good cholesterol.

As triglycerides are metabolized, fragments of these bundles are left circulating in your bloodstream. Doctors now believe these fragments have a tendency to get trapped and form dangerous plaque in artery walls, the same way bad cholesterol does.

In addition, triglycerides have an indirect impact on two other important risk factors for heart disease…

●**Triglyceride levels are inversely correlated to good cholesterol.** Whenever triglyceride levels go up, levels of good cholesterol automatically go down.

●**High triglyceride levels are associated with syndrome X,** a condition marked by obesity, diabetes, hypertension and a dramatically increased risk of heart disease.

Because of these links, a growing number of experts now agree that keeping triglycerides in a healthful range is critical for maintaining cardiovascular health.

HEALTHFUL TRIGLYCERIDE LEVELS

Triglyceride readings are taken after a 10-hour fast. *Doctors currently use the following categories when evaluating triglyceride levels…*

Very high: Above 500 milligrams per deciliter (mg/dL).

High: 200 to 499.

Borderline high: 150 to 199.

Normal: Below 150.

Recent studies, though, indicate that what constitutes a "normal" triglyceride level may have to be reconsidered.

Reason: Triglyceride levels as low as 100 mg/dL have been associated with an increased risk of heart disease.

LOWER YOUR TRIGLYCERIDES

Triglyceride levels will usually drop with just a few simple lifestyle changes…

●**Switch to a low-fat, low-sugar, high-fiber diet.** Because triglycerides are the main way that nature packages fat, levels will fall if you avoid saturated fat, cholesterol and simple sugars (such as in soda and candy)…and eat more fruits and vegetables.

Especially beneficial: Apples, strawberries, oranges, plums, broccoli, green beans, kidney beans, pinto beans, oatmeal, barley and whole-grain bread.

Foods to avoid: Beef, pork, veal, poultry (or remove the skin before cooking), butter, non-skim milk and cheese, egg yolks, organ meats, shrimp, fatty junk foods such as potato chips and processed snack foods, coconut oil and palm oil, cane sugar, honey and sugary juices.

•**Minimize alcohol intake.** Because it's quickly broken down into sugar in the blood-stream, alcohol has a powerful effect on triglyc-eride levels.

Consume no more than two drinks per day. If you already have elevated triglyceride levels, your doctor may advise avoiding alcohol com-pletely until your levels return to normal—or, at most, limiting yourself to one drink per day.

•**Do aerobic exercise every day.** Twenty to 30 minutes of daily walking, cycling or some other form of aerobic exercise will cause more efficient breakdown of triglycerides, and lessen their synthesis. Exercise also boosts your levels of protective HDL cholesterol.

•**Take daily fish-oil capsules.** These con-tain omega-3 fatty acids, which appear to lower triglyceride levels.

Other good sources of omega-3s are salmon, herring and mackerel…and flaxseed oil.

If the above steps don't do the trick: Your doctor may prescribe a triglyceride-lowering drug. *The three main types…*

•**Fibrates,** such as *gemfibrozil* (Lopid), *clofi-brate* (Atromid-S) and *fenofibrate* (Tricor), re-duce triglycerides, boost HDL cholesterol and have a modest effect on LDL cholesterol.

•**Statins,** such as *lovastatin* (Mevacor) and *pravastatin* (Pravachol), work primarily to lower LDL cholesterol but reduce triglyceride levels as well.

•**Niacin (nicotinic acid)** is a form of vita-min B3 that reduces triglycerides when given in high doses (typically one to three grams a day). While niacin is cheap and effective, it may cause side effects, including gastrointestinal dis-tress, increased blood glucose levels and, in 5% of cases, liver inflammation. Otherwise, it can

be an excellent triglyceride-lowering agent and HDL-raising agent.

Caution: Large doses of niacin should be taken only under a doctor's supervision.

What the New Cholesterol Guidelines Mean for You

Robert S. Rosenson, MD, director of the Preventive Car-diology Center at Northwestern University Medical School in Chicago. Dr. Rosenson was a member of the American College of Cardiology committee that helped to formulate the new recommendations. To learn more about these guidelines, visit the National Heart, Lung and Blood Insti-tute Web site at *www.nhlbi.nih.gov.*

Cholesterol—just how low do you need to go? For many people, the answer has recently changed.

Based on new guidelines set by the National Heart, Lung and Blood Institute, the number of Americans who should follow dietary restric-tions increased from 52 million to 65 million. The number of people who should be taking cholesterol-lowering drugs tripled.

Is it time for you to get down to cholesterol-busting business?

LATEST RESEARCH FINDINGS

Since the previous guidelines were issued by the National Cholesterol Education Program (NCEP-II) nine years ago, it has become clear that they weren't stringent enough.

Earlier standards identified only 45% of peo-ple at high risk of dying from heart disease in the following 10 years.

The new guidelines (NCEP-III) incorporate the latest research on heart disease and update advice on how to live a longer, healthier life. More than earlier versions, NCEP-III is based on detailed testing.

Example: In addition to screening for total and "good" cholesterol (high-density lipoprotein, or HDL) every five years, NCEP-III recommends testing for triglycerides—blood fats that can also cause heart disease—and "bad" cholesterol (low-density lipoprotein, or LDL).

The target for total cholesterol remains at less than 200 milligrams per deciliter (mg/dL). An "acceptable" level of HDL cholesterol has gone up, from 35 to 40. Many experts believe the cutoff level should actually be 50 for women, since their HDL levels are normally 10 points higher than those of men.

In all persons with low HDL cholesterol, the primary target is LDL cholesterol. After the LDL cholesterol target is reached, your doctor should suggest interventions, such as weight loss, exercise and/or medication.

In recognition of the role that triglycerides play in the development of heart disease, the new guidelines lower the acceptable level from 200 to 150.

As for LDL cholesterol, most people should aim for a level below 130 (160 was considered acceptable before). The target for those who have already had a heart attack is 100. This level is also recommended for anyone at "high risk" for heart disease, meaning the individual's chances of dying of heart disease or having a heart attack within 10 years is 20% or higher.

KEY RISK FACTORS

Informed physicians have long known that target cholesterol levels depend on many factors. That's why doctors also consider age, family history, other diseases, etc., in deciding when—and how—to reduce cholesterol levels.

NCEP-III standardizes this decision-making process. By using data from the mammoth Framingham Heart Study, begun in 1948, the guidelines identify people who should reduce their cholesterol levels further and faster. *Among the key factors...*

●**Diabetes.** Type 2 (adult-onset) diabetes affects 14 million Americans. The disease doubles heart attack risk in men and triples it in women. Earlier guidelines recommended an LDL level of 130 for people with diabetes. That target level has now been dropped to 100.

●**Metabolic syndrome (Syndrome X).** This common health problem includes abdominal obesity (indicated by a waist larger than 40 inches for men, 35 inches for women)...high blood pressure (above 130/85)...low HDL (less than 40 for men, 50 for women)...elevated blood glucose level (fasting glucose of 110 or above) and triglycerides (150 or above). The condition increases heart disease risk as much as cigarette smoking.

If you suffer from metabolic syndrome, cholesterol abnormalities must be treated in an aggressive manner.

●**Multiple risk factors.** Two or more major risk factors—cigarette smoking, high blood pressure, low HDL cholesterol, middle age, family history of premature heart disease, etc.—demand the same aggressive cholesterol strategies prescribed for heart attack victims.

"TLC" FOR YOUR HEART

The new guidelines—like earlier versions—advocate starting with lifestyle. Recommendations now include a total treatment plan known as therapeutic lifestyle change (TLC).

Controlling fat intake is the most widely used strategy. New guidelines lower the amount of saturated fat in the diet to less than 7% of total calories for all patients.

Total fat allowance is *increased* (from 30% to 35%). This change reflects the findings of recent population studies in Europe, which established that certain fats—especially monounsaturates, such as those found in olive oil—reduce heart disease risk. The increase also incorporates new research showing that too little fat can contribute to other risk factors, such as high triglycerides or low HDL.

In addition, NCEP-III advocates foods that are rich in soluble fiber—cereal grains, beans, fruits and vegetables—for their cholesterol-lowering effects. The guidelines also recommend boosting intake of *stanols* and *sterols*, plant-derived chemicals added to salad dressings and margarines, such as Benecol and Take Control.

There's also more emphasis on weight control and physical activity. Both lower LDL and triglyceride levels and raise HDL. These are particularly important for people who have diabetes or metabolic syndrome.

IS IT TIME FOR MEDICATION?

Lifestyle changes won't work overnight. If your risk for having a heart attack is low, you should give these strategies at least three months to bring your cholesterol profile into an acceptable range.

When risk is high, the guidelines suggest six weeks of diet and exercise—then a return visit to the doctor. If progress isn't being made, it's time for more intensive counseling on exercise and weight control, perhaps nutritional supplements, such as psyllium (Metamucil) and oat bran, and/or a consultation with a dietitian.

If these measures don't help within the second six weeks, it may be time for medication.

Blood Pressure Drugs Are Not All Alike

The calcium channel blockers may be less effective than other blood pressure drugs at preventing heart attack.

A new study suggests that these drugs may contribute to 85,000 heart attacks and cases of heart failure each year. The reason is unknown.

If you take a calcium channel blocker: Ask your doctor if you should switch to an ACE inhibitor, beta blocker or low-dose diuretic. Do not stop taking the drug on your own.

Curt D. Furberg, MD, a professor of public health science at Wake Forest University School of Medicine, Winston-Salem, NC. His analysis of nine studies involving 27,000 patients was presented at a recent meeting of the European Cardiology Society.

New Strategies For Controlling High Blood Pressure

Sheldon G. Sheps, MD, a cardiologist and emeritus professor of medicine at the Mayo Medical School in Rochester, MN. He is the editor of *Mayo Clinic on High Blood Pressure* (Mayo Clinic).

Most people assume that high blood pressure (hypertension) is relatively easy to diagnose and treat. Not so. Even experienced doctors can fail to treat effectively all the complexities of the condition.

To avoid many of the serious health threats associated with hypertension—heart attack, stroke, kidney failure, etc.—here are the latest research findings...

• **Even mild hypertension needs treatment.** Normal blood pressure is 120/80. Traditionally, doctors have treated blood pressure only when readings climb to 140/90 or higher.

But recent research shows that a systolic reading (the top number) of 130 to 139 and a diastolic reading (the bottom number) of 85 to 89 can cause artery damage.*

Any increase in blood pressure needs to be lowered, either with lifestyle changes (a healthful diet, regular exercise, etc.) or medication.

• **Systolic pressure is just as important as diastolic pressure.** Many doctors continue to focus on diastolic pressure because they were taught it was the main cause of organ damage.

Fact: Mildly elevated systolic pressure (140 to 150) needs to be lowered—even if diastolic pressure is normal.

• **"Pulse pressure" may predict heart disease more accurately** than systolic and diastolic readings. Pulse pressure is the numerical difference between systolic and diastolic pressure. Some researchers believe that pulse pressure is even more important than systolic pressure in determining long-term health risks.

A pulse pressure below 50 indicates that the arteries are elastic and healthy. But when arteries are stiff and inelastic, systolic pressure rises and diastolic pressure falls. This increases pulse pressure to 60 or greater.

New medications: Vasopeptide inhibitors target pulse pressure by lowering systolic pressure while having relatively less effect on diastolic pressure. These drugs, currently in clinical trials, should be available by prescription within one year.

• **Blood pressure readings taken in a doctor's office are not always enough.** People who regularly check their blood pressure at home control their hypertension more effectively than those who get only periodic readings in a doctor's office.

Bonus: Monitoring done in your home can detect two common types of faulty blood pressure readings...

*Systolic pressure is the force that's generated when the heart's main pumping chamber contracts. Diastolic pressure is that which occurs between these contractions.

●White-coat hypertension is a spike in blood pressure that occurs when people feel anxiety during a doctor's appointment.

●White-coat normotension is a drop in blood pressure that occurs in people who feel especially relaxed in their doctors' offices (compared with home or work).

Consider at-home monitoring if your blood pressure is mildly elevated during office visits …or if you're being treated for high blood pressure. Your doctor can give you specific recommendations on the frequency. *For accurate home readings…*

●Use an electronic (digital) blood pressure-measuring device. Most models are easy to use. *Cost:* $35 to $400. *Important:* Ask your doctor to measure your arm to determine the proper cuff size. Cuffs that are too small give artificially high readings. Cuffs that are too big give low readings.

●On the days you measure your blood pressure, take two readings in the morning (a few hours after you wake up)…two in the evening…and average the results. Always wait at least a half hour after eating…smoking…or drinking caffeine or alcohol to take your blood pressure. *Important:* Go to the bathroom first. A full bladder elevates readings.

●Bring a log of the readings to your next doctor's appointment. If the readings are unusually high—or are rising over time—call your doctor right away.

●**Salt really does matter.** New research shows that restricting salt intake to 1,500 mg daily—down from the current recommendation of 2,400 mg—can reduce systolic pressure by 11.5 points and diastolic pressure by an average of 5.5 points.

●**Drinking alcohol can raise blood pressure.** Excessive alcohol consumption is thought to contribute to hypertension in one out of 10 people who suffers from this condition.

Men should have fewer than two drinks per day…women, one.

●**Deep breathing helps.** People who practice deep breathing for 15 minutes daily—inhaling through the nose for about four seconds…holding it momentarily…then exhaling through the mouth for four seconds—may reduce their blood pressure.

Helpful: The FDA has approved a prescription device called RespeRate for lowering high blood pressure. The device measures breathing rate, then creates audio-guided exercises to slow breathing down.

More information: Contact the manufacturer, InterCure at 877-988-9388 or on the Web at *www.resperate.com.*

●**Even minor weight loss makes a difference.** In a recent study, 40% of people with hypertension who lost eight to 10 pounds were able to stay off antihypertensive medication.

Key: Exercise regularly, eat less fat and cut your calories.

●**Exercise daily.** Most experts recommend exercising at least three days a week, but new research shows that exercising every day or most days can lower blood pressure by five to 10 points.

Best choices: Aerobic exercises, such as walking, biking or swimming.

Ibuprofen Warning

Ibuprofen, as well as the other nonsteroidal anti-inflammatory drugs (NSAIDs), may trigger congestive heart failure (CHF).

Of more than 1,000 patients—average age 75—those who took NSAIDs were twice as likely to be hospitalized for CHF as those who didn't.

NSAIDs may interfere with substances that regulate blood pressure and kidney function.

Alternative: Acetaminophen may be safer, but talk to your doctor.

Low-dose aspirin has been shown to protect the heart and probably does not have this adverse effect.

David Henry, MD, professor of clinical pharmacology, University of Newcastle, New South Wales, Australia.

Serious Leg Problem Often Goes Undiagnosed

Leg cramps, aches and tired muscles can be symptomatic of a serious leg problem that often goes undiagnosed. *Peripheral artery disease* develops when hardening of the arteries (atherosclerosis) occurs in the leg, often causing poor walking endurance and other disabilities. Long-term problems include an increased risk for heart disease and stroke. In some people, symptoms occur during walking. But many patients have no symptoms.

Self-defense: Screening for people age 55 and older with diabetes or a history of cigarette smoking…and everyone age 70 or older.

This condition can be diagnosed with a test that compares blood pressure in the arms with blood pressure in the ankles.

Mary McGrae McDermott, MD, assistant professor of medicine and preventive medicine at Feinberg School of Medicine, Northwestern University, Chicago.

Bypass Surgery Alternative

Coronary stents—wire mesh tubes inserted during balloon angioplasty to keep arteries open—are just as effective as more invasive bypass surgery in treating heart disease. During a recent one-year study, patients who received stents suffered about the same number of heart attacks and strokes as did patients who underwent bypass surgery.

Bonus: Depending on your circumstances, the stents can cost thousands of dollars less than bypass surgery.

If you have been diagnosed with a coronary blockage: Ask your doctor if angioplasty with stents is an option.

Patrick W. Serruys, MD, professor, department of interventional cardiology heart center at Erasmus University, Rotterdam, the Netherlands.

Monthly Self-Test Helps Prevent Stroke

Frederick E. Munschauer III, MD, director, Research Center for Stroke & Heart Disease, Buffalo.

To evaluate your stroke risk, be sure to perform this simple 60-second pulse test monthly…

•**Turn your left hand palm-side up with the first two fingers of your right hand along the outer edge of the left wrist,** just below where the wrist and thumb meet. Be sure to use only the fingertips, not the flat "fingerprint" surface.

•**Slide your fingertips slowly toward the center of the wrist until you feel a pulse—** between the wrist bone and the tendon. If you reach the center of the wrist, you have gone too far.

•**Press *gently* with your fingertips until you feel the pulse.** Hold for 60 seconds. Note if the pulse is regular and constant—like the ticking of a clock—or irregular.

If you suspect your pulse is irregular, see your physician.

Atrial fibrillation (AF)—a type of irregular heartbeat—causes up to 80,000 strokes each year. Monitoring your pulse rate helps detect AF, which is typically treated with aspirin and/or the blood thinner *warfarin* (Coumadin). Treating AF reduces stroke risk by 70%.

Alzheimer's Self-Defense

If you have high blood pressure, keep a close eye on your cholesterol levels, too. Middle-aged people with hypertension and high cholesterol are *five times* more likely to develop Alzheimer's late in life than other people. Individuals with either high blood pressure or high cholesterol are two to three times more likely to develop Alzheimer's. Treating hypertension and/or high cholesterol with medication, diet and exercise may help lower the risk for coronary heart disease as well as Alzheimer's.

Miia Kivipelto, MD, research fellow, the department of neuroscience and neurology, University of Kuopio, Kuopio, Finland. Her review of health statistics of 1,449 people was published in the *British Medical Journal,* Tavistock Sq., London WC1H 9JR.

Pacemaker for the Brain

A brain pacemaker improves Parkinson's tremors by 90%. The device, roughly the size of a pager, is implanted below the collarbone, and a thin wire is threaded from it to an electrode implanted in the brain. Electrical pulses sent from the pacemaker interrupt the abnormal brain signals that trigger symptoms, such as tremors, rigidity, slowness of movement and walking difficulties.

More information: Contact the National Parkinson Foundation, 800-327-4545, *www.parkin son.org/whatsnew.htm.*

Ali Rezai, MD, head, section of stereotactic and functional neurosurgery, Cleveland Clinic Foundation, OH.

Better Cancer Test

If cancer is suspected, ask your doctor about getting a PET scan. Positron emission tomography (PET) detects and stages the severity of many types of cancer far more effectively than other diagnostic tests, such as computed tomography (CT) and magnetic resonance imaging (MRI). Commonly used in conjunction with other imaging tests, PET is especially useful in detecting any malignancies of the lung, lymph nodes, colon, skin, head, neck, breast, esophagus, testicle and thyroid. In a recent survey of breast cancer patients, doctors changed the course of treatment for 60% of the women after reviewing PET scans. There are 300 PET scanners in use in the US.

Cost of the scan: About $2,000 to $3,500, which is usually covered by insurance.

Johannes Czernin, MD, director of nuclear medicine, University of California at Los Angeles Medical Center.

New Tick Warning

Bites from ticks can cause *tularemia*—a life-threatening disease if not treated promptly with antibiotics. Ticks pick up the bacteria from hares, rabbits and other rodents. About 200 cases are reported in the US each year—mainly in south-central states.

Symptoms: Chills…dry cough…fever…headaches…joint pain…muscle aches…pneumonia…progressive weakness…skin ulcers.

Katherine Feldman, DVM, an epidemic intelligence service officer, National Center for Infectious Diseases, Centers for Disease Control and Prevention, Fort Collins, CO.

Skin Care Self-Defense

Some nonmedical technicians are performing procedures that until recently were performed only by doctors. Many skin care salons and so-called wellness centers are offering laser treatments, chemical peels, micro-dermabrasion and cosmetic treatments for hair and blood vessel removal. But the people handling the equipment may have attended only a one-day training course. When used incorrectly, lasers can cause burns, scars and other injuries.

Self-defense: Make sure there is a doctor on-site. Ask for a test patch…and call for medical attention if a problem occurs.

Harold J. Brody, MD, clinical professor of dermatology, Emory University Medical School, Atlanta.

Little-Known Causes Of Hair Loss

Hair loss can be caused by antidepressants, beta-blockers for high blood pressure, *cimetidine* (Tagamet) for ulcers, *colchicine* for gout, the blood thinner *heparin*, cholesterol-lowering medications and the over-the-counter painkiller *ibuprofen* (Advil).

Other possible causes include deficiencies of zinc, magnesium, protein and/or vitamins B and D.

Good news: Once the cause is identified and corrected, hair loss usually stops.

If you suffer from hair loss: Ask your doctor if it could be caused by medication and/or a nutritional deficiency.

Wilma F. Bergfeld, MD, head of clinical research, department of dermatology, The Cleveland Clinic.

More Effective Diabetes Testing

Diabetes frequently goes undetected because testing is done in the afternoon.

Problem: Blood glucose levels peak in the morning, then drop in the afternoon.

Self-defense: If you experience frequent urination, excessive thirst, increased appetite, rapid, unexplained weight loss and/or blurred vision, talk to your doctor about getting a fasting blood glucose test. The test should be repeated on a different day. At least one of the tests needs to be performed in the morning.

Catherine C. Cowie, PhD, epidemiologist and director of the Type 1 Diabetes Clinical Trials Program, National Institute of Diabetes and Digestive and Kidney Diseases, Bethesda, MD.

Arthritis/Gum Disease Connection

People with rheumatoid arthritis are more than twice as likely as healthy people to develop gum problems. That's because damage caused by the immune system and chronic inflammation are central to both diseases.

Good news: Caught early, gum disease can usually be treated successfully with simple plaque-removing procedures. Red, swollen or bleeding gums are typically the earliest sign of gum disease.

If you suffer from rheumatoid arthritis: Ask your dentist for specific recommendations.

Michael McGuire, DDS, president, American Academy of Periodontology, Chicago.

New Help for Chronic Back Pain

Chronic back pain can be eased in less than 30 minutes via a new outpatient procedure used for people with mildly herniated discs and sciatica. *Nucleoplasty* is faster and safer than other intradiscal procedures. This involves inserting a needle into the disc and releasing radio-frequency energy that heats the area, vaporizing tissue inside the disc. Performed under local anesthesia, nucleoplasty provides, on average, a 70% reduction in pain.

Yung Chen, MD, assistant professor of physical medicine and rehabilitation, Stanford University School of Medicine, and medical director, Stanford Interventional Spine Center, both in Stanford, CA.

Antidepressant Alert

Doctors often misprescribe tranquilizers and antidepressants. Especially among older adults, some of these medications' potentially harmful effects—like urine retention, sedation and confusion—may outweigh their potential benefits. It's estimated that 20% of people age 65 and older take a drug that could be especially dangerous for them.

Self-defense: At least once a year, review with your doctor all over-the-counter and prescription medications you take. Discuss side effects you are experiencing and whether you can reduce the dosage or stop taking the drug.

Important: Never discontinue a medication without consulting your doctor.

Arlene S. Bierman, MD, senior research physician at the Center for Outcomes and Effectiveness Research, Agency for Healthcare Research and Quality, Rockville, MD.

Asthma/Heartburn Link

Asthma sufferers often have chronic gastric reflux—without even knowing it. That's because the "backsplash" of stomach acid into the esophagus can occur without causing symptoms of heartburn. All asthmatics should be screened for reflux symptoms. If reflux, heartburn or other symptoms are present, three months of anti-reflux medication, such as a proton-pump inhibitor, should be considered. If asthma improves, long-term treatment for reflux may be appropriate.

Susan M. Harding, MD, associate professor of medicine, University of Alabama School of Medicine in Birmingham.

Asthma Medication Trap

The very medication that is supposed to relieve asthma attacks can actually trigger them. Certain asthma drugs that are used in nebulizers—devices that deliver the drugs—contain *benzalkonium chloride*. This preservative is used only in *albuterol* (Proventil) and *metaproterenol* (Alupent) solutions in screwcap containers. It is not contained in drugs used in metered-dose inhalers.

If you use asthma medication that contains benzalkonium chloride: Ask your doctor about switching to a drug that is packaged as a single-unit dose in a nonresealable container.

Michael J. Asmus, PharmD, assistant professor of pharmacy practice, University of Florida College of Pharmacy, Gainesville.

The Latest on Laser Eye Surgery

Andrew Caster, MD, clinical professor of ophthalmology at University of California, Los Angeles. He is medical director of Caster Eye Center in Beverly Hills, CA, and author of *The Eye Laser Miracle: The Complete Guide to Better Vision* (Ballantine). He has performed more than 12,000 laser eye surgeries. *www.castervision.com.*

More than one million Americans have undergone vision-correction surgery as a hassle-free alternative to wearing glasses or contact lenses. About 95% see well enough after the surgery to pass a driver's license exam—and 75% achieve "perfect" 20/20 vision.

The most common form of vision-correcting surgery, Laser-Assisted In Situ Keratomileusis (LASIK), is safe and effective—but not for everyone. People with cataracts or certain other eye conditions are poor candidates for it. Insurance companies do not cover it. And despite the advertising hyperbole of some clinics, LASIK doesn't guarantee perfect vision—and isn't free from risks or side effects.

Though the vision-correcting effects of the procedure are permanent, LASIK doesn't stop the natural changing of the eye over time, which may necessitate additional surgery or corrective lenses in the future.

Below, Andrew Caster, MD, clinical professor of ophthalmology at University of California, Los Angeles, answers some questions about the benefits and risks of LASIK…

●What does LASIK do? It is a precise way of changing the curvature of the cornea. To correct nearsightedness, the cornea is flattened. For farsightedness, the curvature is increased. To correct astigmatism, the curvature is equalized.

The 10-minute outpatient procedure uses pulses of ultraviolet laser light to remove microscopic layers of cells from different parts of the cornea. A computer determines the number of light pulses needed to remove exactly the right amount of tissue. It also guides the laser during the operation.

●**What exactly will happen during the surgery?** The patient sits in a reclining chair. A numbing drop is placed in the eye, the surrounding area is cleaned and the eyelid is propped open with an instrument called a lid speculum. The patient is given a mild oral sedative, but he/she remains awake throughout the entire procedure.

The doctor cuts a tiny flap in the cornea, which will allow the laser to shape the cornea from inside.

The patient is instructed to stare at a fixed light during the procedure to steady the eye. There's a ticking sound when the laser fires but no discomfort. Light from the laser is "cold"—it vaporizes, but doesn't burn, the tissue.

Most patients have both eyes treated at the same time, but a few opt to have one eye treated first and the other later, after they have evaluated the results.

●**I've heard it is dangerous to move during the procedure. Is this true?** This used to be a real problem. In fact, the people who couldn't keep their eye focused on a light for 60 seconds were often rejected for surgery.

Today, tracking lasers lock onto and follow the eye as it moves. The equipment I use measures the position of the eye 4,000 times a second. A little bit of head or eye movement does not matter.

Older lasers that lack the tracking feature are still in use at some low-cost vision-correction centers. Ask the doctor if he/she uses a tracking laser. If not, find a doctor who does.

●**How will I feel after the procedure?** Most people are able to return to work and drive the following day. However, there are mild fluctuations in vision for up to three months after the procedure. Most people will also experience dry eyes…mild scratchiness…and glare or "halos" for a few weeks or months.

●**What are the main complications?** The most common problem is when vision after the procedure is not as improved as it should be. This can almost always be corrected with "touch-up" surgery—usually performed from three to 12 months later to adjust the cornea's curvature. Most doctors don't charge extra for this, but ask ahead.

Infections are occasionally a problem, but they're easily prevented by using antibiotic eyedrops for a week after the surgery.

About 2% of patients who undergo the LASIK procedure have long-term visual aberrations, such as glare or ghost images. But the use of newer lasers has reduced this problem to less than 1% of all people who undergo LASIK.

In rare cases—less than one in 10,000—vision is severely impaired and the patient requires a corneal transplant.

●**Who are the best candidates?** People with modest levels of near- or farsightedness or astigmatism. The less tissue that has to be removed from the cornea, the more successful the surgery.

LASIK is not recommended for people age 18 or younger because the cornea is still changing shape. Nor is it a good idea for adults with refractive instability, a condition marked by frequent changes in distance vision. If you need a new prescription for corrective distance lenses every year or two, you probably shouldn't have the LASIK procedure.

Others who shouldn't have LASIK surgery include people with cataracts or certain other eye diseases…those with very thin corneas or extremely large pupils…and women who are pregnant or breast-feeding. Hormonal fluctuations during pregnancy and lactation sometimes change the shape of the cornea.

●**Can LASIK eliminate the need for reading glasses?** Usually not. At this point, LASIK is not a solution for *presbyopia* (Latin for "old eyes"). Lenses normally focus up close by changing shape. By age 45, the lenses have stiffened and the muscle that changes the shape doesn't work as well.

LASIK can create *monovision*, a condition in which one eye is corrected for distance and the other eye for close-up. To see far, the distance eye does the work. To read, the other eye takes over. Because the eyes do not work together, however, it may be difficult to perform certain tasks that require particularly sharp vision, such as threading a needle.

●**A lot of clinics advertise LASIK surgery. How do I pick the best one?** Make sure the surgeon is board-certified in ophthalmology. Ask how many procedures he has performed. You want someone who has done the surgery at least 200 times.

Beware: Most optometrists have financial arrangements with certain eye surgeons or centers and will get a financial benefit if you act on their referrals.

Be wary of discount eye-surgery centers—especially those that use high-pressure sales tactics, such as a discount if you bring a friend or demanding a deposit on your first visit.

The prices at discount centers are tempting. I have seen advertisements for as low as $399 per eye, compared with the average of $1,200 to $1,800 per eye. But the only way to cut costs is to cut corners.

Examples: Some clinics may calibrate their lasers once a day in the morning—but equipment needs to be adjusted for each patient to compensate for changes in room temperature and humidity. Low-cost eye centers are also less likely to give thorough eye exams or take multiple measurements prior to the procedure.

●**Is there anything I should do before and after surgery?** Don't wear soft contact lenses for 10 days before the procedure. If you wear hard or gas-permeable lenses, leave them out for one month for every decade that you've worn them. If you have worn hard contacts for 30 years, for example, don't wear them for three months prior to the surgery. Contacts temporarily change the shape of the cornea. Going without allows the eye to regain its natural curvature.

●**Are there other kinds of laser eye surgery?** About 5% of patients can't have LASIK because of certain eye conditions…or won't because they are concerned about having a flap cut in the cornea. In these cases, two other variations of the procedure may be appropriate, both of which require more healing time than LASIK.

One is Photorefractive Keratectomy (PRK), which uses a laser to alter the cornea but does not involve cutting a flap. A newer variation of PRK, called Laser-Assisted Epithelial Keratomileusis (LASEK), has a slightly faster recovery time than PRK.

Cell Phone Ailment

Frequent cell phone use can cause an ailment more commonly associated with nuns. Scientists are still debating whether cell phone use increases brain cancer risk. But there appears to be no controversy over the occurrence of *chondrodermatitis*, a condition in which tiny, painful, crusty bumps form on the side of the ear.

Culprit: Pressing your cell phone too firmly against the ear. Nuns develop the condition from wearing tight-fitting cloth headpieces (wimples). Symptoms include irritation on the ears.

Helpful: Use the phone less, hold it lightly against your ear and switch ears periodically.

Mervyn Elgart, MD, clinical professor of dermatology, medicine and pediatrics, George Washington University School of Medicine, Washington, DC.

Warning Signs Of Hearing Loss

Christopher Linstrom, MD, chief of neurootology, New York Eye and Ear Infirmary, New York City.

Half of people over age 65 have some degree of hearing loss—but most do not know it.

The most common type of hearing loss is associated with aging (presbyacusis). But since it occurs gradually, in many cases it goes unnoticed for years. *Warning signs…*

●**Frequently asking others to repeat what they've said.**

• **Turning up the volume of the radio** or TV until others complain.

• **Favoring one ear.**

• **Trouble following conversation** in a group setting or amid background noises.

• **Needing to look at a speaker's face** to hear clearly.

• **Ringing or buzzing in the ears.**

Important: Early detection is vital for effective treatment. Have your hearing checked as part of your regular medical checkup.

Brain-Boosting Pills: The Ones That Work... And Those That Don't

Jay Schneider, PhD, professor of neurology, pathology, anatomy and cell biology at Thomas Jefferson University in Philadelphia. He is coauthor of *Brain Candy: Boost Your Brain Power with Vitamins, Supplements, Drugs and Other Substances* (Fireside).

Do you sometimes forget where you parked the car? Or need a little extra time to program the VCR?

As we age, these and other lapses can make us feel that we're losing our mental edge.

That's why the brain-boosting supplements, herbs and drugs are so popular. But do the top sellers *really* work? Are they safe?*

Here's the opinion of one leading expert...

• **Acetyl-L-carnitine.** This over-the-counter (OTC) amino acid is believed to jump-start the brain by helping to produce chemicals that power brain cell activity. Initial studies suggest that taking the supplement may improve memory and attention, even in healthy, young adults.

Acetyl-L-carnitine also may stave off the protein deposits that develop in the brains of early-stage Alzheimer's patients.

Typical daily dosage: 1 g to 3 g.

Caution: Do not confuse acetyl-L-carnitine with DL-carnitine, which can produce severe loss of muscle strength.

*The Food and Drug Administration does not approve herbs or supplements. Always consult your physician before taking any of these products.

• **B vitamins.** Clinical studies show that thiamine (B-1), niacin (B-3) and pyridoxine (B-6) may improve memory and thinking. How do they work? Thiamine enables the body to metabolize carbohydrates, the primary source of energy for brain cells. Niacin appears to improve short-term memory and comprehension. Pyridoxine plays a role in forming several of the brain's neurotransmitters. Taking 20 mg to 50 mg daily of vitamin B-6 has been found to improve mood and memory.

Typical daily dosage: Follow dosage recommendations on the labels of B-complex and individual B vitamins.

Caution: In addition to being potentially toxic to the liver, more than 2 g daily of niacin can cause peptic ulcers and may exacerbate cardiac arrhythmia. More than 200 mg daily of B-6 can be toxic to nerve cells and may interfere with Parkinson's disease drugs.

If you eat plenty of foods that are rich in B-vitamins—organ meats, pork, legumes and nuts—you might not need to take supplements.

• **Fipexide.** This OTC stimulant is said to enhance thinking and learning by increasing levels of the neurotransmitter dopamine in the brain. In a single clinical trial, fipexide did improve mental functioning in a group of older patients with brain disease. However, this stimulant has been known to cause severe liver damage.

• **Gerovital.** This OTC supplement—marketed as an antiaging formula for body and brain—is nothing more than the local anesthetic *procaine*, combined with an antioxidant and a preservative. There is no scientific evidence that Gerovital rejuvenates the mind.

But excessive use can cause tremors, unconsciousness, convulsions, low or high blood pressure and respiratory or cardiac arrest.

• **Ginkgo biloba.** There's good reason this Chinese herb has become our favorite alternative remedy for memory impairment. It works.

Ginkgo has been shown to improve memory in Alzheimer's patients, though the evidence is not as strong in healthy people. Researchers attribute the benefit to the herb's antioxidant and anti-inflammatory properties.

Typical daily dosage: 120 mg to 240 mg.

Caution: Ginkgo inhibits blood clotting. It should not be taken by people on aspirin or blood thinners, such as *warfarin* (Coumadin). Ginkgo should also be avoided by patients facing surgery or anyone with a clotting disorder, such as hemophilia or vitamin K deficiency.

● **Growth hormone.** This protein, secreted by the pituitary gland, promotes cell growth. Sold as a prescription drug, growth hormone is said to prevent physical *and* mental deterioration in adults that have acquired growth hormone deficiency.

However, its effectiveness as an "antiaging" drug is unsubstantiated. The risks are considerable. Growth hormone can cause fluid retention, hypertension and hyperglycemia. This, in turn, can lead to diabetes, high blood pressure and heart disease. It may also stimulate growth of existing tumors, such as colon malignancies.

● **Phenytoin (Dilantin).** Commonly prescribed to treat epilepsy, this anticonvulsant is sometimes falsely promoted as an "IQ-booster." But there are no convincing studies to support this claim.

But there are plenty of data detailing the drug's potential side effects—everything from slurred speech and insomnia to potentially fatal disorders of the liver, blood and thyroid.

● **Phosphatidylserine.** This fat-like substance is one of the several OTC dietary supplements clinically tested on healthy and cognitively impaired adults. It has been shown consistently to improve memory and attention, without causing serious side effects.

Phosphatidylserine seems to enhance communication between the chemical messengers (neurotransmitters) in the brain. It also appears to inhibit synthesis of *cortisol,* a stress hormone that may interfere with thinking and memory.

Typical daily dosage: 100 mg three times a day.

Caution: Phosphatidylserine may slow blood clotting. For this reason, it should be avoided by the same people who are cautioned against taking ginkgo.

● **Piracetam.** This OTC supplement was the first "nootropic" (a drug designed specifically to improve brain function) to be marketed in

Europe. In the US, it can be purchased only from mail-order or Internet retailers.

Piracetam has been widely tested on healthy and cognitively impaired adults.

When combined with memory exercises, it has been shown to lessen age-associated memory loss significantly. To date, there have been no serious side effects reported.

Typical daily dosage: 2,400 mg to 4,800 mg, divided in three doses.

● **Vincamine.** This herbal supplement, which is derived from the periwinkle plant, is said to enhance concentration in healthy adults, and boost memory and attention in patients with impaired brain circulation caused by cerebrovascular disease.

Vincamine does increase the cerebral blood flow, so it may be of some benefit if promptly administered after a stroke. But long-term use can cause life-threatening cardiac arrhythmias, as well as severe sleep disturbances.

How to Fend Off Nasty Germs

Jack Brown, PhD, a professor of molecular biosciences at the University of Kansas, Lawrence. He is the author of *Don't Touch That Doorknob! How Germs Can Zap You and How You Can Zap Back* (Warner).

With new strains of antibiotic-resistant bacteria and the continued threat of biological warfare, many people are taking extraordinary steps to avoid germs.

But there's no need for an obsessive concern about germs—if you take a few simple precautions to protect yourself and your family. *Microbiology expert Jack Brown, PhD, answers some questions below...*

● **We've all heard that hand washing is the best way to prevent the common cold. Does this practice really help?** The *best* way, of course, is to avoid contact with anyone with a cold infection. But with one billion colds occurring in America each year, that's impractical.

The next best protection is to wash your hands often to protect against exposure to germs during routine activities. For example, a cold virus can survive for up to three hours on a dry surface, such as a doorknob. Plain soap eliminates most germs, reducing the possibility that the virus will hopscotch from your hands to your nose, mouth or eyes.

The key is to wash *thoroughly*. Soap all parts of your hands. Scrub between and around the fingers, the palm, the back of the hand and underneath fingernails—for at least 20 seconds. Rinse well. Dry your hands with a disposable towel. Cloth towels can harbor germs.

●**Are "antibacterial" products worth using?** If you use antibacterial products consistently at home or in the workplace, you'll only be encouraging the growth of resistant microorganisms. Experts have already identified a bacterium that's resistant to *triclosan,* a common ingredient in antibacterial products. Plus, you must leave the product on a surface for several minutes for it to work.

Overuse of antibacterial hand soaps can damage the skin, causing a form of eczema, which increases the potential for bacterial infection.

Sanitizing gels, which contain more than 60% alcohol, can dry the skin by removing the natural protective oils. Prudent use of these products is recommended.

●**Is it ever appropriate to use an antibacterial cleaning agent?** These products can be useful in homes where someone has a compromised immune system—a longtime steroid user, a cancer patient on chemotherapy, a person infected with HIV, as well as some infants, pregnant women and older adults.

●**What's the best way to prevent bacterial contamination when preparing food?** Wash your hands after every step in meal preparation, particularly after you handle raw meat. This simple step could eliminate 50% of all food poisoning cases.

Never place any ingredient or food on a surface that's been exposed to raw meat, unless the surface has been thoroughly cleaned. If possible, put the plate or cutting board in the dishwasher. Or use a diluted bleach solution (one tablespoon bleach per gallon of water).

Cook meat thoroughly. Red meat should be at an internal temperature of 160°F…poultry, 170°F to 180°F. To prevent growth of bacteria, I advocate placing hot foods in the refrigerator instead of leaving them out to cool. For rapid cooling, store the food in smaller portions.

Keep your refrigerator between 35°F and 40°F. A recent survey indicated that 60% of Americans do not realize that their refrigerator should be set at that temperature. Sixty-seven percent did not own a refrigerator thermometer …and 70% relied on "feel" to tell if their food was cold enough.

Even if your refrigerator has a built-in thermometer, it is a good idea to have an additional one that you can easily move around inside the refrigerator.

●**How can I avoid infections while traveling abroad?** Learn about your destination before you travel. Find out whether you need any vaccinations from the Centers for Disease Control and Prevention at *www.cdc.gov/travel.* Find out about disease outbreaks from the World Health Organization at *www.who.int.*

When traveling abroad, especially in underdeveloped countries, use only bottled water or water that has been boiled for several minutes. It's also important to not use tap water when brushing your teeth and to avoid eating raw vegetables washed in local water.

●**Is there any way to reduce the chances of acquiring an infection during hospitalization?** Each year, 2.5 million Americans acquire infections during hospitalization, leading to 100,000 deaths. It may *not* be possible to completely protect yourself from infection if you're hospitalized. The best strategy is to ask each nurse and/or physician to wash his/her hands and to clean his stethoscope with alcohol before examining you.

Healthier Barbecuing

Suzanne Havala Hobbs, DrPH, RD, adjunct assistant professor, School of Public Health, University of North Carolina in Chapel Hill. She is author of several books, including *The Natural Kitchen* (Berkley).

When you fire up your grill, be sure to cook foods safely and healthfully. *Simple steps...*

FOOD POISONING DEFENSE

●**Cook meats, poultry and fish thoroughly.** If you precook foods indoors in order to shorten the grilling time, do so immediately before grilling.

Use a meat thermometer to ensure that all fish, poultry and meats—including burgers and hot dogs—reach an internal temperature of 160°F. Whole poultry should reach an internal temperature of 180°F...and poultry parts —wings, legs, etc.—should reach 160°F.

●**Transfer cooked food to a clean serving plate.** Do not let cooked food touch plates or other surfaces that held raw meat. The surfaces may harbor disease-causing bacteria.

●**Keep hot foods hot.** If cooked meats are not going to be eaten immediately, keep them at 140°F or warmer—for up to two hours.

●**Refrigerate any leftovers within two hours**—one hour if the outdoor temperature is 90°F or higher.

REDUCE CANCER RISK

Charring meats creates cancer-causing compounds called nitrosamines. *To keep charring to a minimum...*

●**Wrap food in aluminum foil before you grill.** This prevents direct contact with the flame and minimizes drips that create the smoke that delivers nitrosamines to the cooking meats.

●**Remove visible fat.** When fat drips from meat, flare-ups can cause charring.

●**Precook meats immediately before grilling.** This minimizes time on the grill.

MEATLESS OPTIONS

Consider adding more fruits, vegetables and meatless alternatives to your menus. You will lower the fat and cholesterol content of your meal and boost your fiber. *Good choices...*

●**Tofu hot dogs and veggie burgers.** They often taste great, grill well and take only minutes to cook.

●**Vegetable kabobs.** Skewer whole mushrooms, cherry tomatoes, chunks of onion, bell peppers, eggplant, zucchini and pineapple. Wrap up in foil, and cook until ready. Serve in a pita pocket with some plain yogurt or your favorite salad dressing.

●**Fish.**

●**Fresh produce.** Round out your meals with watermelon, cantaloupe and blueberries, vine-ripened tomatoes and green salads.

Drink All the Milk in Your Cereal Bowl

Vitamins added to cereal are sprayed on, so they dissolve in milk. If you do not finish the milk, you leave nutrients behind.

Prevention, 33 E. Minor St., Emmaus, PA 18098.

2

Dealing with Doctors and Hospitals

The Ultimate Medical Checkup

The managed-care revolution has drastically reduced the amount of time doctors are willing to spend with their patients.

During the typical office visit, your doctor barely has time to investigate troublesome symptoms and check your weight...pulse... heartbeat...blood pressure, etc. That is just not enough.

A thorough exam should also address your overall physical and emotional well-being... diet...lifestyle...and any "silent" symptoms that can increase your risk for health problems.

Most doctors take a medical history, listing current health problems...prescribed medications...allergies, etc. This information is critical.

Helpful: When writing down your concerns, give your doctor additional information that he/ she may fail to include in the medical history...

- **How's your diet?**
- **Are you taking any herbal or dietary supplements?**
- **Do you get enough sleep?**
- **Are you physically active?**
- **Are you experiencing sexual problems?**

Also mention if you smoke, how much alcohol you drink and whether you're having difficulty in your personal relationships. Try to keep the list to one page.

THE PHYSICAL

To save time, doctors often take shortcuts during the physical. This can affect not only your current diagnosis and treatment—but also your future health. *Here are the steps most commonly omitted...*

- **Blood pressure.** This vital sign is typically checked in one arm while the patient is sitting. For a more accurate reading, blood pressure

Leo Galland, MD, director of the Foundation for Integrated Medicine in New York City. Dr. Galland is the author of *Power Healing* (Random House).

should be tested in *both* arms, preferably while you're lying down.

If blood pressure differs by 15% or more between arms, there may be blockages in the large blood vessels.

Important: If you're taking blood pressure medication—or if you get dizzy when you change positions—your doctor should check your blood pressure immediately after you stand up. If blood pressure drops by more than 10%, a change in dosage of blood pressure medication may be needed.

●**Eyes.** Most people visit an ophthalmologist or optometrist. But if you don't see an eye specialist regularly and you're age 40 or older, your internist or family practitioner should measure the pressure on your eyeballs to test for glaucoma and look for lack of lens clarity—an early sign of cataracts.

Bonus: A careful eye exam can also reveal blood vessel narrowing or small hemorrhages on the retina—indicators of vascular conditions that increase your heart disease risk.

●**Hamstrings.** Few doctors test these muscles at the back of the thighs to identify potential back problems. To do so, the doctor should ask you to lie on your back and lift each leg to a 90° angle.

If you can't perform the lift, you may need a stretching program to relax the hamstrings.

●**Lymph nodes.** The lymph nodes in your neck are typically checked, but doctors should also check those in the groin and under arms. Swollen lymph nodes may signal infection. Lumps could indicate cancer.

●**Pulse points.** Your doctor probably checks your pulse in your neck and/or groin—but may skip your feet. If pulse strength differs in these three areas, it can be a sign of peripheral arterial disease.

●**Skin.** Many doctors ignore the skin altogether, assuming that it should be examined by a dermatologist. Not true. The skin should also be checked during a general medical checkup.

To examine your skin, your doctor should ask you to disrobe so he can look for moles on every part of your body, even your scalp and the bottoms of your feet.

If you have moles larger than one-half inch—or if your moles have gotten larger, darkened or changed their shape—you should get a referral to a dermatologist for a melanoma screening.

●**Thyroid.** This butterfly-shaped gland at the base of the neck is often missed during the lymph node exam. By palpating the thyroid, your doctor can screen for thyroid cancer.

FOR WOMEN ONLY

●**Breast and reproductive organs.** Most doctors check the breasts for suspicious lumps, but few doctors show women how to perform monthly exams at home.

Helpful: When performing a self-exam, move all eight fingers, minus the thumbs, up and down instead of in a circle. That way, you will be covering the entire breast.

If you don't see your gynecologist regularly, your physician should also perform rectal and vaginal exams. These exams should be performed simultaneously—it makes it easier to identify suspicious masses.

FOR MEN ONLY

●**Testicles and rectum.** When examining men age 40 or older, most doctors perform a digital rectal exam to screen for prostate cancer. However, they often fail to perform a testicular exam to check for testicular cancer. Your doctor should also teach you how to perform a testicular self-exam.

Beginning at age 50—even earlier if there's a family history of prostate cancer—every man should undergo a prostate-specific antigen (PSA) blood test performed every three years… or more often if abnormalities are found.

LABORATORY TESTS

Routine blood tests include cholesterol levels …liver and kidney function…blood glucose levels…and a white blood cell count. But we now know that other blood tests can be important if a patient shows signs of certain conditions. *These tests include…*

●**C-reactive protein.** An elevated level of this inflammation marker can indicate heart disease risk.

●**Homocysteine.** Elevated levels of this amino acid are associated with heart disease and stroke risk.

Helpful: The B vitamin folate, when taken at 200 mcg to 400 mcg daily, reduces homocysteine levels.

●**Iron.** Elevated levels of this mineral cause iron overload (*hemochromatosis*).

●**Lipoprotein (a).** Elevated levels of this blood protein increase the risk for blood clots.

●**Magnesium.** Low levels of this mineral can bring about fatigue, generalized pain and/or muscle spasms.

●**Zinc.** If you're deficient in this immune-strengthening mineral, you may be prone to frequent infection.

How Much Do You Know About Your Doctor?

John J. Connolly, EdD, a former president of New York Medical College in Valhalla, NY. He copublishes *America's Top Doctors* (Castle Connolly Medical Ltd.), an annual guide that lists the top specialists in a variety of fields, based on each doctor's credentials, experience and assessments by his/her peers.

When choosing a doctor, most people will rely on the recommendation of a friend, family member, coworker or another doctor.

Few of us seek enough specific information from the prospective physicians themselves to predict the quality of care we will receive.

If you don't feel very comfortable speaking directly to a doctor about his/her qualifications, ask to talk to the office manager when you call to make an appointment. This person should be knowledgeable about the doctor's background.

The American Medical Association, *www.ama-assn.org* or 312-464-5000, also provides biographical information about physicians—but the AMA does not judge quality.

To ensure that you have enough information about a doctor, ask him these questions…

●**Are you board-certified?** Whether you're choosing a primary-care doctor or a specialist, board certification is the best indicator of competence and training.

Every medical specialty, including family practice and internal medicine, has a governing board that sets and enforces professional standards. Board certification means the doctor has completed an approved residency program and passed the board's stiff examination.

The American Board of Medical Specialties, *www.abms.org* or 866-275-2267, can tell you if a doctor is board-certified.

●**Where did you complete your residency?** Look for a physician who has at least three years of postgraduate specialty training in a residency program at a major hospital. This ensures that the doctor has gained experience in treating patients under the supervision of leading specialists.

It is fine to inquire where a doctor attended medical school, however, do not place too much emphasis on it. All accredited medical schools meet high standards, requiring graduates to pass standardized tests and compete for prestigious residencies.

A graduate from a foreign medical school must pass the same exam as a US medical school graduate—and complete the same residency requirements—to receive board certification from the appropriate governing board in the US.

●**How long have you been in practice?** If you put a premium on a doctor's clinical experience, you are likely to prefer an older doctor who has been in practice for a number of years.

However, many people prefer doctors who completed their residency within the past five years, assuming they will be more familiar with the latest treatments.

Regardless of whether the doctor is old or young, he should have a lot of experience with your particular condition.

●**With which hospital are you affiliated?** Most doctors have admitting privileges at one or more hospitals. This allows them to admit patients to the hospital and care for them there.

Choose a doctor who has privileges at a major medical center with a good reputation. The very best doctors typically practice at the best hospitals.

Helpful: *U.S. News and World Report* ranks the best US hospitals each year. You can find details at *www.usnews.com.*

CHOOSING A SPECIALIST

For serious medical problems, including those that require surgery, your primary-care physician will often refer you to a specialist. Request more than one recommendation so that you'll have a choice.

Ask these questions to confirm a specialist's qualifications…

●**Are you board-certified in the appropriate subspecialty?** A doctor who is board-certified in a subspecialty has completed additional fellowship training in that area.

Example: A hand surgeon may be an orthopedist or a plastic surgeon who completed fellowship training in hand surgery.

●**How often have you performed this procedure?** Look for a doctor who has performed a procedure, such as laparoscopic surgery or open-heart surgery, as often as every day or every week for several years.

For rare procedures, such as the removal of certain types of brain tumors or liver malignancies, the frequency would be less. The more experience a doctor has performing a procedure, the greater the odds of success.

Caution: Every year, hundreds of physicians are disciplined or put on probation by their state medical authorities for improper behavior, substance abuse, fraud and other problems.

To avoid these doctors, call your state's medical licensing authority (check the state government listings in your phone book) or go to the Web site of the Federation of State Medical Boards at *www.fsmb.org.*

In addition to asking the questions above, patients can receive recommendations from area support groups and branches of national organizations, such as the American Diabetes Association, *www.diabetes.org.*

Use the triangulation method: If three people whose opinion you respect recommend the same doctor, he is likely to be a good choice.

Diagnostic Tests: Some Are More Reliable Than Others

Isadore Rosenfeld, MD, professor of clinical medicine at the Weill Medical College of Cornell University in New York City. He is the author of *Power to the Patient* and *Live Now, Age Later* (both from Warner Books).

Doctors used to have the final word on which tests and treatments patients received. Today, your physician may be advised by a profit-conscious managed-care organization to recommend against costly tests and treatments even if they're in your best interest.

Example: The radionuclide scan or a stress echocardiogram is the best way to diagnose angina. In the former, a tracer dose of radioactive material is injected to evaluate heart activity, both at rest and after exercise. A stress echocardiogram uses ultrasound imaging to detect abnormalities in the heart.

These procedures are especially important because as many as 70% of patients with angina have a normal electrocardiogram (EKG) at rest. An EKG records the electrical impulses of the heart.

Many patients with suspicious chest pain are first given less accurate tests, such as the standard treadmill test, because they are cheaper.

To ensure that you get optimum medical care, insist on the best tests and treatments…

GALLSTONES

When gallstones are diagnosed, some doctors still routinely recommend surgery. But only 2% of gallstone patients develop symptoms that require an operation.

If you have symptoms, such as gas, bloating and recurrent abdominal pain, a diagnosis of gallstones should be confirmed by…

●**Abdominal ultrasound.** This procedure detects stones in 98% of cases. X rays of the abdomen needlessly expose you to radiation.

●**CT scan.** If your doctor is uncertain whether your abdominal symptoms are due to gallstones, disease of the pancreas or even cancer, this is the diagnostic procedure of choice.

For gallstones that must be removed, laparoscopic surgery is preferred. It does not require opening the abdomen. Instead, three small incisions are made in the abdominal wall, through which cameras and surgical instruments are inserted to remove the diseased organ. This causes less discomfort and allows for a faster recovery than "open" abdominal surgery. If your doctor recommends the older procedure, get a second opinion.

HEART DISEASE

Some doctors balk at recommending tests to detect heart disease unless you have a major risk factor, such as smoking, high cholesterol or a family history of heart disease. But even people *without* these factors may be at increased risk for heart problems.

In addition to a medical history and a physical exam, postmenopausal women and all men over 40 should ask their doctor to order an EKG and routine blood tests for kidney function and sugar and cholesterol levels. If your EKG taken at rest is normal, you should have a radionuclide scan or stress echocardiogram.

If you have risk factors, such as high cholesterol and/or a family history of heart disease, ask your doctor to perform…

●**Specialized blood tests.** High levels of the protein *homocysteine* predispose you to heart attack. Homocysteine levels can be lowered by taking 800 micrograms (mcg) of folic acid daily.

High levels of the proteins *alpha lipoprotein (a)* and *C-reactive protein* are also thought to be associated with increased heart attack risk. There's no known way to lower alpha lipoprotein (a) levels. But if your levels are high, it may motivate you to address other risk factors.

Levels of C-reactive protein can be lowered by reducing your total cholesterol through diet or drug therapy.

●**Ultrafast CT scan of the chest.** This sophisticated 10-minute X-ray technique detects the presence of calcium in the coronary arteries and can confirm heart disease risk.

HIGH BLOOD PRESSURE

Screening is essential because hypertension is a silent killer. It rarely causes symptoms until your arteries become blocked or your kidneys are damaged. All adults need to have their blood pressure checked each time they see their doctor—and at least once a year.

●**Home blood pressure monitoring.** If office readings are borderline (slightly above 140/90) or vary widely, buy a blood pressure monitor to check readings at home.

●**Vascular exams.** These tests measure blood flow to the extremities to detect early damage to blood vessels. If hypertension is present, postmenopausal women and men over age 40 should get an ultrasound of the carotid arteries in the neck, along with routine neurological exams.

Unless your blood pressure is very high, you may be able to control it with a low-salt diet, exercise, weight loss and other lifestyle factors. Try this approach before considering drug therapy.

STROKE

Stroke is the third-leading cause of death in the US. Among people who survive a stroke, 70% have residual physical disability.

For anyone suffering stroke symptoms, such as slurred speech, sudden numbness, weakness, confusion, double vision and/or headache, an accurate diagnosis—and immediate treatment—are crucial.

If you suspect you are having a stroke: Have someone take you to the nearest emergency room immediately. *Once there, in addition to a neurological exam, get…*

●**Brain CT scan.** It is performed to detect brain hemorrhaging. If there is no hemorrhaging, clot-dissolving drugs, such as *tissue plasminogen activator*—or tPA (Activase)—should be considered. Stroke patients given tPA are 50% less likely to suffer permanent disability.

THYROID DISEASE

The thyroid gland regulates metabolism. If it is producing too little hormone, you'll have low energy levels and weight gain. If it is producing too much hormone, you'll feel anxious and lose weight. *If you suffer these symptoms, ask for…*

●**Thyroid-stimulating hormone (TSH) blood test.** This test determines if the thyroid is functioning properly. I advise it for everyone over age 50, regardless of symptoms.

• **Ultrasound of the thyroid.** If you or your physician discovers a lump on your thyroid, have an ultrasound to determine if it's a benign cyst. If there's a tumor, your doctor should perform a fine-needle biopsy to determine if the tumor is malignant.

These Genetic Tests Could Save Your Life

Aubrey Milunsky, MD, director of the Center for Human Genetics at Boston University School of Medicine. He is the author of *Your Genetic Destiny: Know Your Genes, Secure Your Health, Save Your Life* (Perseus).

Genes influence much more than appearance and personality. More than 8,600 disorders and traits have been traced to specific genes, and many more are known to involve *several* genes.

But heredity doesn't have to be your destiny. Understanding your genetic makeup will give you a weapon to protect your health. It may even save your life.

Here's what you should know about common hereditary illnesses…

HEMOCHROMATOSIS

One person in 200 has two copies of the defective gene that causes *hemochromatosis*—a condition in which the body stores excessive iron, resulting in potentially fatal damage to the heart, liver and pancreas.

Consider DNA testing if: You experience persistent malaise and joint aches…and a close family member (parent, sibling, aunt, uncle, first cousin, grandparent) suffers from or died of heart failure, diabetes or unexplained cirrhosis of the liver. In advanced stages of hemochromatosis, distinct skin pigmentation appears—you look as if you have a tan even though you haven't been out in the sun.

If the test is positive: Your physician will arrange for you to "donate" a pint of blood once a week for three months…then once every three months. This keeps blood iron levels in check.

PULMONARY EMBOLISM

About 3% to 5% of Caucasians carry defective genes for the blood component *factor V Leiden.* About 2% carry a *prothrombin* gene mutation. These put individuals at risk for sudden death from *pulmonary embolism* (a blood clot in the lung).

Consider DNA testing if: You or a member of your family has suffered either *deep vein thrombosis*—a blood clot in the thigh or calf—or a pulmonary embolism before age 50.

If the test is positive: Women should avoid oral contraceptives. These increase clotting risk. Anyone, male or female, should alert his/her doctor if he will be immobile for a long period of time, such as after surgery—or even on a long plane or car trip.

BREAST CANCER/OVARIAN CANCER

Five to 10 percent of breast cancers are inherited—most through mutations in two specific genes, *BRCA1* and *BRCA2.* A woman who has inherited one of these two genes has an 85% risk of developing breast cancer in her lifetime—and a 40% to 65% risk of developing ovarian cancer.

Consider DNA testing if: Two or more close relatives had breast or ovarian cancer…or one relative had cancer in both breasts.

If the test is positive: Surgical removal of both breasts is an option. This does not *eliminate* cancer risk—some susceptible tissue is left behind—but reduces it to less than 10%. Removal of both ovaries is also an option.

If you opt against surgery: Discuss with your doctor how to watch for early signs of breast and ovarian cancers. He may recommend that you have regular mammograms, ultrasounds, blood tests, etc.

Important: Sons of women with breast cancer who inherit a breast cancer gene mutation are vulnerable. The half who inherit the mutant gene have a greater risk for prostate, intestinal, pancreatic or even breast cancer. Ask your doctor about how to maintain close surveillance of these organs to catch cancer early.

COLON CANCER

One to three percent of colon cancers are caused by *familial polyposis.* In this condition, hundreds—possibly thousands—of growths develop along the intestinal lining. Some of these turn malignant. There are other hereditary forms of colon cancer, too.

Consider DNA testing if: Two members of your family have had colon cancer…or one family member had familial polyposis.

If the test is positive: Removal of the colon is an option. Otherwise, keep close watch by having an annual colonoscopy.

POLYCYSTIC KIDNEY DISEASE

One person in 1,000 has this illness, which causes multiple cysts in the kidneys and leads to hypertension and kidney failure. It also raises the risk of *cerebral aneurysm*—a brain artery dilation (bubble) that is prone to rupture.

Consider DNA testing if: A close relative has the condition.

If the test is positive: Consult your doctor about kidney transplants—you may need one —and about CAT or MRI scans of the brain.

FAMILIAL MEDITERRANEAN FEVER

This disease is characterized by progressive deposits of *amyloid,* a waxy substance, in the kidneys, leading to kidney failure and, if left untreated, death.

Consider DNA testing if: You are of Armenian, Turkish, Arab or Sephardic Jewish descent…and you suffer from intermittent fever, abdominal and chest pain, arthritis or other symptoms that doctors cannot explain.

If the test is positive: Treatment with *colchicine,* an alkaloid medication in tablet form, will prevent serious kidney damage.

EMPHYSEMA

People who do not possess the *alpha-1-antitrypsin* enzyme are prone to emphysema.

Consider DNA testing if: A close family member developed chronic lung disease, particularly if he also had cirrhosis of the liver.

If the test is positive: Avoid smoking as well as prolonged contact with any dust or industrial pollutants.

WHAT ELSE YOU SHOULD KNOW

If you think you have a familial disorder, ask your doctor if he recommends DNA testing. Think carefully about the decision and the treatment options. Be aware that most—but not all—states have legislation prohibiting the use of genetic information when being considered for life or health insurance or employment. A federal bill is pending.

To find a clinical geneticist, call the department of genetics at a university medical center. Or contact the American College of Medical Genetics, 301-530-7127…*www.acmg.net.*

What Hospitals Don't Want You to Know

Timothy McCall, MD, a Boston internist, the author of *Examining Your Doctor: A Patient's Guide to Avoiding Harmful Medical Care* (Citadel Press) and a commentator for the National Public Radio program *Marketplace.*

Hospitals are fighting for their survival. Cutbacks from the federal government and from managed-care plans have reduced their revenue streams. Throughout the US, hospitals are closing, merging or implementing draconian cost-cutting measures.

But it's not just hospitals that are at risk. Corner-cutting also threatens the well-being of patients. *Here's what hospitals don't want to tell you—and what you can do about it…*

•**They're discharging patients "quicker and sicker."** To save money, hospitals are routinely discharging patients much earlier than they used to. If they plan to send you home, be sure you'll have the support services you may need, such as visiting nurses and physical therapists, and that family members will be able to perform any duties expected of them. If you do not feel your condition or home circumstances make discharge safe, alert your doctor. If necessary, file an appeal with your insurer.

•**They've cut their nursing staffs.** Even though doctors get most of the glory, it's the nurses who run hospitals. They monitor your condition, administer medications and make sure medical equipment functions properly. But maintaining a skilled nursing staff is expensive, so hospitals have found it cheaper to substitute "aides," many of whom have very little bedside training.

You have the right to inquire about the qualifications of anyone who will treat you. Ideally, your primary nurse will be a registered nurse (RN). It's best if each nurse working on a typical medical or surgical ward is caring for no more than five patients or no more than two in an intensive-care unit.

If the nurse-to-patient ratio is much higher than that, consider having family members stay with you at all times while you're hospitalized or, if you can afford it, hire a private-duty nurse.

●**They reuse disposable medical equipment.** Some equipment, such as the dialysis catheters, intended for single-use only are routinely cleaned and reused, raising some concerns about infection and product failure. While reusing equipment is not illegal, I recommend requesting that only new equipment be used.

●**They do not report inferior doctors.** Although the law mandates that incompetence or any misconduct among physicians must be reported to the federal government, 60% of hospitals have never filed even a single disciplinary report in the last decade. Part of the reason is that doctors are hospitals' "cash cows." They have the power to direct their patients to competing hospitals, so there's an incentive to not make waves.

Your best bet: Avoid potentially dangerous doctors by learning as much as you can about your condition and medications. The more you know, the better your ability to spot a bad apple.

●**They overwork residents and interns.** Although new regulations cap the work hours of doctors-in-training at 80 hours a week, in the past similar regulations have been routinely violated. If you are admitted to a teaching hospital, ask your resident or intern how many consecutive hours he/she has been working. Thirty-six-hour shifts are still routine. If you're concerned, it's your right to refuse care from anyone who looks too exhausted to provide it.

If you believe a hospital is doing anything that imperils patients, I recommend reporting it to your state's regulatory authority or contacting the not-for-profit Joint Commission on Accreditation of Healthcare Organizations at 800-994-6610 or *www.jcaho.org.* Their E-mail address is *complaint@jcaho.org.*

More from Timothy McCall...

How to Choose the Right Surgeon

Besides the severity of your medical condition, most likely the biggest factor in determining the success of any operation is the surgeon. Obviously, good ones have better technical skills. But they are also more likely to be affiliated with the hospitals and other professionals—such as topflight registered nurses and anesthesiologists—who will increase your odds of a positive outcome. Even so, numerous people simply use whatever surgeon they are assigned by the hospital, their primary-care provider or HMO.

It's not necessary to find the absolute best surgeon—usually, that isn't even possible. Your job is to make a reasonable choice in the time available and—most importantly—to avoid a bad surgeon.

Here's what I suggest...

●**Get a few names to begin your search.** If you have a primary-care doctor you know and trust, ask which surgeon he/she would choose for a loved one—and why. Also ask which surgeons are held in particularly high esteem by their colleagues. The answers may differ.

Remember, doctors sometimes make referrals based on friendship, reciprocal business relationships (you refer to me, I'll refer to you) or institutional affiliations, so it's wise to cast a wider net. If you have friends who work in local hospitals or clinics or who are otherwise in the know, ask them for the scuttlebutt on top surgeons.

●**Check credentials.** If the surgeon is on the faculty of a local medical school or on staff at a respected hospital—both good signs—chances are, he is board-certified. This means the doctor has completed a residency at an accredited hospital and passed a rigorous certifying exam. To find out if a doctor is board-certified, consult the American Board of Medical Specialties' Web site at *www.abms.org* or call 866-275-2267. Also check the fields in which the doctor is certified. For example, a doctor who performs liposuction should be certified in plastic surgery, not just in general surgery or family practice.

● **Ask about the surgeon's experience.** How many times has the doctor performed the operation in question? How many of those procedures were done, say, this year? There's no magic cutoff, but the more a doctor has done, the better. For heart surgery, I'd want a surgeon who does at least 100 a year.

Experience is particularly important for complicated operations, such as heart or brain surgery, and for newer procedures, including some "minimally invasive" laparoscopic operations, with which most doctors may have only limited experience. Ask the doctor what specific training he has had in the procedure you may undergo.

● **Ask about the surgeon's track record.** You want to find out not only how many operations a surgeon has done, but also how his patients have fared. Did they experience any wound infections or need to have the procedure repeated? Which complications have been most common? If a surgeon you're considering bristles at these questions or even declines to answer, look elsewhere.

● **Ask where the operation will be performed.** For heart surgery, you want to be at an institution that does at least 200 a year, according to recent studies. Community hospitals may be fine for routine procedures, such as hernia repair or gallbladder removal. But for complex or rare procedures, you are generally better off at a major teaching hospital.

● **Be suspicious of surgeons who are too "gung-ho."** The surgeons who always want to operate make me nervous. Surgery may *not* be the best option. One of the best orthopedic surgeons I've ever met routinely tries to talk patients out of having any operation he is not convinced will help them. When he recommends surgery, you know you need it.

Six Dangerous Myths About Antibiotics

Stuart B. Levy, MD, president of the Alliance for the Prudent Use of Antibiotics, *www.apua.org*, and director of the Center for Adaptation Genetics and Drug Resistance at Tufts University School of Medicine, both are located in Boston. He is the author of *The Antibiotic Paradox: How the Misuse of Antibiotics Destroys Their Curative Powers* (Perseus Books).

The antibiotic *ciprofloxacin* (Cipro) has been taken by thousands of Americans who may have been exposed to the spores of the bacterium that causes anthrax.

Unfortunately, practically one out of five of these people have suffered side effects, including itching, breathing problems and swelling of the face, neck or throat, according to the Centers for Disease Control and Prevention.

Even though many people think that antibiotics are relatively harmless, they can endanger your health—and the health of your family.

Here are the six most common misconceptions about antibiotics…

***Misconception:* Antibiotics kill viruses.**

Antibiotics attack only bacteria—they do not kill off viruses. Antibiotics are not effective for upper-respiratory viral ailments such as colds, flu and coughs.

***Misconception:* It's a good idea to stockpile antibiotics in case you get sick.**

By stockpiling antibiotics in your home, you may be tempted to take them without a physician's advice.

Self-medication could cause unexpected side effects and propagate resistant bacteria, which can pass to other family members and the rest of your community. Also, taking antibiotics or any drugs that are not stored properly and/or are used after the expiration date can cause liver and kidney damage.

***Misconception:* There's really no harm in taking antibiotics even if you do not need them.**

Any time you take an antibiotic unnecessarily, you risk side effects.

Also, some of the bacteria in your body survive and develop resistance to the drug. These bacteria inevitably pass to other people, creating a pool of antibiotic-resistant bacteria. When someone else develops an infection with antibiotic-resistant bacteria, the drugs may not work.

The only way to prevent this problem is for each of us to use antibiotics *only when necessary*. This means relying on a physician to diagnose your condition and prescribe antibiotics accordingly.

Misconception: It is okay to stop taking antibiotics as soon as your symptoms begin to subside.

You may start feeling better a few days after starting an antibiotic, but you must continue to take the drug for the full course of the prescription.

If you don't, surviving bacteria can reactivate the infection. Taking only a partial course of antibiotics is also more likely to create antibiotic-resistant bacteria.

Misconception: Antibiotic resistance is only a theoretical problem.

Not true. Bacteria have developed resistance to multiple antibiotics. Some bacteria now exist that are resistant to every antibiotic on the market today.

In 1992, less than 10% of US patients infected with *Streptococcus pneumoniae* (which causes pneumococcus pneumonia, ear infections and meningitis) experienced penicillin resistance.

A recent report in *The New England Journal of Medicine* showed that the frequency increased to 21% in 1995 and 25% in 1998. During that time, the bacteria's frequency of resistance to three or more types of antibiotics increased from 9% to 14%.

In hospitals, once-powerful antibiotics, such as methicillin, can no longer be relied upon to kill the common *Staphylococcus aureus* bacterium, which causes life-threatening blood poisoning. In fact, this bacterium is often resistant to whole classes of antibiotics, including *penicillins, cephalosporins, aminoglycosides* and *quinolones*.

Misconception: It's easy for researchers to develop new, stronger antibiotics.

This was true when penicillin was first being widely used back in the 1940s. At that point, scientists knew that pathogenic bacteria died when put in the soil and theorized that the

earth might be a rich source of additional antibacterial chemicals.

They were right. They discovered new antibiotics in soil all over the world.

Now, most of those antibiotics are no longer effective because so many bacteria are resistant to them. As a result, scientists are creating synthetic versions—a process that is much more expensive and time-consuming than finding an antibiotic in nature.

What's more, scientists are finding it difficult to produce synthetic antibiotics to treat drug-resistant strains of bacteria. The days of rapid discovery of new, ever-stronger antibiotic miracle drugs are over.

Best Timing for Medications

William J. Elliott, MD, PhD, a professor of preventive medicine, internal medicine and pharmacology at Rush Medical College of Rush University, Chicago.

Any medication you take will work better when it is taken at the appropriate time of day.

Asthma: A dose of inhaled corticosteroids taken at dinnertime works nearly as well as four doses taken throughout the day. Oral prednisone works better when taken at 3 pm than at 8 am.

Hay fever: Antihistamines are generally more effective when taken in the evening.

High cholesterol: Taken in the evening, most cholesterol-lowering drugs are up to 35% more effective than the very same dose taken in the morning.

Osteoarthritis: Pain is most common in the afternoon and evening, so take medicine in the morning to be sure the highest concentration is in your body when needed.

Rheumatoid arthritis: Pain caused by this condition usually peaks in the morning, so it may be helpful to take this medicine just before your bedtime.

Check with your doctor *before* changing the times you take your current medications.

Goof-Proof Surgery

Before undergoing surgery, write "no"—or ask your surgeon to write it—on the leg, knee, arm, etc., that should *not* be operated on. Many patients are more comforted by writing "no" on a healthy body part than by the more standard practice of writing "yes" on the area requiring surgery. The word "yes" also runs the risk of being washed off when the site is prepared for surgery.

Saul N. Schreiber, MD, an orthopedic surgeon in private practice in Phoenix.

Secrets of Safe, Pain-Free Surgery

Michael J. Murray, MD, PhD, professor and chair of anesthesiology at Mayo Medical School in Jacksonville, FL. He is coauthor of Clinical Anesthesiology (McGraw-Hill).

Most people who need an operation are interested in finding a good surgeon. Few of us focus very much attention on the anesthesiologist.

Anyone who is scheduled to undergo surgery has the right to select the anesthesiologist. But the reality is that the surgeon frequently makes the choice.

Either way, it is a good idea to schedule a talk with the anesthesiologist at least one day before the operation.

Here are seven smart questions to ask...

●**Is the surgical facility equipped for emergencies?** If you're having surgery in a hospital or a hospital-based outpatient clinic, the answer is most likely "yes." Both must meet tough national safety standards established by the Joint Commission on Accreditation of Healthcare Organizations (JCAHO).

In such settings, your chances of anesthesia-related complications are only one in 200,000.

Freestanding outpatient clinics and private physicians' offices aren't scrutinized as closely, and some states don't regulate them at all. Mishaps, while still uncommon, are *four times* more likely to occur here than at a hospital.

●**Will you be in the operating room during the entire surgery?** Your best shot at glitch-free surgery is when a qualified professional is present throughout the procedure to administer the anesthetic and monitor your blood pressure, heart rate, breathing, body temperature and other vital signs.

This can be either an anesthesiologist (a medical doctor who has completed a three-year anesthesia residency) or a certified registered nurse anesthetist who is supervised by a surgeon, physician or an anesthesiologist. Hospitals require that an anesthesiologist or nurse anesthetist be present during all surgeries.

Independent clinics *are not* governed by the same rules. Nurse anesthetists frequently work without supervision. Another possibility is that no one, other than your surgeon, dentist or plastic surgeon, is there to keep tabs on your vital signs.

In such cases, you should be certain that a pulse oximeter is clipped to your finger or to an earlobe to measure the oxygen levels in your bloodstream.

●**Do I have a choice of anesthesia?** For some surgeries, you don't have a choice—you must be asleep. In most other cases, however, you usually can—and should—pick out your type of anesthesia. *Your choices include...*

●General anesthesia is given intravenously or as an inhaled gas. It causes complete unconsciousness. General anesthesia is best used for major surgery, such as open-heart procedures.

●Regional anesthesia includes spinal and epidural anesthesia. It numbs only a section of your body, allowing you to stay awake. Regional anesthesia is often used for childbirth, orthopedic surgery and prostate surgery.

●Local anesthesia is usually reserved for minor procedures that require a pain-block only at the site of surgery. It allows you to stay awake. Local anesthesia is best used for minor surgery, such as hand or foot procedures.

●Monitored anesthesia care (MAC) is often used to supplement local or regional anesthesia. Low doses of sedatives are given intravenously to induce light sleep, but patients remain responsive.

•What do you need to know about my medical history before surgery? Underlying medical problems, such as diabetes, asthma, heart problems or arthritis, as well as prescription medications, over-the-counter pain relievers, like aspirin, and herbal supplements can alter the effectiveness of the anesthetic.

Tell your anesthesiologist *everything*, no matter how trivial or embarrassing. This includes any health condition that has sent you to a doctor within the last two years or requires medication…any family or personal history of anesthesia complications…any bleeding tendencies from taking anticlotting medications, such as aspirin or *warfarin* (Coumadin)…and any allergies (including allergies to particular painkillers—or even to surgical tape).

Smoking, alcohol use and illegal drug use should also be noted, even if you're uncomfortable discussing such things.

Remember, divulging this information could possibly save your life. By knowing your medical conditions, the anesthesiologist will be prepared to treat them should surgical complications arise.

This is also the time to sort through your after-surgery pain-relief options, which include everything from pills to a patient-controlled IV pump. Discuss your preferences with your doctor and anesthesiologist.

•What if I wake up during surgery? You are unlikely to regain full consciousness during your procedure, but occasionally people will become vaguely aware of what's going on around them. If this happens, you will still be anesthetized enough so you won't feel pain.

Chances are your anesthesiologist will notice signs of consciousness, such as rising blood pressure, before you do—and then adjust your anesthesia accordingly.

•Can I take something before surgery to calm my nerves? Absolutely. Your anesthesiologist can administer a tranquilizer, such as *diazepam* (Valium) or *alprazolam* (Xanax), if you request one.

Talk very openly with your anesthesiologist about your fears. Many people who are about to undergo surgery worry about not waking up again. No fear is too silly to mention.

•Will I have side effects from anesthesia? Other than feeling woozy and light-headed, side effects should be minor. If you're in pain after the procedure, ask your anesthesiologist immediately to boost your pain medication or switch to something else. Don't be afraid to speak up.

With general anesthesia, your throat may be mildly sore. That's because a breathing tube is inserted during surgery to assist breathing. The soreness should diminish within 24 hours. To avoid this discomfort, ask if you can use a breathing mask instead of a breathing tube.

Music Soothes Anxiety During Surgery

In a recent study, patients undergoing cataract or glaucoma surgery under local anesthesia suffered less stress and maintained normal blood pressure when they listened to music of their choice.

If you are scheduled for surgery with a local anesthetic: Ask your doctor if you can listen to music during the procedure.

Karen Allen, PhD, research scientist, State University of New York, Buffalo.

Secrets of Speedy Rehabilitation After Stroke, Surgery or Injury

Kristjan T. Ragnarsson, MD, professor and chairman of the department of rehabilitation medicine at Mount Sinai School of Medicine in New York City.

Nearly 70% of Americans will require some form of physical rehabilitation during their lifetimes.

For most people recovering from a serious illness or injury, a program of exercise and other physical therapies is just as important as the medical treatment they receive.

Here are steps that you can take to ensure the success of a rehabilitation program…

●**Ask the doctor who treated your illness or injury for a referral for physical therapy.** Rehabilitation can take place on an inpatient or outpatient basis, depending on your condition. Your doctor should recommend a treatment plan and prescribe a specific number of rehabilitation sessions.

●**Compare facilities.** First, find out which rehabilitation programs are covered by your insurance…check out the reputation of each institution you're considering…then pay each a visit.

Helpful: Ask a staff member if you can speak to some former patients. Visit at least three facilities before selecting one.

Whether inpatient or outpatient, the rehabilitation facility should…

●Provide appropriate therapy—whether it be physical, occupational* or speech.

●Offer a broad range of treatments for your specific problem.

Example: Therapies to treat inflammation and pain often include massage, ultrasound, whirlpool baths, electrical stimulation devices as well as heat sources.

The standard strength-training and aerobic equipment includes free weights and weight-lifting machines, *Thera-Bands* (elastic bands used to train muscles), balance boards, treadmills, exercise bikes

*Occupational therapy helps patients resume activities at home and at work.

and "water treadmills," which allow you to walk or run in a tank of waist-deep water.

●Be within easy commuting distance of your home or office.

●Be clean, well-maintained and have a bright and cheerful ambience.

Important: Inpatient programs should be accredited by the Rehabilitation Accreditation Commission at 520-325-1044 or *www.carf.org*.

●**Check staff credentials.** Licensing varies from state to state, but the supervising therapist should be a registered physical therapist (RPT) or an occupational therapist (OT) with a master's degree.

Helpful: Ask how many years of experience is typical for the facility's RPTs and OTs… and whether they participate in continuing-education programs. Also find out how many patients each therapist is assigned per hour. For optimal care, it should be no more than three.

●**Make sure you have "good chemistry" with your therapy team.** Since physical and occupational therapy involve a great deal of repetition, success depends largely on staying motivated. That is why you should have a good rapport with your team.

Meet briefly with every member of your team before signing up with a facility, and find out each person's area of responsibility. All team members should be friendly, supportive and available.

If you feel the chemistry is not good with one or more members of your team, ask for another therapist or switch facilities.

●**Be sure that you can confidently perform your exercises before returning to home.** Your supervising therapist should be available to answer any questions that may come up later. You should also schedule a follow-up visit with your physician within one month to monitor your progress.

●**Enlist the support of family and friends.** Once your formal rehabilitation is completed, have a relative or friend assist—or "spot"—you during your exercises to keep you motivated… and safe.

●**Address psychological needs.** A physical injury or lengthy illness can trigger a wide range of emotions, from frustration to clinical depression. These feelings can limit your ability to stick with your rehabilitation program.

If negative feelings persist, talk to your doctor about getting psychotherapy. Drug treatment may also be needed.

Secrets of Safer Cosmetic Surgery

Alan M. Engler, MD, an assistant clinical professor of plastic surgery at Albert Einstein College of Medicine in New York City. He is the author of *BodySculpture: Plastic Surgery of the Body for Men and Women* (Hudson Publishing). *www.bodysculpture.com.*

Improved surgical methods have made face-lifts, tummy tucks, liposuction and breast surgery (for women and men) increasingly safe and effective. But complications do occur. These range from adverse anesthesia reactions and infection to botched procedures resulting in permanent disfigurement.

To minimize your risks, take these recommended precautions...

●**Insist on a top-notch surgeon.** This is not as straightforward as it sounds. While family members, friends and colleagues may refer you to a competent internist or even a psychiatrist, most people are exceedingly private when it comes to cosmetic surgery.

Looking in the phone book is a gamble. Anyone with a medical degree can legally perform plastic surgery—no special training or certification is necessary.

Indeed, many doctors who perform cosmetic surgery are actually certified in such fields as dermatology...ear, nose and throat...or ophthalmology. These doctors may be competent cosmetic surgeons, but the fact is that they may never have had to demonstrate this competence before a professional board.

Good place to start: Choose a surgeon who is a member of The American Society for Aesthetic Plastic Surgery (888-272-7711, *www. surgery.org*). Members are certified by the American Board of Plastic Surgery and have demonstrated expertise in cosmetic procedures.

●**Query your doctor.** When it comes to cosmetic surgery, do not rely on a prospective surgeon as your primary source of information. When you arrive for your initial consultation, you should be knowledgeable about the procedure you are interested in.

Read about the procedure in books, magazines and on the Internet. Two helpful sites are *www.surgery.org,* mentioned earlier, and *www.plasticsurgery.org,* sponsored by the American Society of Plastic Surgeons and the Plastic Surgery Educational Foundation.

Come prepared with a short list of questions.

Examples: Which surgical technique do you use for this procedure? May I see photos of your work? How are emergencies handled if they occur?

This will allow you to focus your attention and instincts on deciding if the surgeon (rather than the surgery) is right for you.

Plan on interviewing two or three surgeons —but if you happen to click with the very first one, that may be enough.

●**Be prudent when it comes to anesthesia.** Cosmetic surgery may be done under general anesthesia, regional anesthesia (an epidural) or local anesthesia with or without intravenous sedation. You may have a strong preference for a certain type of anesthesia. But listen to the surgeon's recommendation.

For your own safety, do not insist that the doctor use a form of anesthesia with which he and his team have little experience. If the surgeon seems uncomfortable working with the type of anesthesia that you're determined to have, find another surgeon.

Ideally, the anesthesiologist will be board-certified. To confirm an anesthesiologist's certification, contact the American Board of Medical Specialties, 866-275-2267, *www.abms.org.*

In some parts of the country (particularly in rural areas) or if a surgeon prefers it, anesthesia may be provided by a certified registered nurse anesthetist (CRNA). These are specially trained nurses who deliver anesthetic to more than half the patients who undergo surgery in the US each year.

If a CRNA will administer your anesthetic, check for certification by the Council on Certification of Nurse Anesthetists (800-255-1312, *www.aana.com/crna*).

•**Choose an accredited surgical facility.** Cosmetic surgery may be performed in the hospital, a surgery center or a surgeon's office. If you're over age 60 or have an underlying medical condition, such as heart disease or diabetes, consider having the surgery done in a hospital. It is better equipped to handle emergencies.

For shorter operations (up to four hours) and for relatively healthy patients, the privacy, personalized care and lower costs of an office setting are often preferable.

Crucial: If your surgery will take place in an office, be certain the office is accredited by an independent organization, such as the American Association for Accreditation of Ambulatory Surgery Facilities (888-545-5222, *www.aaaasf.org*). It establishes and oversees stringent quality and safety standards.

•**Reconsider if you have diabetes or a vascular disorder or if you smoke.** Certain plastic surgery procedures, such as face-lifts and tummy tucks, require that the skin and other tissues survive temporarily on a relatively reduced blood supply. There is a higher risk of complications in people with conditions (or habits) that inhibit circulation.

•**Give yourself enough time to recuperate.** Clear your schedule for at least one week following all but the most minor procedures, such as light peels, collagen injections and minor liposuctions. Plan on taking off for at least two weeks for major operations, such as tummy tucks and face-lifts.

Expect some pain and swelling for at least the first few days after surgery. Some patients report only mild discomfort. Others experience severe pain.

Caution: Postoperative fever, shortness of breath, asymmetrical pain (significant pain on only one side of the operative area, such as one breast or one eye), redness or swelling (particularly with breast implants) may indicate infection or excessive bleeding. These symptoms require immediate medical attention.

Make sure you know how to get in touch with your doctor after hours—or which hospital emergency department to go to.

•**Beware outrageous claims.** A face-lift can help you look younger, but it won't stop the clock. Liposuction can improve the appearance of problem areas, but it can't cure obesity, eliminate cellulite or prevent future weight gain.

Before undergoing cosmetic surgery, make sure that you understand what can and cannot be accomplished, how long the results are likely to last and what kind of maintenance might be required.

Be wary of any surgeon who promises to make you look 30 if you are 50 or give you perfectly contoured abdominals when you are grossly overweight. Such promises inevitably lead to disappointment...or worse.

Example: Several years ago, a number of liposuction deaths were linked to excessive removal of fat. Most experts now agree that 10 pounds of fat is about the most that should be removed at one time. More can be removed several months later. The exact amount depends on the patient's height, weight and other factors.

Dramatic results are preferred, but not at the expense of safety.

•**Do *not* get ambushed by hidden costs.** Cosmetic surgery shouldn't leave you shocked when you look at your bill. Ask beforehand what your *total* costs will be, including separate anesthesia or facility fees. Also ask if there is a policy regarding fees if any minor revisions are called for.

Emergency Room Self-Defense

Ted Christopher, MD, chief of the division of emergency medicine at Thomas Jefferson University Hospital in Philadelphia.

Hospital emergency departments (EDs) are busier now than ever. In 1999, there were 103 million ED visits in the US, according to a new study by the Centers for Disease Control and Prevention. That is up from 90 million in 1992—an increase of 35,000 patients a day.

Because of decreasing health-care budgets, examining rooms and equipment are in short supply. Doctors, nurses and technicians are overworked. No wonder the average wait to see a doctor is 49 minutes—with many ED patients waiting hours.

For better emergency care…

●**Call 911 or an ambulance if you suspect heart attack or stroke,** two "time-dependent" conditions that can quickly worsen. Ambulance technicians will begin your care on the way…and you'll be seen by a doctor as soon as you arrive at the hospital.

If your condition isn't truly an emergency, arriving by ambulance won't make a difference, and you could get stuck with the bill. The sickest patients always get taken care of first.

●**Go to the closest hospital if you think you have an emergency.** The majority of all hospital EDs are now being staffed with board-certified emergency physicians. Teaching hospitals are staffed with attending emergency physicians and many residents and interns. In nonteaching hospitals, there will be only one or two doctors on staff. You may spend time waiting in either setting.

●**Don't wait for a referral from your doctor.** It is no longer necessary to bring a referral or get prior approval from your doctor before going to the ED.

Everyone who comes to the ED undergoes *triage.* That's the process by which each patient is evaluated by a nurse to determine how serious his/her condition is and who is to be seen first by a doctor.

●**Know the names and phone numbers of all your doctors**—especially your primary-care physician, but also any specialists you may have seen. Your private doctors often possess medical information that can assist the emergency physician in treating you.

●**Bring all of your medications.** ED staff will learn a lot about your health history simply by reading the labels. If you're going to need drugs, it's vital that the doctors know what medications you're taking.

Helpful: Keep a list of all your medications, along with the details of other health information (serious allergies, for example), on the refrigerator door. If you're unable to talk, the ambulance crew can take the list to the ED.

Even better: Bring the actual bottles—the printed labels are easiest to read.

●**Report changes in symptoms immediately.** Don't suffer in silence in the waiting room. You'll see a doctor more quickly if you inform the staff that your symptoms are getting worse. You should be given medication, if necessary, even before you see a doctor.

3

Simple Remedies for Common Ailments

Doctor-Approved Folk Remedies That Work

While we were growing up in Brooklyn, our mother had an old folk remedy for almost everything when we got sick. And if she did not, our grandmother did.

Folk remedies don't work for everyone, but they are worth a try. They are generally inexpensive, easy to follow, time-tested and safe (the hundreds of remedies in our books have all been doctor-approved). Only the effective remedies are passed down from generation to generation—the rest are left behind.

Everyone knows about prunes for constipation and cranberry juice for urinary-tract infections. *Here are some lesser-known favorites...*

ARTHRITIS

If you are plagued by morning stiffness, put a sleeping bag on your bed and zip yourself in for the night. Your own body heat will be trapped in the sleeping bag and will be evenly distributed.

This seems to be much safer than using an electric blanket or a heating pad and more effective in terms of ease of movement upon waking in the morning.

COMMON COLDS

Garlic, with its chemical compound *allicin,* is a natural antibiotic with antiviral, antifungal and antiseptic properties. It can also act as a decongestant and an expectorant.

So, when you have a bad cold, what is even better than chicken soup? Chicken soup with a clove of minced raw garlic.

GOUT

The classic folk remedy for gout is to eat four ounces of fresh Bing cherries daily. If cherries are not in season, drink bottled cherry juice or buy cherry-juice concentrate (at health food stores) and have one tablespoon three times a

Joan and Lydia Wilen of New York City. The Wilen sisters are authors of a dozen books, including the bestsellers Chicken Soup & Other Folk Remedies *(Ballantine) and* Folk Remedies That Work *(Harper).*

day. You can also eat frozen or canned cherries. While you're at it, add strawberries to your shopping list. They neutralize uric acid, a buildup of which causes this condition.

HANGOVER

To ease the symptoms of a hangover, cut a wedge of lemon and rub it on your armpits. As outrageous as this sounds, it works.

The doctor hired by our publisher to review each remedy in our book wrote in the margin, *Great remedy.*

HAY FEVER

To relieve runny nose, sneezing and itchy, red eyes, chew a one-inch square of honeycomb. Swallow the honey and continue to chew the waxy gum for about 10 minutes, then spit it out.

Buy honeycomb that was collected in your local area so that it contains the same pollen that is causing your symptoms.

Most health food stores carry honeycomb. Check the packaging to be sure that it is from your part of the country.

To help immunize yourself, chew a one-inch square of honeycomb daily, starting a month or two before hay fever season.

Caution: Of course, if you are allergic to honey, do not use this remedy.

HEADACHE

Peel a long, wide (one- to two-inch) strip of lemon rind. Rub the inside of the peel (pith) on your temples. Put the rind across your forehead, securing it in place with a bandage or a handkerchief.

While we were on a television show, the host told us he had a three-day-old headache. Nothing he tried had worked. We put the rind on his forehead and, 20 minutes later, his headache was gone.

INDIGESTION AND GAS

Prepare ginger tea by covering one tablespoon of fresh gingerroot with one cup of just-boiled water. Let it steep for 10 minutes. Strain and drink after a gassy and/or fatty meal. It helps digestion and helps get rid of the gas.

Keep gingerroot in the freezer to make it easier to grate. If the ginger is not frozen, simply cut three or four quarter-sized pieces of the fresh root for your tea. If you don't have fresh ginger, mix one-half teaspoon of ginger powder in one cup of hot water. It is effective but doesn't taste as good.

INSOMNIA

For occasional sleeplessness, cut up a yellow onion into chunks, and put them in a covered jar on your nightstand.

When you are tossing and turning, uncover the jar and take a deep whiff. Close the jar, lie back and think lovely thoughts. You should be asleep within 15 minutes.

In the morning, discard the onion. Do not use the same one night after night.

LEG CRAMPS

Some people wake up in the middle of the night with leg cramps. Others get them after exercising. In either case, place a piece of silverware—a spoon is safest—right on the cramp. The spoon does not have to be sterling—stainless steel will do the trick.

Another cramp solution: Pinch your philtrum—the area between your nose and upper lip—until the cramp is gone. It usually takes just a few seconds. Use this remedy when you don't have a piece of silverware handy.

SORE THROAT

Mix two teaspoons of apple cider vinegar in one glass of warm water. Gargle a mouthful, spit it out, then swallow a mouthful. Keep doing this until you finish the glass. Repeat the entire process every hour. Within three to four hours, the sore throat is usually history.

Additional help: Drink pineapple juice. It contains healing enzymes that soothe irritated throat tissues and may help them heal faster.

STY

As soon as you feel a sty coming on, rub the area a few times with a gold ring. The gold may prevent it from becoming one of those atrocious, full-blown infections that can linger for a week or more.

A few years ago, Joan woke up with a sty on each eye. We were scheduled to do a TV show that day. She took a gold ring and rubbed her lids. By the time we arrived at the studio, both of her eyes were fine.

Eight Ways To Feel More Energetic

Jamison Starbuck, ND, a naturopathic physician in family practice and a lecturer at the University of Montana, both in Missoula. She is past president of the American Association of Naturopathic Physicians and a contributing editor to The Alternative Advisor: The Complete Guide to Natural Therapies and Alternative Treatments *(Time Life).*

If you are over age 40, fatigue is likely to be a frequent complaint. And if you're like many people, your doctor has checked you over and proclaimed that you're fine. "You are just getting older" is the typical refrain.

The obvious solution is to get more sleep. To be productive, most middle-aged adults need at least seven hours each night. But some people get adequate sleep—and still feel tired. If that's the case, don't head for the rocker. *Try these strategies to get more pep...*

•**Drink more water.** It's an old saw, but true. Most folks just don't drink enough water. That's too bad because dehydration makes us sluggish. To determine how many ounces of water you should drink each day, divide your weight in pounds by two. Add an extra eight ounces for every 30 minutes of aerobic exercise you perform, plus an additional eight ounces for every cup of caffeinated coffee, black tea or soda that you consume.

•**Take a daily B-complex vitamin supplement.** The B vitamins provide energy and help maintain healthy muscle and nerve cells. Aging and stress increase our need for these vitamins, while alcohol and caffeine deplete them from our bodies. Take a B supplement daily with breakfast. Make sure it contains at least 50 mg each of B-1, B-3, B-5 and B-6... and 400 micrograms (mcg) each of B-12 and folic acid.

•**Try licorice.** This herb improves immune health, so it's a great tonic for people with fatigue. Use the herb, not the candy. Take one-half teaspoon of tincture daily for up to two months.

Caution: Check with your doctor before trying this—or any—herbal remedy. Licorice is not safe for people with high blood pressure or liver or kidney disease.

If you dislike the taste of licorice: Try schisandra. Like licorice, this herb helps the body to overcome exhaustion by enhancing immune function. Take one-half teaspoon of the tincture daily for up to two months.

•**Exercise.** Starting an exercise program can be very overwhelming if you suffer from fatigue. That's why I recommend some gentle stretching exercises combined with walking. For specific exercises, get a copy of the book *Stretching* written by Bob and Jean Anderson and published by Shelter.

•**Lose weight.** Even a small weight gain is enough to make some people tired. Hard to believe? Imagine strapping a 10-pound bag of sugar to your back and taking it with you everywhere you go. You'll have more energy if you drop unnecessary body weight.

•**Declutter.** Living in a mess—and feeling guilty about it—is tiring. Clutter also distracts the mind, making it more difficult to concentrate. Get just one room—or even one area—organized. You'll get a boost.

•**Pare down your schedule.** Doing less is not easy. But overscheduling is a primary cause of fatigue. If you're often tired, keep a journal of your daily activities for one week. You'll probably find that you are doing more than you think. Is all of it necessary? Is it enjoyable? If not, eliminate some activities and make time for rest and pleasure.

•**Have fun.** We all know that laughter is essential to physical well-being. But, sadly, merriment is a foreign concept for some people. Finding delight in life is energizing. Whether it's mountain climbing or reading in a hammock, find the things that give you a lift and indulge.

More from Jamison Starbuck...

Effective Remedies from Your Kitchen Cabinet

Next time you're searching for relief from an acute ailment, look in your kitchen. Chances are you'll find as many remedies there as in your medicine chest.

Some people are reluctant to consider any home remedies because they must be prepared. But they're worth the effort. Why? With natural medicines, you can avoid potentially harmful constituents, such as dyes, preservatives and synthetic binders that are so common in conventional over-the-counter (OTC) medicines. You can also ensure that the ingredients are fresh or, if you prefer, organic. And home remedies almost always cost less than OTC products.

Here are several conditions for which quick and easy home remedies are effective…

•**Cold.** Try *ginger tea.* Both an antiviral and anti-inflammatory remedy, it helps prevent chills and reduces the buildup of phlegm.

What to do: Peel and thinly slice a two-inch piece of fresh gingerroot (available in the produce section of grocery stores). Put it in a saucepan and cover with 12 ounces of water. Bring to a boil, then gently simmer for seven minutes. Strain, add honey and the juice of one-half fresh lemon. Sip six ounces every three hours.

•**Flu.** For a light, nutritious meal while you are nursing the flu, your best bet is "quick" miso soup. *Miso soup* contains enzymes that assist in fighting viruses.

What to do: Put one heaping tablespoon of miso (available in the refrigerated grocery section of health food stores) in a bowl. Add one thinly sliced raw carrot, then pour in six ounces of boiling water, stirring to dissolve the paste-like miso. Add one garlic clove and a pinch of cayenne. Squeeze in the juice of one-quarter fresh lemon.

•**Sinus congestion.** To clear your nasal and sinus passages, try a steam inhalation with dried *thyme leaves.* Thyme is a good antiseptic and decongestant.

What to do: Pour a quart of boiling water into a bowl. Add a heaping teaspoon of dried thyme leaves. Drape a large, dry cotton towel over your head and hold your face about 12 inches above the bowl. Breathe in the thyme-laced steam for eight minutes. Then gently blow your nose.

•**Bladder infection.** If you experience the early symptoms of a bladder infection—such as pain when urinating or increased frequency—try some parsley tea. Most people think that cranberry juice is their only choice. But parsley, a mild natural diuretic that contains virtually no calories, also flushes the bladder of pesky organisms that can cause infection. It's a good choice for people who don't like cranberry juice. Drink parsley tea alone—or alternate it throughout the day with cranberry juice.

What to do: Bring one quart of water to a boil, turn off the heat and add one cup of fresh parsley, stems and leaves. Cover and steep for 15 minutes. Strain and drink one cup of cool tea over a two-hour period. Repeat the process four hours later. If your symptoms worsen or persist for more than 24 hours, see your health-care provider.

Also from Jamison Starbuck…

Best Cures for Common Skin Problems

If you've got a common skin ailment, such as acne or eczema, chances are you can get rid of it for good—if you are willing to change your diet and lifestyle.

Consider the experience of Nora, one of my patients. She had *lichen planus,* an eruptive, inflammatory skin disorder. Her hands, lower legs and gums were a mess—bloody, cracked and peeling. Working, dressing and even showering were torture.

Medical doctors don't know the cause of lichen planus or, for that matter, many other common skin conditions. They will prescribe hydrocortisone or the antifungal creams and mouthwashes. When these don't help, doctors will try oral antihistamines and corticosteroids.

For three months, Nora applied prescription topical drugs. When none of these worked, she came to me. As part of her treatment plan, I had Nora give up doughnuts, pasta and diet cola. She also replaced her nightly television habit with walking and yoga. In one month, her skin had improved.

In my experience, skin problems are best cured from the "inside out." Though it's often difficult to make dietary and lifestyle changes, this approach to skin conditions is effective about 80% of the time.

For starters, keep a diet diary for one week. Milk, peanuts, wheat, corn, chocolate and/or caffeinated beverages are often the culprits in eczema, a red, moist, itchy rash usually on the hands and face. Though medical doctors don't necessarily agree, adult acne and seborrheic dermatitis, which causes dandruff or scaly patches on the scalp, are associated with fatty foods, such as meat and french fries. If you eat more than one serving per day of any of these foods, there is a good chance it's contributing to your skin problem. Remove these foods from your diet for three weeks, and look for improvement.

As you're removing harmful substances from your body, you should add *gamma linolenic acid* (GLA) and "friendly" intestinal bacteria, such as *lactobacillus acidophilus* and *bifidus*. GLA, a fatty acid that has anti-inflammatory properties, is found in borage oil and evening primrose oil. Take 2,000 mg daily of either oil in capsule form. In addition, take three billion units each of acidophilus and bifidus daily. They help the body to absorb beneficial fatty acids.

To improve the circulation to your skin, exercise for at least 20 minutes daily. Since B vitamins are important in maintaining healthy skin and are quickly depleted during times of stress, take a B-complex daily supplement that contains at least 50 mg of B-6. This can be taken in addition to a multivitamin. To avoid nausea, be sure to take all vitamins with food.

Anxiety will increase inflammation, which just aggravates skin problems. Soothe your nerves—and your skin—by taking a formula of equal parts valerian, hops and chamomile in an alcohol extract. *Dosage:* 60 drops of the mixture in the morning and evening until symptoms improve.

Finally, use a gentle, natural topical remedy to encourage healthy skin growth…

●**Acne:** Tincture of equal parts calendula and goldenseal. Apply directly to acne lesions twice daily after washing with lukewarm water.

●**Eczema:** Calendula salve, in a base of olive oil and vitamin E. Apply several times daily.

●**Seborrheic dermatitis:** Mix six drops of lavender essential oil and one-quarter teaspoon of vitamin E oil—the equivalent of two capsules—into one-half ounce of sesame oil. Apply twice daily to dry patches on the scalp.

Basil Repels Mosquitoes

Rubbing a handful of fresh basil leaves on your skin should protect you from mosquitoes for a few hours. The herb does not contain hazardous chemicals and is less likely than synthetic bug sprays to cause skin irritation. It's also cheaper.

James A. Duke, PhD, a Fulton, Maryland–based author of 25 books including *The Green Pharmacy* (Rodale Press), and past chief of the US Department of Agriculture's medicinal plant laboratory.

Healing Teas

Victoria Zak, award-winning researcher and writer in the health-care field, Holliston, MA. She is the author of *20,000 Secrets of Tea* (Dell). In writing the book, Ms. Zak tested all of the herbs and consulted with herbalists and doctors of naturopathy about their use.

The right kind of teas can really work magic on a wide variety of common illnesses and ailments.

Rule of thumb: Drink a cup of tea one to three times a day until the problem subsides… then use intermittently to maintain health. Experiment to see which herbs or blends work best for you.

Important: Check with your physician before using any herbal treatment—particularly if you are taking prescription medications or are under a doctor's care.

And see your doctor if symptoms persist for more than one week.

Best way to brew: Steep one tea bag in six ounces of boiling water for three minutes. Steep dried herbs or loose tea in a tea infuser for three to five minutes. If you are making your own blend with dried or fresh herbs, use equal parts of the herbs to total one teaspoonful per cup of tea.

To enhance flavor: Add in some honey, lemon, cinnamon, real vanilla extract, a slice of orange or sweet anise…or blend with any fruit tea.

PREMENSTRUAL SYNDROME

Look for the following teas or a blend that contains one or more of these herbs—dandelion…hops…dong quai…feverfew…cramp bark. If you take cramp bark alone, make it a weaker tea and sip it slowly.

HEADACHE

My favorite blend for headaches is feverfew, parsley and milk thistle. Combine equal parts of each herb to total one teaspoonful per cup of tea.

Also effective: Lavender…wood betony… and ginkgo.

COLDS AND FLU

Use a blend of *echinacea* and *elder* teas. You can make it yourself, or buy a premade mix. I like Traditional Medicinals products, available in most health food stores. Take for a maximum of one month…then take a one-month break before starting again.

SLEEP AID

Chamomile is a common sleep aid. Mix it with *vervain* for a stronger blend.

I drink deglycyrrhizinated licorice tea at bedtime—it calms the digestive tract.

UPSET STOMACH

For a digestive disorder: Papaya can work wonders…deglycyrrhizinated licorice also helps.

For motion sickness or nausea: Ginger or peppermint. Drink this tea iced to increase its soothing effects.

Singing Silences Snoring

Even those who can't carry a tune snored less after performing vocal exercises 20 minutes a day for three months.

Theory: Singing tones flabby throat muscles that cause snoring.

If you snore: Before trying singing, ask your doctor about sleep apnea, a potentially dangerous airway disorder that causes sufferers to stop breathing repeatedly during the night. This may require surgery or other treatment.

Edzard Ernst, MD, PhD, head of the department of complementary medicine, University of Exeter, Exeter, England.

Quick Fixes for Problem Feet

Suzanne M. Levine, DPM, a podiatric surgeon at New York Hospital–Cornell Medical Center and a staff physician at Manhattan Eye and Ear Hospital, both in New York City. She is the author of *Your Feet Don't Have to Hurt* (St. Martin's Press) and coauthor of *The Botox Book* (M. Evans and Company). For more on foot problems, go to her Web site, *www.institutebeaute.com.*

Anyone who has ever suffered from athlete's foot knows that antifungal creams usually clear up the condition in about two weeks. What most people don't know is that the medication must be used for a full month to eradicate the fungus.

Like athlete's foot, most foot problems are either caused—or worsened—by the sufferers themselves. *Here are five painful foot ailments and the mistakes that cause them…*

BUNIONS

Millions of American adults undergo surgery each year to remove bunions—bony protrusions that usually appear on the outside of the big toe. Many of these operations could be prevented with proper self-care.

Common mistake: Wearing high heels or shoes with tight toes. This can cause inflammation and swelling, which irritate and worsen the bunions.

To avoid this problem, buy shoes that are not too tight in the toe box. If you are unsure of size, have your feet measured. Many people are wearing shoes that are up to one full size too small.

If you already suffer from bunions, you can reduce the pressure with over-the-counter (OTC) orthotic inserts that support the arch.

If OTC orthotic inserts don't help, you may need prescription orthotics. They work by correcting a person's abnormal gait. *Cost:* $250 to $500.

Wearing snug socks also reduces the friction on bunions.

To relieve painful bunion attacks: Mix up one cup of vinegar in one gallon of warm water, and soak the foot for 15 minutes daily.

Also, wrap ice or a package of frozen peas in a thin towel and apply to the bunion twice a day for 15 minutes. These treatments will reduce swelling and pain.

CALLUSES

Calluses are thick layers of dead skin cells that accumulate in areas of the foot exposed to frequent pressure. High heels or flat shoes can make calluses worse by shifting body weight to the forefoot. Shoes with one-inch heels are preferable because they put less pressure on this part of the foot.

Common mistake: Using the OTC callus-removal products. They don't always work very well—and the active ingredient (*salicylic acid*) can damage healthy skin.

It is often more effective to remove calluses after taking a warm bath or shower.

Very gently abrade the callus with a pumice stone. Before going to bed, apply a moisturizer that contains *copper,* a softening agent that will make calluses easier to remove. *A good choice:* Copper Complex.

If this process doesn't help, ask your doctor about *microdermabrasion.* This new 15- to 30-minute, pain-free outpatient procedure eliminates the need for surgery.

During microdermabrasion, a podiatrist uses aluminum oxide crystals to exfoliate the callus. *Typical cost:* $125 to $200.

CORNS

These kernel-shaped areas of thickened tissue are similar to calluses but usually form at the tips of—or between—toes.

Common mistake: Cutting or roughly abrading corns. This causes more pain and often results in infection.

It's more effective to soak the corn in an Epsom salt solution for 10 minutes. Gently rub the corn with a pumice stone. Repeat the treatment daily until the corn is gone.

FALLEN ARCHES

People develop fallen arches when the feet flatten over time. This happens when aging, weight gain and/or hormonal changes cause loosening of the *plantar fascia* ligaments at the bottom of the feet.

Other people may have inherited a low arch. The condition causes arch pain—often accompanied by heel or ankle pain.

Common mistake: Forgoing physical activity. Inactivity usually worsens the condition.

Arch pain can usually be reduced or eliminated with exercises that stretch the Achilles tendons and the plantar fascia ligaments.

Do each of the following stretches six times, twice daily. Hold each stretch for 30 seconds.

●**Place your right foot on a chair or step.** Keep both heels flat. Lean forward over the chair or step until you feel a stretch in the right calf. Repeat with the left foot.

●**Stand on a step facing the stairs with your feet together.** Move your right foot back until the heel hangs over the edge. Lower the heel until you feel a stretch in the right calf. Repeat with the left foot.

●**Sit in a chair.** Rest your right ankle on your left knee. Gently pull the toes of your right foot upward toward your chest, until you feel a stretch in the arch of the foot. Repeat with the left foot.

People with fallen arches should wear dress shoes with one-inch heels or athletic shoes with built-in arches. Slip-in prescription orthotic inserts are helpful for restoring proper arch and support.

To determine if you have fallen arches: Walk in sand, and look at your footprints. The print of a normal foot has a gap between the heel and the forefoot. However, a fallen arch will have little or no gap.

INGROWN NAILS

Ingrown toenails curve and push into the flesh instead of growing straight over the toe.

The condition causes pain, redness and/or swelling at the ends or sides of the toes.

Common mistake: Trimming nails on a curve. That increases the risk for ingrown nails.

To reduce this risk, soak your feet in warm water, wash thoroughly with soap and trim the nails straight across.

If there is redness or other signs of infection, apply an OTC antibiotic, such as Neosporin.

If pain and redness don't go away after two days: Your doctor may need to remove the portion of nail beneath the skin. This can be done in a 15-minute outpatient procedure.

Relief for Constipation

For relief from constipation, mix one-half cup of unprocessed bran, one-half cup of applesauce and one-third cup of prune juice. Refrigerate the mixture. Take two tablespoons after dinner, followed by a glass of water. If this does not relieve constipation, increase the dose to three or four tablespoons.

More hints: Eat plenty of fresh fruit, vegetables and fiber. If the extra fiber causes you to have excess gas, try the herbal remedy epazote. *Note:* For people with restricted mobility, more fiber can aggravate constipation.

Craig Rubin, MD, professor of internal medicine and chief of geriatrics at the University of Texas Southwestern Medical Center, Dallas.

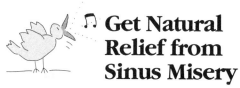 # Get Natural Relief from Sinus Misery

Murray Grossan, MD, an otolaryngologist with the Tower Ear, Nose and Throat Clinic at Cedars-Sinai Medical Center in Los Angeles. He is coauthor of The Sinus Cure: Seven Simple Steps to Relieve Sinusitis and Other Ear, Nose and Throat Conditions *(Ballantine).*

Physicians can be too quick to prescribe decongestants, antibiotics and even surgery as a solution to sinus problems.

Before taking any of these steps, you should be aware that some surprisingly easy remedies are often highly effective. That's something I've discovered again and again in my 35 years of practice as an ear, nose and throat specialist. These natural remedies are also free of the side effects that medication and surgery can cause.

How do these treatments work? Each one focuses on improving function of the *cilia.* Those are the millions of microscopic hairs that line your respiratory tract.

Cilia function like oars, moving 16 times per second to propel mucus—which carries bacteria, dirt, allergens and other toxins—out of your nose, sinuses and chest and into your throat, where it is swallowed.

When your cilia aren't working properly, mucus thickens and gets trapped in your sinuses. That's what leads to congestion and infection. Your cilia may be underactive if you frequently cough, sneeze and/or cough up phlegm. These are all attempts by your body to rid itself of excess mucus.

Here are the very best ways to keep your cilia healthy—*and your sinuses trouble free...*

●**Drink hot tea and hot soup.** Clinical studies conducted at Johns Hopkins University in Baltimore have demonstrated that the antioxidants, flavonoids and polyphenols in hot tea improve nasal symptoms.

Chicken soup, which contains the amino acid *cysteine,* can also be helpful. Both tea and soup keep the mucus membranes hydrated and help thin mucus, making it easier to expel.

Helpful: Drink eight cups of tea or soup every day.

A hot drink is especially beneficial in the early morning. That's because your cilia slow during sleep, allowing inhaled dust to accumulate in your mucus membranes. This can trigger a sneezing or coughing fit when you wake up.

I advise my patients to drink some hot tea in bed each day before rising. This helps get their cilia moving and clears out their respiratory tract.

Smart idea: Purchase a thermos, fill it up with some hot tea before retiring and place it at your bedside.

Hot beverages also help in dry air, which interferes with cilia activity. Because air in most commercial aircraft is particularly hard on people with sinus conditions, I tell my patients to carry tea bags with them at all times when they fly and to order cups of hot water. That way, they can sip tea continuously throughout the flight.

Avoid chilled drinks. Cold liquids inhibit the activity of cilia.

• **Do *not* blow your nose.** Many people blow their nose vigorously when they have sinus congestion. This forces bacteria-filled mucus back into the sinuses, making conditions ripe for a sinus infection. Wipe your nose instead. If you *must* blow your nose, do so as gently as possible.

• **Try papaya enzyme tablets.** Chewable papaya enzyme tablets—sold as food supplements in drugstores and natural food stores—are highly effective at reducing sinus inflammation and swelling.

Helpful: Four times per day, place one tablet between cheek and gum and let it melt.

To enhance the beneficial effect of papaya enzyme, supplement it with *bromelain* tablets (also dissolved between the cheek and gum). Bromelain, an enzyme found in pineapple, helps reduce sinus inflammation.

Clear-Ease brand tablets contain both the papaya enzyme and bromelain.

Helpful: If you take antibiotics, these fruit enzymes will boost their effectiveness.

• **Use saline solution to irrigate nasal passages.** This technique was first practiced by yoga masters 3,000 years ago. It remains one of the most effective tools for keeping your sinuses healthy.

Washing out your nasal passages once or twice a day not only helps keep your cilia hydrated and mucus thinned, but also whisks away bacteria and other toxins.

To make saline solution: Mix one teaspoon of table salt and one-half teaspoon of baking soda into two cups of warm water.

You can also use the *Locke-Ringer's Solution* (sold under the brand name Breathe-Ease) or *Alkalol,* a nonprescription irrigating solution. Both are sold at drugstores.

Caution: Prepared saline solutions that contain additives, particularly the preservative *benzalkonium,* can slow cilia movement.

Saline solution can be administered with a large rubber bulb syringe, a plastic spray bottle or a Neti pot (a ceramic container available in most drugstores and health food stores).

Lean over a sink, tilt your head to one side and squeeze, spray or pour a small amount of the solution directly into one nostril. Allow the liquid to flow out of the other nostril and down your throat. Spit out the drainage, clear your throat and exhale gently through your nose to clear your nasal passages.

• **Keep your surroundings free of dust.** Your cilia have a full-time job clearing your respiratory tract of toxins and allergens. It only makes matters much worse if you live in a dusty environment—amidst all the allergen-producing dust mites that invariably accompany any dust.

To minimize dust…

• Get rid of wall-to-wall carpeting. It's just impossible to clean effectively. Use only throw rugs. Machine-wash them every six weeks.

• Avoid heavy drapes. They, too, tend to collect a lot of dust.

• Use a high-efficiency particulate-arresting (HEPA) air filter in rooms where you spend the most time.

• Encase your mattress and pillows in mite-proof covers. The covers now available are as silky and comfortable as fine sheets.

These products are available from Allergy Control, 800-422-3878, *www.allergycontrol.com* …and National Allergy Supply, 800-522-1448, *www.natlallergy.com.*

How to Cure Stomach Ailments Naturally

Rob Pyke, MD, PhD, a Ridgefield, Connecticut–based internist and a clinical pharmacologist. He is the author of *Dr. Pyke's Natural Way to Complete Stomach Relief— Great Foods and Holistic Methods to Cure Your Upper Digestive Tract Forever* (Prentice Hall).

Whether it's heartburn, an ulcer or reflux disease, stomach distress is so common that many of us simply learn to live with it. Either that, or we pop an over-the-counter (OTC) remedy and hope for the best. Only 10% of people who suffer from stomach problems consult a doctor.

As an internist and clinical pharmacologist, I'm well-versed in the conventional treatment of all gastrointestinal conditions. Prescription drugs are the primary defense. Some doctors also counsel their patients to reduce stress, exercise regularly and lose weight to ease stomach problems.

But in 1994, my views on gastrointestinal ailments changed drastically—when I became the patient.

I was suffering from gastritis, an inflammation of the stomach lining. I also had heartburn and gastroesophageal reflux disease (GERD). That is a condition that results whenever the contents of the stomach "backwash" into the esophagus and cause irritation.

The gastroenterologist I consulted prescribed the medication *omeprazole* (Prilosec). But two weeks later, my condition still had not improved.

A review of the gastrointestinal tract showed hundreds of little holes in my stomach. That was the last straw. I decided to stop being a "passive patient," relying only on what my doctor told me. I researched conventional and alternative treatments and created a self-healing program that addresses the causes—not the symptoms—of stomach problems.

Caution: Before beginning self-treatment, consult a physician about your stomach problem. *This is especially true if you are experiencing...*

● **Stomach pain that lasts** more than one hour twice a week.

● **Loss of appetite** or unwanted weight loss.

● **Blood in your stool** or a darkening of the stool.

● **Vomiting episodes** that produce "coffee grounds" (dark matter that contains blood).

● **Difficulty swallowing.**

● **Pain that occurs when using nonsteroidal anti-inflammatory drugs (NSAIDs)** or while drinking alcohol or eating spicy foods.

SELF-CARE STRATEGIES

In addition to following your physician's advice, here's how to increase your chances of getting relief from stomach problems...

● **Avoid *all* offending foods.** Most people know the worst stomach offenders—hot peppers, peppermint, chocolate, soda, onions and nuts. But there are less obvious triggers, such as butter, milk, ice cream, coffee and tea. These offenders add or promote stomach acid or open the valve from the stomach to the esophagus, which can result in reflux.

● **Eat the right foods.** Artichokes (try out canned artichoke hearts in salad) and sauerkraut nourish friendly digestive-tract bacteria. Low-fat soy milk and yogurt buffer stomach acid. Papaya and pineapple contain helpful digestive enzymes.

● **Eat six small meals each day instead of three large ones.** You'll produce less stomach acid. Reducing meal size also helps to prevent reflux, the "burp up" sensation that occurs when food and stomach acid back up into the esophagus.

● **Drink no more than one cup of a beverage during each meal.** The more you drink, the more likely your food is to back up into the esophagus. Fluids also dilute digestive enzymes, which convert food into molecules that can be easily absorbed by the intestine.

Important: Drink eight eight-ounce cups of water daily. Be sure to drink them between your meals. This helps dilute residual stomach acid.

● **Take at least 15 minutes to eat each meal.** Most of us don't chew our food long enough. This means that large pieces of food enter the stomach, which can promote indigestion and cause the stomach to empty slowly. This results in excess acid and more opportunity for reflux to develop. Thoroughly chewing your food leads to better digestion.

•**Watch your body position.** To prevent indigestion and reflux, stay upright for at least two hours after eating.

To help stomach patients avoid nighttime reflux, many doctors suggest placing wooden blocks under the feet at the head of the bed. This can work—but if you move around, you run the risk of knocking the bed off the blocks.

Better way: Get a five- or six-foot wedge of foam from a medical-supply store. The foam should be four inches thick at the head and gradually taper down. Wrap it in a small mattress cover.

Bonus: The wedge enables you to adjust only your side of the bed without disturbing your partner.

•**Ask your doctor about using vitamin supplements and herbs.** Taking certain vitamins and herbs helps prevent and treat stomach conditions. To decrease stomach acid, consider taking 400 International Units (IU) of vitamin E daily. Vitamin C (250 mg daily in buffered or ester form) helps heal stomach ulcers. Ask your doctor about taking these in addition to a regular multivitamin.

Deglycerizinated licorice, aloe vera and chamomile with catnip can also ease stomach upset. These are available at health food stores as capsules, gels, liquids or tea bags. Follow label instructions.

Quick Herbal Relief For Indigestion

Rosemary is often effective for indigestion, gas and bloating.

For best results: Take as a tea or tincture 15 minutes *before* eating. That helps maximize the effect of the herb's bitter compounds, which promotes the flow of digestive juices.

To prepare the tea: Add one teaspoon of dried rosemary to one cup of boiling water. Steep for 10 minutes, then strain. Or, add 10 to 20 drops of tincture to one cup of water.

Chanchal Cabrera, an herbalist in private practice in Vancouver, BC, and a member of the American Herbalist Guild, Halifax, VA.

Asthma/Allergy Self-Defense

Consider keeping the floors in your home bare if family members are affected by allergies and/or asthma. Rugs tend to trap pollen, mites, mold, animal dander and dust, all of which can trigger breathing problems among susceptible people. Frequent vacuuming simply cannot get rid of all of the irritants that collect in rugs. Bare floors trap fewer irritants and are easier to clean. Families with allergies should consider designing their new homes with hardwood floors, and exposing original hardwood floors in old homes.

Brigitte Johnson, spokesperson, Asthma and Allergy Foundation of America, 1233 W. 20 St. NW, Suite 402, Washington, DC 20036, *www.aafa.org*.

Another Way to Reduce Allergy Symptoms

Indoor allergy symptoms, such as runny nose and itchy throat, will subside when indoor humidity levels are 50% or lower. These levels limit the growth of dust mites and production of their allergens.

To control humidity: Run an air conditioner and dehumidifier to maintain a temperature of approximately 75°F and a humidity level of 48%. A hygrometer that measures these levels can be purchased at hardware stores.

Larry G. Arlian, PhD, professor of biological sciences, microbiology and immunology, Wright State University, Dayton, OH.

Allergy Attack Self-Help

During an allergy attack, apply pressure to the center of the web between the thumb and index finger of one hand. Angle the pressure toward the bone that connects to the index finger. Maintain pressure for two minutes. Take slow, deep breaths. Repeat with the other hand. This stimulates the acupressure points that relieve allergic reactions.

Michael Reed Gach, PhD, director of the Acupressure Institute, Berkeley, CA, *www.acupressure.com*.

Asthma First Aid

Martha V. White, MD, an allergy and asthma specialist at the Institute for Asthma and Allergy, Washington Hospital Center, 11160 Veirs Mill Rd., Suite 414, Wheaton, MD 20895.

Be sure to follow these practical suggestions if you feel an asthma attack coming on...

• **Use asthma medicine as prescribed.**

• **Get away from the trigger**—if you know what is causing the attack. *Example:* A cat.

• **Head for a warm area**—cold will usually worsen an attack.

• **Sit down and try to relax.**

• **Drink something caffeinated,** such as a cola, coffee or black tea. These beverages contain theophylline, which will relax constricted bronchial tubes.

• **Breathe warm, moist air**—take a warm shower...or sit by a pot of boiled water with a towel over your head to trap steam.

If the asthma attack worsens or does not respond to these treatments: Seek medical attention immediately—even if that means going to a hospital emergency room.

Curb Insomnia with a Bedtime Snack

To fall asleep faster, try snacking on cheese and crackers before bedtime.

Like milk—a well-known sleep inducer—cheese is loaded with tryptophan. This amino acid induces the body to make the neurotransmitter serotonin, which has sedative properties.

To keep fat and calories to a minimum: Choose a low-fat cheese.

If insomnia persists: Consult your doctor.

Peter Hauri, PhD, emeritus professor of psychology, Mayo Medical School, and former director of the Mayo Clinic Insomnia Program, both in Rochester, MN.

Easy Wart Treatment

Put duct tape over a wart, and leave it on for seven days. Then uncover the area for 12 hours. Repeat the cycle until the wart falls off. Duct tape keeps moisture in and helps break down wart tissue.

Daniel M. Siegel, MD, associate professor of dermatology, State University of New York at Stony Brook.

4

Getting Fit

Six Ways to Trigger Your Natural Fat Burners

e have trouble shedding excess fat because our bodies and brains have an innate drive to create and store body fat. Combine this tendency with the typical American high-fat diet, and you've got a prescription for weight problems.

Good news: By switching on your natural fat-burning mechanisms, you can counteract the body's fat-storing tendencies…and boost energy levels at the same time.

●**Fat Burner 1: Turn up the light.** To jump-start your metabolism each morning, expose yourself to sunlight by opening the curtains or blinds and standing there for several minutes.

If your bedroom doesn't get direct sun, turn on all the lights.

Alternative: Install full-spectrum lightbulbs —available at hardware and lighting stores.

●**Fat Burner 2: Eat three low-fat meals a day,** with several low-fat snacks in between, and eat breakfast. The more food you consume early, the higher your metabolic rate will be later in the day. Skipping breakfast also encourages bingeing at the end of the day, when your body's tendency to store fat is at its peak.

Follow the "3 plus 4" eating strategy—three low-fat meals a day, plus four low-fat snacks.

Recommended snack times…

●10 am—making it less likely that you'll stuff yourself at lunch.

●3 pm—to head off the desire for a salty snack later in the day.

●5:30 pm—a predinner appetizer, so you won't binge at dinner.

●9 pm—a small snack of fruit or grains, if you desire.

Appropriate snacks include…

Robert K. Cooper, PhD, a researcher, speaker and writer in Ann Arbor, MI, *www.robertkcooper.com.* He is author of several books, including *Low-Fat Living—Turn Off the Fat-Makers, Turn On the Fat-Burners for Longevity, Energy, Weight Loss, Freedom from Disease* (Rodale).

•Whole-grain bread, crackers, bagel or English muffin topped with low-fat cottage cheese, fresh fruit or all-fruit preserves.

•Low-fat granola bar.

•One cup of nonfat plain yogurt with fresh fruit added.

•A cup of nonfat or low-fat soup.

•A whole-grain-bread sandwich with Dijon mustard, nonfat mayonnaise and two slices of turkey or chicken breast (not a good choice for a nighttime snack, however).

•A piece of fresh fruit.

•**Fat Burner 3: Drink eight glasses of water daily.** Most people don't drink enough water to replace fluids lost throughout the day. Dehydration inhibits your body's ability to metabolize fat for energy.

To maximize fat-burning, drink eight eight-ounce glasses of water or an equivalent low-calorie noncaffeinated beverage every day. (Caffeinated drinks act as diuretics, contributing to fluid loss.)

•**Fat Burner 4: Fit in 30 minutes of daily aerobic activity.** Thirty minutes of daily aerobic exercise burns *hundreds* of extra calories each week, while training your body to burn fat more efficiently. Exercising a few minutes at a time is just as beneficial to your health as doing it all at once.

Follow the "Four Fives and a Ten" plan—a five-minute walk just before or after breakfast, another five-minute walk before and after lunch, five minutes of walking or other light activity when you get home and a brisk 10-minute walk or cycle after dinner.

To accelerate fat-burning…

•Add walks of 20 to 30 consecutive minutes, three or four times a week.

•Add in regular strength-training sessions every other day to increase muscle mass.

•**Fat Burner 5: Practice on-the-spot stress reduction.** When you feel frustrated, anxious or upset, your body produces stress-related hormones that promote the storage of body fat. Stress also leads people to overeat and eat foods rich in fat and sugar.

To keep your fat-burning mechanism in full gear, use *diaphragmatic breathing* whenever a stressful situation arises…

•Sit or stand with your shoulders relaxed, your spine straight.

•Place your hands on your stomach just below your rib cage. Slowly inhale through your nose, feeling your abdomen expand slightly downward and forward. As you complete the inhalation, feel your chest expand comfortably.

•Exhale slowly through your mouth, feeling a wave of relaxation flood your abdomen, chest, throat and face.

Other ways to reduce stress…

•Shift your attention to focus on what you can control, rather than what you can't.

•Trigger calming regions of your brain by imagining a "relaxation wave" running through your body—beginning in your face, then passing through your neck and shoulders and down your arms and legs, ending in your fingertips and toes.

•Close your eyes and visualize the people, possessions or memories that you value and love.

•Write to or call someone you love.

•**Fat Burner 6: Get deeper, high-metabolism sleep.** No matter how much shut-eye you get, improving the quality of your sleep will increase the amount of fat you burn at night… and speed the building of new muscle tissue.

For deeper, more restful sleep…

•Switch to a lighter blanket or just a sheet, to allow your normal body thermostat to kick in. (Cooler temperatures increase metabolism.)

•Do light exercise or take a hot bath or shower three hours before bed. This will trigger a drop in body temperature as you're falling asleep, which helps deepen your rest.

•Make your bed a time-free environment. Set an alarm if you must, but turn the clock so you cannot see the face if you wake up during the night.

Surprising Ways to Shed Unwanted Pounds... Easily

Stephanie Dalvit-McPhillips, PhD, a registered dietitian with a doctorate in nutritional biochemistry. Ms. Dalvit-McPhillips has a private counseling practice in Willoughby, OH, where she treats people with weight problems and eating disorders. She is the author of *The Right Bite: Outsmart 43 Scientifically Proven Fat Triggers and Beat the Dieter's Curse* (Fair Winds).

If you've tried every fad diet but failed to reach your ideal weight, stop blaming yourself. No single diet can address all the complex factors that contribute to weight gain.

In two decades of nutrition research and clinical practice, I've identified dozens of hidden triggers that can cause weight gain—in some cases, even *when you don't overeat.*

Some triggers alter your metabolism, causing you to burn fat and calories inefficiently. Others spark irresistible cravings that give way to out-of-control bingeing.

The key is to identify and avoid your personal triggers. *Here are eight that may surprise you...*

SENSORY CUES

Have you ever claimed to put on weight just by looking at food? Well, you may be right.

In a recent Yale University study, insulin levels skyrocketed in hungry individuals exposed to the sight, smell and even the mere mention of charcoal-broiled steaks. Participants' bodies started converting glucose to fat even before they had taken their first bite.

What to do: Don't linger near buffet tables or dessert trays—especially if you are hungry.

LACK OF FIBER

Low-fiber diets typically provide a lot of fat and calories but few nutrients. Such diets also lack bulk, which means you need to eat more to feel full.

High-fiber foods are filling, nutritionally dense and relatively low in fat and refined sugar. High-fiber foods also help stabilize blood glucose and insulin levels.

What to do: Get at least 25 g of fiber in your daily diet. Good sources include whole grains, fruits, vegetables and legumes.

INSUFFICIENT CALORIES

When you limit calories to 1,000 or fewer daily, your body starts to pilfer protein from lean body tissue, destroying the muscle mass necessary to burn fat and calories. You also begin to manufacture an overabundance of *lipoprotein lipase,* an enzyme that stores fat in your cells.

You may drop pounds on an extremely low-calorie diet. But once you resume eating normally, your body will convert what it now perceives as excess calories into fat.

What to do: Don't eat fewer than 1,400 calories daily. Total calories should be divided among several meals and snacks.

DIET FOODS

You may assume that you can eat more if foods are labeled "low-fat" or "lite." Wrong. Despite the catchy labeling, these foods can be packed with sugar *and* calories. "Sugar-free" products may contain aspartame or saccharin—sweeter-than-sugar substitutes that can provoke a sweet tooth.

What to do: Read ingredient and nutrition labels. Avoid foods that derive more than 20% of calories from fat.

SALT AND FLAVOR ENHANCERS

Scientists are not sure why salt triggers compulsive eating. It may trigger hormonal changes that amplify hunger, or we may eat more of the foods we find flavorful.

In addition to salt, food manufacturers can choose from more than 2,000 flavor enhancers to make packaged snacks and meals irresistible. But many of these ingredients, such as monosodium glutamate and ammonium carbonate, may cause you to not only eat more, but also to store more of what you do eat as fat.

What to do: Avoid salt and foods with artificial flavor-boosters. Use lemon, herbs, balsamic vinegar and no-salt substitutes.

THIRST

People frequently confuse thirst for hunger. What's more, we neglect to count the calories we drink. For example, most 12-ounce sodas contain 150 calories.

What to do: Before surrendering to cravings, drink a glass of water—then reassess your hunger. When choosing beverages, stick to water or herbal tea.

CAFFEINE AND NICOTINE

Often trumpeted as appetite suppressants, caffeine and nicotine actually *increase* hunger and cravings in certain individuals.

Both substances trigger our fight-or-flight response. This causes glucose to flood into the bloodstream, providing quick energy and *temporarily* suppressing appetite. But as blood glucose levels rise, so do insulin levels.

Result: Within one hour of consuming caffeine (even as little as one cup of coffee) or nicotine, glucose levels take a nose-dive. This leaves you ravenous.

Worrisome: Secondhand smoke. People exposed to smoke experience the same fluctuations in blood sugar, but—unlike a smoker—won't light up when they feel hunger.

What to do: Avoid caffeine for three months. Are you able to forgo that midmorning donut? Have you shed pounds? If so, caffeine is a trigger to be avoided. Nicotine should be eliminated—weight-gain trigger or not. Talk to your doctor about quitting smoking...and avoid secondhand smoke.

NOT ENOUGH SLEEP

Sleep-deprived people may increase their daily calorie consumption by as much as 15%, according to research conducted at Emory University School of Medicine in Atlanta.

What to do: Strive for eight hours of sleep a night.

Calcium Promotes Weight Loss

In one recent finding, women whose diets contained 1,000 mg of calcium per day lost more body fat than women whose diets were lower in calcium. This finding was strongest in women who ate fewer than 1,800 calories a day.

Theory: Low calcium raises levels of parathyroid hormone and the active form of vitamin D. This causes calcium to accumulate in fat cells and makes it harder for fat to break down.

Roseann Lyle, PhD, associate professor in the department of health, kinesiology and leisure studies, Purdue University, West Lafayette, IN, and leader of a study of 54 women, reported in *Tufts University Health & Nutrition Letter.*

How Three Big Losers Keep the Weight Off

Phyllis Ingram, an in-house temporary employee for a book and magazine publisher.
Diane Walton, a financial analyst and personal trainer.
Joanna Williams, a book designer.

What is the key to losing weight and keeping it off? *Here are secrets from three people who know from personal experience...*

PHYLLIS INGRAM, 54

Four years ago, I weighed 225 pounds. I had tried every diet out there. I lost some weight but always gained it back—plus more.

The turning point: My health was deteriorating. I had low energy and trouble climbing stairs. On a vacation to Florida, I found it difficult to get around.

•**I started practicing portion control**—having only one cup of pasta instead of filling my plate, for example. In the first week, I really thought I was in hell. But my body gradually adjusted to the change.

•**To prevent mindless "grazing," I write down everything I eat.**

•**I start out every day with a high-fiber breakfast.** That fills me up *and* helps control my cravings all day long. I mix Kashi GoLean with All-Bran cereal—that's 22 grams of fiber right there.

•**I take low-calorie frozen meals to work** and heat them in the microwave. When I want a snack, I have a fat-free yogurt or sugar-free Jell-O or pudding.

Challenging: I love chocolate, so I didn't even try to give it up. *Instead:* I place a single piece of dark chocolate in my mouth and let it dissolve. The flavor lingers, so I don't want more than a piece or two.

For exercise, I ride a stationary bike in the gym or my road bike four days a week. This provides a good workout without stressing my knees or hips. The weekend before I turned 53, I rode my bike from Salisbury, Maryland, to Assateague Island and back—100 miles in eight hours.

Today: I weigh 175. I have lost about 50 pounds in 18 months, and have dropped from size 26 to a size 14. My goal is to get down to 155 pounds, which is what I weighed 30 years ago.

DIANE WALTON, 35

I had been heavy all my life—even as a teenager. In junior high and high school, at 5' 5" I fluctuated between 165 and 190 pounds. I was active in sports, but my eating habits were bad. I tried every diet in the book. I even took grapefruit pills because I thought they would boost my metabolism.

The turning point: When I weighed myself and saw 200 on the scale. That wasn't a number I wanted to see.

•**I then started working out on a stair-stepper every morning.** At first, I could barely do two minutes. But I always tried to go a little longer and eventually got up to 45 minutes. Now I do some kind of daily aerobic exercise—spinning…running on a treadmill …or aerobics.

•**I lift weights three days a week at the gym I belong to.** I started my weight training on Cybex machines, then switched to a combination of free weights and machines.

Exercising was hard at first. Soon, though, it got easier, and the results were dramatic. When I first started, my body was 45% fat. That dropped to 31% three months after I started lifting weights.

I now eat lots of fruits and vegetables. I eat my main meal at lunch and have a light supper. *Other tricks…*

•**On weekends, I eat whatever I want,** so I don't feel deprived. But I still watch portion sizes.

•**I buy packaged or frozen vegetables** because they're easy to prepare.

•**I avoid foods with any added fat.** That includes bread with butter and vegetables with rich sauces.

•**When I crave something "sinful,"** like ice cream, I plan for it by eating less during the day.

Today: I weigh 145 pounds. I have maintained that weight for three years.

I used to view dieting and exercise as temporary solutions. Now I know that they require a lifetime commitment.

I became so enthusiastic about fitness that I am now a personal trainer. My clients really listen to me because they know I understand what they're going through.

JOANNA WILLIAMS, 28

After college, I took a position as a creative designer. After a few years of this mostly sedentary work, I was 30 pounds heavier. My clothes were slowly getting tighter, and I had to buy larger sizes.

The turning point: I am only 5' 3", and when I hit a size 10 and 145 pounds, I knew I had to do something. Plus, my wedding was coming up. When I looked at old pictures, I hardly recognized myself.

I joined Weight Watchers. I quickly learned I was consuming a huge number of calories— a lot more than I was burning off with what exercise I was doing. Plus, I was not making healthy choices about what I was eating. *To cut back…*

•**I ate more slowly** and started waiting at least 30 minutes before going back for seconds. Most of the time, I found that I didn't need seconds.

•**I was never very fond of vegetables,** but I started trying new things and found that I really liked squash, peas and zucchini.

•**At the beginning of each week,** I stocked up on salad fixings and healthy snacks. That way, I would be sure to have nutritious, low-calorie ingredients on hand.

•**At work, doughnuts, cookies or cakes are always to be found.** Rather than give them up altogether, I let myself have a taste— but I wouldn't finish anything.

Challenging: My husband is a meat-and-potatoes guy. After my eating habits changed, I often found myself making two meals—one for him and a lower-calorie meal for me. Now that he has begun to try new foods, things are easier.

When we are having steak or any other rich food, I take a small serving...and fill up on the salad, grains or vegetables.

I had tried exercise before but found it so boring that I always gave it up. Then I discovered kick-boxing. I also started lifting weights twice a week. That's when the weight really started coming off.

Today: I weigh 120 pounds. I backslide now and then—I gained five pounds on a recent vacation—but I always get right back to my exercise and diet routines. They have become integral to my life.

Feed Cravings Wisely

Satisfy mood-induced cravings for sweets with fruit or high-fiber, whole-grain snacks. Avoid candy or refined-flour baked goods.

Reason: Products containing refined sugar give you a fast energy buzz as your blood-sugar level rises. But the resulting insulin rush causes blood sugar—and mood—to slump again. The sugar in fruit is absorbed gradually, and fiber slows down absorption, helping to prevent food-linked mood shifts.

Hilary Boyd, West London, England–based registered general nurse and the author of *Banishing the Blues* (Mitchell Beazley).

More on Food Cravings

Food cravings do vary by gender. About 25% of women have cravings, but only 13% of men do. Women experience cravings when depressed or bored, while men tend to get them when they're happy.

Self-defense: If you crave a sweet, you're probably tired. A desire for salty foods usually means you need a nutritious meal.

Lionel Lafay, PhD, researcher at the French Agency of Food Health Safety, Maisons-Alfort, France.

Asian Weight-Loss Secret

Stop eating when you are 80% full. Elders on the Japanese island of Okinawa call this *hara hachi bu*—and it helps them eat 10% to 40% fewer calories than Americans consume.

Rationale: It takes the stomach 20 minutes to signal the brain that it is full. Stopping when you are almost full—and waiting 20 minutes—helps your body feel satisfied without eating additional food.

Helpful: At the first faint sign of fullness, put down your utensils, and leave the table.

Barbara Rolls, PhD, nutrition professor, Pennsylvania State University, University Park, and coauthor of *The Volumetrics Weight-Control Plan* (Quill).

High-Protein Diet Danger

High-protein diets may encourage the formation of kidney stones. Studies show that a high-protein diet will result in acidic, calcium-rich urine. These conditions encourage the formation of kidney stones.

Instead: Dieters should find a balanced diet that allows them to lose weight...and drink plenty of water, too.

Shalini Reddy, MD, assistant professor of clinical medicine, primary care group, University of Chicago.

Time Bombs—Hidden Salt, Sugar and Fat in Everyday Foods

John McDougall, MD, founder and medical director of the McDougall Program in Santa Rosa, CA, www.drmcdougall.com. He is the author of 10 books, including The McDougall Program for Women: What Every Woman Needs to Know to Be Healthy for Life *(Plume).*

Even "good" eaters will compromise their health with poor dietary habits—and they often don't even realize it.

Most dangerous culprits: Salt, sugar and fat. Make the appropriate changes to avoid these "hidden" ingredients to reduce your risk of disease.

HIDDEN SALT

Table salt and high-sodium ingredients flavor and preserve everything—from pudding and cake mix...to salad dressing and frozen entrées...to canned food and condiments.

About 20% of the population is sodium-sensitive, suffering from increased blood pressure or fluid retention due to excess sodium. Excess sodium also causes bones to release calcium and therefore contributes to the development of osteoporosis.

The average American has 3,000 mg to 5,000 mg of sodium per day. Aim for no more than 2,000 mg per day. People with congestive heart failure, gout, hypertension and kidney problems should avoid foods with added salt.

Sodium is added in various forms, including monosodium glutamate (MSG)...sodium bicarbonate...sodium chloride (table salt)...and sodium nitrate.

One cup of soup can easily contain 800 mg to 1,000 mg of sodium, and a few handfuls of chips can contain up to 400 mg. Read labels to compare the sodium content of similar products. *Other strategies...*

●**Buy foods in their natural states.** Avoid processed foods. They are likely to have lots of added sodium.

●**Do not add salt while cooking.** If you must add salt, use it sparingly on the surface when you're ready to eat—don't mix it in. Your tongue will detect the salt and you will be satisfied without a lot of it laced throughout the dish.

●**Use lemon juice, lime juice, vinegar and extra herbs and spices to flavor foods.** All add punch without extra sodium. Add a few squirts or pinches to cooked greens, low-sodium tomato juice and low-sodium soup.

HIDDEN SUGAR

Refined and even natural sugars are added to everything—from baby food and breakfast cereal...to pasta sauce and processed foods. On food labels, sugar is listed in many ways—as sucrose, fructose, high-fructose corn syrup, fruit juice concentrate, honey, molasses, maple syrup and others. An ingredient ending in *-ose* is usually a form of sugar.

If you are overweight, eating excess sugar can slow weight loss or even cause weight gain. Dried fruit, fruit juice and foods flavored with added sugar are concentrated in calories. All sugar—whether refined or natural—can contribute to elevated blood triglyceride levels, a risk factor for heart disease.

Sugar-avoidance strategies...

●**Eat fresh fruit.** Limit processed fruit products, such as fruit juices and canned and dried fruits. I advise my patients to eat no more than three servings of fruit per day...or one serving per day for maximum weight loss.

●**Think of fruit as dessert.** Fruit is a wonderful source of vitamins, minerals and health-supporting phytochemicals as well as fiber. Make fresh fruit the sweet ending to a meal. Skip fattening desserts, which are devoid of nutritional benefits.

●**Add sugar to the surface.** As with salt, a little sugar on the surface of food adds flavor without many extra calories. A bowl of cooked oatmeal topped with a teaspoon of brown sugar is satisfying and contains less sugar than many presweetened packaged varieties.

Likewise, you can buy unsweetened cold breakfast cereals and drizzle a bit of honey on top. You will get much less sugar than in presweetened cereal.

HIDDEN FAT

Fat is added to processed foods to enhance the flavor and texture and blend ingredients. Everyone needs to monitor fat intake. In addition to obesity, consuming dietary fat promotes cancer, coronary artery disease and diabetes. Both animal and plant fats are a concern.

I advise *no* added fat. Those who need to lose weight should also avoid high-fat plant foods, such as avocados, nuts, olives, seeds and soy products.

Food manufacturers list fat on labels in different ways...

●**Mono- and diglycerides.** These fats are added to bread and other baked goods to soften them.

●**Hydrogenated fat (trans fatty acids).** Commonly used in margarine and processed foods, it raises blood cholesterol levels even more than butter and cream.

●**"Fat-free."** Foods that contain less than one-half gram of fat per serving can be labeled "fat-free." The trouble is that many standard "servings" are small by consumers' standards. If you eat several servings of a so-called fat-free food, you may be consuming a fair amount of total fat.

●**Choice of fats.** Foods are often labeled with *possible* fat sources. A product label might say, "may contain soybean and/or cottonseed oil." Manufacturers can then use whichever fat is most cost-effective for them.

Fat self-defense strategies...

●**Eat fresh foods.** Baked potatoes, steamed vegetables and cooked rice do not have any extra fat unless you put it there.

●**Choose wisely.** Eat less meat and fewer dairy products and more whole grains and fresh fruits and vegetables.

●**Cook and bake from scratch**—to control the amount of fat used.

Examples: Use only nonstick cookware... experiment with decreasing the amount of fat in recipes...substitute mashed bananas, unsweetened applesauce or prune paste for fat.

Breaking The Sugar Habit

Nancy Appleton, PhD, a researcher and nutritional consultant in Santa Monica, CA. She is the author of *Lick the Sugar Habit* and *Lick the Sugar Habit Counter* (both Penguin Putnam).

The average American consumes more than 20 teaspoons of refined sugar each day. That's 20% more than the amount we consumed a decade ago.

If you think tooth decay and weight gain are the only health consequences, think again.

By replacing fruits and vegetables and other nutrient-dense, disease-fighting foods, sugary foods and beverages can cause increased blood sugar (glucose) levels and obesity. These conditions can lead, in turn, to chronic health problems, such as heart disease, high blood pressure and diabetes.

Cakes, cookies, candy and ice cream aren't the only sources of refined sugar. It can also be found in the seemingly wholesome foods and beverages, such as muffins, flavored instant oatmeal, canned sweet potatoes and even old-fashioned lemonade.

For some people, sugar—like alcohol or tobacco—can be addictive.

Example: Sugar addicts time their meals and snacks so they have some form of sugar in their body at all times. They crave sugar and experience the withdrawal symptoms, such as fatigue, headache, depression or shaking, if they stop eating sugar "cold turkey."

That's why it's important for sugar addicts to *slowly* reduce the sugar in their diets.

Whether you're a "sugarholic" or an average American who consumes too much sugar—often unknowingly—your long-term health will benefit if you gradually reduce your intake. *Here's how...*

●**Read the Nutrition Facts panel on food labels.** A healthy person can metabolize 8 g (two teaspoons) of sugar at one time. Stay away from foods that contain more than 8 g of sugar per serving.

This means foregoing soft drinks and many fruit juices, which average about 40 g (10 teaspoons) of sugar per 12-ounce serving.

•**Avoid foods and drinks containing artificial sweeteners.** Even though artificially sweetened foods don't contain sugar, they can stimulate your sweet tooth. Instead of diet soda, for example, opt for tap or mineral water with a spritz of lemon.

•**Use *half* as much sugar.** Start by cutting back on what you normally add to your coffee, tea, cereal, etc.

Also halve the amount of sugar you use in recipes. Because sugar adds tenderness to dough and golden-brown surfaces to baked goods, some recipes may not survive without it.

What to do: Switch to recipes that can be made without sugar. Its absence won't affect the texture of many foods.

Example: Fruit pies made with fully ripened fruit taste plenty sweet without the half cup—or more—of sugar frequently called for in the recipe.

Gradually reduce your sugar intake until the taste buds adjust. If you are a sugar addict, try eliminating sugar altogether.

•**Satisfy sugar cravings.** Fruit is your best choice. Besides nutrients and disease-fighting plant chemicals known as *phytochemicals*, fruit provides fiber. This slows the absorption of sugar into your bloodstream.

Fruit won't give you the same energy rush that you get from refined sugar. That's partly what makes sugar so addictive for some people.

Once you are accustomed to eating fruit instead of, say, cookies or candy, add vegetables to your snacking repertoire.

Steam some white potatoes, sweet potatoes, squash and other vegetables containing complex carbohydrates.

Complex carbohydrates are converted into sugar in your digestive tract. This provides a steady flow of sugar into the bloodstream.

Keep these foods in your refrigerator along with fresh green and red pepper strips, jicama, carrots and celery.

Helpful: Brush your teeth when you crave sugar. Most toothpastes contain artificial sweetener. It often satisfies a craving.

•**Don't keep sugar-laden foods in your home.** That way, if you need a sugar fix, you'll be forced to go to the store to feed your habit.

This delaying tactic will give you time to change your mind and temper—if not lessen—the urge.

Sugar cravings often subside within 15 minutes. If you still must have sugar after you've traveled to a store, buy the smallest size of whatever it is you crave—and enjoy it. Then throw out what you don't eat…or give it away.

•**Be aware of psychological stress.** Is there something that's making you anxious? Are you putting that sweet morsel in your mouth to calm emotional upset?

Rather than opening the refrigerator, try exercising, writing in a journal, deep breathing, yoga, listening to music, praying or meditating —anything that helps alleviate stress.

Once you've successfully eliminated—or at least cut back on—your sugar consumption, you'll begin to appreciate the natural sweetness of many healthful foods. A carrot or a piece of fruit will taste as good as candy once did.

Obesity Can Cause Vitamin D Deficiency

In a recent study, vitamin D levels were 57% lower in obese adults than in lean individuals.

Problem: The vitamin D gets trapped in fat, increasing the risk for osteoporosis as well as other ailments.

If you're overweight or on a diet: Eat vitamin D-rich foods, such as dairy products and salmon…take a daily supplement containing 400 international units (IU) of vitamin D…and spend five minutes in sunlight two to three times a week.

Jacobo Wortsman, MD, a professor of internal medicine, Southern Illinois University School of Medicine in Springfield.

Diabetic Workout Drink

Diabetics should choose milk or a sports drink over water when exercising. In a recent study, volunteers with juvenile-onset (type 1) diabetes who drank water before, during and after exercising developed low blood sugar. Glucose levels remained normal or increased in those who drank whole or skim milk or a sports drink, such as Gatorade.

Theory: Milk contains carbohydrates and other nutrients that may provide calories for an extended time. Sports drinks contain an effective mix of carbohydrates and electrolytes.

Peter A. Farrel, PhD, professor of physiology and director, Noll Physiological Research Center, Pennsylvania State University, University Park.

New York City Firefighter's 30-Minute Workout

Michael Stefano, a captain in the New York City Fire Department and a certified personal trainer, *www.fire fightersworkout.com.* He is the author of *The Firefighter's Workout Book* (Quill).

To become a New York City firefighter, the recruits must carry a 150-pound dummy up and down a flight of stairs…scale an eight-foot wall…and run a mile in less than six minutes. To do all that, you would have to work out hours every day, right? Wrong.

I met the challenge after following my own 30-minute, every-other-day workout program. It strengthens muscles, fights fat and doesn't require fancy exercise equipment. The key is to work more than one muscle group at a time—and to keep the workout intensity high.*

MUSCLE STRENGTHENERS

For each of the following, do three sets, resting for one to two minutes between sets. Use the first set as a warm-up with roughly half the weight or exertion you would use in a

*Be sure to see your physician before starting any exercise program.

full set. If the exercise calls for dumbbells, use enough weight so that you become tired after eight repetitions.

●**Squats.** These strengthen the entire lower body, including the quadriceps, hamstrings, gluteals and lower back.

Stand with feet shoulder-width apart, holding dumbbells at your sides. Swing the weights forward as you bend at the knees and hips until you are in a sitting position, thighs parallel to the floor. Be sure knees do not extend beyond toes and buttocks don't drop below knees when lowering. Do eight squats per set.

●**Bent arm rows.** These work the back, shoulders and biceps.

With a dumbbell in your right hand, stand with your right foot on the floor and your left knee on a bench or step roughly knee-level in height. Bend at the waist, and place your left hand on the bench for support, so your upper body is parallel to the floor. Lift the dumbbell up to your right hip, then let your arm return to a dangling position. Do three sets of eight for each arm.

●**Push-ups.** These strengthen chest, shoulders, arms and abdominals.

Lie face down on the floor with both hands underneath you, elbows bent. Slowly raise your body. If you have trouble, do a modified push-up—knees instead of toes on the floor—until you're stronger. Aim for 20 push-ups per set.

●**Crunches.** These tighten the stomach and oblique muscles.

Lie with your back on the floor. Keep your knees partially bent and feet flat on the floor. With arms folded across your chest, slowly raise your torso 45°. For added difficulty, clasp hands behind your head. Aim for 30 crunches per set.

To prevent low-back pain and maximize the effectiveness of the movement, concentrate on pressing your lower back into the floor, reducing the arch area between spine and floor.

STRETCHES

These can be done after the strengthening exercises or during the rests between sets. Hold each one for 30 seconds.

●**Chest stretch.** Stand in front of a doorway with each of your arms extending beyond the doorjamb. Step forward, allowing the doorjamb to pull your arms back.

●**Shoulder stretch.** Hold your right arm in front of your body parallel to the ground at shoulder level. Bend at the elbow, as if you were about to grab your left shoulder. Use your left hand to push your right elbow toward your body, with your right hand passing over the left shoulder. Repeat for the left arm.

●**Triangle stretch.** Stand with feet spread shoulder-width apart, arms in a T position in relation to your trunk. Then bend at the waist, reaching for your right leg with your right arm and pointing your left arm upward. Repeat to the left.

●**Hamstring step stretch.** Place your right foot on a step, with your left foot on the ground 12 inches back. Slowly bend the left knee, creating a stretch in the back of the right leg. Repeat with the left leg.

To intensify the stretch: Bend slightly at the waist, and place your hands on the thigh of the stretched leg.

●**Calf stretch.** Stand facing a wall, three to four feet away, with hands on the wall. With your heels firmly planted on the floor, lean in toward the wall.

Better Than Walking... Fitness Walking

Therese Iknoian, an exercise physiologist and walking instructor in Grass Valley, CA. She is the author of *Walking Fast—Techniques and Workouts for High-Level Fitness and Performance* (Human Kinetics). For more tips, visit *www.totalfitnessnetwork.com.*

A casual daily walk of 30 minutes can reduce your risk for cardiovascular disease and diabetes—and increase your life span.

Fast "fitness" walking brings even greater benefits. You'll slim your waistline, improve muscle tone and increase your endurance. Plus, fast walking is fun! *But first...*

ASSESS YOUR HEALTH

Fast walking puts extra strain on your cardiovascular system. Be sure to get the OK from your doctor before starting a fitness walking program. *Undergo a complete physical exam especially if you...*

●**Are mostly sedentary.**

●**Smoke cigarettes.**

●**Have a medical history of heart disease or chest pain.**

●**Have a family member who was diagnosed with heart disease before age 50.**

●**Have diabetes or high blood sugar,** or blood pressure of 140/90 or above.

●**Have joint pain that generally worsens with exercise.**

●**Are taking medication that may interfere with your ability to exercise**—such as for diabetes or high blood pressure.

MIND AND FEET

Walking faster requires concentrating on your walking form. Start by evaluating your normal walking style.

Find a stretch of open sidewalk where you can watch yourself in shop windows. Or have a friend videotape you walking. Make sure that he/she films your entire body, including your feet. Pay special attention to the swing of your arms and the movement of your hips—how you walk normally.

Fitness walking should *not* be done in tennis shoes, aerobics shoes or cross-trainers—they aren't built for straight-ahead movement and walking-specific foot impact.

Instead: Spend at least $50 on a pair of shoes designed strictly for walking...or a pair of lightweight running shoes with a low heel. The shoe should bend easily across the ball of the foot when you flex it in your hand.

HONE YOUR TECHNIQUE

Pick a smooth walking route—a clear sidewalk, a bike path, a running track or an open field. *Do several 30-second bursts of fast walking, keeping these points in mind...*

●**Keep your arms bent at the elbows at a 90-degree angle.** Swing your arms from the shoulder at a faster-than-normal tempo.

When you swing your arms faster, your legs automatically move faster, too.

● **Hold your elbows close to your body.** Concentrate on a strong backswing, pulling your fist all the way back to the hipbone. Don't overdo the forward motion of your arms— reaching out in front of you robs your walking stride of power.

● **Keep your chin pulled in.** Make sure your ears are positioned directly in line with your shoulders.

● **Resist the urge to lean forward.** Keep yourself tall with tight abdominals.

● **Land on your heel, and roll forward onto the ball of your foot.** Keep your toes pointed straight ahead.

● **Keep the area from just below your rib cage to your hipbones as relaxed as possible.** As you stride, imagine that your legs start at your waist.

● **Don't take big steps.** Try to glide as if you are on wheels, taking shorter, quicker steps.

SUPPLEMENTAL EXERCISES

To avoid sticking out your elbows: Practice walking close to a hedge or wall. Keep your elbows tucked in on that side to avoid hitting the barrier.

For a quicker stride: Mark off a 10- to 30-yard section of sidewalk, street or track. Walk this stretch as fast as you can, counting your steps. Repeat several times. Try to increase the number of steps with each repetition.

Practice pushing yourself: Walk up a short hill several times, being careful not to lean forward from the waist.

To limber up your walking muscles: Try out the following…

● **Hip stretch.** Sit on the floor with the right leg straight in front of you and the left knee bent with the foot on the floor to the outside of the right leg. Sit up straight. Use the right arm to pull the bent left knee to your body. Gently rotate the right shoulder to the left knee. Hold for 15 to 30 seconds, then switch legs and repeat.

● **Lower-back stretch.** Lie on your back. Grasp behind your right knee with both hands. Use a towel if you have trouble reaching with your hands. Pull your knee to your chest so you feel a slight stretch in your lower back and upper hips. Hold for 15 to 30 seconds. Switch legs and repeat.

DEVELOP A WALKING PROGRAM

Once you've mastered the technique, start incorporating fast fitness walking into your regular daily walks.

After warming up for five to 10 minutes, pick an object a short distance away—such as a mailbox or a telephone pole—and walk as fast as you can until you reach it. Then return to your normal walking pace. Repeat this several times.

Over the next few weeks, gradually increase the length of these "speed bursts" until you're able to hold a fast pace for a minute or two at a time.

Next, do a three-minute session of fast walking in the middle of your workout. Every other day, add a little time to it, until you can walk fast for five minutes with good form and without stopping.

When you've accomplished this, begin adding a second fast walk right after the first, with a minute or two of slow walking in between to recover. Do this every other day until you can manage to perform two or more five-minute stretches back to back. As a final step, try to eliminate the "rest period," and walk fast for 10 or more minutes straight.

Continue fitting in 10 minutes of fast walking into your regular walks every other day. This can be done all in one stretch…or you can break up the 10 minutes into smaller pieces for variety.

On one or two days per week, add three to six "speed bursts" of one minute, alternated with one to two minutes of easier walking. Don't overdo it—you should always have one easy workout after every hard workout. Once a week, walk for 45 to 60 minutes at a steady, brisk pace—this will help increase endurance.

Enlist a training partner for some workouts: Walking fast is even more fun when you share the experience with a friend or your spouse—and you'll both come away from your fitness walks feeling trimmer, stronger and more energetic.

Strength Training: Simple 20-Minute Plan Brings Big Improvements

Wayne Westcott, PhD, fitness director, South Shore YMCA, Quincy, MA. He is coauthor of *Strength Training Past 50—For Fitness and Performance Through the Years* (Human Kinetics).

Many people think that strength training is only for young people or athletes. In fact, people over age 50 stand to gain the most from strength training. *Even men and women in their 80s can get huge benefits from lifting weights...*

- **Increased muscle mass.**
- **Increased metabolic rate,** making it easier to reduce body fat.
- **Increased bone density.**
- **Improved glucose metabolism.**
- **Quicker digestion.**
- **Reduced blood pressure.**
- **Lower cholesterol levels.**

Best of all, you can get these benefits quickly and safely in your own home. The strength-training program outlined below takes only 20 minutes per session.

GETTING STARTED

Before starting any strength-training program, get clearance from your doctor. If you have a preexisting condition, such as heart disease, diabetes or low back pain, he/she may suggest some training modifications.

Once you have your doctor's go-ahead, you'll need two adjustable dumbbells with locks and 75 pounds of weight plates...

- **Four 10-pound plates**
- **Four five-pound plates**
- **Four 2.5-pound plates**
- **Four 1.25-pound plates**

These can be obtained at a sporting-goods store for about $45 to $80.

You will also require a flat, padded weight-lifting bench. *Cost:* About $100.

Place the bench and weights in an uncluttered area. Then dress in comfortable, loose-fitting clothing and athletic shoes, and you're ready to begin.

FOR MAXIMUM BENEFIT

Always warm up with five minutes of easy walking or cycling. *Other important strategies...*

- **For each strength-training session,** do eight to 12 repetitions of each exercise. If the twelfth repetition feels easy, add 2.5 to five pounds of weight to each dumbbell. If you can't do eight repetitions, subtract 2.5 to five pounds from each dumbbell.
- **Do two to three strength-training sessions a week** on nonconsecutive days.
- **Perform each exercise smoothly,** at a controlled speed. Take two seconds for the lifting phase, and another four seconds to lower the weight back to starting position.
- **Once 12 repetitions of a given exercise feels easy for two sessions in a row,** add 2.5 pounds to each dumbbell.
- **Rest three minutes between exercises.**
- **Drink plenty of water** before, during and after each strength-training session.
- **If your muscles feel sore for more than two days,** check with your doctor before doing another session.

Caution: Holding your breath while lifting weights can cause a dangerous rise in blood pressure. Breathe smoothly at all times. Exhale as you lift the weight, and inhale as you lower it.

A TRAINING PLAN

- **Dumbbell squat** (works the fronts and backs of thighs). Grasp a dumbbell in each hand. Stand with palms facing inward and feet about hip-width apart. Looking straight ahead, slowly lower your hips down and back. *Note:* To avoid injury, it is important that your knees do not extend beyond your feet. If balance is a problem, position your buttocks against a wall for support. Slowly straighten your knees and hips, exhaling as you do, until you're standing upright again.

Typical Starting Weight

Age	50–59	60–69	70–79
Men	25 lbs.	20 lbs.	15 lbs.
Women	12.5 lbs.	10 lbs.	7.5 lbs.

- **Chest press** (works chest, shoulders, backs of arms). Lie on your back on the weight bench with your legs straddling the bench, knees bent

90 degrees with feet flat on the floor. With arms bent at the elbow, grasp both dumbbells so that they rest naturally at your shoulders. Push them up in unison until your arms are extended over your chest, with elbows slightly flexed.

Slowly lower the dumbbells together until your upper arms are parallel to the floor. Then slowly push them back to the starting position, exhaling as you lift them.

Typical Starting Weight

Age	50–59	60–69	70–79
Men	25 lbs.	20 lbs.	15 lbs.
Women	10 lbs.	7.5 lbs.	5 lbs.

●**Dumbbell one-arm row** (works the upper back, shoulders, fronts of arms). Grasp a dumbbell in your right hand. Support your weight by placing your left hand and knee on the weight bench. Keep your right leg straight and your right foot flat on the floor.

With your right palm facing inward, slowly lift the dumbbell to your chest, keeping your back straight and exhaling as you do. Then slowly lower the dumbbell to starting position. Do this eight to 12 times, then switch sides and repeat.

Typical Starting Weight

Age	50–59	60–69	70–79
Men	25 lbs.	20 lbs.	15 lbs.
Women	10 lbs.	7.5 lbs.	5 lbs.

●**Dumbbell press** (works the shoulders and backs of arms). Sit upright with legs straddling the weight bench, feet flat on the floor. Grasp both dumbbells with palms turned forward and held at shoulder height.

Slowly lift the dumbbells in unison until your arms are fully extended straight over your shoulders, exhaling as you do. Slowly lower the dumbbells to starting position.

Typical Starting Weight

Age	50–59	60–69	70–79
Men	20 lbs.	15 lbs.	10 lbs.
Women	10 lbs.	7.5 lbs.	5 lbs.

●**Trunk curl** (works the midsection). Lie on your back on a mat or carpeted floor, with your knees bent and your feet flat on the floor. Place your hands loosely behind your head. Slowly raise your shoulders about 30 degrees off the floor, exhaling as you do. Then slowly lower your shoulders to the floor.

●**Dumbbell curl** (works the fronts of arms). Stand with feet hip-width apart. Grasp a dumbbell in each hand with arms straight down, palms facing inward. Lift both dumbbells upward to your shoulders by rotating your wrists until your palms face your chest, exhaling as you do. Then slowly lower both dumbbells to starting position.

Typical Starting Weight

Age	50–59	60–69	70–79
Men	15 lbs.	12.5 lbs.	10 lbs.
Women	10 lbs.	7.5 lbs.	5 lbs.

●**Dumbbell triceps extension** (works the backs of arms). Grasp one dumbbell with both hands, and stand with feet hip-width apart. Lift the dumbbell until your arms are fully extended straight overhead. Inhale as you slowly bend your arm and lower the dumbbell behind your head, toward the base of your neck. Then lift the dumbbell back to the starting position, exhaling as you do.

Typical Starting Weight

Age	50–59	60–69	70–79
Men	20 lbs.	17.5 lbs.	15 lbs.
Women	10 lbs.	7.5 lbs.	5 lbs.

Yoga for Everyone

Miriam Austin, the author of *Yoga for Wimps: Poses for the Flexibly Impaired* (Sterling). She is a yoga teacher in Otis, MA.

Many people think you must be super-flexible to do yoga. That's simply not the case.

When I first started taking yoga 20 years ago, the poses proved too difficult since I had so many athletic injuries. Luckily, I found a teacher who helped me modify the poses so that they are easy enough for any beginner.

These yoga poses reduce stress, relieve lower back pain, enhance athletic ability and boost your sense of well-being.

The following seven poses do not require a lengthy workout session. They can be performed between your daily activities. You can use them for a light workout—or as a stepping stone to more advanced poses or a formal yoga class.*

If you've never tried yoga, here's how to get started…

• **Perform all of the poses in bare or stocking feet.**

• **Keep two towels handy** for poses that require extra support.

• **Begin and end each pose slowly.**

• **Relax and breathe normally** while holding each pose.

• **Never do any movement that causes you pain.**

CHAIR STRETCH

This is a great pose to relax your back and shoulders. When you're feeling tense, use it to stretch out your back—or as a break during shopping or sightseeing.

Sit in a chair with your feet placed slightly wider than your hips. Bend forward at the waist, relaxing your entire body. When you're leaning all the way forward, grasp each elbow with the opposing hand and drop your head in the space between your knees.

Relax your neck completely. Hold the pose for one minute.

KITCHEN COUNTER POSE

This pose relieves back pain by stretching out the lower and upper back. You can do it while waiting for your coffee or tea to brew in the morning.

Place a folded towel on your kitchen countertop. Stand with your hips pressed against the side of the counter. The countertop edge should be even with the bend in your hip crease. (If you're too low, stand on your toes or on a phone book…too high, bend your knees.)

Lean over the counter. Place your head and crossed arms on the towel with your head turned to one side. Rest in this position for five minutes.

*To find a teacher in your area, visit the *Yoga Journal* Web site at *www.yogajournal.com.*

If your neck feels tight, do this facedown instead, resting your forehead on your arms or rolled towel.

RECLINING HAMSTRING STRETCH

This pose limbers up your walking muscles by stretching the backs of your thighs. I recommend doing it before you get out of bed each morning.

Lie on your back with your legs extended. Place the midpoint of a man's necktie under the ball of your right foot and grasp the ends in either hand. Holding the tie, lift your right leg toward the ceiling, keeping your leg straight and your toes flexed in toward you. Hold for 30 seconds. Switch legs and repeat. Then place both feet in the tie and stretch for 60 seconds.

ROCK THE BABY

This chair exercise is a terrific way to loosen a stiff hip or to stretch out your hips before more strenuous exercise, such as walking, jogging or bicycling. It also helps relieve lower back pain.

Sit in the middle of the chair seat, holding your back straight. Bring your right leg up to your chest, grasping your knee in your right hand and your foot in your left hand.

Bring your calf as close as possible to your chest, keeping it parallel to the floor. Move your right leg from side to side as though you were rocking a baby. Do this for 30 seconds. Switch legs and repeat.

DOWNWARD FACING DOG

This is one of the most famous yoga poses. It stretches and strengthens your legs, torso, arms and shoulders. When you're feeling tired or stressed, perform this exercise in the kitchen or at your desk.

Place the back of a chair against the wall. Kneel two feet in front of the chair and place your hands on the sides of the seat.

Keeping your arms straight, slowly raise up on your toes, by straightening your knees. Your torso should angle downward. Hold for 20 seconds, lengthening your back as much as possible.

STAFF POSE

This is a great way to stretch your legs and hips before and after physical activity, such as skiing, running or racquet sports.

Lie on your back with your buttocks as close to the wall as possible. Extend your legs straight up the wall. As you're doing this, straighten your knees and flex your feet toward you. Hold the pose for another 20 seconds.

To stretch your hips *and* inner thighs, slowly open your legs as far as you comfortably can and flex your feet toward you.

Remember, gravity is your friend. Allow it to ease your legs wider as the muscles relax. Hold for 30 seconds. To take pressure off your inner thighs, do this pose with a rolled-up towel placed between the outside of each upper thigh and the floor.

PASSIVE BACK BEND

This pose is perfect for unwinding at the end of the day. It stretches and strengthens the back and allows more oxygen into the lungs.

Roll up a large towel. Lie on your back. Place the roll under your upper back, behind your breast-bone. Extend arms and legs straight outward. Relax and breathe naturally.

Rest as long as you want. I like to stay in this pose for at least 20 minutes. To enhance the relaxation effect, cover your eyes with a small towel and insert earplugs.

Yoga illustrations by Shawn Banner.

Get Fit Fast with 10-Minute Workouts

Glenn A. Gaesser, PhD, professor of exercise physiology and faculty adviser of the cardiovascular health and fitness program, University of Virginia, Charlottesville. He is coauthor of *The Spark: The Revolutionary New Plan to Get Fit and Lose Weight 10 Minutes at a Time* (Fireside).

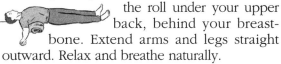

The biggest misconception about exercise is that it must be done for long periods of time in order to be effective. Unfortunately, I may be partly to blame for that mistaken belief.

In 1998, my colleagues and I at the American College of Sports Medicine issued new fitness guidelines. We recommended 20 to 60 minutes of aerobics, three to five times weekly, plus regular strengthening and stretching exercises.

Only later did it occur to me that these guidelines might actually *discourage* fitness—that people unable to dedicate up to an hour to each exercise session might never get off the couch.

But was there an effective alternative? In 2000, I launched a study to determine whether two or three 10-minute workouts, performed on most days of the week, could substantially improve fitness. Forty mostly sedentary adults, ages 32 to 68, enrolled in the program. *After only three weeks, the participants averaged...*

●**A three-pound weight loss** (that is a healthy and *sustainable* drop of one pound per week).

●**A doubling of their strength and muscular endurance.**

●**A 15-point drop in total cholesterol levels.** Participants who started in the high-risk range for cholesterol (240 points and above) experienced an average 34-point drop in total cholesterol.

Result: The group as a whole reduced their heart disease risk by 20%, while high-risk members lowered their risk by nearly 40%.

10-MINUTE WORKOUTS

Regardless of your current fitness level, you can benefit from brief, high-intensity workouts —what I call "sparks." Sparks can be incorporated into your existing program or used as a fitness routine on their own.

Aim to do two or three 10-minute sparks daily, for a total of 15 a week. Half should be aerobic workouts, with the other half divided between strengthening and stretching exercises.

Intensity is crucial. As endurance, strength and flexibility increase, you'll want to move faster...lift more weight...and stretch farther so that your brief workouts remain challenging.

AEROBIC SPARK

Brisk walking, running, cycling, jumping rope or fast dancing—any activity that gets your heart and lungs pumping—is great aerobic exercise.

Begin your aerobic workouts with a slow, two-minute warm-up (walking or a slower version of any activity you choose), build to near-peak intensity for minutes three through nine, then return to an easy pace for a final 60-second cooldown.

Near-peak intensity means you're breathing hard and would have trouble holding a normal conversation. Remember, you must set a pace you can sustain for five to six minutes. If you're gasping for air, slow down.

STRENGTHENING SPARK

Strengthening exercises should be done at high intensity for the duration of the workout.

For the upper-body exercises, choose hand weights that make you *work* for the last two repetitions of any 10- to 15-rep set. If you are breezing right through your sets, increase the weight, not the repetitions.

For the lower-body exercises done without weights, increase the repetitions to keep the routine challenging.

Here's a 10-minute strengthening workout you can do almost anywhere. Aim to do the workout every other day. For each exercise, perform two sets of 10 to 15 repetitions, resting for 30 seconds between sets.

●**Minutes 1 to 2: Biceps curl.** Stand

straight, arms at your sides, hands facing in, gripping weights. Slowly curl the weights up to your shoulders, turning your arms so that your hands face your chest. Slowly lower your arms to starting position.

●**Minutes 3 to 4: Upper-arm presses.** Stand straight, arms bent at elbow, palms facing out, gripping a weight in each hand. Very slowly lift your weights straight up above your head, palms still facing out. Slowly lower weights back to shoulder level.

●**Minutes 5 to 6: Upper body.** While sitting on the edge of a chair, hold your back straight and put your feet flat on the floor. Balance hand weights on the tops of your legs, palms facing down. Then slowly raise your elbows to shoulder height. Hold

for two seconds, palms facing down. Slowly lower elbows back to your sides.

●**Minutes 7 to 8: Lower body.** While sitting

on the edge of a chair, hold your back straight and put your feet flat on the floor. Clasp your arms across your chest. Inhale and rise slowly out of the chair, keeping your back extremely straight and your arms crossed so that you use only your buttocks and thighs. Slowly lower yourself back into the chair.

●**Minute 9: Abdomen.** Sit on the edge of a chair and lower your torso so that your shoulders touch the back of the chair. Extend your legs, knees slightly bent, right ankle crossed over left. Lower your left heel to the floor. Grasping the sides of the chair, inhale and slowly raise your legs until they are parallel to the floor, using only your abdominal muscles.

Do *not* strain your arms or neck. Hold for three seconds. Exhale and slowly lower your feet to the floor. After completing a set, repeat with left ankle crossed over right.

●**Minute 10: Back track.** Stand in a slight lunge position—right foot back and straight, heel on floor, left foot forward with knee slightly bent. With your arms at your sides, exhale and slowly move your arms straight out and over your head.

Bend your left knee as much as you can, without bending your right leg or lifting your right foot off the floor. Inhale as you slowly reverse the move, returning to your starting position. After completing a set, switch leg positions and repeat.

FLEXIBILITY SPARK

Flexibility exercises should stretch your muscles, not strain them. If you feel sharp pain, stop.

Here is a 10-minute stretching session. Aim to do the stretches every other day. For each exercise, hold the stretch for 30 seconds. Rest for 15 to 30 seconds between each repetition.

● **Minutes 1 to 3: The pelvic rock.** Lie on your back, knees bent, feet flat on the floor. Slowly lift your torso, keeping your head, shoulders and feet on the floor. Hold for 30 seconds. Slowly lower your body to the floor. Repeat three times.

● **Minutes 4 to 6: The rag doll.** Stand with feet straight, arms at your sides, knees slightly bent. Inhale deeply. Exhale, while slowly bending your body at the waist. Let your head hang loose as your fingers reach for the floor. Hold for 30 seconds. Slowly roll back up. Inhale. Repeat three times.

● **Minutes 7 to 10: The cat.** Get on all fours, hips tucked in, head aligned with your back and face down. Slowly inhale. Lift your head up and arch your back. Hold for 30 seconds. Exhale slowly, while rounding your back and lowering your head toward the floor. Hold for 30 seconds. Inhale and return to the starting position. Repeat four times.

Workout illustrations by Shawn Banner.

Muscle Loss Prevention

Muscle mass in the average adult declines by more than six pounds per decade. The rate of muscle loss accelerates after age 45.

Good news: Age-related muscle loss can be prevented and even reversed by exercising 30 to 50 minutes a day four or five days a week.

Best: A fitness routine that encompasses stretching, weight lifting and aerobic activity.

William J. Evans, PhD, professor of geriatrics, physiology and nutrition, University of Arkansas for Medical Sciences, Little Rock.

Benefits of a Fitness Trainer

Get results from exercise, faster *and* more easily by hiring a fitness trainer.

Recent study: Two groups of men began a fitness program. One group exercised under the supervision of a fitness trainer. The other group worked out on their own.

Result: Those who worked with a trainer became 30% to 45% stronger than the solo exercisers—and achieved results 30% faster.

Trainers charge as little as $20 an hour. Most YMCAs/YWCAs and health clubs have trainers on staff.

Scott Mazzetti, doctoral fellow and instructor, Human Performance Laboratory, study author, Ball State University, Muncie, IN.

5

Better Health Naturally

Longevity Boosters From the World's Longest-Lived People

The residents of Okinawa, an island chain of Japan, are among the healthiest and longest-lived people in the world. Okinawa has more 100-year-olds than anywhere else—33.6 per 100,000 people, compared with approximately 10 per 100,000 in the US.

The 25-year Okinawa Centenarian Study discovered that, compared with Americans, Okinawans have...

●**80% lower risk of breast and prostate cancers.**

●**50% lower risk of colon and ovarian cancers.**

●**40% fewer hip fractures.**

●**Minimal risk of heart disease.**

What's the secret to the Okinawans' longevity —and what can we do to achieve the same healthful vigor? *The following factors are especially important...*

ACCEPTING ATTITUDE

While many Americans have Type A personalities, Okinawans believe that life's travails will work themselves out. The average American might be said to suffer from *hurry sickness.* Okinawans prefer to work at their own pace, referred to locally as *Okinawa Time.* They don't ignore stress...but they rarely internalize it.

Stress signals your body to secrete large amounts of *cortisol* and other stress hormones. That damages the heart and blood vessels and accelerates bone loss.

To reduce stress: Don't take on more than you can handle...take advantage of flextime at work...don't get worked up about things you can't change, such as traffic jams or rude behavior...practice deep breathing and meditation.

Bradley J. Willcox, MD, principal investigator of geriatrics, Pacific Health Research Institute, Honolulu, HI and assistant professor of geriatrics, University of Hawaii. He is also coauthor of *The Okinawa Program: How the World's Longest-Lived People Achieve Everlasting Health—and How You Can Too* (Crown).

LOW-CALORIE INTAKE

Okinawans consume an average of 1,900 calories a day, compared with 2,500 for Americans. Studies have shown that animals given a diet with 40% fewer calories than the diets of free-feeding animals live about 50% longer.

Reason: Harmful oxygen molecules (free radicals) are created every time the body metabolizes food for energy. Because the Okinawans take in fewer calories, their lifetime exposure to free radicals—which damage cells in the arteries, brain and other parts of the body—is reduced.

PLANT-BASED DIET

About 98% of the *traditional* Okinawan diet consists of sweet potatoes, soy-based foods, grains, fruits and vegetables. This is supplemented by a small amount of fish (and lean pork on special occasions). These plant foods contain *phytonutrients*—chemical compounds that reduce free radical damage. A plant-based diet is also high in fiber, which lowers cholesterol and reduces the risk of diabetes, breast cancer and heart disease. The *current* Okinawan diet is about 80% plant food.

Wok advantage: The Okinawans' style of cooking is high-heat stir-frying in a wok, which requires little oil. They typically stir-fry with canola oil, which is high in heart-healthy monounsaturated fat and omega-3 fatty acids. These fatty acids lower levels of LDL (bad) cholesterol while increasing levels of HDL (good) cholesterol.

SOY FOODS

Elderly Okinawans eat an average of two servings of soy foods daily—such as tofu, miso soup and soybean sprouts. Soy is rich in flavonoids, chemical compounds that reduce the tendency of LDL to stick to arteries, thereby reducing the risk of heart disease or stroke. Soy foods may also protect against cancer…menopausal discomfort (such as hot flashes)…and osteoporosis. You don't have to eat a lot of soy foods to get similar benefits. One daily serving of tofu (about three ounces) or soy milk (eight ounces) may be protective.

FISH

Fish harvested from the waters surrounding Okinawa is an integral part of the daily diet. The omega-3 fatty acids in fish "thin" the blood and reduce the risk of clots—the main cause of heart attack.

Omega-3s also inhibit the body's production of inflammatory chemicals called *prostaglandins.* That may lower the risk of inflammatory conditions, such as arthritis and the bowel disorder Crohn's disease.

Americans can get similar benefits by eating fish at least three times a week. Cold-water fish —salmon, mackerel, tuna—contain the largest amounts of omega-3s. Fish oil supplements are a worthwhile alternative for people who are "fish phobic."

HEALTHY WEIGHT

The traditional Okinawan diet is low in fat and processed foods, as well as calories—so obesity is rare in elder Okinawans. This means their risk of weight-related health problems, such as diabetes, heart disease and cancer, is much lower than that of Americans. This is in stark contrast to younger Okinawans, who eat a more Westernized diet and have the highest obesity levels in Japan.

Postmenopausal bonus: After menopause, a woman's main source of estrogen is no longer the ovaries, but extraglandular tissues, mainly body fat. Women who maintain a healthful weight produce less estrogen, which reduces the risk for breast cancer.

JASMINE TEA

Okinawans drink about three cups of jasmine tea daily. It contains more antioxidant flavonoids than black tea. Those antioxidants may reduce risk for heart disease as well as some cancers.

NOT SMOKING

In the US, hundreds of thousands of people die from smoking-related diseases annually. Few elderly Okinawans have ever smoked… although one man interviewed for the study took up smoking when he was 100. He got bored with it and quit the next year. About 60% of younger Okinawan men now smoke.

EXERCISE

People are healthiest when they combine aerobic, strengthening and flexibility exercises. Okinawans often get all three by practicing martial arts or a traditional style of dance that resembles tai chi. *Smart regimen…*

- **Swimming, biking, jogging, etc.** for at least 30 minutes three times weekly.

- **Lifting weights** at least 20 minutes twice a week.

- **Flexibility exercises**—yoga or stretching —whenever you can and certainly after each aerobic or strength-training session.

SOCIAL LINKS

Moai is the Okinawan word that means "meeting for a common purpose." Groups of friends, colleagues or relatives get together at least once a month to talk…share gossip…and provide emotional or even financial support.

People who maintain active social networks live longer and are less likely to get sick. When they do get sick, they recover more quickly if they have the support of friends.

SPIRITUALITY AND RELIGION

People who have spiritual or religious beliefs live longer than those who don't. Spirituality and religion are a part of daily life in Okinawa. People pray daily for health and peace. They look out for one another in a "help thy neighbor" ethic called *Yuimaru.* Moderation is a key cultural value.

Women are the religious leaders in Okinawa. They also tend to have very high levels of life satisfaction and respect as they age.

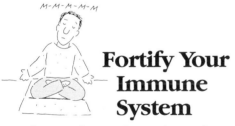

M-M-M-M-M

Fortify Your Immune System

Andrew L. Rubman, ND, associate professor of clinical medicine at the College of Naturopathic Medicine, University of Bridgeport, and director, Southbury Clinic for Traditional Medicines, both in Connecticut.

A healthy immune system can help to fight off pathogens, including bacteria and viruses, and may improve resistance to anthrax bacteria, smallpox viruses and other germs.

The following supplements boost immunity and are generally safe for most everyone. For dosages, read the label or discuss with your doctor. Check with your pediatrician for children's dosages. Pregnant and breast-feeding women should consult their obstetricians before taking any supplements.

- **Bio-Vegetarian,** a combination of vitamins and minerals. Priority One Health and Nutrition, 800-443-2039…*www.priorityonevitamins.com.* $17.50* for 60 tablets.

- **Aqua Sel,** which contains the mineral selenium. T.E. Neesby, 800-633-7294. $10.50 for 15 ml.

To protect and help detoxify the liver and digestive tract…

- **Lipall-Plus,** a vitamin and herb supplement. Anabolic Laboratories, 800-445-6849… *www.anaboliclabs.com.* $8.30 for 90 tablets.

- **Anabolic Milk Thistle.** Anabolic Laboratories, 800-445-6849…*www.anaboliclabs.com.* $6.45 for 50 capsules.

Also important: Exercise regularly…minimize stress…eat plenty of fresh fruits and vegetables…and reduce intake of wheat-based products.

Emergency food supply: Freeze servings of egg-drop soup made with a chicken-stock base. This is a compact source of fresh water, protein, vital fat, vitamins and minerals. *Classic recipe: www.globalgourmet.com/food/special/ 2001/joy/eggdrop.html.*

*Prices subject to change.

Little-Known Risks from Popular Herbal Remedies

Joe Graedon, a Durham, North Carolina–based pharmacologist, and his wife, Teresa Graedon, PhD, authors of several books, including *The People's Pharmacy Guide to Home and Herbal Remedies* (St. Martin's Griffin). Their Web site, *www.peoplespharmacy.org,* provides information about the uses and side effects of herbs and drugs.

Most people assume that herbal remedies are inherently safer than drugs because they're "natural"…and because they've been in use for thousands of years.

Herbs *are* less likely to cause dangerous side effects. But as the use of medicinal herbs increases, so does the risk of harm.

Here are the eight most commonly used medicinal herbs—in alphabetical order—and important precautions to take if you use them…

BLACK COHOSH

It is used to relieve symptoms of menopause—hot flashes, night sweats and mood changes. Women who are using hormone-replacement therapy should not take black cohosh—it is an unnecessary duplication of effort.

CASCARA SAGRADA

Also known as *sacred bark*, this laxative works by stimulating intestinal contractions.

Risks: Cascara sagrada can cause severe diarrhea, which depletes essential minerals from the body. It can be dangerous when combined with other types of electrolyte-depleting drugs, such as diuretics.

Better choice: Bulk-forming laxatives that contain psyllium seed or methylcellulose.

Better still: Eat more foods that are high in bulk-forming fiber—such as fruits, vegetables and legumes (beans, peas, etc.).

EPHEDRA

Also called *ma huang*, ephedra is commonly found in diet pills and "energy boosters."

Risks: Taking ephedra in combination with MAO-inhibitor antidepressants (Marplan, Nardil, Parnate, etc.) can cause dangerously high blood pressure. Ephedra is also dangerous when combined with certain heart medications, migraine drugs or caffeine.

There have been cases of stroke and cardiac arrest in ephedra users. Many doctors say ephedra shouldn't be available over the counter.

GARLIC

Garlic is used to lower cholesterol…prevent blood clots…lower high blood pressure…and as an antifungal.

The effectiveness of garlic capsules versus fresh garlic remains an unresolved issue.

Risks: Garlic may increase the risk of internal bleeding in those taking anticoagulant medications, such as *warfarin* (Coumadin).

Bottom line: You would have to eat a lot of garlic before experiencing any problems. But if you already take a blood-thinner, garlic supplements could be dangerous.

GINKGO BILOBA

It is used to improve circulation…possibly delay mental declines that are associated with Alzheimer's disease…and reverse some sexual side effects associated with depression.

Risks: In people taking blood-thinning medications, ginkgo may increase the risk of internal bleeding because it inhibits blood clotting.

Like the herb ginseng, ginkgo slows the body's ability to metabolize drugs. If you take *atorvastatin* (Lipitor) for lowering cholesterol or *nifedipine* (Procardia) for controlling high blood pressure, do not take ginkgo. Doing so could result in a dangerous buildup of the drugs in the bloodstream.

GREEN TEA

It has antioxidant and antibacterial properties that are believed to reduce cancer risk and may reduce the incidence of gum disease. Habitual drinkers may have lower cholesterol levels as well.

Risks: In theory, the vitamin K in green tea could reduce the effectiveness of anticoagulants, such as warfarin. But you would have to drink a lot of tea before this could happen.

The tannins in green tea can also block the absorption of iron—a problem for women with anemia.

Important: Supplements that contain concentrated green tea are more likely to cause problems than the beverage itself. It's best to *drink* green tea.

LICORICE

It speeds healing of ulcers, inflammatory bowel disease and other inflammatory conditions of the digestive tract.

Licorice inhibits the secretion of stomach acid and increases production of *prostaglandins*, which protect tissues in the digestive tract.

Risks: Regular use of licorice can deplete potassium from the body, especially when combined with diuretics such as *furosemide* (Lasix). Low levels of potassium are particularly dangerous if you are taking the heart medication *digoxin* (Lanoxin), as this may result in dangerous heart-rhythm disturbances (arrhythmias).

Excessive black licorice use may also bring on increased blood pressure…fluid retention…reduced sex drive…and hormonal imbalances.

Safer: *Deglycyrrhizinated* licorice has been stripped of a harmful component to reduce the risk of side effects.

ST. JOHN'S WORT

St. John's wort appears to be as effective as prescription antidepressants for mild to moderate depression.

Risks: Combining St. John's wort with an antidepressant can cause irritability, muscle contractions, anxiety and/or panic. It may also cause photosensitivity, so do not spend a lot of time out in bright light. Sunglasses will not help.

St. John's wort may also reduce the effectiveness of oral contraceptives. Women who take St. John's wort while using birth-control pills may be more vulnerable to an unplanned pregnancy.

And St. John's wort can decrease the effectiveness of certain medications used to control the AIDS virus.

It is best to avoid combining St. John's wort with other medications unless you have discussed your specific situation with a naturopath, herbalist or knowledgeable physician.

For More Nutrition From Your Veggies...

Vegetables cooked quickly with high heat will retain more of their nutrients.

Helpful: Avoid overcooking. Microwave or sauté veggies on high heat until they are just tender...slice vegetables thinly so they will cook faster...heat the pan before adding the vegetables...stir them constantly so they'll cook evenly ...pour any leftover liquid over the vegetables— it's packed with vitamins and minerals.

Joan Carter, RD, instructor, department of pediatrics at Baylor College of Medicine, Houston, and spokesperson, American Dietetic Association, Chicago.

Natural Vitamin E Is Better

The natural forms of vitamin E, *gamma tocopherol* and *d-alpha tocopherol*, are needed by the body (and are present in grains). Synthetic vitamin E, *dl-alpha tocopherol*, can cause internal bleeding, including a hemorrhagic stroke. If you take vitamin E supplements, be sure to take the natural form.

The late Victor Herbert, MD, JD, former professor of medicine, Mount Sinai–New York University Health Systems & Bronx VA Medical Center, New York City.

Cook Your Pasta Al Dente

Pasta that's slightly firm has a lower Glycemic Index (GI) than pasta cooked until soft. Foods with low GIs are absorbed into the bloodstream more slowly than high-GI foods and do not cause your blood sugar to rise as quickly. Slower absorption may protect against weight gain, heart disease and diabetes.

Natural Health, 70 Lincoln St., Boston 02111.

Let Oregano Help Keep You Healthy

Ounce for ounce, oregano has 42 times more antioxidant activity than apples... 30 times more than potatoes...and 12 times more than oranges. One tablespoon of fresh oregano (or one-half teaspoon dried oregano) contains the same amount of antioxidants as one medium-sized apple.

Other antioxidant-packed herbs are chives, coriander, dill, parsley, sage and thyme.

Helpful: Add herbs to hot water for a potent tea...or sprinkle them on lean meats and vegetables.

Shiow Y. Wang, PhD, a plant physiologist and biochemist, US Department of Agriculture, Beltsville, MD. Her study was published in the Journal of Agriculture and Food Chemistry, 1 Shields Ave., Davis, CA 95616.

The Omega-3 Solution— Fatty Acids Fight Heart Disease, Arthritis And Obesity

Andrew L. Stoll, MD, director of the psychopharmacology research laboratory at McLean Hospital, and assistant professor of psychiatry at Harvard Medical School, both in Boston. He is the author of *The Omega-3 Connection* (Simon & Schuster).

In Japan and other nations where fish is a dietary staple, many disease rates are significantly lower than in Western countries.

Omega-3 fatty acids—lipid compounds that are a major constituent of fish oil—receive much of the credit for this difference.

Many people now take omega-3 supplements to reduce their risk for heart disease, rheumatoid arthritis, obesity and other health problems. But do omega-3s really deliver all these salutary effects?

Below, distinguished researcher Andrew L. Stoll, MD, gives us the facts…

●**Why are omega-3 fatty acids important?** Essential fatty acids are dietary constituents that promote good health.

In addition to omega-3, there's another essential fatty acid known as omega-6. For optimum health, we need to consume roughly the same amount of omega-3s and omega-6s.

But Americans eat small quantities of fish and even less omega-3-containing plants, such as flax and the salad green purslane. Instead, our diets are loaded with omega-6-rich oils— corn, sunflower and most oils in processed foods. We eat 10 to 20 times more omega-6s than omega-3s.

●**Why is this unhealthful?** Omega-3s contain *eicosapentaenoic acid* (EPA). When we consume this beneficial fat, much of it gets converted into *eicosanoids*, hormone-like substances that direct the inflammatory response and other functions within the immune system, heart and brain.

Omega-6s contain the fatty acid *arachidonic acid*. This substance also turns into eicosanoids —but with a critical difference.

Omega-6 eicosanoids are strongly inflammatory. On the other hand, omega-3 eicosanoids are only slightly inflammatory or, in some instances, anti-inflammatory.

That's why balance is so important. Without it, uncontrolled inflammatory responses can damage virtually any organ system in the body.

●**How do omega-3s protect the heart?** By offsetting omega-6s, omega-3s reduce *atherosclerosis* (hardening of the arteries). Without omega-3s, omega-6s can inflame and damage coronary arteries, allowing plaque buildup.

Omega-3s also raise levels of high-density lipoprotein (HDL), which transports plaque-causing cholesterol out of the body.

EPA prevents blood platelets from sticking together, reducing the risk for clotting.

Omega-3s also help to inhibit *arrhythmia* (erratic heartbeat), the leading factor in fatal heart attacks. Research shows that at least 1 g daily of omega-3s reduces the heart patient's risk for sudden death by 30%.

●**How do omega-3s help prevent obesity and diabetes?** Obesity is a diabetes risk factor. Omega-3s are the only fats that may actually promote weight loss, since they cause the body to burn calories. Plus, people who eat omega-3-rich foods or take supplements often report fewer cravings for other more fattening foods, such as ice cream, butter and cookies.

Omega-3s fight diabetes by making the body's insulin receptors more responsive. In adult-onset (type 2) diabetes, the body's insulin receptors fail. This can lead to a dangerously high level of blood sugar.

●**What about diseases of the immune system?** The highly inflammatory eicosanoids produced by omega-6s are great infection fighters. But when left unchecked by omega-3s, they can damage healthy tissue.

In the digestive disorder known as Crohn's disease, the gut becomes inflamed…in rheumatoid arthritis, it's the joints…in asthma, the airways are inflamed.

In a remarkable Italian study published in *The New England Journal of Medicine*, 60% of Crohn's patients who took 2.7 g of fish oil supplements daily went into remission for more than one year. No medication has proven to be more effective in treating Crohn's disease.

Studies have also indicated that omega-3s reduce the inflammation of rheumatoid arthritis and asthma.

•Do omega-3s help fight other diseases? Research conducted at Brigham and Women's Hospital in Boston indicated that omega-3s block abnormal brain cell signaling in patients who have bipolar disorder (manic depression). Therefore, omega-3s can be a powerful adjunct in treating this illness.

Many bipolar patients who take the antidepressant *lithium* (Lithonate) and other mood stabilizers, such as *divalproex* (Depakote) and *lamotrigine* (Lamictal), improve initially but then later relapse. Omega-3s can enhance the drug's effectiveness and may allow some people to reduce their dosage.

If you're on a mood stabilizer: Do not alter the dose without your doctor's approval. Stopping these medicines abruptly can make the illness worse.

•How much omega-3 does a healthy person need? To maintain health, 1 g to 2 g a day. But it's difficult to get that much in food alone. You would have to consume, say, a large salmon steak daily.

You should certainly try to eat more omega-3-rich foods, such as salmon, tuna, mackerel, sardines…wild game meats, including buffalo and venison…flax…purslane…and walnuts. Add one to two servings a day of these foods to your diet. Still, you may not get enough omega-3s in dietary sources. To ensure adequate intake, take a daily 1 g to 2 g supplement.

•How do I choose the right supplement? Look for distilled fish oil capsules that have an omega-3 concentration of 50% or more.

Quality supplements cost more, but they do enable you to take fewer and smaller pills, without the fishy aftertaste you often get with other brands.

•What do you recommend for vegetarians? Flaxseed oil is a good option for strict vegetarians or those allergic to fish. Consume one-half tablespoon of this plant-based omega-3 every day.

Some people will take flaxseed oil straight. Others can't tolerate the strong taste. However, it's virtually imperceptible when used in waffle batter and other recipes.

•Do omega-3 supplements have any side effects? Omega-3s may inhibit blood clotting. If you're taking a blood thinner, such as *warfarin* (Coumadin), or high-dose aspirin, check with your doctor before starting a regimen of omega-3 supplements.

Some people experience stomach upset, but this usually goes away within seven days. You'll be less likely to have this problem if you use a quality supplement…take it with food…and divide your daily intake among two or three equal doses.

By the way, it's a good idea to take vitamins C and E with omega-3s. These antioxidant vitamins scavenge disease-causing molecules known as "free radicals." Once free radicals are eliminated, omega-3s can do their job.

I typically recommend 800 international units (IU) of vitamin E and 1,000 mg of vitamin C daily. In addition to other benefits, your colds won't last as long.

Cold-Water Therapy Stabilizes Blood Pressure… Reduces Pain… And More

Alexa Fleckenstein, MD, a board-certified internist who practices traditional and complementary medicine in the Boston area. Dr. Fleckenstein holds a German subspecialty degree in natural medicine.

For most Americans, a steaming hot bath or shower is a daily routine. But for the past 150 years, numerous Europeans have used invigorating *cold* showers and swims to promote good health.

Scientific evidence and numerous case histories support the use of "cold-water therapy" as an adjunct to standard treatments for frequent colds, insomnia, high blood pressure—even cancer and other serious disorders.

HOW IT BEGAN

Cold-water therapy was first popularized in Germany by the priest Sebastian Kneipp (1821–1897). In the winter of 1849, Kneipp successfully battled then-incurable tuberculosis by plunging several times weekly into the frigid Danube River. His 1886 book, *My Water Cure,* became an international best-seller.

THE MECHANISM

When practiced for at least four weeks, cold-water therapy...

●**Stabilizes blood pressure.** Cold water triggers the *autonomic nervous system*—which controls involuntary functions, such as heartbeat and breathing—to raise blood pressure, increase heart rate and constrict blood vessels.

The autonomic responses strengthen with each exposure. This stabilizes blood pressure, improves circulation and balances other bodily functions, such as the sleep/wake cycle.

●**Enhances immunity.** Cold water triggers the release of *cytokines* and other hormone-like substances that are key to immune function.

Recent finding: Breast cancer patients who underwent cold-water therapy for four weeks experienced significant gains in their levels of disease-fighting white blood cells, according to a German study.

●**Reduces pain.** Cold causes the body to release *endorphins*, hormones with proven pain-fighting properties.

●**Improves moods.** Cold water activates sensory nerves that lead to the brain. A cold, exhilarating shower can be emotionally uplifting and prime a person for new experiences.

THE REGIMEN

To gain the benefits of cold-water therapy at home, begin with your usual warm shower. When you're finished, step out of the water stream and turn off the hot water. Leave the cold water running.*

Start by wetting your feet first. Next, expose the hands and face.

*Water temperature should be about 60°F. In all but the hottest areas, water straight from the cold faucet will do. If your water is not cold enough to give you a good jolt, enhance the effect by air-drying—rather than towel-drying—your body.

Important: Jumping in all at once may hinder circulation.

Finally, step under the shower. Let the cold water run over your scalp, face, the front of your body, then down your back. You can begin with a shower that lasts only a couple of seconds.

After one month, the entire process should last no more than 40 seconds. Work up to whatever is comfortable for you.

If you can't tolerate the cold: Keep the water cold but expose only your feet, hands and face. Gradually increase the duration and area of exposure.

Caution: People who are very thin or frail may be unable to tolerate cold showers in the beginning. If you do not feel warm and invigorated after the shower, decrease the length of your next cold shower.

If you still don't feel warm within minutes, forgo cold showers. Instead, condition your body with cold sponge baths of the feet, hands, face—and then the rest of your body—after your warm shower.

Do not try cold-water therapy if you suffer from an acute illness, such as severe back pain ...have hardening of the arteries (atherosclerosis)...Raynaud's disease...or have high blood pressure not controlled by medication.

Cold water causes a spike in blood pressure, which can be dangerous for those with conditions such as unmanaged hypertension.

The therapy can be safely used to reduce mildly elevated blood pressure (150/100 and below) or to raise low blood pressure.

If you have questions about your blood pressure: See your doctor for a blood pressure test before starting a cold-water regimen.

Natural Remedies for Arthritis Pain

James M. Rippe, MD, associate professor of medicine at the Tufts University School of Medicine in Boston. Dr. Rippe is the founder and director of the Rippe Lifestyle Institute in Shrewsbury, MA, and the author of 18 books, including *The Joint Health Prescription* (Rodale).

More than half of Americans over age 40 are dealing with some type of joint problem, from stiffness to arthritis pain. In people over age 60, joint problems account for more than 50% of all cases of disability.

In the past, doctors typically relied on the painkilling drugs to treat joint ailments. But these medications do not solve the underlying problems. *Here's how to get lasting relief...*

EXERCISE

A decade ago, doctors told their patients with joint pain to avoid exercise. We now know from dozens of studies that regular exercise is one of the *best* things you can do for your joints.

The perfect exercise program for healthy joints will include aerobics and stretching as well as strengthening...

•**Aerobics.** The safest workouts are low-impact activities such as walking, swimming and bicycling.

Avoid running, step aerobics and jumping rope. They could cause joint injury.

•**Stretching.** Do head rolls, shoulder rolls and hamstring stretches.

•**Strengthening.** Use dumbbells or weight machines. Stretching and strengthening exercises help cushion and stabilize the joints.

To start an exercise program: Perform 10 minutes of aerobic exercises a day. Every week, increase that time by five minutes until you are getting 30 minutes of moderate aerobic activity every day. Do stretching exercises every morning and night. Strengthening exercises should be done every other day.

You do *not* have to do all your daily exercise at one time—as long as you accumulate 30 minutes of activity throughout the day. Gardening, housework and taking the stairs all count.

Caution: If you already have arthritis or another serious joint condition, such as a prior injury, have your doctor and/or physical therapist recommend appropriate exercises for you. Anyone who has been sedentary should consult a doctor before beginning an exercise program.

WEIGHT LOSS AND NUTRITION

If you are overweight, losing even 10 pounds will reduce wear and tear on your joints. Even if you are not overweight, proper nutrition can help keep your joints healthy.

Be skeptical of any "arthritis diet" that claims to cure joint pain by promoting a single type of food or eliminating whole categories of foods. *Instead, just follow basic principles of good nutrition...*

•**Avoid unhealthy fats.** A high-fat diet triggers inflammation—a key component of joint problems. This is especially true of saturated fat (found in many animal products, such as red meat) and omega-6 fatty acids (found in many processed foods and vegetable oils).

Helpful: Substitute monounsaturated fats, such as olive oil and canola oil. Eat foods rich in "good" omega-3 fatty acids, such as nuts, flaxseed and cold-water fish, including salmon and mackerel. These foods help fight inflammation.

•**Eat more vitamin-rich foods.** Fruits and vegetables are good sources of antioxidant vitamins. Antioxidants will neutralize the free radicals, which damage cells and contribute to joint inflammation.

Also, certain vitamins may act directly on joints. Vitamin C is involved in the production of collagen, a component of cartilage and connective tissue. Beta-carotene and vitamins D and K help in the development of strong bones.

For more information on healthy eating and nutrition, contact the American Dietetic Association, 800-877-1600, *www.eatright.org.*

SUPPLEMENTS

Research suggests that certain supplements can help relieve joint problems. *Ask your doctor whether any of the following supplements are right for you...**

•**Vitamins.** Even though food is the best way to get your vitamins, it's a good idea to

*Supplements can interact with other drugs, so tell all your doctors what you are taking.

take a multivitamin supplement to make sure you are getting *all* the vitamins you need. These include beta-carotene and vitamins C, D and E. Vitamin E is especially hard to get in sufficient quantities from food.

●**Gelatin.** It contains *glycine* and *proline,* two amino acids that are important for rebuilding cartilage. These amino acids are found in products made with hydrolyzed collagen protein (such as Knox NutraJoint). Such products dissolve in juice without congealing—unlike cooking gelatin. *Typical daily dosage:* 10 g.

●**Glucosamine.** This sugar is one of the building blocks of cartilage. Increasing evidence suggests that glucosamine helps relieve arthritis pain and stiffness—without major side effects. *Typical daily dosage:* 1,500 mg.

●**Chondroitin.** Naturally present in cartilage, chondroitin is believed to guard against destructive enzymes. *Typical daily dosage:* 1,200 mg. A number of supplements combine glucosamine and chondroitin.

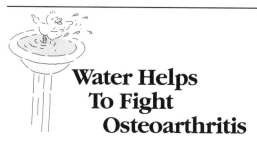

Water Helps To Fight Osteoarthritis

Osteoarthritis pain may be a symptom of dehydration in the joint. Increasing water intake often improves the condition after about four weeks—the time needed to rehydrate the body. Drink half your body weight in ounces.

Example: If you weigh 160 pounds, drink 80 ounces—10 eight-ounce glasses. Drink more during the summer, when humidity is high, or when exercising.

Ronald Lawrence, MD, PhD, a founding member of the International Association for the Study of Pain, Seattle, and coauthor of *Preventing Arthritis* (Putnam).

Wine May Protect Against Arthritis

Two compounds in white wine as well as extra-virgin olive oil—*Tyrosol* and *caffeic acid*—help regulate the release of cytokines, chemical messengers in the body's immune system. Cytokines trigger the inflammation associated with rheumatoid arthritis.

Self-defense: Ask your doctor about drinking white wine—and eating an olive oil-rich diet —to help prevent rheumatoid arthritis.

Alberto A. E. Bertelli, MD, PhD, researcher, department of human anatomy, University of Milan.

Eat Prunes to Prevent Bone Loss

In a new finding, 58 postmenopausal women who consumed about 12 prunes per day for three months showed higher blood levels of enzymes and growth factors indicative of bone formation than women who did not eat prunes.

Theory: The polyphenolic compounds and other nutrients in prunes act as antioxidants to curb bone loss. Although women were studied, researchers believe that men can gain the same beneficial effects from eating prunes.

Bonus: Those studied suffered no significant gastrointestinal side effects.

Baharm H. Arjmandi, PhD, RD, a professor of nutritional sciences and gerontology at the Oklahoma State University, Stillwater.

The Ultimate Cholesterol-Lowering Diet

John McDougall, MD, founder and medical director of the McDougall Program in Santa Rosa, CA, *www.drmcdougall.com*. He is the author of 10 books, including *The McDougall Program for a Healthy Heart: A Lifesaving Approach to Preventing and Treating Heart Disease* (Plume).

The importance of lowering cholesterol levels was underscored again last year, when the National Institutes of Health (NIH) released the new guidelines calling for aggressive treatment for total cholesterol levels of 240 or higher.

NIH recommended aiming for a level of 200 or below.

With my patients, I go even further—I work with them to achieve and maintain a total cholesterol level *no higher than 150.* This is the point where heart disease stops progressing and begins to reverse itself. This is also a level of cholesterol where the risk of dying from heart disease is almost zero. If you settle for a total cholesterol of 200 instead, you still subject your arteries to toxins and plaque buildup—and risk a heart attack.

Here is how I helped my high-cholesterol patients get their levels under control...

CUT OUT ANIMAL PRODUCTS

The single most effective way to lower your blood cholesterol is to stop eating foods that contain cholesterol. In other words, *avoid all animal products*—red meat, poultry, shellfish, fish, eggs, dairy products and foods made with them.

As far as the health of your arteries is concerned, there is no "safe" amount in regard to the consumption of animal products.

Forbidden foods (many of which have long been perceived as permissible) include...

●**Fish and fowl.** Studies show that these foods will raise cholesterol just as surely as beef or pork.

●**Low-fat or skim milk,** cheese or other dairy products. Even when the fat is taken out, the animal proteins in these foods can raise cholesterol levels and damage the artery walls.

●**"Free" fats such as margarine,** corn oil, olive oil and canola oil. These fats are easily oxidized in the bloodstream, making plaque likely to build up on artery walls.

If you follow a strict vegetarian diet for several months, you can lower your cholesterol levels by 25% or more. At the same time, blood levels of triglycerides, homocysteine, uric acid and other heart disease risk factors will also decline.

VEGETARIAN DELIGHTS

Giving up animal products does not mean you must eat poorly. The foods in my program are varied and delicious. They provide all needed nutrients in optimal amounts.

You can eat *all you want* of the following...

●**Whole grains,** including barley, brown rice, buckwheat, bulgur, corn, oatmeal and wheat, as well as noodles that are made from these sources.

●**Potatoes,** sweet potatoes and yams.

●**Root vegetables,** including beets, carrots and turnips.

●**Squashes,** such as acorn, buttercup and zucchini squash.

●**Beans and peas,** including chickpeas, green peas, kidney beans, lentils as well as string beans.

●**Other vegetables,** such as broccoli, brussels sprouts, cabbage, celery, the darker lettuces, spinach, cucumbers, okra, onions, peppers and mushrooms.

●**Mild spices** and cooking herbs.

Eat only limited amounts of fruit and fruit juice (no more than three servings a day), sugar and other sweeteners, salt and fatty plant foods, such as peanut butter, seed spreads, avocados, olives and soybean products—including tofu. Simple sugars, even fruit and juice, raise cholesterol and triglycerides.

HEART-HEALTHY MENU PLAN

There are many excellent vegetarian cookbooks to choose from, but you don't have to be a gourmet to prepare heart-healthful meals. Start with potatoes, rice, beans or spaghetti, then add some low-fat, plant-based sauces and soups. Throw in a salad and bread, and you've got a meal. *Other tips...*

• **For breakfast,** toast, bagels, oatmeal, cereals, hash browns and pancakes (all made from the right ingredients) are all fine. Use rice milk or soy milk on cold cereal.

• **Sauté food in soy sauce,** wine or sherry, vinegar (rice or balsamic), vegetarian Worcestershire sauce, salsa, or lemon or lime juice.

• **Eat until you're satisfied...**and eat as often as you need to.

• **To boost feelings of fullness,** include beans and peas in your meals.

A typical day's menu might include...

Breakfast: Pancakes, oatmeal, French toast or a breakfast tortilla.

Lunch: Vegetable soup, along with a vegetarian sandwich or a veggie burger.

Dinner: Bean burritos, mu-shu vegetables over rice, chili and rice, or spaghetti with marinara sauce, along with some fresh bread and a chickpea salad.

After a week or two on this diet, most people find themselves craving healthful foods—and not missing all that poisonous dietary fat.

CHOLESTEROL-LOWERING DRUGS

With a high-risk patient—someone who's had a heart attack or appears headed for a heart attack, coronary bypass or angioplasty—I would not wait several months to "see what happens." If his/her total cholesterol hasn't fallen to 150 after 10 days of healthful eating, I suggest supplementing the diet with drugs.

Between a vegetarian diet and cholesterol-lowering medication, virtually anyone's cholesterol can be brought down to 150.

First, try out some of the natural cholesterol-lowering "medications"...

• **Garlic** (up to 800 mg, or one clove a day).

• **Oat bran** (two ounces a day) or oatmeal (three ounces, dry weight, a day).

• **Vitamin C** (2,000 mg a day).

• **Vitamin E** (dry form, 400 IU a day).

• **Beta-carotene** (25,000 IU a day).

• **Gugulipid.** Recently, I have been recommending this Indian herb (500 to 1,500 mg, three times a day).

• **Immediate-release niacin** is yet another potentially useful medication. But it can damage the liver, so it should be taken only under a doctor's supervision.

If the patient doesn't respond, I typically prescribe *simvastatin* (Zocor), *pravastatin* (Pravachol), *lovastatin* (Mevacor) or *fluvastatin* (Lescol). Since my patient may have to take this medication for years, it's important to match him with the drug that's most effective, but with the fewest side effects.

EXERCISE AND GOOD HABITS

While exercise isn't as crucial as diet, a brisk walk of at least 20 minutes each day benefits your heart and arteries in many ways.

Exercise trains the heart to beat more efficiently...increases levels of HDL (good) cholesterol...lowers levels of triglycerides...increases oxygen flow to your heart, brain, muscles and other tissues...and boosts the immune system.

As if you didn't know: Don't smoke. Limit coffee consumption (both regular and decaffeinated raise cholesterol levels about 10%). Drink alcohol moderately if at all. Your arteries will thank you.

Apple Juice Fights Heart Disease

Drinking as little as 12 ounces a day of apple juice reduced oxidation of LDL (bad) cholesterol by 20%, compared with 9% in people who ate two whole apples a day. LDL cholesterol oxidization triggers the formation of plaque on coronary artery walls. Researchers theorize that the antioxidant flavonoids found in apples and apple juice are responsible for this beneficial effect. However, they are uncertain why the juice was more effective.

Dianne Hyson, PhD, RD, a staff research associate, department of nutrition, University of California, Davis. Her study was published in the *Journal of Medicinal Food,* 2159 Avenida de la Playa, La Jolla, CA 92037.

Breakfast Cereal May Help Prevent Heart Attack

A 10-year study of 68,000 women found that those who ate breakfast cereal at least five times a week had a 19% lower risk for coronary heart disease than did those who did not eat cereal. Researchers attributed health benefits to the fiber in the cereal and concluded that women may need fiber more than men.

Alicja Wolk, DMSc, professor of nutritional epidemiology, Karolinska Institute, Department of Medical Epidemiology, 17177 Stockholm, Sweden.

Eat Your Way to Lower Blood Pressure

Michael F. Roizen, MD, dean, School of Medicine at SUNY Upstate School of Medicine, Syracuse, NY. He is author of Real Age: Are You as Young as You Can Be? (Cliff Street) and The Real Age Diet: Make Yourself Younger with What You Eat (Harper). www.realage.com.

High blood pressure is more than a leading cause of heart disease and stroke. It is also a major factor in memory loss, wrinkling of the skin, impotence and decreased sexual response in women. Most Americans have blood pressure well over the ideal of 115/75. In fact, less than 10% of those over age 50 have ideal pressure.

While many people require medication, a diet rich in fruits, vegetables, fiber, calcium and potassium has been proven to reduce blood pressure...

•**Eat two to four servings of fruits and three to five servings of vegetables each day.** A colorful variety is best.

•**Up to 25% of daily calories should come from healthful fat** (monounsaturated and polyunsaturated). These are found in olive, canola and flaxseed oils...avocados...unsalted nuts...and fish. When you cook, use oil sparingly. A mere half-teaspoon per meal contains all the necessary nutrients.

•**Eat one clove of garlic and as much onion as you can tolerate each day.** These contain flavonoids, which help the arteries to resist hardening.

•**Avoid saturated fat, found in all animal products.** Eat red meat no more than once a week. An hour before eating a fatty meal, take 400 mg of vitamin C and 400 IU of vitamin E. These may contribute to healthier arteries.

•**Get 1,200 mg of calcium daily**—and 400 IU of vitamin D to help with absorption.

•**Make exercise part of your "daily diet."** I start hypertension patients with 30 minutes of walking a day. After three weeks, they add 10 minutes of weight lifting three times a week. Any exercise is good exercise...and some is better than none.

Chromium Deficiency Increases Your Heart Attack Risk

Chromium, an essential heavy metal, has already been shown to help control blood sugar in people with type 2 (adult-onset) diabetes. And now there's evidence that it may lessen heart attack risk.

Recent finding: The average concentration of chromium in heart attack victims was significantly lower than levels in a control group.

Good sources of chromium: Whole-grain products, green beans, bran cereals and brewer's yeast. The long-term effectiveness and safety of chromium supplements are unknown.

Eliseo Guallar, PhD, assistant professor of epidemiology, Johns Hopkins University School of Public Health, Baltimore.

Proven Ways to Reduce Your Risk of 12 Common Cancers

Cynthia Stein, MD, MPH, research fellow in cancer prevention at the Center for Cancer Prevention at Harvard School of Public Health, Boston. The Center's Web site, *www.yourcancerrisk.harvard.edu*, helps individuals evaluate their risks of different types of cancer.

Cancer is now the second-leading cause of death in the United States, after heart disease, and kills one in four Americans. Each year, more than one million new cases are diagnosed. Some cancer risk factors—family history, age, ethnicity, etc.—can't be changed. *But you can lower your risk of developing cancer by making basic lifestyle changes...*

- **Don't smoke.**

- **Eat a healthy diet.**

- **Maintain a healthy weight.**

- **Get regular physical activity.**

- **Limit alcohol consumption.**

- **Protect yourself from the sun.**

- **Avoid sexually transmitted infections.**

As much as 50% of cancers in this country could be prevented. *Here are some specific steps you can take to decrease your risk of the most common ones...*

PROSTATE CANCER

More than 198,000 new cases are diagnosed annually. *Risk reducers...*

- **Limit the amount of animal fat in your diet.** Men who eat fewer than five servings a day of meat, milk, cheese, etc. have a lower risk of prostate cancer. One serving, which is four ounces, is about the size of a deck of playing cards.

A great deal of research is being done to identify the factors in animal fat that increase prostate cancer risk. One explanation may be that animal fat can affect different hormone levels, increasing cancer risk.

- **Eat one or more servings daily of tomatoes or tomato-based foods,** such as tomato juice and spaghetti sauce. One serving equals one-half cup of whole or chopped tomatoes or sauce, or three-quarters of a cup of tomato juice. Tomatoes are rich in the antioxidant *lycopene*, which may protect the prostate from cancerous cells. Other fruits and vegetables contain lycopene, but tomatoes are the best source.

- **Talk to your doctor about screening tests,** especially if you are at high risk—African-Americans and men with a close relative who had prostate cancer at a young age are at increased risk.

BREAST CANCER

More than 190,000 American women are diagnosed with breast cancer every year. Although the overwhelming majority of people with breast cancer are women, about 1,500 American men are also diagnosed with this disease each year. *Risk reducers...*

- **Eat at least three servings of vegetables daily.** A serving equals one cup of green, leafy vegetables or one-half cup of other vegetables, cooked beans or peas. There are many vitamins and nutrients in vegetables that may reduce the risk of different types of cancers. Specifically, low levels of vitamin A have been associated with breast cancer risk.

- **Limit your alcohol intake.** Alcohol may affect levels of estrogen and other hormones, increasing the risk of breast cancer. Women who have less than one drink per day have a lower risk of breast cancer. One drink is equal to a can of beer, a glass of wine or a shot of liquor.

- **Get regular screening.** All women should get clinical breast exams regularly and should start getting mammograms at age 50 (earlier if there is a strong family history or other risk factors).

LUNG CANCER

Lung cancer is the third most common cancer in the US but the leading cause of cancer death. Nearly 170,000 cases are diagnosed annually. *Risk reducers...*

- **Do not smoke**—and avoid secondhand smoke. Tobacco smoke causes 90% of lung cancer cases. Quitting not only decreases the risk of lung cancer, it also reduces the risk of heart disease, stroke and cancers of the mouth, esophagus, pancreas, kidney, bladder, cervix and colon.

•**Eat a diet rich in fruits and vegetables.** They have many cancer-fighting ingredients, including vitamins A and C. People who eat three or more servings per day have a lower risk of lung cancer. One serving equals one cup of leafy greens…one medium-sized fruit …one-half cup of cut fruit or vegetables…or one-third cup of juice.

Although fruits and vegetables can help protect against many kinds of cancer, nothing will decrease your risk of lung cancer nearly as much as avoiding tobacco smoke.

COLORECTAL CANCER

Cancer of the colon and rectum is currently the second-leading cause of cancer deaths in the US. More than 130,000 new cases are diagnosed every year. *Risk reducers…*

•**Maintain a healthy weight.** Researchers have found that people who maintain a healthy weight have a lower risk of colon cancer. This may be because weight affects different hormone levels in the body.

•**Limit the amount of red meat in your diet.** People who eat less than one serving per day of beef, pork, lamb or veal have a lower risk of colon cancer. One serving is about four ounces. Cooked meat contains chemicals that may increase cancerous cells.

•**Avoid alcohol.** As with breast cancer, it has been found that people who have less than one alcoholic drink per day have a lower risk of colon cancer. Alcohol decreases levels of folate, a B vitamin that may provide protection against cancer.

•**Take a daily multivitamin.** It should contain 400 IU of folate. *Also:* Eat folate-rich foods, such as spinach, asparagus, beans, peas and fortified cereals.

•**Exercise at least 30 minutes each day.** There are many benefits to physical activity. One way it may help against colon cancer is by speeding up the movement of waste through the body.

•**Get screened.** Screening allows early discovery and removal of polyps—small growths that can become cancerous. People who are screened regularly have a lower risk of colon cancer. Ask your doctor about the appropriate screening frequency for you.

BLADDER CANCER

More than 54,000 new cases are diagnosed every year. It most commonly afflicts men. *Risk reducers…*

•**If you smoke, quit now.** Tobacco contains more than 40 carcinogens. Many of these can concentrate in the urine and damage cells lining the bladder walls. As little as one cigarette per day can increase your cancer risk. Quit, and the risk drops almost immediately.

•**Beware of workplace chemicals,** especially those used in the rubber, aluminum and dye industries. Chemicals including aromatic amines have been linked to an increase in bladder cancer. Adequate safety equipment—gloves, respirators, protective suits and eye protection —is essential.

MELANOMA

The deadliest form of skin cancer, melanoma strikes more than 50,000 Americans each year. Other forms of skin cancer like basal cell and squamous cell are more common (more than one million cases per year) but also more easily treated. *Risk reducers…*

•**Use sunblock.** Avoid prolonged sun exposure, especially between 10 am and 4 pm. Wear a hat, sunglasses and long sleeves as often as possible. Always use sunblock with a sun protection factor (SPF) of 15 or higher. Reapply often, especially if you have been in the water or perspiring.

•**Protect your children.** As much as 80% of lifetime sun exposure can occur before age 21. Sunburns early in life increase the risk of skin cancer in later years. Don't let your children go outside without sunblock, a hat and protective cover.

UTERINE CANCER

Also called endometrial cancer, this is the most common cancer of the female reproductive tract. About 36,000 cases are diagnosed annually. *Risk reducer…*

●**Maintain a healthy weight.** High levels of estrogen, especially after menopause, can increase the risk of uterine cancer. And excess fat increases the amount of estrogen in a woman's body.

KIDNEY CANCER

It strikes about 30,000 Americans annually. *Risk reducers....*

●**Don't smoke.** Many of the same carcinogens that damage the bladder also increase kidney cancer risk.

●**Maintain a healthy weight.** In addition to the other benefits of a healthy weight, people who are not overweight also have a lower risk of kidney cancer.

PANCREATIC CANCER

This type of cancer strikes about 29,000 Americans every year. It is often diagnosed at a late stage because there may be no early warning signs. Survival rates are terrible—20% at one year...4% at five years, according to the American Cancer Society. *Risk reducers...*

●**Eat at least three servings of vegetables every day.** Vegetables may protect against cancer in different ways. One way they may protect against pancreatic cancer is by adding fiber to the diet.

●**Don't smoke.** People who smoke have a higher risk of pancreatic cancer than do non-smokers. The chemicals in tobacco smoke will cause cell damage throughout the body, increasing the risk of many types of cancer and other diseases, such as heart disease and stroke.

OVARIAN CANCER

Each year, it strikes 23,000 American women. Like pancreatic cancer, the disease is often difficult to detect and, in many cases, spreads prior to the diagnosis. *Risk reducers...*

●**Breast-feeding,** which can cause a woman to ovulate (produce an egg) less frequently, may help decrease ovarian cancer risk.

●**Taking birth control pills for at least five years** can also decrease the risk of ovarian cancer. They may be protective by preventing ovulation.

However, there are also risks involved in taking oral contraceptives, and a woman should discuss the risks and benefits with her doctor.

STOMACH CANCER

There are more than 20,000 new cases every year. *Risk reducers...*

●**Eat three or more daily servings of fruit.** One vitamin in fruit that may be particularly helpful is vitamin C. Low levels have been associated with stomach cancer.

●**Limit salt intake.** High salt content may affect the lining of the stomach, and thereby increase the risk of cancer. Large amounts of salt are often found in processed foods, soups and sauces.

CERVICAL CANCER

Cervical cancer tends to grow slowly, which is why it can often be prevented or treated successfully when detected early with a Pap test. About 13,000 American women are diagnosed with cervical cancer annually. *Risk reducers...*

●**Use safer-sex practices**—condoms, abstinence or monogamy. Women who are exposed to sexually transmitted infections, especially certain types of the human papillomavirus (HPV) —and especially at young ages—have a higher risk. The infections may cause cell changes that lead to cervical cancer.

●**Do not smoke.** Again, the chemicals in tobacco smoke cause cell damage and increase the risk of cancer.

●**Have regular Pap tests.** Pap tests can identify changes in cells before they become cancerous. Women who have regular Pap tests have a lower risk of cervical cancer.

New Hope For Cancer Patients

Mistletoe extract may provide new hope for cancer patients. In a study, 396 patients received conventional therapy plus injections of *Iscador*—the extract actress Suzanne Somers is using to fight breast cancer. This increased average survival time for breast, colon and other solid tumor cancers to 4.25 years, versus three years for the 396 patients who received chemotherapy and/or radiation but no Iscador. Consult your oncologist for information.

David Riley, MD, editor in chief of *Alternative Therapies in Health and Medicine*, which published the 27-year study by researchers at the Institute of Preventive Medicine in Heidelberg, Germany.

Cancer Fighter on A Sandwich

Broccoli sprouts are rich in a compound that provides significant protection against breast and colon cancers. Sprouts grown from certain broccoli seeds contain up to 50 times more of this compound—sulforaphane glucosinolate (SGS)—than mature broccoli.

Caution: The amount of SGS in broccoli sprouts varies widely.

BroccoSprouts, a brand developed at Johns Hopkins University, is guaranteed to have 20 times the SGS of mature broccoli on an ounce-for-ounce basis. Check your local supermarket.

Paul Talalay, MD, pharmacologist at Johns Hopkins University, Brassica Chemoprotection Laboratory, 725 N. Wolfe St., Baltimore 21205.

Don't Overdose on Soy

High levels of phytoestrogens called isoflavones found in soy may *increase* breast cancer risk. And excessive soy consumption can interfere with thyroid function. Moderate soy consumption—through foods, not supplements—can lower cholesterol levels and reduce breast cancer risk.

Most people can get the benefits of soy's isoflavones from tofu (one-half cup), soy milk (one cup), soy protein (one-half cup cooked) or roasted soy nuts (one ounce). One serving per day will provide up to 50 milligrams of isoflavones—a safe and healthful amount.

Andrew Weil, MD, the director of the Foundation for Integrative Medicine, Vail, AZ.

Apples and Tomatoes For Healthier Lungs

Tomatoes and apples may help your lungs stay healthy. The people who ate tomatoes three times a week and five or more apples a week had slower age-related declines in lung function than those who did not eat these foods, a recent study found. Even smokers did significantly better on lung function tests if they ate plenty of tomatoes and apples.

Theory: Researchers believe the particular combination of antioxidants found in these foods provides the beneficial effect.

Sarah Lewis, PhD, senior lecturer in respiratory epidemiology, Nottingham University, England.

Love Your Liver— How to Care for Your Second-Largest Organ

James L. Boyer, MD, professor of medicine and director, Liver Center at Yale University School of Medicine in New Haven, CT.

The liver is the body's second-largest internal organ by weight (the brain is the largest). It removes toxic substances ingested, inhaled or absorbed through the skin …fights off invading bacteria and viruses… produces clotting factors, blood proteins, bile for digestion and more than 1,000 enzymes… stores iron and glucose needed for energy… and metabolizes cholesterol.

LIVER FITNESS PROGRAM

•**Go easy on alcohol.** Limit beer, liquor or wine to two drinks a day. More than two, especially for women, may harm the liver. Do not drink at all when taking certain medications, such as *acetaminophen* (Tylenol). Alcohol diminishes the liver's ability to metabolize many drugs—even over-the-counter products.

•**Use medication cautiously.** Don't take antibiotics for the sniffles—they fight bacterial infection, not viruses. Check with your physician about any herbal supplements—they may be toxic and/or contaminated due to poor manufacturing conditions.

Always ask about drug side effects. And don't combine medications without your doctor's approval.

●**Limit chemical exposure.** Use aerosol cleaners, chemicals such as carbon tetrachloride and paint sprays only in well-ventilated areas…and be sure to wear a mask, available in hardware stores.

●**Eat wisely.** A balanced diet helps maintain the health of your liver and your gallbladder, which stores bile.

●Avoid fatty foods. High fat consumption raises the risk of gallstones.

●Minimize salt intake.

●Maintain your ideal weight. Obesity is directly linked to gallbladder disorders and may cause fat buildup in the liver. Protein malnutrition can also produce fat buildup.

●Exercise daily.

DISEASE SELF-DEFENSE

There are numerous types of liver disease, including the following…

●**Hepatitis A (HAV).** Sources are contaminated water, food (particularly shellfish) and eating utensils. HAV does not cause chronic liver problems. Symptoms may include nausea, vomiting, fatigue and jaundice.

●**Hepatitis B (HBV).** Transmitted sexually and through exposure to infected blood and other bodily fluids, HBV may lead to other liver complications, such as chronic hepatitis, cirrhosis and even liver cancer.

Both HAV and HBV normally last only a few weeks. And they can be completely prevented with vaccines, which are advised for those in health-related or day-care fields and anyone traveling to developing countries. A vaccine for HBV is now recommended for all children.

●**Hepatitis C (HCV).** Transmitted through exposure to blood, intravenous drug users are at highest risk. HCV can lead to chronic—and potentially fatal—liver infections in 10% to 20% of infected individuals. Older males with HCV who also abuse alcohol have the greatest chance of developing cirrhosis.

●**Cirrhosis.** When scar tissue replaces damaged cells, limiting blood flow and handicapping liver function, the liver becomes cirrhotic. The most common causes of cirrhosis in the US are infection with HCV and heavy drinking. Cirrhosis has also been traced to congenital disease (occurring since birth), environmental toxins, autoimmune reactions and parasitic infection.

DETECT TROUBLE

While we do know what causes many liver disorders, few people can pinpoint the origin or onset of their ailment.

The liver can continue to perform despite some damage—so there may be no warning until effective treatment is impossible. *Symptoms of possible problems include…*

●**Chronic fatigue.**

●**Nausea or loss of appetite.**

●**Jaundice,** the yellow discoloration of skin or eyes.

●**Abdominal swelling** or severe abdominal pain.

●**Chronic itching.**

●**Very dark urine or pale stools.**

Precautions: Have your doctor check your liver as part of your annual physical. Blood tests measure liver function and indicate the presence of disease. You may also require ultrasound and CAT scans or a needle biopsy.

How to Prevent Stomach Ulcers

Stomach ulcer risk can be reduced by up to 50% by exercising.

Theory: Exercise helps prevent ulcers by reducing stomach acid secretion, improving immune function and relieving stress.

The more you work out—and the greater the intensity—the lower the risk.

Caroline Macera, PhD, researcher, physical activity and health branch, Centers for Disease Control and Prevention, Atlanta.

Sleep Right to Avoid Kidney Stones

Sleeping in one position for too long may increase your kidney stone risk.

Recent study: Among people with kidney stones, those who slept mostly on their right side had an 82% chance of forming stones on that side. Left-sided sleepers had a 70% chance of developing left-sided stones.

Self-defense: If you typically sleep on one side, consider varying your sleep position.

Marshall Stoller, MD, professor of urology, University of California, San Francisco, School of Medicine. His study of 110 patients with recurrent kidney stones was published in the *Journal of Urology,* 1120 N. Charles St., Baltimore 21201.

Better Eyesight Protection

Eyesight can be protected by taking vitamin and mineral supplements.

Recent finding: People who took 500 mg of vitamin C, 400 international units (IU) of vitamin E, 25,000 IU of beta carotene and 80 mg of zinc had a 25% lower risk for age-related macular degeneration (AMD) than people who did not take these supplements. AMD is a leading cause of blindness.

If you are age 55 or older: See your eye doctor to determine your risk of developing AMD and whether taking these vitamins and minerals might be beneficial for you.

Emily Chew, MD, deputy director of epidemiology and clinical research, National Eye Institute, Bethesda, MD.

Cinnamon for Lower Blood Sugar

Cinnamon helps keep blood glucose under control. Adding one teaspoon of ground cinnamon—not cinnamon flavoring—to your daily diet will boost the body's synthesis of glucose-burning enzymes.

Smart idea: Add cinnamon to juices and other drinks, oatmeal, casseroles, etc.

Richard Anderson, PhD, lead scientist, Human Nutrition Research Center, US Department of Agriculture, Beltsville, MD.

Back Pain Relief Without Surgery or Drugs

Douglas R. Johnson, MD, medical director of the inpatient rehabilitation unit at Charlton Memorial Hospital in Fall River, MA.

Ronald D. Siegel, PsyD, psychologist and clinical faculty member of Harvard Medical School, Boston.

They are the coauthors of *Back Sense: A Revolutionary Approach to Halting the Cycle of Chronic Back Pain* (Broadway). *www.backsense.org.*

One in 40 adult Americans is disabled by chronic back problems. In fact, back pain is second only to colds and flu as the main reason for doctor visits.

For years, doctors assumed that an aching back was the result of problems in the spine, such as herniated or "slipped" disks or misaligned vertebrae. The latest scientific evidence shows that these conditions, while often present, are rarely the cause of pain. Only about one in 200 cases actually requires medical or surgical treatment.

Most back pain is caused by nothing more than muscle tension. The muscles surrounding the spine may hurt, but the spine itself is usually fine.

Caution: If your back pain lasts for more than four weeks or if you have a fever…trouble with your bowel or bladder…weakness in the legs…weight loss…or decreased appetite, see a physician to rule out potentially serious problems, such as a spinal infection, a tumor or damage to the spine.

BREAKING THE PAIN CYCLE

Chronic back pain usually begins with a slight injury—for example, straining your back while working in the yard. The muscles respond to the injury by contracting. The resulting pain can be excruciating.

People naturally get anxious when they're in pain. And anxiety compounds the problem. It further contracts the muscles, increasing the pain...and makes back pain sufferers reluctant to move their bodies—tightening the muscles even more. The pain causes stress...which causes more muscle tension...which causes more pain...and so on. *Here's how to break the cycle...*

●**Don't inhibit your movements.** Some doctors still recommend bed rest and avoidance of normal activities, such as vacuuming...carrying laundry...walking the dog, etc. *Big mistake.*

People who follow this advice tend to get worse, not better, because muscles that don't move tighten up. The more anxiety people feel about performing their usual activities, the more intense the pain. Resuming activities may hurt at first, but you're not damaging anything—you're returning the muscles to normal function. Take *ibuprofen* (Advil) or *acetaminophen* (Tylenol) to relieve pain.

Also exercise regularly. It warms up and relaxes the muscles—and reduces stress.

Best aerobic activities for back pain sufferers include walking, swimming and bicycling.

Yoga and stretching also help. Several times a day, bend forward at the waist...let gravity bring your fingers toward the floor...and hold the stretch for about 20 seconds.

Eventually, try to pick things up off the floor during this stretch. Start with something light, like a magazine. Then use heavier items, like a hardcover book or several books.

●**Take a stress inventory.** Simply acknowledging the stress in your life—even if you do nothing to change it—can reduce the intensity of back pain.

To ease stress, make a list of its causes—a difficult boss, a hectic schedule, a loved one with medical problems—or keep a journal, noting things that upset you. Talk with friends or family about what's bothering you.

●**Practice mindfulness.** This form of meditation helps reduce tension by focusing all your attention on the present moment instead of worrying about the future or past.

Several times a day, make a conscious effort to concentrate on the here and now—the smell of coffee brewing...the sounds of children playing outside...the sensation of your feet touching the floor, etc.

To employ mindfulness when you experience pain: Sit quietly for 20 minutes...pay attention to the sensation of your stomach rising when you inhale and falling when you exhale. Allow yourself to feel the pain sensations in your body.

Bringing your complete attention to the present moment without fighting the pain can help break the pain cycle.

Useful Web Sites

Alternative Treatment

☐ Alternative Medicine Magazine
www.alternativemedicine.com

Features about all the latest health care issues and news about alternative treatments.

☐ Experimental Trials
www.herbalgram.org

This site, from the American Botanical Council, discusses experimental trials on botanical or herbal medicines.

☐ Herbal Healing for Pets
www.wic.net/waltzark

An on-line encyclopedia of alternative treatments for your pet—everything from itching and fleas to diarrhea and carsickness. Click on "Herbal Healing for Pets."

☐ Herb Research Foundation
www.herbs.org

Information about medicinal plants and how you can get the most benefit from them.

Consumer Information

☐ Clinical Trials
http://clinicaltrials.gov

The US National Institutes of Health's site, offering current information about clinical research studies.

☐ Eldercare Locator
www.eldercare.gov

The on-line Eldercare Locator, a service of the US Administration on Aging, helps seniors and their caregivers find local services.

☐ Nursing Home Quality
www.nccnhr.org

The National Citizens' Coalition for Nursing Home Reform's site assists you in locating a nursing home that offers quality care.

☐ People's Medical Society
www.peoplesmed.org

Want to learn how to beat the health care system? This site is dedicated to educating consumers about health care and medical rights.

☐ Healthfinder
www.healthfinder.gov

At this Web site of the US Department of Health and Human Services, you'll find information on diseases…insurance…health organizations…hospitals…and many other topics.

Conditions

☐ Asthma and Allergies
http://allergy.mcg.edu

Learn all about allergies and asthma. You can also take an asthma screening test.

☐ Arthritis
www.arthritis.org

Loaded with information and support for people who suffer from arthritis.

☐ Eating Disorders
www.nationaleatingdisorders.org

Help for all eating disorders, including anorexia nervosa, bulimia nervosa and binge-eating.

☐ Panic Attacks
www.adaa.org

The Anxiety Disorders Association of America can help you find a cognitive-behavioral therapist.

Nutrition

☐ Eat Right
www.eatright.org

The American Dietetic Association offers comprehensive nutrition information on everything from diets to calorie measurements.

Nutrition Information
www.nal.usda.gov/fnic/foodcomp
The National Nutrient Database will help you understand food values.

Vegetarian Resource Group
www.vrg.org
Offers practical hints for vegetarian meal planning and articles relevant to vegetarian nutrition.

Self-Help

Al-Anon
www.al-anon.org
A nonprofit organization helping families and friends of alcoholics recover from the effects of living with an alcoholic.

Alcoholics Anonymous
www.alcoholics-anonymous.org
This self-supporting, nondenominational organization is open to anyone who wants to do something about his or her drinking problem.

Domestic Violence
www.ndvh.org
Crisis-intervention information on domestic violence as well as referrals to local service providers.

Mental Health
www.mentalhelp.net
Created by psychologists and mental-health professionals, this site offers information on diseases, symptoms, treatments, resources and more.

Children's Health

Asthma and Children
www.epa.gov/children
Insert "asthma" in the search box. Click on the *EPA Children's Environmental Health Yearbook* and then on "Table of Contents."

Attention-Deficit/Hyperactivity Disorder
www.chadd.org
Information on ADD/HD. Find support groups, answers to frequently asked questions and research information.

Children's Health Page
http://gazissax.best.vwh.net/chealth.html
Links to many helpful resources related to your children's health.

Help Kids Cope with Violence
www.nimh.nih.gov
The National Institute of Mental Health offers up-to-date information on helping children who have suffered trauma. Click on "For the Public," then on "Children & Violence."

Children's Mental Health
www.nmha.org
If you are concerned that your child has a mental disorder, go to the National Mental Health Association's Web site. Type "Children" in the search box.

Vaccination Basics
www.fda.gov/fdac/reprints/vaccine.html
Up-to-date information on what type of immunizations your children need and when.

Women's Health

Fertility
www.asrm.org
For a referral to a fertility counselor in your area, visit this Web site of the American Society for Reproductive Medicine.

National Women's Health Information Center
www.4woman.org
Directs you to a wide variety of women's health-related material.

6
Savvy Money Moves

Break Bad Money Habits…Now

There are very few decisions that people make in regard to their money and investments that are based upon real logic.

As investors, we tend to overreact to the latest news flash rather than base decisions on objective—but less interesting—statistical data.

As consumers, we make major purchases based on fleeting impulses. Impulse shopping gives us a feeling of empowerment—that is, until we get the credit card statement.

The key to breaking bad money habits is recognizing when our instincts lead us astray—and then making a conscious decision to focus on facts.

BUYING A HOME

Many people search for months or years for their perfect house. Then they make an offer and hold their breath. But deciding on your "dream house" without weighing other options weakens your bargaining position. Because you are afraid to lose the house, you're likely to offer too much or jump on the first counteroffer.

Negotiating power comes from clearly sizing up all your alternatives. The less regret you have at the possibility of walking away, the greater your willingness to wait for the other party to compromise.

Strategy: Set a rational price—above which you would rather spend money on a different opportunity than pay a higher sum for the home.

BUYING A CAR

Jim wanted to pay about $10,000 for a used car. He found one he liked at a dealership. The salesman hoped to sell the car for $12,500. He quoted the price as $15,000, then suggested they split the difference. Jim didn't want to be unreasonable, so he agreed.

Max Bazerman, PhD, Jesse Isador Straus professor of business administration at Harvard Business School in Boston. He is the author of *Smart Money Decisions: Why You Do What You Do with Money and How to Change for the Better* (Wiley) and coauthor of *You Can't Enlarge the Pie* (Basic), with Jon Baron and Katie Shonk.

Reality: A 50-50 split is arbitrary. Use it only when it's to your advantage.

If you wind up on the wrong side of a 50-50 split, think about splitting the difference of the difference.

Jim should have said to the car salesman, "Thanks for your flexibility, but $15,000 is way too high and $12,500 is also more than I can afford. I told you I was looking to pay closer to $10,000. But to save myself the time and effort of going to another car lot, what if we go 50-50 on your second offer? I'll pay $11,250."

INVESTING

When I give seminars for Fortune 500 executives about decision making, I ask them to assign themselves a percentile ranking in various skills, with 50% being average. Stock market investing always scores in the 70s. These business executives fancy themselves investment experts, yet even most *professional* money managers fail to beat the market averages. *Strategies...*

●**Put most of your money in low-cost index funds** until you prove you can do a better job of picking individual stocks or actively managed funds. After at least one year, assess the performance of your actively managed portfolio. Were you able to beat the index after expenses and taxes? Few people do.

●**Make it expensive and logistically difficult to trade stocks.** University of California finance professors Terence Odean and Brad Barber have demonstrated that the more easily investors can trade, the more their emotions interfere with their decisions. Portfolio returns of investors at traditional brokerage houses who switch to on-line trading drop by an average of 3.6%.

●**If you lose money on a high-risk stock, resist the urge to recoup your losses by risking more money on the same stock.** A stock you bought at $20 may not be a great bargain at $10 if the drop in price was due to a dramatic decline in earnings or a loss of market share. Instead, examine the stock as if you never owned it. Is this an investment you want to be in...or are there better opportunities?

GENERAL PURCHASES

Melissa spent five hours researching on the Internet to save $20 on the purchase of a VCR. Yet she would consider it ludicrous to work at any job that paid $4 an hour.

Better: Set parameters on how much your time is worth before you start trying to save money on a purchase—unless you find bargain hunting pleasurable. Use your time constraints as a tool.

Salespeople know that the more time they spend with you, the more money you are likely to spend. Tell the salesperson you have exactly a certain number of minutes to shop. The more valuable your time seems to the salesperson, the more pressure he/she is under to make concessions.

BUYING WARRANTIES

About 40% of people who shop for electronics and appliances purchase extended warranties. Only 10% of warranties are exercised. Why? We overestimate the likelihood that the product will fail. One horror story from a salesperson has a far greater effect on our attitudes than statistical data. *Better...*

●**Before making a warranty decision, ask the salesperson,** "How often are claims made on this warranty?...Under what circumstances would a loss not be covered?...Am I already covered for this potential loss through other insurance?"

●**Skip insurance for any potential loss that is affordable.**

SALARY NEGOTIATION

Denise had a job for which she was paid $50,000 a year. She knew people with equal skills were earning at least $75,000.

When she interviewed for a new job, Denise explained what her salary was and why she deserved much more. The interviewer agreed, but pointed out that the company's policy restricted him from offering new hires more than 15% above their old salaries, in this case $57,500 a year.

Strategy: Instead of letting her old salary dictate the parameters of the entire negotiation, Denise should have created "anchors" that would have kept her close to her desired outcome.

When asked about her previous salary, Denise should have responded, "I'm interested in showing what I can do for you and finding out what my services are worth to your firm."

This way, she could have anchored off a salary that the interviewer provided first or suggested an average figure for the industry.

Most Dangerous Financial-Services Rip-Offs

Scott Borchert, director of enforcement, Minnesota Department of Commerce, St. Paul. He is enforcement section chairperson and was elected to the board of directors of the Washington, DC–based North American Securities Administrators Association (NASAA), a watchdog group that protects investors. It is made up of members of securities regulatory agencies from each state. *www.nasaa.org.*

Beginning with the passage of the Glass-Steagall Act in 1933, the federal government prohibited all banks, insurance companies and securities firms from competing in one another's businesses.

In November of 1999, Congress repealed the Glass-Steagall Act, and the resulting deregulation has brought cheaper, more convenient financial products and services. But the deregulation has also created an environment ripe for rip-offs.

Result: $10 billion a year in losses due to consumer fraud.

Risky investments are sold by insurance agents and securities brokers. *State regulators have received the most complaints about these five investments...*

PROMISSORY NOTES

Promissory notes are short-term-debt instruments used most often by start-up companies for short-term borrowing. A loophole in securities laws exempts certain promissory notes from regulatory scrutiny.

Typical deal: The investor lends the start-up company capital for a nine-month term in exchange for up to 15% *per month* in interest. Those returns are said to be guaranteed because the start-up is backed and bonded by an insurance company.

Problem: In many cases, the start-up fails and the insurance company proves to be a phony or disreputable offshore entity. The investors will receive no interest, and they may lose all or part of their principal.

To protect yourself...

●**Check that your insurance agent or adviser has a multiyear track record with promissory notes.** Ask for documented evidence of just how much money his/her clients have made using them. If you are an inexperienced investor, it might be best to avoid promissory notes altogether.

●**Invest directly in the note.** Don't let your money be pooled with that of other clients because you will have little control over how it is managed.

●**Find out who is issuing the note.** Research the background of the corporation at Web sites such as *www.hoovers.com.* Choose a company that is regulated in your state in case problems arise or you have to go to court.

ENERGY-RELATED SECURITIES

Unlicensed stock dealers are profiting from panic over the energy crisis by selling—often over the Internet—phony public ownership shares in everything from natural gas fields to oil-exploration firms. *To protect yourself...*

●**Invest only in equities you can research on your own.** Check the company's Web site and prospectus. The information should match data on file with the US Securities and Exchange Commission (SEC), 800-732-0330...*www.sec.gov/edgar.shtml.* Pay attention to the forms S-1 (prospectus), 10-K (annual report) and 10-Q (quarterly report). If the company is not public and has no SEC filings, inquire about it with your state securities regulator. Contact the North American Securities Administrators Association (NASAA). 202-737-0900...*www.nasaa.org.*

●**Investigate your investment adviser/salesperson.** He should be registered with your state's securities agency and the National Association of Securities Dealers (NASD). For disciplinary histories, contact NASD Regulation at 800-289-9999...*www.nasd.com.*

●**Watch for the telltale signs of a scam.** *Common phrases...*

●This investment is IRS-approved (the IRS does not approve investments for IRAs).

●We will match your investment.

●This is a pre-IPO offering.

●This is an offshore and tax-free investment (Americans must still pay taxes on any investments that are offshore).

Other warning signs: You are required to pay a fee before being permitted to view the list of *exclusive offerings*…you are asked to submit financial information on-line to determine whether you're an *accredited investor*… you are required to make the investment within the next 24 or 48 hours.

ONE-YEAR CALLABLE CDs

Callable CDs have become popular because they are federally insured and offer higher yields than traditional CDs.

Problem: Few investors understand how they work. Callable CDs usually have 10- or 20-year maturities.

Example: A bank might decide to call—or terminate—a high-yield CD if interest rates fall. CD holders would then have to reinvest their money at lower rates.

To protect yourself: Get the CD's maturity date *in writing*. Confirm the interest rate you will receive…and when and how the rate can change. Find out what the penalties are for early withdrawal and costs associated with selling before maturity.

VIATICAL SETTLEMENTS

Viatical settlements are lump-sum payments given to terminally ill people in exchange for the death benefits of their insurance policies. The cash handed over to patients—roughly half the policy value—often helps cover medical costs and living expenses. Viaticals are legal. Investors profit from the insurance proceeds when the individual dies.

Problem: Viatical settlements are pitched as safe, but they can be quite risky.

Investors get no return until after the insured dies. Perversely, any medical advances could substantially prolong the life of the insured, postponing profits to the investor.

If the viatical company becomes insolvent, an investor could lose his/her entire investment.

Because viatical settlements are not traditional securities, they are not regulated by the state securities commissioners.

Only sophisticated investors should consider viaticals. For more information, contact The Viatical and Life Settlement Association of America, 407-894-3797…*www.viatical.org.*

SPOT SECONDARY OFFERINGS

When a publicly traded company needs to raise some additional money, it makes a secondary—or "follow-on"—offering to investors. An underwriter's brokers promote the offering for several weeks to give investors time to evaluate the deal.

"Spot secondary offerings" are quick deals that occur without promotion. Investors are called by brokers the morning before trading starts. Stock prices are set at a discount of a few pennies from the previous day's closing.

Problem: You must decide almost instantly if you want in on the deal.

These are not recommended for the individual investor.

Can't-Lose Plan for Making Money Grow

Marshall Loeb, a New York City–based author of *52 Weeks to Financial Fitness: The Week-by-Week Plan for Making Your Money Grow* (Crown Business). The former editor of *Fortune, Money* and *Columbia Journalism Review,* he is now a columnist for CBSMarketwatch.com.

Getting into financial shape is a little like getting into physical shape. It requires discipline every day, especially in these trying times. *Take these steps, no matter what the markets are doing…*

●**Set up a sensible filing system.** Most people keep too many documents and fail to protect the important ones.

Income tax records: Save 1099s, W2s and other tax forms as well as records that support your deductions (canceled checks for business expenses, acknowledgments for charitable donations, etc.) for at least six years.

Helpful resource: IRS Publication 552, *Recordkeeping for Individuals.* 800-TAX-FORM *…www.irs.gov.* Free.

Real estate records: Save supporting documents from when you purchased your home, such as inspection results. Keep receipts for capital improvement projects or any work that adds to the value of your home (an upgraded roof, renovated kitchen, home additions, etc.). The costs of these can be deducted from your profit when you sell your home, reducing the tax bite if your gain exceeds the exclusion amount.

Investment records: Records of contributions, distributions and rollovers for IRAs or other retirement plans.

Records to keep in a safe-deposit box…

●Real estate records, including the deed to your home and mortgage contract.

●Certificates for shares in a cooperative residence or time-share.

●Receipts for insured valuables (jewelry, furs, etc.) along with photos/videos of the items for insurance purposes.

●Certificates of ownership for stocks, bonds and other securities.

●List and copies of insurance policies along with your agents' names and phone numbers.

●Car titles.

●Marriage certificate.

●Birth certificates and/or adoption papers.

●Passports.

●Social Security cards and other vital documents that would be difficult or time-consuming to replace.

Caution: Don't keep your power of attorney or will in a safe-deposit box. Many states make it difficult for heirs or family members to open it. Instead, leave the originals of these documents with your lawyer.

Records you can throw out…

●Monthly brokerage account and mutual fund statements, after you have received your annual statements.

●Investment transaction reports, six years after you sell the assets.

●Expired insurance policies.

●Old wills, powers of attorney and living wills (keeping old versions may lead to confusion about your wishes).

●Pay stubs after you receive your annual W-2 from your employer.

●Receipts and canceled checks that are over one year old (exception—those needed for tax reasons should be kept for at least six years).

●**Buy inflation-indexed US savings bonds (I bonds).** They pay a fixed rate of return plus an additional increment to compensate for inflation, all guaranteed by the US Treasury, so they are a good place to put part of your savings.

Advantages: No state or local income tax on interest. No federal income tax until bonds are redeemed after as many as 30 years. Plus, no federal income tax when proceeds are used to fund college or vocational school if your income is up to $57,600 for single filers and $86,400 for joint filers in 2002 ($58,500 and $87,750 in 2003).

Most banks and savings institutions sell the I bonds in denominations of $50 to $10,000. You can also buy them at *www.savingsbonds.gov.*

●**Fund a Coverdell Education Savings Account (formerly called Education IRA)** *and* **a 529 plan** for each child's educational needs. The new tax laws let you invest in both at the same time.

Helpful resource: 800-400-9113…*www.savingforcollege.com.*

Caution: A 529 plan may affect financial-aid eligibility. If you think your child may qualify for aid, talk to a financial adviser before using a 529 plan.

●**Make saving on taxes a year-round goal.** At year-end, there's very little even the most skilled tax professional can do to save you money. *Instead…*

●Keep wages in the family. If you are self-employed or have a sideline business, put your children under age 18 on the payroll. They must be paid at a fair market rate. You needn't withhold Social Security or Medicare taxes on their wages. Earnings of up to $4,700 in 2002 ($4,750 in 2003) are not subject to federal income tax. Anything above that will be taxed at the child's rate, usually 10% or 15%. And you can deduct his/her wages from your net income.

●Make some gifts to charity. You have until December 31 to write off gifts on your 2003 tax return, even if the checks aren't cashed until after January 1, 2004.

• Buy six-month Treasury bills after July. Even though you will receive interest in the current tax year, you do not need to include it on your federal tax return until the year in which the T-bill matures.

• If you are married, file separate state tax returns if it saves you money. Normally, spouses file joint federal *and* state returns. But some states let married couples file separately even if they file jointly on the federal return.

• Reduce taxes on dividends. Sell a stock after a dividend is declared but before it is paid. During this period, the dividend is reflected in the price of the stock. The sale qualifies for the 20% capital gains rate, provided that you have owned the stock for at least one year and a day. If you sell after you receive the dividend, it is taxed as ordinary income.

Useful books on tax-saving strategies: *J.K. Lasser's New Rules for Retirement and Tax* and *The Ernst & Young Tax Guide* (both published by Wiley).

• **Don't overlook key deductions.**

• Expenses related to volunteer work. You can deduct costs of traveling to meetings, fund-raisers and other events at 14 cents per mile if you drive, as well as parking fees and tolls, bus and taxi fares…and out-of-pocket costs—for phone calls, stationery, stamps and uniforms.

• Student-loan interest. You can write off up to $2,500 of interest annually. For full deductibility, your adjusted gross income (AGI) must be less than $50,000 ($100,000 for couples) in 2002 and 2003.

• **Bunch miscellaneous expenses**—union or professional dues…tax-preparation and investment advisory fees…legal and accounting fees…costs of job uniforms and tools…job-related education expenses…and the costs of business publications and books.

These expenses can be written off to the extent that they exceed 2% of your AGI. If you are close to that threshold, pay next year's expenses by December 31 of this year.

• **Write off points if you refinance your home.** Points usually must be deducted over the life of a mortgage. But if you refinance the loan on your principal residence, you can usually deduct all the points on your previous mortgage that you haven't written off in previous years.

• **Buy your parents' home or condominium, and lease it back to them.** This can be a win-win situation. When your parents sell their home, they can exclude up to $500,000 of the gain from their taxable income. You get to enjoy the tax benefits of being a landlord—the deductions for mortgage interest, maintenance and depreciation.

Important: The IRS insists that you sign a formal lease with your parents. Document that you are charging them a fair market rent by asking a local real estate broker for a *written* estimate of what rental amount the property should command.

Shrewd Ways To Protect Your Assets Against a Lawsuit

Gideon Rothschild, Esq., CPA, a partner in the law firm Moses & Singer LLP, 1301 Avenue of the Americas, New York City 10019, *www.mosessinger.com.*

We really do live in a litigious society. Even if you've done nothing wrong, you can find yourself the target of a ruinous lawsuit. But if you act *before* anyone sues, you can protect your assets. The sooner you act, the more options you have.

YOUR HOLDINGS

Look to see where you are most vulnerable to a lawsuit. These areas should be the focus of your asset-protection plans. *Consider…*

• **Your business interests.** To what extent are your personal assets vulnerable as a result of your owning and/or running a business? Have you personally guaranteed any of your corporation's debts?

Strategy: If you are a general partner of a business, consider transforming that ownership interest into a limited liability company (LLC). Having the LLC act as the general partner will protect your personal assets.

• **Your personal life.** To what extent are you personally vulnerable as a result of your marital status? If you are married, what impact would divorce have on your assets? Be sure to consider state property rights (such as community property), prenuptial agreements and other arrangements.

Beware: The wealthier you are, the more vulnerable you are to personal lawsuits arising from car accidents and injuries that occur on your property.

YOUR INSURANCE

Insurance is your first line of defense against a lawsuit. *Two reasons:* The policy will pay off if you're found liable. And the insurance company may be required to defend you—saving you costly legal fees.

Review the policies you now hold. Make sure you're covered for every future legal action you may be exposed to. *Key policies to have…*

●**Umbrella policy.** It supplements the coverage under your homeowner's and car insurance policies. Such a policy typically provides an additional $1 million to $10 million in coverage. The greater your personal wealth, the bigger your umbrella policy should be.

●**D&O coverage.** If you serve as a corporate director or officer—or a member of the board of directors of a nonprofit organization—make sure you're covered for actions against directors and officers. Ask to see a copy of the policy before agreeing to serve in such positions.

●**Malpractice insurance.** If you are a doctor, lawyer or other professional who may be the object of a malpractice suit, make sure you understand the extent of your policy's coverage—the types of legal actions it will and will not cover.

CHANGE OF OWNERSHIP

How are your assets owned? The way you hold title to property can make it less vulnerable to creditors' claims. *Consider these changes…*

●**Transfer assets to your spouse or children.** Assuming the transfers are made before a problem arises, this strategy should fully protect the assets.

●**Change title of jointly owned assets into "tenancy by the entirety."** When real estate is held in tenancy by the entirety, the creditors of one spouse can't get at the assets of the other.

In a few states (such as Florida, Pennsylvania and Virginia), tenancy by the entirety can be used for more than just real estate. In those states, it can, for instance, be used to protect brokerage accounts.

●**Create family limited partnerships to own securities.** While this strategy does not fully protect the holdings, it makes it more difficult for creditors to reach them.

Alternative: Set up a charitable remainder trust to own the securities. You can receive an income for life from the trust, with the assets then passing to the charity. Tax-wise, you obtain an immediate income tax deduction for the value of the charity's remainder interest.

For asset protection purposes, creditors may be able to reach your income interest in a charitable remainder trust—but probably only for a limited number of years (typically a judgment runs for 10 years). If this happens, you will at least have protected the remaining years of income and all of the underlying trust assets.

●**Set up a limited liability company to own any real estate now held in your name.** Then, if any legal action arises from the real estate, your personal assets will be protected.

BANKRUPTCY EXEMPTIONS

Federal and state bankruptcy laws let you protect certain assets from creditors—even if your financial situation is so dire that you must file for bankruptcy.

●**Homestead protection.** Most states provide some protection from creditors for the equity in your home. A handful of states provide generous protection. Florida, for example, completely exempts a home from creditors' claims, even if it's purchased on the eve of bankruptcy.

●**Retirement plans and IRAs.** Federal law exempts assets in qualified retirement plans from claims of creditors. The extent of asset protection for IRAs and other nonqualified plans (including Roth IRAs) varies from state to state. For a listing by state of exemptions available, visit the Web site, *www.mosessinger.com/ resources/protecting.shtml.*

●**Annuities and life insurance.** Some degree of protection is offered in some states. Check your state's law. For a listing by state of exemptions that are available, visit *www.mosess inger.com/resources/creditprotec.shtml.*

Note: Federal bankruptcy reform, which failed to be enacted in summer 2001, would have limited some exemptions—such as complete homestead exemptions. It remains to be seen whether Congress will again take up bankruptcy reform. For a listing of state exemptions, visit the Web site above.

ASSET PROTECTION TRUST

Asset protection trusts are designed to give you unfettered access to your funds while protecting them from creditors' claims. The trusts are "self-settled," meaning you set them up with your own assets, and you remain as beneficiary.

Important: Asset protection trusts do *not* provide tax savings...

●For income tax purposes, since you continue to be the "owner" of the trust, you're taxed on trust earnings.

●For estate tax purposes, unless the transfer is treated as a completed gift subject to gift tax, the assets must be included in your taxable estate.

●**Domestic asset protection trusts.** Asset protection trusts—in which you are both the grantor (or "settlor") and the beneficiary—can now be set up in Alaska, Delaware, Nevada and Rhode Island. (Colorado also allows self-settled "spendthrift trusts," but does not provide as broad protection for settlors as the other four states.) Unlike other self-settled trusts, state law in these jurisdictions provides protection for these trusts.

How much protection do they offer? Residents of these states can obtain protection for assets held in these trusts. It is not clear, however, whether nonresidents can achieve the same asset protection by setting up a trust in one of these states. For example, it is unclear whether a resident of New York who sets up a Delaware asset protection trust will have his/her assets fully protected in case of court action arising in New York.

●**Offshore asset protection trusts.** Two dozen foreign jurisdictions cater to Americans who want to set up asset protection trusts. The most popular sites now being used—Cook Islands, Nevis, St. Lucia and St. Vincent.

Caution: Beware of offshore trust scams promising asset protection and no federal income taxes. At *www.irs.gov,* the IRS lists scams it has uncovered. The Financial & Tax Fraud Education Associates, Inc. Web site, *www.quatloos.com,* also lists offshore scams to avoid.

How to Stay Out of Debt

Mary Hunt, author of *Debt-Proof Living* (Broadman & Holman) and publisher of *Cheapskate Monthly,* Box 2135, Paramount, CA 90723, *www.cheapskatemonthly.com.*

The average US family owes more than $8,000 on credit cards alone. Consumers seldom fall deep into debt all at once. Instead, their expenses outpace their income little by little until the balance becomes unmanageable. Once that happens, they have to make lifestyle changes to get out from under.

You don't have to be a tightwad to prevent debt overload. *Simple strategies...*

●**Identify situations in which you lack financial willpower.** Take preemptive action based on these behavior patterns. *Examples...*

●Catalogs. Fill out order forms for what you want, then put them aside. One week later, allow yourself to send away for whatever you can actually remember, without looking at the forms. You wind up buying only what is important.

Also: Try to find the items locally to avoid shipping-and-handling costs.

●Supermarket impulse buys. Put any items that are not on your shopping list in the shopping cart's child seat. Before checkout, choose just one item from the child seat. If you find a great bargain, take something off your list to accommodate the good deal.

●Long-distance telephone service. Cancel unrestricted services if you can't control your calls. Use prepaid phone cards instead. Using a phone card is like using cash, so you tend to be more careful about your phone time. Warehouse discount clubs now sell cards for around four cents per minute. Beware—some sell for 50 cents a minute.

•Pay cash—even for big purchases. It may be inconvenient, but it forces you to prioritize. It's the single best way to eliminate impulse buying. Cash customers spend 30% less on shopping sprees than those who pay with plastic.

If you need extra security, keep a $100 traveler's check in your wallet instead of a credit card. You are less likely to break the traveler's check for an impulse purchase.

•Set up a monthly spending plan...

•Log how much you spend each day for one month. Use one index card per day. Put the date at the top and make two columns—"What" and "How Much." Don't cheat or neglect to incorporate bargains. Include everything you spend.

•Create a spending record. Analyze your daily logs, and group expenses into categories—groceries, clothing, entertainment, etc. Most people have about 20 categories. Total the amount in each.

•Figure out your income for each month—including salary, dividends, interest and other types of income.

•Subtract monthly expenses from income. Most Americans live on close to 110% of their monthly incomes. You're likely to face debt problems if your expenses are more than 80% of your monthly income.

•Analyze the logs to identify problem areas. Create new targets so that your expenses won't exceed income.

•Draw up a new log for the second month with expense goals by category. Again, track all expenses. And again, see if you are spending too much...and identify places to cut back. Repeat this process until you reach your spending goals.

•Budget for large expenses. Car brakes wear down over time. But instead of saving regularly for the inevitable brake job, most people seem surprised by the large bill. Everything has a limited life—washing machines and other appliances, the roof on your house, etc.

Solution: Set up a "Freedom Account" to better prepare for unexpected, irregular or intermittent expenses. Fill a binder with individual pages, and allot one category per page. *How it should work...*

☐ Review your checking account for the past 12 months—to find expenses that did not recur regularly. *Common:* Auto maintenance, insurance

premiums, clothing, property taxes, vacation, holiday/special-occasion gifts, home repairs and appliance replacement.

☐ Add up expenses for each category, then divide by 12 to figure out how much you need to contribute each month.

Example: If you have $1,000 a year in car repairs, you need to contribute about $83 a month.

☐ To save for these expenses, open a second checking account that pays interest or a money market account that offers checking. *My favorite:* USAA Money Market. No minimum requirement as long as you make an automatic deposit of at least $50 a month. 877-632-3002.

☐ Authorize automatic deposits to transfer the monthly total of your irregular expenses from your regular checking account into your "Freedom Account."

Smart: Create a category called "insurance deductibles." Deposit a specified amount each month until the balance is equal to the annual deductibles on health, homeowner's and auto insurance plans. By year-end, if I haven't drawn on my deductibles at all, I keep adding money and authorize my insurance agent to increase the deductibles in exchange for lower premiums. If I never have to use the deductibles, the money is still earning interest.

Example: If your deductible is $500, save that amount as quickly as possible ($50 a month for 10 months), then hold off and start funding something else.

Large expenses that occur every several years—new car, painting a house—should have a category, too. When you save the amount required, stop funding them. Once the funds are used up, resume saving.

•**Track credit card balances weekly.** Most credit card companies will provide you with a password to get up-to-date account information on their Web sites. Seeing your outstanding balance will help you avoid taking on debt.

EASY AREAS TO CUT BACK

•**Food outside the home.** The typical family spends only half its food budget at supermarkets. Restaurants are the single biggest budget wreckers. The rest is spent at fast-food places, coffee bars, etc.

•**Automobile expenses...**

•Tires. Ask the tire shop if it has *take-offs*—new tires that end up in inventory if a new-car buyer decides to replace his/her tires with special ones. *Cost:* About 50% less than original price.

●Gasoline. Not all gas stations or grades of gasoline are the same. Try different grades and stations. Keep track of your mileage, and use the grades and stations that give you the very best mileage per dollar.

●Movie rentals. Save money on video rentals by borrowing movies—free—from the library.

More from Mary Hunt...

Easy Ways to Pay Off Your Debts

How to pay off all of your debts *without* increasing the amount you have to pay each month...

●**Stop incurring new debt.** If you do not stop buying on credit, you will *never* pay off your debts.

●**Total up all of your current monthly required minimum payments** on all your debts and credit cards. Commit to paying this total amount each month until all your debts are paid off.

●**List your debts in order of the number of months it will take to pay them.** Put the shortest term debts at the top of the list.

●**When the shortest-term debt is paid off,** add the amount that you paid on it each month to the amount that you're paying on the next shortest-term debt.

●**When the second debt is paid off,** add the amount that you paid on the first two debts to what you pay on the third debt...and so on.

Lower Bank Fees

Reduce or even eliminate any banking fees, with these practical tips...

●**Never bounce a check**—that can cost $25 or more. Consider an overdraft account to cover overdrawn funds.

●**Use your bank's ATMs**—or find a bank that refunds nonbranch surcharges, which can cost $4 each.

●**Get cash back when you make purchases with your ATM card**—many stores allow this without a fee.

●**Instead of keeping a high checking account balance to get low interest**—find a non-interest-bearing account with no minimum or a very low one. Consider investing the difference in a mutual fund.

Helpful: Search *www.bankrate.com* for the best account rates.

Edward Mrkvicka, Jr., president of Reliance Enterprises, Inc., financial consulting company, 22115 O'Connell Rd., Marengo, IL 60152, and author of *Your Bank Is Ripping You Off* (St. Martin's).

More from Edward Mrkvicka...

Smarter Bill Paying

Pay your bills well in advance to avoid late charges. Allow at least three days for your account to be credited when paying on-line and five days when paying by mail. *Paying in person?* Do not assume your payment will be posted the same day—it may be posted the next day.

Helpful: If your cash flow makes it hard to meet creditors' payment deadlines, ask to move the deadlines.

Example: A credit card company may move your due date from the first to the 15th.

Better Banking

If you bounce even one check, you could be denied a checking account at a new bank. Most banks will report bounced checks to the interbank service ChexSystems. If you later apply for a new account at another bank that uses ChexSystems, it may refuse you—for up to five years.

Self-defense: Set up overdraft protection to ensure all checks clear.

Ric Edelman, CFS, chairman of Edelman Financial Services, Inc., Fairfax, VA, and author of *Financial Security in Troubled Times* (Harper). *www.ricedelman.com.*

Bank Floats Are Being Eliminated

Large banks are eliminating *float*—the time between when you write a check and when the funds are deducted from your account. Many people write checks against paychecks that will be deposited a few days later. But many banks now link check-processing systems to ATM networks. That allows almost immediate deduction of funds from checking accounts. But funds you deposit directly are not necessarily immediately available to you.

Self-defense: Ask about your bank's float policy…and do not write checks against funds that are not yet in your account.

Woody Tyner, senior vice president of BB&T Corp., financial holding company, Winston-Salem, NC.

Dangers of Joint Accounts

Do you and your partner share any joint accounts? *If the answer is "yes," be aware of these traps…*

●**Each owner is exposed to the other person's potential liabilities.**

●**Joint accounts can increase estate, gift and capital gains taxes.**

●**It is more difficult to divide assets in the event of divorce.**

Better ways to hold assets: In a trust, limited liability company or family limited partnership…as tenants in common, which means each person technically owns only part of the property. Consult with your lawyer or financial adviser.

Robert Klueger, an attorney specializing in tax and asset-protection planning, Boldra & Klueger, Encino, CA, and author of *A Guide to Asset Protection: How to Keep What's Legally Yours* (Wiley).

What to Do with a Cash Windfall

If you receive an inheritance or other cash windfall, do not prepay your mortgage. A 7% mortgage has an after-tax cost of only about 5% for those taxpayers in the highest tax brackets because the interest is tax deductible.

Instead: Pay off credit card debt or other nondeductible consumer loans…fully fund your IRA or 401(k) plan…pay up your life insurance or disability policy…and build a cash reserve of three to six months for expenses.

If you've covered all of these bases, invest the money, possibly using the gains to pay down your loan over time. Even safe investments, such as CDs, can earn more than the 5% your mortgage might cost.

Keith Gumbinger, vice president of HSH Associates, financial publishers of mortgage information, Butler, NJ, *www.hsh.com.*

Credit Card Billing Dates Do Matter

If you have many bills due at the start of the month, ask your credit card issuers to bill you on a date that coordinates with when you receive your paycheck. Also, know your credit card's closing cycle. You can then make a major purchase right after that month's closing date and have almost two months to pay, with no interest.

Example: If your card cycle closes on the 15th, make a major purchase on the 16th. It will appear on the following month's bill, and you will then have an additional grace period before payment is due.

Note: This will only work if you pay your credit card bills in full each month and don't carry a balance.

Gerri Detweiler, education adviser, Myvesta.org, nonprofit financial assistance organization, Rockville, MD.

Best Ways to Fix Credit-Report Problems

Eric Gertler, the president and CEO of Privista, privacy and credit-management consultants in New York City, *www.privista.com.*

If you have proof that an item on your credit report is incorrect, contact the creditor or lender. Every creditor is required under the federal Fair Credit Reporting Act to send updates to credit-reporting agencies, usually within 30 days.

In a letter, state the disputed item...how it is inaccurate...and how it should be fixed. Always include your full name and account number and copies of original documents. Send correspondence *return receipt requested.*

If you can't resolve a problem with a lender or creditor, get a copy of your credit report from the reporting agencies...

●**Equifax,** 800-685-1111, *www.equifax.com.*

●**Experian,** 888-397-3742, *www.experian. com.*

●**TransUnion,** 800-916-8800, *www.trans union.com.*

It is easiest to send written documentation of the inaccuracy to one of the credit-reporting agencies. It will make changes to your report if its investigation proves you correct. The other agencies will eventually pick up the corrected information, but to ensure prompt correction, contact all agencies directly.

Ask the agencies to send your corrected report to every company that received an inaccurate report in the past six months (or two years for employers who have requested your credit report).

If you can't resolve a disputed item, write up an explanation of up to 100 words. The credit agency should make this part of your file. If you believe a creditor or credit-reporting agency has not responded fairly or promptly to your situation, contact the Federal Trade Commission at 877-382-4357 or *www.ftc.gov.*

Caution: Steer clear of credit-repair companies that guarantee to "clean up" your credit report—they can't. By law, negative information may be removed only if it is inaccurate or the reporting period—seven years or, in the case of bankruptcy, 10 years—has expired.

Unnecessary Credit Card Services

Credit card services you should not think twice about...

●**Job-loss protection**—pays the minimum monthly amount and then only under certain conditions.

●**Registries** that list all your cards in case they are lost or stolen—it is just as easy to keep the card and phone numbers yourself.

●**Platinum and gold cards**—worthwhile only if the frills are worth more to you than their extra cost.

●**Life insurance**—will pay off your balance if you die, but costs much more than term insurance.

●**Disability coverage**—pays only the minimum amount per month if you become disabled, and there are waiting periods of up to several months.

Nancy Lloyd, former Federal Reserve Board economist and author of *Simple Money Solutions* (Random House).

How Many Credit Cards Do You Need?

The average family today has 15 credit cards. Having that many cards encourages overspending and multiplies the risk that you'll be victimized by credit card fraud.

Best: Have two cards per adult. One card should carry the lowest rate obtainable and be used to pay off major charges over time. Use the other to make charges of convenience that you pay off in full every month. It should have no annual fee but may carry a higher interest rate, since you won't incur it. Make charges on this card also to earn bonuses, such as frequent-flier miles.

Special case: Get an additional card if you frequently make business charges—to help keep records separate.

Robert McKinley, CEO, CardWeb.com, a research firm that tracks the US credit card industry, Frederick, MD.

How to Cut Credit Card Costs

Four simple things you can do to lower your credit card costs…

•**When offered a low interest rate,** check how long it is in effect—many run for only a few months.

•**Look around for a grace period**—without any interest—for making payments.

•**If a card offer includes special features,** such as no annual fee or a low fixed rate, find out if your current cards already offer them—many issuers have the same enhancements.

•**If a new offer really is better,** call your current issuer and ask it to match the offer.

Rob and Terry Adams, both longtime bargain hunters in Panama City Beach, FL, and authors of *The Bargain Hunter's Field Guide* (Avebury).

Forgotten Assets In Divorce

Harvey I. Sladkus, Esq., who has more than three decades of experience as a matrimonial lawyer, including many high-profile and celebrity cases, of counsel to the law firm of Todtman, Nachamie, Spizz and Johns, PC, 425 Park Ave., New York City 10022. He is a fellow of the American and International Academies of Matrimonial Lawyers.

People going through a divorce will often become irrational in negotiations, ignoring crucial financial issues—as well as substantial assets.

Each state has its own laws on divorce…

Equitable distribution: In the 40 *equitable-distribution* states, the spouses are required to exchange sworn statements of their net worth and their budgetary requirements, so a judge can determine who gets what.

Equal divisions: The community property divorce laws prevail in nine states—Arizona, California, Idaho, Louisiana, Nevada, New Mexico, Texas, Washington and Wisconsin. Assets acquired during marriage are divided equally between spouses.

Title state: In the lone *title state*—Mississippi—each spouse keeps only the property that is in his/her name. The court divides the rest.

ASSETS TO INCLUDE

•**Stock options.** There are two philosophies about options—which one prevails generally depends on state law…

•Reward for past service. If the parties were married when options were earned, the spouse would be entitled to a share of their future value.

•Incentive to remain with a company. A spouse would not be entitled to a share of the gains if the employee were to exercise options after the marriage ended.

•**Cash value of paid-up whole-life insurance policies** can be substantial.

•**Retirement plans—pensions, Social Security benefits and 401(k)s.** These assets are tricky to divide. A judge might award a husband 90% of the value of his pension, figuring the wife did not contribute to this future benefit—and then balance things by increasing the wife's share of other assets.

•**Pets are often treated like children.**

•**Gifts.** In equitable-distribution states, gifts from a third party given to a couple jointly *during* marriage are usually divided equally.

That's not true for gifts made before marriage (the wife keeps the $25,000 diamond engagement ring)—or gifts or inheritances received by one spouse from third parties during the marriage. Interspousal gifts are considered *marital* property in many states.

•**Professional licenses and degrees.** Everyone knows of someone who helped put his/her spouse through medical school, only to be cast aside later. These spouses are entitled to a property division that reflects the financial value of the degree as well as the value of a practice generated by that degree.

●**Vacation homes.** If the partners do not wish to sell a prized beachfront condominium, they may wind up splitting use of the place... or even renting to a third party and dividing the rental income.

●**Fine art, jewelry, boats, collectibles, cars, planes, season tickets to sporting and cultural events.**

●**Spouse's business.** If someone started and built the business during a long marriage, the spouse may be entitled to a substantial share of this marital property.

If one spouse inherited a successful business from a parent and merely acted as a caretaker, the other spouse may not be able to claim a portion of its value.

●**Hidden assets.** Secret safe-deposit boxes that hold hundreds of thousands of dollars are common. And many people hold secret property or offshore accounts.

SELF-DEFENSE

Locating and valuing family assets after a marriage dissolves often requires expert assistance. When assets are large, it is better to turn to an accountant, actuary, appraiser or private investigator, rather than just a lawyer. These professionals charge up to $400 an hour. Their fees, which typically may total near $25,000, can exceed legal costs.

If your marriage is in trouble, ascertain as early as possible the location and value of all of your spouse's assets.

Have a private investigator discreetly look for hidden brokerage or bank accounts and safe-deposit boxes in the spouse's name or in someone else's name but to which the spouse has access. It is much easier to do this while you are still married.

To avoid problems down the road—even in marriages that are currently happy—it may be prudent for the less affluent spouse to put marital property in joint names whenever this is legally permissible.

Find the Right Financial Adviser, Accountant And Insurance Agent

Charles A. Jaffe, nationally syndicated financial columnist for *The Boston Globe.* He is author of *The Right Way to Hire Financial Help: A Complete Guide to Choosing and Managing Brokers, Financial Planners, Insurance Agents, Lawyers, Tax Preparers, Bankers, and Real Estate Agents* (MIT).

No one wants to pay for financial help. And today with so much information designed especially for the do-it-yourselfer, you don't have to.

But an adviser can be worthwhile if you do not have time to create a financial plan—and the discipline to stick to it—or you don't feel confident and can't afford to mess up major money decisions.

My rules for hiring a financial adviser, tax accountant or insurance agent...

GENERAL GUIDELINES

●**Recruit an adviser before you need one.** This allows you time to research candidates, make a selection and build trust. If you wait until a crisis, you may be too distraught to call the shots.

●**Consider at least three candidates.** Get recommendations from friends, colleagues or the professional associations cited on the next page. Interview each first by telephone to make sure you fit his/her typical client profile. Discuss your advice requirements.

●**Do a background check with state regulatory authorities and professional associations** before your meeting. Check out the company also. You don't want even the most reputable person at a disreputable firm.

●**Conduct a 30-minute initial in-person interview.** If an adviser won't do this interview for free, put him last on your list of candidates and cancel if you find a winner first. Do the adviser's demeanor and level of service meet your expectations? Is he willing to work with other financial specialists? If he provides more than one service, is he comfortable with having only one slice of your business?

●**Check with two references.** *Questions to ask...*

　●Was this professional able to help you understand complex topics...or did he try to convince you that he's the expert and you should just trust him?

　●Did he follow your instructions...and are you satisfied with the results?

　●Has his service ever disappointed you? If so, what did he do about it?

●**Set the ground rules for fees/billing.** Put the details in writing on what you will get for your money...how fees are charged...and how disputes will be resolved. Determine whether quick calls—for instance, when the stock market dives—are billable. Appropriate guidelines vary by profession.

Make sure your spouse/partner approves of —and feels comfortable with—the professional you hire.

HIRING A FINANCIAL ADVISER
●**Where to find one...**

　●Financial Planning Association, 800-282-7526...*www.fpanet.org.*

　●National Association of Personal Financial Advisors, 888-333-6659...*www.napfa.org.*

●**Important credentials.** A CFP (Certified Financial Planner). Advisers who concentrate on securities selection may have the more prestigious CFA (Chartered Financial Analyst).

●**Lowdown on fees.** Fee-only advisers, who make no commission on your investments, are preferable. Most charge a percentage of assets under management (usually between 0.5% and 2% annually). However, if you have an isolated problem or portfolio decision, then consider an adviser who charges a flat hourly rate ($100 to $300 per hour).

Many advisers also charge a one-time fee of $1,000 or more to create a financial plan. If you have less than $100,000, you might have to choose only from the pool of commissioned advisers and brokers.

●**Red flags...**

　●Anyone who tells you he can definitely "beat the market." Instead, he should strive for a diversified portfolio that enables you to reach agreed-upon, long-term goals.

　●An adviser who promises personalized service but has more than 60 clients. He can't give you regular attention...and he's likely to palm off a lot of work on subordinates.

　●Potential conflicts of interest. If he suggests other financial professionals, ask if there is any fee-sharing arrangement.

　●Transaction confirmations and account statements sent only to your adviser. Without a paper trail, you have little recourse if anything goes wrong.

●**Background checks.** Check with your state's securities regulator for the adviser's Form ADV, which would include any disciplinary history.

HIRING AN ACCOUNTANT OR TAX PREPARER
●**Where to find one...**

　●Accreditation Council for Accountancy and Taxation, 888-289-7763...*www.acatcredentials.org.*

　●National Association of Enrolled Agents, 800-424-4339...*www.naea.org.*

　•Your state Society of CPAs.

●**Important credentials.** For tax preparers, an ATP (Accredited Tax Preparer) and ATA (Accredited Tax Advisor)...for accountants, a CPA (Certified Public Accountant)...for enrolled agents, EA.

●**Lowdown on fees.** Stick with tax preparers who charge an hourly rate. A flat fee per return encourages them to pump out work quickly. Plan on paying $100 or more for a walk-in national chain as opposed to $500 or more for a CPA who may provide a variety of financial services in addition to tax preparation and guidance throughout the year.

●**Strategies...**

　●Consider an enrolled agent if you desire more expertise and attention than a walk-in chain provides, but don't need a full-service CPA. Generally, these are former IRS employees who have passed comprehensive exams and are trained in all areas of tax preparation.

　●Ask about his approach to deductions. Are you comfortable with how aggressive he is? I know a tax preparer who refused to file home-office deductions because it was a red flag for audits. Since my home office was legitimate, I felt he was too conservative and didn't hire him.

• Clarify your preparer's function if you get audited. Not every tax preparer is allowed to represent clients in audits. If you fear being audited, you want an adviser who has the appropriate experience.

• Find out what percentage of his clients were audited in the last year. If it's more than 1%, be wary. Get written assurances that the adviser will pay penalties and interest due if he miscalculates your return, causing you to underpay.

• **Background checks.** For tax preparers, the Accreditation Council for Accountancy and Taxation (888-289-7763... *www.acatcredentials. org*). For accountants, the American Institute of Certified Public Accountants (888-777-7077... *www.aicpa.org/index.htm*).

HIRING AN INSURANCE AGENT
• **Where to find one...**

• American Institute for Chartered Property Casualty Underwriters, 800-644-2101... *www. aicpcu.org*.

• Society of Financial Service Professionals, 888-243-2258... *www.financialpro.org*.

• Your state's independent insurance agents association.

• **Important credentials.** For life insurance agents, a CLU (Chartered Life Underwriter) or membership in the National Association of Life Underwriters (NALU)...for property and liability insurers, a CPCU (Chartered Property Casualty Underwriter).

• **Lowdown on fees.** With rare exceptions, insurance sellers work on commission. Since commissions are paid by the insurer, you will not save by choosing one agent over another. Concentrate on finding the best life/property/liability policies at the most reasonable prices.

• **Decide what kind of agent...**

• *Captive agents* work for only one insurer, but they have more experience and knowledge about the provisions of policies. If you are more concerned with service than price, consider a captive agent.

• *Independent agents* represent a number of insurance companies and may be more willing to lobby on your behalf if they believe an insurer mishandled your claim.

• **Pay particular attention to references.** Can you speak with your agent on a weekend? Will he walk you through the claims process... or leave it up to the adjuster? Is he helpful in reducing the costs? Will he unbundle standard policies to see if you're better off with a menu of services customized to your needs?

• **Choose someone in your community** if all other factors are equal. You want to hire someone who is concerned about preserving his reputation.

• **Background checks.** Your state's insurance commissioner can tell you about any complaints or disciplinary problems. Also, try the Society of Financial Service Professionals, 888-243-2258... *www.financialpro.org*.

Consider: Going to an insurer who sells directly to the public if low price is your objective. Prices are lower, but because it's an emerging industry with new options every day, you'll need to do more research. For more information, go to *www.quotesmith.com* or *www.insweb.com*.

Inside Insurance

How to Fight Your Insurer...and Win

 on't throw up your hands when your health, auto or home insurance company denies a claim. *There are ways to fight back...*

HEALTH INSURANCE
Nancy Davenport

More than half of all Americans will have a disagreement with their medical insurers someday. Problems often develop when you're not able to use a specific health-care provider...or obtain approval for a specific treatment...or when a bill is "kicked back"—unpaid—from the insurance company after treatment.

When a health claim is denied, the patient's health-care provider normally handles the first stage of the appeals process. If the appeal is rejected, the patient needs to play an active role in further appeals.

●**Find out why the claim was rejected.** *It is usually because...*

●The treatment was not preauthorized, as required by the plan.

●The claim was not coded correctly by the insurance provider.

●The insurance company believes that your treatment was not medically necessary.

●The insurance company regards the treatment as experimental.

●The insurance policy specifically excludes that particular treatment.

●The health-care provider is not included in the plan.

Nancy Davenport, founding executive director of Patient Advocate Foundation, 753 Thimble Shoals Blvd., Suite B, Newport News, VA 23606, *www.patientadvocate. org*. The foundation publishes *The Managed Care Answer Guide* and *Your Guide to the Appeals Process*.

William Shernoff, senior partner at Shernoff, Bidart & Darras, a law firm specializing in bad-faith insurance litigation on behalf of consumers, 600 S. Indian Hill Blvd., Claremont, CA 91711. He is the author of *Fight Back & Win: How to Get Your HMO and Health Insurance to Pay Up* (Capital).

If you did not receive written notice of the denial, call the insurance company and request one. Without such documentation, you will have no foundation for an appeal.

●**Get a copy of your actual health insurance policy.** An estimated 40% of people facing rejected claims do not have this document. If you're insured through work, request a copy of the policy from your employer's human resources department.

●**Enlist help.** With the written denial and health-plan documents in hand, it is time to seek professional help. Our nonprofit organization can provide references (800-532-5274)...or check our Web site for a list of resources in your region (*http://data.patientadvocate.org*).

●**Keep an eye on the calendar.** Every insurance policy has a limited window for filing appeals, generally 30 to 90 days from the date of rejection. After the deadline, it becomes substantially more difficult—or even impossible—to appeal.

●**Address the reason for the insurer's rejection in your appeal.**

●If the insurer says a procedure is medically unnecessary—find statistics showing the procedure may extend or improve quality of life. Also provide encouraging statistics from clinical trials.

●If the insurer claims that a medical procedure is experimental—you, your health-care provider or your lawyer must prove otherwise, by citing studies on the subject published in well-regarded, peer-reviewed medical journals. Enlist the help of your health-care provider.

●If the insurer excludes the procedure— file a compassionate appeal and cite facts to support exceptions.

Important: Doctors' appeals of rejected claims are most likely to fail when they focus on medical ethics and opinion and neglect what the insurance companies like—hard proof.

AUTO & HOMEOWNER'S INSURANCE
William Shernoff

●**Depend on your agent.** When you are shopping for auto or homeowner's insurance, one downside of buying through a discount direct-sales arrangement is that you will not have an agent in your corner.

An agent might be affiliated with the insurance company. But since he/she is paid in commissions, his loyalties lie with customers. The more successful the agent is, the more powerful an advocate he is. The last thing the company wants to do is anger one of its revenue generators. If you run into any static, get help early. One call from an agent saying, "This is a good customer" or "I told him this was covered" goes a long way.

●**Don't get scared off by technicalities.** Meet deadlines and know precisely what your policy covers. But do not panic if you are denied a claim because of a missed deadline or misinterpretation of complex contractual language. Courts have consistently sided in favor of policyholders in these situations. A technicality should not be enough to prevent a legitimate claim.

●**Fight even the smaller things.** If you believe your insurance company is trying to cheat you, it might be worth fighting over even minor problems.

Example: A client who fought a $48 claim refusal wound up winning a $4.5 million judgment. The jury wanted to punish the insurer for its lack of ethics.

This is extreme, but anyone who believes an insurance company is doing him wrong should consider standing up to it.

●**Contact your state's department of insurance before you go to court**—but don't be surprised if it sides with the insurance company. Every state has an office that handles consumer insurance problems—the phone numbers are listed in my book or your phone book's state government listings.

The advice is generally free. Unfortunately, many state insurance commissioners go on to high-paying jobs with insurance companies, so they tend to side with the companies.

California, Illinois and New York all have slightly better records. But even in these states, there are problems.

●**Get everything in writing.** In order for you to contest an insurance company's decision, you need the specific reasons for their decision on paper.

• **Move up the ladder.** Send a summary of the problem, with *copies* of relevant documents—not originals—to the insurance company's "Claims Department Manager." Send all correspondence by certified mail, with return receipt requested.

In most states, insurance companies are required by law to respond to complaints. If you don't hear back within three weeks, send a second letter with copies of everything you initially sent.

If that doesn't get you satisfaction, write to the insurance company's president—you can find the address in A.M. Best Company's *Rating Book of Insurance Companies,* available in public libraries or at *www.ambest.com.*

If you still can't resolve your problem, consult a lawyer on a contingency basis. In most states, the insurance company may have to pay punitive damages if you can show its conduct was flagrant.

Helpful: Even if you can't bring the insurance company around to your way of thinking, it might provide further explanation for its decision. These details could prove useful if you eventually take the insurance company to court.

Get the Most Out of Your Insurance Plan

Scott Bellin, manager of administrative services at Thesco Benefits, LLC, an employee benefits broker and consultant, 320 W. 57 St., New York City 10019.

When it comes to insurance benefits, employees are enjoying more flexibility than ever. But the array of options can be daunting. *Here's how to get the most out of your employer's plan...*

LIFE INSURANCE

• **Buy supplemental group life insurance when you first enroll.** It is much cheaper than an individual policy—plus you don't have to undergo a medical exam or fill out health-related questionnaires. If you elect supplemental coverage at a later date, you will be subject to evidence of insurability.

Note: You owe taxes on employer coverage with benefits greater than $50,000. Tax is scaled by age and rated by cost per $1,000 of protection per month. *Under age 25:* Tax is 5¢ per $1,000. *Ages 45 to 49:* 15¢. *Over age 70:* $2.06.

LONG-TERM DISABILITY

• **Pay the premiums yourself**—if your employer gives you that option.

Reason: The benefits are tax free in the event the policy pays off. If the employer pays the premiums, the federal government taxes you on the benefits.

Example: If you're now in the 30% tax bracket and employer-paid coverage provides you with $10,000 a month, you would receive only $7,000 after tax.

Disability premiums within group policies are more affordable than if you buy the policy yourself.

FLEXIBLE-SPENDING ACCOUNTS

• **Dependent care.** These plans allow you to place pretax money into an account to pay for child care.

Trap: If you run afoul of the rules, you could be responsible for taxes on money in the account plus penalties. Your caregiver must pay taxes, and you must pay taxes as the employer.

• **Health care.** Use pretax money to pay for out-of-pocket medical expenses—deductibles, co-payments, eyeglasses, etc.—not covered by insurance. All these expenses must be incurred within the plan year for which the deductions are elected. Unused funds are forfeited. If the employee leaves, he/she can only submit claims through the termination date.

DENTAL PLANS

• **Choose a dental plan based on your out-of-network needs.** *Dental HMO plans versus indemnity/PPO plans...*

Dental HMO: In this plan, you're treated by a managed-care primary dentist who can refer you to a specialist. Most coverage is 100% reimbursable. *Best for:* Those who have major dental problems or don't have a favorite dentist.

Indemnity: Higher annual premiums, but you can see any dentist. Reimbursement can range from 100% for simple preventive work to 50% for major work.

Preferred Provider Organization (PPO): Offers the freedom of indemnity plans and a network of dentists who charge "contractor" rates, typically 25% below normal.

MEDICAL PLANS

•**Choose between *high-cost* and *low-cost* managed-care plans,** based on how often you and your family consult doctors who are out of the plan's network. Many employers offer both types.

Low-cost plan: Typically, a $1,000 annual deductible with 70% reimbursement on your first $10,000. After $10,000, the reimbursement is 100%. Premiums vary, based on employer, location, etc.—but generally, they are $200 to $400 a month for single coverage. Some employees get the low-cost plan through their companies for free. Opt for it if you rarely visit doctors or are sure you will only go to the in-network providers.

High-cost plan: Typically, a $200 annual deductible with 80% reimbursement on your first $5,000...and 100% reimbursement after that. High annual premiums—$300 to $900 a month for single coverage. Opt for it if you have a favorite doctor who is not affiliated with your insurer's network or you know you will need a specialist for a medical condition.

Self-defense: Buy from a trusted agent... and have your attorney read over the policy carefully before you sign.

Chris Cooper, certified financial planner and geriatric-care manager. He is president of Chris Cooper & Co., Inc., and ElderCare Advocates Inc., both of these organizations are located in Toledo.

Medical Mistakes And Medicare

Medicare patients are entitled to information about doctors' mistakes, says a new court decision.

After a woman died of cancer, her husband alleged that her death was caused by doctors who misdiagnosed the wife's condition as an abscess, appendicitis, bladder infection and "old woman's pain." The government investigated but—citing Medicare regulations—refused to tell the husband what it found. He sued.

Court: These regulations are invalid. Medicare must disclose the results of the review and of all other reviews held in cases in which a patient or family member claimed medical mistakes or poor care.

Public Citizen v. Dept. of Health and Human Services, DC, Dist. of Columbia, No. 00-0731 (ESH).

Long-Term-Care Plans Can Be Very Tricky

Long-term-care policies may not provide anything like the coverage you expect to get— because of tricky wording.

Before buying a policy, make sure that you understand exactly what it does and does not cover...and how benefits are calculated.

Example: If you need care only three days a week and it costs $200/day, you might expect the $600 weekly cost to be covered by a policy with a $100/day limit. But some insurers pay $100/day only on days you actually receive care—so you get only $300 for the three days and have to pay $300/week yourself.

Life Insurance Buyers Beware

Glenn Daily, a fee-only insurance analyst in New York City. www.glenndaily.com.

Never buy a whole-life insurance policy that has no cash value. Most agent-sold policies have no cash value due to high loads. Without a cash value, if you decide to drop the policy, you won't be able to do a tax-free exchange to an annuity.

Result: A lost opportunity for some tax-free earnings.

A true story: One year ago, a retired couple paid an initial premium of $48,100 (the cost basis) for a $5 million second-to-die life insurance policy. They didn't want to pay another premium to keep it in force. The policy had no cash value because of a high surrender charge.

Upon request, the couple's insurance company waived the surrender charge and created a small cash value, which then enabled the couple to do a tax-free exchange into an annuity offered by the same company. Their contributions to the annuity can now earn almost $48,100 free of income tax because of the cost basis carried over from the unwanted life insurance policy. Without a cash value, they would have lost this valuable benefit.

Strategy: Before you buy a policy, read the contract carefully and insist on a cash surrender value at all times. If you want to drop an existing policy with no cash value, ask the insurer to waive a small amount of the surrender charge to create a cash value.

More from Glenn Daily...

Life Insurance Smarts

To save on life insurance ask your agent about *blending,* which involves substituting lower-commission term insurance for a portion of the face amount of a whole-life policy. Blending can result in a higher cash value and death benefit—for the same premium.

Example: In 1992, one business owner bought a $2 million second-to-die, whole-life policy with a $40,000 annual premium. The agent set up the policy as 50% whole-life and 50% term without discussing alternatives. If the policy had been set up as 25% whole-life and 75% term with the same annual premium, the cash value would be almost $100,000 higher today and the death benefit would be the same or higher.

Note: Because blending can result in a lower commission for the agent, he/she may not offer it unless you ask.

If you own a cash value policy: Ask the insurer if it can be improved upon by correcting the blend from the date of issue.

How Much Life Insurance Do You *Really* Need?

J.J. MacNab, CFP, CLU, principal, Insurance Barometer LLC, insurance analysis company, Bethesda, MD, *www. deathandtaxes.com.*

Anyone who has dependents but is not independently wealthy requires life insurance. The difficult question is— *just how much?*

Before the Internet, consumers had to rely on agents to determine insurance needs and quote prices from several companies—and then had to pay hefty commissions of 50% to 140% of the first year's policy premium.

Consumers can buy their insurance commission free by phone or even on-line. But those who have special considerations, such as chronic health problems or complex financial needs, are still better off using an agent.

HOW MUCH IS ENOUGH?

It can take several hours to gather the financial information needed for these calculations. *Calculate the insurance needs for each spouse— assuming loss of each spouse's income and benefits/services to the household...*

●**Add up present and future debts and expenses,** such as mortgages, car payments and costs of children's college tuitions, weddings, etc., up to retirement. Don't forget the less obvious costs—such as an expensive vacation—and a possible future loss of income.

Example: If a stay-at-home spouse died, the working spouse would have to pay for day care and/or reduce his/her own working time and income.

●**Sum up invested assets**—savings, including 401(k)s and IRAs...other investments... future Social Security and pension benefits.

●**Subtract assets from long- and short-term debts** to arrive at how much insurance you will need.

Plug the required figures into one of the on-line calculators at *www.insweb.com* or *www.insurance.com* to determine how much insurance you should buy.

THE MEDICAL EXAM

Once you've chosen a policy, the insurer will require a 20- to 30-minute physical exam and typically reply to you in four to six weeks.

If you're in good health—you will probably pay the same premium rate you had been quoted on-line or by an agent.

If you have had particular diseases or chronic conditions—such as cancer, diabetes, high blood pressure, a history of heart attacks, severe depression, drug addiction or alcoholism—ask an agent to help you find an insurer that is willing to accept you.

TYPES OF INSURANCE

●**Term insurance.** This type is structured to provide up to 20 years of coverage for financial needs that will end at a foreseeable point, such as mortgage payments and children's future college tuition costs. The typical person needs between $100,000 and $1 million of term insurance.

Example I: Based on his needs, a 38-year-old married man with two children, in a management position paying $60,000 a year, requires at least $300,000 of term insurance. For a 20-year policy, he would pay a $245 annual premium. The premium on a $500,000 policy might cost $375 a year. The man's stay-at-home spouse might need $150,000 at a premium of $133 a year.

Example II: A 60-year-old man who wants to pay off a $350,000 mortgage would pay a premium for a 10-year term of $566 a year.

Strategies…

●Buy term insurance that guarantees your premium rate for the full length of your policy. It only costs 10% to 15% more than a standard policy, varying by age.

●Consider buying insurance with a longer duration than you think you will require—20 years instead of 10 years, for example. The policy will last long enough to cover an unforeseen increase in your insurance needs.

●**Permanent insurance.** These policies will last at least 20 years and insure long-term needs—future estate taxes, costs of caring for a disabled child, business needs, etc.

Example III: An employee stands to inherit a portion of a company after the owner's death. In order to have the cash needed to buy the widow's portion, he/she could purchase a long-term policy on the owner's life.

Example IV: A 70-year-old widow has as her primary asset an IRA, which will incur taxes of between 40% and 70% at her death. Life insurance can be paid for by taking IRA withdrawals, and the death benefit will cover the taxes when she dies.

Permanent policies carry higher premiums than term insurance in the early years of coverage. The extra money goes into a side fund that builds cash value. In later years, its earnings can offset insurance costs.

What it costs: In Example I, the 38-year-old's $300,000 policy would cost him $2,000 instead of $245. In Example II, the 60-year-old's $350,000 policy would cost him $12,250 instead of $566.

Three main types of permanent policies…

●Whole life. You pay a fixed, lifelong premium. Money placed in the side fund pays a fixed dividend. Suitable for those with little appetite for risk.

●Universal life. A popular form of permanent insurance, it offers high flexibility with moderate risk. Side funds are invested in long-term bonds. If interest rates remain stable or rise, the bond returns can offset the policy cost, making it less expensive than whole life. If rates drop significantly, the premium will rise.

●Variable universal life. This type of policy has the highest risk and the greatest possible gain. Its side fund is invested in mutual fund–like accounts offered by the insurer, so the premium is flexible. It will fall if the funds do well—and rise if they don't. Investors need to choose and monitor their own funds. Unlike most variable annuities, variable life insurance has a death benefit that exceeds its cash value.

IMPORTANT FEATURES

●**Guaranteed renewability.** Offered with all term and permanent policies, it allows for renewals at a guaranteed premium without a physical exam. No extra cost.

●**Convertibility.** The option to convert a term policy to a permanent life policy up to a specified age without another medical exam. Important to have in case you become ill later on. No extra cost.

•**Waiver of premium.** Available with term and permanent life insurance. The fee for this option can be substantial (the premium might increase from $375 to $455 a year). But it lets you keep your life insurance without paying a premium if you become disabled.

•**Guaranteed insurability.** This permanent insurance option lets you increase your coverage at a guaranteed premium without a medical exam. Useful for coverage of future estate taxes for clients under age 45. There's no extra charge.

•**No-load insurance.** Buyers incur no surrender charges if they cash out of this type of policy within the first few years. Buyers of fully loaded products pay high surrender charges if they cash out during the first 15 to 20 years.

The phrase *no-load insurance* applies to permanent insurance. Term insurance has no cash value and thus no surrender charges.

Variable Life Insurance Trap

Costs may go up for variable life insurance—or the policy may not last as long —when investment values go down. In a level-death-benefit policy, a rising account value lowers the "amount at risk"—the difference between the death benefit and the account value—which, in turn, lowers insurance charges. Conversely, a falling account value increases insurance charges, which can have a snowball effect if prolonged.

Better for most people: Term insurance and mutual funds rather than a variable policy.

James Hunt, a life insurance actuary for the Consumer Federation of America, 1424 16 St. NW, Washington, DC 20036, *www.consumerfed.org.*

The Weakest Links in Home and Auto Insurance

Lynn Knauf, policy manager at Alliance of American Insurers, an organization of 325 property-casualty insurers, 3025 Highland Pkwy., Downers Grove, IL 60515. She was previously a senior property claims adjuster for a national insurance company.

Madelyn Flannagan, vice president of research and education for Independent Insurance Agents of America, a consumer advocacy organization at 127 S. Peyton St., Alexandria, VA 22314.

In reaction to the events of September 11, 2001, some insurance companies decided to exclude coverage for terrorist acts. Others are waiting to see if the government agrees to play a role if there are future attacks.

While you cannot plan for such unlikely events, you can close up common—and potentially expensive—gaps in homeowner's and auto policies...

HOME INSURANCE
Lynn Knauf

•**Coverage for floods.** The Federal government's Federal Emergency Management Agency (FEMA) provides flood insurance, but it must be purchased through your insurance agent. It is recommended if you live in a flood-prone area.

Cost: Discuss how much coverage you require with your agent.

•**Sewer and drain coverage.** A typical homeowner's policy will not cover the damage from water that backs up through sewers or drains or if your sump pump stops working. Sewer and drain coverage is worthwhile if you have a finished basement with furniture or appliances that may be damaged by water.

•**Valuables.** Most policies cap the amount that will be paid for certain valuables that are stolen. For additional coverage, purchase riders.

•Jewelry and silver. Standard insurance policies have a $1,000 maximum payout for jewelry...$2,500 for silver. Items may need to be reappraised every five years if they appreciate in value.

•Fine art. Standard coverage is included within the personal property or "contents" coverage of your policy. Items of unusual value need to be appraised and covered by a fine arts floater.

A floater or rider includes coverage for any breakage and provides proof of the item's existence and its true value.

•Home office/business equipment. Standard insurance policies have a maximum payout for stolen or damaged items—and less for items that are stolen outside the home, such as laptop computers. If you operate a part-time business out of your home, you may have no liability coverage for business-related claims.

•**Enhanced policies.** Numerous insurance companies provide enhanced policies with broader coverage, including higher sublimits on items such as jewelry and replacement cost coverage on most personal property.

These policies may also include added coverage for lost jewelry (subject to a limit) and coverage for spoiled food resulting from a power outage. Extended replacement cost for the dwelling is also included with these policies.

•**Replacement cost coverage on contents.** Most homeowner's policies include coverage for your personal property or contents at "actual cash value"—that is, the cost to replace the item less the depreciation.

Ask your insurance company about upgrading your coverage to a "replacement cost on contents settlement."

AUTO INSURANCE
Madelyn Flannagan

•**Gaps in car leases/loans.** If your car is totaled, your insurance pays the cash value of the car—which, in the case of an expensive car, could be thousands of dollars less than the amount that you still owe.

This rider covers the difference between the loan or lease balance and the car's value. This rider is worthwhile if you have a large loan or lease a vehicle at the end of a model year.

•**Additional drivers.** Your claim may be denied if someone who drives your car on a regular basis is involved in an accident. You are required to give your insurer the driver's license numbers and dates of birth of anyone driving your car regularly.

Examples: Your nanny…your son, who uses the car when he is home from college.

Listing additional drivers may not raise your premiums as long as they have good driving records. Check with your agent or insurer.

•**Business use.** Notify your insurance company if your car is used for business. Business use is excluded from a liability standpoint in most policies. Most states define a "regular" business as one that generates more than $250 a year in income directly from your vehicle.

Examples: Your teenager uses the car to deliver pizzas…your spouse runs a weekly shuttle service for children for a fee…you transport equipment to mow lawns part-time on the weekends.

Cost to add liability coverage for business use: Will vary depending on how much you use your car for business. Ask your agent or insurer.

•**Rental cars.** If you are in an accident, most policies will pay for repairs to the actual rental car—not incidental charges, which can cost several hundred dollars.

Example: You can be liable for the lost rental revenue while the car is being replaced or for the cost of storing the damaged car until it can be fixed.

Auto insurers do not offer riders to cover incidental charges for rental cars. Some credit cards offer this. If yours does not, take the additional insurance that rental car companies offer. *Cost:* About $15/day and up, depending on the state in which you rent the car.

If you rent a vehicle for more than 30 days, your insurance plan may not cover any damage to the car. Ask your insurer about *extended non-owned coverage.*

•**Divorce.** If a divorced man and woman hold a policy and one has an accident, the other may share liability.

•**Children.** Kids are not automatically covered when they get their driver's licenses. You must notify the carrier. If you don't and the child is in an accident, you can be retroactively billed or dropped by the insurer.

Spend Less on Car Insurance

J. Robert Hunter, former Texas insurance commissioner and currently the director of insurance with the Consumer Federation of America at 1424 16 St. NW, Washington, DC 20036, *www.consumerfed.org.*

Some features of auto coverage are required, some are desirable and some are a waste of money. By putting your money only in the coverage that makes sense for you, you can shrink your auto insurance premiums dramatically.

Caution: Do not cut back to the point where your family—and your assets—are inadequately protected.

REQUIRED COVERAGE

Most states require "bodily injury liability insurance." This covers medical treatment for injury caused by you to your passengers, as well as to other drivers and their passengers—even pedestrians.

What we suggest…

• **At least $100,000 per person** per accident of bodily injury coverage.

• **Property damage coverage.** This covers repairing or replacing other motorists' cars and property.

• **Coverage for collision.** If you lease or finance your car, you are required to carry coverage to handle damage to it. You can *choose* to carry collision coverage if you own your car outright (see next column).

• **Comprehensive insurance.** Covers theft of your vehicle and damage to it (other than by way of accident). Again, if you lease or finance your car, you're required to carry comprehensive coverage. It's optional if you own the car.

SAVINGS STRATEGIES

Insurance premiums vary from company to company…and from policy to policy. It is essential to comparison shop.

Several Web sites show sample rates to assist you. It is best to see if your state insurance department Web pages list this information—most do.

Other cost cutters…

• **Increase your deductible.** If you carry collision and/or comprehensive coverage, you should raise your deductible. Decide how much you can afford to pay out-of-pocket.

Example: Increasing the deductible from $200 to $500 on collision and/or comprehensive coverage can lower the cost of this coverage by almost 30%.

• **Drop collision coverage.** If your car is worth less than $3,000, you'll pay more in premiums over time than you'd ever collect, even if the car were totaled. To determine your car's value, check the *Kelley Blue Book*.

• **Buy a car that is unlikely to be stolen.** Or one with low repair expenses. Cars with high theft rates or which are expensive to repair have high insurance costs. Ask your insurance agent before buying.

• **Drop towing coverage.** This only pays if an accident renders your vehicle undrivable. If you are a member of an auto club, such as AAA, you don't need this coverage, since they provide this service.

• **Drop glass coverage.** This feature covers the full cost of replacing broken glass, without a deductible. Sometimes it's built in to the comprehensive premium. If not, it can add 20% to auto insurance costs.

MAXIMIZE YOUR DISCOUNTS

Most insurance companies offer various discounts. *But beware:* Some insurance companies with the highest prices offer the largest discounts—but still end up high in overall price. Make sure you get all the discounts you are entitled to, but shop around for the lowest price after discounts are applied. *You're eligible if you…*

• **Drive less than 10 miles to work.** Allstate, for example, discounts if you drive less than 7,500 miles annually. Other companies differ, so check with your insurer.

• **Drive a car that has safety equipment—** automatic seat belts, air bags, antilock brakes.

• **Have had no accidents or tickets within the last three to five years.** Taking a driver training course can also result in savings—one course may cut premiums for several years.

●**Insure more than one car on your policy**—or insure your home with the same insurance carrier that insures your car.

●**Are in a special category.** If you fit a certain profile, you're eligible for discounts. *Check out the following categories...*

●Age 50-plus and belonging to AARP. The Hartford's AARP Auto Insurance Program, *http://aarp.thehartford.com*, offers AARP members discounts of up to 40%. But shop around since their rates are frequently not the lowest.

●Teachers who belong to a state education association or the National Education Association, *www.nea.org*, can get a 10% to 15% discount from Horace Mann Insurance Company, *www.horacemann.com*, in most states.

●In some Western states, individuals with a college degree in certain engineering or science-related fields can get a discount from the 21st Century Group, *www.i21.com*, and Argonaut Insurance Company, *www.argonautgroup.com*.

●Active and retired armed services personnel can save by going to USAA, *www.usaa.com*.

Bonus: If you decide to buy insurance online through the Progressive Insurance Co., *www.progressive.com*, or Reliance Direct Insurance Co., *www.reliancedirect.com*, you'll get a nominal discount in addition to any others.

More from J. Robert Hunter...

Insurance You Can Do Without

There are some types of insurance that are just not worth the cost...

●**Mortgage protection insurance:** It is cheaper to buy term life insurance to pay off your mortgage and other debts.

●**Funeral insurance:** Expensive and inefficient. Again, term life insurance is the better way to go because you can buy many times as much coverage for the same cost.

Worth considering...

●**Trip-cancellation insurance**—if you pay up front for an expensive vacation.

●**Flood and earthquake insurance**—if you live in areas in which these natural disasters are likely.

Make Sure Homeowner's Insurance Covers Mold Damage

Steven Dobreff, a partner in the law firm of Dobreff & Dobreff in Warren, MI, and an expert in mold litigation.

The health risks from mold include respiratory problems, rashes, headaches, even neurological damage. Most policies will exclude such coverage if the damage results from shoddy home construction or condensation from normal water usage. *And:* Some insurers are redrafting policies in an attempt to exclude all mold claims.

Self-defense: Review new or existing policies. Before submitting a mold claim, consult a lawyer about rights under your policy, and document the damage and repair costs. If your claim is headed for litigation, you will need expert witnesses to support your case.

Examples: An epidemiologist to deal with the environmental exposure issues...pulmonary (lung) specialist...your family physician...building engineer or inspector...damage appraiser.

If you suspect a problem: Ask your local health department or hospital for a list of industrial hygienists who can test your home.

8

Tax Traps and Opportunities

Thanks

Opportunities in the 2002 Tax Act

he *Job Creation and Worker Assistance Act of 2002* was signed into law on March 9, 2002. It provides $38.7 billion in tax incentives—primarily for businesses. But it also contains important new tax breaks for individuals.

FOR INDIVIDUALS

●**AMT relief.** The rule allowing personal tax credits—such as the dependent care credit and education credits—to offset regular income tax *and* the alternative minimum tax has been extended to include 2002 and 2003. This rule formerly applied only to 2001 returns.

After 2003, unless Congress decides to take additional action, only the child tax credit and the adoption credit can be used to offset AMT liability. Taxpayers who are faced with the AMT will lose the benefit of their other personal tax credits.

●**Larger tax-free foster care payments.** The definition of "foster care payments" that can be excluded from income has been broadened to include payments not only by a state, but also by a foster care placement agency. Similarly, the definition of a "foster care individual" has been broadened to include a person of any age placed by a qualified foster care placement agency. (The age 18 restriction has been removed.) These changes started in 2002.

●**Archer Medical Savings Accounts (MSAs)** —set to expire at the end of 2002—have been extended through 2003.

●**New write-off for teachers' expenses.** Elementary and secondary school teachers who spend their own money on supplies and equipment can deduct up to $250 per year as an adjustment to gross income. They need not itemize to claim this write-off, which applies only for 2002 and 2003.

Sidney Kess, attorney and CPA, 10 Rockefeller Plaza, Suite 909, New York City 10020. Mr. Kess is coauthor/consulting editor of *Financial and Estate Planning* and coauthor of *1040 Preparation, 2003 Edition* (both from CCH).

FOR BUSINESS

●Bonus first-year depreciation deduction.

An additional 30% first-year depreciation deduction can be taken for property acquired after September 10, 2001, and before September 11, 2004, as long as it's placed in service before January 1, 2005.

This bonus write-off is in addition to any of the first-year expensing deductions a business is entitled to claim.

Example: In August 2002, X Corp. bought and placed in service equipment costing $50,000. Assume that X Corp. is entitled to claim a first-year expensing deduction of $24,000. Because of the new law, it can also write off bonus depreciation of $7,800 (30% of $50,000 minus $24,000). Thus, the total first-year write-off for the $50,000 of equipment is $31,800 ($24,000 plus $7,800).

The balance of the cost—$18,200—can be depreciated over the equipment's recovery period starting with a depreciation allowance for 2002.

●Luxury cars.

For automobiles costing more than $15,300, there is a dollar limit on what can be written off each year. This regular limit is $3,060 for the first year if the car was placed in service in 2002. The new law increases the first-year write-off for cars placed in service after September 10, 2001, and before September 11, 2004, by an additional $4,600, raising the cost of a car to $17,409 before the cap is triggered.

Example: In August 2002, you place in service a car costing $25,000 that you use entirely for business. Your first-year write-off is $7,660 ($3,060 plus $4,600).

●Longer carryback of net operating losses (NOLs).

Net operating losses arising in tax years ending in 2001 and 2002 can now be carried back *five years* instead of two. This extension of the carryback period can provide an immediate infusion of cash as a refund for taxpayers with substantial NOLs.

If you do *not* want this extended carryback period, you must elect to apply the old two-year limit. The election is irrevocable.

You may wish to waive the five-year period in some situations. This might be the case if you were in a lower tax bracket in the three extra years that qualify for carryback than you expect to be in future years. (A net operating loss is worth more at higher tax rates.)

Example: In 2002, you had an NOL of $50,000. In 1997, 1998, and 1999 (the three extra carryback years), you were in the 15% tax bracket. You anticipate your business being profitable in 2003 and thereafter—when you'll be in a tax bracket over 25%. In this situation, you might want to forgo the three additional years so that any NOL can be used in the future against your higher tax bracket.

For AMT purposes, the NOL deduction is increased to 100% (instead of the old 90% limit).

●Electronic 1099s.

The new tax law allows information returns (1099s) to be sent electronically to taxpayers who received payments from the business. *Required:* The recipients of payments must consent to receiving their 1099 information returns electronically.

Note: 1099s can already be sent out to the IRS electronically, so you may now be set up for this method of sending forms to recipients. All you will have to do is add the recipients' E-mail addresses to your present system.

MORE GOOD NEWS

●Extensions of expired provisions.

The new law extends for two years (in most cases) several tax credits that had expired at the end of 2001. *These include…*

●The work opportunity credit.

●The welfare-to-work credit.

●Certain energy incentives (such as the credit for producing electricity from wind, biomass or poultry litter, or buying an electric car).

●Technical corrections.

The new tax law corrects certain problems in previous legislation, including…

●The deduction for SEPs in 2002 has been changed to match the 25% contribution limit.

●Catch-up contributions to qualifying plans and IRAs can be made starting at the beginning of the year, as long as the individual turns age 50 by year-end.

More from Sidney Kess…

Audit Triggers

Any one of the following items could flag your return for an audit…

●A math error or factual mistake,

such as the wrong Social Security number—the IRS believes simple errors are indications of more serious ones.

- **Neglecting to declare self-employment income** for which you received Form 1099—IRS computers will cross-check.

- **Earning more than $100,000.**

- **Writing a protest note on your return.**

- **Stating your hobby is a business** after declaring a loss year after year.

Also from Sidney Kess...

Kiddie Tax Trap

The investment income of a child under age 14 is taxed at the top tax rate of his/her parents. To get around this so-called "kiddie tax," it is common to give growth assets that do not pay current income—such as growth stocks—to such a child, then have the child sell them and pay tax on the gain at his own low rate after reaching age 14.

Trap: The kiddie tax does not let a parent deduct investment losses of a child under age 14—losses can be deducted only by the child. Growth assets often are volatile in value, and if a child takes a loss on an investment, there may be no effective way to deduct it.

Consider this risk when forming your family investment strategies.

Deciphering The 2001 Tax Relief Act

C. Clinton Stretch, tax principal and director of tax policy at Deloitte & Touche LLP, 555 12 St. NW, Suite 500, Washington, DC 20004.

The *Tax Relief Act of 2001* provides the largest tax cut in close to 20 years—$1.35 trillion. But the act is also one of the most complex.

Key changes—and traps to avoid...

TAX RATES

Overall rates will be reduced by about 10% between now and 2006. The 15% tax bracket has been reduced to 10% for the first $12,000 of taxable income of married couples, $10,000 of income for households and $6,000 of income for other single persons.

Rate reductions will take place according to this schedule...

TAX-BRACKET RATES

2002/03	2004/05	2006 & Beyond
38.6%	37.6%	35%
35.0%	34.0%	33%
30.0%	29.0%	28%
27.0%	26.0%	25%

MORE INCOME TAX SAVERS

- **Increased child tax credit.**

New levels...

Year	Credit
2002-2004	$600
2005-2008	$700
2009	$800
2010 and beyond	$1,000

- **Repeal of *hidden* taxes.** High-income individuals now face hidden taxes that increase effective tax rates...

- Both joint and single filers have their itemized deductions reduced by 3% of the amount by which their adjusted gross income (AGI) exceeds $137,300 for 2002 ($139,500 in 2003). That effectively increases their tax rate by as much as 3%.

- Personal exemptions are phased out as AGI rises from $137,300 to $259,800 on a single return ($139,500 to $262,000 in 2003)...and from $206,000 to $328,500 on a joint return ($209,250 to $331,750 in 2003), additionally increasing the effective tax rate.

The new law gradually phases out these two "penalties" starting in 2006 and eliminates them in 2010.

- **Reduction of the marriage penalty.** The marriage penalty means that two-earner married couples have higher taxes than single filers with the same incomes. But again, relief is deferred. *Beginning in 2005...*

- The standard deduction for joint filers will increase each year until 2009, when it reaches a level of twice the single standard deduction.

- The size of the 15% tax bracket for joint filers will increase each year until 2008, when it will be double that of the 15% bracket for singles.

These changes will eliminate the marriage penalty for lower-income filers subject to the 15%

rate who take the standard deduction. There will be a lesser penalty for those who itemize deductions and/or are in higher brackets.

AMT TRAP

Many high-income individuals and a growing number of middle-income individuals will find tax savings from the new law reduced or even eliminated by the alternative minimum tax (AMT). The AMT is a tax calculation required for high-income individuals. The final tax owed is the *larger* of that owed under regular or AMT rules. It has never been indexed for inflation, so AMT hits more people every year.

The new law increases the amount of income exempt from the AMT to $49,000 from $45,000 for joint filers…and to $35,750 from $33,750 for singles. This increase runs through 2004.

Result: Even though there is a slight rise in the AMT exemption, the new law will reduce "regular" tax liability to less than AMT liability for millions of Americans who will be subject to AMT for the first time.

Important: AMT will likely hit those who deduct large amounts of state and local taxes, especially in high-tax states, and who also claim "preference items" and certain adjustments, such as deductions for accelerated depreciation or tax-deferred gains on incentive stock options.

To learn more, go to the IRS Web site at *www. irs.gov* and enter "AMT" in the first search box.

RETIREMENT SAVINGS

●**Larger IRA contributions.** *Maximum IRA contributions are increased…*

Year	Contribution
2002-2004	$3,000
2005-2007	$4,000
2008 and beyond	$5,000

Those age 50 or older are allowed to make annual "catch-up" contributions of $500 from 2002 to 2005…and of $1,000 in 2006 and after.

●**Larger 401(k) contributions.** The limit on 401(k) contributions is increased gradually to $15,000 in 2006. *New limits…*

Year	Contribution
2002	$11,000
2003	$12,000
2004	$13,000
2005	$14,000
2006 and beyond	$15,000

Again, those age 50 or older can make "catch-up" contributions. *Limits…*

Year	Contribution
2002	$1,000
2003	$2,000
2004	$3,000
2005	$4,000
2006 and beyond	$5,000

Other employer-provided qualified retirement plans will also have their contribution limits increased. And a new "Roth 401(k)" that is taxed similarly to a Roth IRA will become available in 2006. Here, the employee's salary contributions are designated as after-tax contributions. Earnings can be withdrawn tax free after five years provided that certain conditions are met.

EDUCATION SAVINGS

The new law expands tax breaks for education and creates new ones.

●**Coverdell Education Savings Accounts** (formerly called education IRAs) are expanded. The annual contribution limit was increased from $500 to $2,000 starting in 2002, with 2002 contributions permitted through April 15, 2003. Moreover, education IRAs can now be used tax free to pay kindergarten through 12th-grade education expenses and expenses of state-approved home schooling instead of only college costs.

●**New college tuition deduction.** Up to $3,000 of college tuition is deductible in 2002 …and $4,000 in 2003. The maximum deduction is permitted on joint returns with less than $130,000 of AGI and single returns with less than $65,000 of AGI. Use the deduction soon. It goes away in 2006.

●**Longer interest deduction on student loans** to cover the life of a loan, not just the first 60 months.

●**More employer-provided assistance.** Up to $5,250 of tax-free aid can now be provided to employees for graduate and undergraduate study.

●**State-sponsored 529 college savings plans.** The new law makes withdrawals *tax free* when they are used for qualified expenditures. Formerly, they were taxed at the child's tax rate.

The legislation also allows 529 plans to be set up by private colleges and universities for prepaying tuition.

ESTATE TAX

The repeal of the estate tax is enacted by the new law…but not until 2010—and only for that one year! Before then, exempt amounts are increased and tax rates are modestly reduced.

The estate-tax-exempt amount increases from $1 million in 2002 and 2003 to $1.5 million for 2004…$2 million for 2006…$3.5 million for 2009, before repeal in 2010. The gift-tax-exempt amount increased to $1 million in 2002, but no further.

The top estate tax rate is reduced from 50% in 2002 to 49% in 2003, declining by one percentage point each year to 45% in 2007, where it stays until repeal.

Important: Consult a tax adviser to update wills and estate plans.

FUTURE TRAPS

Because many provisions of the new law contain deferred effective dates and premature expiration dates—in fact, the *entire law* expires by its terms in 2011—*continuous* tax planning is a must.

Tax Savers from Taxpayers Who Beat the IRS

The following recent taxpayer victories over the IRS may help you reduce *your* tax bill this year…

COSMETIC SURGERY DEDUCTIBLE

A woman who was treated for obesity and lost 100 pounds was left with loose skin. She underwent plastic surgery to remove it. Her health insurer said the procedure was "cosmetic" and did not pay for it. When she deducted the surgery as a medical expense, the IRS said cosmetic surgery was not deductible.

Court: Surgery that is *merely* cosmetic and not medically necessary is not deductible. But in this case, the loose skin was painful and prone to sores and infection. Removing it was essential in order to alleviate the health risks of obesity. The surgery is deductible.

Cynthia S. Al-Murshidi, TC Summary Opinion 2001-185.

REFUND AFTER DEADLINE

A tax return contained mathematical errors that caused the IRS to reduce the requested refund. After the statute-of-limitations deadline for claiming a refund had passed, the taxpayer then filed a corrected return claiming the full refund amount.

Decision: The first return was valid despite all its mathematical mistakes, and the full refund is allowed.

IRS Service Center Advice 200108041.

IRS IGNORED BACKUP

The IRS told a taxpayer that it would disallow his deductions if he did not provide additional documents to support them. He gave the IRS what it asked for—but it disallowed the deductions anyway and sent a tax-deficiency notice. Sometime later, the IRS reviewed the paperwork, agreed that no tax was due and dropped the assessment. By that time, the taxpayer had hired a lawyer to contest the case in Tax Court, so he asked to have his legal fees reimbursed.

Court: The IRS acted unreasonably when it assessed the tax without reading the requested documentation. The IRS must pay the taxpayer's legal bills.

Phuong K. Nguyen, TC Memo 2001-41.

"INNOCENT SPOUSE" STATUS FOR DECEASED'S ESTATE

A couple filed a joint tax return that claimed deductions from the husband's investment in a partnership. After the wife died, the IRS disallowed these deductions. To enable the wife's estate to escape the tax bill that resulted from the husband's poor investment, its executor claimed "innocent spouse" status for it—as the wife could have claimed for herself were she still alive.

Ruling: The executor is allowed to request "innocent spouse" relief. The IRS will then review the request under its normal criteria for granting or refusing such relief, as it would have if the wife had requested the relief herself.

IRS Legal Memorandum 200149010.

IRS MISSED DEADLINE

Ten years after one taxpayer deducted a donation to an IRS-approved charity, the IRS sent a letter demanding detailed information about it. The letter gave only 21 days to reply and did not explain the nature of the inquiry.

When the taxpayer responded that he had only a general recollection of the gift, the IRS accused him of committing tax fraud…disallowed his deduction…added interest and fraud penalties that quadrupled the total tax bill…and said the statute of limitations did not protect him because of the fraud.

Court: The IRS gave no justification for its very late tax assessment or the fraud charge. So the three-year limitation period does apply. The tax was lifted—and the IRS must pay the taxpayer's legal bills.

Thomas Johnson, DC CD Ca., No. CV 00461 R (Ex); 87 AFTR2d Par. 2001-1047.

EX-WIFE BEATS IRS TO HUSBAND'S PENSION

A divorce decree awarded a man's pension account to his wife. Nevertheless, the IRS levied on it to collect his back taxes. The wife then served a Qualified Domestic Relations Order (QDRO) on the pension's trustees, as required by federal pension law, to notify them that the assets were hers.

The IRS said that its levy on the account predated the QDRO, so it should get paid first.

Court: The divorce decree gave the ex-wife a lien on her husband's pension, and it predated the IRS action. The later issuance of the QDRO merely clarified the wife's rights.

Cooper Industries Inc. v. Jacqueline M. Compagnoni, DC SD Tex., No. H-00-0702; 88 AFTR2d Par. 2001-5303.

LOTTERY WINNER'S ESTATE WINS, TOO

An individual died shortly after winning a multimillion dollar lottery prize payable over 20 years. The IRS valued the prize for estate tax purposes, using the valuation rules that apply to a normal annuity, and arrived at a value of $4 million. The estate protested that the valuation was too high because it did not reflect restrictions against transferring the prize payments.

Court: For the estate. Lottery rules that prohibited any sale or transfer of prize payments substantially reduced their market value. So the estate tax value was cut in half—to $2 million.

Rosa Shackleford, CA-9, No. 99-17541; 88 AFTR2d Par. 2001-5250.

IRS CANNOT ORALLY ALTER AGREEMENT

A married couple entered into a compromise agreement with the IRS covering their joint taxes. The husband also entered into a separate compromise agreement covering employment taxes he owed.

An IRS agent told the couple verbally that if either agreement was breached, the other one would be defaulted. When the husband failed to make payments on his agreement, the IRS defaulted the joint agreement—even though it had already been paid off in full. Of course, the couple protested.

Ruling: The Tax Code and IRS regulations require all terms of a compromise agreement to be in writing. The oral condition is invalid, and the joint agreement remains in effect.

IRS Field Service Advice 200130043.

The General Rule May Not Be Best for You

Lisa N. Collins, CPA/PFS, vice president and director of tax services at Harding, Shymanski & Co., PC, Evansville, IN, and the author of *The Complete Idiot's Guide to Tax Deductions* (Alpha). Ms. Collins is a member of the steering committee of the American Institute of Certified Public Accountants' Tax Strategies for the High Income Individual Conference.

Tax experts are quick to quote the "general rule" that applies in various situations. But sometimes it's better to ignore these general rules, and do the opposite. *Here are some examples…*

STRATEGIES FOR INDIVIDUALS

●**Deferral of income.** It is the generally accepted practice to defer as much income as possible into subsequent tax years. By doing so, you'll postpone current tax on that income.

Deferral makes a lot of sense today, when tax rates are falling. Not only will tax be postponed, but the deferred income will be taxed at lower rates.

But, in some situations, accelerating income into the *current* year is the better strategy.

Taxpayers should accelerate their income when they...

...are subject to the alternative minimum tax (AMT) and are in a tax bracket above 28% for regular income tax. Income for AMT purposes is taxed at only 28%. Any income you accelerate will be taxed at this rate rather than your higher regular income tax rate.

...have deductions, credits or carryovers that could be claimed only if income were accelerated. These write-offs will offset the accelerated income (or the tax on that income).

●**Deferred compensation.** Executives are usually advised to arrange with their employer to defer year-end bonuses and other compensation into their retirement years, if possible, when they should be in a lower tax bracket.

But deferral does *not* make sense if...

...there is any concern about the company's survival. *Problem with deferred compensation:* For the deferral to be effective for tax purposes, the arrangement must be an unsecured promise by the company to make payment. The funds remain subject to the claims of the company's general creditors if the company runs into trouble. *Impact:* Your deferred compensation could be lost in bankruptcy.

...you believe you can earn more on the money by investing it yourself than the company will pay. For example, the company may credit an annual amount of interest on the deferred compensation, but if you can earn more than this rate, it's better to take the money, pay the tax now and invest for the future.

●**IRA distributions.** The general advice is to take only minimum distributions from traditional IRAs. That way, the funds can continue to grow on a tax-deferred basis. You're told not to take money until age 70½ (the required beginning date for distributions), and then only enough to avoid penalty.

But it's better to take more than the required amounts if...

...you intend to make substantial charitable donations. Bigger IRA distributions will increase your adjusted gross income, allowing a greater current deduction for the charitable donations. The deduction will help offset the income resulting from the IRA distribution.

...you are in a low tax bracket. For example, a person who retires at age 60 may have most of his/her money tied up in a rollover IRA account and little or no other income. Such a person probably should take distributions right away—even though not legally required—because this income will be taxed at low rates.

Note: After age 59½, IRA withdrawals are no longer subject to an early distribution penalty.

●**The dependency exemption.** Parents can claim a dependency exemption for a child who is under age 19 (or under age 24 and a full-time student), regardless of the child's income.

In the case of divorced parents, the dependency exemption automatically belongs to the custodial parent. But the custodial parent can waive the exemption in favor of the noncustodial parent—who is often the parent providing the greater share of support. Divorce decrees often require such a waiver, and this is the general rule.

*But...*the custodial parent should not waive the exemption if the noncustodial parent is a high-income taxpayer subject to the phase-out of the exemption. In 2002, the exemption is phased out when AGI exceeds $137,300 for a single parent who is not a head of household. This figure increases to $139,500 in 2003.

Starting in 2006, the phase-out of personal exemptions for high-income taxpayers starts to disappear and is eliminated entirely by 2010.

●**State and local taxes.** The general rule is that before the end of the year you should pay any state and local taxes otherwise due the following January. *Reason:* To increase write-offs for the current year.

*But...*you should *not* prepay state and local taxes if you are subject to the alternative minimum tax. These taxes are *not* deductible for AMT purposes.

STRATEGIES FOR BUSINESS

●**Depreciation.** The general counsel is to claim accelerated depreciation to boost business write-offs. But doing so can dilute the benefit of the write-offs and, in some cases, trigger AMT.

●Start-up businesses should "save" depreciation deductions for future years by opting for slower current depreciation.

• Don't elect first-year expensing (Section 179 deduction) in a year when the business has an operating loss. This deduction can only be claimed when there is an equal amount of taxable income (although unused expensing can be carried forward). Instead, claim depreciation to spread the write-offs into profitable years.

• **Net operating losses (NOLs).** The general rule requires NOLs to be carried back (generally two years, but five years for NOLs in 2001 and 2002) and then forward for up to 20 years. A carryback produces an immediate cash infusion for the business. But taxpayers can elect not to claim the carryback and instead only carry NOLs forward. This election should be considered when…

…you expect to be in a higher tax bracket in the future. This will allow the NOLs to effectively save more tax dollars.

…you were married during a carryback year. *Example:* A taxpayer generating an NOL was married in a carryback year but is single in the loss year. Waiving the carryback avoids complicated computations and possible dealings with his former spouse.

STRATEGIES FOR INVESTORS

• **Capital gains and losses.** The standard advice is to postpone the realization of capital gains until assets have been held for more than one year. This makes the gains long-term capital gains, which are taxed at favorable rates. But waiting isn't always necessary.

If you have capital losses—long term or short term—you don't have to wait out the year to realize long-term gains. You can use short-term gains—as well as long-term gains—to offset your capital losses.

• **Savings bonds.** Taxpayers owning US savings bonds generally opt to postpone reporting income until the bonds are cashed in, or they mature. But reporting interest currently may be wise when the bondholder…

…dies early in the year. The accrued interest on the bonds may be taxed at low rates if the decedent had very little or no other income in the year he died. *Reason:* In the year of death, a decedent can claim a full standard deduction (if not itemizing deductions) and a full personal exemption—no proration required.

…is a child over age 13. Once a child is beyond the kiddie tax, income is taxed at his low rates—10% or 15%. A child with modest income may pay no tax on the interest.

Caution: If the child has been deferring interest until age 13 and his adviser now wants him to report it currently, the child must file for a change in accounting method. Automatic IRS consent procedures simplify this action.

• **Installment sales.** The general rule is to use the installment method to report gain on sales of assets for which payment will be received in more than one year. But electing out of installment reporting is advisable when…

…you have capital losses to offset the gain. *Reminder:* Don't overlook any carryover capital losses that you can use to offset the gain.

…the seller dies in the same year as the sale, before payments have been received. Electing out of the installment sale method causes the entire gain to be taxed on the final tax return of the decedent. The income tax obligation will reduce the estate tax (because it is a liability of the decedent).

If the gain is not reported on the final tax return, the heirs must pay income tax on the installment gain (because it is income in respect of a decedent). This is in addition to paying estate tax on the value of the installment note.

IRS Won't Tax Frequent-Flier Miles

Addressing a long-unresolved question, the IRS now says it will not claim that income is understated when an individual personally uses frequent-flier miles attributable to business or official travel without including their value in income. It also reports that any future change in this position will apply only prospectively, and will not affect past treatment of such miles.

Caution: The IRS says this position does not apply to miles that are converted to cash, when miles are paid as compensation or when miles are used for any tax-avoidance purpose.

Details: IRS Announcement 2002-18; IRB 2002-10,1.

Best Tax Strategies For Owners Of Vacation Homes

Edward D. Fulbright, CPA/PFS, and Genevia Fulbright, CPA, Fulbright & Fulbright, CPA, PA at 5410 Hwy. 55, Suite AC, Durham, NC 27707, *www.moneyful.com*. Mr. Fulbright is the host and producer of *Mastering Your Money* on NPR station WNCU-FM.

If you own a vacation home, you will get more satisfaction out of your time there by knowing you're making the most of possible tax breaks.

RESIDENTIAL TAX BREAKS

A vacation home is considered a residence. *Owners are entitled to the same tax advantages that apply to a primary residence...*

●**Deductible mortgage interest.** For your primary residence and one vacation home, you can deduct the combined interest on mortgages of up to $1 million.

In addition, you can deduct the interest on a home-equity credit line of up to $100,000, secured by that second home.

Mortgage points on the original purchase of the vacation home are 100% deductible. Points on refinanced loans must be written off over the life of the loan unless they are used for capital improvements.

●**Property taxes.** Local property taxes also are deductible.

●**Tax-favored sales.** If you sell a vacation home you've owned more than one year and on which you've never claimed depreciation, any gain will be long-term, taxed no higher than 20%. The cost of capital improvements you've made to the home can be added to your tax cost (basis), reducing the tax if you sell the home.

Retirement strategy I: If you think you'll be in the 15% tax bracket after retirement, wait until then to sell your vacation home. As long as you've owned the home more than five years, you'll owe only 8% tax on any gains.

Retirement strategy II: Sell an appreciated primary residence and pocket up to $250,000 worth of tax-free capital gains ($500,000 if married, filing jointly). Then, move into your vacation home and live there full-time.

After living in the latter home for two years, you can sell it and claim another $250,000 (or $500,000) tax-free gain.

THE 14-DAY FREEBIE

You may rent your vacation home to others as well as use it yourself. If so, the tax treatment depends on how often you rent it.

A unique provision of the Tax Code was supposedly enacted originally to benefit home owners in Augusta, Georgia, site of the annual Masters golf tournament. Under this rule, owners can rent out a home (including a vacation home) for up to 14 days per year without having to declare any taxable income.

This opportunity for tax-free income may be especially appealing if you own a vacation home in a resort area or near a major sports venue. You might collect thousands of dollars without owing tax or losing any tax benefits.

If you're a principal in a business or professional practice, rent your vacation home to the company for a retreat or a management meeting. *If you do...*

●**Your company can deduct the payment,** as long as it's reasonable given the length of the meeting and the time of the year.

●**You won't pick up any taxable income** on your personal return if you observe the 14-day limit.

Trap: A sole proprietorship may not be able to deduct this rental expense if the proprietor owns the vacation home.

Strategy: Transfer the property into the name of the nonbusiness-owner spouse.

LONGER-TERM TAX BREAKS

If you rent your vacation home for more than 14 days, another set of rules will determine whether it's taxed as a residence or as rental property.

If your personal use of a vacation home is more than 14 days or 10% of the total days that it's rented at a fair price (whichever is greater), that home will be taxed as a residence.

Example: You rent out your beach house for 180 days a year. If your personal use is 18 days or fewer this year, the house is a rental property. If your personal use is 19 days or more, it's a residence.

You'll have to report income if you rent your vacation home more than 14 days per year. However, you can offset this taxable income with expenses you incur.

Examples: An allocable share of interest and property tax…similar allocations to repairs and insurance…advertising…depreciation.

For a vacation home classified as a residence, expenses can be taken only up to the amount of rental income. Excess expenses can be carried forward to years in which rental income exceeds expenses.

Example: You receive $10,000 in rent this year. Expenses total $12,000. You'd owe no tax on your rental income while the excess $2,000 carries forward.

RENTAL PROPERTY

If your personal use is no more than 14 days and you rent your vacation home more than 14 days, you have a rental property. Even if your personal use is more than 14 days, you have a rental property if personal use is no more than 10% of rental days.

Example: You use your vacation home 15 days this year. If you rent the home for at least 151 days, it's a rental property.

You can increase the number of days you can use your vacation home by doing repairs. Repair days do *not* count as personal days.

With rental property, expenses can offset rental income. Moreover, those expenses may include travel to a distant vacation home classified as rental property.

If expenses related to your rental property exceed rental income, losses may be deductible.

Example: With $10,000 worth of income and $12,000 worth of expenses, you would have a $2,000 loss to deduct against other income.

Trap: The "passive activity" rules restrict such losses to $25,000 per year (unless there is income from other passive activities).

Most taxpayers lose $1 worth of passive loss deductions for each $2 their adjusted gross income (AGI) tops $100,000. At $150,000 of AGI, no passive losses are deductible.

Example: Your AGI is $110,000, $10,000 over the threshold. You'd lose $5,000 in permissible passive-loss deductions, bringing the maximum down to $20,000.

With a passive loss of $2,000, as described above, you'd need AGI no higher than $146,000 for a full deduction.

ENDGAMES

Vacation home owners who rent out their property may well have two sets of loss carryforwards—one from rental property years and one from residential years. These carryforwards can't be combined.

Strategy: In the years before you intend to sell the home, make a concerted effort to increase rental income.

Rent the property out for more days, perhaps setting low rents to attract tenants. As long as you use the rental property yourself more than 10% of the rental days, the property will qualify as a residence.

Result: Carryforwards from years the property was classified as a residence can be used up.

If you have used a short-term mortgage to acquire your vacation home, interest deductions will disappear eventually. Then you can deduct more operating expenses, including expenses from prior years.

Strategy: Stop using the property yourself in the year of sale. That turns the house into a rental property.

When you sell a rental property, all passive losses are fully deductible—including loss carryforwards. It doesn't matter how high your AGI is that year.

Result: You can write off all the accumulated passive losses.

SWAPPING HOMES

Instead of selling your vacation home, consider entering into a like-kind exchange when it is considered a rental property.

Strategy: Exchange the property for a rental home in the area where you live, and rent it out to others for 24 months. After 24 months, you may convert this rental home to your primary residence for two years and then sell it.

On this sale you will be able to exclude $250,000 worth of capital gains ($500,000 if married, filing jointly).

Home Advantage

Take the exclusion of capital gains on home sales, regardless of your age—even if you don't buy another home. Any person who has owned and lived in a home as the principal residence for at least two of the last five years pays no tax on the first $250,000 of profit from selling the home. A couple pays no tax on the first $500,000. You could sell the house, retain the money and pay no tax. The house does not have to be in both spouses' names for both to take the exclusion.

Joseph F. Gelband, attorney specializing in tax law and estate planning, Larchmont, NY.

Finance Your Boat or RV With a Home-Equity Loan

Tax-deductible boat or recreational vehicle (RV) financing is possible. If you finance a boat or RV with a home-equity loan, you get a deduction—home-equity loan interest up to $100,000 is usually deductible.

Also: A boat or an RV with sleeping, cooking and toilet facilities may qualify as a second home—making the loan deductible under the same terms as a mortgage on a vacation home.

Caution: Be sure the loan is secured by the boat or RV if you're planning to take mortgage-interest deductions.

Randy Bruce Blaustein, Esq., senior tax partner, R.B. Blaustein & Co., 155 E. 31 St., New York City 10016. Mr. Blaustein is author of How to Do Business with the IRS *(Prentice Hall).*

More from Randy Bruce Blaustein...

How to Get the IRS to Forgive Tax Debt

It is difficult—but not impossible—to get the IRS to forgive tax debts. *An offer in compromise* allows you to settle unpaid tax liabilities for less than the full amount due (including interest and penalties). The IRS generally agrees to forgive a tax liability only if there is a question as to the amount of tax owed and whether you could ever pay the full amount, given your income and assets. A compromise also might be granted if you suffer a financial hardship, such as the loss of your home.

Important: The IRS considers your spouse's income and assets in determining eligibility for an offer in compromise.

Details: Check out IRS Publication 594, *The IRS Collection Process,* at *www.irs.gov.*

Also from Randy Bruce Blaustein...

When Your Accountant Commits Tax Fraud

Some accountants—even CPAs—take very aggressive positions on their client's returns which, for all practical purposes, amount to tax fraud. Sometimes the accountant is cavalier. Sometimes he/she is wrongly applying the tax law to reduce or eliminate tax. The problem for you arises when the IRS picks your tax return for examination.

Best approach: Do not use the accountant who prepared the return to represent you. Engage a knowledgeable tax attorney who knows how to minimize the chances of having a routine tax audit snowball into a criminal investigation.

Finally from Randy Bruce Blaustein...

What the IRS Looks for When It Audits Entertainment Expenses

Revenue agents believe that business entertainment expenses are an abuse area. They eagerly challenge deductions claimed for meals, tickets to sporting events and other entertainment costs. Even if you do have the required receipt to support payment of the expense, the agent may question whether the expense is reasonable—as opposed to lavish. He/she will also question the business purpose of the expense. Be prepared to explain how the person you entertained brought you new business or has the potential to generate additional business.

Trap: A sharp revenue agent will ask your permission to contact one or more of the people you claim to have taken to dinner. The agent wants to make sure you're not trying to deduct a personal expense. Don't go along with it! Generally it's unwise to grant such permission. Most times, the agent will back down.

Tax Form Loopholes

Edward Mendlowitz, CPA, partner in the accounting firm of Mendlowitz Weitsen, LLP, CPAs, Two Pennsylvania Plaza, Suite 1500, New York City 10121.

Most people simply try to get the numbers right when they fill out their tax returns. But there is a lot more to this. Making strategic decisions can save you money, and, if you're careful, can reduce the odds of an IRS audit. *Consider these strategies...*

FOR INDIVIDUAL TAXPAYERS

Loophole: **Make a Section 83(b) election when exercising any unvested incentive stock options.** The election has to be made within 30 days of the exercise and will lower your alternative minimum tax (AMT) liability.

Making a Section 83(b) election means you owe AMT—in the year you make the election—on the difference between the exercise price for the options and the fair market value of the shares.

If you don't make the election, the AMT is calculated on the difference between the price you pay for the options and the fair market value of the shares when they vest.

Strategy: If you expect the shares to increase substantially in value, exercise incentive stock options as soon as possible. That way, you minimize the difference between the exercise price and the shares' market value.

Loophole: **File a gift tax return for gifts used to pay insurance premiums.** File the return even though it is not legally required.

When you give money to a trust to pay insurance premiums, no gift tax return is required if you give no more than $11,000 in 2003 and no grandchildren are involved (as long as the recipient signs a "Crummey" letter, making the payment a gift of a present interest).

If the IRS determines in a subsequent estate tax audit that the letter was inadequate, no statute of limitations will have run. The donor or his/her estate could be liable for tax on the gifts.

Better: Filing a gift tax return blocks the IRS from assessing taxes after the three-year statute of limitations runs.

Loophole: **Don't take valuation discounts on Form 709 for small gifts.** When you take a valuation discount for a gift, you must check the box on the gift tax return and include full disclosure of the reasons for the discount.

If you don't take a discount, the box is not checked off and you will decrease the chances of an audit. You should compare the benefits of avoiding an audit with the higher gift valuation.

Loophole: **Enter Form 1099 information on Schedules B and D of your tax return—even if it's wrong.** The IRS cross-checks the totals that are shown on Schedules B and D—reflecting capital gains, dividends and interest income—with the amounts banks, brokers and other payors report on Forms 1099. If the amounts differ, an IRS notice is automatically generated.

If there's a mistake on a 1099: Enter the 1099 figure on your tax return. Then subtract the erroneous amount to end up with your real total. Attach an explanatory letter to your return.

Loophole: **Claim no more than nine withholding exemptions on Form W-4.** When you claim 10 or more withholding allowances, or exemptions from withholding, a copy of the Form W-4 must be sent to the IRS, where agents can check whether the exemptions are valid and possibly generate correspondence.

Loophole: **Make a tardy generation-skipping transfer election.** In general, grandparents who set up trusts for grandchildren can take a $1.12 million lifetime exemption in 2003, adjusted for inflation, for their collective gifts. When Form 709 is filed on time, the value of the gift is determined when the gift (or transfer) was actually made. When you make a late election, the value is determined when you filed the late return and elected to offset the gift's value against the lifetime exemption.

So, making a post-April 15 election saves money when the value of the gift decreases after you make it, such as a whole-life insurance policy premium.

Trap: If you don't make a timely election and the insured dies, the full face value of the policy's face could be considered a generation-skipping transfer. That could create an enormous tax bill.

Loophole: Keep the total of your money in foreign bank accounts below $10,000. You must file a Form TD F 90-22.1 when the aggregate of foreign bank accounts in which you hold money and accounts from which you have check-signing power (even though the money is not yours) exceeds $10,000. Filing the form opens the accounts up for IRS scrutiny.

FOR BUSINESS TAXPAYERS

Loophole: Choose a low-audit business code number to put on the company's Schedule C. The IRS targets for audit certain types of businesses and industries. When your business could legitimately fit into more than one category, choose the business code number that is not on the IRS's hit list. For example, a car wash can possibly be called an auto service center.

Loophole: Attach an "election schedule" for a controlled group of corporations to the corporation's Form 1120. When you run a controlled group of corporations (more than one corporation under common ownership), you must attach to the business's tax return an election schedule that includes an apportionment plan for certain tax items (e.g., the AMT exemption). Otherwise, the IRS automatically allocates all exemptions and the benefits of the lower tax brackets equally among all the companies in the group.

Strategy: When you have a controlled group that includes dormant and active businesses, allocate all the exemptions and tax breaks to the active business.

Loophole: Report a fair market value appraisal on Form 1120S when you switch your C corporation to an S corporation. This will reduce the taxes owed on any built-in gains.

Businesses that convert from C corporation to S corporation status must value the business's assets as of the date of the conversion. If assets are sold within 10 years, profits are realized as if the C status were still in effect to the extent of any built-in gains as of that date, i.e., the S corporation pays the tax.

Strategy: When you get a preconversion *fair market value* appraisal, the valuation is generally lower than what the assets could be sold for, saving taxes if the assets are sold before the 10-year deadline.

More from Edward Mendlowitz...

Remarriage Tax Loopholes

People who remarry should take the time to examine the tax-planning and estate-planning consequences of their action...

RETIREMENT ACCOUNTS

●**Who will inherit your company pension and retirement accounts after your remarriage?** Federal law requires that spouses who will not inherit at least half of their spouse's pension and retirement accounts waive their rights to the money *in writing*. But very few individuals who remarry bother to ask for a written waiver, and that can lead to unintended consequences.

Example: One divorced man names his children from his first marriage as beneficiaries of his retirement accounts. When he remarries, he makes no changes to those accounts. So, when he dies, his new wife will be entitled to inherit 50% of the accounts.

Loophole: Ask your new spouse to sign a separate agreement governing pension money immediately *after* the marriage.

Trap: A prenuptial agreement waiving a share of a pension is not binding because it was signed before the marriage. *Note:* No waiver is necessary for IRAs.

●**Will your pension payout choices still make sense?** Typically, for payout, you can choose a "one-life annuity," which would make payments to you for life. Or you can choose a "two-life annuity," which would make smaller payments during your lifetime but continue to pay your spouse until he/she dies.

In many second marriages, it isn't necessary to provide lifetime payments to the surviving spouse, who could very well be covered under a pension plan from his first marriage.

Loophole: Buy a term-certain, fixed-premium life insurance policy that will pay the children the amount they otherwise would have received from the pension payments after your death. When you must cover a second spouse under your pension plan, make sure your children from your first marriage don't lose financially.

Example: After you die, your spouse will receive $5,000 a month in pension payments over his lifetime. You can make that up to your children by naming them beneficiaries of a 10-year term fixed-premium life insurance policy that pays them the present value of $5,000 a month in a lump sum.

ESTATE PLANNING

●**Will your new extended family be adequately covered by your will?** Many people neglect to prepare new wills when they remarry. However, most states have laws that automatically give a portion of an estate outright to a surviving spouse.

Loophole: Set up a *qualified terminable interest property* (QTIP) trust for a new spouse. This type of trust will provide income solely to the spouse over his lifetime. At your death, trust assets are distributed to your children or other beneficiaries designated under your will.

●**Does your will specify whether the estate tax should be apportioned against each bequest or paid from your residuary estate?** Estate tax apportionment has become increasingly important as the amount of money in pension and IRA accounts increases.

Reason: Retirement account assets pass outside the taxable estate. Without apportionment, nonretirement account beneficiaries would pay the full amount of the estate tax on assets inherited by the retirement account beneficiaries.

Apportionment requires that beneficiaries pay their share of the taxes according to how much they inherit. Otherwise, taxes are paid from the remaining estate assets.

Loophole: Estate tax apportionment must be taken into account when planning out your estate so that your net bequests will be what you want them to be.

●**Can you minimize taxes by allocating value-discounted estate assets to various beneficiaries?** Estate tax valuation discounts apply to family partnerships, corporate stock and other assets in which the decedent owns a noncontrolling interest. Discounted assets carry reduced estate tax liability.

Strategy: Use undiscounted assets to fund a QTIP trust for your surviving spouse, and give discounted assets to children on which estate tax is to be paid. There is no current tax on the assets left to the spouse.

Example: You own $5 million in securities plus a family partnership worth $5 million before discounting, or gross estate assets totaling $10 million. Because of estate tax valuation adjustments, the partnership is valued at $3.5 million, so the taxable estate equals $8.5 million. You leave "half" the taxable estate ($4.25 million) to your children and the balance in trust for your spouse.

Question: Should you leave the securities in trust, or the partnership shares?

If you leave the partnership shares, your spouse gets assets valued at $3.5 million for tax purposes but worth $5 million for cash flow purposes.

To make up the 50% split, you would have to add another $750,000, so your spouse gets assets worth $4.25 million, but lifetime income generated by $5.75 million. The children would get $4.25 million of assets that would be further reduced by the estate taxes.

What to do: Leave the discounted assets to the children to avoid a drastic distortion in their net bequests.

Loophole: Fund a QTIP during your lifetime with trust provisions that mirror the provisions in your will.

Finally from Edward Mendlowitz...

Financial Planning Loopholes

Financial planning is a booming part of my practice. People know that taxes will have an impact on any financial moves they make, so they come to an accountant for guidance—a person who can give both planning and tax advice. *Some of the tax-saving strategies I recommend...*

Loophole: **Shelter part-time business income in a tax-deferred retirement plan.** You won't pay tax on the money you put into the plan until you take it out. There are several plans to choose from. *What I tell my clients...*

• **You can contribute up to $40,000 in 2002 and 2003** to a defined-contribution plan. The deduction cannot exceed 25% of compensation (or for self-employed individuals, 20% of net earnings from self-employment).

• **If your net income from a part-time business is less than $35,000,** you may be better off with a SIMPLE plan, to which you can contribute up to $7,000 a year or $7,500 if age 50 or older by year-end (your net income must be at least the amount of the contribution) for 2002 ($8,000, or $9,000 if 50 or older in 2003).

Caution: You must have set up a SIMPLE plan by October 1, 2003, in order to take deductions for 2003.

• **If you are over age 50,** consider setting up a defined-benefit plan, which may permit deductible contributions much larger than the $40,000 cap for defined-contribution plans.

• **Don't miss the deadline.** With the exception of SIMPLE plans, you have until December 31 to create a qualified retirement plan for the year. If you do miss the deadline, SEPs can be set up until the extended due date of your return.

Loophole: **Deduct the full market value of appreciated securities donated to charity.** You get a market value deduction for such donations, and avoid paying tax on the appreciation.

Important: To get the full write-off, make sure you have owned the securities for more than 12 months. Otherwise, your deduction will be limited to your tax cost (basis) in the securities.

Loophole: **Account for future taxes when transferring shares in a family business as part of a divorce settlement.** There are no tax consequences when stock in a closely held company is transferred from one spouse to the other as part of a divorce settlement.

However, the person receiving these shares takes the same tax cost as the person transferring them, along with any built-in capital gains. The recipient must pay tax on gains when he/she disposes of the stock.

My advice: Figure in taxes when valuing the shares for purposes of the settlement.

Example: Boris transferred 10,000 shares in his company to Natasha during their divorce. Boris paid $100 each for shares that are now worth $250 apiece. Because of the $150 per share built-in gain, the shares are worth only $2.2 million to Natasha ($2.5 million market value minus the $300,000 capital gains tax). Natasha should use the after-tax $2.2 million amount in working out the property settlement.

Loophole: **Maximize mutual fund after-tax profits by tracking dividends that you reinvest in the fund.** Keep a folder for each fund you hold, and file copies of the interim and annual statements you receive from the fund company in the appropriate folder.

You must pay tax each year on any dividends from your fund—even if you receive no cash from the fund because you automatically reinvest the dividends.

Trap: If you don't keep track, you will pay tax on the dividends *twice*—when the dividends are paid and again when you sell those shares.

Tax saver: Add reinvested dividends and capital gains distributions to your tax cost (basis) in your fund shares. Because capital gains taxes are owed on the difference between the selling price and your tax cost, increasing the tax cost reduces your tax bill.

Example: You invest $20,000 in Fund X. During the three years you own it, the fund pays a total of $5,000 in dividends that you reinvest. When you sell the shares for $30,000, you owe tax on a gain of $5,000, not $10,000.

Loophole: **Receive a full deduction for donated art.** *To get the full deduction...*

• **You must get a valuation** from an independent appraiser, if donated art is worth more than $5,000.

• **The art must be used for the charity's basic purpose.**

Example: Donate antique glass items to a retirement center, where they will be placed on display to enhance the residents' environment.

Loophole: **Have shares of stock in your employer's company that are held in a 401(k) plan distributed directly to you rather than rolled over to an IRA.** Employees who receive shares of corporate stock that have been contributed to their 401(k) account have two choices when it comes to taking the shares out of the plan. *They are...*

• **Roll over the shares into an IRA** and pay no tax, or...

•**Have the shares distributed** to them (the employees) and pay taxes...and possibly owe an early withdrawal penalty.

When you roll over company stock into an IRA, you or your IRA beneficiaries will pay tax on the full value of the shares when they are eventually withdrawn from the account. IRA distributions are taxed at ordinary income rates —up to 38.6% in 2002 and 2003.

Better: Have the company stock in a 401(k) plan distributed directly to you, and pay tax at the time of distribution. The tax will be based on actual value of the shares *at the time they were put into the plan* and not their value when you received them. If the stock has greatly appreciated, and you hold the shares for more than one year, the sales proceeds will be taxed at favorable long-term capital gains rates.

Loophole: Minimize your capital gains taxes by determining the most favorable method of calculating your profits when you sell shares of stock or mutual funds. The IRS requires you to use the FIFO (first-in, first-out) method to figure your gain on securities sales—unless you elect a different method. FIFO assumes that the shares you sold were the first ones you bought—usually the ones with the lowest cost and the highest built-in gains.

Better: Choose the *specific identification* method. When you identify the shares you are selling, you can pick which ones to sell to control the amount of tax you pay.

Keep detailed records when you buy shares of stock and mutual funds—purchase date, price per share and number of shares—so you can sell those that will produce the lowest taxable gain. When you sell them, designate in writing which shares are to be sold by the date of purchase.

Loophole: Convert a regular IRA to a Roth IRA. Unlike regular IRAs, Roth IRA withdrawals are tax free. To be eligible to convert, your adjusted gross income (without the conversion amount) for the year must be $100,000 or less.

Downside: To gain the benefit of tax-free withdrawals, you must pay tax on the amount you convert from the regular IRA to the Roth.

How to Dodge The Alternative Minimum Tax

Ralph Anderson, CPA, senior vice president, Executive Monetary Management, a division of Neuberger Berman, 200 E. 42 St., New York City 10017.

The more than one million taxpayers who have been paying the alternative minimum tax (AMT) will receive little benefit from the new tax law. Even worse, the law will make many more taxpayers subject to the AMT in the coming years.

Important: Estimate your AMT exposure *now*. That way, if you face risk of the AMT, you can take steps to avoid it, reduce its cost or even take advantage of it.

TWO CALCULATIONS

The AMT calculation is one that every individual must work through, in addition to the calculation of tax under normal rules.

The final tax due is the *larger* of that calculated under both sets of rules.

The AMT was created in 1978 to prevent a small number of high-income individuals from avoiding income tax entirely through the use of deductions, tax credits and other "tax preference items."

The tax brackets and other items under the regular income tax have all been indexed for inflation since 1986. Not so with the AMT tax brackets and exemptions.

Result: Inflation has subjected a growing number of taxpayers to the AMT every year, and the AMT is hitting larger numbers of middle-income taxpayers. In 2000, 1.3 million taxpayers paid the AMT.

NEW AMT TRAPS

Because the new law reduces the tax bill computed under normal rules without reducing that computed under AMT rules, it will push many more people into owing AMT.

Under prior law, the number of taxpayers subject to the AMT was expected to reach 20 million by the year 2010. Under the new law, it is expected to grow to *36 million*.

Those who *become* subject to the AMT will get less tax savings than they otherwise would.

Individuals who are *already* subject to the AMT will get little tax savings under the new law, since it does almost nothing to reduce tax computed under AMT rules.

It is not difficult to identify the risk of incurring the AMT, and to make a rough calculation of the amount of possible AMT liability for yourself. But rules for calculating the AMT are complex. To accurately project your AMT liability, see an expert.

PREFERENCES & ADJUSTMENTS

Liability for the AMT results when specified preference and adjustment items that reduce tax under normal rules become too large relative to total income. *Items that frequently cause AMT liability…*

●**Deduction of state and local income and property taxes** by residents in high-tax states.

●**Miscellaneous itemized deductions,** in particular, itemized deductions of employee business expenses.

●**Incentive stock options (ISOs).**

●**Accelerated depreciation.**

As these items suggest, the persons most likely to incur AMT are…

●**High-income individuals** who live in the states that have steep personal income tax or property tax rates, including Massachusetts and New York.

●**Executives** who have large employee business expense deductions and/or who exercise their ISOs.

●**Owners of business proprietorships** and pass-through entities, like S corporations, partnerships and limited liability companies.

These owners may report on their personal returns business deductions for depreciation and state and local taxes that lead to AMT liability. This is a problem especially when business income for the year is low.

If you expect to claim on your return large amounts for any of the four items listed above, *or* if you fit into any of the profiles, also listed above, you risk incurring the AMT.

ESTIMATING YOUR AMT

To estimate your AMT liability, take the following steps…

●**Start with your tax return for the prior year.** Adjust the numbers on it for the current year using your best estimates.

●**Take the number for "taxable income" that appears on page two of the return.** *Add to this number…*

●The deduction for state and local income and property taxes.

●Miscellaneous itemized deductions.

●The "bargain element" of all ISOs you expect to acquire—that is, the amount by which the value of the stock acquired exceeds the price you pay for it.

●The amount by which the deductions for accelerated depreciation that you expect to claim exceed what straight-line depreciation would be on the same assets.

The number resulting from this process is your AMT income (AMTI).

●**Subtract your AMT exemption.** You initially are entitled to a $49,000 AMT exemption on a joint return, or $35,750 on a single return.

●**If AMTI, as calculated above, exceeds $150,000 on a joint return,** or $75,000 on a single return, *reduce* your exemption by 25% of the excess.

This phase-out leaves no exemption when your AMTI exceeds $346,000 on a joint return or $218,000 on a single return, and a reduced exemption when AMTI is at intermediate levels.

Persons who have AMTI of more than these amounts receive no benefit from the increased exemptions in the new law.

●**Apply the higher AMT tax rate**—a flat 28%—to the balance of AMTI. The result is your *estimated* AMT. (*Actual* AMT is based on 26% and 28% rates, depending on AMTI.)

●**Project your regular income tax** under normal rules. If your estimated AMT is larger, you will owe it instead.

PLANNING AHEAD

If you expect to owe AMT for this year—or be close to doing so—have an expert review your AMT situation.

AMT liability may be affected by many other preference and adjustment items besides the four most commonly incurred ones that are mentioned here.

With some planning, it may be possible to take steps to avoid or reduce AMT. *How...*

●**Residents of high-tax states** can avoid the common tactic of prepaying state and local taxes by year-end to get a federal deduction for them.

Example: State estimated income tax generally is due on January 15 for the fourth quarter of the year, with any unpaid balance due with the tax return filed on April 15. Many taxpayers routinely make these payments by the prior December 31 to get a deduction a year earlier on the federal return. This strategy backfires on those who owe AMT.

●**Executives who own ISOs** can minimize the AMT they owe by planning the number of options that they exercise, as well as the timing of the exercise.

They may also defer incurring deductible employee business expenses until the next year —instead of the typical practice of accelerating them into the current year.

●**Owners of pass-through business entities** can plan to minimize AMT.

Example: Instead of placing new business equipment in service by December 31 to get six months of accelerated depreciation for it, delay placing it in service until January 1—reducing accelerated depreciation.

BENEFITING FROM THE AMT

High-income individuals who can't escape the AMT are sometimes able to benefit from it.

Reason: The AMT tax rate of 28% is lower than the top personal rates of 30%, 35% and 38.6% for 2003.

Those who otherwise would be in the top brackets may reduce their tax bracket rates by accelerating income—such as distributions from a business—into a current year when they are subject to the 28% AMT rate, from a later year when they would owe a higher tax rate.

Making the Most of Interest Expense Deductions

Gail T. Winawer, CPA, managing director, American Express Tax and Business Services Inc., 1185 Avenue of the Americas, New York City 10036.

The way to minimize the after-tax cost of borrowing is to maximize your deduction for interest expense. *How...*

YOUR DEBT PORTFOLIO

Start by reviewing your total borrowing and considering it in terms of a "debt portfolio."

Objective: To allocate your total borrowing among different kinds of debt in the manner that gives you the biggest total interest deduction.

Key: Money is "fungible"—no matter how you get it, you can use it for any purpose.

If you want to borrow to finance, say, a consumer purchase, it's not necessary to take out a consumer loan to do so. You can instead borrow to finance some expenditure of another kind—such as an investment or business purchase—and use the cash you save to purchase the consumer item.

Result: Both the amount you borrow and the amount that you spend are unchanged—but you increase your interest deduction by borrowing more money in a manner that produces deductible interest.

Going forward, adjust your debt portfolio by planning new borrowing to be of a type that generates deductible interest. Also—consider taking advantage of today's low rates to pay off old nondeductible debt, replacing it with new tax-favored financing.

PLANNING OPPORTUNITIES

The best planning opportunities for generating interest deductions exist with mortgage interest, investment interest and business interest. College loan interest also is deductible, but the deduction is subject to so many restrictions that planning opportunities for it are limited.

Consumer interest—such as interest charged on credit cards to finance consumer purchases

—is not deductible. Seek to make it as small a part of your debt portfolio as possible.

The deduction rules to use in planning…

●**Mortgage interest** is deductible on up to $1 million of borrowing used to acquire or improve a residence.

The deduction can be divided between two residences. If you have a vacation home, you can deduct mortgage interest for it as well as for your primary residence. If you have more than two residences, you can claim the deduction for your primary residence and the second residence of your choice—and you can change that choice each year.

In addition, interest is deductible on up to $100,000 of home-equity borrowing, regardless of the purpose for which the borrowed funds are used.

Rule: To generate deductible mortgage interest, a loan must be secured by a residence. It is not enough to use a loan to buy or improve a home, if the loan is not secured by the home.

●**Investment interest** is deductible up to the amount of your net investment income. That equals your investment income—including dividends, interest and short-term capital gains—minus your investment expenses.

Excess investment interest may be carried forward to be deducted in future years, without limitation.

Tactic: If your investment interest expense exceeds investment income, one may elect to treat long-term capital gains as short-term gains and deduct investment income against them.

Doing so yields a current deduction rather than a deferred one—but the deduction produces tax savings at only a maximum 20% rate, instead of at higher ordinary tax rates.

Rule: To produce an interest deduction, borrowed funds must be used to purchase an investment and be traceable to it. If you commingle borrowed funds with other funds in your checking account, you may lose the deduction—so keep borrowed investment funds in a segregated account.

●**Business interest** is deductible without limit when incurred as a business expense and reported on Schedule C of your tax return.

You can have this deduction if you operate a business proprietorship either full time or as a sideline. If you are an owner of a pass-through entity such as an S corporation, limited liability company or partnership, you should borrow the funds yourself.

Example of debt portfolio planning: Say you intend to purchase a $20,000 automobile for personal use. If you use an auto loan to do so, you will get no interest deduction. *But you may be able to obtain an interest deduction by…*

●Using a $20,000 home-equity loan to buy the vehicle or…

●Borrowing to finance a $20,000 investment or business expenditure instead of paying cash—and using the cash saved to buy the car.

HOME BORROWING

This may be your most powerful method of reducing interest cost. Deduction rules are generous, and home-secured loans often carry lower interest rates than other kinds of loans. *Some opportunities…*

●**Home-equity borrowing exceeding $100,000 is deductible as…**

●Business interest, if borrowed funds are used for a business purpose.

●Investment interest, if borrowed funds can be traced to the purchase of an investment.

Advantages: By using a home as security for a business or investment loan, you may get a lower interest rate—or obtain funds you couldn't get at all otherwise.

●**Home-equity borrowing up to $100,000 can be used for any purpose.** You can use such loans to refinance expensive and nondeductible credit card debt, or to finance new consumer purchases.

Caution: Beware of paying down a home mortgage too quickly. Many home owners prepay their mortgages to increase their financial security and reduce the total interest they will pay on the mortgage over the years. But by prepaying your mortgage, you may significantly reduce the total deductible borrowing available to you.

If you prepay a mortgage to the point that your equity in your home exceeds $100,000 (the maximum home-equity loan for which interest is deductible), you won't be able to borrow against the excess with deductible interest even if you need the money.

Your home mortgage may just be your least expensive debt after taxes. Other debt, such as credit card debt, may incur much higher rates and not be deductible.

Best: When prepaying debt, start with your most costly debt first. Your home mortgage may be last on the list.

REFINANCING

If you increase the amount of the loan outstanding when refinancing a home loan to take advantage of a lower interest rate, deductibility depends on the amount refinanced and how you use the proceeds. If the excess is used to substantially improve the home, it can be treated as acquisition debt (subject to the $1 million limit). If it is used for other purposes (such as to pay off credit card balances), it can be treated as home equity debt (up to the $100,000 limit). Interest on any excess amount is nondeductible.

Example: You have a $300,000 mortgage balance on a home worth $575,000. When refinancing your mortgage to obtain a lower interest rate, you increase the balance to $450,000 and use the excess to pay off credit card debt, as well as other personal expenses. Of that amount, $300,000 (the replacement of your outstanding balance) is treated as deductible acquisition debt, while $100,000 is treated as deductible home equity debt, but interest on the remaining $50,000 is nondeductible.

FAILING TO SECURE

A loan not secured by a residence does not produce deductible mortgage interest.

Example: Parents lend a child $20,000 to make a down payment on a home. Even though the money is used to buy the home, the child cannot deduct mortgage interest on the loan unless it is secured by the home just as the primary mortgage is.

INVESTMENT BORROWING

Deduction rules for investment borrowing are the *opposite* of those for home-equity borrowing—the loan need not be secured by an investment, but it must be spent on an investment—except for tax-exempt securities.

If a parent lends funds to a child who uses them to make investments, the child can deduct interest paid to the parent on the loan under normal investment interest rules.

Important: Intrafamily loans must have reasonable terms, be documented and the terms must be followed—or you risk having the IRS treat them as gifts.

BUSINESS BORROWING

Interest on this is deductible without limit if borrowed funds are used for legitimate business purposes. An undocumented loan, or one whose terms are not followed, may be deemed by the IRS to be an equity investment—disallowing all interest.

Note: Borrowing money to buy stock in a business is treated as investment borrowing and the deduction is subject to the investment interest limitations mentioned previously.

Better Year-End Charitable Giving

Conrad Teitell, Esq., partner at Cummings & Lockwood, Four Stamford Plaza, Stamford, CT 06904.

The recent decline in tax rates and other tax law changes will have only a minor impact on charitable giving. Saving taxes is rarely the main motivation for making charitable contributions. Most people give out of a desire to benefit humankind, not to save taxes.

However, the tax savings generated by charitable contributions enables donors to give away more than they might otherwise have thought possible. *Examples...*

●**A donor in the 38.6% tax bracket in 2003 who gives $10,000 cash,** can actually give $16,285 and then be out-of-pocket only $10,000 after factoring in the tax savings from the deduction.

●**A donor in the 38.6% tax bracket in 2003 who gives long-term stock worth $10,000** that has appreciated from $5,000, is really giving only $5,140 out-of-pocket. He's saving $4,860 in taxes. There is a $3,860 tax savings from the donation ($10,000 x 38.6%), as well as a capital gains tax avoidance of $1,000 (20% of the $5,000 of appreciation).

BE ON TIME

When making year-end donations, keep an eye on the calendar. *Key rules to observe...*

●**Checks and donations of stock sent by US mail** are considered to be made on time for 2002 returns if they were postmarked no later than December 31, 2002.

Caution: If you used a private carrier, such as UPS, on December 31, you will *not* get a deduction for 2002. The IRS's "timely mailed, timely filed" ruling only applies to tax returns—not to charitable contributions.

Best: Send checks and gifts of stock by certified or registered mail (return receipt requested) until the last day of the year. Or, send them via private carrier a few days *before* year-end.

●**Donations charged to your credit card before the end of the year** are effective in 2002 even though the credit card bill isn't paid until 2003.

Caution: Don't wait until the last minute to make gifts of mutual fund shares. It can take three or four weeks for the funds to make the appropriate transfers to the charity.

Each fund has its own rules for transfers. Call your fund well before December 31.

GET SUBSTANTIATION

Charitable donations of more than a certain amount must be backed up by proof…

●**Acknowledgment.** The tax law requires donors giving $250 or more at one time to get an "acknowledgment" from the charity. A canceled check is *not* sufficient proof of the gift.

The charity must acknowledge receipt of the gift and the fact that no goods or services were given in return.*

The donor—not the charity—is penalized for failing to get an acknowledgment…

●A deduction is not considered valid without an acknowledgment.

●The acknowledgment must be in your hands by the *earlier* of your filing the return, or the return's due date.

Bottom line: Don't file your return until you have the acknowledgment. If you haven't received an acknowledgment by the due date of the return, obtain a filing extension to gain more time to receive the acknowledgment.

Early filers: If making year-end donations by check and planning to file early, write on the back of the check, "Endorsement of this

---

*If some goods or services were given, the charity must state their value. This amount is subtracted from the gift to yield the deductible amount.

check constitutes a charitable gift of [insert the amount of the check], and the charity acknowledges that no goods or services were given in connection with this gift."

While this technique has not yet been approved by the IRS as a method of acknowledgment, it is arguably a backup if the charity fails to give you a receipt.

●**Appraisals.** Gifts of property, aside from the publicly traded securities worth more than $5,000 ($10,000 for the closely held securities), must include a "qualified written appraisal." An appraisal summary on Form 8283 needs to be attached to your return. Again, failure to obtain the appraisal invalidates the deduction—even if the value of the donation isn't in question.

CONTROL

If you do know how much you want to give, but are not sure of the charity you want to benefit, consider the following forms of giving…

●**Community foundations.** Local community foundations (public charities) allow donors to spread their charitable contributions over several organizations.

●**Donor-advised funds.** Commercial charitable funds, like those offered by Vanguard and Fidelity, allow donors to "suggest" the organizations that will receive the funds. The donor's suggestions generally are followed. Check out the minimum fund contributions, usually $10,000 to $25,000.

●**Private foundations.** The ultimate way to control the disbursement of charitable funds is to set up your own foundation.

Donors who set up these foundations retain control and have an opportunity to involve their children in a tradition of philanthropy.

Charitable Deduction Smarts

A filing extension may save charitable contribution deductions.

Why: Deductions claimed for gifts to charity may be disallowed if the required documentation isn't obtained by the time the tax return is filed. For a gift of $250 or more, the taxpayer must obtain a written acknowledgment from the charity that states the amount of the donation and the value of anything the charity may have provided in return. The acknowledgment must be obtained by the date the tax return is filed, or its due date *including extensions,* whichever is earlier.

Retain the acknowledgment for your files in case of an audit. For a noncash gift, IRS rules for obtaining an appraisal of the property must be followed as well.

Key: Check to see that you have all of the required gift documentation. If you don't, get a filing extension to obtain more time.

Irving L. Blackman, CPA, founding partner, Blackman Kallick Bartelstein, LLP, 300 S. Riverside Plaza, Chicago 60606, *www.taxsecretsofthewealthy.com.*

Car Donation Advertisements May Be Misleading

A ds that promise a tax deduction for donating a car to charity often fail to reveal that deductions are available only to taxpayers who itemize, as only a minority do. Many ads also imply that a vehicle's full blue book value is deductible regardless of its condition, when only market value of the specific car is.

Key: Ads that disclose these deduction limits are the mark of a bona fide deduction program. Others may come under IRS scrutiny.

Marcus S. Owens, former director of the IRS Exempt Organization Division, now partner at Caplin & Drysdale, Washington, DC, as well as board member of the Better Business Bureau Wise Giving Alliance.

Huge Tax Help for Your Parents

Alan S. Zipp, Esq., CPA, 932 Hungerford Dr., Suite 13, Rockville, MD 20850. Mr. Zipp is an instructor of income tax courses for the American Institute of CPAs. He specializes in the income tax problems of individuals and small businesses.

Y our parents (or one parent) may want to stay in the house where they've lived for years—but may also need to tap their home equity in order to live comfortably.

You can help them out by buying the home and then renting it back to them. You enjoy the tax benefits of owning investment property, in addition to deductions for mortgage interest and property taxes. Your parents will have cash to support their lifestyle as well as the opportunity to stay in their home.

Your parents may have run out of homeowners' tax breaks…

● **If they've been in the house for many years,** the mortgage may be paid off, or nearly paid off. As the owners, they might be getting little or no deductions for mortgage interest.

● **Any mortgage interest or property tax deductions** your parents now take may have very little value, if they're in a low tax bracket in retirement.

● **Your parents (like many seniors) may not even itemize deductions**—so they'd be getting no tax benefit from home ownership.

But a sale-leaseback presents your parents and you with substantial new tax breaks.

TAX-FREE GAINS

It's often better for one child rather than a group of children to buy the house from the parents. This helps reduce disputes among the siblings and other complications. A fair value should be paid for the house—to avoid hard feelings among the other children.

Loophole: Home owners (your parents) can sell a principal residence and avoid tax on up to $500,000 worth of gain, if a joint return is filed. Single filers can avoid tax on up to $250,000 worth of gain.

If a sale-leaseback is arranged so that the profit falls under the $250,000 or $500,000 limit, no capital gains tax will be due.

Example: Nancy White, a widow with a basis of $200,000 in her house, might sell it to her son, Dan White, for $450,000 without triggering any tax. Then Nancy can live in the house indefinitely, paying rent to Dan.

The IRS might claim that the house was undervalued and that the difference was a taxable gift. In the above example, the IRS might argue that the house was really worth $600,000 at the time of sale, so Nancy gave Dan a gift of $150,000—the $600,000 value of the house minus the $450,000 selling price.

Self-defense: To demonstrate the value of a house at the time of the sale, collect current newspaper listings, showing asking prices of similar homes.

For extra protection against an IRS attack, get a professional appraisal to support the price actually paid. With the amount of tax money at stake, an independent appraisal is cheap insurance.

Another good way to reduce your exposure to an IRS challenge is to indicate that the sale-leaseback resulted in a small gift. This tactic may block an audit.

In the above example, where the selling price was $450,000, Nancy could file a gift tax return, explaining that she made an $11,000 gift to her son because the house was worth $461,000.

To avoid IRS complications, attach an explanation and whatever documentation is available to support the value placed on the house.

If you report a small gift, keep in mind that gifts of up to $11,000 a year ($22,000 joint) are free of gift tax.

Audit free: Under current law, the IRS has only three years to audit a gift tax return and challenge a valuation, provided the gift has been adequately disclosed. If you get by the three-year limit, you won't have to worry about a challenge far in the future.

FAIR DEALING

To claim the tax benefits of owning investment property, your parents must pay you a fair rent.

You can even give your parents a break on "fair market value" rent by charging less. You can do this because when renting to relatives, you will likely realize savings in maintenance and management fees.

Suppose the house is in a neighborhood where similar houses rent for $1,000 per month. You can rent the house to your parents for $800 per month—a 20% discount—and still claim the tax benefits.

Trap: If the rent is too low, the IRS can say that your parents' stay in the house is personal use for you, the new owner. In that case, tax benefits will be limited to deductions for property taxes and mortgage interest—the same as they would be if you used the property as a vacation home.

As long as the rent is fair and the house is considered rental property, however, you also can take deductions for depreciation and operating expenses—utilities, maintenance, insurance, repairs, supplies, etc.

Travel expenses also may be deductible. If you go to visit your rental property, some or even all of your expenses can be written off as investment property monitoring—but the deductions must be reasonable in relation to the income generated by the property.

Bonus: Residential properties placed in service can be depreciated over 27.5 years.

You *can't* depreciate the cost of the property allocated to land. Be sure the house sale comes with an appraisal allocating the price paid for depreciable improvements.

If you provide new furnishings and appliances, you can depreciate those items separately over a shorter time period.

WINNING FROM LOSSES

All of these deductions can offset the rental income you receive from your parents. Therefore, most or even all of this income can be tax sheltered.

Your deductions might even exceed the rental income, generating a loss that may be deductible, in whole or in part, if your adjusted gross income (AGI) is less than $150,000.

Limitation: In general, you can deduct your losses up to $25,000 per year, as long as your AGI is less than $100,000. As your AGI exceeds that, your ability to deduct losses is reduced, dwindling to zero when your AGI reaches $150,000.

Suspended (unused) passive losses eventually can be deducted when the house is sold.

If you buy your parents' home for cash, and thus take no interest deduction, your income from the property may exceed deductions—so "passive" income will be generated.

Passive losses—such as unusable losses from old tax shelters—can offset this passive income.

EXIT STRATEGIES

Aside from all the tax and financial consequences, other factors need to be taken into consideration with a sale-leaseback. You should sign a lease with your parents, as you would with any other tenant.

The lease might state that your parents are responsible for the routine maintenance of the house…and for preserving its marketability. Putting the terms of the agreement on paper will help if disputes arise.

Eventually, your parents no longer will be able to live in the house. At that point, you can sell it, rent to another tenant or move in. After you've lived there at least two years, you'll qualify for another $250,000 or $500,000 capital gains exclusion on a subsequent sale.

Loopholes In the Nanny Tax

Barbara Weltman, Esq., practices in Millwood, NY, *www.bwideas.com*. She is author of many books, including *J.K. Lasser's New Rules for Small Business Taxes* (Wiley) and *Bottom Line's Very Shrewd Money Book* (Bottom Line Books).

If you employ household help, you should know that it is not necessary to pay "nanny tax" for the following…

●**Household work by your child** under age 21 or your parent.

●**A household employee under age 18** whose principal occupation does not include domestic work—such as a student who works as a part-time baby-sitter.

●**Any worker employed by a firm** that assigns the job and pays the worker (cleaning service, etc.).

●**A worker who comes in once a week,** whose total *daily* payment is less than $25, such as a maid to whom you pay $6 an hour for four hours on Fridays.

In general, nanny tax—income tax withholding on wages, plus the employer and employee share of Social Security and Medicare (FICA) taxes and federal unemployment tax—must be paid for a domestic worker (baby-sitter, housekeeper, chef, home health aide, chauffeur).

For 2002, you need to pay FICA if annual wages for a domestic worker are $1,300 or more ($1,400 in 2003). You don't have to withhold income tax, but you do have to pay unemployment tax if you paid cash wages of $1,000 or more to one or more workers in any calendar quarter.

Information: IRS Publication 926, *Household Employers Tax Guide*. 800-829-3676… *www.irs.gov.*

How to Avoid Internet Tax Scams

Frederick W. Daily, tax attorney at 741 Tyner Way, Incline Village, NV 89451. Mr. Daily is author of *Stand Up to the IRS* (Nolo.com).

Internet tax fraud is *exploding*, far outpacing the attempts of the IRS and other law-enforcement agencies to stop it. In fact, scam artists often cite the lack of law-enforcement action against them as proof of the legitimacy of their schemes.

Recent hearings before the US Senate Finance Committee confirmed the alarming scope and fast-growing nature of the problem.

The Internet has become an ideal tool for marketing tax hoaxes. Scam artists sell their schemes to millions via E-mail and sophisticated Web sites.

Phony tax shelters that once targeted only small numbers of the wealthy or fringe groups are now being mass-marketed to millions.

TAX SHELTER SCAM

The most frequently marketed scam on the Internet today is the "pure trust." It purports to let an individual retain full control of his/her assets while avoiding all taxes related to them.

A pure trust is really a series of bogus trust arrangements that the scam artist sells.

One witness at the hearings, Robert L. Sommers, a tax attorney who operates the *www.tax prophet.com* tax information Web site, described a typical trust arrangement...

•**Trust #1/Business Trust**—contains an individual's business assets (allegedly transferred to it on a tax-free basis). When this trust generates income, it is subject to self-employment taxes. *But the income is supposedly eliminated by...*

•**Trust #2/Siphon Trust**—created to lease or sell equipment, services and inventory to the business trust at inflated prices, siphoning off the income that would otherwise be subject to tax. So the self-employment tax is allegedly eliminated. *Then...*

•**Trust #3/Personal Residence Trust**—is set up to own the individual's home and receive the income of the siphon trust. The siphon trust will now supposedly escape being subject to income tax since it is offset by inflated depreciation deductions claimed by the trust for the home...and by payments that are made by the trust to the individual for living in the home as a "caretaker."

As part of the caretaker's package, he gets to live in the home tax free and the trust pays his family's medical and educational expenses, deducting them as business expenses.

None of this is legal. It's all a shell game to confuse the scam victim, with many variations for persons in different circumstances.

But scam artists have been hugely successful at selling these—for fees of $20,000 or more. The IRS estimates 250,000 bogus pure trusts existed in 1999 and the number has increased since then.

OTHER INTERNET SCAMS

Another witness at the hearings, J.J. MacNab, who operates the *www.deathandtaxes.com* Web site, testified that the references to pure trusts and related scam trusts she found on the Internet grew from 1,418 in March 2000 to 7,814 in March 2001. That's an increase of 550% in just one year!

Pure trusts are far from the only bogus tax scheme being sold on the Internet, MacNab testified. *Other widespread Internet tax scams...*

•**Drop-out-of-the-tax-system scam.** Here, employers are told that it is legal to stop withholding tax from employee pay. Employees are told that it is legal for them to stop reporting their income. The scam artist charges a hefty fee for instructing *how* to do this. This new scam is spreading rapidly.

•**Foreign accounts scams.** These tell individuals that they can escape taxes by placing funds in foreign bank accounts or investing in foreign insurance companies or trusts.

•**Personal charity scams.** Using these, people are urged to deduct contributions to "charities" they set up to support themselves.

WHY SCAMS SELL

These scams sell because...

•**Marketing is sophisticated**. Scam artists use modern marketing techniques to identify individuals most susceptible to their offers—then bombard them with E-mail solicitations.

•**Tax scams are run as businesses.** The Internet has enabled scam artists to build *sales forces* with multilevel marketing (MLM) schemes.

How: The scam victim not only buys the bogus tax shelter product for himself but also tries to sell it to others—while paying the scam artist for materials needed to do so.

The victim thinks he's making money two ways—by eliminating his own tax bill *and* starting a business.

In fact, he's *losing* money two ways. He's incurring a back tax bill plus penalties *and* losing the investment he gives to the scam promoter for the materials he sells to others.

This is a classic pyramid scheme. To make back the cost of his "business investment," the scam artist must solicit several others to sell the scheme on his behalf while making payments to the scam artist. But soon there aren't enough "others" to go around—just as with a chain letter—and the chance to make money is gone.

In the meantime, the scam artist now has an aggressive sales force of individuals who are trying to make a lot of money by selling the tax scam for him.

●**Presentations are convincing.** Scam Web sites often feature slick graphics. They cite the Constitution, laws and judges that purportedly support their claims.

Scam sites also emphasize false claims that have emotional impact on their targeted audiences, such as…

●Paying taxes is voluntary—even the IRS says so.

●The wealthy save taxes this way—so you should, too.

●It's your God-given right not to pay taxes.

●The audit lottery odds are so long you will never get caught.

●The IRS is weak. Even if you are caught, Congress will protect you.

●Taxation is not constitutional—the 16th Amendment was never ratified.

●A government conspiracy is hiding the truth that you don't have to pay taxes.

●Everyone cheats—so you're a chump if you don't.

WEAK IRS ENFORCEMENT

Another major reason for the rapid spread of the scams is the lack of any visible action taken against them.

Scam artists operate openly on the Internet and almost nothing ever happens to them.

Yet another witness at the recent hearings, Aaron B., lost thousands and thousands of dollars after buying into a bogus tax shelter pyramid scheme.

After realizing that he had been scammed, Aaron B. reported full details of the operation —including the names and addresses of its main operators—to the IRS, FBI, Federal Trade Commission, the attorneys general of several states and other law-enforcement agencies. Nobody did anything. The scam operation continued until the day of his Senate testimony.

Problem: The IRS is continuing to combat Internet tax fraud with the same old, slow strategies it used to fight fraud in pre-Internet days…

●**IRS undercover investigation procedures take years** to secure evidence of fraud.

●**While the IRS has obtained criminal convictions of scam promoters,** it has done almost nothing to stop the marketing of scams. Even after scam operators have been arrested or fled as fugitives from the law, their Web sites often continue operating.

●**The IRS's own "marketing effort" to counter the scams** has amounted to little more than printing a few little-read brochures. These are available from *www.irs.gov.*

WHAT TO DO

At the recent Senate hearings, experts testified that the IRS and other law-enforcement agencies must reorganize to attack the scam artists on "Internet time."

This means finding ways to quickly…

●**Close down scam Internet marketing operations,** and…

●**Broadly distribute educational materials** that counter scam artists' claims.

In the meantime, taxpayers are warned to beware of all tax-eliminating opportunities that they learn of by E-mail or on the Web. If a tax shelter claim sounds too good to be true, it probably is.

More from Frederick Daily…

Audit Know-How

If you are being audited by the IRS, send your accountant or attorney to the meeting —he/she knows the rules and is less likely to become emotional. *If you insist on attending…*

●**Do not fill in any silences.** Auditors may deliberately pause to give you time to say something incriminating.

●**Answer only what is asked.** Do not volunteer information.

●**Be polite.**

●**Tell the truth.** Auditors sometimes will test people by asking questions to which they already know the answers.

●**Dress normally.** Don't dress at a less expensive level than you usually do.

Some IRS Forms Are Very Dangerous To File...Ever

Martin S. Kaplan, CPA, Geller, Marzano & Co., CPAs, PC, 225 W. 34 St., Suite 700, New York City 10122. He is coauthor of *What the IRS Doesn't Want You to Know* (Villard).

Just how much does the IRS know about you? Nothing, in most cases, except what is reported to it on the information returns, such as W-2s, K-1s or 1099s, and what you tell it yourself.

So a key rule of limiting your audit exposure is *never tell the IRS anything you don't have to.* This means not filing IRS forms you don't have to file. *Here are the five optional forms you should never file...*

• **Form 5213,** *Election To Postpone Determination As To Whether the Presumption Applies That an Activity Is Engaged in for Profit.* Imagine that you've launched your own business—either full time or as a sideline. The majority of new businesses incur start-up losses—sometimes for years.

But business losses are deductible against other income. If you own your business as a proprietorship or a pass-through entity (partnership, limited liability company or S corporation), you will be able to get a tax subsidy for such losses by deducting them against other income.

Snag: Losses are deductible against other income only if they derive from an activity you pursue with a *profit motive.* If the IRS decides your continuing losses indicate there is no profit motive, it may disallow your deduction for them by ruling that your business is really just a hobby.

Such a ruling is especially likely if your business is a sideline that the IRS thinks you are using as a tax shelter, or if it involves a long-time avocation, such as collecting, writing, photography, etc.

Don't fall for the lure: If you file Form 5213 when you start the business, the IRS will not examine your profit motive for five years in most cases. Then you will be *presumed* to have a profit motive if the business was profitable for three of those five years. Even if the business fails to meet that test, you can still save your loss deductions by documenting a profit motive with evidence such as a credible business plan, proof of the hours you worked, good business records, etc.

So filing Form 5213 may *sound* like a good deal—you escape audits for five years, get that long to make your business profitable and your loss deductions are safe in the meantime.

But filing the form puts the IRS *on notice* that you have started a new business and *asks* for an audit five years in the future. It also allows the IRS to audit business income and expenses for all five years, instead of the normal three years.

If you do not file this form, you probably won't be audited at all. If the IRS notices the business losses you deduct, it probably will think they come from an established business, not a new one with "profit motive" issues. Even if you are audited, you will have to meet the very same tests to prove a profit motive that you would if you had filed the form—except the IRS will be limited to auditing three years.

• **Form 8275,** *Disclosure Statement.* The IRS says you should file this with your tax return to disclose any questionable or "gray area" deductions or positions on it, and to provide your justifications for taking them (such as an IRS ruling or a court case you rely on).

If you do file this form and your return is audited, and the item is subsequently disallowed, the IRS maintains it won't add a penalty to the taxes and interest you owe.

But why tell the IRS about the questionable items on your return? This form just saves the IRS the trouble of finding them on its own.

If you don't file the form and are audited, you will be in exactly the same legal position regarding the examined items that you would be in if you had filed the form—only you are more likely to be audited if you do file it.

The slight potential savings of an avoided penalty isn't worth the increased risk of incurring an audit and of having to pay back taxes and interest.

• **Form 8082,** *Notice of Inconsistent Treatment or Administrative Adjustment Request (AAR).* If you receive income from a pass-through entity or trust or estate, you will receive a K-1 information return. This form reports your share of its income and expenses that are to be reported on your return.

Snag: If you disagree with the way an amount has been reported on your K-1, you can't just change it on your return. Instead, the IRS says you should file Form 8082 to explain why you think the amount reported is wrong.

You are raising a red flag to the IRS that there's a problem with your return—and that you disagree with the manager of the entity, and others who are involved with it, about how it should be handled. You are asking for an audit for yourself—and possibly for everyone else involved with the entity.

Better strategy: As soon as you get your K-1, examine it. If there is a problem, ask the issuing entity's managers for a corrected K-1 before you file your return.

If there's no time to do that, file your return using the data on the errant K-1, then straighten out the problem, get a corrected K-1 and file an amended tax return.

●**Form 872-A,** *Special Consent to Extend Time to Assess Tax.* When the IRS conducts an audit, it often runs up against the three-year deadline within which it must assess tax.

At that point, the IRS auditor may ask you to agree to an extension of the assessment period. If you object, the auditor may threaten to disallow every questionable item on your return and send a deficiency notice, forcing you to go to Tax Court to save your deductions.

This is the time to negotiate. The IRS auditor wants the case closed. If it stays open and goes to Tax Court, the IRS might lose—especially now that the low-cost Small Case Division of Tax Court is a viable option for taxpayers in most cases like this.

You should be able to negotiate a *limited* extension. This will give the IRS extra time— one year, perhaps—to complete the audit, while limiting the areas on the return that will remain open to audit.

To agree to such a limited extension, sign IRS Form 872, *Consent to Extend Time to Assess Tax.*

Do *not* sign Form 872-A, *Special Consent to Extend Time to Assess Tax.* The name is almost

the same, but this form gives the IRS an extra *10 years* to conduct the audit.

Caution: When signing the consent, be sure the auditor doesn't mistakenly hand you the wrong form—it happens.

●**Form SS-8,** *Determination of Worker Status for Purposes of Federal Employment Taxes and Income Tax Withholding.* One of the hottest audit topics now is the tax status of workers hired as independent contractors—and whether they are really employees.

The IRS says that both businesses and individuals can fill out and file a questionnaire, Form SS-8, which determines a worker's status.

Trap: Filing this form can lead to huge problems for the company and its workers. Not surprisingly, the IRS is likely to declare that workers treated as independent contractors are in fact employees. *Results...*

●A company can face a major back tax bill, in addition to complications with state taxes and benefit plans.

●Workers recategorized as employees may lose their self-employed retirement plans, business deductions and the other tax benefits of being self-employed.

Warning: An individual may file this form thinking only of himself/herself, but it may cause the IRS to examine other workers in the company.

Better: Whether you are an employer or an independent contractor, any question regarding employment status is better referred to a tax professional. He can review the situation and recommend a remedy that will not subject the business to IRS scrutiny.

Wrong Information From the IRS Could Cost You Big

In a recent government survey, IRS representatives gave incorrect answers nearly three-quarters of the time at walk-in sites set up to help taxpayers. The IRS admits to a 50% error rate. If you use incorrect IRS information when filing, the IRS still considers you at fault and can assess interest and penalties—plus any additional tax due.

Self-defense: Pay a tax practitioner to do your return if it is complicated or you are uncomfortable doing it yourself.

Marvin Michelman, CPA, director and specialist in IRS practice and procedure, Deloitte & Touche LLP, Two World Financial Center, New York City 10281.

Proven Way to Avoid IRS Penalties

If you use a professional to prepare your tax return, not only will it be less likely to contain errors that could result in penalties, you may also escape penalties for any errors that it *does* contain.

Example: When one business proprietor claimed several deductions that proved to be erroneous, the IRS sought to impose negligence penalties as well as back taxes.

Tax Court: The individual had provided all his records to a reputable tax professional and had relied on the professional's advice when preparing his return. So he had acted responsibly, and the penalty was lifted.

Kevin P. Osborne, TC Memo 2002-11.

Innocent Spouse Limitation

The IRS says that when innocent spouse status is granted to one spouse, relieving that spouse from liability for the other spouse's taxes on a joint tax return, the relief works only one way. The other spouse's liability on the joint return is not affected.

So despite relief granted to one spouse, the second spouse remains fully liable for all taxes owed by both spouses on the joint return.

IRS Legal Memorandum 200027052.

How Credit Card Companies Are Helping the IRS

Credit card companies are helping the IRS catch tax evaders by providing information about customers who have offshore accounts. MasterCard has turned over information on 230,000 accounts, American Express has just agreed to provide similar information and Visa is expected to reach an agreement soon. All of this is part of an IRS program to identify persons who open foreign bank accounts to avoid paying tax on income earned in them.

IRS Press Release, March 25, 2002.

Millions Overpay Taxes by Failing to Itemize

Each year, only about 30% of taxpayers itemize deductions—but more should.

A new study finds that as many as 2.2 million filers could have cut their tax bills by claiming itemized deductions (for items such as mortgage interest, property taxes, state and local taxes, and charitable contributions). But they, or their preparers, failed to do so and used the simpler standard deduction instead. Their overpayments may have totaled almost $1 billion.

If you didn't itemize a return within the last three years, check to see if the total itemized deductions you could have claimed exceeded the standard deduction. If so, file IRS Form 1040X, *Amended US Individual Income Tax Return,* to take your extra deductions now— and get a tax refund.

General Accounting Office report GAO-02-509, *Further Estimates of Taxpayers Who May Have Overpaid Federal Taxes by Not Itemizing, www.gao.gov.*

Four Myths About The IRS

Donald W. MacPherson, head attorney of The Mac-Pherson Group, PC, which practices in criminal, tax and bankruptcy law, 3404 W. Cheryl Dr., Phoenix 85051, *www.beatirs.com.*

Don't believe everything you hear about the IRS—especially these four myths, which the IRS wants you to believe because they serve its interests...

Myth: The IRS has become "kinder and gentler." The number of IRS audits and collection actions, including liens and levies, has fallen in recent years. But this is attributable more to IRS staffing problems than any new kinder-and-gentler attitude toward taxpayers.

Reality: The IRS has been reorganizing since the *IRS Restructuring Act of 1998.* And while it has been moving people from old jobs into training for new ones, old and new positions alike have been understaffed.

The IRS is getting over this problem. Already the number of collection actions is rising. The audit rate will, too, perhaps with a vengeance.

Myth: You need receipts for all of your deductions.

Reality: If you are audited and lack records for deductions, you may still be able to keep them.

It's best to have full records. But under the Cohan rule, the Tax Court may permit deductions for undocumented expenditures when it is clear that they must have been incurred.

Example: Suppose your business records of utility bills, phone charges and equipment depreciation were lost in an accident. But you can show through your sworn statement that you must have incurred them while running your business.

Under the Cohan rule, the court will let you deduct a reasonable estimate of them—and you can tell an IRS auditor that. You can also support deductions with persuasive secondary evidence, even if not actual proof.

Example: A bill that you received for an expense and a checkbook register entry showing a payment in that amount, even if you have no canceled check or receipt.

Checkbook registers are easy documentation to keep. Save them all in a safe place *forever.*

Beware: The Tax Code requires specific documentation to deduct meal, entertainment and travel expenses. The Cohan rule won't help with them.

Myth: Writing to your Congressperson won't help.

Reality: The IRS has become more politically sensitive as a result of the *IRS Restructuring Act* and the Congressional hearings that led up to it. If you feel you are being treated unfairly by the IRS, it just might pay to alert your political representatives.

Write about your case to your representative and senators, as well as to the top IRS officers, including the IRS Commissioner and National Taxpayer Advocate.

Include in each letter a listing of all the others you are writing to—doing so helps motivate IRS personnel to take action on your case before they get an inquiry from the higher-ups or politicians.

Myth: The Taxpayer Advocate is your advocate.

Reality: The Taxpayer Advocate's Office is little more than the old Problems Resolution Office with a new name.

It can be helpful in resolving administrative and red-tape problems (such as miscredited payments). Plus, the independence of local Taxpayer Advocates in IRS district offices has been increased by having them report to the National Taxpayer Advocate instead of the local IRS executives.

However, the Taxpayer Advocate is *not* an advocate for taxpayers. The National Taxpayer Advocate reports to the IRS Commissioner, and local offices of the Taxpayer Advocate are staffed by lifetime IRS employees—not by workers with experience advocating on behalf of taxpayers against the IRS. The Taxpayer Advocate *can* be a useful resource. But keep your expectations realistic.

9

Smart Investment Strategies

Turn Your Lunch Money Into $1 Million with Stock Index Funds

There are many reasons why a single index fund is the only investment you'll ever need, claims trading whiz Wayne Wagner.

●**Why should investors use index funds rather than actively managed mutual funds?** Because they work. In 14 of the 20 years from 1980 through 1999, index funds simply did better than the average equity fund. *Two reasons...*

●US stock markets are efficient. With so many investors and money managers following financial news, most stocks remain near their "fair" price. It's extremely difficult for a mutual fund manager to exploit price differences consistently. Index funds don't waste time trying to do better than the market. They just try to match it.

●Lower expenses. Index funds don't need expensive research staffs to make investment

decisions—they trade to stay in lockstep with the index. Most index funds pass along those savings to investors.

Some S&P 500 index funds charge as little as 0.18% per year, while the typical actively managed domestic equity mutual fund has an expense ratio of 1.4%. That difference adds up over time.

Example: Assume that you invested $180 per month in two funds that each gained 10% a year over the next 40 years—before expenses. But one's annual expense ratio was 0.18%...the other's was 1.4%. The low-expense fund would earn more than $1.07 million...the high-expense fund, less than $749,000.

●**Any other advantages?** *Yes, there are several outlined below...*

●Simplicity. The biggest reason people do not invest isn't the fear or lack of money. They simply don't know what to do. Strategies don't

---

Wayne Wagner, chairman, Plexus Group, a Los Angeles-based consulting firm that advises money managers and brokerage firms. He is a coauthor of *Millionaire: The Best Explanation of How an Index Fund Can Turn Your Lunch Money into a Fortune* (Renaissance).

get any simpler than regular investments in an S&P 500 index fund.

• No worries about picking the right funds, stocks or fund managers.

• No hassles. With actively managed mutual funds, investors are warned to make sure that the fund's performance isn't slipping and its focus isn't changing. And they're told to rebalance their portfolios at least once a year. There's no need to do either with a single fund.

• Isn't it dangerous to put all your money into one fund? With an actively managed fund, it would be dangerous. But S&P 500 index funds don't zig or zag. They serve as a proxy for the US stock market.

If you owned a portfolio of only stocks, not mutual funds—and that portfolio contained shares of 500 of the country's largest firms—no one would say you were taking a risk. They would say you had an extremely diversified portfolio. The same is true for an index fund.

• Why haven't all investors turned to index funds? Brokers earn big commissions—and fund companies can charge much higher management fees—for the actively managed funds, so their funds are marketed aggressively. Besides, index funds are not glamorous. At any given time, one sector leads the market, so certain managed funds will post some eye-popping returns—short term. When your friends are swapping stock tips, no one is going to be impressed with your index fund.

• Should investors also use bond index funds? Bonds simply can't offer the returns that long-term investors need.

For the 75 years through 2000, 30-year US Treasury bonds have had an average annual return of 5.3%. Large-cap stocks, on the other hand, have earned 11%, according to Ibbotson Associates. If you invest $180 a month over 40 years, that is the difference between more than $200,000 and more than $1.2 million.

• How should investors go about selecting an S&P 500 index fund? Choose the lowest-cost fund. Also check the minimum initial investment required.

• What about the small-cap or foreign indexes? There's nothing wrong with investing in other stock market indexes in addition to the S&P 500. But expenses will be higher—because of higher trading costs—and they might not provide the diversification that you expect. Investing in more than one fund also means you would have to rebalance at least once a year to return to your target asset allocation.

• Are exchange-traded index derivatives a good idea? These funds, which include Standard & Poor's Depositary Receipts (SPDRs), have lower annual expenses than index mutual funds, but investors must pay a commission when they purchase shares. If you purchase shares every month, that can add up. In the end, it's probably best to stick with regular index funds.

• Is it a good idea to invest in an S&P 500 fund when the market is volatile? Timing is largely irrelevant. Even professional investors are not good at predicting when to invest. If anything, it's better to start out at a time when the market has been struggling. Since shares are relatively cheap, you'll own more by the time things start turning.

• What about investors who don't have 40 years until retirement? It is hard to save when time is limited. Many people want to become millionaires. If you have 25 years, you'll have to invest $805 a month—instead of $180—assuming a 10% annual return, to reach $1 million by age 65. With 20 years, that jumps to $1,382 a month. With 15 years, it's $2,491. That does *not* mean an S&P 500 index fund isn't the way to go. If you're starting late, you need the big returns that come from stocks.

• Shouldn't older investors be more conservative? If you already have enough to retire on, sure. But if you're nearing retirement and you don't have enough, you can't afford that luxury.

People these days are living so long that they shouldn't expect to retire at age 65 and have just five or 10 years in retirement. I am 62, and my money is still 100% in stocks. When I actually move into my retirement years, I will start to slowly shift some assets into a bond index fund.

The Enron Aftermath: What Investors Must Know Now

Edward Mendlowitz, CPA, partner in the accounting firm of Mendlowitz Weitsen, LLP, CPAs, Two Pennsylvania Plaza, Suite 1500, New York City 10121.

The grim lesson of the Enron mess is that the system that was supposed to protect investors broke down.

Enron used quirky accounting to conceal mounting losses from its core business of selling energy...and secretive, off-balance-sheet partnerships to conceal its mounting debt. The abuses at Enron were so blatant that they should have been obvious to everyone monitoring the company. Yet none of the entities that might have blown the whistle did so. *Some examples...*

● **Arthur Andersen LLP,** Enron's independent outside auditor either missed or deliberately overlooked what was happening inside the company. At the very least, it did not do satisfactory work in accordance with professional accounting standards.

● **Credit-rating agencies** are supposed to measure the financial health of businesses. They should have caught Enron's problems.

● **Major Wall Street brokerage firms** employ highly trained analysts whose job it is to probe the finances, cost structure and debt burden of the companies they cover. Virtually all of the major firms still had Enron as a "buy" right up until it declared bankruptcy.

● **Mutual and pension fund managers** are paid big bucks to do independent analyses of the companies in which they invest public money. They obviously did not do their homework on Enron.

● **Securities and Exchange Commission (SEC)** is responsible for reviewing the financial statements of public companies. If the SEC had done its job, it probably would have uncovered the off-balance-sheet financing that triggered the mess.

TAKE RESPONSIBILITY

Investors must now take total responsibility for their own investment safety. *Here's how...*

● **Avoid individual stocks completely—** unless you are an experienced investor who is willing to do a lot of research on each company. Otherwise, invest only in mutual funds. Stick to broad-based funds—those invested in many industries—or index funds. Avoid funds that focus on only a single hot market sector.

An index fund manager must invest so that the fund tracks its index. You won't have to worry that the manager may put your money at risk by chasing a hot stock that could quickly blow up.

Index alternative: Exchange-Traded Funds (ETFs) act like mutual funds but trade like common stocks. ETFs are available for every major market index, including the S&P 500, and for most foreign markets. They are slightly more tax efficient than mutual funds, and their fees are usually lower. But you will have to pay a commission to trade them.

Virtually all ETFs trade on the American Stock Exchange (AMEX). You will find a complete listing of ETFs at the AMEX Web site, *www.amex.com.*

● **Diversify.** Never let any one asset make up more than 15% of your portfolio. Even indexes may not provide enough diversification.

Example: Common sense says the S&P 500 index would provide more diversification than the Dow 30 industrials. But because of the way the S&P 500 is calculated, just 15 to 20 stocks dominate its performance, while the Dow is driven equally by all 30 stocks. On that basis, the Dow offers more diversification.

Index strategy: Purchase one fund or ETF based on the S&P 500...and another based on the Dow...and one or two more investments linked to indexes, such as the Russell 2000 or NASDAQ 100.

● **Keep your "can't-lose" money absolutely safe.** Keep money that you will need within three to five years for a specific purpose—a down payment on a house or college bills—in short-term US Treasury securities, bank CDs or money market mutual funds.

IF YOU WANT TO OWN STOCKS

Own at least 15 stocks to reduce risk. *For each stock, look at the company's annual report to find out…*

●**How the company makes money.** Whatever it sells, how many did it sell last year and the year before?

Where to look: Income Statement.

●**The company's debt situation.** Does the company owe any money? If so, how much? When must the debt be repaid? What happens if the debt isn't repaid in a timely fashion? A company's current finances may look great— but if it has a lot of long-term debt coming due in two years and profits don't hold up, it could be in serious trouble.

Where to look: Balance Sheet.

●**If the company has off-balance-sheet debt.** Because Enron set up private energy-trading partnerships, huge debts never showed up on the balance sheet. The debts must be repaid whether or not they are shown on the balance sheet.

Where to look: Notes to the financial statement in a category called "Commitments and Contingencies."

●**How much cash the company generates.** A company can use accounting tricks to inflate profits. If the profits are real, they will turn up as cash in the company's books. Is growth in cash flow steady or improving compared with the previous two years? Is growth in cash flow approximately proportionate to growth in reported profits? Beware of any company that reports $1 billion in profits but only a $100 million increase in cash flow.

Where to look: Statement of Cash Flows.

●**If the company is playing games with the profit-and-loss statement.** Basic profits come from sales. But other items could affect profits—gains or losses on conversions of foreign currencies…on restructuring the business …on business investments…on acquisitions… and even on the performance of the company's pension fund. Beware if the major part of the company's profits each year comes from extraordinary items.

Where to look: The section of the annual report called "Other Comprehensive Income."

Big Tax Opportunities For Investors

Michael Andreola, CPA, partner, BDO Seidman, LLP, 330 Madison Ave., New York City 10017.

The 2001 tax law changes, phased in over the next several years, will have a major impact on your investment decisions.

IMPACT OF LOWER RATES

Before the *2001 Tax Relief Act*, rates ranged from 15% to 39.6%. *Under the new law:* Rates will range from 10% to 35% by 2006.

Winners: Active traders whose income is in the form of short-term capital gains—taxed at ordinary income rates, which are falling.

Winners: Investments that pay taxable interest and dividends. They are more attractive. This income, too, is taxed at ordinary income rates. *Examples:* Treasury and corporate bonds, mortgage-backed securities, dividend-paying stocks such as real estate investment trusts (REITs).

Losers: Municipal bonds. Tax-exempt interest is much less appealing when you are in a 35% bracket by 2006, as opposed to a 38.6% bracket in 2003.

AMT: The 2001 tax law increases the number of taxpayers subject to the alternative minimum tax (AMT).

Losers: Some municipal bonds pay interest that's taxable for individuals caught in the AMT. Those bonds will lose allure, as will bond funds that hold such munis.

ENHANCED INCOME SHIFTING

The law introduced a new 10% tax rate. It covers up to $12,000 of taxable income on a joint return, $6,000 for singles.

Impact: The strategy of shifting any yield-oriented investments to your children is even more effective now.

Example: You hold $100,000 in a taxable bond fund. Over several years, you and your spouse transfer the fund shares to your 15-year-old daughter. At a 6% yield, she would receive $6,000 in interest and owe only $600 in tax. Ultimately, she could use the money to pay for college, make a down payment on a home, etc.

IMPACT ON DEDUCTIONS

Declining tax rates make itemized deductions less valuable. How will this devaluation affect investors?

●**Deductible interest on margin loans** (if you qualify for the deduction) won't be as valuable. Investing on margin will be less attractive.

●**Home mortgage interest deductions** also lose ground. If you have been weighing mortgage prepayments against using the cash for investing, the scales now tip toward paying down your home loan.

●**Investment-related deductions** such as advisory fees may be written off as miscellaneous itemized deductions under some circumstances. The allowable deductions will be devalued, so you may want to renegotiate your fee arrangements with your adviser.

Although lower tax rates devalue itemized deductions, another provision in the new tax law repeals the old law's reduction in itemized deductions of high-income taxpayers. This repeal makes itemized deductions *more* attractive to some investors. Repeal doesn't begin until 2006, and won't be fully effective until 2010.

For now, the loss of itemized deductions and the lowering of marginal tax rates work *against* itemized deductions.

INVESTING FOR RETIREMENT

Starting in 2002, the new tax law increased the amount that can be contributed to virtually every type of retirement plan. *Examples...*

●**IRA (and Roth IRA) maximums went up** from $2,000 in 2001 to $3,000 in 2002 and 2003 and will eventually reach $5,000 in 2008.

●**401(k) maximums changed** from $10,500 in 2001 to $11,000 in 2002, $12,000 in 2003, and will reach $15,000 by the year 2006.

●**SEP plans permitted contributions** of up to 15% of compensation in 2001. The compensation ceiling rose from $170,000 to $200,000 in 2002, and the percentage limit to 25%. That pushes up the maximum deduction for contributions from $25,500 to $40,000—the dollar limit on defined-contribution plans. The same limits apply in 2003.

●**Similar increases have been approved** for the following plans—SIMPLE, defined-benefit and profit-sharing.

●**Catch-up contributions.** In addition to the above increases, people who are age 50 and older can now make extra contributions to their retirement plans.

Investment strategy: In coming years, it's likely you will be doing much more of your investing inside rather than outside of a retirement plan.

Example: Joanne, age 52, has a financial plan that calls for her to invest $30,000 per year. In 2003, she invests $14,000 ($12,000 plus a $2,000 catch-up contribution) in her 401(k) and $16,000 outside of her plan. In 2006, she'll be able to invest $20,000 ($15,000 plus a $5,000 catch-up contribution) in her 401(k), on a tax-deferred basis, and $10,000 on the outside.

As more investing is done inside retirement plans, there will be less emphasis on growth stocks. Why take the risk if you won't enjoy the favorable tax treatment of long-term capital gains? Less-risky, income-oriented investments will become more popular.

Loser: Variable annuities will become less attractive as retirement investments. These contracts offer mutual fund-like investments along with tax deferral, but with no up-front deduction.

As more money goes into the retirement plans mentioned above (which allow you to invest with pretax rather than after-tax dollars), less money will be placed in variable annuities.

Winner: Converting your regular IRA to a Roth IRA will become less painful. Such conversions are taxable as ordinary income, so the lower tax rates will reduce the tax bill.

Strategy: If the bear market devalued your traditional IRA, consider a Roth conversion. Your income can't be greater than $100,000, though.

Future attraction: In 2006, the traditional 401(k)s will be joined by Roth 401(k)s. As with Roth IRAs, contributions will be made with after-tax contributions.

Opportunity: Tax-free, rather than taxable, income upon withdrawal.

INVESTING FOR COLLEGE

If you're investing for a youngster's education, the new tax law may have a great impact on your strategy.

●**Section 529 plans.** Named after a section of the Tax Code, these plans are offered by most states. The money that you invest is handled by professionals and the earnings buildup is untaxed.

Winner: Effective in 2002, all withdrawals from state-sponsored 529 plans are tax free, as long as the money is spent on higher education. This makes investing for college through a 529 plan a big winner.

Catch: Like all provisions of the new law, tax-free withdrawals will be permitted after 2010 only if this tax break is extended.

Does this mean you should avoid investing for a younger child? Not necessarily. Even if this new law is annulled—an unlikely possibility—529 plans will revert to prior law, under which withdrawals will be taxed at the student's presumably lower tax rate.

●**Coverdell education savings accounts.** The other big investment change is the emergence of Coverdell education savings accounts as an important choice for educational funding. Like 529 plans, Coverdell education savings accounts receive nondeductible contributions and provide tax-free money for education.

Under prior law, contributions were capped at $500 per student per year. Now the limit is $2,000 per year, so you can build a sizable fund.

Even so, you can put a lot less into a Coverdell education savings account than into a 529 plan, where contribution limits may reach into six figures. *Other differences...*

●Control. You make the investment decisions with a Coverdell education savings account. With 529 plans, you turn your money over to managers hired by the state.

●Income limits. While 529 plans are open to all, Coverdell education savings accounts can't be funded by high-income individuals. However, a lower income friend or relative (even a child) can put money into a youngster's Coverdell education savings account.

●Breadth. Coverdell education savings accounts can now be used to pay for all levels of education, starting in kindergarten—public and private. Section 529 plans can pay only for undergraduate and graduate schools.

Doubling up: Today, you can fund both a Coverdell education savings account *and* a 529 plan for your kids—so investing for college can be twice as tax advantaged.

Making Up for Big Market Losses

Jonathan Clements, personal finance columnist for *The Wall Street Journal* and author of *25 Myths You've Got to Avoid If You Want to Manage Your Money Right: The New Rules of Financial Success* (Simon & Schuster).

Those whose retirement nest eggs have lost ground might want to consider the following three ways to get themselves back on track...

●**Invest fresh savings.** If you can, bolster your retirement portfolio by adding in more shares, which can be purchased now at good prices. Also, rebalance within your stock portfolio to maintain your target percentages in each category. This will force you to sell what has appreciated and to take advantage of lower share prices in other sectors.

●**Get help from dividends.** Take advantage of falling share prices by reinvesting all of your dividends.

●**Try value averaging.** This is a combination of dollar cost averaging (investing the same amount regularly every month) and rebalancing. It was developed by Michael Edleson, chief economist of the NASDAQ Stock Market and former Harvard Business School professor.

How it works: You try to make your portfolio grow by a specified amount each month. Instead of investing a flat $100 every month, for example, if the first $100 falls to, say, $95 during the month, you would make a contribution of $105 the second month.

In months where portfolio growth was more than $100, you might not invest the next month, or you might even sell some shares. Historically, this strategy has produced even better results than dollar cost averaging.

How to Pick Stocks Like the Pros

Jon D. Markman, Redmond, Washington–based managing editor of the Web site CNBC on MSN Money, *http://moneycentral.msn.com*. He is author of *Online Investing: How to Find the Right Stocks at the Right Time* (Microsoft).

For many investors, choosing stocks is anything but scientific. Ideas can come from family members or friends…talking heads on television…or a gut feeling.

Professionals rely on stock screens to generate and help them review thousands of investment ideas. With the array of free Internet tools now available, individuals can, too.

These search engine-like programs let you quickly sift through data on publicly traded companies to find stocks that fit specific criteria—and weed out ones that don't. Result? A much more disciplined way to invest.

STARTING OUT

● **Decide on the criteria you want before you screen for stocks.** Otherwise, it is easy to be overwhelmed by the hundreds of possible valuation measurements you can use.

Look at the stocks you already own and with which you are happy. Examine the financial attributes of those companies. Do they have low price-to-earnings ratios (P/Es)? Do they pay generous dividends?

● **Consider the strategies used by stock fund managers and investors you respect.** Financial publications print interviews with top money managers, who often go into great detail about the characteristics they look for.

Example: One of the world's best-known value investors, Warren Buffett, looks for high profit margins, high return on equity, limited debt and strong free cash flow.

Resources: Stock Market Wizards: Interviews with America's Top Stock Traders by Jack D. Schwager (HarperBusiness)…and *Contrarian Investment Strategies, The Next Generation: Beat the Market by Going Against the Crowd* by David N. Dreman (Simon & Schuster).

USING SCREENS ON-LINE

Go to one of the free financial Web sites, such as…

● http://moneycentral.msn.com/investor/finder/customstocks.asp

● www.stockscreener.com

● www.quicken.com/investments/stocks/search/full

Choose among the industry, size and valuation measurements. Create a list of companies that meet your standards based on the screens. You can look at up to 100 matches at a time. Save the screens you generate for later use, or export them to a portfolio-tracking Web site such as *http://portfolio.morningstar.com* or *www.forbes.com/portfolio*.

POPULAR STOCK-SCREEN CRITERIA

The following criteria are commonly available on most financial-screening Web sites…

● **P/E lower than industry average.**

● **Stock price above its 50-day moving average.**

● **Five-year earnings growth greater than 10%.**

● **Pretax profit margins greater than the industry average.**

● **Other valuation ratios lower than the industry average**—price-to-sales…price-to-cash-flow.

● P/E to Growth (PEG) ratio. Calculated by dividing P/E by the growth in earnings per share. Pick companies that have PEGs of less than 1.5.

● Return on equity that is higher than the industry average or greater than 10%.

● Debt-to-equity ratio that is less than the industry average or 5%.

SAVVIER SCREENING

Screens should select only reputable, liquid and well-researched companies. *To ensure this, every stock should meet these criteria…*

● **Market capitalization** (number of shares outstanding times the share price) that is over $500 million.

● **Covered by Wall Street analysts.**

● **Cost more than $5/share.**

● **Trading volume of at least 200,000 shares a day** so you can easily get in and out of a position.

Remember: Screens are a starting point. Use them to create manageable lists of *potential*

stock purchases. To narrow your choices, rely on qualitative research and fundamental analysis.

Examples: If you are concerned about the quality of the company's management, read their annual and quarterly reports to see how honest and efficient the CEO is about admitting mistakes and correcting them. If you are worried about a company's high debt level, call its investor relations officer and ask why the debt is so high and what the business is doing to pay it down.

USEFUL PREFAB SCREENS

To avoid the time and complexity of putting together your own criteria, these sites provide screens created by financial experts…

● **http://moneycentral.msn.com/investor/ finder/predefstocks.asp.** This site offers six preset screens, including ones for finding large-cap growth stocks and the highest-yielding stocks in the S&P 500 index.

● **www.marketscreen.com.** This subscription site enables you to obtain market overviews, chart stock prices, spot trends and put together lists of stocks based on other criteria.

● **www.quicken.com.** Go to the Web site, then click on "Investing" and follow their prompts to the different categories. You'll find screens based on Warren Buffett's return-on-equity and low-debt-to-equity strategies…and growth strategies from the National Association of Investors Corporation (NAIC). This nonprofit organization serves over 30,000 amateur clubs around the country. It focuses on five-year-earnings growth and pretax profit margins.

Five Broker Fibs That Can Cost You Big

Mark Dempsey, a former broker with Merrill Lynch & Co. and currently a financial journalist in Dallas. He is author of *Robbing You Blind* (Morrow) and *Tricks of the Trade* (JIST Works).

Even though more than 70% of investors use full-service brokerages or advisers, few investors get their money's worth from the fees they pay.

To receive what you really need from Wall Street, you have to learn the brokers' dirty little secrets. *Be leery if your broker makes any of the following statements…*

"I'm a trained professional, skilled in investing your money."

Although a broker must pass a variety of licensing exams, there is no minimum education requirement—not even a high school diploma. Brokerage firms don't look for investment expertise…they look for sales ability.

Example: In just a few weeks, one of my best friends went from selling women's underwear to managing money at a very prestigious brokerage firm.

Self-defense: Check the broker's résumé. Ask about his/her education…previous work experience…and how long and where he has worked in the brokerage industry.

You can also check out your broker with the National Association of Securities Dealers Regulation, 800-289-9999…*www.nasdr.com.*

Finally, ask for references from the broker's clients—but don't let glowing reviews excuse poor performance.

"Your account will always get my individual attention."

A typical broker who has been in the business for any time at all will have 300 to 400 accounts. He might have the time to actively manage 10% of them.

Unless you are bringing in what the broker thinks is big money, you'll only get boilerplate recommendations from the firm's research department, with little or no personal attention from the broker.

When there is news about a stock, the broker will call his biggest clients first, telling them how to act on the news. If you are not one of those clients, you'll get called late in the day—if at all.

Self-defense: Keep on top of company-specific financial news. Many financial publications, including *The Wall Street Journal*, have a company index.

Useful resource: To listen in on conference calls between corporations and Wall Street analysts—*www.bestcalls.com.*

When big news affects one of your holdings or a stock you have been watching, call your broker.

Even better: Call whenever you feel like it, just to ask how things are going and what's new. That makes you stand out from the broker's other clients.

If you have family or friends who do business with the firm, let your broker know. This implies that unsatisfactory service could affect other accounts.

"I'm recommending this stock (or fund) because it's perfect for you."

Brokers often recommend specific stocks because the brokerage firm has a position in the stock that it wants to unload…it is underwriting securities for that company…or the broker is trying to win a sales contest. Remember, the broker's value to his firm depends not on whether he makes money for you, but on whether he generates enough commissions or fees for his employer.

Self-defense: Don't take any recommendation at face value. Ask for a research report. Such reports must state if the firm has an underwriting relationship with the company issuing the stock. Be wary if there is one.

"Our fees and commissions are fixed. There is nothing I can do about them."

Brokerage commissions haven't been fixed in more than 25 years. Within reason, *every* commission and fee the firm charges is negotiable.

You'll usually be asked to pay a fee for managing your account…to provide a minimum balance to open the account…and to pay a commission on each trade. The broker almost certainly can cut account fees and commissions by 20% to 40%—and accept a smaller opening balance—without getting approval from his manager.

Your bargaining power is strongest when you open the account. Make sure all fees and commissions are spelled out in advance. Ask about discounts. Don't open the account until you get the discounts you want.

"If you want mutual funds, it is best to buy them from me."

You don't need a broker to buy many available mutual funds. If you do want him/her to choose funds for you, watch your As, Bs and Cs.

Full-service brokerage houses will sell you load funds, which carry sales charges. Regardless of share class, the investment portfolio is the same. However, the commission costs can vary widely.

Many brokers push a fund's Class B shares, with the pitch being that they have no up-front load. What you may not be told is that expenses tend to be higher on Class B shares than on Class A shares, which have a 3% to 5.75% front-end load. Worse still, you will pay a hefty charge if you sell B shares in fewer than four to seven years.

Even costlier long term are C shares because they carry a 1% annual fee ad infinitum, but usually no up-front load.

Self-defense: Make sure you understand all the sales charges before you buy a fund from a broker. Check out the annual expenses for the class of fund shares you intend to buy.

With more than 13,000 mutual funds from which to choose, there is no compelling reason to buy a load fund. Consider buying no-load funds on your own, including low-cost index funds.

Beware of Portfolio Pumping

Near the end of each quarter and at year-end, some fund managers buy extra shares of stocks they own. This drives up the stock price and makes their funds' performances look better. The Securities and Exchange Commission has brought only one case of portfolio pumping. But some watchdog groups are arguing for greater fund disclosure to reveal if and when it takes place.

Self-defense: Don't buy mutual funds on the last day of the quarter—and make sure you are not inadvertently doing this through your automatic paycheck deductions. Don't focus on annual or quarterly returns. Returns that end on nonquarter-ends are more informative because they do not reflect this transitory boost.

David K. Musto, PhD, assistant professor of finance, Wharton School of the University of Pennsylvania in Philadelphia, and coauthor of a report on fund performance near the end of reporting periods.

How to Spot Warning Signs In Annual Reports

Howard Schilit, PhD, founder of the Center for Financial Research & Analysis, an independent research organization that reviews financial reports of public companies, 6001 Montrose Rd., Rockville, MD 20852. He is also author of *Financial Shenanigans: How to Detect Accounting Gimmicks and Fraud in Financial Reports* (McGraw-Hill).

More and more companies are engaging in financial shenanigans to boost earnings or camouflage deteriorating business. This can be disastrous to shareholders.

Investors should ignore the glossy photos and upbeat pie charts at the front of annual reports. But pay close attention to the detailed financial statements in the second half.

You don't have to be a math whiz to assess profitability, growth and stability—or to identify warning signs that a stock is set for a precipitous decline.

FINDING INFORMATION

Annual reports, also known as 10-Ks, usually can be found on company Web sites. You can also download them from the US Securities and Exchange Commission's Web site, *www.sec.gov/ edgar.shtml*.

Most annual reports give detailed financial information for the past three years. Watch for numbers that are out of proportion or inconsistent with historical norms for the company.

Example: Cisco Systems, Inc., reported that from July 2000 to January 2001, its inventories more than doubled, from $1.2 billion to $2.5 billion. This red flag signaled that routers and other inventory were piling up and not selling. Cisco stock lost 52.7% in 2001.

STEP 1: ANALYZE CASH FLOW

The *Cash Flow Statement* of the annual report will indicate how much money is coming into the company and being paid out. *Check the following...*

•**Does net cash from operations closely track net income?** If cash flow lags behind net income (the amount of money the company is making after expenses and taxes), it can mean operating problems. Perhaps the company's customers are paying too slowly... or its inventory is getting bloated.

•**Is net cash from operations growing steadily?** A healthy company generates a lot of cash flow, enabling it to grow its business... make acquisitions...buy back stock...or pay off debt.

Example: Microsoft Corp. has weathered its legal troubles in part because it generated $13.4 billion in cash flow from operations in 2001.

•**Is debt ballooning?** You can find how much debt the company has—and how it is paying it down—in the subsection of the Cash Flow Statement called *Financing Activities*. There is nothing wrong with debt as long as it is growing proportionally with sales and earnings. If it is growing faster, the company could be heading for trouble.

STEP 2: ANALYZE INCOME

The *Income Statement* tracks major sources of revenue—products, services and investments—as well as expenses, such as costs for production or research and development. *Check the following...*

•**Are profits increasing because the company is really doing well?** Growth in profits is not automatically a sign of a healthy company. Ideally, profits should come from boosting sales or reducing production costs. Make sure profits aren't from a one-time special occurrence, such as a sale of assets.

•**Is the company taking any write-offs against earnings?** It is common for companies to write off the estimated future cost of laying off employees or closing a plant—costs the company may actually pay over several years. *Result:* Profits look depressed in the year they are recorded, and future earnings look much brighter.

Be wary if a company is writing off their accounts receivable. This is an indication that sales may be inflated.

Example: A company may record a large sale on its books only to find out later that the customer has gone into bankruptcy and can't pay.

STEP 3: EXAMINE THE BALANCE SHEET

The *Balance Sheet* is like a snapshot of the company's financial position. It shows what the company owns (assets)...what it owes (liabilities)…and what shareholders own (shareholder's equity). *Check the following…*

●**How fast are sales growing in relation to assets?** If sales—found on the Income Statement—are up 10%, assets on the balance sheet should be growing at roughly the same rate. For instance, inventory levels growing much faster than sales indicate that either the company has overproduced or demand is shrinking.

●**Are there new accounts on the balance sheet that don't seem to make sense?** Companies sometimes list expenses in creative ways.

Example: In its 1997 fiscal year, America Online, Inc., had a $385 million asset on its balance sheet called *deferred subscriber acquisition costs.* It was a fancy description for new-subscriber advertising costs—something that should have been charged against income as an expense.

STEP 4: ASSESS YOUR FINDINGS

Once you have identified any irregularities, check out the *Management's Discussion and Analysis of Financial Condition,* also known as the MD&A. This section includes management's take on the competition and industry trends that can affect business. It should also offer explanations for any figures that seem out of line.

If it does not, phone the investor relations department at the company. Ask for an explanation from a senior financial person. As a shareholder or prospective shareholder, your concerns should be taken seriously. If you're not satisfied with the explanation, take your business elsewhere.

Helpful: For more on how to read an annual report, go to *www.ameritrade.com/educationv2/fhtml/learning/readannrpts.fhtml.*

Stock-Buying Tip

Check a company's credit rating before buying its stock. To attract bond investors, the lower-rated companies may pay interest rates that are three or more percentage points higher than those of top-rated companies. This burden can hurt growth prospects for the companies'

stock. Whether you buy stocks or bonds, stick to companies with an improving credit outlook from rating agencies such as Moody's and Standard & Poor's.

Abraham Gulkowitz, economic consultant in New York City and editor, The PunchLine, *twice-monthly newsletter on the global financial outlook, abe@gulkowitz.com.*

Better IPO Investing

The average return on initial public offering (IPO) stocks during their first five years of trading is about 4% lower than the average return for companies that have been around for longer.

Self-defense: If you want to buy stock in a company that has just made an initial public offering, wait several months, then evaluate the company as you would more established firms.

Jay Ritter, PhD, professor of finance who has studied IPO performance, University of Florida, Gainesville.

Turn Stock Market Lemons into Tax-Saving Lemonade

Dennis Kroner, CPA/PFS, president of Pitt, Ryan & Linnear, Ltd., 150 N. Wacker Dr., Chicago 60606. A tax and financial adviser to business owners, Mr. Kroner is a former chairman of the American Institute of Certified Public Accountants, Personal Financial Specialist Credential and Examination Committee.

Most investors are now holding stocks and/or stock funds that trade at prices far below what they initially paid.

Good news: A long-term program of loss harvesting can help force Uncle Sam to share your pain. It's a low-risk way to improve stock market results.

YOUR LOSS PICTURE

Losses on stocks (or stock funds) are considered capital losses.

Short-term capital losses occur when shares are held 12 months or less. Long-term capital losses occur when shares are held more than 12 months.

Preparing a balance sheet: Each calendar year, separately net your short-term capital gains and losses as well as your long-term gains and losses. Then net short-term gain or loss is netted against net long-term gain or loss.

Exception: Do not include gains or losses taken inside tax-deferred retirement accounts.

If this balance sheet shows that you had a net capital gain for the year, you will owe tax. Long-term gains merit favorable tax rates. Short-term gains are taxed at ordinary income rates.

Net losses offer tax advantages…

●**Each year, up to $3,000 worth of losses** may be written off against salary and other ordinary income (though Congress may vote to increase this limit).

●**Net losses in excess of $3,000** may be carried forward into future years. The losses can be used to offset future capital gains and any excess written off against ordinary income at the rate of $3,000 per year.

STRATEGY SESSION

The simplest form of tax-loss planning involves year-end trading. Your goal is to end the year with a $3,000 net capital loss.

Example: In early December, you tally your trades for the year. So far, you have $20,000 in net realized gains. At an assumed 24% rate (federal and state), you would owe $4,800 in tax.

Sell enough stocks or mutual funds before year-end to realize $23,000 of losses. Now you have a $3,000 net capital loss for the year.

Assuming an effective 40% tax bracket, you will have a $1,200 tax savings on your return rather than a $4,800 tax obligation. Your total tax savings equals $6,000.

More harvesting: When figuring out your expected capital gains for the year, don't forget to include distributions from mutual funds. Call your mutual fund companies to get estimates of the short- and long-term payouts.

YEAR-ROUND HARVEST

A more sophisticated form of this plan calls for you to harvest losses continually throughout the year, rather than wait until December.

Whenever you buy a stock or stock fund, set a price at which you'll take a loss.

Example: You buy GE shares at $40 and set $35 as a selling point. If GE falls to $35, you'll sell your shares. You might enter a "stop-loss" order with your broker to sell at $35.

By harvesting losses throughout the year, you will build up a substantial bank of capital losses. *Such a strategy offers several advantages…*

●**Flexibility.** With a bank of losses, you can take capital gains whenever you wish. You do not have to let tax results determine investment decisions.

Moreover, you can't be certain that you will have a capital loss of exactly $23,000 to take this year, as in an earlier example. Harvesting losses regularly ensures that you'll have a $3,000 loss to deduct each year.

Key: You may have capital gains from other sources such as hedge funds, venture capital, real estate, closely held business interests, etc.

The losses that you harvest can offset taxable gains from these activities.

●**Discipline.** Many investors are reluctant to take trading losses, studies have shown. They hold on in the hopes of breaking even. If you take losses regularly, you won't sit on losing stocks as they become worthless, or nearly so.

●**Portfolio improvement.** Cutting losses and letting the winners ride is a proven way of building wealth in an investment portfolio.

Selling losers while holding winners is also extremely tax efficient.

●**Reinvestment success.** If you sell losers regularly, you'll have the sales proceeds to reinvest on a periodic basis. In practice, you'll be doing more selling and reinvesting during periods when the stock market turns down.

This strategy will enable you to do more buying when the market is lower. Long term, a buy-low strategy is likely to build wealth.

In essence, taking losses on a regular basis and reinvesting periodically is a form of dollar-cost averaging—a proven strategy for lowering your overall cost per share.

•**Extra tax savings.** Transforming capital gains to capital losses will then reduce your adjusted gross income (AGI). A lower AGI, in turn, will help cut your taxes in other areas.

Examples: You may get more tax savings from personal exemptions and itemized deductions.

A strategy of taking trading losses will lower the estimated taxes you'll owe each quarter. These tax savings can be invested in stocks each quarter, further building up your investment portfolio.

REINVESTMENT RULES

When you sell stocks or mutual funds at a loss, you must be careful how you reinvest the proceeds.

Trap: If you buy the same securities (or substantially identical securities) within 30 days, the tax loss won't count. This means there's a 61-day window during which you can't buy back what you sold.

There are several ways to avoid this "wash-sale" problem…

•**Wait for 31 days, then buy back what you sold.** You may have to pay more if the stock has appreciated.

•**Buy a similar (but not identical) stock or stock fund.** After selling shares in one large-cap fund, for example, you can buy in a different large-cap fund right away. Your portfolio won't look much different and you'll have a tax loss in your bank.

•**Buy *before* selling.** Suppose you want to sell GM stock, but don't want to own Ford instead. You could buy the same number of GM shares you own, wait at least 31 days, then sell your original GM shares. The wash-sale rules won't apply.

Each time you sell stocks at a loss, your reinvestment is a new investment decision. You can invest in another stock or industry, if that seems more appealing at the time.

THE $100,000 QUESTION

The above strategies all apply to taxable accounts. However, a weak stock market may be useful for retirement plans, too.

Strategy: Convert a regular IRA to a Roth IRA. You can do this with any regular IRA, including one you have rolled over from an employer-sponsored retirement plan.

Required: Your AGI can't exceed $100,000 in the year you're converting a regular IRA to a Roth IRA.

Five years after a conversion, all withdrawals from a Roth IRA will be tax free, as long as you are at least age 59½.

Trap: Converting a regular IRA to a Roth IRA triggers the deferred income tax on the full amount of the regular IRA account.

Converting after a bear market has trimmed your IRA will trim your tax bill.

Example: If you convert a $300,000 IRA to a Roth IRA, you'll pick up $300,000 in taxable income. If a bear market has cut that IRA's value to $200,000, you'll pick up only $200,000 in income.

Then, if the market rebounds and your Roth IRA grows to $300,000, $400,000 or more, all of that growth can be tax free.

"Worthless" Stock Does Have Value

Stock from a defunct company *does* have value. You have a tax loss based on what you originally paid for it. Know the exact date when the stock became worthless to establish your loss.

Also: Think through what you can learn from having owned the stock. Why did you buy this stock in the first place? What went wrong? Why didn't you sell it before it lost its value? Use the answers to these questions to make better investments in the future.

John Markese, president of the American Association of Individual Investors, 625 N. Michigan Ave., Chicago 60611, *www.aaii.com*.

Too Much Diversification?

You cannot be too diversified in terms of asset allocation—spreading money between stocks, bonds, commodities, real estate, cash, etc. But in the stock portion of your portfolio, as the legendary Peter Lynch has said, diversification can turn into *deworsification* if you buy too many stocks. Then, your portfolio will mirror the market as a whole, and you'd be better off in terms of fees and expenses to buy one broad-based index fund. For an individual stock portfolio, 20 to 25 stocks offer about the right amount of diversification for most investors.

Ralph Acampora, CMT, managing director, director of technical research, Prudential Securities Inc., One New York Plaza, New York City 10292.

Signs That a Mutual Fund May Close

Be on the lookout for the following indications that a mutual fund is in trouble...

●**Low asset base**—compare the fund's dollar value with that of its competitors.

●**The parent company has a history of liquidations**—these organizations are more likely to close funds in the future.

●**It is a small fund family**—instead of closing a fund, a large fund group may merge it into another with similar objectives.

●**Consistently poor performance** versus its peers.

●**Poor category performance**—most liquidations happen in sectors in which all funds are hit hard and only the strongest survive.

Good news: Typically you can claim a tax loss on a fund that closes—which can help offset gains in the rest of your portfolio.

John Rekenthaler, president of on-line advice at Morningstar Inc., global investment information firm, 225 W. Wacker Dr., Chicago 60606, *www.morningstar.com.*

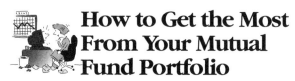

How to Get the Most From Your Mutual Fund Portfolio

Charles A. Jaffe, nationally syndicated financial columnist for *The Boston Globe.* He is the author of several books, including *Chuck Jaffe's Lifetime Guide to Mutual Funds* (Perseus).

Mutual fund investing was supposed to be so simple. But it has now become very complicated.

There are more than 13,000 funds—index funds that track broad market benchmarks...actively managed stock funds that trade frenetically...fund "supermarkets" for one-stop shopping...mutual fund look-alikes...and lifestyle funds for different types of investors.

Six simple ways to get the most out of your fund portfolio...

SHOP THE "SUPERMARKETS"

Discount brokerages are a convenient way to buy, monitor and switch among funds from different fund families. When you want to buy or sell, you contact the supermarket rather than the fund companies.

Advantage...

●**Only one statement.** That's a major time-saver at tax time, when you would otherwise have to calculate capital gains and dividend distributions from multiple funds.

Disadvantages...

●**Cost.** Supermarkets charge a transaction fee on every trade, sometimes even when you invest in a no-load fund. This can be $39 and up or a percentage of the amount invested.

Most provide some no-transaction-fee (NTF) funds and don't charge account maintenance fees if you maintain a minimum balance—typically $5,000 to $25,000.

Other fees: Some supermarkets will charge account setup fees ($15 to $50)...transfer fees (up to $15) for moving funds you already own into the brokerage.

●**Lack of fund choice.** Not all fund families are available through all supermarkets. Before you sign on, find out how many of the funds that you are interested in—or already own—are available.

Examples: Ameritrade, E*Trade and Datek offer few, if any, Fidelity funds. Datek doesn't offer Vanguard funds.

Best fund selection…

- **Fidelity,** 800-343-3548…*www.fidelity.com.*

- **Schwab,** which offers the widest assortment of NTF mutual funds, 800-225-8570…*www.schwab.com.*

- **Vanguard,** 800-523-7731…*www.vanguard.com.*

CONSIDER LIFESTYLE FUNDS

Specifically designed for investors in different age groups, these funds shift their asset allocations over time, becoming more conservative as the investor approaches retirement. Similar approaches are used for Section 529 college tuition savings plans.

This concept makes sense as long as you don't own any other funds. If you do, make sure they don't duplicate holdings in the lifestyle funds.

Resources: Compare the securities overlap among funds for free at *www.maxfunds.com* and *www.morningstar.com.*

KEEP COSTS DOWN

- **Index using exchange traded funds (ETFs).** Low-cost index funds have annual expenses of less than 0.20%. ETFs, the newer alternative, can be even cheaper if you don't dollar-cost average.

Like the index funds, ETFs own baskets of stocks that track a given index. But like stocks, they can be traded throughout the day…and can be bought on margin or sold short.

ETFs are a little more tax efficient than index funds because of how they process the dividends received from stocks in the portfolio.

Beware: Ease of trading may encourage you to trade more often.

- **Watch out for fees.** Despite explosive growth in assets, average fund expenses have increased, largely because of marketing and administrative costs. The expenses have been fairly stable in funds with more than $100 million in assets.

Never buy a fund that has above-average expenses for its category. The average expense ratio of large-cap funds is 1.4% of assets…

small-cap funds, 1.5%…international funds, 1.7%…bond funds, 1%.

Some load funds have lower expenses than funds without sales charges, and many can be purchased without loads through supermarkets.

DON'T OVERDIVERSIFY

You can be diversified with just four funds —a total stock market index fund…an international stock fund…a general bond fund… and a money market fund.

For more depth: Consider a portfolio with the following types of funds…

- **Large-cap growth**
- **Large-cap value**
- **Small-cap growth**
- **Small-cap value**
- **International growth**
- **International value**
- **Bond fund**
- **Money market fund**
- **One or two sector funds** (focused on such industries as energy and banking)

If you own more than a dozen funds, the overlap causes your combined funds to perform like a single index fund, but at a much higher cost.

WATCH OUT FOR TAXES

On average, taxes reduce a fund's return by 2% to 3%. That's a compelling reason to buy tax-efficient funds for taxable accounts. As many investors learned in the past few years, it is possible to have a net loss on a fund yet owe taxes on the gains the fund realized during the year.

Good news: The SEC now requires funds to disclose information on after-tax returns.

In general, the more a fund churns through its portfolio, the greater the potential to realize gains. But some tax-efficient funds have high turnover because they sell losers quickly, using the loss to offset gains on sales of winners.

Best bet: Take a look at turnover and past tax efficiency.

MAKE USE OF THE WEB

The Web has made research and portfolio tracking easier than ever. *My favorite sites…*

- **www.fundsinteractive.com**

- **www.morningstar.com**
- **www.vanguard.com,** particularly its "plain talk" library of general investing information.

---

10 Scary Mutual Fund Tax Traps

Robert Willens, CPA, managing director at Lehman Brothers Inc., 745 Seventh Ave., New York City 10019.

You can boost your mutual fund returns by staying away from these 10 major tax traps…

Trap: **Buying a fund just before it declares a capital gains distribution.** Distributions are taxable to shareholders of record as of the distribution date. They're taxable even if reinvested in the fund. In fact, even if you did not own shares when the fund earned its gains, you'll pay tax on the distribution if you own shares on the distribution date.

Caution: The value of your shares will decline in an amount equal to the distribution. If you buy some shares just before the distribution, your original investment, after taxes, will shrink immediately.

Self-defense: Be sure to wait until after the fund makes its distribution to buy shares. Call the fund or check its Web site to learn the exact distribution date.

If you're planning to sell fund shares, sell before the distribution date. This maximizes the sale price.

Trap: **Not owning tax-managed funds.** Mutual funds are required to distribute at least 90% of their total income to shareholders. Shareholders must pay tax on these income distributions. This reduces your after-tax return.

Self-defense: Research funds that are "tax managed" or "tax efficient." These funds limit their buying and selling. The ultimate practitioners of this are index funds. They buy low-dividend, high-growth stocks, postpone selling to qualify for long-term capital gains rates, sell their most costly shares first and take losses strategically.

Caution: Some funds are advertised as "tax managed" or "tax efficient," but their history

indicates otherwise. Before investing, study a fund's distribution history.

The SEC requires pretax and after-tax returns to be included in every fund prospectus.

Trap: **Losing tax deductions by reinvesting sales proceeds in the same fund within 30 days.** If you sell shares in a mutual fund and buy shares in the same fund within 30 days before or after the original sale, you can't deduct the loss. The "wash-sale" rule prohibits it.

Caution: You can fall into the wash-sale trap if you automatically reinvest dividends in a fund within the wash-sale period.

Self-defense: To secure the loss, invest the proceeds in a similar, but not identical, fund—one with similar investment objectives and a similar performance record. You can avoid the wash-sale rule by waiting 31 days to reinvest in shares of the original fund. If you reinvested dividends, you needn't defer the entire loss—only the amount of the loss equal to the dividends.

Trap: **Buying municipal funds that own large amounts of AMT bonds.** "Private purpose" municipal bonds pay interest that is free from regular income tax but subject to the alternative minimum tax (AMT). If so, the interest earned by your municipal bond fund might be taxable.

Self-defense: If you know you'll be hit by the AMT, determine what percentage of the fund's portfolio is invested in private purpose bonds before you buy into it. If you don't pay AMT, increase your income slightly by investing in a fund that has large holdings of higher-yielding private purpose bonds.

Trap: **Investing in municipal funds that buy "discount" bonds.** Bonds that are sold for less than face value are bought by some municipal bond funds. When held to maturity, the difference between the purchase price and the maturity price is taxable as ordinary income—not as capital gains.

Self-defense: Before buying, check to see if the fund owns "discount" bonds.

Trap: **Paying double taxes on your mutual fund dividends.** If you're careless in your record keeping, you'll pay taxes twice—when the dividends are paid and when you sell your shares.

Self-defense: Keep good records. Add reinvested amounts to your basis in the fund shares. Increasing your basis reduces your tax bill when you sell. When shares are received by gift, document the donor's tax basis—this carries over to you.

***Trap:* Paying capital gains tax on municipal bond fund distributions.** Most income earned by municipal bond funds is tax free, but a gain on the sale of the bonds is not. If a fund manager earns capital gains by selling bonds, it may be passed on to the fund's shareholders.

Self-defense: Before you purchase a municipal bond fund, look at the "turnover ratio" found in the fee table in the fund's prospectus. A large turnover ratio indicates a high frequency of buys and sells that can lead to taxable capital gains.

***Trap:* Failing to recognize that phone switches among funds are taxable transactions.** Most fund families let you switch money among their stock, bond and money market funds by phone. Many investors don't realize that a switch is a taxable sale. The IRS considers it a sale of the first fund when you move money between funds—even if you reinvest all the money in the second fund. You owe taxes on any gains the sale produces.

Self-defense: Before making a telephone switch, decide whether it makes sense tax-wise.

***Trap:* Not designating which shares you're selling when you sell part of your holdings in a fund.** The method you use to determine the basis in these shares will affect your gain or loss. If you acquired shares at different prices and times and you don't specifically identify the shares you're selling, the IRS assumes you're selling on a first-in first-out basis—the earliest shares acquired are the first ones you sold.

Self-defense: You can "specifically designate" to your mutual fund company or broker which shares you're selling. *Required:* Written confirmation of the sale identifying the shares sold.

This method is best for cutting taxes since you can pick which shares to sell for the best tax impact. But it requires extensive record keeping—both for sale and purchase and for shares acquired through dividend reinvestment.

Designation is more important than ever in view of a second, lower capital gains rate on shares held more than five years that went into effect on January 1, 2001. The new, extra-long-term capital gains tax rate is 18% instead of 20%. For taxpayers in the 10% or 15% bracket, the new capital gains tax rate is only 8%.

Example: Assume an investor in Fund X is in the 15% tax bracket, acquired shares at various times, and is now selling off some shares. If he/she designates shares acquired in 1993 as the ones being sold, he pays only 8% tax on his gain.

***Trap:* Not deducting investing expenses.** These are deductible as "miscellaneous expenses" to the extent they exceed 2% of your adjusted gross income (AGI).

You can deduct subscriptions to investment-related publications, investment advice, management services and postage and telephone costs related to investing.

Costs related to buying or selling a fund—either a front- or back-end load—are not deductible. If you paid a fee to buy a no-load fund through a discount broker, add the fee to your basis to reduce your capital gains when you sell.

Taxes and Mutual Funds: New Research Tool for Astute Investors

Thomas E. Faust, Jr., CFA, chief investment officer at Eaton Vance Corp., 255 State St., Boston 02109.

Mutual funds must now report *after-tax* as well as pretax returns. This new method of reporting a fund's performance—mandated by the US Securities and Exchange Commission (SEC)—went into effect in February 2002. It will make it easier to compare funds so you can decide which ones to buy and where to hold them.

Before the new rules, mutual fund performance reports included only pretax numbers. Now, you will be able to see what your earnings from your mutual funds will be after you have paid your tax bill.

LESS THAN MEETS THE EYE

At many funds, there is a tremendous disparity between pretax and after-tax returns.

Example: ABC Mutual Fund has an excellent record, returning 16.6% per year for the past 10 years. Assuming that John Jones invested $10,000 in this fund 10 years ago, he would have nearly $47,000 today. Right?

No. That return is *pretax.* Assume that Jones has been in the top federal tax bracket each year and lives in a state with no income tax. After-tax, John's return has been 11.3%, not 16.6%. Instead of nearly $47,000, John would have just over $29,000 (assuming he used the mutual fund to pay the tax).

Over this 10-year span, more than 37% of John's return disappears into the pockets of the tax collector.

The average mutual fund investor gives up about 25% of his/her pretax earnings to federal income taxes, according to the SEC. State and local taxes take their own bite, too.

TAXING MATTERS

What accounts for such big losses to taxes?

• **Gains on sale.** When mutual fund shares are sold at a profit, tax is due on the short- or long-term capital gains.

• **Income dividends.** When interest or dividends are passed through to shareholders, tax is due.

• **Capital gains distributions.** Mutual funds must net realized gains against realized losses. When net gains are distributed to investors, tax is due.

Capital gains distributions are taxable even if they're reinvested in the same fund.

Depending on the holding period of the securities by the fund, some distributions are taxed as short-term gains, at ordinary income rates of up to 38.6% in 2003. This applies even to long-term fund investors.

Shelter: No tax is levied on mutual funds held in a tax-deferred retirement account. Taxes are deferred until money is withdrawn.

BEFORE AND AFTER

The new SEC rules apply to all the mutual funds except money market funds and funds used exclusively in tax-deferred retirement plans. *All other funds must report results in the following three ways...*

• **Pretax.** These returns assume all distributions have been reinvested in additional fund shares but no taxes have been paid.

• **After-tax for continuing shareholders.** Again, reinvestment of distributions is assumed. *However, it also is assumed that all distributions have been taxed...*

• Income distributions are assumed to have been taxed at the highest ordinary tax rate for that year.

• Short-term capital gains distributions are assumed to have been taxed the same as ordinary income.

• Long-term gains are assumed to have been taxed at the highest rate for such gains.

• **After-tax for selling shareholders.** The same rules apply for calculating assumed tax obligations. Also, it is assumed that the fund has been sold and any capital gains tax has been paid.

Key: Few investors have been in the highest ordinary income tax bracket, so published after-tax returns may be understated.

Published after-tax returns do *not* include state and local taxes. The under and overstatements of tax obligations may cancel each other out so that the published returns are reasonably close to the real experience of many investors.

TIMELY RETURNS

The pretax and after-tax returns described in this article must be reported for several time periods, depending upon how long the fund has been in existence...

• **Funds more than 10 years old** must report for the previous one, five and 10 years.

• **Funds five to 10 years old** must report for the previous one and five years and for the life of the fund.

• **Funds less than five years old** must report for the latest year and for the life of the fund.

All mutual funds must include this information in the "Risks and Returns" section of each new prospectus.

Funds that bill themselves as "tax-managed," "tax-efficient," etc., must include these reports in their advertising and sales materials whenever they mention prior returns.

SIFTING THE STATISTICS

Now that the data are becoming available, how can you use them?

Long-term view: Just as you should not invest in a mutual fund because of its one-year return, so you shouldn't give much weight to a fund's one-year tax efficiency.

The five-year and, especially, the 10-year tax-efficiency numbers are more meaningful.

Example: Two funds have 10% pretax returns for the previous 10 years. Fund X has a 9% after-tax return for existing investors. Fund Y has a 7% after-tax return.

Fund X, with a 90% tax efficiency, may be considered more tax efficient than Fund Y, with a 70% tax efficiency.

Key: You can't predict with certainty future returns from past results. The same holds true for a fund's tax efficiency.

High tax efficiency can be either intentional (the result of how a fund is managed) or it can be unintentional, reflecting strong cash inflows that dilute required distributions or other temporary factors.

Funds that are intentionally tax efficient usually have an objective of generating after-tax returns. To meet this goal, fund managers use strategies such as low turnover of securities or taking losses to offset realized gains.

Important: Read the fund's prospectus before you invest. Pay close attention to both the fund's investment objective (does it mention after-tax returns?) and the table showing pretax and after-tax returns.

IMPLICATIONS FOR INVESTORS

●**For tax-deferred retirement plans.** The after-tax numbers don't matter too much. You should select a fund that you expect will generate a substantial pretax return for a given level of risk.

●**For taxable investments.** Take a look at the long-term after-tax numbers, rather than looking at the pretax numbers, when examining a fund's return. Those are the numbers you should use to compare funds.

●**For placement questions.** *You may be considering several funds for both tax-deferred retirement and taxable accounts...*

●Put the least tax-efficient funds inside your retirement plan. A fund such as ABC, described earlier, which has excellent pretax but mediocre after-tax returns, will benefit from the tax shelter.

●Hold the most tax-efficient funds outside of your retirement plan. Some mutual funds, including tax-managed funds, have long-term tax efficiencies of more than 90%. Holding such funds in a tax-deferred account will effectively waste the tax shelter.

The new rules can help you decide which mutual funds are best held inside a tax-deferred retirement account and which ones won't deliver tax headaches if owned directly.

Mutual Fund Wisdom

Scott Cooley, senior analyst...Catherine Hickey, analyst ...Kunal Kapoor, senior analyst...Christopher Traulsen, senior mutual fund analyst...and Gregg Wolper, senior analyst at Morningstar, Inc., provider of mutual fund and other investment information, 225 W. Wacker Dr., Chicago 60606, *www.morningstar.com.*

With more than 13,000 mutual funds now available, choosing funds has become as tricky as picking stocks.

Below, analysts at Morningstar answer some questions about new trends in investing...

●**Is there any tax benefit if I invest in a fund that has posted big losses?** Yes. The funds' future gains can be offset by those losses, reducing potential capital gains distributed by the fund to investors.

To view potential capital gains and losses: Type the fund's name or ticker symbol into the quote box at Morningstar.com...click on the "Tax Analysis" tab. The number is the aggregate figure (gains minus losses).

●**Is it better for funds to own fewer stocks?** "Focused funds" do not necessarily deliver better returns than diversified funds. The average three-year performance of mutual funds with 30 or fewer holdings was no better than that of funds that held many more stocks, according to a recent analysis. *And:* Focused funds were more divergent—good ones were much better than their peers, while the bad ones were much worse.

Bottom line: Evaluate focused funds more carefully than other funds.

●**Should I sell a fund if it changes managers?** Not necessarily. Our studies have shown that mutual fund winners stay winners even after a manager shift. And poor performers continue to trail their peers after a manager leaves.

Trap: Selling a mutual fund can trigger severe tax consequences.

Better: Consider selling a fund that has been underperforming others in the same category for more than two years.

●**How important is a fund's investment style?*** Stock funds that adhere to a particular style have lower returns than more flexible funds. Style "impurity" should not deter investors who are comfortable with the risk and potential overlap with other investments.

Reason: Funds with wider guidelines are free to move appropriately as the market conditions dictate.

●**Many socially responsible funds were hit hard by the tech bust. Do any of them have low exposures to technology?** Most of the socially responsible mutual funds are heavily weighted in technology stocks, but they stay away from other industries—such as gun manufacturing and tobacco.

Reason: Technology companies are among the "greenest" and most employee-friendly.

*Common investment styles: Large-cap growth…small-cap value, etc.

When to Leave a Fund

Many investors are finding that they can't handle a fund's returns dropping by 20% even though they thought they could.

Good advice: If a sector fund (a fund that invests in only one industry) falls by that much, get out. However, a solid, well-diversified fund (invested in at least three sectors) will probably come back from a 15% to 20% loss. Consider its five-year record.

One good reason to leave any fund: When a fund manager deviates significantly from the performance of his/her peer group or benchmark. At a minimum, ask why.

Vern Hayden, CFP, president of the Hayden Financial Group LLP, 830 Post Rd. E., Westport, CT 06880.

Long-Term CD Warning

Beware of investing in long-term certificates of deposit (CDs). Unscrupulous brokerage firms and scammers are taking advantage of the reputation of CDs for safety to sell high-yield CDs with maturities as long as 20 years.

Trap: Investors can't get their money back before the CDs mature. Seniors who are dazzled by the high interest rate may effectively give their money away for the rest of their lives when they buy such CDs.

Trick: CDs often are advertised as having "no penalty for early withdrawal" when they have no provision for early withdrawal at all.

Arthur Levitt, former chairman of the US Securities and Exchange Commission, Washington, DC.

Municipal Bond Investors Can Dodge the AMT Trap—Here's How…

Clifford Gladson, manager of USAA Intermediate-Term Fund, a national tax-exempt municipal bond fund offered by USAA Investment Management Co., San Antonio, TX.

Investors in high tax brackets often invest in municipal bonds or municipal bond funds to reduce their tax burden.

In some instances, though, supposedly tax-exempt bond interest turns out to be taxable.

Reason: Alternative minimum tax (AMT).

AMT CREEP

The AMT—designed to prevent wealthy individuals from paying little or no income tax—is spreading to middle-income taxpayers.

In 1987, only 140,000 personal tax returns were subject to the AMT. By 2001, that number was around 1.4 million.

In what has been called a "tax time bomb," the number of individuals paying the AMT is projected to skyrocket to 35.5 million in 2010, according to the Congressional Joint Committee on Taxation.

A change introduced by the *Tax Relief Act of 2001* provides only limited relief. As a result of this law, regular income tax rates fall, but AMT rates remain constant. *Impact:* The lower marginal income tax rates may expose more taxpayers to the AMT.

In addition, while the tax brackets of regular income tax are indexed for inflation, the income threshold for the AMT is not indexed.

The taxpayer always loses. In our tax system, you pay whichever is *greater*—your regular tax bill or the AMT.

Example 1: Joe Smith owes $60,000 on his AMT and $70,000 on his regular tax—so he pays the regular income tax.

Example 2: Betty Jones owes $80,000 on her regular tax and $90,000 on her AMT—so she pays the AMT.

LOWER RATES, HIGHER TAXES

Why are the totals different in the two tax systems described?

The AMT starts with your regular taxable income and makes several adjustments, eliminating some of the deductions and credits you've taken.

This larger amount is then multiplied by relatively low flat rates. On the joint return, AMT income up to $175,000 (after a $49,000 exemption) is subject to a 26% tax—everything over that is taxed at 28%.

The new tax law includes many provisions designed to decrease your regular income tax bill but does little to reduce your AMT. *Main changes to the AMT…*

•**The AMT exemption has increased** by $2,000 for single filers and by $4,000 for joint filers. *Problem:* These additional exemption amounts will expire after 2004, unless Congress takes further action.

•**The *Tax Relief Act of 2001*** allows the child tax credit to be claimed against the AMT.

•**AMT offsets of refundable credits** have been repealed.

THE WORLD OF MUNIs

Since more people are likely to be paying the AMT in future years, more unsuspecting municipal bond investors will be hurt.

Background: In the 1980s, federal tax law created a class of "AMT munis" for some "private activity" municipal bonds. These bonds typically are used by companies to finance state and local infrastructure projects, and are subject to the AMT.

These private-purpose muni bonds might be issued to pay for local infrastructure projects, such as a sports stadium or a waste recycling facility, that benefit a privately owned company or partnership.

AMT munis carry slightly higher yields than the truly tax-free munis of comparable quality and maturity.

As long as you pay regular income tax rather than the AMT, an individual investor can pocket the extra yield.

But if you are subject to the AMT, the interest on such bonds becomes taxable rather than remaining tax exempt.

Example: Investors in AMT munis might be paying tax on a 5.2% yield rather than paying no tax on a non-AMT muni with a 5% yield.

What to do: Avoid the purchase of private-purpose bonds if you are frequently subject to the AMT.

Monitor your portfolio: If you're not paying the AMT now and you hold short-term munis, there's not much to worry about. But if you're buying long-term munis—perhaps to help fund a child's education—be careful about AMT bonds. That applies to zero-coupon munis as well as to munis that pay current interest.

Trap: A zero-coupon muni only pays interest at maturity. However, if you are subject to the AMT and own an AMT municipal bond, you must pay taxes on the income accumulation even though it has not yet been received.

FUND WATCH

The same concerns also apply to municipal bonds held through mutual funds. Some municipal bond funds own significant amounts of AMT bonds because such holdings push up their yields.

Example: Mutual fund ABC holds 35% of its assets in AMT bonds. If you invest in a fund with 35% AMT holdings, then 35% of the income dividends will be subject to the AMT.

Municipal bond issuers must disclose if the interest is subject to the AMT, so read the official statement before investing.

Strategy: Mutual funds and closed-end funds are required to disclose their holdings of AMT bonds. Screen muni funds thoroughly before buying them, and monitor them regularly thereafter.

Municipal money market funds are affected, too. Some hold substantial amounts of paper that are subject to the AMT. That means that some of the interest income may not be tax exempt after all.

"High-yield" muni funds may hold large amounts of AMT bonds. If muni funds bear the label "tax free," they must keep their AMT exposure below 20%.

In general, the taxpayers most subject to the AMT are those who pay sizable amounts of state and local taxes…claim large miscellaneous itemized deductions…exercise incentive stock options (ISOs)…and claim a large number of dependents.

If you're in the above group, avoid AMT munis and funds holding such bonds. If you are not now and not likely to be subject to the AMT, consider buying AMT munis for the extra yield.

Laddered Bonds for More Stability

Laddered bonds provide stability in volatile markets. Laddering a portfolio means buying and holding equal amounts of fixed-income securities with maturities that range from one to 20 years. Rising interest rates reduce the value of existing bonds, especially those with long maturities. But in a laddered portfolio, the risk is mitigated because proceeds from maturing bonds are used to buy new bonds at the lower price.

Note: It is safest to ladder with US Treasury securities, available through a broker or through the Treasury Department, 800-722-2678, *www.treasurydirect.gov.*

If you ladder with municipal or corporate bonds, choose *noncallable* bonds—those that can't be repaid by the issuer prior to maturity. Otherwise your higher-rate bonds may be called and you may be forced to reinvest at lower rates.

George Strickland, a municipal bond portfolio manager at Thornburg Investment Management, Sante Fe, NM, which manages $2 billion in bond portfolios.

Blue Chip Criteria

A blue chip stock should meet five of the following six criteria—an S&P "A" category ranking…20 or more years of uninterrupted dividends…the dividend has been increased at least five times in the last 12 years…earnings have improved in at least seven of the last 12 years…at least five million shares outstanding…the stock is owned by at least 80 institutional investors.

Gregory Weiss, editor of *Investment Quality Trends,* 7440 Girard Ave., Suite 4, La Jolla, CA 92037.

10

Consumer Know-How

How You Can Get Total Customer Satisfaction

It's amazing what stores and businesses will do to keep you happy. If you have a bad experience, let the business know. Request compensation. You'll be financially better off and feel better, too. That's because *asking* is psychologically healthier than simply stewing about the injustice or just complaining.

Remember—if you don't ask, the answer is *always* "no."

●**Honey works better than vinegar.** Venting anger makes people respond defensively. It's particularly ineffective when the person you're talking to wasn't responsible for the problem in the first place.

Try, "I wonder if you can help me." Turn the person into a friend who will assist you because your cause is just. Indicate that you're dissatisfied, but make it clear that you're reasonable.

Begin the process in person or by phone. Writing a letter should be your last resort.

Reason: Many people plan to send a letter but never get around to writing it. Calling is easier and more personal.

●**Specify the desired remedy.** When a clothing store forgot to remove the plastic anti-theft device on a dress I purchased, I had to drive 20 minutes out of my way to bring it back. I asked to be compensated for my time—and received a $25 gift certificate.

When a national chain store kept a friend waiting two hours for the delivery of an appliance, he requested that the store pay his $25 hourly wage for those two lost hours. Otherwise, he said, the deal was off and they could take the appliance back where it came from. He got his $50.

●**Nothing is too outrageous to ask for.** Years ago, I bought a bank certificate of deposit (CD) that paid 5%. Soon afterward, the rate on similar CDs jumped to 6%. I was not very happy.

Barbara Rollin, a consumer advocate in San Diego and the author of *Ask! The Revolutionary New Guide for Getting Total Customer Satisfaction* (St. Martin's Griffin). Learn more about her techniques at *www.askexchange.com.*

Such things happen all the time, of course, and most people take them in stride. I don't. I called my bank and asked them to raise the rate on my CD. They did.

When the rates continued to rise, I called again. They raised my rate again.

Banks and other financial institutions can be especially accommodating when you request a better deal. If you are paying high interest on a credit card, call to request a lower rate.

Similarly, many credit card issuers are willing to waive their annual fees for good customers.

●**Don't take "no" for an answer.** If the first person you speak to turns you down, call back an hour later and talk with someone else. If you get two negative responses, ask for a supervisor. At that level, you're almost guaranteed to get the help you need.

You may have more leverage with a national chain than with a single-store operation. One of the few times I did *not* get what I wanted was at a bed-and-breakfast in the Boston area. National chains recognize that you'll have many future opportunities to use—or avoid—their services. *Examples...*

●A four-star hotel chain once stuck my husband and me in a room that was filled with dust. When I asked for help, they moved us to the executive floor at no extra charge. It was cleaner and nicer up there.

●A rental agency once gave us a car with an ashtray full of cigarettes—this after we had requested a nonsmoking vehicle! Because we were in a rush and had to take the car as it was, we suffered with the vehicle. To make things right, the agency took one day's charge, the extra gasoline charge and an additional $100 off the bill. Instead of berating the woman at the desk for what the company had done to me, I had merely asked, "What can you do to compensate me for a bad experience?" I'm still a customer.

●**Ask...even when the rules aren't in your favor.** Recently I bought chairs at a home-furnishings store, and they went on sale at 40% off a month later. I asked to have 40% taken off my bill—and it was. *Other examples...*

●I've had repairs done free of charge even though the warranty had expired.

●I've received sale prices even when I've left the "required" coupon at home.

●I've returned goods even though I could not locate my sales receipt.

●I've learned that stores that don't advertise "we'll match any price," sometimes do. I wanted a pair of Birkenstock sandals and saw a great price at a store 40 minutes away. Well, it wasn't worth the drive. So, I told my local department store about the price—and it matched the deal. Salespeople have much more discretion than many shoppers realize.

●**Whatever else happens, never hesitate to speak up.** You may think you're being a pain in the neck, but that's not the way many successful businesses see it.

Sometimes I've told the owner of a good restaurant that a certain dish was subpar. He has been glad to get the feedback and has usually refunded the cost of the item. And why not? Put yourself in his shoes. His nightmare is a customer who doesn't complain—but never comes back.

●**Don't settle for the first offer.** A first offer is only that. Getting a $15 gift certificate is nice, but $25 is nicer.

Complain on the Web

On-line consumer complaint sites let you vent frustrations, see messages from other customers and possibly get a response from the company that made you angry. Some sites encourage companies to check complaints and post responses. Others are message boards that companies may not review.

Check out: *www.baddealings.com...www. ecomplaints.com...www.thecomplaintstation. com...www.planetfeedback.com.*

Dana Blankenhorn, writer and Internet consultant at a-clue.com, 215 Winter Ave., Atlanta 30317.

Live Well on Less—The American Dream On a Shoestring

Vicki Robin, a Seattle-based author who lectures on frugality and simplicity, *www.newroadmap.org*. She is the coauthor of *Your Money or Your Life: Transforming Your Relationship with Money and Achieving Financial Independence* (Penguin USA).

Trace the word "frugality" back to its Latin roots and you may be surprised to discover that it does not mean being cheap. It means enjoying the virtue of getting good value from everything you have in life.

The key to frugality is to consciously reduce expenses so you can use your time, money and energy most effectively.

10 MONEY-SAVING PRINCIPLES

1. Don't go shopping unless you really need something. For many people, shopping has become a pastime, if not an addiction.

2. Live within your means. Purchase only what you can afford. Hold off until you have enough money to pay cash. This will save you interest charges and provide a waiting period during which you may decide you can do perfectly well without the item.

3. Take care of what you have. That includes your health and your possessions.

4. Don't throw out anything if it is still usable for a purpose other than what it was originally intended for.

5. Do it yourself. Rather than paying other people, learn to do your own taxes...replace broken glass...repair your roof...and perform other vital tasks. If the job is too big, learn enough about it to choose the right person—and make sure he/she does it effectively as well as economically.

6. Plan ahead. Buy what you need at your convenience and at a lower price than you would have to pay in an emergency.

Be aware of when you are likely to run out of household items...when your car tires are becoming worn...the prices of items so you can recognize a bargain when it comes along.

7. Research your purchases so you buy the items most appropriate for your purposes. *Example:* Buy one pot that can serve multiple uses rather than multiple single-task pots. For long-term use, look for durability and quality. Cheap products end up costing more because they wear out rapidly.

8. Hunt for bargains. Before buying, comparison shop. When you are in the store, ask if there is a discount for seniors or for paying cash. Don't be afraid to bargain.

9. Buy secondhand. If you have not yet explored thrift stores and garage sales, start doing so now. You may be surprised at the high quality and low prices.

Caution: Know the regular prices for items you buy, or you may end up paying too much.

10. Stop trying to impress other people. Satisfy your own needs, not your expectations of what others will think. Chances are, people around you are so busy trying to impress you that they probably won't notice what you are doing. The best impression you can give them over the years will be how much you have managed to save.

SAVINGS STRATEGIES

• **Minimize interest costs and finance charges.** Pay off all your credit cards and keep only one for emergencies...avoid interest by paying cash for all purchases, even the major ones, such as your car...pay down your mortgage as quickly as possible...get a free checking account.

• **Minimize transportation costs.** Get by with one car and keep it as long as possible... use car pools and/or public transportation whenever possible...keep careful track of auto expenses for preventive maintenance and early warnings of problems...do basic auto maintenance yourself and find a reliable and affordable mechanic for what you cannot do...shop around for auto insurance and drop unnecessary coverage.

• **Minimize medical costs.** Don't smoke... keep fit with exercise and a healthful diet and get enough sleep...comparison shop for medical insurance, drugs and medical tests…increase the deductible on your major medical policy.

●**Minimize housing costs.** Rent out space in your home…rent out your vacation home when you are not using it…house-sit.

●**Minimize shopping costs.** Go to the store less often…scan supermarket ads for the very best values…make a list and stick to it…use coupons…buy in bulk…check the prices of items reduced for quick sale…avoid convenience foods.

●**Minimize vacation costs.** Take vacations close to home…camp instead of staying in motels…buy airline tickets well in advance… arrange your schedule to meet requirements for cut-rate tickets. *Example:* Fly midweek and stay over Saturday night.

●**Minimize socializing and entertainment costs.** Have potlucks rather than dinner parties …serve guests your usual meals rather than exotic, expensive dishes…invite friends over to have dessert and watch a video…when you go to the movies, choose a matinee…go to the theater free by volunteering to be an usher at local events…eat out less often.

●**Instead of buying expensive items, share.** You can borrow tools and swap gardening and other services. Many items, such as books, magazines and videos can be borrowed from your local public library.

●**Minimize gift expenses.** Limit grandchildren's holiday presents to one gift per child… purchase gifts at garage sales and save them for appropriate occasions…make gifts yourself… give services—like baby-sitting, massages, dishwashing for a week—instead of things.

Painless Ways to Save

Angie Zalewski, Austin, Texas–based cofounder of the Frugal Family Network, Inc., an organization that offers workshops, a newsletter and other information on helping families live creatively within their means, *www.frugal familynetwork.com*. She is coauthor of *Cheap Talk with the Frugal Friends* (Starburst).

If you have been "downsized" or are simply smarting from the economic slowdown, here are ways to start saving money…

CUT BACK ON THE STUFF THAT HURTS THE LEAST

If you are not using it, you will not miss it. *Some examples…*

●**Unnecessary phone services.** You may have charges on your phone bill for call forwarding, call waiting and other features that you simply don't use or need.

●**Gym membership that you haven't used in six months.** Stay in shape for free by walking or jogging.

●**Deluxe cable-TV package** when you watch only a few network shows. Drop down to basic cable, and you'll save as much as $40 per month—or cancel it completely.

●**High-speed Internet access.** You might be spending $55 or more a month for a cable modem connection or Digital Subscriber Line (DSL). Few people need more than a dial-up Internet connection. If you shop around, you can find decent Internet Service Providers (ISPs) that charge around $10 a month, less than half of what you would pay for big ISPs, such as America Online or Earthlink.

Example: Juno (800-879-5866 or on the Web at *www.juno.com*).

ELIMINATE EXCESS

●**Cut down on renting videos and buying recorded music.** Most libraries offer a wide selection of videos and music—for free. If you ask, they can generally request videos from other branches as well.

●**Eat out less.** Pack your own lunch every day or at least a few times a week.

●**Keep your car longer.** If you are happy with it, keep it for as long as you can instead of trading it in every few years.

CHANGE YOUR GROCERY-BUYING HABITS

I cut my family of four's grocery bill from $400 a month to $135 without skipping meals or desserts or giving up things we like. *Here's how to save...*

●**Reduce your meat consumption...**or buy less expensive cuts. Meat is one of the most expensive items in many diets. Boneless/skinless chicken breasts are about $3.89 per pound, compared with whole fryer chickens, which may be as low as $0.39 per pound. Cook the whole bird, remove the meat and combine it with a "meal stretcher," such as beans, potatoes, pasta or rice. You can create wonderful meals, including chicken divan, beef stroganoff and Texas chili, with these "meal stretchers."

Also, look for meat marked "for quick sale," meaning that it is close to its expiration date. It is still good but often half the price.

●**Buy prebagged produce.** A 10-pound bag of potatoes can cost the same as three loose potatoes.

●**Try store brands.** Big manufacturers make private-label products for stores. They are often the same as the brand-name items but about 25% cheaper.

●**Avoid single-serving foods.** Juice boxes and other ready-to-eat food items are far more expensive than bottled juice that you put in a small container or carrots that you cut yourself and stick in a plastic bag.

●**Look beyond grocery stores.** Discount stores, such as Wal-Mart and Target, sell some foods for as much as two-thirds less than traditional supermarkets.

DO IT YOURSELF

●**Take care of your pet yourself.** The next time you take your pet to the groomer, ask a lot of questions. If your pet is docile, try trimming its fur to save on professional grooming services. Depending on the animal's size, many people can even use regular hair shears.

My brother uses a beard trimmer on his toy poodle. For our large border collie/German shepherd, we have invested in pet shears, which will pay for themselves in fewer than two uses.

●**Mix your own cleaning products.** Water, ammonia, vinegar and baking soda are the basic ingredients in practically all cleaning products. But don't simply combine them. *Use these "recipes"...*

Glass cleaner: Mix one cup of white vinegar and two cups of water in a spray bottle.

Toilet bowl cleaner: Pour in one tablespoon of vinegar and a bit of baking soda.

Floor cleaner: Combine one-half cup of ammonia and one gallon of water.

●**Trim your children's hair.** At the very least, cut their bangs to stretch out the interval between visits to the salon.

Also: Numerous chain salons and beauty schools have training days when they cut hair for free or a very low price. Call and ask.

●**Make your own baby food.** Steam peas or other vegetables and fruits, and purée in a food processor. Put well-cooked meat through a food processor or baby-food grinder, and serve immediately or freeze.

●**Save on everyday/play clothes.** Create a swapping network with family and friends. When your children outgrow their clothes, offer the nicest items to someone with smaller children. You will get a reputation as someone who likes to recycle. And if you need something, put the word out. If someone offers you something, take it. Even if you don't need it, you might know someone who does.

●**Clean out your closet.** Take the better brands of clothing to a consignment store. You will probably get about a quarter of the retail price—tax free.

●**Shop at thrift stores.** Those run by hospitals or symphonies are usually cheaper than better-known thrift outlets, such as those run by Goodwill.

Best Questions for Savvy Shoppers to Ask

Dorothy Leeds, a New York City–based motivational speaker and communications consultant for many Fortune 500 companies, *www.dorothyleeds.com.* She is the author of *The 7 Powers of Questions* (Perigee).

Shoppers can get more for their money simply by knowing what to ask. *Some of the best questions…*

●**May I speak to the manager?** Whatever you want—a better deal, a return that stretches the rules, free gift wrapping—the odds are better if you ask the person in charge. A sales associate is bound by store policy. A manager can bend the rules.

●**What can you do for a big spender?** Recently, I spent a lot of money in a clothing store. Before I made my purchases, I asked what the store would do for me if I bought everything I had selected. They threw in $100 worth of free merchandise.

Helpful: Be polite, not demanding, when you ask for extras. You're more likely to get what you want.

●**Can you show me something else?** The more time that a salesperson spends with you, the more anxious he/she is to make the sale—particularly if a commission is involved. If you have the time to linger over a decision, it might just land you a better deal.

●**Will this item go on sale soon? Was it on sale recently?** If a store will soon mark down an item—or if it had been reduced and is now back to regular price—there is a good chance you can get the sale price now.

●**What new features will the next generation of this product include? When will it arrive?** Certain products, such as electronics and computer goods, are continually being updated. Ask the salesperson if the item in the store is likely to be replaced by a new model soon.

If the new model includes features you like, consider waiting. If you don't need the extra bells and whistles, prices on the remaining stock will probably be marked down as the delivery date on the new item approaches. You might even be able to negotiate a better deal that day.

On-Line Shopping Know-How

If an on-line merchant shuts down while owing you money or merchandise, you may never get a refund.

If you paid by credit card: Contact the card company to credit your account.

Or, the Better Business Bureau (BBB) at *www.bbb.org*, in the city in which the company is based may help. If the firm has gone bankrupt, you are simply one creditor among many and may get nothing back after several years.

Safest when shopping on-line: Check out the merchant before buying. Look for the BBB Online Reliability seal on the Web site. Don't assume that larger firms are safer—some have failed, while some of the smaller ones serve customers well.

Holly Cherico, vice president of the Council of Better Business Bureaus, 4200 Wilson Blvd., Suite 800, Arlington, VA 22203.

Researching Recalls

Ken Giles, spokesperson for the Consumer Product Safety Commission, Washington, DC.

Half of all product recalls are for children's products—toys, furniture and recreational products, such as swings and bicycles. The Consumer Product Safety Commission (CPSC) announces as many as 300 recalls a year.

Self-defense: Once a month, call the CPSC (800-638-2772) or visit its Web site, *www.cpsc.gov.* Search by product name to find out if a specific item has been recalled…or sign up for the CPSC's

E-mail subscription list to get all recall notices automatically.

Especially important: Search the Web site thoroughly before purchasing items at thrift stores or garage sales.

Caution: Toys for children under age three should have no small parts that could be swallowed. Be careful of older siblings' toys that could be dangerous to a younger child. When buying electrical products, always look for safety seals from the Underwriters Laboratories (UL) or ETL Semko (ETL).

The Biggest Bargain Store In the US

For terrific bargains on an almost unlimited range of items, be sure to visit the airlines' Unclaimed Baggage Center in Scottsboro, Alabama, or check them out on the Internet at *www.unclaimedbaggage.com.*

On sale: Luggage, clothing, sporting goods, watches, cameras, jewelry, artwork, collectibles—plus unexpected items, such as a candlestick that is shaped like a cobra, or an erhu (a traditional Chinese stringed instrument), other musical instruments, toys.

Many items for sale are "like new" or in pristine condition. All have gone unclaimed by travelers on US airlines.

The store even has an "unclaimed cargo" section for unclaimed business shipments.

If you will be in the Atlanta, Nashville, Memphis or Birmingham area, a visit to the store can be a side trip that is both fun and rewarding.

Get yourself put on a list to be notified of special events—such as sales of artwork—by visiting the Center's Web site or by calling 256-259-1525.

How to Get More for Everything You Sell On-Line

Malcolm Katt, an antiques dealer and owner of the Millwood Gallery in Millwood, NY. Mr. Katt is an eBay PowerSeller.

The Internet has now become the world's largest marketplace. eBay alone has more than 46.1 million registered users and closes nearly four million auction listings each day. It has hundreds of thousands of regular sellers. About 50,000 of these are "PowerSellers," doing a minimum of $2,000 a month in sales.

Techniques that will help you compete in this vast arena…

STUDY AUCTION SITES

To develop a good feel for how the top on-line sellers conduct business, find an item at an auction site that appeals to you. *Answer the following questions…*

● **How did the item attract your attention?**

● **Was there anything in the title or description** that would encourage you to bid?

● **What payment and shipping methods** were offered?

RESEARCH PRICES

To get top dollar, you must know what others have paid…

● **Use guidebooks for collectibles as a starting point.** These gather actual retail prices from auctions, shows, shops and the Internet. Don't use them as your only source for pricing since some of the prices may be antiquated even by the time the book is printed.

● **Kovels** (*www.kovels.com*) has a database of more than 200,000 appraiser-approved values.

PICK A SITE WITH HEAVY TRAFFIC

The greater the number of people who see your item, the more potential bidders.

Run a search at *www.bidfind.com* to see where the most traffic is for the item you wish to sell—this site tracks auctions on more than 450 sites. *The top three on-line auction sites (at press time) are…*

● **eBay** (*www.ebay.com*).

- **Yahoo!** (*www.auctions.yahoo.com*).
- **Amazon** (*www.auctions.amazon.com*).

Strategy: Check out specialty sites. For example, if you're selling a rare comic book, you might use Mile High Comics (*www.milehigh comics.com*) instead of the "big three" auction sites. You'll attract more knowledgeable bidders and higher prices.

WRITE YOUR COPY

- **Make titles descriptive.** How you describe an item is the most important aspect of a listing. You have to do it in no more than 45 characters. When prospective buyers browse listings, all they see is the title. It must be clear and enticing.

Caution: Don't waste any characters on superlatives like beautiful, special or wonderful.

- **Check your spelling.** If you misspell any words, potential buyers won't find your item because the search engines will not pick it up. Don't misspell "Wedgwood" as "Wedgewood," for example.

Strategy: Use the singular form of a word —for instance, medal, not medals. Search engines make the distinction, and most buyers and sellers use the singular.

- **Use keywords that will be picked up by the site's search engine.** Include as many search words in the title as possible. *For example, if you are listing a silver cake knife, the following words are search words:* Tiffany… Olympian…sterling…cake…knife.

Strategy: Search engines ignore certain symbols, so you gain extra characters by using them. For example, using "&" instead of "and" saves three characters because the "&" isn't picked up by search engines.

- **Write a complete and accurate description.** Doing this dramatically increases the odds of a sale.

Rule of thumb: Keep your description to under 500 words so you won't chance losing the reader's interest.

- **Be honest about size, color, name of the maker, pattern and any imperfections.** Describe any problem in detail. Being open at the outset will save you headaches later. If the item is "mint," say so. Mint means perfect. If an item has a slight scratch, chip or nick, or a part is missing, it isn't mint.

- **Make descriptions attractive, and easy and enjoyable to read.** Design your descriptions to look like your favorite magazine. Avoid long blocks of text. Experiment with typefaces and colors to create a description that dazzles potential bidders.

- **Offer a money-back guarantee.** This reassures buyers. You'll get more bids and very few returns.

Strategy: Rather than composing your description on-line, type it in your word processing program and then copy and paste it in the auction site's description box.

POST DIGITAL PHOTOS

To get a high closing bid for an item, post its picture…

- **Display every side or angle.** This will minimize the number of bidder questions.

- **Don't hide defects or problems.** Buyers who bid with full knowledge of a problem are less likely to return the item.

You'll need a digital camera to get decent pictures. You can buy one that does the job for about $250. Canon, Casio, Olympus and Sony all have good models.

Buy a camera that produces at least 1.3 megapixel images. The higher the resolution, the better the picture quality.

Strategy: When posting a product, avoid fancy graphics, background colors or music that slows the download. Interested bidders might not wait around.

THE AUCTION

- **Open the bidding at 10% of what you think an item is worth.** Use reserve auctions sparingly—bidders don't like them. (In a reserve auction, you set a hidden minimum price that you'll sell an item for.)

- **End your auction at a time when most bidders are on-line.** While auctions typically run for seven days, most of the bidding takes place in the last three hours. You can specify the hour and minute when the auction ends.

Best auction times: Lunch hours (between noon and 2 pm) and between 8 pm and midnight (Eastern Standard Time) during the workweek. Some on-line sellers actually prefer early Sunday evenings.

Take into account the different time zones so you can be available to answer E-mail questions during the last three hours of your auction.

PAYMENT

•**Offer several payment options.** Accepting charge cards greatly increases sales. Payments by money order or personal check are fine—you'll build goodwill and expand your customer base.

Use secure payment services such as PayPal (*www.paypal.com*) and Billpoint (*www.bill point.com*). These services allow buyers to send credit card or bank account information over the Internet.

•**Include shipping charges and insurance (if desired).** Learn the cost of postage and insurance so you can accurately recover these costs from the buyer. You'll find information at the US Postal Service Web site at *www.usps.com*.

AFTER THE AUCTION

•**Follow up.** Send a congratulatory E-mail to the high bidder within 24 hours of the auction close. Arrange payment and obtain shipping instructions. If payment is made by check, E-mail the buyer when it's received and again when the item is shipped (after the check has cleared the bank).

•**Ship at once.** Customers will appreciate it, and you'll avoid handling extra E-mail inquiries asking, "Where's my item?"

•**Solicit positive feedback.** Feedback from satisfied buyers encourages other buyers to bid for your items. Buyers check the site's feedback ratings to make sure you've lived up to your part of the deal—"shipped promptly," "handled problems reasonably," etc.

Strategy: Include in the item's package a slip asking the buyer to post positive feedback on the auction site. Include the item number and your user ID to ensure a proper listing.

Better Jewelry Shopping

To differentiate between real and fake metal, hold a magnet next to the item. Gold and most platinum alloys are not magnetic. Iron, some stainless steel and cobalt platinum—often used for casting—are. While cobalt platinum is not an inferior quality metal, cast-made items may not be as durable as those that are hand- or machine-made.

Renée Newman, Los Angeles–based gemologist and author of Gold & Platinum Jewelry Buying Guide *(International Jewelry).*

Get a Guarantee On Antiques

Antiques dealers are not always sure of the age or quality of what they sell. If asked, reputable dealers will provide a guarantee as well as include a detailed description of the item, when it was made and what parts—if any —have been repaired or replaced. The guarantee should promise a full refund if the item turns out to be different from what you or the dealer thought it was.

Leigh Keno, antiques dealer, Leigh Keno American Antiques, New York City, and author of Hidden Treasures *(Warner).*

Secrets of Better Buying and Selling at Auctions

Harry L. Rinker, a syndicated columnist who writes about antiques and collectibles in Emmaus, PA. He is the author of more than a dozen books, the latest of which is The Official Rinker Price Guide to Collectibles *(House of Collectibles).*

Whether you are buying or selling, whether you are going on-line or making the traditional auction house circuit, here's how you can gain more with much less pain...

ON-LINE AUCTIONS

On-line auctions give you access to items from all over the world. Bidding is fun. But there are problems involving security, lack of direct contact between buyer and seller and the hard-to-regulate nature of the on-line auction process.

If buying or selling on-line…

•**Focus on large sites with heavy traffic.** You're more likely to find what you want and you may do better price-wise than you would on a smaller site.

Run a search at *www.bidfind.com* to see where the most auction traffic is for the item you wish to buy or sell. This company tracks auctions on more than 450 sites.

•**Check various auction sites.** Person-to-person auctions, such as those on eBay and Amazon.com, have the greatest diversity of items for sale.

On commercial sites, such as uBid.com, companies sell their goods in an auction format.

Don't overlook real-time Webcasts. These are live auction "netcasts." Buyers bid from the auction room or from the Web. Several traditional auction houses, such as Butterfields, run Webcast auctions. There are even sites that will do all the bidding for you such as *www2. icollector.com.*

WHAT MAKES A GOOD SITE

In addition to heavy traffic, look for…

•**A secure link whenever credit card information is entered.** You'll know the site is secure if you see a padlock symbol at the bottom of the screen. Some sites run the line, "This is a secure site."

•**Clearly defined dispute policy.** eBay, for example, outlines the precise procedure to follow in the event of a dispute.

•**Fraud protection.** Does the site reimburse you for some of your loss in the event of fraud?

•**A rating system for sellers and buyers.** That way, you'll know the track record of the person you're trading with.

•**Clearly stated fees and commissions.** Selling on-line is inexpensive because buyers pay no fees. Sellers should expect to pay two fees—a per-item listing/insertion fee (usually from 30 cents to about $3) and a final value/completion fee that varies depending on the amount of the winning bid (typically up to 5% for items to $25, 1.25% for items over $1,000).

•**Access to escrow services.** For a small fee, a third party—the escrow agent—holds the payment from the buyer in trust until the seller sends the merchandise. The fee runs from $2.50 for items up to $100 to 4% for items up to $25,000.

Using an escrow service protects the seller against credit card fraud and insufficient funds. It also allows the buyer to inspect the goods before the seller is paid.

BETTER SELLING

Selling at an on-line auction is easy, but to get the most for your items, keep the following in mind…

•**Write up a clear, concise description of your item.** Be very specific. In headlines, use key words that will appear in the site's search engine.

•**Post digital pictures of your item.** Potential buyers are more likely to bid on items with accompanying photos.

•**Set your opening bid as low as possible.** Also, price your items "off-dollar." Buyers respond better to $19.99 than $20.

•**Research the price for your item.** At *www.bidxs.com,* you can search prices at 300 auction sites.

•**Set a hidden "reserve" price for the item.** This is the price below which you will not go.

•**Schedule your auction to attract the most bidders.** *Best:* Allow it to run over two weekends. Most bidding takes place in the last three hours.

•**Be honest about damage to items.** This will turn off some bidders, but save you the headache of having to accept returns and refund payments.

BETTER BUYING

Be sure to check out the seller's rating. Take note of any negative feedback from other buyers. *Also important…*

•**Not all auctions offer bargains.** Be a wise consumer—investigate retail valuations.

•**Carefully check the item's description and photographs for any damage.** At commercial sites, determine if the goods are used or refurbished.

•**Set your maximum bid and stick to it.** With the ease of on-line bidding, it is easy to get seduced into paying more than you are comfortable with.

TRADITIONAL AUCTIONS

Auction houses are the primary source for quality pieces. The traditional firms—such as Sotheby's (*www.sothebys.com*) and Christie's (*www.christies.com*)—use their departmental specialists (who cover categories from Aboriginal art to Russian icons) to share their expertise with collectors.

The world of the auction house is significantly different from the world of on-line auctions. Although low-end sales (less than $20,000) occur at Sotheby's Arcade auctions and elsewhere, most items are sold for top dollar, and "trophy collecting" or buying an object for sale at any price is common.

For buyers…

•**Get a copy of the sales catalog.** It will contain pictures and descriptions. Make sure you understand the "conditions of sale" and "terms of guarantee."

•**Examine items carefully in person, if possible.** Items are sold "as is," so be sure to attend the auction preview. Upon request, a specialist can provide a condition report if you can't attend in person. The best advice a specialist can give you is what not to buy.

•**Understand the buyer's premium.** This is what you owe the auction house and can be as high as 17.5% of the purchase price.

For sellers…

•**Find out if the auction house specializes in your type of item.** If you're selling rare stamps, for example, you might want to check out Robert A. Siegel Auction Galleries (*http:// siegelauctions.com*).

To locate auctions and auctioneers worldwide, visit *www.auctionguide.com*. For auctions by category, try *www.internetauctionlist.com*.

•**Research what your item may yield at auction.** An estimate is only a guide for prospective bidders. It should not be relied upon as a prediction of the actual selling price. A reasonable estimate encourages bidding.

•**Understand the auction process.** It can take two to three months or more from the time your item is consigned to the house—for research, cataloging and photography—until the actual auction. It can take about 30 days after the sale to receive your proceeds. An on-line auction, on the other hand, typically takes only a week or two.

•**Understand the seller's commission.** It can run 10% to 15% of the sale price, plus possible charges for insurance, illustration, restoration and shipping.

How to Avoid Rip-Offs On Repairs

Chuck Whitlock, an investigative reporter located in Washougal, WA, *www.chuckwhitlock.com*. He is author of many books on white-collar crime, including *Mediscams* (Renaissance), and his work has been featured on television shows such as *Hard Copy* and *The Oprah Winfrey Show*.

To minimize your exposure to repair rip-offs, follow this helpful advice from consumer advocate, Chuck Whitlock…

•**Be wary of repair people who come to your door.** Most legitimate repair businesses have clients come to them.

•**Avoid one-day-only deals.** If the price isn't good after today, then something fishy is going on.

•**Get a second opinion.** Never take an unknown repairperson's word that you need major repairs without first having someone else confirm the diagnosis.

Helpful: Get at least two quotes in writing, and make sure they include a complete description of the work to be done.

•**Don't be bullied when a repairperson warns you of an emergency.** Many scam artists try to rush their victims into making panicky decisions.

●**Know your warranties.** Most household appliances are protected by long-term warranties. You may be able to get the manufacturer to fix them free or at a discount. Keep warranties and guarantees for future reference.

●**Insist that all new materials be used.** *Examples:* Make sure *diluted* driveway sealant is not used. Ask the car mechanic to use only the factory-approved replacement parts and to return the old parts to you.

●**Ask for local references—and phone them.** Call your local Better Business Bureau to see if the repairperson has any complaints pending…contact the contractor's state licensing board to check his/her license and reputation…make sure he and any other workers who will be on your property are licensed and bonded—and ask for proof.

●**Insist that the repairperson return one month after the work is finished** to make any adjustments.

Repair It Yourself

Before repairing a costly item—such as a lawn tractor or projection TV—check the troubleshooting section of the owner's manual *and* the manufacturer's Web site. You can sometimes make the simple repairs yourself. However, *do not* void the warranty.

Calling the company for advice can be frustrating and time-consuming—but if you do get through, the company may offer to fix or replace the item for free. If this does not work, consider factory or authorized service, with technicians trained on the latest equipment. Look in the *Yellow Pages* under "Technicians."

Consumer Reports, 101 Truman Ave., Yonkers, NY 10703, *www.consumerreports.org.*

The *Right* Way to Pay a Contractor

Do *not* accept a boilerplate agreement from the American Institute of Architects or any other contractor-provided agreement. You or—if the job is big—your lawyer should create a payment schedule in which you put 10% down and pay another 80% in stages as parts of the job are finished. Keep the remaining 10%—at least—until every item on the walk-through punch list is completed. Make sure you get a warranty of at least one year on the work.

Stephen Elder, home inspector and home-repair specialist, Pittsboro, NC.

Lumens vs. Watts

New high-efficiency lightbulbs are being rated according to the amount of electricity (wattage) they use and the amount of light (lumens) they produce. A bulb that produces more lumens with fewer watts is more efficient.

Example: A 60-watt, 1,080-lumen bulb will be brighter and cost less to use than a 75-watt, 1,000-lumen bulb.

Where to Retire, 1502 Augusta, Suite 415, Houston 77057.

How to Cut Heating Costs

Heating and air-conditioning ducts that are leaky can increase utility bills by as much as 30%. For about $300, an energy consultant can do a pressure test to locate leaks. For an additional cost, he/she can seal them.

To find a consultant: Ask your gas or electric company…call a reputable insulation contractor…get in touch with the department of energy in your state.

Caution: Always check references before hiring anyone.

Bill Keith, owner of Tri-Star Remodeling, St. John, IN, and host of the *Home Tips Show,* a Midwestern cable-TV program. *www.billkeith.com.*

Better Utility Budgeting

Ask your utility company about flexible billing options. *Budget billing* allows you to spread the cost of energy over a time period established by your utility. You may be subject to periodic adjustments, or "true ups," to reconcile your bill for changes in usage, weather or energy prices. With *flat billing*, you pay a pre-determined amount for your gas or electric that is guaranteed every month for up to one year. Different from traditional budget bills, there are no adjustments required—no matter what happens with the weather or energy prices.

Resources: Get an interactive home energy checkup at *www.ase.org/checkup.* Also get free advice from an energy efficiency expert at *www.eren.doe.gov/askanenergyexpert.* And for even more ways to lower your energy costs, go to the Web site, *www.homeenergysaver.lbl.gov.*

Doug Laderer, vice president for WeatherWise USA, provider of services that reduce weather-related financial risk for utility companies and their customers, One North Shore Center, 12 Federal St., Suite 230, Pittsburgh 15212, *www.weatherwiseusa.com.*

How to Save on Electricity

Time-of-day electricity pricing can save you money without limiting your use of appliances. Some utility companies reward customers with lower rates if they avoid using appliances during peak periods. Instead, use your appliances after 8 pm during the week, when power use is low. Time-of-day pricing is now available in most states. Ask your local utility if it offers such a program.

Steven Rosenstock, a researcher for the Edison Electric Institute, Washington, DC.

Best Ways to Cut Energy Bills

To trim your energy bill, try out some of these suggestions…

•**Set your water heater to "warm" (120°F)** and wrap it with an insulating blanket.

•**Use the energy-saving settings** on your refrigerator, dishwasher, washing machine and clothes dryer.

•**Replace old appliances** with new energy-efficient models.

•**Clean or replace furnace, air conditioner and heat-pump filters.** Check manufacturers' instructions.

•**Seal air leaks**—such as any gaps around chimneys, recessed lights in insulated ceilings and unfinished spaces behind your cupboards and cabinets.

•**Install a programmable thermostat** to control temperature.

American Council for an Energy-Efficient Economy, *www.aceee.org.*

Beware of "Free" Internet Access

Free Internet access isn't always free. *How to protect yourself…*

•**Find out how long the trial period will last.** If a company offers 500 free hours and the trial period is one month, you would have to be on-line more than 16 hours per day in order to reach 500 hours. But some firms start the clock as soon as you sign up.

•**Understand the cancellation policies.** Some services will permit on-line cancellation. Others require a phone call—and may be difficult to reach.

•**Be sure a provider has local access numbers**—so you avoid long-distance calls.

Helpful: A Federal Trade Commission alert on free Internet service offers, available at *www.ftc.gov/bcp/conline/pubs/alerts/freeispalrt.htm.*

Brenda Mack, public affairs specialist, Federal Trade Commission, 600 Pennsylvania Ave. NW, Washington, DC 20580.

Save on Dry-Cleaning Bills

Home dry-cleaning kits can extend the time between professional dry cleanings—but they don't replace the cleanings. Use them for garments that are hard to hand-wash…small blankets and bedspreads…draperies…sweaters …and dry-clean-only blouses. Follow directions carefully, and remove clothes from the dryer bag immediately. *Cost:* $10 to $15.

Linda Cobb, an Arizona-based cleaning expert and the author of *Talking Dirty Laundry with the Queen of Clean* (Pocket). *www.queenofclean.com.*

Great Gifts That Don't Cost A Bundle

Steve Rhode, president and cofounder of Myvesta.org, a nonprofit financial services organization, Six Taft Ct., Rockville, MD 20850.

To give memorable gifts, you *don't* have to spend a lot. You must simply *personalize* what you give so the recipients feel how much you care.

Every year, Myvesta.org, a national, nonprofit organization dedicated to helping people get out of debt, invites consumers to submit their most creative ways to save money on gift giving for birthdays, anniversaries and other special occasions. *Some recent winners…*

● **Special interest kits** for the recipient's favorite activity. If your dad loves to fish, his kit might include adhesive bandages, beef jerky, candy, sunglasses, matches and his favorite steel leader hooks.

● **Framed photographs** of your loved one's home during the seasons.

● **Address boulder.** Get a large rock at the local quarry. Paint the recipient's house number on it with fluorescent paint. He/she will think about you every time he drives up to his home.

● **Trade in frequent-flier miles for magazine subscriptions and other gifts,** such as home appliances or luggage. Many airlines now send out gift brochures with items costing as little as 500 miles.

GIFTS FOR KIDS

● **Personalized picture.** Use heavy paper and crayons or markers to write adjectives for each letter of a child's name.

Example: Jenna—J is for *Joyous…*E is for *Exciting…*N is for *Neat,* etc.

● **Coupon gift book.** Each book contains 14 coupons—one for each month plus Valentine's Day and a birthday. Make each coupon redeemable for whatever you choose. The front of each coupon has your favorite saying or advice…the back has space for a thank-you note.

To redeem the coupon, the child must present it to you each month, recite the saying or advice and tell you what it means. He must also fill out the thank-you note on the back.

Free and Low-Cost Alternatives to High-Priced Legal Help

Bahman Eslamboly, Esq., partner in the law firm of Eslamboly & Barlavi, which specializes in accident, injury and workers' compensation cases, 6100 Wilshire Blvd., Los Angeles 90048. His firm runs the Web site *www. lawguru.com,* a free legal resource for people acting as their own attorneys as well as for legal professionals.

Turned off by attorneys and their exorbitant legal fees, more people are opting to represent themselves in a wide range of legal matters. The savings can be substantial.

Example: Filing a no-fault divorce on your own costs about $400…through lawyers, $1,800 or more.

What can you realistically handle yourself? When do you really need an attorney? *Attorney Bahman Eslamboly gives some answers…*

WHEN TO USE A PROFESSIONAL

The following situations are too complex to handle yourself…

● **Prenuptial agreements.** Each of the parties should retain his/her own attorney. If this is not done, your spouse could easily dispute the prenup on the grounds that he was not properly represented and did not understand what he was signing.

●**Criminal cases.** Mounting an adequate defense requires legal expertise and knowledge of civil liberties, police procedures, etc.

HANDLE YOURSELF

●**Small-claims court.** Municipal and county courthouses often provide on-site advocates to offer procedural advice. Small-claims court covers civil cases seeking up to $15,000—but the amount will vary from state to state. *Helpful resources to try...*

Free advice on how to file a suit: Go to your state or county Web page...or find the phone number of your municipal or county courthouse in the blue pages of your telephone book.

For general guidance on suing in small-claims court...

●*www.courttv.com.* Then click on "Legal Help" and go to the "Consumer Law Center."

●*Everybody's Guide to Small Claims Court, National Edition* by Ralph E. Warner (Nolo).

If you win your case, ask the court to "certify" the judgment. The form is available from the district-court clerk. This allows you to file papers to have the defendant's wages or bank account "garnished" or to put a lien on any real estate he owns.

Alternative: Sell your judgment to a local collections agency. Expect to get 50 cents on the dollar or less.

●**Workers' compensation disputes.** Individuals can handle the simple cases, such as those involving minor bodily injuries resulting from employer negligence.

For a legal guide to workers' comp disputes, go to *http://employment-law.freeadvice.com.* Click on "Workers Comp."

See an attorney if...

●You are seeking large, additional penalties.

●You were demoted or fired because of an injury.

●Your case involves technical legal matters —for example, the injury involved defective equipment, which could introduce product-liability issues.

●**Demand/complaint letters.** Disputes are often easy to resolve if you present the facts thoroughly in a well-written letter. But send it via certified mail to establish a paper trail if you decide to sue.

Useful resource: Shocked, Appalled, and Dismayed! How to Write Letters of Complaint That Get Results by Ellen Phillips (Vintage).

●**Landlord–tenant disputes.** Check out *www.references–etc.com/rental_legal.html,* which sells legal guides for tenants ($13 to $22).

Other simple-to-handle situations that do not require professional legal advice: Car leases...apartment rental leases.

CUT COSTS BY DOING SOME WORK YOURSELF

Save substantially in the situations below by obtaining and filling out legal forms yourself. Then pay an attorney or a paralegal to review the documents and make sure they are complete and comply with state and local laws.

●**No-fault divorce.** *Divorce Yourself: The National No-Fault Divorce Kit* by Dan Sitarz (Nova), provides the details on handling an uncontested divorce in every state. You will probably need more extensive legal advice if you have child custody issues...or complex joint holdings...or your spouse has hired his own attorney.

●**Personal bankruptcy.** Filing yourself is quite easy if you have relatively few (six or fewer) creditors and debts that total less than $100,000. Most bankruptcies fall under federal law, but be sure to check with an attorney about additional state requirements.

Useful resource: Debt Free: The National Bankruptcy Kit by Dan Sitarz (Nova).

●**Wills, living wills, powers of attorney.** The estate-planning software, with forms and detailed instructions to make your own will, is inexpensive.

My favorite brand: Family Lawyer 2003 Wills & Estates (Broderbund, $19.99*). This software produces wills, powers of attorney, trusts, living wills and advance directives that you fill out with the help of a question-and-answer format. 800-395-0277...*www.learningco.com* or *www.broderbund.com.*

*Price subject to change.

Consult a professional if you have extensive property holdings or a large portfolio that could cause tax liability issues. These documents must be completed in accordance with state law to be valid.

Important...

•Do not ask a beneficiary to be a witness. The will may be legal, but the beneficiary could lose his/her legacy. Another party could challenge the will in court based on this fact.

•Do not keep your will in a safe-deposit box. Some states require safe-deposit boxes to be sealed when the holder dies, which slows down the inheritance process. Instead, keep your original will with your attorney and a copy at home in a fire-safe box.

•Review your will every three years and more often if there is major new tax legislation or a change in your family status.

•Revise your will if you move between a community-property state, where most assets acquired during marriage are jointly owned, and a common-law state, where the assets are owned by the person who obtains them.

MORE RESOURCES

•**Prepaid legal plans** provide an array of legal services, from simple documents, such as wills and cease and desist letters, to representation in court cases.

How they work: You pay a monthly fee for access to a network of licensed, general-practice lawyers. Choose from several types of coverage. *Fee:* $14 and up plus an enrollment fee. For more information, go to *www.prepaid legal.com* or *www.legalplans.com.*

•**On-line legal services** streamline the process to cut costs.

How they work: You complete extensive on-line questionnaires. Your documents are prepared for a flat fee. *Standard savings:* 50% to 85% less than seeing an attorney in person. For more information, go to *www.mycounsel. com* or *www.legalzoom.com.*

•**Free legal information and forms that are geared to nonlawyers...**

•*http://law.about.com.* Information on dozens of legal topics. There are comprehensive pointers to state and local legal resources.

•*www.legal.net.* Information for consumers and legal professionals.

•*www.halt.org.* Operated by a nonprofit, nonpartisan group.

•*www.legalpulse.com.* Provides legal advice and documents.

•*www.legalengine.com.* On-line legal self-help guides.

•*www.findforms.com* and *www.uslegal forms.com.* Thousands of state-specific legal forms. *Cost:* $10 and up per packet.

•**Nolo Press** publishes more than 200 self-help legal books, covering subjects from neighbors to dogs. 800-728-3555...*www.nolo.com.*

Fitness Club Savings

Discounts on fitness club membership are offered by many health insurance plans. Plans typically have negotiated discounts of 10% to 40%. For details, check the insurer's Web site or call your customer service representative.

Walter Cherniak, public relations manager, Aetna, US Healthcare, Heath Insurance, Washington, DC.

How to Block Telemarketing Calls

Nancy Dunnan, a financial adviser and author based in New York City. She is the author of *How to Invest $50–$5,000* (HarperCollins).

There are several good options for blocking those annoying telemarketing calls. *Exercise them all...*

•**The Privacy Rights Clearinghouse** (*www. privacyrights.org*) offers advice on how to get telemarketers to stop calling. On the home page, click on "Fact Sheets" and then #5, "Telemarketing: Whatever Happened to a Quiet Evening at Home?"

•**The Direct Marketing Association** (*www. the-dma.org*) maintains a telephone preference list. Add your name to the list, and you will no longer receive calls from companies that belong to the association.

Important: Your name remains on the list for five years. Let the association know if you move or change your phone number.

●**State do-not-call services.** The Direct Marketing Association also maintains a list of the states that currently operate their own do-not-call services. Visit *www.the-dma.org/government/donotcalllists.shtml.*

Don't Get Hung Up On Big Cell Phone Problems

Penelope Stetz, former district manager with cell phone manufacturer Motorola and currently owner of PhoneTech Wireless Consultants in Euclid, OH, *www.wirelesswhiz.com.* She is the author of several books on cell phones, including *The Cell Phone Handbook* and *The Cell Phone Buyer's Guide* (both from Aegis).

While cell phones are useful, they can be infuriating. *How to minimize common cell phone complaints...*

SPOTTY COVERAGE

Slick promotional maps from the six major providers suggest excellent coverage from coast to coast. Don't be fooled. Problems tend to be localized. The service provider that works well for your friend across town or two states away might be terrible for you. Since you may be locked into a service agreement for at least one year, you don't want to choose a provider with poor coverage in your area.

Strategy: Borrow phones from friends—or ask the sales agent at each provider for a trial phone—for a day. Make calls from your home, office, the roads you take to work or anywhere you expect to do a lot of calling. Note your success rate with each service provider. Ask friends who live or work near you if they have had a lot of fast busy signals. This indicates the network is overloaded in those regions.

SHORT-LIVED BATTERIES

Most cell phones come with nickel cadmium or nickel metal hydride batteries—but *lithium* batteries offer twice the talk time as nickel for the same size battery. When purchasing your phone, ask about the cost to upgrade to lithium. You will get a better deal if you agree to a longer-term commitment.

For an *existing* phone, buy a lithium battery from your phone's manufacturer. Some aftermarket batteries are poor quality, and using one might void your phone's warranty. A lithium battery costs $25 to $85, depending on capacity.

Important: Make sure the battery charger can be used with lithium batteries—some are only for nickel batteries.

HIGH COST FOR EMERGENCY-ONLY SERVICE

The average cell phone service costs hundreds of dollars a year. That is a big deterrent for people who only want a cell phone as an emergency lifeline.

Better: Ask providers about *analog plans* or other low-cost alternatives to digital service. In some regions, such plans are available for only about $15/month if you sign up for a year—and may include a free phone.

Save even more money with a prepaid phone plan—you buy minutes when you need them. While the minutes are relatively expensive—10 minutes might cost $5 or more—it is still a good deal if you don't use the phone much.

Caution: Prepaid minutes expire if not used in 30 to 90 days—unless you purchase more minutes before the expiration date.

Even cheaper alternative: By law, any inactive cell phone can be used to call 9-1-1. So if you want a cell phone only for extreme emergencies—not to call the auto club or a friend when your car breaks down—you do not need to pay for service at all. Ask family and friends if they have an old cell phone you could use.

Important: Do not throw an emergency phone in the glove compartment and then forget about it. The battery needs recharging at least once a week.

Save Money Every Day

Ellie Kay, the "Coupon Queen," a writer located in Alamogordo, NM, *www.elliekay.com*. Her latest book is *How to Save Money Every Day* (Bethany House).

Here are some of the "coupon queen's" favorite secrets for significantly cutting costs every day…

FOOD

●**Coupons.** Every true penny-pincher clips coupons. *Another source:* Search the manufacturer's Web site for coupon offers there.

Twice as good: Double coupons. If your supermarket does not offer them, get friends to sign a petition saying they would patronize the supermarket more frequently if it offered double coupons.

Show this to the store manager. If he/she is reluctant, suggest that he try offering double coupons only on the slowest day of the week —and see if sales increase.

●**Milk, meat and produce.** Coupons are seldom available for these staples, but you can save by buying when they are on sale.

Stock up on meat specials and freeze…and take advantage of stores that match prices offered in competitors' ads. Many Wal-Mart superstores will do this. To save on fruit and vegetables, ask for a discount on imperfect produce. You may have to cut out some bruises, but what's left is perfectly good.

Even better: If you live close to a wholesale produce supplier, its rejects are apt to be in better shape than those available at the retailer.

●**Food co-ops.** If you get 10 people together who make a regular monthly order, you can form a co-op to buy produce from a wholesaler. Members must pay up front and always take their order—or find someone else to take it.

FURNITURE AND APPLIANCES

Before buying furniture, ask yourself: "Do I need it? Can I afford it? How am I going to pay for it?" Write down your dream list, and then take it to a furniture store. Compare the amount of cash that you have to spend with the cost of what you want to buy. Factor in the interest you will pay if you buy on credit.

Example: The new furniture you desire costs $10,000 more than you have in cash. Suppose you use store credit to pay for it. If you make the monthly minimum payment at typical interest rates of 18% to 22%, your new furniture will end up costing you $26,000. It would take you more than 33 years to pay off that debt.

Here are some alternatives…

●**The Internet.** Many furniture manufacturers list outlet stores on their Web sites. Search for the price of the pieces you want. Go back to the store and ask if it can match the prices.

Or print out a list of all the furniture distributors within a 100-mile radius. Call them and ask for their best price. Then go back to your local store and give it a chance to match it.

Finally, ask if it can *beat* that price by throwing in free delivery, free fabric treatment, etc. *Potential savings:* Up to 50%.

●**Furniture craftsmen.** Local craftsmen often build custom furniture for less than the retail price. Locate craftsmen by asking at local lumberyards, antique stores and furniture repair shops…or look in the *Yellow Pages* under "Custom Builders" and "Furniture Designers."

Before calling for an estimate, make sure that you know exactly what you want in terms of type and quality of wood, style, finish, fabric and price range. Ask to see samples and references…how long it will take…and if the craftsman can suggest a less costly alternative.

●**Model homes.** Make an offer for furniture and appliances in model homes.

Caution: The furniture displayed in model homes is usually smaller than regular furniture— to make the homes appear bigger.

●**Floor models.** Some appliance dealers and department stores sell floor models at a discount. These appliances usually still carry a new appliance guarantee. If they have minor cosmetic damage, you may be able to reduce the price even more.

●**Secondhand merchandise.** Check out local secondhand stores, garage sales and classified ads. Inspect old furniture for quality and condition. Consider reupholstering.

Check ads for used merchandise on bulletin boards in supermarkets, libraries, churches and workplaces—and post your own ad.

Useful Web Sites

For Consumers

☐ Appliance Repair Clinic
www.repairclinic.com

Troubleshooting and repair information for 16 appliances, from refrigerators to washing machines.

☐ Backpack Safety
www.backpacksafe.com

Guidelines on purchasing the right backpack for your child to avoid slouching, back pain, muscle strain and stress on the body.

☐ Bargains On-Line
www.bargaindog.com

Tracks 15 categories of merchandise and sends out weekly E-mail letters about deals.

☐ Car-Buying Skills
http://money.cnn.com/pf/101/lessons/17

Learn how to improve your car-purchasing skills and save money at this practical site.

☐ Consumer Action
www.pueblo.gsa.gov

Get the contact numbers of your city, county or state consumer-protection office. Go to "Consumer Help," then click on "Attorneys Gen."

☐ Credit Repair Scams
www.attorneygeneral.gov/pei/bcp.cfm

Get the facts on credit-repair scams at this US government Web site.

☐ Free Shipping
www.freeshipping.com

Maintains a list of over 1,000 on-line retailers offering good deals on shipping.

☐ Phone Bargains
www.getconnected.com

Compare and shop for great deals on wireless phones, Internet connections, long-distance or local telephone service and cable or satellite TV.

Insurance

☐ Health Insurance On-Line
www.ehealthinsurance.com

This national on-line broker has access to thousands of health plans across the country and provides free comparison quotes.

☐ Compare Rates On-Line
www.insurance.com

Provides articles and expert information on all types of insurance. You can also shop for insurance products and quickly compare rates and policy terms from a select group of the nation's leading carriers.

☐ Insurance Fraud
www.insurancefraud.org

Learn about insurance fraud, an $80-billion crime wave, and what you can do to avoid it.

☐ Insurance Quotes
www.intelliquote.com

Compare more than 200 insurance companies. Health, home, car and other insurance quotes are available.

☐ Long-Term-Care Insurance
www.kiplinger.com

Learn more about buying long-term-care insurance at this helpful site provided by Kiplinger. In the search box type "Long-Term-Care Insurance," then scroll down.

Investments

☐ Teens and Investing
www.fool.com/teens

At this fun site, teens can ask questions about money and talk about money and investing with other teens.

☐ US Treasury Securities On-Line
www.treasurydirect.gov

Buy US Treasury securities directly over the Internet and eliminate a broker's fee.

Personal Finance

☐ Budget Organizer
www.homemoneyhelp.com

Get a budget form, bill summary form, ledger and budget stretcher free at this Web site.

☐ Consumer Loans
www.hsh.com

Provides up-to-the-minute mortgage rates as well as credit, payment, refinancing and other calculators.

☐ Debtors Anonymous
www.debtorsanonymous.org

Help and other valuable information on compulsive spending.

☐ Debt Work Out
www.debtworkout.com

For those considering bankruptcy, this easy-to-understand Web site gives alternatives.

☐ Grandparents' Finance Center
www.igrandparents.com

These fun games will help you teach your grandchildren all about money. Click on "Finance" under "Grand Topics."

☐ Find an Appraiser
www.isa-appraisers.org

Learn what questions to ask before hiring a property appraiser, and what the appraisal report should and shouldn't include.

Taxes

☐ Charitable Contributions
www.irs.gov

The IRS maintains a list of organizations that are approved for deductible charitable contributions. Type in "Cumulative List of Organizations" in the first search box.

☐ Gifts in Kind International
www.giftsinkind.org

Instead of throwing away old computer equipment, give it to charity and get a tax deduction. This refers you to organizations that accept such equipment.

☐ Tax-Friendly States
www.kiplinger.com

Some states are more tax-friendly toward retirees than others. Learn more by typing "Tax-Friendly States" in the search box, then scrolling down to "Where You Stay—What You Pay."

☐ Tax Links
http://users.visi.net/~gillco/ tax_links.htm

Contains links to government tax Web sites, as well as other sites with information on tax breaks and tax laws.

☐ More Tax Help
www.taxgaga.com

Articles about taxes and education, marriage, retirement, death and more. Ask a tax question, find a tax pro or file on-line.

11

Financing Retirement

Smart Ways to Tap Into Your Retirement Nest Egg

**M**any people spend their working lives building up retirement savings accounts—then make one of two devastating mistakes when they withdraw their money from those accounts…

•**They withdraw too much too soon**—leaving their retirement funds badly eroded somewhere down the line.

•**They withdraw too little too late**—leaving a big estate to their children, but pinching pennies while still alive.

HOW TO HANDLE WITHDRAWALS

•**Start your withdrawal planning today.** What throws some people off track is thinking that they should be planning for retirement, when they really should be planning to maintain financial independence.

Result: They start taking withdrawals from their retirement accounts on the date that they retire, whether they need to or not.

Retirement is only a date on a calendar. It doesn't mean that all your income immediately dries up and you are instantly forced to tap into your nest egg—you only do that when you must to maintain your lifestyle.

Important: When you are working, your financial independence comes from the salary you earn. When you retire, it comes from your pension, Social Security benefits and, perhaps, income from a postretirement job.

Withdraw from retirement savings accounts only when other sources of income fall short and you need that money in order to remain financially independent.

•**Calculate how much income you will need in retirement.** That is where people really can get into trouble. They use a formula

Ronald Yolles, attorney and chartered financial analyst, Yolles Samrah Investment Management, Inc., 3000 Town Center, Suite 2550, Southfield, MI 48075. He is coauthor of *You're Retired, Now What? Money Skills for a Comfortable Retirement* and *Getting Started in Retirement Planning* (Wiley).

from a broker or a financial magazine that says they can get by on 60% or 70% of preretirement income. They build their withdrawal strategy around that magic number.

Reality: There is no such thing today as a "standard" retirement and no magic number to tell you how much you'll need in retirement.

Recently, a colleague and I interviewed more than 100 people and found almost no one who was retiring in the traditional sense of retirement—doing a little gardening, playing a little golf. People are staying incredibly active well into their 70s and 80s—traveling more, buying second homes, working at postretirement jobs or volunteering.

Your spending could go down when you retire, but just as easily it could go up because you are traveling more and helping the kids with their expenses.

●**Don't rely on any magic number.** Prepare a budget that represents your *best guess* about your expenses in retirement…

●How much will you travel?

●Will you help a child buy a home?

●Are you planning to pay for your favorite grandchild's education?

●Will you work after retirement…and how much can you realistically expect to earn?

Consider the first year or two of your retirement as a period of testing and learning. Then take another look at the budget and adjust it as necessary.

●**Delay withdrawals until the last possible minute.** Every day that you delay taking withdrawals from your retirement accounts—IRAs and 401(k) plans—is another day that tax-sheltered compounding keeps your retirement savings growing.

Strategy: If you can, wait until age 70½ to begin making withdrawals. That's when the law says you must start. If you can't wait that long—wait until you really need the money.

●**Before you tap tax-sheltered accounts, withdraw from your taxable investment accounts.** Doing so preserves tax sheltering for as long as possible.

Gains in taxable accounts are taxed at the capital gains rate (maximum 20%). All withdrawals from tax-sheltered accounts are taxed

as ordinary income (maximum 38.6% in 2003). Hang on to that tax advantage as long as it is possible.

●**When you start withdrawing, withdraw the minimum.** Even if you wait till age 70½ to start withdrawals, withdraw the minimum that's allowed by law.

Helpful: Calculating the allowable minimum withdrawal is complicated, so you'll probably want some help from an attorney, CPA or financial planner.

Under new IRS rules, the Minimum Distribution Incidental Benefit (MDIB) method is used to calculate minimum withdrawals. This uses the joint life expectancy of the IRA owner and a hypothetical person 10 years younger than the owner as the period over which distributions must be taken.

Key: Under the new rules, this method is used even if there's no beneficiary or the beneficiary is not 10 years younger.

Exception: IRA owners who have a spouse more than 10 years younger than themselves will be able to calculate required distributions over their actual joint life expectancies—which will work even better than using the MDIB method.

●**Make the most of Social Security.** The one exception to the last-minute approach to withdrawals applies to Social Security.

You can get a bigger payout by waiting until your normal retirement age (e.g., 65 and two months for those born in 1938).

Our advice: Don't wait. Take the money as early as possible, especially if you're not working—at age 62 if you can. We have worked through scenarios for hundreds of clients. In more than 90% of the cases, it makes sense to start Social Security payments as early as possible, instead of waiting for a bigger payout down the road.

●**Include investment planning in retirement planning.** The most overlooked aspect of withdrawal planning is how to change your approach to investing once you start to make significant withdrawals.

The need for growth investments doesn't change when you retire. With people living longer, the best strategy is to continue to invest heavily in common stocks for their superior long-term-growth potential. But once you start withdrawing from retirement accounts, market volatility will become your enemy. You need to dampen it as much as possible.

Reason: The money for withdrawals comes from selling the investments in your retirement accounts. The more you must sell in a down market, the quicker you'll go through your retirement nest egg.

Since 1926, 24% of the five-year periods in the stock market have produced returns that were either negative or lower than the return on fixed-income investments. That's too risky, once you begin taking withdrawals.

Strategy: Dampen the volatility by shifting more of your retirement accounts into bonds.

Until retirement, I advocate keeping your allocation 70% stocks, 25% bonds and 5% cash. Once you begin withdrawing from retirement savings, shift to 50% stocks, 40% bonds and 10% cash.

How Much Money Will You Need When You Retire?

Nancy Dunnan, a financial adviser and author based in New York City. She is the author of *How to Invest $50–$5,000* (HarperCollins).

To determine how much money you will need to retire, add up all your expenses for last year. Subtract those you think you won't have in retirement, such as business clothes, commuting costs and FICA taxes… and add in possible postretirement expenses, such as health insurance. Perhaps you'll travel more in your free time.

Once you reach this theoretical retirement expense amount, live on it for three months. This is an imperfect experiment, but it will give you some sense of how comfortable you are living on a given amount of money.

Next, add up your Social Security benefits (if you haven't received your annual statement, get an estimate by calling 800-772-1213 or at

www.ssa.gov), pension, 401(k) and IRA, investments and savings accounts.

Once you have done this number crunching, fine-tune your plan using the T. Rowe Price Retirement Income Calculator, "Will Your Retirement Assets Last Your Lifetime?" You can find it at *www.troweprice.com/ric.*

Five Big Retirement Plan Pitfalls… And How to Avoid Them

Melvin L. Maisel, president and CEO, Stabilization Plans for Business, Inc., White Plains, NY. The firm advises companies on retirement plans. Mr. Maisel is also chairman, Cornerstone Bancorp, Stamford, CT.

Qualified retirement plans are a wonderful way to build retirement savings on a tax-advantaged basis. However, the law is complex and riddled with numerous pitfalls.

Pitfall 1: **Using the company's preprinted beneficiary forms.** Companies typically provide employees with forms on which to name beneficiaries for their accounts. These forms usually have a space only two to three inches long for correctly specifying choices, such as the contingent beneficiaries—people who will inherit the accounts if your primary beneficiaries predecease you.

Problem: The beneficiary designation form may name minor children or grandchildren as contingent beneficiaries. This can lead to disastrous consequences. It may involve the surrogate's court in the distribution of benefits. This complication could be prevented if the form instead provided room to name a trust under the terms of your will for the benefit of these minors.

Solution: Have an estate planner draw up a beneficiary designation form for you.

Make sure your plan's sponsor accepts such a form. If this is unacceptable, have the estate planner tell you what you should write on the company form.

189

If the custodial agreement of a brokerage firm or mutual fund company refuses to let you use your own beneficiary designation form for an IRA, find a company that does.

***Pitfall 2:* Starting distributions before you have to.** You must begin to take money out of your IRA no later than April 1 of the year after the year you reach age 70½. Qualified retirement plans have the same age-70½ requirement, but if you're still working at that age, your company must allow you to put off distributions until you actually retire. This may be well beyond age 70½.

Problem: This right to postpone distributions beyond age 70½ does not apply if you own more than 5% of the company at any time after turning age 66½. Ownership by a spouse, child or parent is attributed to you and counts in determining your ownership percentage.

Solution: If you started taking money out of a qualified plan at retirement age because you thought you had to, but continued to work, ask the plan administrator to stop distributions.

***Pitfall 3:* Assuming a prenuptial agreement that contains a spousal waiver of benefits protects children and grandchildren.** In second marriages, the new spouse typically agrees to forgo retirement plan benefits in favor of the participant's children from the prior marriage. But a fiancé signing a prenuptial agreement is not a "spouse," so the purported waiver isn't valid.

What to do: Wait until *after* the wedding to execute the spousal waiver. This can be done by signing a retirement plan form or by executing a postnuptial agreement that contains the same elements required in a waiver—the name of the plan and the benefits being waived.

***Pitfall 4:* Not rolling over a distribution from a qualified plan to an IRA as soon as possible.** If the plan allows for an "in-service" distribution (while you're still employed), don't wait until you leave the company to make the rollover.

Reason: If you die with your benefits still in the qualified plan and those benefits are payable to anyone other than your surviving spouse (the only person permitted to make a rollover to avoid immediate taxation), or if the rollover is not completed prior to your spouse's death, the benefits must be distributed in a lump sum to your beneficiaries.

Result: The benefits are immediately taxable and the chance to affect income tax savings for future generations is lost forever.

What to do: Ask the plan administrator if you're permitted to take distributions while still working at the company. If so, roll over benefits to an IRA.

***Pitfall 5:* Failing to claim an income tax deduction for the federal estate tax paid on inherited retirement plan benefits.** If you inherit an IRA or other qualified plan that was subject to federal estate tax, you are entitled to an income tax deduction for a portion of the federal estate tax that was paid, typically at the top tax rate.

You can deduct that portion of federal estate tax attributable to the benefits that are included in your income. The deduction is a miscellaneous itemized deduction (not subject to the 2% floor).

Double deduction requirement: You may qualify for another deduction if the primary beneficiary dies with a taxable estate and you are the contingent beneficiary. A contingent beneficiary who inherits the balance of the retirement benefits can claim a deduction with respect to the federal estate tax on the plan participant's estate and the primary beneficiary's.

Example: A daughter inherits an IRA from her mother. The daughter dies, and her son inherits the balance of the grandmother's IRA. Since the IRA was taxed in both the grandmother's and daughter's estate, the son can claim a deduction for each of the sets of estate taxes paid.

What to do: If you failed to take a deduction for which you were eligible, file an amended return. Generally, you have three years from the due date of the return to do so.

New IRA Rules Bring Big Opportunities...but Even Bigger Traps

Seymour Goldberg, Esq., CPA, senior partner, Goldberg & Goldberg, PC, One Huntington Quadrangle, Melville, NY 11737, *www.goldbergira.com*. One of the nation's leading authorities on IRA distributions, Mr. Goldberg is author of *The New IRA Distribution Rules* (IRG).

New IRS rules for IRAs make it much easier to manage the distributions and beneficiary designations. But beware. While the rules are generally pro-taxpayer, they create *new traps* that may prove costly for anyone who overlooks them.

When you're revising your estate plan to take advantage of the new rules, be sure to avoid these common traps...

THE GAP PERIOD

The biggest trap in the new IRA rules is the *gap period* regarding beneficiary designations.

The new rules help taxpayers by allowing IRA beneficiary designations to be modified as late as September 30 of the year following the year in which the IRA owner dies. *How...*

●**By having a beneficiary give up all rights to the IRA** so that it passes to a contingent beneficiary.

●**By dividing an IRA** with multiple beneficiaries into separate accounts.

●**By fully paying off a beneficiary with a zero life expectancy**—such as a charity or estate—so that another beneficiary, if any, can take payments over his/her full life expectancy.

But here's the trap. According to the new rules, when a named beneficiary dies before December 31 of the year following the year in which the IRA owner dies, IRA distributions *cannot* be made over that beneficiary's life expectancy as of the date of the IRA owner's death (as they could under prior rules).

Instead, a zero life expectancy applies, so the IRA must be distributed...

●**Generally, under the five-year rule,** if the owner of the IRA had not yet reached the *required beginning date (RBD)* of age 70½ for minimum annual distributions.

●**Over the IRA owner's life expectancy at the date of death,** if the IRA owner had reached his RBD.

This can have a large impact on the way the IRA is taxed—at a great cost to the IRA owner's family.

Reason: An IRA beneficiary who can take distributions from it during his own full life expectancy may earn decades of tax-deferred investment returns. These are lost when the IRA is paid out over the shorter term.

Example: An individual names his son as his IRA beneficiary, then dies during calendar 2002 when the son is age 40. Under the new rules, the IRA can be distributed to the son over the son's remaining 43.6-year life expectancy—earning more than four decades of tax-deferred investment returns for the son's family—if the son lives to September 30, 2003.

But if the son dies before September 30, 2003, the IRA must then be distributed over a much shorter period of time. *If the IRA-owning parent...*

●Had not reached his RBD, generally the distributions must be taken according to the five-year rule.

●Had reached his RBD, the IRA must be distributed over the parent's life expectancy just before death. For instance, if the parent was age 73, over 14.8 years.

In either case, decades of tax-favored investment returns are lost to the son's family.

Contrast: Under prior IRS rules, the IRA could be distributed over the son's 43.6-year life expectancy as long as the son lived past the father's date of death—even if he did die within the next year. So the new rules are much worse than the old rules for the son's family.

BACKUP PLAN

To ensure there is a beneficiary on September 30 of the year after death, name a contingent beneficiary. The IRA then will pass to the contingent beneficiary, such as a grandchild of the owner, who may take distributions over his full life expectancy.

MORE NEW IRA TRAPS

●**Trust trap.** Another trap is created in the new rules in situations where an IRA is payable to a trust.

In these cases, the new rules require the trustee to deliver a copy of the trust papers to the IRA's custodian by September 30 of the year following the IRA owner's death.

Note: Trusts that failed in the past to provide the necessary documentation have until October 31, 2003 to act.

If documentation requirements are not met, the beneficiaries are deemed to have a zero life expectancy, and the IRA must be fully distributed to the trust under the five-year rule or over the IRA owner's life expectancy (as described earlier). Again, *decades* of tax-favored investment returns may be lost.

Caution: This penalty applies even if the papers weren't delivered on time simply because someone was unaware of this new rule.

If the proposed reduction or elimination of the estate tax is enacted, more trusts will be used with IRAs—IRAs will be able to hold more funds without incurring estate tax, and trusts will be valuable in managing the disposition of the IRA assets.

●**Surviving spouse trap.** Yet another trap arises when one spouse dies and leaves an IRA to the other spouse as a beneficiary.

If the deceased spouse reached age 70½ or older and hadn't taken his required IRA distribution for the year of his death, the new rules say that the surviving spouse must take that required distribution before rolling over the funds from the deceased spouse's IRA into her own IRA. The distribution amount for the year of death can't be rolled over into the surviving spouse's IRA.

Neglecting to take the required distribution amount from the decedent's IRA may result in a steep excise tax penalty. Taking such a distribution for the year of the IRA owner's death was not required under the old rules—so the new requirement may be a costly surprise.

PLANNING DIFFICULTIES

The real problem in the new IRA rules is that while it may seem unlikely that the aforementioned problems will apply in your case, you can't tell in advance. That makes it difficult to plan.

Example: If you name a child as your IRA beneficiary, it may be unlikely that the child will die before September 30 of the year following your death. But if he does, it may cost your family hundreds of thousands or even millions of dollars.

If you pay your IRA to a trust, a paperwork foul-up could devastate your estate plan the same way.

Helpful: You and your adviser can read the full text of the new IRS rules for IRAs by entering "REG-108697-02" in the first search box at *www. irs.gov.* Then click on "Retirement Plans."

After reviewing the rules, revise your estate plan to make the most of them—while also taking explicit steps to avoid the new traps.

IRA Contribution Trap

A potential trap faces taxpayers who seek to take advantage of new, increased contribution limits for IRAs and qualified retirement plans.

Snag: Some states have not amended their laws to comply with the new federal law to allow the contributions. For instance, at this writing, California has not amended its law to bring it into line with the new federal law regarding either IRAs or qualified plans such as 401(k)s.

Danger: The contributions now allowed under federal law may not be permitted at the state level, and can result in penalties. Even worse, employer-sponsored plans may be disqualified for violating state law.

In the past, most states complied with federal law in the end—but not always. Check with your adviser.

Meloni Hallock, CPA/PFS, tax partner, Ernst & Young LLP, 725 S. Figueroa St., Los Angeles 90017.

How to Take Early Penalty-Free Withdrawals From Retirement Accounts

James Blinka, CPA, tax partner, BDO Seidman, LLP, Two Plaza E., 330 E. Killbourn Ave., Milwaukee 53202.

Anyone who takes money out of an IRA or other tax-deferred retirement plan will owe income tax, assuming the account was funded with deductible contributions.

In most situations, you will also owe a 10% penalty tax on withdrawals before age 59½. If you take out $10,000 at age 54, for example, you would have to pay a $1,000 penalty.

But there are some exceptions to the early withdrawal penalty. If you really must take an early withdrawal, use one of the following methods to avoid the 10% penalty tax bite.

UNIVERSAL EXCEPTIONS

The following exceptions apply to all tax-deferred retirement plans…

●**Death.** If you inherit a retirement account, you won't face the 10% penalty. That's true no matter how old you are.

●**Disability.** Again, the 10% penalty does not apply if you cannot work and need to make a withdrawal.

How can you prove to the IRS that you are disabled? In most cases, you should be receiving disability checks from Social Security or from an insurance policy.

Smart 1040 strategy: Attach an explanation to your tax return, clearly stating that you are receiving disability benefits and that the 10% penalty should not apply.

●**Medical bills.** The 10% penalty will not apply to money spent for deductible medical expenses in excess of 7.5% of your adjusted gross income (AGI).

●**Substantially equal periodic payments (SEPPs).** Avoid the 10% penalty by withdrawing annual amounts based on your life expectancy.

These payments must continue for at least five years or until age 59½, whichever comes later.

Caution: If you don't maintain the SEPPs until the later of five years or until age 59½, you will owe the 10% penalty tax on all withdrawals, retroactively.

EMPLOYER-SPONSORED PLANS

The following two exceptions to the 10% early withdrawal penalty apply only to withdrawals from 401(k)s, profit-sharing plans and other qualified retirement plans.

●**Separation from service.** If you leave your employer, you can take money from your retirement account and not pay a penalty.

Requirement: The separation must occur no earlier than the year you reach age 55.

●**Qualified domestic relations orders (QDROs).** In a divorce or marital separation, a QDRO is an order to the plan administrator to transfer part of one spouse's account to the other spouse. Such a transfer won't be subject to tax. But subsequent withdrawals from an employer-sponsored plan under a QDRO before age 59½ will not be subject to a penalty.

Implication: You can give or receive alimony or child support from an employer-sponsored retirement plan, penalty free, as long as those payments are required by a QDRO.

Don't take the money out of a plan and then give it to your spouse. The IRS looks harshly on that approach, applying income tax under the theory that you took a distribution. Money should go directly to the beneficiary of the QDRO, as required.

IRA EXCEPTIONS

The separation-from-service and QDRO exceptions do not apply to early distributions from IRAs. *On the other hand, there are escape hatches that are only for IRAs…*

●**Higher education.** Distributions from IRAs to pay post-high-school expenses are exempt from the 10% penalty.

Eligible expenses: Tuition, room and board, fees, books, supplies and necessary equipment.

These qualifying expenses can be used to pay for your education or that of your spouse, your children or your grandchildren.

●**Health insurance.** After you are out of work for 12 consecutive weeks, you can take money from an IRA to keep your health insurance in force, penalty free.

After you're back at work, you won't owe a penalty on IRA withdrawals used to pay health insurance premiums for the next 60 days.

●**Purchasing a first home.** You may take penalty-free withdrawals up to $10,000 for a first-time home purchase.

Required: You cannot have had an ownership interest in a residence during the previous two years. The $10,000 is a lifetime limit.

ROTH IRAs

If you're withdrawing money from a Roth IRA before age 59½, you'll owe the penalty on the amount that is attributable to your earnings inside the Roth IRA, but not to your original contributions.

Exceptions: Death, disability and first-time home buyer up to $10,000.

THE SEPP SOLUTION

Some of the exceptions listed above (death, disability, divorce) apply only in specific circumstances. However, IRA owners can make use of the SEPP exception at any time. Participants in other plans can use SEPPs after separation from service.

SEPP rules are so flexible that you can take out almost any amount needed, penalty free, as long as your account balance is large enough. *Three methods permitted by the IRS…*

●**Life expectancy.** You withdraw money based on your life expectancy, according to IRS tables. For example, if your life expectancy is 40 years, you'd calculate ¼₀ (2.5%) of your plan balance and withdraw that much each year.

●**Amortization.** You calculate that your initial plan balance will grow by a reasonable rate, perhaps 6% or 7% per year. The higher the assumed rate, the greater the penalty-free withdrawals permitted. This method permits much higher withdrawals than the life expectancy method.

●**Annuitization.** This complicated calculation, incorporating annuity factors and present values, allows you to withdraw a bit more than with the amortization method.

With each method, you can name a beneficiary in order to withdraw a smaller amount each year, if desired. You also can split your account to come up with the desired result.

Example: You have a $600,000 IRA and you wish to withdraw $2,500 per month. However, if the SEPP rules (amortization method) require that you withdraw $3,750 per month from a $600,000 IRA, you'd be paying tax on an unneeded $1,250 a month.

Solution: Split your $600,000 IRA into a $400,000 IRA and a $200,000 IRA, tax free. Then take distributions from the $400,000 IRA, pulling out the $2,500 per month that you need, using the amortization method. In your other $200,000 IRA, you can continue the tax-free buildup.

How 401(k)s Can Team Up With Roth IRAs

Glenn Frank, CPA/PFS, CFP, vice president at Tanager Financial Services, Inc., 800 South St., Suite 195, Waltham, MA 02453. He teaches postgraduate courses in portfolio construction at nearby Bentley College.

The *Tax Relief Act* increased the amount taxpayers can contribute to 401(k) and similar retirement plans.

In 2003, you can contribute up to $12,000 to a 401(k) plan. Then the ceiling will increase by $1,000 per year, reaching $15,000 in 2006.

A catch-up bonus: In addition, 401(k) participants age 50 or older can contribute an extra $2,000 in 2003. This amount will increase by $1,000 each year until it reaches $5,000 in 2006.

After 2006, both the regular and the catch-up caps will be indexed to inflation.

MIX AND MATCH

As a result of these changes, 401(k) plans will offer more shelter than they did in the past. Before you automatically max out your 401(k) contribution, however, consider putting a Roth IRA into the mix. You may be better off limiting your 401(k) contribution and maximizing contributions to a Roth IRA.

Strategy: Fund your 401(k) as much as necessary to get the greatest possible employer match, then put your next dollars into a Roth IRA.

Example: Your employer promises you a 50% match on 401(k) contributions up to 6% of your pay. Your base salary is $90,000, so the maximum match is $2,700. Following the above strategy, contribute at least $5,400 to your 401(k), 6% of your salary. You'll get a $2,700 match—50% of $5,400.

The employer matching contribution is part of your compensation package. If you don't contribute enough to get the full match, you are passing up part of your pay.

ROTH IRA REWARDS

Suppose, in the above example, that you want to save more than $5,400 per year for your retirement. Your next dollars should go into a Roth IRA, rather than into your 401(k) account.

Roth limits: In 2003, contributions of up to $3,000 can be made to a Roth IRA. That cap rises to $4,000 in 2005 and $5,000 in 2008, after which it will be linked to inflation.

To contribute the maximum amount to a Roth, income can't exceed $95,000 ($150,000 on a joint return). At slightly higher income levels, you can make a partial contribution.

Catch-up contributions: The 50-and-up bonus contribution to Roth IRAs is $500 a year in 2003 to 2005 and $1,000 thereafter (there's no indexing for this limit).

Payoff: Roth contributions are not deductible. However, all Roth IRA withdrawals may be tax free. You can take tax-free withdrawals from a Roth IRA after five years, provided you're at least 59½ years old.

CONQUERING THE TAXMAN

Why is a Roth IRA contribution better than an unmatched contribution to a 401(k)? You could, after all, put your $3,000 into your 401(k) rather than a Roth. *Here are the main reasons why it's better…*

●**Tax-free versus tax-deferred.** An unmatched 401(k) contribution reduces your income up front, but taxes will be owed eventually on the deferred salary as well as on all the earnings. What's more, that tax will be owed at ordinary income tax rates. Roth IRA withdrawals may, by contrast, be completely tax free.

●**No required distributions.** The more you contribute to a 401(k), the more money you must withdraw (and the more tax you must pay) after age 70½.

Roth IRAs are exempt from the required lifetime minimum distribution rules. This extra flexibility gives you even more time to get the benefit of tax-free compounding.

●**Penalty-free payouts.** With a 401(k) plan, withdrawals before age 59½ probably will be subject to a 10% early withdrawal penalty in addition to ordinary income tax. With a Roth IRA, you can withdraw the amount that you have contributed at any time, tax free and penalty free.

Example: From age 35 to 50, you contribute $66,000 to a Roth IRA, which grows to $125,000. If you need cash then, you can pull out as much as $66,000 and owe no tax or penalties. If you withdraw $66,000, the other $59,000 can continue to grow tax free.

●**Investment flexibility.** Most 401(k) plans have limited investment options. With Roth IRAs, you can select your own investments.

●**Lower fees.** Investments inside of 401(k) plans may be burdened with higher expenses, which can decrease returns over the long term. With a Roth IRA, you're able to seek out low-cost investments.

Strategy: Hold the investments with the highest expected total return in the Roth IRA to avoid tax on those returns. The greater the investment returns, the greater the benefit of long-term tax-free compounding.

Although it's difficult to say precisely which investments will pay off most, stocks (especially small-company stocks) historically have posted the best long-term results.

Investing in a Roth IRA each year is really a form of dollar-cost averaging. This strategy is a proven means of reducing your price per share in the equities market.

If you decide to invest Roth IRA money in certain attractive mutual funds, arrange for monthly transfers from your bank account to the fund, to ensure true dollar-cost averaging.

HAPPIER ENDINGS

What if you max out your employer match and your Roth IRA contribution, and still have more to invest? Where should that money go?

Example: George Jones wants to invest $10,000 in 2003 for his retirement. He contributes $3,000 to his 401(k), to get the maximum employer match, plus $3,000 to max his Roth IRA. Thus, he has another $4,000 to invest.

Strategy: Assume George is reaching the income limits for maximum Roth contributions and is in a relatively high tax bracket. If so, he may want to put the extra $4,000 into his 401(k) to get the up-front income reduction.

Under the new law, tax rates will drop in future years. Increasing 401(k) contributions will give George valuable deductions when available. If his tax bracket drops after he retires, he might be shifting income from a high to a low bracket.

On the other hand, suppose George is in the early stages of his career, expecting his income to rise considerably over the years. He may want to invest the extra $4,000 outside of his 401(k).

In a low bracket, the up-front income reduction will be less valuable. Deferring $4,000 in a 15% bracket saves only $600. That $4,000, plus all the accumulated earnings, may be taxed at a much higher rate when it's withdrawn in the future.

By investing that $4,000 outside his 401(k), George can choose among many tax-advantaged alternatives, such as no-dividend stocks and tax-managed mutual funds. Any long-term capital gains can ultimately be cashed in at favorable tax rates.

CRUNCHING THE NUMBERS

Say you're in the 15% bracket. You can contribute an unmatched $4,000 to your 401(k) this year, saving you $600 in taxes. You can put that $600 into a tax-efficient investment account.

Alternatively, you can put $4,000 of after-tax income into a tax-efficient investment account.

Assume that all investments earn 9% per year, over 30 years, and that no taxes are due in the interim. If you're in the 35% tax bracket 30 years from now, you'd be slightly ahead with the tax-efficient outside fund rather than the unmatched 401(k) plus the outside fund.

Changing assumptions can change the outcome. For example, assuming a 25% withdrawal tax rate, the $4,000 unmatched 401(k) plus the $600 outside fund become the better choice. But if you're going to spend your 401(k) tax savings

rather than invest in an outside fund, you may be better off without an unmatched 401(k).

No matter what assumptions you use, you have more withdrawal options outside of a 401(k). On the outside, you do not have to worry about early withdrawal penalties or minimum required distributions.

Bottom line: The value of an unmatched 401(k) contribution lies in tax deferral, so the longer the better. However, you should be cautious about deferring tax if you're likely to be in a higher tax bracket when the money is withdrawn.

Retirement Planning Savvy

Robert S. Keebler, CPA, MST, partner, Virchow, Krause & Co., LLP, 1400 Lombardi Ave., Suite 200, Green Bay, WI 54304. Mr. Keebler is author of *A CPA's Guide to Making the Most of the New IRA* (American Institute of CPAs).

Many corporations today have a 401(k) or other tax-deferred retirement plan for employees.

Opportunity: Contribute as much as the plan allows, for maximum tax-deferred wealth buildup. If it's possible, make additional non-deductible contributions.

Trap: Many corporations pressure executives to load up on company stock with retirement plan contributions. If it is possible, use your retirement plan contributions to help in the diversification of your portfolio.

To make the most of your plan's tax deferral: Use the plan to hold high-turnover mutual funds and actively traded stocks.

Don't waste your retirement plan's tax deferral on low-dividend stocks and funds that you intend to hold forever. Those stocks will never generate much of a tax bill, so you might as well hold them in a taxable account.

If you keep tax-efficient holdings outside of a plan, any appreciation will qualify for favorable capital gains rates. Gains taken within a plan will eventually be taxed at the higher ordinary income rates, when money is withdrawn.

Hottest Retirement Places Now

Kenneth A. Stern, CFP, president of the firm, Asset Planning Solutions in San Diego, CA. He is author of *50 Fabulous Places to Retire in America* (Career Press).

If relocation is part of your plan for retirement, don't rush into it. Before making a decision, consider the "four Cs" that make a place suitable for your particular lifestyle.

Crime: Is the community safe?

Climate: What kind of weather and seasonal changes do you enjoy? Don't assume that the place you love to visit in summer will be equally agreeable in the winter.

Cost of living: Can you afford to live there? Can you find work/business opportunities there if planning on a postretirement career?

Culture: Do the local residents share your same interests?

Where people are retiring to now…

NORTHWEST

●**Eugene, Oregon.** Located 110 miles from Portland, it's close to the ocean and the mountains. It has a moderate year-round climate and offers a variety of outdoor activities, including world-class skiing, river rafting, hiking and fishing. Local colleges provide great continuing-education programs.

Drawbacks: Occasional air-quality problems…above-average living costs, including taxes and medical expenses.

●**Medford, Oregon.** Situated about 170 miles from Eugene, Medford is a small, laid-back town with plenty of outdoor recreational opportunities, including golfing, skiing, fishing or just enjoying the mountains or picturesque Oregon coast. A world-renowned Shakespeare Festival is held each year in Ashland.

Other advantages: Below-average living costs…affordable housing…part-time jobs and start-up entrepreneurial business opportunities.

●**Bellingham, Washington.** In the North Cascades region, this bayside community offers outdoor recreation in the nearby Pacific Ocean and Cascade Mountains, including fishing, skiing, kayaking and golf…as well as many trails for jogging and walking while enjoying the spectacular natural beauty of the Pacific Northwest.

This small, relaxed community also offers the cultural amenities of a university town (Western Washington University).

Drawbacks: Very wet—170 rainy days a year…limited job opportunities.

FLORIDA

●**Ocala.** Located in north central Florida, about 40 miles from Gainesville, it's one of the world centers for thoroughbred horse breeding. It offers plenty of outdoor recreational activities without crowds of tourists.

Other advantages: Below-average housing and living costs.

Drawbacks: No public transportation and limited shopping.

●**Kissimmee.** Located in central Florida— 18 miles from Orlando, so your grandchildren won't need any persuading to come visit you. Apart from nearby Disney World and other attractions, Kissimmee offers boating and fishing on the Chain of Lakes, and lots of wildlife.

Drawback: Floods of tourists.

LAS VEGAS

The self-styled entertainment capital has no income tax, inheritance tax or estate tax. Las Vegas has more than 320 days a year of sun and low humidity, year-round golf and tennis, and nearby state and national parks and skiing, hiking and canoeing. There are also many cultural offerings, along with excellent health care and senior services.

Drawbacks: July and August temperatures often exceed 105 degrees…traffic…crime.

THE SOUTHWEST

●**Austin, Texas.** The state capital of Texas is a rapidly growing metropolis with year-round outdoor recreation, a rich cultural environment and impressive health-care facilities.

Drawback: Hot summers.

●**Brownsville, Texas.** Situated in the Lower Rio Grande Valley in southeast Texas, it has a Mexican heritage and a multicultural lifestyle. The cost of living is well below average. Matamoros, Mexico, with even lower prices, is a much larger city within walking distance.

Other advantages: Superb hunting, fishing and bird-watching.

Drawbacks: Hot, humid summers...heavy cross-border traffic and crime problems—particularly car theft.

● **Las Cruces, New Mexico.** Located on the southern border of the state, it's about 45 miles from El Paso, Texas. Las Cruces is surrounded by fabulous landscapes, including the Organ Mountains, the Chihuahua Desert and the Rio Grande. It offers great entertainment, arts, recreation and cultural attractions, beautiful weather, wonderful shopping and dining—all at affordable prices.

Drawback: Springtime dust storms.

RETIREMENT ABROAD

If you do not mind a major culture change and really want to stretch your retirement dollars, consider moving abroad...

● **Mexico.** Some of the places now attracting an increasing number of Americans include Tijuana, comfortably close to San Diego...and Rosarito, about 200 miles down the Pacific coastline. One thousand miles further south is Puerto Vallarta, a charming coastal resort.

● **Costa Rica.** San Jose, the country's capital, has a lot to offer, including a climate milder than Florida's, the lowest crime rate of any foreign community that's popular among US expatriates, and friendly people—most of whom speak English.

● **The Bahamas.** Nassau, a tropical paradise, is now an offshore banking haven attracting an increasing number of retirees. You don't need to worry about learning a new language in this English-speaking nation.

THE RELOCATION DECISION

Even if a particular community seems ideal at first sight, don't buy until you have spent time there on several occasions—and during different seasons. If it still appeals to you, rent for a year before you buy a new home, to be sure you are in the right place.

Happier Postretirement Living

Postretirement life satisfaction depends more on a person's social network than on health or wealth. New retirees need a social network more than they did when working—to listen to their concerns, provide emotional support and let them know they are still valued.

Problem: Many people's social interactions occur primarily at work. After retirement, those interactions must be found elsewhere.

Caution: Before relocating, consider whether you will enjoy the sorts of people you would be living near.

Mitch Anthony, Rochester, Minnesota–based author of *The New Retirementality: Planning Your Life and Living Your Dreams...At Any Age You Want* (Dearborn Trade).

12

Better Estate Protection

Estate Planning Needs Much More Attention *Now*

Many people believe the new tax law's "repeal" of the estate tax means that they do not need to worry about their estate planning anymore.

Reality: The new law reduces the estate tax—and ultimately repeals it in 2010. But the estate tax is immediately reinstated the following year.

Common strategies, such as use of life insurance, may still be necessary for nontax reasons.

Examples: To provide for your surviving spouse and dependents...to fund a business buyout agreement.

KEY CHANGES TO MAKE NOW

●**Adjust your will and estate plan to reflect the new tax rules.** The top estate tax rate fell from 55% in 2001 to 50% in 2002 to 49% in 2003...and then falls one percentage point annually until 2007, when it reaches 45%.

Estate tax exemption: The amount of assets exempt from estate tax increases gradually from $675,000 in 2001 to $3.5 million in 2009.

In 2001, a married couple could leave up to $1.35 million tax free by having each spouse make full use of his/her exempt amount. In 2003, this amount for a couple increased to $2 million, and it will gradually rise to $7 million in 2009.

Strategy: Each spouse must own enough property *separately.* This may require changing assets from joint to individual ownership—*even your home.*

Gift tax exemption: The amount of lifetime gifts that is exempt from *gift tax* increased from $675,000 in 2001 to $1 million in 2002—and remains at that level permanently. This means that additional tax-free gifts can be made to

David S. Rhine, CPA, regional director, family wealth planning at Sagemark Consulting, a division of Lincoln Financial Advisors Corp., registered investment adviser, 395 W. Passaic St., Rochelle Park, NJ 07662.

most taxpayers—even to those people who have already used up their entire exemption amount (because of the way in which gift taxes are figured, the additional gift amount comes to about $302,000).

Note: The gift tax does not just go away. Even after 2010, the year of the "demise" of the estate tax, the exclusion will remain at $1 million, and gifts in excess of that amount will be taxed at the maximum income tax rate.

Beneficiary trap: Many wills use standard "formula clauses" designed to minimize tax under the prior law. Have your estate attorney modify these formula clauses, if necessary.

Example: A parent's will leaves "the maximum amount that can pass tax free" to a trust for his children. If his total assets were $5 million, he had made no prior gifts and died in 2001, the trust would have received $675,000 and his spouse would have received $4,325,000. If he doesn't change his will and were to die in 2006, the trust would get $2 million and his spouse would get $3 million. In 2009, the trust would get $3.5 million and his spouse would get only $1.5 million.

●**Beware of the new "inheritance" tax.** Many people think repealing the estate tax will eliminate *all* tax on inherited property. In fact, the estate tax is replaced with new *capital gains taxes* that may substantially offset estate tax savings.

Currently, the basis used to determine gain or loss on the sale of an inherited property is increased to market value at the date of death, eliminating its taxable gain to heirs.

The new law generally repeals application of a "stepped-up basis" to inherited property. Heirs will inherit property with "carryover basis" from the decedent instead—taxing the entire gain.

There is some relief in the new law. An executor may apply up to $1.3 million of basis increase to assets in an individual's estate. An additional $3 million increase is available for property passing to the surviving spouse, but using that relief may leave more to your spouse than you intended.

Strategy: To calculate gain on assets you have in your estate, your heirs will need basis records that may go back years. These need to document acquisition cost, cost of improvements and depreciation. If cost records don't exist, heirs may face capital gains tax on *100%* of the sale proceeds. If the potential capital gain is large enough, life insurance may be appropriate.

●**Charitable gifts.** If you wish to make bequests, fund them with traditional IRAs—since their distributions are taxable—and low-basis, highly appreciated assets, such as stocks.

Leave cash and recently purchased, high-basis assets to heirs, since capital gains taxes on them will be lower.

More from David Rhine...

Tricky Trusts

Trusts are powerful tools for estate planning and tax reduction. But they are subject to complex legal and tax rules. Mistakes are costly.

TRUST MYTHS

Myth: **A trust can let you avoid income tax.**

The IRS's *number-one* enforcement target today is "abusive trusts"—used to avoid tax on normal income, such as salary, or to deduct personal expenses, such as children's education costs.

These trusts are being sold aggressively by promoters who prey on Americans' desire to escape taxes.

Example: The trust promoter promises that salary can be made tax free by having one's employer pay it to a trust.

While it may be possible to shift certain income from one person to another, someone will owe tax on the income. Trusts that receive income may owe income tax at higher rates than individuals would.

The overall IRS audit rate has fallen to a historic low, however the IRS has *stepped up* its targeting of abusive trusts. It is obtaining criminal convictions of those who sell them and those who use them.

Red flag: The promoter claims, "The IRS doesn't want you to know about this…" Or, "This is so new that your accountant won't have heard of it."

Resource: Visit the "Individuals" section of the IRS Web site at *www.irs.gov.* Or visit the IRS Criminal Investigation Web site at *www.treas. gov/irs/ci.*

Myth: **Living trusts reduce estate taxes.**

Living trusts have numerous legitimate uses. These popular trusts become irrevocable upon death to assume ownership of assets and manage them according to your wishes.

- Assets placed in a living trust escape probate. That means they may be distributed to heirs more quickly than if they pass through your will.

- The terms of a living trust are private. Wills become public documents when probated.

People mistakenly believe that, because the assets in a living trust do not pass through a probate estate, they escape estate taxes.

Reality: When you die, all of your assets will be included in your taxable estate—whether in a living trust or not. While there may be good reasons to establish a living trust, escaping estate tax is not one of them. The very same tax-saving provisions of your will can be incorporated in a living trust.

Myth: **Making large gifts to children through a Uniform Gifts to Minors Act (UGMA) or a Uniform Transfers to Minors Act (UTMA) account is a good substitute for a trust.**

Numerous banks, brokers and other financial institutions will let you open a low-cost UGMA/UTMA account in a child's name to make gifts to the child without incurring the cost of setting up a trust.

Trap: A UGMA/UTMA account distributes proceeds to the child when he/she reaches the age of legal majority, which is as low as 18 in some states. The child may use the proceeds in any way he wishes—regardless of the desire of parents, grandparents or others who have funded the account.

Safer alternatives…

If small amounts are involved: Keep the account yourself…then give money to the child when you are sure he will use it wisely.

If large amounts are involved: Set up a customized trust. Have the funds managed on the child's behalf—or on behalf of other heirs, if the child disqualifies himself from receiving them.

Myth: **Annual gifts made to a trust are always free of gift tax.**

The annual gift tax exclusion lets individuals make annual gifts of up to $11,000 to as many recipients as desired, free of gift tax in 2003. By using your annual exclusion on a series of gifts over several years—and transferring the assets to a trust—one can substantially reduce a taxable estate. That's especially true if gifts are of appreciating property, such as the shares in a private business.

Trap: To qualify for the gift tax exclusion, a gift must be made to an individual and be completed. If you make gifts to a trust that benefits a group of people—or that may "cut off" a beneficiary—the exclusion won't apply.

Example: You make gifts to a trust on the condition that it be paid to the child if he gets married by age 30. If he is not married by age 30, the trust will pay the same funds to other family members. The gifts to the trust do not qualify for the gift tax exclusion because they are conditional—the child may not receive them…others may.

Better: Use your lifetime exemption amount of $1 million to fund gifts to a trust that will provide benefits to a group of your family members or provide conditional benefits.

Myth: **It pays to use a "college savings" trust to fund college costs.**

Instead of having a trust pay college tuition, pay it yourself as a tax-free gift to the child. Then make an additional $11,000 gift ($22,000 if both parents are giving) to the trust. You'll decrease your future estate by the maximum amount and increase the child's welfare.

Reason: Payments made directly to educational institutions and medical facilities on behalf of another individual are not subject to gift tax.

Example: You can give $11,000 to a grandchild using your annual gift tax exclusion…pay $20,000 of his college tuition…and pay $5,000 in medical bills to a hospital that treated him, all without incurring gift tax.

Myth: **Family members generally make the best trustees.**

Selecting the right trustee to manage a trust is important, especially if he will have discretion to allocate—or withhold—distributions to family members.

Dilemma: A trustee who is a family member —or is close to certain family members—may be seen as self-interested or partisan. But a trustee who is unfamiliar with the family may lack the knowledge to make wise decisions.

Option: Designate more than one trustee, so that together they have the knowledge and skills—including investment sophistication—needed to manage the trust. There should be an odd number of trustees in order to avoid a deadlock. Be sure to specify the procedures for group decision making.

Name a substitute trustee in case one of the original ones becomes unable to continue in the role.

Also from David Rhine...

Avoiding the Five Biggest Pitfalls of Custodial Accounts

Parents and grandparents can very conveniently make gifts to young children using the *Uniform Gifts to Minors Act* (UGMA) or the *Uniform Transfers to Minors Act* (UTMA), whichever law applies in their state.

These "custodial accounts" are set up under the child's Social Security number with an adult acting as custodian of the money. There are no attorney's fees or other costs for setting up the account. They are simple and cheap and can serve family estate-planning purposes. But they carry a number of serious traps for the unwary.

Trap: Hidden estate taxes. If the parent or grandparent names himself/herself as custodian of the account, the funds still in the account will be included in his estate when he dies. If the reason for setting up the account was to cut estate taxes, this objective will backfire.

A better way: The donor should designate someone other than himself as custodian. The donor can even name his spouse. *Caution:* The spouse that's named as custodian will control the account if the marriage gets rocky. A grandparent can name the child's parent as custodian to keep the account from being included in the grandparent's estate.

If the wrong person has already been designated as custodian, the desired change can be made by completing the requisite paperwork with the account's financial institution.

Trap: Loss of control over funds. Funds in a custodial account remain in the account until the child reaches age 18 or 21 (depending on state law). At that time, all of the money falls under the child's control. While the funds may have been intended as an education fund or for some other noble purpose, there is no way to prevent a child from using the money on an expensive car or a wild expenditure.

A better way: When modest amounts are involved—a $25 birthday gift or a $50 holiday present—custodial accounts are an easy way to handle the money.

But where large amounts are concerned—$11,000/$22,000 annual gifts in 2003 and the like—it may be preferable to use a formal trust so that the child cannot obtain complete control at 18 or 21. Instead, the funds can be held in the trust for as long as desired (with the trustee retaining control) while being used for the child's benefit.

Trap: Loss of college financial aid. Many people set up custodial accounts as a vehicle to save for their child's college education. For those expecting to require financial aid, this strategy is flawed. The financial aid formulas colleges use count funds that are in the child's name more heavily than funds that are in the parent's name.

Result: A custodial account may limit a child's eligibility for financial aid.

A better way: Parents and grandparents can save the funds in their own accounts to enable a child to qualify for aid. Then, if they are financially able to help, parents or grandparents can pay college tuition directly. Such gifts are not limited by any dollar amount and can be made in addition to the annual limit on tax-free gifts ($11,000/$22,000).

Trap: Possibility of a liability suit. The custodian is required by law to hold the funds in the account for the benefit of the child. As a practical matter, however, a custodian often deals with the funds as his own, especially when it's the custodian who put the money into the account. Where there is family acrimony, the custodian may be brought to court on charges of mismanagement of the funds.

Example: After a bitter divorce, the wife accuses the husband of using money in custodial accounts to meet his child support payments or other personal expenses.

A better way: Respect the fact that the funds belong absolutely to the child. Keep good records of how funds have been spent. Understand that the money cannot be used to satisfy a parent's legal obligation of supporting the child.

Trap: **Setting up a custodial account for asset protection.** It may not work. A minor child generally isn't liable for debts or other obligations. However, once the minor reaches the age of majority and gets control over the assets in the custodial account, his assets will become subject to the claims of creditors. An accident, a lawsuit or a divorce can expose these assets to creditor claims.

A better way: Use a trust rather than a custodial account for asset protection. Funds in the trust can be made largely creditor-proof.

Finally from David Rhine...

Filing a Gift Return Can Block an Audit

Consider filing a gift tax return even when you don't have to.

Why: Doing so starts the three-year statute of limitations running to limit the time the IRS has to challenge the value of the gift.

Example: You make a gift of property (such as a collectible or shares in a family business) to a child. You determine its value is less than $11,000, the amount of the annual gift tax exclusion, so you don't have to file a gift tax return. But then the property appreciates greatly in value.

Looking back more than three years later, the IRS may conclude the original gift was worth more than $11,000. If you *didn't* file a gift tax return, the IRS can challenge the valuation. If you did, the IRS is out of luck.

Caution: The return must be complete and include an appraisal when required.

Smart Planning for Gift Recipients

Robert E. Harrison, attorney and CPA, chairman, tax consulting services, Eisner LLP, 750 Third Ave., New York City 10017.

Don't forget about planning for income taxes whenever you're the recipient of a gift of property. To compute the future gain or loss that will result from the disposition of the gift property for income tax purposes, you will need some information about the property from the gift maker. *Why...*

• **In computing gain on a disposition of the property,** the gift maker's basis in it carries over to the recipient.

• **In computing a loss on a disposition,** the recipient's basis is the lower of the gift maker's basis in the property or its fair market value on the date of the gift.

• **If the gift maker incurred gift tax on the transfer,** a portion of the tax may be added to the recipient's basis in the property.

How much: Basis may be increased by a percentage of the gift tax that equals the percentage that appreciation represents in the property's total fair market value.

Example: A person makes a gift of a property worth $100,000 in which he has a basis of $60,000, and upon which $45,000 of gift tax is due. The $40,000 of appreciation equals 40% of the property's market value. Therefore, $18,000 (40% of the gift tax) can be added to the $60,000 "carryover" basis, to give the gift recipient a basis of $78,000 in the property.

• **The gift maker's holding period carries over to the recipient.**

Impact: To compute future income taxes, the gift recipient needs documentation of the gift maker's basis in the property, its actual market value on the date of the gift, the amount of any gift tax paid on it and the gift maker's holding period in it. If the information is not readily available, reconstruct lost records to the extent that this is possible.

Note: Starting in 2010, donors must provide information about their gift to the recipient in order to avoid penalty.

Estate Tax Break

Many high-net-worth individuals can reduce inheritance and gift taxes by using a limited liability company (LLC). Place assets—such as real estate or closely held business interests—in an LLC and then give your heirs nonvoting, nontransferable interests. Because of voting and other restrictions, the IRS allows you to value the gifts of LLC interests at approximately 35% less than the value of the LLC's assets. That means you can put $1 million of assets into an LLC, give heirs 99% of all interests in the LLC and the gift will be only $643,500 —not $990,000 and less than the $1 million exemption amount.

Cynthia Della Torre, Esq., Kemp Klein Umphrey & Endelman, PC, Columbia Ctr., Suite 600, 201 W. Big Beaver Rd., Troy, MI 48084.

Before You Leave All Your Money to Your Kids...Read This!

Michael Stolper, president of Stolper & Co., financial consulting firm to foundations and high-net-worth families, 600 W. Broadway, San Diego 92101.

The days of leaving every penny to your children are disappearing. More and more of my clients, from middle-income to well-to-do, are choosing *not* to leave children or grandchildren the bulk of their estates.

Their concern: Passing along their fortunes does not pass along their values.

I urge my clients to deal with inheritance issues as soon as their net worth reaches the mid-six figures.

●**Decide what makes you feel good *and* responsible.** No matter how you allocate your resources, someone will feel hurt. It is fruitless to try to figure out what amount of money will make your children happy. *Instead, consider...*

●Your needs while you are still alive. Before you make decisions about giving away money while you're living, figure out how much you will need to retain your independence.

Example: A client needed income of $100,000 a year during his retirement to maintain his lifestyle. That meant his savings would have to generate $150,000 in income before taxes. Assuming a conservative 5% return on his money after inflation for the next 30 years, he required a lump sum of $3 million.

●The impact of inheritance money on your children, given their personalities and relationships with one another.

●Your values. Ask each child about his/her plans for the inheritance. If you disagree, leave money specifically for what you consider priorities—funding your grandchildren's educations, for example.

●Your feelings and financial commitment to nonfamily beneficiaries—friends, charities, etc.

●**Tell your heirs your plans early on** if you decide to leave only a limited amount to them. The natural impulse is to avoid dissension by keeping your wishes private until after your death. But an inheritance that is less than expected hurts more when it comes as a complete surprise. If you set the rules now, your children will know what to expect.

How to tell them: Speak to them in your home, not in an attorney's office or a public place. Say, "I have thought a lot about this and want to explain my rationale for what I have chosen to do. I hope you can be comfortable with how I want to order my affairs."

SLICING THE PIE

●**Make it equitable.** Whatever money you do leave your children should be divided equally and be subject to the same restrictions.

It may seem fair to give more to the child who is a struggling artist than to the successful businessman...or to put money in a trust for an irresponsible child. But nothing is more divisive to sibling relationships than a parent favoring one child over another.

●**Do not use incentives to change an heir's behavior after you die.** Many people like to impose specific personal conditions on beneficiaries, such as a child holding down a job or getting married before he receives any money. These carrot-and-stick schemes rarely work. By preventing your child from taking charge of his own life, these conditions breed deep resentment.

●**Give money in stages** if you are worried your heirs will quickly squander their inheritances. Set up a trust through an estate attorney to pay out inheritance money over your child's life cycle. For example, on a $1 million inheritance, he may receive $50,000 at the age of 21…$250,000 at 35…and the remainder after 40. This works well because people tend to handle money more responsibly as they age.

●**Consider involving children in charitable giving** while you are alive by starting a charitable trust.

Example: A client let his child act as the trustee and decide what charities would get income from the trust. This benefited everyone. My client got an annual gift tax break, which reflected the discount value of the donation. His child practiced handling large sums of money and became involved with charitable causes and the community.

Resource: For a database of more than 850,000 federally approved charities, visit *www.guidestar.com.*

There are no limits on how much you can give to a charity. But make sure the IRS recognizes your trust as an organization that has tax-exempt, nonprofit status.

Recommended reading: Immortality Made Easy by Paul Rampell (Parthenon)…*The Rich Die Richer and You Can Too* by William D. Zabel (Wiley).

taxes, you may need twice as much. Remember, federal estate tax isn't scheduled to be repealed until 2010 and may never be—and state death taxes continue to apply.

Also, income earned on the assets is subject to income tax at top rates—and the assets are "tied up." You can't spend them *and* bequeath them, too.

If you wish to make several such bequests, these problems are multiplied.

Alternative: Fund the bequest to the child with a $1 million life insurance policy held in a life insurance trust. *Why…*

●**A properly structured trust will be estate tax free**—reducing the assets you need by as much as half and cutting the IRS out of the deal.

●**Investment income** earned within the insurance policy will be tax free.

●**The dollar cost is very low** since the value of the policy is leveraged through tax savings.

Example: A married couple, both age 60, find they can buy a $1 million second-to-die life insurance policy (that pays on the death of the survivor) for an annual premium of about $13,000 a year for 15 years. They place the policy in a life insurance trust benefiting a child. Policy premiums are gift tax free, due to the couple's annual joint gift tax exclusion ($22,000 in 2003).

Payoff: The child will receive $1 million tax free at a maximum cash cost to the couple of only $195,000. And the after-tax cost may be as much as 50% less, as the $195,000 is removed from their taxable estate.

Make Your Heirs Rich At No Cost to You

Irving L. Blackman, CPA, founding partner, Blackman Kallick Bartelstein, LLP, 300 S. Riverside Plaza, Chicago 60606, *www.taxsecretsofthewealthy.com.*

If you want to make a major bequest to a child or grandchild, the smart way to do it may be to use life insurance instead of a bequest of property.

Say you want to leave $1 million to a grandchild. First you need at least that much in assets—and, after federal and local estate

When It's Best to Name Grandchildren as IRA Beneficiaries

Ed Slott, CPA, E. Slott & Co., CPAs, 100 Merrick Rd., Suite 200 E, Rockville Centre, NY 11570, *www.irahelp.com.* A practicing CPA for more than 20 years, Mr. Slott is a nationally recognized IRA distributions expert. He is publisher of *Ed Slott's IRA Advisor.* 800-663-1340.

Who should be named the beneficiary of your IRA? *Some guidance from a renowned IRA expert…*

First choice: Your spouse. He/she can roll over an inherited regular IRA or Roth IRA and name new beneficiaries.

Second choice: If you have children but no spouse, you'll probably name your child or children. After your death, these designated beneficiaries can spread out tax-free distributions over their life expectancies.

GRANDCHILDREN IN TRUST

Your children may be wealthy in their own right. Nevertheless, if they inherit a regular IRA, they will have to take minimum required distributions and pay the tax on them.

With either a regular or a Roth IRA, the cash from minimum required distributions will pile up...and may be subject to estate tax when your children die.

Solution: Instead of naming your children as beneficiaries, leave your IRA to your grandchild or grandchildren. This will give the account an extra generation of tax-deferred (regular IRA) or tax-free (Roth IRA) compounding.

What if you don't yet know whether to leave your IRA to your children or your grandchildren? Suppose your children are now in their 30s, working on their careers. By the time they inherit your IRA, years in the future, they may or may not need the additional cash.

Thanks to final IRS regulations issued in 2002, you now have a great deal of flexibility. You can name your children as beneficiaries and your grandchildren as *contingent* beneficiaries.

After your death, your children will have nine months to decide whether they'll need the IRA. If not, they can disclaim (give up) the inherited IRA, letting it pass to the next generation.

Alternative: You can name a trust as contingent beneficiary with your grandchildren as trust beneficiaries. The trustee will see that distributions are stretched out over your grandchildren's long life expectancies.

Example: A grandchild who inherits an IRA at age 15 will have an additional 67.9-year life expectancy for minimum required distributions. In year one, only 1.47% of the inherited account need be withdrawn. The other 98.53% can stay in the IRA.

Other benefits in naming a trust...

● **A trust can provide that your as-yet-unborn grandchildren will become IRA beneficiaries.**

● **Although income tax rates are high if money is retained in a trust,** that won't be a problem if the trust holds a tax-free Roth IRA.

GENERATION-SKIPPING TAX

If you leave an IRA to your grandchildren—outright or in trust—such bequests are subject to the generation-skipping transfer tax (GST)...on top of any estate tax due.

In 2003, the GST tax rate is 50%. This rate will gradually drop to 45% by 2007, disappear in 2010, and then reappear (at 55%) in 2011.

Good news: Each taxpayer is entitled to a $1,120,000 GST tax exemption in 2003. Starting in 2004, the GST tax exemption will increase to match with the estate tax exemption.

Example: Joe Smith dies in 2003, leaving $1.8 million to his grandson. Joe has not used up any of his GST tax exemption. Thus, $1.12 million would be exempt from GST tax while the other $680,000 would be taxed at 50%.

Any GST tax that has to be paid will be in addition to the federal gift or estate tax. In a worst-case scenario, grandparent-to-grandchild IRA bequests will be subject to estate tax and GST tax. Both rates will be around 50%. For example, leaving a $4 million Roth IRA to your grandchild might generate $3 million—or even more—in transfer taxes (estate and GST).

Most people will be wary of paying the GST tax. However, after all the number crunching, a family will come out ahead by stretching distributions over an extra generation. This result is likely even if a large GST tax must be paid.

The advantage (grandchild bequest vs. child bequest) is greater with a Roth IRA, because distributions will be tax free. This tactic also will be a wealth-builder if a regular IRA is used and the deferred distributions are taxable.

Key: The GST tax should be paid from non-IRA funds. This will keep the IRA intact for greater future growth.

EXTRA EFFORT

Why does it make sense to leave an IRA to a grandchild, even though your family will have to pay generation-skipping transfer tax? Because of tax deferral.

Suppose your son inherits your IRA when he is age 59. He'll have 26 years of compounding. But if your son's daughter inherits at age 23, she will have 60 years to stretch out distributions. That's an extra 34 years.

What's more, paying a GST tax may be pre-paying an estate tax on a smaller amount.

Example: At your death, when your son is age 59, you leave a $2 million IRA. If he disclaims in favor of your granddaughter, a GST tax will be due —and that could cost about $1 million.

Suppose that your son does not disclaim the IRA and takes distributions over his 25-year life expectancy. Those distributions, along with compound earnings, might add $8 million to your son's estate—and add $4 million to the estate tax.

Result: Paying the GST tax costs $1 million upfront, but saves your family $4 million down the road.

OUTSIDE CHANCE

As mentioned, leaving a Roth IRA to a grandchild may be an especially powerful strategy. That's because your grandchild will have an extra generation of income-tax-free buildup.

Required for Roth conversions…

• **Your income must be no greater than $100,000** in the year that you convert your regular IRA to a Roth.

• **You must possess substantial liquid assets** outside of the IRA in order to pay the tax on conversion.

Reason: Converting a $1 million IRA to a Roth IRA might add $400,000 to your income tax bill for the year. If you tap your Roth IRA to pay that tax bill, you would only have $600,000 left, for tax-free compounding.

More tax: You'll pay a 10% penalty if you convert before age 59½.

This strategy works best if you can pay the income tax bill from other non-IRA assets. Paying the income tax on a Roth IRA conversion removes substantial assets from your taxable estate without triggering a gift tax.

BILLION-DOLLAR BUILDUP

The real-life example below puts this strategy in perspective…

• **Paul Jones is wealthy enough to hold a $14 million regular IRA** and enough liquid assets to pay the income tax due on a Roth IRA conversion.

• **Paul has a substantial net operating loss,** which can reduce his adjusted gross income below $100,000 for the year, permitting the Roth IRA conversion.

• **Paul's advisers assume an 8% pretax return** on that account.

• **A $15 million GST tax payment is forecast** at the time of Paul's death, when the IRA is assumed to hold $30 million.

• **Paul's grandchild would then be 19,** able to stretch out distributions over an additional 64-year life expectancy.

Bottom line: Today's $14 million IRA may provide about $1.7 billion to Paul and his family, over 74 years.

Contrast: Leaving the IRA to Paul's son, age 59, who would have a 26-year stretchout, would avoid the GST tax and generate $700 million for the family.

In this scenario, the difference is an extra billion dollars, despite paying the GST tax.

Bequeath Your IRA To Charity

It has now become easier to name a charity as the beneficiary of your IRA or qualified retirement account.

Example: New IRS rules no longer require you to calculate minimum required distributions using a single life expectancy when a charity is an IRA or plan beneficiary. *Impact:* You can leave more money in such an account longer when it has a charitable beneficiary.

Strategy: If you leave an IRA or retirement account to heirs, they will owe income tax on distributions from it. So if you are planning to make a bequest to charity, you may do best by leaving the IRA or plan account to it, and leaving to heirs cash or other assets that they can take income tax free.

Seymour Goldberg, Esq., CPA, senior partner, Goldberg & Goldberg, PC, One Huntington Quadrangle, Melville, NY 11737, *www.goldbergira.com.*

Estate and Tax Planning Strategies for Unmarried Couples

Laurence I. Foster, CPA/PFS, former partner and currently consultant at Eisner LLP, 750 Third Ave., New York City 10017. Mr. Foster is former chairman, estate planning committee, New York State Society of Certified Public Accountants.

The federal tax and estate laws are written largely with married couples and single people in mind. Unmarried couples often have to take special steps to achieve what laws *automatically* provide to married couples.

PLANNING KEYS

A single person with a significant other has no legal "spouse" who usually inherits his/her estate and makes decisions on his behalf in event of incapacity.

An unmarried individual may have a legal "next of kin," but that may *not* be the person the individual wants to be his heir, or to be making decisions on his behalf.

Trap 1: If the single person is part of an unmarried couple, the next of kin may take actions contrary to the interests of the other member of the couple.

Trap 2: By law, the next of kin may become an unmarried person's sole heir. That can leave the surviving member of an unmarried couple completely disinherited.

Trap 3: The next of kin may obtain power of disposition over an incapacitated unmarried person's affairs, with power to cut off the other member of the couple.

If children—and sometimes even pets—are involved, potential conflicts may be even worse.

Vital: Unmarried individuals must have wills to direct the disposition of their assets. And they must prepare additional estate planning documents to direct their affairs in case of incapacity. These may include a health-care proxy, living will and durable power of attorney. All should be prepared by attorneys who specialize in the field and who know local law.

The documents also should provide for the guardianship and support of any minor children of the individuals.

Be sure that up-to-date beneficiary designations are made for insurance policies, pension plans, IRAs and investment accounts.

Trouble saver: Check to see if financial institutions have their own forms for documents, such as powers of attorney, that may give control over assets held by them. If so, use them.

Why: A financial institution might be suspicious if a nonrelative shows up to claim a client's accounts using an unfamiliar form. Delays and conflicts could result.

Benefits trap: Unmarried couples should take special care with employer-provided benefits, such as pensions.

Federal benefits law grants special rights to spouses, which may continue on even after divorce, while not providing the same rights to unmarried partners. One member of an unmarried couple may not be legally entitled to the expected pension benefits earned by the other.

Example: Very few company pension plans permit the surviving partner of a deceased unmarried worker to inherit the worker's vested pension benefits.

Carefully examine the status of retirement and other benefits with an expert. Develop a strategy to overcome this potential problem.

ESTATE TAX PLANNING

The federal estate tax continues on until at least 2010, despite its "repeal" in the new law. Unmarrieds are at a big disadvantage regarding estate tax because they have…

…one personal exempt amount, as opposed to two for couples.

…no unlimited marital deduction, to use to pass any amount to a spouse tax free.

Unmarrieds must take extra care with their estate tax planning.

Key: The amount of an individual's estate that is exempt from estate tax will increase from $1 million in 2003 to $3.5 million in 2009.

A married couple can utilize two exempt amounts by having a spouse make separate bequests in the exempt amount, while leaving the remainder of the estate to the other spouse, who can use a second exempt amount. As a result, the married couple can make total tax-free bequests rising from $2 million in 2003 to $7 million in 2009.

An unmarried individual with assets exceeding the exempt amount who wishes to avoid estate tax must reduce his estate by making transfers before death—such as by making tax-free gifts. *Strategies...*

●**The new tax law increased the dollar amount of lifetime gifts** one can make free of gift tax to $1 million in 2002 and thereafter.

●**The annual gift tax exclusion lets you make annual tax-free gifts** of up to $11,000 each to any number of recipients. These do not count against the $1 million lifetime limit.

Through a program of gift giving—especially of appreciating assets—an individual may reduce an estate to below the exempt amount.

Couples' trap: One member of an unmarried couple may be much wealthier than the other. If the wealthier member dies first and leaves everything to the other, his assets will be reduced by estate tax before passing to the survivor—reducing the survivor's wealth.

In addition, the assets will be subject to estate tax a second time when the survivor dies.

Strategy: A program of tax-free gifts made by the wealthier member to the other can be used to equalize wealth between them. In addition, the wealthier member can pay the medical expenses and tuition of the other. *Results...*

●Each member of the couple may come to own enough separate assets to use up a full personal exempt amount—matching the situation of a married couple.

●The less wealthy member of the couple gains more financial security from the gifts. Owning more wealth personally makes the individual less dependent on receiving a bequest should his partner die—and less vulnerable to challenges to such a bequest that may be made by third parties.

INCOME TAX PLANNING

The members of an unmarried couple also may have unequal incomes—leaving one paying a higher income tax rate than the other.

By shifting income from the higher-income to the lower-income member, an unmarried couple may equalize income and pay a lower combined tax rate overall. *How...*

●**Gifts of investment assets may move investment income** from high tax bracket rates into a lower tax bracket.

●**If the higher-income member owns a business,** hiring the lower-income member to work in it may produce a high-bracket business deduction for wages while having the wages taxed at a lower tax rate.

SECURITY

When the two people who comprise an unmarried couple have unequal wealth, the less wealthy individual may come to depend on the support of the other. He may become financially vulnerable should the wealthier member decide to end the relationship.

Trap: Unmarried couples do *not* have the legal rights to property division and support that married persons do—unless a palimony suit is instituted.

If the couple equalizes their wealth with gifts from the wealthier partner to the less wealthy one, there's a risk the latter will end the relationship after taking the gifts.

Security strategies: The interests of both partners can be protected by having the wealthier individual place assets in a trust for the benefit of the other. The trust can be designed to control the final disposition of assets according to certain terms and conditions.

Similarly, certain assets—such as business interests and real estate—may be held in a partnership formed by a couple. The partnership agreement can set the rights and obligations of both parties to the property, as well as control its ultimate disposition, much as a partnership-by-marriage would. *Note:* Gift tax may be due on certain transfers.

Important: Trusts and agreements should be drafted by an attorney who is an expert on the local laws governing such matters.

More from Laurence Foster...

What *Not* to Mention in Your Will

When preparing your will, do not mention the items that already have beneficiary designations, such as...

●**Trusts**
●**Life insurance policies**

●**Savings/investment accounts, including retirement plans.**

Distribution of these items is determined by the designation, not by anything you say in your will.

Exception: If you set up a bypass trust to leave money to grandchildren, your will must indicate how much of the estate will go to fund the trust.

Given the changing tax law, it is best to use a specific amount or percentage of assets, rather than designating "the maximum allowed by law."

For your personal effects, such as clothing, write an accompanying letter detailing who should receive each item. If you change your mind, it is much simpler to write a new letter than to redo your will. Give a copy of the letter to your lawyer.

Estate Planning Action Plan

The new tax law makes significant changes in the estate tax. Update your will and estate plan in light of them.

Key: Even if you won't owe estate tax, be sure to revise your will and estate plan periodically to accommodate changing personal and family circumstances.

Also update your beneficiary designations for your employer retirement plans, IRA accounts, life insurance policies, etc.

Best: If your estate adviser doesn't already call on you to check these items every other year or so, ask him/her to do so.

Kathleen O'Blennis, Esq., estate planner, The Castleman Law Firm, 5870 Stoneridge Mall Rd., Suite 207, Pleasanton, CA 94588.

What You Must Know About Being an Executor

Sanford J. Schlesinger, Esq., partner and head of the wills and estates department at the law firm Kaye Scholer LLP, 425 Park Ave., New York City 10022.

An executor's job is to ensure that the final wishes of the deceased are carried out. Being named executor is an honor, but it may not be the job for you.

Payoff: Helping the family and, in many cases, receiving an executor's fee set by state law or the terms of the will.

As an executor, you must...

●**Locate the deceased's will and file it with the appropriate court.** Only after the will has been formally accepted by the court can you be appointed the representative of the estate.

Caution: If you're named as executor under the will, your responsibility for protecting the assets of the estate starts *before* the court makes it official.

Don't let heirs come into the deceased's home and pick it clean before you've had a chance to inventory personal effects and determine their value.

●**Gather and protect assets.** This means handling securities as a conservative investor would. The estate needs cash to pay taxes and other costs. Typically, it's wise for the executor to convert some assets to cash for this purpose.

Do *not* let a declining stock market deter you from selling assets. One executor was reluctant to sell while stock prices fell. When he later sold off assets at even lower prices to raise needed cash, he was sued by beneficiaries for breaching his responsibilities.

●**Notify the beneficiaries named in the will.** Also notify, depending on state law, individuals who might have a legal right to challenge the will—such as those who would inherit under state law if there had been no will.

●**Obtain several copies of the death certificate.** You'll need them when dealing with banks, brokerage firms, life insurance companies and others.

•**Arrange for the payment of the estate's liabilities.** These include bank loans, auto loans and outstanding bills.

•**File for benefits.** These include those from Social Security (*www.ssa.gov*), Veterans Benefits Administration (*www.vba.va.gov*), fraternal organizations, civil service organizations and former employers. Also file for life insurance payable to the estate.

•**Set up banking and brokerage accounts for the estate.** You'll especially need a checking account to pay funeral expenses, taxes, legal fees and other administrative costs.

•**File estate tax returns where required.** This often entails getting appraisals for various assets to complete the returns. Income tax returns may also be necessary.

•**Wind things up.** File an accounting of assets, liabilities and payments with the court if necessary to end the estate and be discharged from the executor's position.

COMMON PROBLEMS

As executor, you may be personally liable (for unpaid estate taxes, etc.) if you distribute assets before taxes and other estate obligations are satisfied. *Traps to avoid...*

•**Failing to locate assets.** You must inventory and place a value on everything in the estate, by appraisal if necessary.

This includes jewelry, art and antiques, personal effects, residences, business property, cars, stocks, bonds, life insurance policies owned by the deceased or payable to the estate, bank accounts, the contents of safe-deposit boxes, IRAs and qualified retirement plan benefits.

Best: Have the deceased's mail forwarded to you to check on statements about investments and bills relating to assets.

If assets turn up *after* the estate is settled, the estate may have to be reopened—with some or all of the same formalities as in the initial process.

•**Failing to file tax returns.** For 2002 and 2003, an estate valued at $1 million or less as of the date of death is exempt from federal estate tax (and may also be exempt from state death taxes).

Even if no tax will be due—if everything is left to a spouse, for example—a return must still be filed if the $1 million valuation threshold is exceeded.

The estate may also have to file income tax returns if it receives income in excess of $600 for the tax year—from dividends or bond interest—during the probate period.

•**Using your own funds to pay estate expenses.** An executor has no legal responsibility to do this. These expenses should be paid by the estate.

WHEN TO ASK FOR HELP

The responsibilities of being an executor can seem overwhelming. *Get assistance from...*

•**An attorney** qualified in estate administration to handle probate and administration.

•**An accountant** to put together the estate tax return.

•**An insurance broker** experienced in filing insurance claims.

The upside of getting professional help is that there's less for you to do (although you remain responsible for and must sign court documents, tax returns, etc.).

But—professionals will be paid with money from the estate, leaving less for heirs. *To help you decide...*

•**Use professionals if the estate is complex**—sizable assets, complex assets, disgruntled heirs, an ambiguous will or guardianship of young children.

•**Do it yourself if the estate is simple**—a house, bank account, insurance policy and no squabbling heirs, for example. The clerk of the probate court can assist you with filing papers yourself.

If small enough, the estate may even qualify for a simplified probate process.

WHEN TO SAY "NO"

•**When you lack the time and/or skills to meet the responsibilities.** The estate may be too complex for you to handle without professional help.

•**When your relationship with the heirs is strained.** For example, if you are named co-executor with your brother and sister and you've always been the loser in sibling battles, you may want to decline the appointment. With multiple executors, the majority usually rules. You don't want to be the minority—again.

•When there's a conflict of interest—for example, the deceased is your business partner, whose share you'd like to purchase.

Proper Power of Attorney Filing

Draft a power of attorney, and send it to financial institutions and other organizations that may have to honor it in the future. Some firms will not accept a power of attorney unless it is prepared in a certain way or additional forms are filed. Find out the requirements now to avoid possible problems later.

Jonathan Pond, president, Financial Planning Information, Inc., Watertown, MA, and the author of Your Money Matters: 21 Tips for Achieving Financial Security in the 21st Century *(Perigee).*

Correct Timing of Year-End Gifts

Make year-end gifts to family members early enough for the checks to clear the bank before year-end. And tell recipients to deposit checks promptly, so they do clear by year-end.

Why: Gifts made by check generally are not final until the check clears the bank, because the maker of the gift can stop payment on the check until then. The courts have upheld gifts in cases where checks were cashed or deposited by the recipient before year-end even though they didn't clear until later—but there's no reason to invite IRS scrutiny.

When checks are not deposited until after year-end, gift treatment may be disallowed—resulting in the loss of your gift tax exclusion.

Robert Rosano, ED NY, No. 97-CV-5361 (JS); 84 AFTR2d ¶99-5391 [Doc 1999-32489].

Useful Web Sites

Financial Planning

☐ Compute Your Net Worth

http://finance.yahoo.com

Compute your net worth by filling out a form provided on-line.

☐ Family Financial Planning

www.msmoney.com

Create a financial plan that works for your family, whether you are just starting out or planning to retire. Click on "Life Planning."

☐ Financial Planning Goals

http://us.etrade.com/e/t/plan/getstarted

Get help setting your retirement or education savings goals.

☐ For the Basics

www.metlife.com

Offers information on a variety of financial topics, including choosing a financial adviser, planning your estate, making a will, creating a budget and more. Click on "Meeting Life," then "Financial."

☐ Money Goals

http://money.cnn.com/pf/101/lessons/1

Helps you clearly define your money goals so you can start working toward them.

☐ Prudential Life Insurance Investments

www.prudential.com/finplanning

Information on life insurance. Click on "Life Insurance Planning – A Useful Tool."

☐ Salomon Smith Barney Calculators

www.salomonsmithbarney.com

All kinds of financial calculators—loan and mortgage, Roth vs. traditional IRA, investment and more. Go to "Tools," then click on "Financial Planning Tools."

Investing

☐ Annuities

www.annuitysite.com

Answers all your questions about annuities—different types, benefits, how to choose, etc.

☐ Bonds

http://university.smartmoney.com

Explains how bonds work. Click on "Investing 101," then scroll down to "Bonds."

☐ Financial Forecast Center

www.forecasts.org/info/stock.htm

Want to find out more about the stock market before investing? Here you'll learn how stocks work and how to buy them.

☐ Mutual Fund Watcher

www.funddemocracy.com

Articles on mutual fund practices, policies and rules that are harmful to shareholders. Keep up-to-date on the latest scams.

☐ Investing Without a Broker

www.weidnerinvest.com

Learn about long-term investing that doesn't require the use of a broker. Plus, you'll get ideas on children's investments, retirement planning, family-wealth building, reducing taxes and more.

☐ IRA Help

www.irahelp.com

How to protect your IRAs, 401(k)s and other retirement accounts from the IRS.

☐ Roth IRA Basics

www.rothira.com

Learn all about Roth IRAs. The site includes articles, calculators, the latest news and more.

☐ Janus Mutual Funds
www.janus.com

Find out more about mutual funds and how they can help you achieve your investment goals. Also includes Web links. Click on "Investing Basics."

☐ Mid-Cap Funds
www.firstamericanfunds.com

Discover how the mid-cap funds can provide growth potential for your portfolio. Click on "Mutual Funds," then go to "Mid-Cap Funds."

☐ Researcher's Top Picks
www.morningstar.com

Simply click on "Our Favorite Stocks," under the category "Stock Research."

☐ Mutual Fund Investor's Center
www.mfea.com

Designed as a resource for investors who want to use mutual funds to achieve their financial goals, this site has a large collection of investing calculators, Web site links, fund listings and planning, tracking and monitoring tools.

☐ Portfolio Management
www.thomsonfn.com

Thomson Financial Solutions provides a comprehensive portfolio-management tool to help you meet your wealth objectives. Click on "Portfolio."

☐ Ric Edelman's Advice
www.ricedelman.com

Ric Edelman, a well-known and respected financial adviser, gives his Top 40 tips for investing. Click on "Financial Basics," then scroll down.

☐ Socially Responsible Funds
www.efund.com

At Citizens Funds, you'll find a family of socially responsible no-load funds for an array of investment objectives. Click on "Individual Investors," then on "Socially Responsible Funds."

☐ American Express Financial
http://americanexpress.com

Advice on investing, banking and loans, insurance, retirement and more. Click on "Financial Services."

Retirement

☐ Retirement Planning
http://academy.retire.cigna.com

Plan for a more financially secure and rewarding retirement by taking this free on-line course. Click on "Getting Your Retirement Plan Underway."

☐ Social Security On-Line
www.ssa.gov

Here you can apply for Social Security benefits, request a Medicare replacement card, get Medicare and Medicaid information and more.

☐ Retirement Locations
www.retirenet.com

Find the right retirement home, anywhere in the country...by size, price, location or any combination of factors.

Estate Planning

☐ Estate Planning Links
www.estateplanninglinks.com

Contains hundreds of links to estate planning, elder law, tax and related Web sites.

Seniors

☐ AARP's Tax-Aide
www.aarp.org/taxaide/is.html

Free tax help from trained volunteers for those who are age 60 and over (from February 1 to April 15). Find a help center near you at this Web site.

☐ Modern Maturity
www.modernmaturity.org

Information to help you enjoy your health, wealth and leisure time. Read some articles, play the games and take part in on-line discussions.

☐ Seniors' Rights
www.seniorlaw.com

Covers elder law issues, Medicare, Medicaid, estate planning, trusts and the rights of the elderly and disabled.

13

Smarter Travel

You're Never Too Old for Adventure Travel

Even if you're over age 50 it doesn't mean you have to give up outdoor adventure. Some of the most exciting adventures are not hugely expensive, and don't require much physical stamina either. *My favorites...*

LEARN TO SCUBA DIVE

Scuba diving is a great escape for people of all ages. With modern fins, you can glide underwater with minimal effort. While air tanks are heavy, once you're in the water, you will essentially be weightless. Divemasters will help you check out your equipment and guide you to underwater attractions.

Learning to dive usually requires lessons over a few weekends.

Typical cost: About $250 to $450.

Instruction is offered by shops that sell diving equipment, YMCAs and some universities.

Look in the *Yellow Pages* under "Diving" and "Scuba," or get in touch with the Professional Association of Diving Instructors (800-729-7234 or *www.padi.com*).

Once you learn how, try a scuba vacation in the Florida Keys or Cayman Islands, where undersea life abounds.

Typical cost: About $45 to $85 for a half-day dive trip. Equipment rental costs extra.

Some scuba tour operators provide a chance to dive alongside dolphins. Among my most favorite operators is Underwater Explorers Society (800-992-3483 or *www.unexso.com*).

RIDE IN A HOT AIR BALLOON

If you have never risen silently above the trees to see the world as birds see it, hot air ballooning can be an unforgettable thrill.

To participate, check out the dozens of regional balloon clubs. The Balloon Federation of

Paul McMenamin, the author of *National Geographic Ultimate Adventure Sourcebook* (National Geographic Society). Mr. McMenamin is an adventure consultant in Santa Barbara, CA.

America (515-961-8809 or *www.bfa.net*) publishes a directory of members. You can also find a balloon ride company in the *Yellow Pages*.

Typical cost: $139 to $169 per person for a one-hour flight, often with brunch included.

A good place to try ballooning is at one of the many balloon festivals. The annual International Balloon Fiesta, held in Albuquerque, New Mexico, takes place every fall. One of the top balloon tour operators in that area is World Balloon (800-351-9588, *www.worldballoon.com*).

TOUR IN A RECREATIONAL VEHICLE

For about $130 a day, plus gasoline, you can rent an RV and enjoy the advantages *without* the responsibility of ownership. And, for a standard two-axle RV, you won't need a special driver's license.

Most RV rental companies offer one-way arrangements, so you can rent a vehicle in one city and drop it off in another.

My favorite RV excursion: Rent an RV in Las Vegas, then circle through the Zion, Bryce Canyon and Arches National Parks in Utah, and conclude with Monument Valley and the Grand Canyon or Lake Powell in Arizona. These parks offer some of the most spectacular scenery in the US.

Cruise America is one of the major RV rental companies in the US (800-327-7799 or *www.cruiseamerica.com*).

GO ON AN ARCHAEOLOGICAL DIG

Archaeologists always need volunteers to help them uncover fossils and artifacts—from mammoth bones to ancient relics.

Working on an expedition puts you in contact with dedicated people and lets you see places that you might not otherwise visit.

One organization that sponsors volunteer programs is Earthwatch Institute, which runs various programs throughout the world (800-776-0188 or *www.earthwatch.org*).

Caution: Archaeological volunteer work can be strenuous. Before signing up, ask about the level of exertion required.

GO ON AN AFRICAN SAFARI

Safaris can cost less than you might think—especially if you choose a safari company that operates its own camps.

Typical cost: As low as $300 a day plus airfare—though $400 and up a day (excluding the airfare) is typical.

Two top safari companies are Abercrombie & Kent (800-323-7308 or *www.abercrombiekent.com*) and Overseas Adventure Travel (800-955-1925 or *www.oattravel.com*).

Kenya, South Africa and Zambia are safe as long as you stay with the safari group. Before departing, consult the US Department of State (202-663-1225 or *http://travel.state.gov*), which provides information about all countries, consular information sheets and travel warnings.

The department also advises travelers on vaccinations and other health requirements.

TAKE A RIVERBOAT TRIP

Sailing on a canal boat down a waterway in France, Holland, Belgium, England, Ireland or Scotland offers a leisurely way to see the countryside, sample the food and meet the locals.

You can hire a cabin cruiser as small as 22 feet in length, which is adequate for up to four people. But it's more common to hire a larger vessel for up to 12 passengers. In addition to a captain, these barges usually come with an onboard chef who specializes in the local cuisine.

Typical cost: About $300 to $650 and up a day per person.

Barge tour operators include Le Boat (800-992-0291 or *www.leboat.com*) and eWaterways (800-546-4777 or *www.ewaterways.com*).

Among riverboat tours in the US, some of the most exciting are on the Columbia River, which marks the border between Oregon and Washington. The breathtaking views are the same ones that Lewis and Clark saw nearly 200 years ago.

Riverboat operators include Sternwheeler Columbia Gorge & Marine Park (800-643-1354 or *www.sternwheeler.com*).

Fun Family Getaways for Toddlers to Teens

Susan Farewell, a Westport, Connecticut–based travel writer. She is the author of several books, including *Quick Escapes from New York City* (Globe Pequot) and *Hidden New England* (Ulysses).

You've got a five-year-old who is in total ecstasy just climbing the monkey bars at your local playground and a teenager who finds everything a bore. Where do you go for a family vacation everyone can enjoy?

DUDE RANCH

Horseback riding is just one of the many activities you will find at ranches. There are rodeos, fishing, tennis, hiking, even spa treatments. Come sundown, you can participate in chuck wagon dinners, square dances, yodeling contests and bonfires.

To find a ranch that's a good fit for your family, contact The Dude Ranchers' Association, 307-587-2339 or *www.duderanch.org.*

INN-TO-INN BIKING

Biking is great fun for an active family. Kid-oriented companies offer trips that even young children can take. Just attach a child's trailer to the back of your bike. For children who can ride by themselves, there are kid-sized itineraries—with extended routes for parents—plus children's menus and activities. Companies provide bikes and helmets, schedule meals and arrange for a van to carry luggage to inns each night.

Backroads has itineraries around the world. 800-462-2848 or *www.backroads.com.*

RIDE THE RAPIDS

Many outfitters and river guides take inexperienced rafters down some of America's most beautiful rivers. The minimum age ranges from five to seven. Each company has its own style regarding pace, meals and campsites.

Example: Some outfitters set up camp and cook all the meals, while others expect guests to participate. Trips can range from one day to longer than a week.

My favorite outfitters…

● **American River Tourist Association,** 800-323-2782 or *www.arta.org.*

● **Dvorak's Kayak & Rafting Expeditions,** 800-824-3795 or *www.dvorakexpeditions.com.*

● **Outdoor Adventure River Specialists (OARS),** 800-346-6277 or *www.oars.com.*

HEAD FOR CAMP

You don't have to be a child to go to camp. Family camps, which offer programs for adults and children of all ages, are becoming increasingly popular.

One standout is the Tyler Place Family Resort in Highgate Springs, Vermont (802-868-4000 or *www.tylerplace.com*). Guests can stay in cottages or lodge suites and can choose from biking, hiking, kayaking, canoeing, waterskiing and tennis. The kids join their age groups, which meet from 8:30 am to 1:30 pm and again from 5:30 pm to 8:30 pm. Activities include swimming, pony rides, camping and cookouts.

HIT THE SLOPES

Ski areas are tailor-made for families. They have ski school for kids as young as age three …camp or day care for younger children…and slopes for older kids and adults. Other activities include skating, sledding, swimming and tennis …plus child-friendly restaurants.

Here are some family ski areas that have the terrain and facilities to please all ages…

● **Breckenridge, Colorado,** 800-789-7669 or *www.breckenridge.snow.com.*

● **Squaw Valley, Lake Tahoe, California,** 800-403-0206 or *www.squaw.com.*

● **Waterville Valley, New Hampshire,** 800-468-2553 or *www.waterville.com.*

For an Inexpensive Foreign Vacation…

Consider visiting Canada for a cheaper foreign vacation. The favorable US–Canadian exchange rate makes travel north a bargain. Two hot destinations are Muskoka, a region of luxury resorts, golf courses, shoreline condos and crystal lakes, two hours from Toronto Airport (golf packages and other tour packages are available)…and French speaking Quebec, on the scenic St. Lawrence River.

Rudy Maxa, publisher, *Rudy Maxa's Traveler,* 1322 18 St. NW, Suite 310, Washington, DC 20036, *www.rudy maxa.com.*

More from Rudy Maxa…

Better Luggage Security

Put your cell phone number—and nothing else—on a luggage tag. *Or:* Use just your E-mail address—not your home address—on luggage, if you will be able to access E-mail while traveling.

Reasons: Thieves monitoring the airport will not be able to find out your home address.

Enjoy the World Outside Disney World

Herbert J. Teison, retired editor, *Travel Smart,* 40 Beechdale Rd., Dobbs Ferry, NY 10522.

If you are planning to take a trip to Disney World, be sure you make the most of the many opportunities that exist in the surrounding area…

LODGING

Staying inside the park keeps you close to the rides—but will cost much more. It also limits you to Disney restaurants and makes it hard to take advantage of outside attractions.

Off-site hotels generally offer more for the money, plus a broader range of facilities and dining. They also save you from "overdosing" on Mickey.

Many hotels offer their own attractions.

Example: The Hotels of the Marriott Village—about one mile from the Magic Kingdom—are home to "Arthur," star of the PBS cartoon series that is a favorite of many children.

ATTRACTIONS

Non-Disney attractions well worth considering include…

- **Cypress Gardens,** where flowers bloom 365 days a year.
- **Ripley's Believe It or Not! Odditorium.**
- **Sea World Aquarium.**
- **Sea World's Discovery Cove,** where you can swim with dolphins.
- **Universal's "Island of Adventure,"** with tropical-themed movie rides like Jurassic Park.
- **Universal's "Ride the Movies" attractions.**

Free Orlando Magic Cards are available to help you save on hotels, restaurants and attractions throughout the area. Persons over age 50 can obtain extra savings with the *Mature Traveler's Guide.* Call 800-646-2087 or visit *www. orlandoinfo.com* for information on both.

More from Herbert Teison…

Keeping Safe When Staying in Hotels

To minimize risk of being the victim of theft or robbery when you are staying in a hotel…

- **Learn the type of hotel it is** when you make your reservation. No-frills establishments charge less, but may lack enough staff to watch the premises.
- **When you check in,** don't let others hear your room number.
- **Don't flash cash,** jewelry or other expensive items.
- **Deposit all valuables** in the hotel or in-room safe.
- **Don't take a room that opens directly on to a pool area,** central garden or terrace from which someone could gain entry—or a thief could make an easy escape. *Better:* A room on the third floor or higher—but not so high that it can't be reached by a fire ladder (about 13 floors).
- **Ask a bellhop or other hotel employee to accompany you** when you take your bags to your room.
- **Lock the door when you leave your room**—no matter how briefly you'll be out. (Be sure to take your key or key card with you.) Double-lock the room while in it. Keep windows and adjoining doors locked.

●**Don't let anyone enter the room** without verifying who he/she is. If the person claims to be providing a hotel service that you haven't ordered, call the front desk to verify it.

●**Don't hang the "maid service" sign on your door when you aren't in**—this advertises that the room is empty. Instead, call housekeeping or speak with the housekeeper directly.

Check out the extent to which your existing insurance coverage protects you while traveling. Homeowner's insurance and credit cards *may* provide protection—but know the limits. If they are insufficient, obtain supplemental coverage.

Also from Herbert Teison...

Save on Car Rentals

If you're renting for less than one week, you will get the cheapest rates at a major company—Avis, Budget, Hertz, National or Thrifty. *For rentals of one week or longer:* You may do better with a small, local company.

●**Ask about discounts for members of national organizations** (such as AAA or AARP)...frequent-flier programs...or credit card affinity programs.

●**See if your employer has negotiated a corporate rate** that you are entitled to use.

●**Beware of fees for an extra driver** and one-way rentals with big drop-off charges.

●**Check the basic rental rate** against advertised discounts.

●**If you're forced to take a compact when you reserved a sedan,** ask for a 10% discount.

●**Pick up the car downtown** to save on airport surcharges.

●**Don't take Collision Damage Waiver (CDW) insurance** if your personal auto policy or major credit card covers it.

●**Return the car with a full tank of gas.**

Finally from Herbert Teison...

Sail Through Airport Security

Getting through tightened airport security does not have to be an ordeal. Follow these helpful suggestions and you'll sail through...

●**Remove all metal from your person.** That includes shoes with taps and belts with metal, braces worn for medical reasons.

If you have any surgically implanted metal or you wear a metal brace, get a note from your physician. Give the note to the security guard before being scanned.

●**Don't wrap presents.** You may be asked to open them. Send wrapped presents ahead by mail.

●**Clean out all carry-on bags of anything that could be suspicious**—corkscrews, manicure scissors, nail files, any kind of knives, etc.

●**Give yourself extra time.** That way, if you—or the people ahead of you—are detained, you won't feel the irritation of time pressure.

Good idea: Before leaving for the airport, examine the full list of items prohibited from carry-on luggage and from the persons of travelers. It's on the FAA Web site at *www.faa.gov.* Click on "Security Tips for Air Travelers."

Airplane Anxiety Self-Defense

Mary Schiavo, Esq., former Inspector General at the US Department of Transportation, now a partner in the law firm of Baum, Hedlund, Aristei, Guilford & Schiavo, Los Angeles. She is author of *Flying Blind, Flying Safe* (available through the National Air Disaster Alliance/Foundation, *www.planesafe.org*).

Barton Blinder, MD, PhD, clinical professor of psychiatry and human behavior, College of Medicine, University of California/Irvine, and a psychiatrist in private practice, Newport Beach, CA.

Airplane travel is unnerving these days, but crashes are still statistically rare. *To maximize safety and minimize stress...*

AIRPLANE SAFETY
Mary Schiavo

●**Fly the major carriers** from developed countries that...

●Do even more than the US government requires for security. The government does not track this information. Ask the airlines directly—it's something they boast about. You want a 100% bag-to-passenger match.

•Have newer airplanes—with average age under 10 years. US examples—Continental, Jet-Blue and Southwest. Many of the major foreign carriers also have young fleets—including JAL, Lufthansa and Qantas.

Note: The newer models are risky in their first two years, when the glitches are still being resolved. However, all models now in service are past this risky period.

Next to impossible: Finding out in advance the exact plane you will be flying.

•**Avoid flying in bad weather,** one of the biggest risk factors for an accident.

•**Fly nonstop.** Most accidents occur during takeoff or landing.

FLIGHT ANXIETY
Barton Blinder

•**Plan your itinerary carefully.** Avoid peak travel times. Use secondary airports rather than major ones. Give yourself plenty of time to get through security checks.

•**Do relaxation exercises** starting two days before and during your flight.

•**Avoid antianxiety medications.** They can impair mental and physical function.

•**Keep your mind occupied** with interesting reading or paperwork.

•**Keep in touch with family and friends.** Call from the airport or plane.

•**Remind yourself that the real risk of danger remains extremely low.**

Best Senior Discount Airfares

Southwest Airlines offers special fares for seniors with the highest fare capped at $129 one-way.* You could end up with as much as 65% off. Eligibility age is 65 plus.

Discounts for companions: Alaska Airlines offers a 10% senior discount on regular fares for people age 62 and older—and will allow the discount for a person under age 62 who travels with a senior.

Jens Jurgen, editor, *Travel Companion Exchange,* Box 833, Amityville, NY 11701, *www.travelcompanions.com.*

*Price subject to change.

How to Find Cheap Airfare

For the lowest airfare, have a travel agent check airline reservation systems over the weekend, when fare changes are posted. Take an off-peak flight—late-night, midday and midweek flights have more sale seats available. If you just miss a sales deadline, find a reservations desk or travel agent in a different time zone—where the deadline has not yet passed. Call Directory Assistance for the airline's local reservations number in a city in that time zone—the airline should honor it.

Laura E. Quarantiello, California-based freelance writer and author of *Air-Ways: The Insider's Guide to Air Travel* (Tiare).

 # Another Low-Airfare Strategy

To get the lowest possible airfare, ask the travel agent *more than once.* In a recent survey only 51% of travel agents disclosed all low-fare flights when first asked. An additional 12% gave the information when asked again. Twenty-five percent of agents *never* gave information on all low-cost flights.

Self-defense: Work with the same reliable agent regularly…check prices on the airlines' Web sites even if an agent handles your bookings.

Survey of 840 travel agents by *Consumer Reports Travel Letter,* 101 Truman Ave., Yonkers, NY 10703.

Airport Parking Bargain

Near-airport parking can be a better deal than parking at the airport. Airport lots tend to be crowded and inconvenient, with slow and intermittent shuttle service. Near-airport lots usually charge a little more than long-term airport lots, but they provide faster and more convenient service. Some near-airport facilities offer valet parking. Others will wash and detail your vehicle while you are away—or even change the oil.

Martin Nesbitt, president, The Parking Spot, Chicago-based operator of near-airport lots in eight US cities, quoted in National Geographic Traveler, *1145 17 St. NW, Washington, DC 20036.*

Let Your Hotel Buy Your Gasoline

Independent hotels nationwide are providing special incentives to travelers who frequent them through the FrequentDriverMiles.com program.

Most participating hotels will reimburse you for a gasoline receipt dated the day you arrive (they buy your gas). Others provide discounts on room rates based on the number of miles you drive to get there.

Other incentives are available, as well as bargain rates to guests who book rooms through the program's Web site.

Member hotels are located in 21 states, with more joining quickly. Hotels are in all categories of quality and price range.

To find a hotel near your destination and get a good deal, visit *www.frequentdrivermiles.com.*

Don't Waste Frequent-Flier Miles

Don't let unused frequent-flier miles go to waste. Many hotel chains will allow guests to apply frequent-flier miles to their bills. Or consider donating miles to charity—contact your airline for information. Be aware that this donation is not tax deductible. You can also visit *www.milepoint.com* to use your miles to purchase merchandise.

If you think the airline that issued your miles might go out of business, go to *www.privilege flyer.com,* which offers an insurance plan to redeem unused frequent-flier miles.

Randy Petersen, publisher, InsideFlyer, *1930 Frequent Flyer Pt., Colorado Springs 80915.*

Home-Exchange Vacations

Roy Prince, owner of HomeExchange.com, featuring listings in more than 80 countries, Santa Barbara, CA.

Looking for a less expensive vacation? Consider exchanging homes. This type of service is provided in California, New York, Paris, London and other locations.

Advantages: You eliminate hotel costs and, often, car-rental fees—a car sometimes comes with the house—and save money on eating out.

To find a home exchange: Post your own ad and answer ads for a fee on home-exchange Web sites, such as *www.homeexchange.com… www.exchangehomes.com…www.digsville.com.*

Before exchanging: Build trust with your exchange partner with lots of pretrip communication…mention any concerns up front—if, for example, you don't permit any smoking in your home. Exchange partners should sign a written agreement and—for final assurance of commitment—exchange copies of their airline tickets. Exchangers who stay in your home for up to 30 days are considered guests and should be covered by your homeowner's insurance—verify this with your insurer. For any periods that are longer than 30 days, ask your insurance company about additional coverage.

221

Another Hotel Alternative

When a vacation stay will exceed a week, consider renting an apartment or condo. It may be not only less expensive but more convenient than a hotel.

Example: You'll have your own kitchen, so you'll be able to eat what and when you want at less cost than if you rely on restaurants. Many apartments and condos are in buildings with doormen, concierge and housekeeping services—just like hotels. In some areas, they come with customary extras—in Hawaii often with a car, in Mexico with a housekeeper or cook.

The only snag for most travelers is learning about the available rentals, so check with your travel agent.

The Mature Traveler, Box 1543, Wildomar, CA 92595.

Shrewd Ways Into a "Booked" Restaurant

Mark Brenner, author of *Tipping for Success: Secrets for How to Get In and Get Great Service* (Brenmark House) and founder of Brenmark House, a marketing solutions think tank for companies that require branding, marketing, sales and advertising strategies, Sherman Oaks, CA, *www.brenmarkhouse.com.*

Anyone can get a last-minute reservation at a popular restaurant that is booked solid—*if* you know what to say and how to tip.

Here's what to do when you call at the last minute and are told no tables are available…

●**Ask to speak with the maitre d'.** Get his/her name before your call is transferred.

●**When the maitre d' picks up, address him by his first name,** and give your own full name. That creates the impression that you have been to the restaurant before and know him.

●**Give your name, and say with empathy, "I know how busy you are tonight.** But if you could find a way to have a table

for me at 8 pm, I would be happy to take care of you the right way." This language may feel uncomfortable or cagey, but it is the language that service professionals recognize.

Helpful: Never mention a dollar figure—it is offensive and demeans his craft. Be precise in what you want. Otherwise you could end up eating at 5 pm or midnight.

●**If the answer is still no, take one last shot.** Say, "I don't mind waiting in the bar for a bit if it would help you out." Your flexibility lets him know that you are experienced and not unreasonable.

●**If you get a table, tip the maitre d' discreetly** (no one should ever see). Give him the folded bill(s) in your handshake.

The tip amount depends on the caliber of the restaurant, how badly you want to get in and how hard the maitre d' had to work to get you the table—$10 is enough for a good restaurant on a typical night…$20 to $50 for more extreme circumstances, such as conventions, holidays, etc.

VALET PARKING: KEEPING YOUR CAR UP FRONT

When your waiter hands you your check, hand him/her your valet ticket stub, and ask him to give it to the valet, so that your car is waiting up front by the time you pay the bill and leave the restaurant.

Travel Alone Without Being Alone

Nadine Nardi Davidson, travel consultant for Travel Store, Inc., Los Angeles, and the author of several books, including *Traveling With Others Without Wishing They'd Stayed Home* (Prince Publishing).

If you've never traveled alone, you may want to ease into the experience. *Start off with one of the following…*

●**Cruise.** An easy way to travel alone. You can enjoy the company of others at meals, during activities or sitting by the pool.

●**Escorted tour.** Join a tour of 10 to 40 people led by a professional guide—enjoy company by day and a room of your own during the night.

Advantages: Rooms and dining arrangements are booked for you. The itinerary is preset so you don't have to concern yourself about directions or bus or train schedules.

Drawbacks: Time is regimented. Free time is minimal.

Tour rates are based on double occupancy, so you'll pay a bit more when you travel alone. To get a cheaper rate, agree to share a room on the trip. Some tours may match you up with a fellow traveler.

Elderhostel arranges group tours specifically for people age 55 or older (877-426-8056 or *www.elderhostel.org*).

●**Hosted tour.** You fly on your own to your destination, but you're met at the airport and driven to a hotel where a room has been reserved for you. Once there, you're on your own. One or two group tours of the cities may be included in the package.

●**All-inclusive resorts**—such as Beaches (800-467-8737) and Club Med (800-258-2633) —will match you up with a roommate if you wish. *Included:* Airfare, accommodations, meals, entertainment, sports instruction, etc.

Dining is typically family-style, so there are plenty of opportunities to meet people.

More Help for Solo Travelers

Singles who travel face a world of double-occupancy tours and inflated prices. But a new guide to single-friendly tour companies and solo travel opportunities is available at *www.travelaloneandloveit.com*. The site links up to resources for single travelers, answers questions, has an E-mail newsletter and recommends single-friendly destinations, hotels, restaurants and travel agents.

Basic Travel-Medicine Kit

For a basic travel-medicine kit, include cold remedy…insect repellent containing DEET …sunblock with at least SPF 15…lip balm… foot-care products, such as blister pads and athlete's foot treatment…diarrhea remedy, such as *loperamide* (Imodium AD)…pain reliever, such as *acetaminophen* (Tylenol) or *ibuprofen* (Advil) …an antibiotic ointment, such as Neosporin… bandages, gauze and adhesive tape…tweezers …scissors…laxatives…thermometer.

Women should carry tampons or sanitary napkins…and medication for yeast infections. Keep everything—prescription and over-the-counter—in their original containers. Pack in carry-on luggage so there is no risk of loss.

If you must carry needles, syringes or other prescription medications: Get a letter from your doctor describing your diagnosis and the reasons you are using these products.

Mary Nettleman, MD, division chairperson, general internal medicine, associate dean for primary care and professor of medicine, Virginia Commonwealth University, Richmond.

Medical Emergencies Overseas—It Pays to Be Prepared

Louise Weiss, an award-winning travel writer based in New York City. She is a contributor to many travel books and publications and the author of *Access to the World: A Travel Guide for the Handicapped* (Henry Holt).

Just imagine for a moment that on your much anticipated dream vacation to Paris, France…

●**You fall on the steps of the Metro and break a hip.**

●You don't speak French.

●You don't know how you're going to pay for hip surgery.

●You worry about the quality of care you will receive.

• You find out it can cost $10,000 or more to be evacuated back to the US.

This is not likely to happen, of course. But what if you *did* have to deal with a medical emergency overseas?

GETTING HELP

Contact the US embassy or consulate. *A consular officer will...*

• **Find English-speaking doctors or dentists** and direct you to the other medical services you need.

• **Contact your family and/or friends back home.**

• **Arrange for the transfer of funds** from the US to cover your medical costs.

If you have an American Express Gold or Platinum card, use its free Global Assist Hotline to find emergency medical referrals. MasterCard Gold and Platinum cards offer a Travel Services Medical Assistance Program, which provides similar travel services.

WHO PAYS?

Don't assume that your health insurance will cover medical expenses abroad. Ditto for the US government. Medicare provides no coverage for hospitalizations or other medical costs outside the US.

Self-defense: Check your existing coverage —*before* you travel. Your health insurance may provide reimbursement for "customary and reasonable" medical claims abroad. But generally, you must pay the bills and seek reimbursement after you return home.

Supplemental Medicare (Medigap) policies— policies C through J—provide some foreign travel emergency coverage. This insurance— which you can buy from an insurance company—will pay 80% of medically necessary foreign emergency care above a $250 deductible. If you're age 65 or older and travel a lot, you may want to carry a Medigap policy just for this coverage.

Health insurance policies that cover the cost of medical evacuation are few and far between.

If your insurance doesn't cover all medical costs on overseas trips, consider buying a special travel medical insurance policy. For a few extra dollars a day—usually about $3 to $5— you can carry short-term coverage (typically 15 days to 12 months) for overseas hospital costs and other medical charges.

Important: Emergency evacuation insurance has to be obtained separately. If your own insurance covers foreign medical costs but not evacuation costs, buy a policy for this type of emergency medical assistance.

Ask your travel agent about short-term medical coverage and medical assistance insurance. *Also check out the following...*

• **US State Department** at *http://travel.state. gov/medical.html.*

• **WorldTravelCenter.com.**

PREVENTIVE MEASURES

• **Be fully immunized for your destinations.** Learn about suggested immunizations at the Centers for Disease Control and Prevention international travel hot line (800-311-3435... *www.cdc.gov*).

Do not assume immunization information from embassies of the countries you will travel to is accurate or complete.

Not all vaccines or necessary medications are available from your family doctor. You may have to call a travel medicine clinic. Look in your local phone book under "Travel Medicine" or call a local medical center.

• **Take all your medications and medical devices with you when you travel.** Keep them in your carry-on bag. Make sure you have *more than enough* of each type of medication for the scheduled length of the trip in case of travel delays.

Helpful: Keep pills, especially narcotics, in their original containers. That helps you to avoid questions about whether or not they are legal drugs.

• **Take copies of prescriptions.** Also take a doctor's letter explaining any special treatment you require if you become ill.

• **Take a list of English-speaking doctors and dentists.** To obtain a list for your destination, contact the Office of Overseas Citizens Services, Bureau of Consular Affairs, Rm. 4811, Washington, DC 20520, *www.travel.state.gov/ overseas_citizens.html* or the International Association for Medical Assistance to Travellers at *www.iamat.org.*

You can sign up on-line for free (a donation is requested) and obtain a booklet listing English-speaking doctors as well as charts detailing climate and food sanitation conditions in 1,400 cities worldwide.

If you have a chronic medical condition, consider getting a Medic Alert tag that contains all your relevant medical information. Call 800-432-5378. *Cost:* About $35.

•**Drink only bottled water.** Do this even if you are told the local water is safe to drink. Avoid ice cubes…and, depending on where you are traveling, peel fresh fruits and vegetables that may have been washed in local water.

•**Carry medical emergency phone numbers in your wallet.** These numbers should include your doctor's and travel agent's.

Also carry the telephone number of the local US consulate…just in case.

More from Louise Weiss…

Helpful Travel Tip

Whenever you travel, bring along your travel agent's contact numbers. If you lose your tickets, need to change flights, find that your hotel reservation has been lost or encounter any similar problem, your travel agent probably can save you a good deal of time and irritation.

Best: Carry your travel agent's phone number, fax number and E-mail address.

How to Minimize Travel Hassles

Carry various forms of identification with you to reduce travel hassles.

Safest: In addition to your driver's license, take your passport (even if flying domestically), a copy of your birth certificate and your Social Security card.

For children: Also carry a family photo that shows you holding your ID and standing with your child.

Even when you are not traveling: It is a good idea to carry a copy of your passport next to your driver's license. If you don't drive, get a state-issued ID card. And carry *another* photo ID, such as a work ID.

Kevin McKeown, a security expert in Washington, DC, and author of *Your Secrets Are My Business* (Plume).

Faster Passports

Get a passport within about two weeks—instead of the normal six—by using the State Department's expedited passport service. *Cost:* $35,* plus a fee for overnight delivery. This cost is in addition to the basic government rates, which are $60 for a new passport and $40 for renewals.

For even faster delivery—in three days or less—use a private expediter service. *Cost:* Typically $100 or more.

Helpful: The State Department's "Passport Services" Web page provides all the forms and information needed to get a passport and tells where to apply for one at a location near you. Click on "How to Get Your Passport in a Hurry" for expedited service, and on "Passport Agencies" for a list of private expediters. *www.travel.state.gov/passport_services.html.*

For superfast service, you can try one of the on-line passport sites like Passport Express, *www.passportexpress.com* or American Passport Express, *www.americanpassport.com.* They can get a passport to you one day after receiving your travel documents. *Cost:* Up to $150 more than it would cost you to get a passport on your own.

*Prices subject to change.

Travel Advice from the Man Who Has Been Almost Everywhere

Gig Gwin, chairman and owner of Gwin's Travel in Kirkwood, MO. He has traveled to every country in the world. He has covered 2,250,000 miles and taken more than 2,300 flights. He is a member of the Travelers' Century Club, which requires visiting at least 100 countries.

Travel can be just as frustrating as it is rewarding. To minimize the many hassles and help you get the most out of your trip—*just follow the basics...*

●**Limit the number of bags you carry.** It's best to fit everything into one carry-on with wheels.

●**Don't travel with expensive jewelry—** even if you're going to fancy events. It is too risky. Consider wearing an obviously cheap watch—particularly if you are traveling to a developing country.

●**Take US cash and credit cards.** Though banks tell us to carry traveler's checks, you can avoid long lines at cash-changing places by carrying lots of dollars. Don't use bills larger than $20.

When packing, divide cash among your wallet or purse...briefcase or carry-on...and suitcase. Use credit cards for big purchases.

●**Allow plenty of time.** Don't rush to make flights, check out of hotels, meet people, etc. Having extra time will keep you in a better frame of mind.

●**Join an airline club if you travel frequently on one airline.** You'll have an oasis in which to wait for flights.

●**Be productive on the plane.** The chunks of time you have on flights and in waiting areas offer opportunities to tackle long-term projects. Redo your address book...write holiday cards...organize your photo album.

●**Learn some local phrases.** *Most useful:* The local greeting...the words for "please" and "thank you."

●**Study a local map** to get your bearings before hitting the streets.

●**Keep your cool.** When things are not going according to plan, lower your voice... organize your mind...and be polite—very polite. It works.

Great Small Towns Worth Visiting

For a weekend getaway, try visiting one of these charming small towns with historic significance...

●**Beaufort, South Carolina,** with impressive historic buildings.

●**Bonaparte, Iowa,** a preserved mill town from the early 1900s.

●**Calistoga, California,** in the Napa Valley.

●**Doylestown, Pennsylvania,** which offers Revolutionary War attractions in addition to a well-preserved downtown.

●**Eureka Springs, Arkansas,** a Victorian village and spa town.

●**Jacksonville, Oregon,** with meticulously restored brick and wooden buildings.

●**Staunton, Virginia,** with a compact, architecturally rich downtown.

Richard Moe, president, the National Trust for Historic Preservation, 1785 Massachusetts Ave. NW, Washington, DC 20036.

14

Funtime

Coaching Kids: Opportunities to Teach and Learn

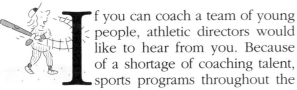

If you can coach a team of young people, athletic directors would like to hear from you. Because of a shortage of coaching talent, sports programs throughout the country are looking for volunteers.

Coaching can be your opportunity to help young people develop teamwork, discipline and other life skills. While it's often an asset to have played a sport yourself, on-the-field experience is rarely essential.

For younger athletes, an effective coach will become a mentor who can provide the attention that parents can't always provide in today's hectic society.

Working with young players...

●**Provides an opportunity to impart experience and values.**

●**Keeps you on your toes** and in touch with the next generation.

●**Promotes good health.**

●**Helps you maintain the skills you've learned** as a parent or in business.

Above all, coaching is fun and can be personally rewarding. For me, a smile of gratitude from a young athlete brings a feeling of energy that lasts for days.

GETTING STARTED

To learn about coaching opportunities in your area, contact the directors of local sports organizations, including public and private schools, the Y's (YMCA, YWCA, YMHA, YWHA), Little League and similar groups, city and county recreation departments and civic organizations that often sponsor sports leagues.

Note: Many of these groups are understaffed. Even though a sports organization may

Richard Rhodes, president of the American Coaching Institute, 18925 Eleanor Ln., Cottonwood, CA 96022, *www.acisport.com.* He is a coach and coauthor, with Steven Hayward, of *Basic Coaching Skills: Building Leadership in Youth Sports* (Griffith).

227

desperately need more coaches, you may have to make several phone calls to find someone to explain the application process.

If you're interested in coaching a particular sport, make contact at least *three months* before the start of the season. It often takes that long to join the group and be assigned to a team.

Coaches are in demand for: Basketball, soccer, football, softball, baseball, track, volleyball, wrestling, golf and hockey, as well as strength training and rugby.

Sports organizations also need volunteers to help with administrative and behind-the-scenes work, including the handling of score books, equipment maintenance, accounting, fund-raising, advertising, public relations and organizing picnics.

Expect the organization you choose to check you out much as a for-profit company would screen a job applicant. You'll typically be asked to supply references and employment history.

COACHING SKILLS

An effective coach must have…

- **Organization and planning ability.**
- **Communications skills.**
- **Patience.**
- **Ability to convince others that hard work pays off.**

If you're unsure about whether your skills are adequate, several organizations provide training for coaches…

- **American Coaching Institute,** 530-347-9215 or *www.acisport.com.*
- **American Sport Education Program,** 800-747-5698 or *www.asep.com.*
- **National Alliance for Youth Sports,** 561-684-1141 or *www.nays.org.*

Look for a program that follows the "National Standards for Athletic Coaches" adopted by the National Association for Sport and Physical Education (800-213-7193 or *www.aahperd.org/NASPE*).

Typical: A basic four-hour coaching course that covers the teaching of fundamental skills, teamwork, motivation and the difference between coaching girls and boys.

Girls are just as competitive as boys, but they are usually more attentive to a coach's instructions. It's not unusual to see a boy persist in using the wrong technique for, say, free throw shots, even though his shots always go wild. Girls are more likely to take advice and correct bad habits fast.

TAKING TO THE FIELD

Don't be overly concerned about not having great athletic talent yourself. Explain what has to be done, then ask one or two kids who have learned the skill to demonstrate it to the others. Young people often become bored by a coach who spends an entire training session demonstrating all the techniques himself.

One big challenge is maintaining discipline and focus.

Strategy: At each practice session, give players the goal of learning three new skills and reviewing skills taught in previous sessions.

Example: During practice, teach a breathing technique in swimming. At the next practice, ask the children to review what they learned before moving on to another lesson.

You might divide the team up into three squads. Assign each a different skill to practice. Then rotate the assignments.

You'll soon discover that kids often learn best through simple metaphors.

Example: In teaching the proper stance and bat swing in softball, I often compare it with squashing a bug with the front foot and kicking over a can with the back foot. It's the kind of language the kids understand and remember.

THE BIG LESSONS

In addition to the physical skills, effective coaches teach…

- **How to develop a competitive edge.** A competitive edge doesn't come just from a player's physical ability. It is also the result of knowledge—of the sport, of opponents and of the player's own ability.
- **How to think long term.** Most children need to be taught that long-term improvement matters more than a quick victory.
- **Tolerance.** Without tolerance, athletes put themselves at a disadvantage—particularly in choosing teammates and in cooperating with the variety of people involved in almost any sports organization.
- **How to lose.** Effective coaches teach players how to learn from a loss…and how to use loss to build self-discipline.

●**Goal setting.** Ambitious young athletes often make the mistake of setting unattainably high goals. A helpful coach will steer them toward a series of increasingly difficult—but achievable—objectives.

●**Perseverance.** Young people today are bombarded with so many activities and entertainment opportunities that it's often difficult for them to stay focused on goals. Coaches provide the encouragement that keeps these players on target.

●**Courtesy.** It might be disappearing in some sports, but off the field it's still an asset that most winners have in abundance.

Choosing a Puppy

To be sure you get a puppy with a good temperament, follow these helpful tips…

●**Toss some crumpled paper away from it**—the puppy should show interest in the paper by running over to examine it.

●**Pick up the puppy,** turn it upside down and cradle it in your arms—it should relax and enjoy a tummy rub.

●**With the puppy upside down,** hold its toes firmly, not harshly, between your thumb and forefinger—the puppy should accept this without becoming aggressive.

●**When the puppy is calm on the floor,** bang a metal pot at least two feet away—it should be startled but should not cower or be excessively frightened.

Richard B. Ford, DVM, professor of medicine, College of Veterinary Medicine, North Carolina State University in Raleigh.

Secrets of Successful Book Groups

Ellen Slezak, a freelance writer based in Los Angeles. She is the editor of *The Book Group Book: A Thoughtful Guide to Forming and Enjoying a Stimulating Book Discussion Group* (Chicago Review). Her first collection of short stories is *Last Year's Jesus* (Hyperion).

The novelist Margaret Atwood calls book groups a graduate seminar, encounter group and good old-fashioned village-pump gossip session all rolled up into one. She's absolutely right.

I have sat in on two dozen book groups all over the US and Canada. I've been in touch with dozens more. *Let me share some of their experiences to help your group find its voice…*

●**Don't admit just anyone.** New members in a 20-year-old book group in Stockton, California, must be civil, well informed, intellectually honest and self-confident. Every potential member is invited to one meeting only. If group reaction is favorable, membership is offered a few days later.

Important: Include enough members so that a hearty discussion is possible when a few members are absent, but not so many that everyone won't have ample opportunities to contribute. A good number is 10 to 12.

●**Rotate leadership.** Doing so prevents any individual from dominating the group while keeping all members vested in its success.

The leader should keep a keen eye out for anyone who needs help wedging their voice into the discussion.

●**Don't allow sweeping praise or condemnation.** View each book and author with respect, not adulation.

Example: A discussion that opens with a general wave of disapproval may be broadened if you ask aloud a question that you wondered about while reading the book.

●**Listen to "the quiet voice."** It was true in school and it's true in book groups, the loudest and wordiest don't always have the most to say. One book group member noted, "If you just want to listen to yourself, stay home."

●**Make the structure suit the group.** Formulate a system that works for you. There are no rules.

Example: Most groups meet monthly. But there are exceptions. The Fairview Lake (Pennsylvania) Book Group, all age 60 to 80, is a summer book group that meets weekly. The reading list, exclusively of paperbacks of fewer than 300 pages, is mailed to group members in November.

CHOOSING BOOKS

What I think of as "the oldest living book group," established by members of The League of Women Voters in Los Angeles, has been going strong for 34 years. *Their book-choosing rules...*

●**Whoever chooses a book must have read it first.**

●**The book must lend itself to discussion.**

●**Even a single strong objection vetoes the book.**

The exception that proves the rule: The group's founder resisted *The Bridges of Madison County* so intensely that she quit when it was chosen. (But the resulting meeting was lively and hilarious.)

PITFALLS

Every problem has a solution, book clubbers say. *Watch out for...*

●**Slackness.** Insist that every attendee read the entire book. Exceptions can be made for personal emergencies, but consistently absorbing material from the group without contributing is quickly resented.

●**The diva.** You know her (or him) well. She monopolizes the discussion, insists that everyone read her recommendations and wants to meet when it's convenient for her. Confront her —don't ignore her.

What not to do: One book group in Los Angeles was hamstrung by the screenwriter-playwright who founded it. Compared with her glamorous life, she made it clear, others' problems and successes were peanuts. In distress, they stopped meeting. When the diva moved away, the group reconvened.

●**Overeating.** Some book groups, finding food too distracting, have eliminated culinary extravaganzas. *Cookies may fuel your discussions, but don't let the feeding get frenzied unless you want it to...*

●Some groups plan the meeting's meal around each book's theme.

●A San Antonio, Texas, group meets from noon to 2 pm, brown bags in hand, at Trinity University, which provides beverages and a meeting room.

●An Ann Arbor, Michigan, group meets "for 90 minutes of low-brow discussion followed by a high-calorie dessert."

●**Drinking.** DUI (discussing under the influence) can be fun unless it goes too far.

A group in Toronto started at a bar when a man demonstrated that James Joyce's *Finnegans Wake* could be understood only when read aloud. Discussions of other Irish writers, then nonIrish ones, followed.

"A glass or two loosens the tongue and gets the gab flowing," one member says.

Though the group still likes to meet in bars, its consumption of alcoholic beverages has declined significantly.

ENRICHMENT FOR LIFE

Groups can fall apart, but many good ones survive for decades, forging lasting friendships. Group members often tell me, "It's more than just a book group."

One Illinois book group member says she depends on "the community and communion, the varied viewpoints, the deeper understandings of two of my favorite pastimes—reading and conversation."

The characters in the books you read will become honorary members of the group. You'll love or hate them, gossip about them and compare their foibles as if they lived in your world. In a way, they do.

FAVORITE BOOKS

Here are some favorites of the Vicar's Landing Book Club in Ponte Vedra Beach, Florida:

●**Fiction...**

  ●*Cold Mountain* by Charles Frazier.

  ●*Memoirs of a Geisha* by Arthur Golden.

  ● *The House of Mirth* by Edith Wharton.

●**Nonfiction...**

  ●*Lewis & Clark: Voyage of Discovery* by Stephen E. Ambrose.

  ● *The Greatest Generation* by Tom Brokaw.

  ●*Madame Curie: A Biography* by Eva Curie.

More Successful Parties

For better party planning put food and drinks at opposite ends of the room so people mingle. Plan on three drinks per person for a three-hour party. Stock sparkling cider for non-drinkers and 15 pounds of ice for every 10 people. Hors d'oeuvres should be small enough to fit on cocktail napkins. If you are serving four types of hors d'oeuvres, count on each guest eating three of each. The typical guest will use three napkins. Light bathrooms with candles so glaring fluorescents are not needed. To signal the end of the party, offer coffee and sweets.

Siobhan Haber, party planner, Flaherty Miller Events, New York City.

Better Toasts

An effective toast is brief, simple and tailored to the occasion. Plan what to say so that it has an opening, a body and a conclusion. Do not try to be funny—be dignified. Avoid clichés, but use quotations or poetry. And don't use note cards.

To overcome stage fright: Visualize yourself making the toast.

Terry McCann, executive director, Toastmasters International, which teaches public speaking and leadership skills, Rancho Santa Margarita, CA, *www.toastmasters.org*.

Music to Make the Mood

Rick Hansberry, entertainment coordinator and professional disc jockey for more than 25 years, Lancaster, PA.

To set the right mood, try out some of the following musical recommendations for your next special occasion…

•**Birthday parties.** Start with pieces from the year the celebrant was born, then move through their milestone years—graduations, wedding, etc.

•**Cocktail parties.** As guests arrive, play smooth jazz—upbeat but not overbearing.

Examples: Peter White, George Benson.

For a relaxed rhythm, blend in soft reggae—Bob Marley, UB40, Fugees, Freddie McGreggor.

Later: Try out the Motown sound (Smokey Robinson, the Temptations, the Four Tops)…and classic pop (James Taylor, Billy Joel).

•**Anniversary, wedding and other milestone occasions.** During dinner, play music from the Classical period (Beethoven, Haydn, Mozart) or music from the Baroque era (Bach, Handel, Vivaldi).

The New Age artists like George Winston and John Tesh work well after the meal.

Favorite songs to dance to at anniversaries: Kenny Rogers's *Through the Years*…Anne Murray's *Could I Have This Dance?*…Heatwave's *Always and Forever*…Shania Twain's *You're Still the One*.

Popular songs for brides and grooms: Lone Star's *Amazed*…98°'s *I Do (Cherish You)*.

Best Way to Clean a CD

A common compact disc (CD) cleaning mistake is to wipe the playing side in a circular motion. If scratches occur while wiping this way, the disc is likely to skip. Instead, wipe in a straight line—starting from the hole of the disc to the outer rim.

Tony Sachs, owner of the music store NYCD at 426 Amsterdam Ave. in New York City 10024.

Restaurant Reviewer's Dining-Out Secrets

Steven Shaw, a New York City–based food critic for *Commentary* magazine and others. His Web site is *www.fatguy.com*. He is author of *The Menu New York* (Ten Speed).

Before you make any future restaurant reservations, get some inside advice on eating out from a well-known New York City food critic…

•**Never order fish on Monday**—odds are, it was fresh on Saturday.

•**Best time to make a dinner reservation** at a popular restaurant is about six hours before you want to eat. That is when cancellations start coming in.

•**Avoid dining out on holidays.** Restaurants are so overbooked that they will often charge double for the same meals they serve every day. *Better:* Have your special meal the day before or after the holiday.

•**Become a regular.** The best restaurant is the one at which you are known.

•**Go out for lunch.** Restaurants that are always full for dinner are often desperate for midday business and may charge you half as much then for the same menu items.

•**Avoid new restaurants for at least three months**—while they are working out the kinks.

•**Be nice.** It's the surest way for you to get good service.

How to Have Fun Gambling On-Line

Bill Haywood, Ohio-based author of *Beat WebCasinos.com: A Shrewd Player's Guide to Internet Gambling* (RGE).

Choosing an on-line casino can be a bit like selecting an auto mechanic. There are plenty of honest ones out there—but it can be tough to know which one to trust.

The industry has attracted some shady operators who are quite willing to do whatever they can to take your money.

If you want to gamble on-line, here's how to do it right…

USE A REPUTABLE CASINO

•**Stick with established Internet casinos.** The Omnicasino (*www.omnicasino.com*), Casino-on-Net (*www.888.com*) and the Mayan Casino (*www.mayancasino.com*) all have solid track records.

•**Check the software.** A casino is usually reputable if it uses software by Boss, CryptoLogic, Microgaming or World Gaming (originally Starnet).

For a list of casinos by software: Go to *www.winneronline.com*.

•**Visit Internet chat rooms** for the latest buzz on a casino in the on-line gambling community. Try *www.gamemasteronline.com* or *www.winneronline.com*.

•**Make sure the casino has a toll-free number** in case you have a problem. Dial the number before you gamble to confirm that it connects you to a person, not a recording.

•**Try out the casino.** Most on-line casinos let you play for free—some for as long as you like, others for a limited time. If the casino doesn't allow any free time, go elsewhere.

TRY AN ON-LINE PAYMENT COMPANY

To place a bet on-line, you need to put up money on a credit card with the casino. If you win, you receive your winnings via the mail, a bank wire or a credit to your account with the casino or with an on-line payment company.

Many Internet gamblers are rightfully concerned about releasing credit card numbers to Internet casinos. Reputable, independent on-line payment organizations—such as FirePay (*www.firepay.com*)…PayPal (*www.paypal.com*)…and NetTeller (*www.jackhenry.com/netteller*)—can act as intermediaries. At the casino's Web site, read the directions under "Setting up an Account" to see what forms of payment the casino will accept.

LOOK FOR NEW-ACCOUNT BONUSES

Casinos often offer bonuses for new customers—as much as 20% of the amount the customer puts up. But you can't just set up an account and then cash out for a profit. Casinos have many rules governing these bonuses.

Example: A casino might require new players to make bets totaling the amount they originally deposited before their bonuses vest. You may be required to leave the money in for a certain time...or you may have to request the bonus by a deadline. Read the requirements carefully to make sure you know what you are getting into.

Be aware that casinos are not pleased when new account holders do just enough to qualify for the bonus and then try to cash out. One common complaint among Internet gamblers is that casinos—even the reputable ones—sometimes withhold bonuses even when all the requirements are met. This is not legal, but because most Internet companies are based overseas, it is not easy to enforce.

KNOW THE ODDS

Whether you play on-line or in a land-based casino, some games stack the odds in the house's favor. The house has a 5% advantage at roulette...as much as 15% at slots...and 29% at keno.*

The odds are better with other games. The house has only a 2% to 3% advantage over the typical blackjack player. Advanced players can cut that to one-half of a percent.

With video poker, the house advantage can also be as low as one-half of a percent. To master the game, read *Video Poker–Optimum Play* by Dan Paymar (ConJelCo).

A craps player who sticks with simple *pass/don't pass* and *come/don't come* bets faces odds only slightly more than 1% in the house's favor.

Baccarat is probably the best choice for the novice gambler. It is easy to learn—and, like craps, the odds are only slightly more than 1% against the gambler.

Internet poker—different from video poker—is a recent development. You play against other players, not the house—and the casino takes a cut of the pot. Visit *www.poker.com* or *www.paradisepoker.com.*

COMPLAIN IF YOU RUN INTO TROUBLE

If the casino is slow to pay, complain via phone and E-mail. Make it clear you are not going away quietly.

*All odds from *www.thewizardofodds.com.*

If you get no satisfaction within two weeks, E-mail the ombudsman at Gambling Grumbles (*www.gambling.com/grumbles/front*).

Another good resource, The Online Players Association (*www.casinogazette.com*), has a blacklist of bad casinos and will follow up on complaints. You can also post any complaints in gambling chat rooms.

WARNING

On-line gamblers are more likely than land-based casino players to be problem gamblers. If you have ever lost more than you could afford at a land-based casino, avoid Internet casinos. If you think you need help, call the National Council on Problem Gambling's confidential 24-hour help line, 800-522-4700 or contact them on the Web at *www.ncpgambling.org.*

How to Get on a Game Show—and Win

Dan Avila, Los Angeles–based photographer and charter member of The Jipters, a nationwide on-line group of TV game-show contestants and aspiring contestants. In addition to Jeopardy!, *he has appeared on many shows, including* The Joker's Wild *and* Greed.

When I became a *Jeopardy!* champion in 1991, my winnings totaled a mere $5,300. Today, the game shows give away millions.

It is no longer enough to be a whiz at trivia. Here's how to boost your chances of getting on a game show and smart strategies to up your winnings...

LAYING THE GROUNDWORK

●**Pick out a show that is suited to your strengths.** I excel at quick recall, so *Jeopardy!* was a good fit for me. If you are a shopping maven, you might prefer *The Price Is Right.*

ACING THE AUDITION

●**Smile to impress the producers.** You want to make an upbeat, energetic impression.

Also important: Prepare short, interesting and articulate answers to the two common questions game-show producers ask—"Tell me a little about yourself?" and "What would you do if you won a lot of money on this show?"

GETTING READY TO PLAY

●**Once you are picked for the game, do not just focus on getting the right answers.** Strategize. Do your best to simulate game conditions. Videotape several episodes of the show, and watch each twice—once to play and keep score...and again to evaluate how you could have played more effectively.

Example: On *Jeopardy!*, timing is key. Any contestant who rings in before the host, Alex Trebek, finishes reading the answer is automatically locked out for one-fifth of a second—and a fraction of a second can make a difference between winning and losing.

Prior to appearing on the show, I spent time practicing my clicking-in technique. So I was then able to concentrate on Trebek's voice and the last word of each answer before I buzzed.

●**Brush up on pop culture.** Early rounds of game shows and the low-money questions are often drawn from show business, sports and other trivia. Flip through such publications as *Entertainment Weekly...People...*and *TV Guide.*

What you need to know: Notable celebrities...movies...and television shows.

●**Cozy up to an encyclopedia.** Purchase a pocket encyclopedia or a world almanac. Use it as a study guide.

For later rounds, you will need to be well versed in history, geography and literature.

Specifics you may need to know: State and world capitals...US presidents' biographies...US and world literature (basic plot lines and major characters)...world leaders (past and present)...Latin and Greek roots of words.

Another resource: 10,000 Answers: The Ultimate Trivia Encyclopedia by Stanley Newman and Hal Fittipaldi (Random House).

●**Make risk/reward decisions before the taping.** When the cameras are rolling and the audience is clapping, it's hard to intelligently decide how big a chance to take.

Example: On *Who Wants to Be a Millionaire*, if I were to reach the $125,000 level and could narrow the answer down to two choices, I would guess.

But if I reached the $250,000 level, I would only answer if I was sure I had it right.

●**Keep your mouth closed when it can hurt you.** The biggest way to get yourself into trouble on any game show is to ring in and make blind guesses...or to blurt out your responses even when you're not sure that you really have the correct answers.

MAKING CONTACT

Auditions can be costly if you don't live in one of the cities where they are held.

If you are selected as a finalist, some shows will pay for your airfare and hotel.

For information about the following popular game shows...

●**Jeopardy!.** 310-244-5367...*http://jeopardy. station.sony.com.*

●**Weakest Link.** 800-390-1001...*www. weakestlink.com.*

For information about other game shows, visit *http://tvgameshows.net.* Follow the links to shows for tryout information.

Most of the network game shows today will not permit you to be a contestant if you have recently appeared on any other game show—typically within the past 12 months.

Every game show has different rules, but most post their regulations on-line.

Tricks for Taking Perfect Pictures

David Joel, a Chicago-based commercial photographer whose clients include IBM, Sara Lee and other Fortune 500 companies. Along with his father (award-winning Life photographer Yale Joel), he is founder of The28thfloor.com, a Web site that provides critiques and technical information for all levels of photographers.

You don't need expensive camera equipment or majestic scenery to take beautiful pictures.

The secret: Take time to look at the people and the environment around you in fresh ways.

●**Photograph what you know.** Look for interesting patterns—a line of trees stretching up the road...rocks along a path...the interplay of light and shadow on a school playground.

●**Experiment with light.** Noontime sun produces shadows—perfect for creating drama. For a softer look, take pictures in early morning or late afternoon.

Photographers often wait for cloudy days to take flattering portraits. The light—known as "open shade"—can hide wrinkles, making people appear younger.

●**Keep portrait backgrounds simple.** The point of interest should be the person, not the background. Arrange your subject in front of a brick wall…against an open sky …in an empty field.

●**Slow down.** People don't look natural when you just grab your camera and start firing away. Give them time to relax. Watch their body language. Even slight body movements—the tilt of a shoulder…a jutting chin …a slight change of posture—make pictures more dynamic.

●**Try different angles.** Do anything but stand directly in front of your subjects. Climb up on a stepladder, so your subjects are below you. Or kneel down and shoot upward.

●**Scatter your subjects.** When taking group pictures, have some people stand close to the camera, others farther away. There's no reason for any of your portraits to look like high school pictures.

Movies to Lift Your Mood

Gary Solomon, PhD, a professor of psychology at Community College of Southern Nevada, Henderson. He is author of *The Motion Picture Prescription* (Aslan) and *Reel Therapy* (Lebhar-Friedman).

If a picture is worth a thousand words, then a film is worth trillions. Movies help us to understand our problems…and discover new ways of coping.

Regardless of what you're experiencing—addiction, failed love, conflicts with your children, etc.—the right movie usually can help you feel better.

Here are some movies that my research has shown to be particularly useful during difficult times…

SADNESS

There's no question about it—laughter is healing. When I see people feeling down, I recommend *When Harry Met Sally…City Slickers* …or *Sleepless in Seattle*. It's almost impossible to watch these movies without feeling better.

Important: Humor should be positive. For example, in the original *The Nutty Professor*, Jerry Lewis is such a nice, oafish guy that it's impossible not to like him. In the Eddie Murphy remake, the humor is more spiteful than good-natured.

RELATIONSHIP PROBLEMS

Watch *About Last Night…* Starring Rob Lowe and Demi Moore, it shows the dangers of falling in love too quickly…and the emotional devastation that occurs when lovers discover they really don't know each other very well.

The passion of a new relationship does not last. Time passes…emotions mature…bodies change. This movie demonstrates we all have to find ways to keep relationships alive and vital.

LONELINESS

Terms of Endearment explores the richness of a mature love. The cautious courtship and coming together of stars Shirley MacLaine and Jack Nicholson remind us that life and love don't end at age 40. This film also addresses universal family issues—what happens when parents and children don't communicate and when they deceive each other.

In *The Kid*, Bruce Willis is a high-powered consultant who meets himself as an eight-year-old. Together, they explore his childhood and he rediscovers his essential self.

TROUBLED TEENS

Watch *East of Eden*, starring James Dean, with your teenager. Every teen will identify with Dean's brooding alienation…and the fact that his heart is in the right place even when he does "bad" things. Parents will see how important it is to accept their children as individuals.

SUBSTANCE ABUSE

If you or someone you love is struggling with alcoholism or drugs, take out *The Boost*. James Woods plays a corporate executive who loses everything as he descends into addiction. I once worked with a young cocaine user. He recognized that the drug was destroying his life but couldn't give it up. After I convinced him to watch *The Boost*, he finally sought help for his habit.

DEATH AND DYING

Steel Magnolias touchingly explores how a mother copes with the death of her daughter. Watching it will bring all of your emotions to the surface.

In our culture, when a loved one dies, we often feel as if we should be on our feet the next day. That seldom happens. In movies like *Steel Magnolias* and *On Golden Pond*, we see what happens as people come to terms with death.

Better Volunteering

To get the most from volunteer work, find situations that give you personal contact with people who need help.

Examples: Spend two hours each week giving one-to-one assistance. Help strangers, not people you already know. Use skills you already have, or work with a group that provides training in skills you want to develop.

Redford Williams, MD, director of the Duke University Behavioral Medicine Research Center, Durham, NC, and coauthor of *Anger Kills: 17 Strategies for Controlling the Hostility That Can Harm Your Health* (HarperPaperbacks).

Cashless Creativity

Focus on the things you enjoy and figure out how to get them for little or no cash.

Examples: If you love theater, volunteer as an usher so you can see plays. If you are a writer with a taste for fine dining, ask restaurants if you can do their promotional materials in exchange for meals. If you have few possessions but love grand houses, ask owners if you can house-sit for them while they travel.

Deborah Knuckey, writer, speaker and money coach in Washington, DC, and author of *The Ms. Spent Money Guide* (Wiley).

15

On the Road

Never Get Taken Again— The New Rules for Buying A Car

An educated buyer can save as much as $5,000 more than an uneducated buyer on an average-priced new automobile.

To be an educated buyer, avoid the following traps…

Trap: **Showing too much enthusiasm.** If you act too excited, the salesperson will know that he/she has something you want…and that you'll pay top dollar. Keep your enthusiasm in check until you've completed the transaction.

Trap: **Buying in haste.** Take your time to comparison shop. Use the Internet car-buying sites to help you decide how much to pay for a car. Do not feel that you must buy on your very first visit to the dealership. If you take your time and are willing to walk away from an unacceptable bid, the price will fall.

Trap: **Giving a deposit before the dealer approves your offer.** A deposit at this point in negotiations is simply a means to keep you around longer while trying to convince you to pay more.

Trap: **Being pressured into leasing when you want to purchase.** Dealerships make much more profit leasing a vehicle than they do selling it. Therefore, they try to convert buyers into lessees.

Perhaps leasing is what you would prefer— it may be cheaper for you if you are shopping for a business car. But don't decide to lease without mulling over the financial implications.

Trap: **Trading in your old car without knowing its value.** A dealership will give as little as possible for your trade-in car. But you can get a bit more by knowing the car's true value. Clean up the trade-in and then shop it around—offering it to several used-car dealers. Your vehicle's real trade-in value is the highest

Remar Sutton, president and cofounder, Consumer Task Force for Automotive Issues, Inc., in Atlanta, and author of *Don't Get Taken Every Time* (Penguin).

237

amount you are offered for it. Don't accept anything less.

Trap: **Financing through the dealership before considering all your options.** Take a copy of the dealer's filled-in contract to your bank or credit union to compare costs. If the dealer refuses to give you a copy of the financing agreement, odds are it's not the cheapest.

HELP FOR USED-CAR BUYERS

The same strategies for buying a new car apply to buying a used car—but there's even more to think about. *To avoid rip-offs...*

• **Have a mechanic check the car before you buy it.** Use a diagnostic center or an independent service shop. A complete checkup will cost about $125.

• **Make sure that necessary repairs are included in the purchase price.** Negotiate with the seller to include the cost of any repairs your mechanic deems necessary.

Example: If a seller wants $8,000, but the vehicle needs $1,000 in repairs, do not pay more than $7,000.

• **Forget about the asking price.** Bargain *up* from the loan value—not *down* from the asking price. The loan value is what a bank or credit union will lend you on the vehicle. If the loan value is $6,000, but the seller is asking $8,000, negotiate up from $6,000.

• **Don't talk warranty until *after* settling on a selling price.** You want at minimum a 30-day, 100% drivetrain warranty. Never accept a 50/50 warranty where the dealer pays only half of warranty-covered expenses. The warranty should pay 100% of covered expenses. Keep in mind that the price of an extended service contract agreement is negotiable.

• **Shop around for financing.** Rates are usually much higher for financing used cars than rates for new vehicles. If a new car can be financed at 8% a year, a two-year-old car might have a 15% financing rate at the dealer.

Just as with a new car, get a copy of the proposed finance contract and see what your bank or credit union will offer you.

USING THE INTERNET

It's *possible* to buy a car on the Internet, but it's hard to negotiate a good price. For many people, dealerships remain the cheapest place to buy. Still, the Internet is the best place to find out how much you should pay for a car. *Helpful Web sites...*

• **Edmunds.com** (*www.edmunds.com*) is the best place to get pricing information for a new car.

• **Kelley Blue Book** (*www.kbb.com*) lists how much a used vehicle is worth—the blue book cost.

• **Cars.com** (*www.cars.com*) gives the dealer invoice price and "target price"—the price you should aim for in negotiations with the automobile dealer.

• **CarFax** (*www.carfax.com*) lets you run a "lemon check" to see if the car you want to buy has a history of problems.

• **National Highway Traffic Safety Administration** (*www.nhtsa.gov*) shows the results of government safety tests.

• **AutoByTel.com** (*www.autobytel.com*) is a car-buying site that directs you to the dealership that has the car you're looking for.

• **CarsDirect.com** (*www.carsdirect.com*)—another buying site—acts as a broker for you rather than directing you to a car dealer.

• **Microsoft Car Point** (*www.carpoint.com*) has information on new and used cars, including consumer articles offering buying tips.

• **ConsumerGuide.com** (*www.consumerguide.com*) is the best overall guide to used cars on the Web. It offers pricing information as well as recall and repair records.

• **Consumer Reports** (*www.consumerreports.com*) offers unbiased information about cars and pricing. Its $12* new-car price service includes current rebate figures, dealer incentives and dealer invoice prices, the manufacturer's suggested retail price (MSRP) as well as the latest safety ratings.

*Price subject to change.

Free Cars

Free cars are available from a company that uses them as travelling billboards. Free-Car Media of Los Angeles (*http://drivers.freecar media.com*) gives motorists two free years of use of a car that is wrapped in advertising slogans. Car users pay for insurance and fuel.

Objective: To have their cars seen in big cities. More than 70,000 people are on a waiting list for the cars.

Alternative: Autowraps (*www.autowraps. com*) pays people up to $400/month to have ads placed on cars they already own.

Reported in *The New York Times.*

Time to Buy A New Car?

Bob Cerullo, certified master mechanic, owner of an automotive diagnostic center in Queens, NY, and the author of *What's Wrong with My Car?* (Plume). He is a columnist for *AMI Auto World* and *Motor* magazines.

If your car is more than a few years old, you may be wondering if it's time to trade it in for something newer. *To help you decide…*

•**Have the car inspected by an independent mechanic—someone you trust.** This means someone who isn't trying to sell you a new car. *Cost:* $99 to $199.

Go to an inspection center that is certified by the Car Care Council. This nonprofit organization educates motorists on car maintenance and safety. Contact them at 419-734-5343 or *www.certifiedinspection.org.*

Here are three common signs that suggest problems are too costly to repair…

•Blue smoke coming from the tailpipe. This indicates serious trouble with the valves or rings. *Repair cost:* $1,500 to $3,000.

•Engine knock in a high-mileage car. This may be indicative of worn bearings and necessitate a complete engine overhaul. *Repair cost:* $2,500 to $4,000.

•Rusting. Major rust spots can weaken the structure…and smaller body rust spots also reduce the value of the car.

•**Find out how much your car is worth.** Go to *www.kbb.com* and use its free service to determine your vehicle's *Kelley Blue Book* value. Deduct the estimated cost of repairs from the book value to determine the car's worth.

If the cost of required repairs to your vehicle greatly exceeds the book value, consider trading it in or selling it.

Avoid Extended Car Warranties

Vehicles are much more reliable than they used to be. Extended warranties are huge profit centers for dealers. If you do buy a car with poor reliability ratings or one that hasn't yet been rated by *Consumer Reports,* consider extended coverage. But even in this case, shop around—other dealers might offer better coverage for less.

Caution: Insist on a contract offered by the auto manufacturer, since it is easier to make claims against the carmaker than against third parties.

Robert Gentile, analyst, *Consumer Reports* New–Used Car Price Service, Consumers Union of United States in Yonkers, NY, *www.consumerreports.com.*

Best Way to Pay for a Car

Even 0% financing has hidden costs—dealers will not negotiate as low a price for a financed car as for one being bought for cash.

Effective negotiating: At the free on-line sites such as *www.edmunds.com* and *www.car point.com*, you can find out the invoice price, dealer incentives and manufacturer rebates for the car you want. Offer the dealer the invoice minus manufacturer incentives. Paying cash makes it much more likely that you will get the best deal.

Ross Levin, CFP, president, Accredited Investors Inc., investment management firm, Edina, MN, and author of *The Wealth Management Index* (McGraw-Hill).

Best Places to Buy A Used Car

The most dependable used cars come from those people who take meticulous care of all their possessions—houses, vehicles and everything else. If you are looking for a car and hear that one is being sold by a friend— or the friend of a friend—who is such a person, check it out as soon as possible. These vehicles are usually snapped up quickly.

Certified preowned cars from dealers pose less risk to buyers, but they cost more. On a $10,000 car, you will pay $300 to $500 more by going to a dealer. A two-year-old certified Toyota Camry—or similar top-ranked brand— will cost you as much as a new vehicle from a less expensive manufacturer. The latter may be a better buy for you.

Ashly Knapp, CEO, AutoAdvisor.com, nationwide vehicle-buying and consulting service, Seattle.

Used-Car Buyers Beware

David Solomon, certified master auto technician and president, Nutz & Boltz, automotive information membership organization, Butler, MD, *www.motorminute.com.*

Some dangerous problems to look out for in a used car *before* you make the decision to purchase one…

• **Cars that have been salvaged from floods or repaired after accidents.** Or cars that were declared lemons and repurchased by car manufacturers to be resold on car lots.

Self-defense: Have the car inspected by a trusted mechanic. Most service shops offer used-car check services. *Cost:* $50 to $100.

Research the vehicle's history at *www.carfax.com* or *www.autocheck.com.* Simply type in the car's Vehicle Identification Number (VIN) for a complete report. The report will disclose discrepancies and retitled salvaged vehicles. You will find the VIN on the driver's-side dashboard of the automobile or inside the driver's-side door. *Cost:* About $15.

• **Air bags and antilock brake systems that have been replaced with used parts—** or, in the case of air bags, simply not replaced and a dummy cover put in the dashboard.

Self-defense: Make sure the dashboard indicator bulb works by having a technician check it with a scan tool during the used-car check.

• **Unpublicized recalls and secret warranties** indicating safety problems.

More from David Solomon…

Must-Have Emergency Car Tool

An automatic center punch for breaking car windows can be a lifesaver. Store it in the driver's door side pocket or the glove compartment. Press the tool against the window until glass breaks. It is especially important for cars with electric windows and doors, which may not work after a crash. *Cost:* About $15 and up. Available at hardware stores or on-line.

Also from David Solomon…

Pumping Gas May Be Lethal

Static electricity can cause fires at the gas pump—particularly in winter. Getting in and out of a vehicle builds up an electrical charge. And winterized fuels—which have increased alcohol content to help cars start in cold weather—are more volatile and can be ignited by a stray spark.

Self-defense: If you pump your own gas, stay outside when filling up, even if it is cold. When filling up a gas container, keep it on the ground. Get back into the car only after shutting off the pump and paying for your purchase.

Finally from David Solomon...

Spark Plug Warning

Long-life spark plugs can cause engine damage. Spark plugs that are advertised as lasting for 100,000 miles may do so only under ideal driving conditions. In the five to 10 years it takes to accumulate these miles, these plugs may become frozen in place, damaging the cylinder head. Worn plugs can also harm the ignition system.

Self-defense: Replace plugs every 60,000 miles. *Best ones:* Bosch Platinum+4. *Cost:* About $5.85 each.

SUV Safe-Driving Strategies

Bud Stanley, partner, Stevens Advanced Driver Training, Merrimack, NH. The firm teaches advanced driving skills to members of corporate driving fleets and law-enforcement agencies in the US and Canada.

Sport-utility vehicles (SUVs) have become the transportation of choice for millions of Americans. They are roomy—and seemingly safer than smaller vehicles.

But the SUVs are two to three times more likely than cars to roll over in accidents. They are also nearly three times more likely to be involved in accidents that result in fatalities to their occupants.

An SUV's high center of gravity makes it "tippy," and the truck-style suspension limits maneuverability in emergencies. *To make driving an SUV safer...*

•**Brake before hard turns.** Most rollovers occur when drivers turn the steering wheel suddenly. To avoid obstacles, hit the brakes hard. Maintain pressure without pumping the pedal. Then steer to safety.

•**Don't be overconfident when driving on snowy, icy or wet roads.** The four-wheel drive on most SUVs improves traction when starting to move—but not once the vehicle is under way on treacherous roads.

Warning: It is easier to lose control of an SUV than a car on snow, ice or wet pavement.

•**Slow down in windy conditions.** Tall vehicles are more likely to tip over in gusty conditions than automobiles with lower centers of gravity.

•**Allow extra distance from the car in front of you.** With cars, a three-second gap is acceptable. With SUVs, you need four seconds. The extra weight of SUVs requires additional stopping or steering time, especially on curves.

To time the gap: When the car in front of you passes a fixed point, such as a road sign or a telephone pole, count the seconds until you reach the same point.

•**Don't let teens drive SUVs.** Their reflexes are faster than those of adults—they tend to overreact and to steer abruptly in emergencies, causing rollovers.

•**Seat heavy passengers in the second row of seats.** Putting too much weight at the front or rear of an SUV reduces maneuverability and stability. It is also best to try to stow luggage and other heavy items in the center of the SUV, between the front and rear axles—and not on the roof rack.

•**Adjust side mirrors outward.** If you can see the tail end of your own vehicle in the mirror, there is probably a large blind spot that will hide cars.

•**Wear a seatbelt.** SUVs give people a false sense of invincibility. If there is a crash or a rollover, SUV drivers are more likely than car drivers to be ejected if they are not wearing their seatbelts.

Another reason to wear seatbelts: They help prevent accidents by keeping the driver from shifting inside the car. On test courses, drivers without seatbelts started knocking over cones almost immediately. They were shifting around too much to maintain control of the vehicle, even at low speeds.

Secrets of Safer Driving

For safer driving, be sure to follow these helpful suggestions…

●**Do head, shoulder and trunk warm-up exercises** before you drive so you can easily turn your head to see blind spots.

●**Get regular vision and hearing check-ups**—annually or at least every two years.

●**Consider staying off the highways and avoid peak-traffic times.** Use slower-speed roads and travel at off-peak hours.

●**Avoid driving at night and in inclement weather.**

●**Stay focused.** Do not use your cell phone while the vehicle is in motion or engage in any other distracting activities—drinking, eating, applying makeup, etc.

●**Take a defensive driving course.**

Al Tetta, traffic-safety specialist, Automobile Club of New York, Garden City, quoted in *The New York Times*.

Garage Hazards That Can Ruin Your Car

McKeel Hagerty, president, Hagerty Classic Insurance, Traverse City, MI. The firm insures collectible automobiles.

If you think that keeping your car garaged will guarantee its safety, then think again. The number of claims for damage in home garages is shocking.

SECRETS OF SAFE GARAGING

●**Keep the area above and around your car clear.** Rakes, shovels, tools, bikes, etc. can all damage a car if they fall.

●**Install a smoke detector**—especially if the furnace is in your garage.

●**Never store flammables near a vehicle.** Keep all such items—including lawn mowers, snowblowers and other gas-powered equipment as well as paint and solvents—at least five feet away from a car.

●**Keep car windows closed.** We regularly receive claims for damage from animals such as raccoons, squirrels, mice and even household pets that got inside a car.

●**Keep the car covered to guard against scratches.** Use a thick cover to prevent claw marks from animals that may find a way into your garage.

My favorite resource: California Car Cover, 800-423-5525…*www.calcarcover.com*.

●**Remove heavy snow from the garage roof.** We get a lot of roof-collapse claims in the Snowbelt states.

●**Get proper insurance.** Homeowner's insurance does not cover a garaged car—even a collectible car that is not driven.

Minimum: Comprehensive coverage. This will insure against damage even when a car is not in motion.

●**Think like a thief.** Be sure the garage is locked, cover windows, and set the car alarm. Consider an alarm for the garage.

Traffic Accident Self-Defense

If you're involved in a traffic accident, document the situation immediately. Take notes about what you were doing, what you saw and felt, who was with you, what the time was, what weather conditions were like and anything you heard other people say. Get a list of witnesses and their contact information for both insurance and legal purposes.

Brian O'Neill, president, Insurance Institute for Highway Safety, 1005 N. Glebe Rd., Arlington, VA 22201.

16

Home and Family Matters

Questions Never to Ask Your Children or Grandchildren

Many questions parents ask their children are guaranteed *not* to get constructive answers. Sometimes the questions can be downright destructive. *Here are some questions to avoid...*

TODDLERS & PRESCHOOLERS

•**Did you...(break the vase, get mud on the couch, smear strawberry jam on the wall)?** You may be using this question to teach your child to take responsibility for his/her behavior, but very young children do not think this way. They have trouble distinguishing fantasy from reality.

That's why a three-year-old who has jam all over his face can give you a look of complete innocence and say, "It wasn't me."

They will also confuse *doing* something bad with *being* someone bad—and they do not want to be bad.

Better: Point out what happened, and help your child correct the situation. "I see you smeared strawberry jam on the wall. That's not good. Help me clean it off."

•**Why did you...(hit your brother, break the toy)?** This requires abstract thinking skills that a preschooler hasn't developed yet. All you are likely to get in response is a blank stare or "I don't know."

Better: Respond to the obvious emotion the child is showing. "I can see you're upset. Hitting is not allowed. Let's find a different way to show your brother that you're angry."

•**What did you do (in preschool, at Jenny's house) today?** This question is too vague for young children. They are unable to determine what is important enough to share.

Lawrence Kutner, PhD, clinical psychologist and lecturer on psychology at Harvard Medical School in Boston, and codirector of the Harvard Center for Mental Health and Media. He lectures widely on parent–child communication. *www.drkutner.com.*

Better: Ask specific questions—"Did you sing a song? Did you take a nap? Did you play with a friend?"

ELEMENTARY SCHOOL AGE/PRETEENS

●**Why can't you (get good grades, work harder, play soccer) like Mike?** Preadolescents are quite sensitive about their social status. Being compared with their friends or siblings can be extremely painful. The message that comes through is, "I don't accept you." If you do get an answer, it won't be enlightening because it will focus on something outside the child's control.

Examples: "Because he's smart and I'm stupid...Because the teacher likes him."

Better: Focus in on the underlying issue without making comparisons—"I'm concerned about your grades. Let's talk about what you can do to improve them."

●**Why don't you have more friends?** Although you may only want to help, this question makes a child feel embarrassed and defensive. Remember—the *number* of friends your child has may be irrelevant. *Quality* of friendships is more important.

Better: Explore the issue in a nonaccusatory way. "Tell me, what do you think makes a good friend? What things do you do that make you a good friend? How can you approach someone new to become a friend?"

TEENAGERS

●**When did you come home last night?** This sets up a battle of wills. You wind up arguing over whether your child got home at 11 pm or midnight, whether he lost track of the time or couldn't find a phone to call you, etc....and avoid discussing deeper concerns, such as what your teenager is doing when he's out late.

Better: Cut to the chase. Say, "When you're out late, I'm concerned that you may be drinking or doing something else that could get you into real trouble. Let's talk about that."

●**What do you see in that creep?** Your child knows that you don't really want the answer—you want to browbeat her into ending the romantic relationship. She feels the obligation to justify her behavior...and your disapproval is more likely to drive her toward the person.

Better: "I can see you have really strong feelings for Sean. I don't know him well, but I can't see what you see. Help me understand why you care about him."

If she feels you are genuinely open, she may articulate his bad qualities as well as his attractive ones...and begin questioning the relationship herself.

●**What makes you such a know-it-all?** It's normal for teenagers to think they know everything. This inescapably hostile question is designed to make a point, not to gather information. It cuts off communication.

Although it is tempting in the heat of the moment to call your child a know-it-all (or worse), restrain yourself.

Better: Acknowledge that your child is developing sophisticated thinking skills and that you are interested in his opinion. "I realize you are not the little boy you were. Tell me more about why you have this opinion."

ADULT CHILDREN

●**When are you going to get married/ have kids? Why don't you get a better job? How much money are you making?** These nosy questions imply that you want the same kind of control over your kids as when they were younger. It's just as disrespectful to ask your kids these questions as it would be to ask a friend or neighbor.

Better: Wait for your child to share this information when and if he is ready.

●**Why don't you call me more often?** This question is manipulative—it implies that there's something wrong with your child. It also misses the point. The real issue is not about reasons why—it's that you miss being in contact.

Better: "I really enjoy talking to you. Is it OK if I call you? What is the best time for me to phone?"

How to Raise An Upbeat Child

Cheryl K. Olson, MPH, associate director of Harvard Medical School Center for Mental Health and Media, Boston. Her research focuses on helping schoolteachers identify depression in children.

S ome kids are born cranky and irritable— it's simply their temperament. But even upbeat kids have their down moments. *To help your kids stay positive...*

● **Ease children's anxiety about their safety and the safety of those around them.** Point out that disasters, such as terrorist attacks, are rare. When my 12-year-old son was very concerned about terrorists dropping nuclear bombs, I explained how hard it is to obtain those materials and actually use them.

Younger children need to be reassured that their parents, aunts, uncles and grandparents will always be there to take care of them.

Limit children's exposure to the news. When kids read about a plane crash or hear about one on TV, for example, they think these types of events happen often. Also, don't share your own anxieties with them.

Example: If you have to fly for a business trip, don't express to your children any concerns you might have about flying. If they're worried for your safety, explain that plane crashes almost never happen.

● **Create a diversion to shake off a bad mood.** If your child is feeling blue, offer to read him/her a book...play a game he enjoys ...put on some upbeat music. See if you can make him laugh.

● **Encourage kids to find a bright spot in the day.** Recently, my son began dreading school because gym, which he does not like, is his first class of the day. I suggested that instead of focusing on gym he think about his after-school activities, which he thoroughly enjoys. Knowing that he had an "island of happiness" to look forward to—even though it was much later in the day—helped him get through the tough moments.

● **Help them to stop *awfulizing.*** Some kids take a single negative event and turn it into an awful generalization.

Example I: Your child gets a bad grade on a spelling test. Instead of seeing it as an isolated event, he complains, "I'm always getting bad grades." Point out the reality to your child—"You got a 93 on the biology test last week." Then together, brainstorm ways he can improve his spelling grades in the future. If the reality is that he does get bad grades often, point out the other things he does well—and, again, talk through ways he might improve his grades.

Example II: Your daughter wants to run for the student council but won't because she says she is not popular. Your response could be, "You don't have to be the most popular kid to get elected, but you do have to be someone the kids know." Then strategize ways your daughter could get to know others better—perhaps by joining clubs or volunteering at school functions.

● **Don't set up your child to fail.** Sometimes, we pressure our children to do things they're not good at in the hope that they'll get better at them. This can backfire.

Example: If your 10-year-old is nervous about swimming, signing him up for the swim team may be putting too much pressure on him. Instead, encourage him to take swimming lessons at his own pace. He can then join a competitive team in a sport in which he has more confidence, such as tennis or basketball.

What to Teach Your Kids Before They Leave Home

Adele Scheele, PhD, director of The Career Center at California State University in Northridge, *www.career inspired.com.* She is author of *Jumpstart Your Career in College* (Kaplan).

W hether your children go to college right after high school or take a few years off for work or to explore the world, they'll face a steep learning curve. They will be making many decisions for the first time—and living with the mistakes.

Schools rarely teach the *life skills*—using credit cards responsibly...making friends in new places…reading the fine print on contracts, etc.—that kids need to become responsible adults.

Before your children pack their bags and walk out the door, here are important things they should know…

FINANCIAL LESSONS

●**Pay off credit cards monthly—no matter what.** Once kids turn 18, every bank will start sending them credit card offers. They could be deep in debt in just a few months if they're not careful.

Trap: Young people often look at the low minimum payments on credit card bills and think they're getting a bargain. They don't realize how much things really cost when they're paying an annual percentage rate of 18%.

●**Set *no-exception* budgets.** Kids have to learn to live within their means—even if that means doing without "necessities" they used to take for granted. Remind your children to factor in *everything*—rent…utilities…clothes…meals…popcorn and soda at the movies, etc.

Temptation will certainly beckon. Children need to learn that giving in to temptation now usually means that they will have to give up something important later.

●**Follow the *$100 rule.*** Encourage your children to consult you before buying anything that costs more than $100. Remind them that the terms for credit purchases are deliberately made to look attractive. The hard truth is often buried in the fine print.

Example: You can get a cell phone for almost nothing—but only if you sign a service contract that costs hundreds of dollars a year.

PERSONAL LESSONS

●**Stay socially active.** Drama clubs…photography workshops…ceramic classes, etc. are great places to meet people in no-pressure settings. When moving to a new area, classes and hobbies make it possible to have a busy social life outside of smoky (and expensive) bars. Remind kids to read campus or community newspapers. These usually list inexpensive or free extracurricular activities.

●**Maintain personal boundaries.** Peer pressure does not lessen when children leave home, especially when they're living in dorm rooms or sharing apartments with friends.

Remind kids that they don't have to do anything that makes them feel uncomfortable—drinking…smoking…staying out all night…spending foolishly, etc.

Example: Suppose your daughter has a roommate who drinks in the dorm—against the school's rules. Rather than risk embarrassment by taking a personal stand, she can simply say, "My parents won't pay my bills here if I get caught with alcohol." She'll get the message across while putting the blame on *you.*

●**Find a mentor.** In high school, talking to teachers is often seen as apple-polishing. In college, it's a shortcut to success. In the working world, it's a key to opportunities. When you ask successful people how they got ahead, they invariably give credit to early mentors.

●**Be prepared for emotional dips.** Children who leave home for the first time often have a difficult transition period. They may gain weight…avoid going out…have trouble sleeping, etc.

Helpful: I tell my students that if someone were videotaping them over the years, they would be amazed at their developing skills and emotional and intellectual growth. It can boost their confidence to understand that how they feel now is temporary. Talking with a psychologist can also be helpful.

●**Learn how to cook the basics.** Teenagers don't believe it, but there will come a time when a handful of potato chips and a soda won't seem like a nutritious meal. Everyone should know a few kitchen basics before leaving home—how to roast a chicken…cook spaghetti and a simple sauce…combine greens for a quick salad.

●**Remind them that you'll be there when they need you.** Many parents start to back off when children leave home because they don't want to interfere, but this approach can leave the kids feeling very isolated.

Important: It is also your children's responsibility to stay in touch with you. I advise making this a condition of receiving their rent checks or other perks. A weekly phone call just might be enough…although it's also important for them to come home several times a year.

How to Help Your Elderly Parents Help Themselves

Joseph A. Ilardo, PhD, and Carole R. Rothman, PhD, codirectors of the Center for Adult Children of the Elderly in Scarsdale, NY. They are the coauthors of *Are Your Parents Driving You Crazy? How to Resolve the Most Common Dilemmas with Aging Parents* (VanderWyk and Burnham).

Do you have an elderly parent you are worried about? Approximately seven million Americans do. *Here are the best ways to help your parents...*

CLARIFY THE PROBLEM

●**Does everyone agree a problem exists?** If not, it may be impossible to get people to work together.

Example: A 91-year-old woman often eats ice cream for dinner. Her daughter thinks her diet is inappropriate. But her physician is satisfied with the elderly woman's health and weight—and she eats healthfully at breakfast and lunch.

●**What will happen if you do nothing?** If there are minimal consequences, then forcing a premature action can cause more problems.

●**What is your motive?** Are you trying to satisfy your parents' needs—or your own?

Example: You and your siblings have been rivals for your parents' affection. You take on the role of the "good child" by insisting that your elderly father move in with you—though he prefers to live on his own.

HOW TO SOLVE PROBLEMS

●**Ask permission before making changes or suggestions.** Instead of saying, "I'm going to arrange for grocery delivery," say, "Would you like help arranging grocery delivery?"

●**Take time to understand your parents' feelings.** You think your mother should move into a nursing home. She seems to agree, but you sense resistance. Ask her to talk more about her feelings. Why is she cool to the idea?

●**Use "I" messages.** These personal statements of feeling are free of blame and less likely to evoke anger.

Example: Your father refuses home health assistance. This places a burden on you. If you say,

"You're being inconsiderate, Dad," you only create a war of wills. Instead, tell him how his behavior is affecting you. Say, "I'm upset with this situation, Dad. It's hard for me to take care of my own kids when I spend so much time here."

You can also use more forceful "I" messages to be firm without being insulting. Say, "I must take care of my children and cannot serve as your housekeeper."

●**Set limits** if your parent is manipulative or bullying. *Suggestions...*

●Tell him/her you do not want to argue. Explain that you will resume talking after he calms down.

●Take notes. Say, "I want to understand your concerns. Tell me again what you are worried about. I'm going to take notes." This calms him down because he knows you are taking his words seriously.

●Use selective "you" messages. These can put the brakes on out-of-control exchanges. Say, "You are out of line, Dad. Please, stop shouting." Or, "You may be able to frighten others by raising your voice. But that doesn't work with me."

●**Solicit the help of a third party whom your parent respects**—a clergyman, attorney, doctor, therapist, etc. Say, "Dad, you and I keep going around and around about this. Would you be willing to chat with your physician about it?"

●**Accept partial solutions.** You can fall short of your ideal but still accomplish the goal.

Example: Your mother is bouncing checks. When you offer to pay bills for her, she accuses you of trying to control her money. Since your real goal is to stabilize her finances, you could offer to hire an accountant to help her once a month. Or ask her to collect all her bills each week so you can "do the math part."

●**Bow out.** If your mother's house is a mess but she refuses your repeated offers to get cleaning help, don't fight her. Say, "Mom, I've done all I can. I'm here to help if you change your mind." When the pressure is off, she may wind up doing what you want anyway.

●**Join a support group.** Caregiver groups help adult children cope with guilt, anger and sadness. To locate a group in your area, call a local hospital or senior center. Or contact your local Office of the Aging—find it in the blue pages under *County Offices* or through your state's social services department.

Important: If your parents' safety is in danger, you may need to call the police or your state's adult protective social services department (reached, in most cases, through your state's social services department).

CASE STUDY:
ELDERLY PARENT IS A DANGEROUS DRIVER

An 87-year-old man had several minor accidents. His son suggested he give up driving. His father accused him of putting him out to pasture. The son thought about how his father would feel if he could no longer drive. It would limit his freedom. He would also lose self-esteem and a sense of belonging in the community.

The son said, "Dad, I know you have been driving since you were 16 and have always been proud of your skills. But yesterday, Mrs. Jones was upset that you sideswiped her car. I know you agreed to pay for the damage, but this kind of thing never used to happen.

"I would feel awful if you hurt yourself or someone else. I imagine you are upset about this, too. We really need to find a way to keep this from happening again."

The son offered his father alternatives…

●**Take public transportation.**

●**Hire a driver** to be on call three afternoons a week.

●**Retake his driver's test.** The son promised to stop pestering his father if he passed—but would continue to monitor his dad's driving.

The elderly man agreed to the first solution. If he had not accepted any of them, the son was prepared to approach his father's physician with accident reports, etc. Many elderly patients agree to stop driving if it's "doctor's orders."

What to Look For in an Assisted-Living Facility

Karen Love, founder and chairman of the Consumer Consortium on Assisted Living, a nonprofit organization that's devoted to representing the needs of consumers in assisted-living facilities, Falls Church, VA, *www.ccal.org.*

Be extremely careful when selecting an assisted-living facility for yourself or a family member. Some facilities have the same staffing and resident-neglect problems found in many nursing homes.

To choose the best—and safest—facility…

●**Assess your—or your family member's needs**—physical, financial and lifestyle.

●**Consult the National Association of Professional Geriatric Care Managers** (*www.caremanager.org*) to locate a professional who can help you.

●**Tour as many facilities as you can,** and ask the community affairs or public relations manager about the things that are most important to you, such as staffing and medication administration. A checklist of important questions is available at *www.ccal.org.*

For your three top contenders: Return to each facility unannounced at least once. Ask the residents what they like and dislike. Talk with staff members to see if they are friendly and knowledgeable. Sample a meal. Read the most recent annual licensing inspection report, which the facility should have available, to see if it was cited for any deficiencies and if they were corrected.

Important: Facilities may ask for up to $10,000 up front—make sure the money is refundable, at least on a prorated basis, in case the new resident is unhappy there. Read the contract carefully.

Note: About 85% of assisted-care residents pay out of their own pockets. Medicare does not pay for assisted living, but private long-term-care policies may. Medicaid policies vary by state.

Better In-Law Relations

Accept the differences between you and your in-laws and respect them, but *don't* feel you have to give in to them all the time. Consider in-laws as friends, with whom relationships may develop quickly or slowly—you don't have to love them and vice versa. Do not expect your spouse to solve in-law problems for you.

Lee Schnebly, MEd, a mental-health and marriage counselor, Tucson, AZ, and the author of Being Happy Being Married: A Guide to Building a Better Relationship *(Fisher).*

Uncovering Your Family History on the Internet

Pamela Rice Hahn, Celina, Ohio–based author of The Unofficial Guide to Online Genealogy *(IDG/Hungry Minds). www.genealogytips.com.*

The Internet offers a treasure trove of genealogical data—directories of surnames, birth records, marriage records, military records, ships' passenger lists, census records, immigration records and much more.

There are even family history sites that contain family trees, wills, photographs, etc.

WHERE TO START

One way to begin your search is by entering your surname into a search engine like Yahoo! (*www.yahoo.com*). But unless your name is unusual, thousands of listings will come up. Searching all the listings is time-consuming and generally unrewarding.

Better way: Use genealogy-specific directories and search engines. An excellent directory is DMOZ Open Directory Project (*http://dmoz.org/Society/Genealogy*). It's organized into categories, such as "obituaries," "adoption search" and "military genealogy." If you're unsure which category to use, search the entire directory by name.

Surname-specific Web directories will list family Web pages but won't list them all—you will need to go to genealogy-specific search engines for more. These work like regular search engines, but look only for sites pertaining to genealogy and family history (Helm's Genealogy Toolbox at *www.genealogytoolbox.com,* for example).

EXPANDING YOUR SEARCH

There are Web sites from all over the world containing information of interest to family tree researchers...

•**The USGenWeb Project** (*www.usgenweb.com*). This site provides links to every state and county genealogical Web site in the US, plus it has copies of census records, wills and other public documents.

Bonus: You'll find information on how to research your family tree, find names, genealogy, vocabulary, census records and more.

•**American Family Immigration History Center** (*www.ellisislandrecords.org*). Search passenger records (and even see original manifests) from ships that brought more than 22 million immigrants to Ellis Island between 1892 and 1924.

•**Family Search Internet Genealogy Service** (*www.familysearch.org*). This is the on-line version of the Church of Jesus Christ of Latter-Day Saints Family History Center—but listings aren't limited to Mormons.

•**Roots Web Surname List** (*www.rootsweb.com*). The oldest and largest free on-line genealogy site, it provides a registry of more than a million surnames. Search by surname and location...and contact the person who submitted the surname to share research.

•**US Federal Land Patent Records** (*www.blm.gov*). The US Bureau of Land Management provides an on-line database of more than two million federal land title records issued between 1820 and 1908.

•**Cemetery Records Online** (*www.internment.net*). This site contains close to 3 million records from almost 6,000 cemeteries all over the world.

•**World Connect Project** (*http://worldconnect.rootsweb.com*). Here you will find a database of family trees submitted by thousands of researchers—there are more than 200 million ancestor names. With your family tree posted here, other researchers with common ancestors will find you.

●**Olive Tree Genealogy** (*www.olivetree genealogy.com*). Here are passenger lists from ships sailing as far back as the 1400s, as well as links to other passenger lists on the Internet.

●**US National Archives and Records Administration** (*www.nara.gov*). Links to Enemy Alien Registration Affidavits, World War II Draft Registration Records and Indian Bounty Land Applications.

Caution: Information you discover on-line is *not* always accurate. Look for a citation showing where the information originated. Never accept information as valid until you verify it.

Helpful: The quickest way to make progress in genealogical research is to communicate with others. *Do this by…*

●Joining a mailing list, which is similar to an E-mail party line.

●Posting a message to a message board—a computerized version of the old-fashioned bulletin board.

●Building your own genealogy Web site which will attract others with information about your ancestors.

YOUR OWN WEB SITE

If you publish your findings on your own family history Web site, you'll get help with your search from genealogists all over the world. They'll view your data, answer your questions and help to fill in the missing information in your family tree.

Genealogical information on the Internet is sent and received through Genealogical Data Communication (GEDCOM) files. This file format allows information that was entered into one genealogy program to be read and used by another program. It is necessary to convert your genealogical database to a GEDCOM file.

There are dozens of automatic conversion software programs which can convert your GEDCOM files into pages suitable for the Web. *Among the best…*

●**Legacy Family Tree** (*www.legacyfamily tree.com*).

●**Master Genealogist** (*www.whollygenes. com*).

Next, line up the server to host your Web page. RootsWeb.com will give you *free* unlimited space to store your Web pages. It will help you decide what information to include on your Web site and how to arrange it, how to put together your own Web pages and send them to the server.

Important: Link up your Web site to the relevant surname, county, state and/or country resources. That way, the users interested in the information on your Web site will see the link and find you.

HELPFUL GUIDELINES

The National Genealogical Society (*www.ngs genealogy.org*) offers these guidelines for publishing Web pages on the Internet…

●**Explain the purpose of your Web site.**

●**Provide complete contact information,** including your name and E-mail address.

●**Respect copyright, attributions, privacy** and the sharing of sensitive information.

●**Have unambiguous source citations.**

●**Identify transcribed, excerpted or abstracted data.**

Whatever you do, update the site at frequent intervals, changing the content to keep the information current and the links valid.

Finding Household Help You Can Trust

J.J. "Jack" Luna, who spent 11 years eluding capture by the police as a secret humanitarian operative in Franco's Spain. He now works as an international security consultant. *www.howtobeinvisible.com*. He is author of *How to Be Invisible: A Step-by-Step Guide to Protecting Your Assets, Your Identity and Your Life* (St. Martin's).

If you employ household help—whether a nanny, a baby-sitter, a once-a-week cleaning service or a full-time maid—you put yourself at risk.

Domestic employees know your schedule, your home security system and the location of all your valuables. Should they be so inclined,

they could dig through your files to learn your Social Security and bank account numbers.

Hiring domestic help through a reputable cleaning service or employment agency offers you scant protection. Even if these companies do background checks on their employees—and many of them do not—a clean police record might not tell the whole story.

Domestic employees sometimes keep themselves free from suspicion by passing on what they find out about you to their confederates. These partners then perform the actual stealing, while the domestic employees keep their noses clean.

To safeguard your home…

●**Ask friends for referrals.** Your friends should have used the cleaning service or employee for at least one year. Be wary if your friends had a break-in either during or after that employee's tenure—whether or not those crimes were traced back to the employee.

●**Avoid hiring help from the "Situation Wanted" section of the classifieds.** Reliable employees usually get enough work via word of mouth.

●**Check all references.** You know this, of course, but surprisingly few people check references thoroughly.

When you speak to former employers, ask if they know where else this employee worked and call those references, too. Ask if they would hire him/her again.

●**Use a "nanny-cam."** A motion-sensitive camera pointed at a desk or jewelry box can catch dishonest employees in the act. Baby-product stores and security companies offer a wide range of nanny-cams—from a few hundred to a few thousand dollars. They can be hidden in everything from wall clocks to the eyes of teddy bears.

●**When a new employee starts, stay for his entire first visit**—and for as many future visits as possible. Treat him with respect. Employees are less likely to steal from employers they know and like.

●**Stop in unexpectedly from time to time.** This makes it hard for an employee to predict when you will be around, which makes planning a crime more difficult.

●**Avoid temptation.** Whenever possible, stow valuables out of sight, preferably in a home safe.

Is Your Home Making You Sick???

Lynn Marie Bower, a multiple chemical sensitivity sufferer and cofounder of The Healthy House Institute, a Bloomington, Indiana–based information resource on household products, electromagnetic fields and other environmental factors. 430 N. Sewell Rd., Bloomington, IN 47408, www.hhinst.com. She is author of Creating a Healthy Household and The Healthy House Answer Book (Healthy House Institute).

The potential problems associated with any prolonged exposure to chemicals in modern homes and offices has made many architects, engineers and health-conscious individuals increasingly aware of *sick building syndrome* and *multiple chemical sensitivity (MCS)*. Sufferers develop maladies that range from allergy-like symptoms to more serious diseases, such as asthma and cancer.

My problems started about 20 years ago, when my husband and I began to renovate a run-down 1850s farmhouse. As the work progressed, my health deteriorated. By the time we completed the remodeling six years later, I was bedridden with a variety of maladies—gastrointestinal problems, breathing difficulty, light sensitivity, balance and memory difficulties and more.

For a long time, we didn't know what was wrong. Then I saw a TV news segment about a woman who could not live in her new house. She said she had MCS, and that led us to research the condition.

In the journey since then, my husband and I have built a series of "healthy" homes from all-natural materials. Now, nearly 20 years later, I feel much better, although I am still highly sensitive to many commonly used chemicals.

Few people ever have symptoms as severe as I did. But a more healthful home or office environment is good even for nonchemically sensitive people.

Whenever you buy a product, consider its health attributes—in addition to price, performance and appearance. *The basics…*

CLEANING/LAUNDERING

●**Use simple, unscented, low-toxicity home-cleaning and washing products**—general-purpose cleaners…dishwashing liquids…window cleaners. Products are often sold in health food stores. Some can be homemade.

●For a scrubbing cleanser use baking soda and a damp sponge.

●Mix up a brass cleaner with some table salt and vinegar.

●For a window or vinyl floor cleaner use white vinegar and water.

●**Avoid scented products,** which often trigger allergic and asthmatic reactions.

●**Dust with a damp cotton-flannel cloth** or an electrostatically charged synthetic dusting cloth. Dust particles will cling tightly to these.

●**Vacuum often**—consider doing so once a week for every household member and pet in your family. For example, a household with two adults, two children and a dog should be vacuumed five times a week.

A central vacuum system is best because it expels dust outdoors. If using a portable vacuum, choose one with a HEPA filter.

●**Wash bed linens**—including sheets and mattress pads—once a week…and pillows, blankets, comforters and quilts every three months, to eliminate dust mites.

●**Change your bathroom towels every other day.**

●**Change kitchen towels daily.**

●**Purchase machine-washable clothes**—to prevent inhaling the dry-cleaning solution *perchloroethylene.* This solution is believed to be carcinogenic.

If you have dry-cleaned clothes: Remove plastic. Hang outside for several hours to minimize perchloroethylene.

DECORATING MATERIALS

●**Pillows, mattresses, sheets and towels should be cotton, wool or hemp.**

Favorite catalogs: Cuddledown of Maine (800-323-6793…*www.cuddledown.com*)…

Garnet Hill (800-870-3513…*www.garnethill. com*)…The Company Store (800-285-DOWN …*www.thecompanystore.com*).

●**Avoid wall-to-wall carpeting.** Having hard-surface floors, such as ceramic tile or hardwood, is healthier.

●**Use low-odor, water-based paints and finishes.** Oil-based paints and finishes contain high levels of petroleum-derived volatile organic compounds, which are believed to harm the respiratory and central nervous systems and to be carcinogenic. They also need toxic solvent for cleanup.

●**Use washable, natural-fabric slipcovers** over upholstered furniture.

PERSONAL CARE

●**Choose unscented, all-natural, hypoallergenic cosmetics** and personal-care products. Some brands to try include Aubrey Organics (800-282-7394…*www.aubreyorganics. com*)…Tom's of Maine (800-367-8667…*www. tomsofmaine.com*). Use odorless natural crystals for body deodorant.

KITCHEN APPLIANCES

●**Keep a minimum number of appliances so cabinets are easier to clean.** Don't leave appliances on a counter to collect dust.

●**Choose glass, stainless steel, ceramic and enameled cast-iron cookware.** These are the least reactive—meaning their components will not leach into food and don't need nonstick coatings.

●**Use an electric stove rather than gas.** Natural gas releases combustion by-products, including carbon dioxide. If you cannot do without a gas stove, have a powerful range hood that vents outdoors…and open a window when cooking. Better electric cooktops are made of smooth-surface radiant glass. They are easy to clean and produce virtually no odor when heated.

●**Keep the refrigerator clean.** Dust cooling coils once a month so dust won't decrease the refrigerator's efficiency or blow into your kitchen. Once a week, clean the inside of the refrigerator…once a month, clean the drip pan underneath it.

WATER AND AIR

●**Filter water** coming out of your kitchen and bathroom sinks and shower heads to remove chlorine.

●**Store your drinking water in a glass or ceramic pitcher or bottle.**

●**Use a dehumidifier** to prevent high humidity (over 40%) and mold growth.

●**Repair leaking pipes, gutters, damp basements and foundations** to remove the excess moisture that can lead to mold growth and pest infestation.

●**Install a general ventilation system,** such as a heat recovery ventilator (HRV). It removes heat from outgoing air and transfers it to incoming air. Spot ventilation systems should be placed in the bathroom, laundry room and kitchen.

Note: Using air filters is inadequate. Filters cannot remove all contaminants…or remove moisture…or create oxygen.

School Bus Warning

Toxic diesel fumes can increase cancer risk and exacerbate asthma and other breathing problems. In a recent study, exhaust levels inside diesel buses were 23 to 46 times *higher* than levels considered a significant cancer risk.

Worst place: Back of a bus more than 10 years old (age is indicated on a plaque above the inside windshield).

Ask the driver to keep windows open…and encourage your child to sit toward the front.

Gina Solomon, MD, MPH, a senior scientist at the Natural Resources Defense Council, San Francisco.

Clothes Dryer Danger

Clothes dryers cause 15,000 fires a year—and about $75 million in property damage. Blocked lint traps are the major cause.

Self-defense: Clean up the lint filter after each use, and vacuum dust and lint from the exhaust regularly. Vent the dryer properly. The exhaust vent pipe should not be restricted, and the outdoor vent flap should open when the dryer operates. Do not leave a dryer running when you leave the house or are sleeping. Have dryers professionally installed and maintained according to manufacturers' instructions.

Margie Coloian, public affairs manager, National Fire Protection Association, One Batterymarch Park, Quincy, MA 02269.

Don't Let Emergencies Catch You Off Guard

Find a plumber, electrician or other repairperson *before* you are hit by an emergency.

Ask neighbors, friends, real estate agents, tradesmen and counter personnel at the local hardware store for referrals.

Have the repairperson work on a small, nonemergency job to see if he/she is really reliable. Then, when an emergency occurs—such as a water leak or storm damage—you'll have the name and number of someone to call. You'll be a known customer, and the repairperson will be more likely to put you near the top of his list when you need him most.

Stephen Elder, home inspector and home-repair specialist, Pittsboro, NC.

Are Your Papers In Order?

Martin Shenkman, CPA, JD, estate attorney and financial planner, New York City, *www.laweasy.com.* He is the author of *The Complete Living Trust Program* (Wiley).

Be sure the following important documents are in order for the benefit and safety of your loved ones…

●**Will** to direct the disposition of your assets, name a guardian and executor.

•**Durable power of attorney** naming someone to handle your financial affairs if you are incapacitated.

•**Medical power of attorney** naming who will make medical decisions for you if you're incapacitated.

•**Living will** expressing your wishes regarding life-saving care.

•**Balance sheet** listing all of your assets, investments and insurance policies.

•**Prenuptial agreement** if you marry and you have family from a prior marriage, or own a business you wish to protect from a possible marital dispute.

•**Child emergency medical form,** if you have minor children, to authorize medical care.

•**Beneficiary designation forms** for IRAs, insurance, etc., to assure that the right people are the recipients.

Your Complete Guide to Purchasing a Home

Edith Lank, syndicated real estate columnist for Tribune Media Services in Rochester, NY. She is author of *The Homebuyer's Kit* and *The Home Seller's Kit* (both from Kaplan).

Whether you're a first-timer or a seasoned buyer, the following guide provides some invaluable tips for purchasing a home...

RESEARCH THE LOCATION

Before you make an appointment to view a home, evaluate the neighborhood carefully. Even if you don't have young children, consider the quality of the school district—a weak district can drive down property values.

A good real estate agent or builder can provide data on per-pupil expenditures in each district, average high school SAT scores and the percentage of college-bound graduates.

Other considerations...

•**Toxic waste.** Environmental audits, common in commercial property purchases, are rare in residential purchases, mainly because of the expense. Ask the seller and your broker if there are any waste sites nearby. Also do your own research. You can start with the Environmental Protection Agency (EPA) Web site (*www.epa.gov*), where you can look up hazardous waste sites in the area.

•**Power lines.** Scientists are still debating the potentially harmful effects of electromagnetic radiation from power sources, particularly on children. Be aware that nearby power lines could affect your resale value.

•**Radon and asbestos.** The EPA considers radon—a colorless, odorless gas—second only to cigarette smoke as a cause of lung cancer. Adequate ventilation can solve the problem.

Asbestos, a flame retardant, was commonly used in houses built before 1975. Intact, it's not a problem—but crumbling particles can lead to lung disease and even cancer. It should be removed by a professional service.

•**Lead.** High levels of lead can cause irreversible mental and physical damage in children. Test for lead in paint and tap water before buying a home built prior to 1978.

Important: The seller must allow you to test for lead in the water. Test water early in the morning because lead from soldering may flush out after water is run for 15 seconds. *For information on lead testing:* Contact the National Lead Information Center at 800-424-5323 or *www.epa.gov/lead/nlic.htm.*

•**Local culture.** Buy a few issues of a community newspaper to get a sense of regional politics, crime levels and other important issues.

USE A BUYER'S BROKER

In most places, you can hire a buyer's broker to represent your interests. You may pay that broker a retainer and/or a percentage of the purchase price. Buyer's brokers are legally obligated to work for you, follow your instructions, keep your information confidential and help you get the deal you want.

Resource: National Association of Exclusive Buyer Agents, 407-767-7700, *www.naeba.org.*

With a traditional seller's broker, the seller pays most or all of the commission.

The broker who listed the home is legally bound to pass on to the seller relevant financial information about you, including your upper spending limits.

That doesn't mean a seller's broker can't be useful in finding you the right home and walking you through the process. *But if you are working with a seller's broker...*

●**Don't reveal the highest price you're willing to pay.** Instead, give a ballpark figure.

●**Ask whether the seller knows of any defects** in the property. He/she is legally required to provide this information.

Both buyer's and seller's brokers will have access to a multiple-listing system, enabling them to show all houses in an area that are not exclusive listings.

KEEP A LOG

If you see more than a few homes in one day, they can become a blur. *To keep track...*

●**List all your criteria.** Before your first appointment, list home features in order of importance—must have...nice to have...and doesn't matter.

Key considerations: Proximity to work/transportation...condition of house...number of bedrooms and bathrooms...garage and storage requirements...yard, deck or patio...den or family room...eat-in kitchen...home office.

●**Keep track of what you've seen.**

●Keep the listing sheets provided by the broker. These may have pictures and detail the number, kind and size of rooms...property features...and views. The listing sheet will also provide the asking price, names of the schools and taxes.

●Take pictures or videos of the houses.

●Make a worksheet listing features of each home that you did or did not like. Rate them from one (least desirable) to 10 (most desirable). Total the rating for each house to compare it with others. Include price...lot size...style of home...etc.

●Note nearby amenities. Mark local parks, schools, shopping areas and other points of interest on a map.

●**Ask neighbors about local concerns and problems,** such as snow removal, parking, traffic and noise.

LIKELY BARGAINS

●**Homes with sloppy housekeeping.** If cars are parked and toys strewn on the lawn,

furniture is old and wallpaper is peeling, the house may sit on the market for a long time and fetch a lower price when it eventually sells. But if the structure, neighborhood and size meet your needs, snatch it up. It's a lot easier to fix cosmetic problems than to replace a roof or add a bathroom.

●**Distressed sellers.** Home owners who need to move in a hurry because of a new job, divorce or death in the family will often accept a lower price. If time is of the essence, the seller may instruct the broker to convey the urgency as a selling point.

●**Developers with excess inventory.** A developer may have overbuilt or lost a prospective sale at the last minute, making him eager to sell.

Telltale sign: A number of empty properties in a development that have been listed for a while.

●**A modest house in an upscale neighborhood.** You can renovate or add on to it and greatly enhance its value. Buying a trophy house in a less desirable neighborhood is rarely a good investment.

If you find a bargain, act fast.

POTENTIAL PITFALLS

Most newer homes meet state and local building codes, but houses that are more than 20 years old may have serious problems.

Some states require home inspectors to be licensed. If your state doesn't, look for inspectors who belong to the American Society of Home Inspectors, 800-743-2744, *www.ashi.com.*

Your inspector should look for...

●**User-friendly maintenance.** Are there built-in sprinklers and self-storing storm windows? Are the gutters properly installed and lined to keep water off the house? Are the drainpipes securely fastened? How soon will the house need painting, siding or a new roof?

●**Adequate outlets.** Older houses tend to have minimal electrical service. Ideally, you want one outlet every 12 feet in larger rooms.

●**Plumbing.** If you prefer older homes, look for an updated system in which galvanized pipes have been replaced with copper ones. Galvanized pipes can corrode and clog, especially the horizontal pipes that carry hot water from the water heater.

● **Basement water.** If the basement is being used for storage, it's a good sign that it's dry. Check the bottom of the furnace and water heater for trouble signs—rust or a patch of newer paint.

● **Other potential hazards.** Termites… improper insulation in the colder regions of the country.

WEB RESOURCES

The Web is a valuable research tool…

● **www.realtor.com.** Sponsored by the National Association of Realtors, this site has extensive listings, including pictures and virtual tours of many residences. Its sister site, *www.homebuilder.com*, has listings of newly built homes.

● **International Real Estate Digest** (*www.ired.com*) and the Inman News Service (*www.inman.com*) provide news on markets, rates, buying and building trends.

● **Realty Times** (*www.realtytimes.com*) offers community profiles, news and advice to consumers.

How to Afford More of a Home Than You Think You Can Afford

James R. Avedisian, CPA, an attorney specializing in estate and family tax planning, 924 W. Fremont Ave., Sunnyvale, CA 94087.

The shaky stock market has left people looking for safe places to invest. Real estate may be just the thing. Homes and apartments have continued to appreciate in value even as the market has declined.

What if you lack the funds to buy and carry the kind of home you want? For help with the monthly expenses, you might consider taking in a tenant. In addition to the extra income, there are some significant tax advantages in this kind of arrangement.

For help with the down payment, consider these options…

● **Take a no-interest loan from a family member.** No-interest loans up to $100,000 are not taxed if the money is used for the down payment on a personal residence (and the borrower's net investment income totals $1,000 or less).

Caution: Check with your bank to make sure such a loan won't disqualify you from getting a mortgage.

● **Find a co-owner.** A parent, for example, might be able to come up with some or all of the down payment. For young home buyers, a co-owner can provide the creditworthiness to get a mortgage.

Trap: The tax law will consider such an arrangement a passive activity on the co-owner's part. The co-owner's ability to write off related expenses is subject to the passive activity loss (PAL) rules.

● **Accept gifts from family members.** Married individuals can give up to $22,000 a year without having to worry about gift tax.

● **Borrow from your 401(k).** The tax law permits you to borrow up to 50% from your account balance—up to a maximum of $50,000 —to buy your first house or apartment.

FINDING A TENANT

Now that you have secured a source of financing, look for a single-family residence or a condominium with at least two bedrooms. Ideally, each bedroom should have its own bathroom. Many new condos are built with twin master bedroom suites.

Then locate a tenant—through word of mouth or advertising. Carefully interview the prospects. Obtain references if it's someone you do not know well. Make sure your lifestyles are compatible.

Fix a rent that's reasonable for the use of your home. Remember, the tenant is not only using a bedroom, but also sharing the kitchen and other common areas. What is reasonable rent? Look in the newspaper for comparable rentals…or check with a local realtor.

Be sure to obtain a security deposit (equal to at least one month's rent) to cover you if the tenant leaves before the end of the lease and you have to find a new tenant.

Worst-case scenario: A tenant who stays to the end of the lease but damages your home.

Put all the terms of your arrangement with the tenant into a lease. For example, if you're sharing utilities, make sure the lease obligates your tenant for this expense.

Also: Rent on a month-to-month basis—or no more than one year—to protect yourself if the tenant doesn't work out.

HELP FROM UNCLE SAM

When you own rental property, tax write-offs offset the rent. If your write-offs equal your rent, you won't pay any income tax on the rent. You can use all the rental income to cover the costs of maintaining the home. *Deductible rental expenses include...*

- **Mortgage interest.**
- **Real estate taxes.**
- **Homeowner's association fees.**
- **Insurance.**
- **Repairs.**
- **Depreciation.**

How is the depreciation figured in this situation? On the entire home? Half the home? Something else? The IRS offers no firm guidance on this point.

Clearly, taking depreciation on the entire home would not be warranted since you use it as your personal residence. But a reasonable argument could be made for depreciating half of the home—the part the tenant is entitled to use. At the very least, you would be able to depreciate the bedroom to which the tenant has exclusive use.

Limits on write-offs in excess of rental income: The vacation home rules limit write-offs other than mortgage interest and real estate taxes. Your write-offs can't exceed your rental income. Do these rules apply to this situation? Again, there is no definitive answer.

The vacation home rules do *not* apply to the portion of a unit used exclusively as a hotel, motel, inn or similar establishment. This so-called "bed-and-breakfast" exception is clearly analogous to the rental arrangement in which the tenant has the exclusive use of a bedroom and all other common areas. If this is the case, your home may be considered a "similar establishment" excludable from the vacation home rules.

If the vacation rules don't apply, excess write-offs are considered passive activity losses. These losses are deductible currently only to the extent of passive activity income. Suspended losses may be carried forward to future years to offset passive activity income and may be claimed in full (without regard to passive activity income) in the year the home is sold.

DOWN THE ROAD

Sharing a home you own with a tenant provides great flexibility for you, no matter what the future brings...

- **You can continue to take in tenants if you still need the rental income.**

- **You can terminate the arrangement at the end of the lease** if you can afford to meet the housing costs on your own. For someone who is just starting out in the workforce, salary increases may make this a possibility.

- **If you marry, your spouse can move in and share costs.**

- **You can "trade up,"** that is, sell the home to buy a more expensive residence. If you've paid down the mortgage and/or the home's value has appreciated, you may have a larger down payment for your next home.

Key tax break: Up to $250,000 of gain realized on the sale of a home can be excluded from income if you're single and have owned and used the home as your main residence for at least two of five years before the sale. That figure is $500,000 on a joint return provided your spouse meets the two-year use test.

This exclusion applies only to the portion of the home used for personal use. It does not apply to the rental portion of the house—probably half of the residence in the arrangement described above.

Depreciation wrinkle: Any depreciation that has been taken is subject to "recapture" when the home is sold. The amount of depreciation you've taken is brought back onto your return and taxed at a rate of 25%.

• You can sell the home to move into a continuing-care facility should you no longer be able to live on your own. The home sale rules will again apply to the portion of the home treated as your personal residence—with depreciation recapture on any depreciation that has been taken.

• You can keep it as a rental unit if you can afford to live elsewhere—for example, if you marry and move into your spouse's residence. Once the home converts completely to rental income, write-offs for the entire unit are governed by the passive activity loss rules.

What Is Your Home Really Worth?

Diana Jacob, master senior appraiser and director of education, National Association of Master Appraisers, a trade group based in San Antonio.

Most people already know—or they're able to quickly find out—how much money is in their checking, savings and investment accounts.

But few people know how to determine the value of what may be their single largest asset—their homes.

The most common reason to determine a home's value is to price it for sale. You may also want to know the value for insurance or tax purposes or to obtain a home-equity loan or line of credit.

Different kinds of appraisals will yield different results.

Do not count on on-line appraisal services. Free on-line services take a random sample of sales in the area and use a statistical analysis to estimate value.

Sales data used by on-line services are culled from public records. Since the computerized logging of the data sometimes lags actual sales by many months, on-line appraisals can be out of sync with market conditions. Moreover, with an on-line appraisal, no one ever actually looks at the property.

WAYS TO ASSESS VALUE

• Read newspaper listings to find out what similarly sized homes in the neighborhood are selling for.

Caution: Sales listings will represent the *seller's* idea of what a house is worth—which is often exaggerated.

• Review the assessed value of your home on municipal tax rolls. If you cannot find your most recent tax bill, ask your local tax assessor to provide the information.

Caution: As a rule, tax assessments reflect only a percentage of actual market value. Even though the ratio of assessed value to market value is generally known—the official assessment might represent 80% of market value—assessments still may not produce accurate market values. Also, a house's value may have increased since its last assessment.

While knowing the assessed value of a home may not be useful in determining a sale price, a review may reveal that the house is actually *overassessed*.

Example: If a garage has been removed from the property.

Moneysaver: If the assessed value of your home seems inflated, ask your local tax authority how you can appeal to have your taxes lowered.

• Consult a real estate agent. Anyone can obtain a "comparative market analysis" from a local real estate agent. This can give you an idea of the value of the house if you are thinking about seeking a home-equity loan or eventually selling your home. The agent will review a number of recent sales of similar houses—or "comparables"—and estimate the value for your home.

Caution: The real estate agent is hoping to list the property for sale—and is competing with other agents to do so. It is not unusual for him/her to err on the high side.

• Hire an appraiser. This is the best way to get an accurate, up-to-date assessment of what a house is really worth. *Cost:* About $300, depending on location.

An individual would generally seek out an appraiser when a property needs to be sold to settle an estate…he/she is appearing before a tax appeals board...he is selling his home directly, without a real estate agent...etc.

An appraiser must certify that he/she has no present or future interest in the property or the parties involved. He has nothing to gain or lose by telling you what your property is really worth.

An appraiser considers the size, style and condition of the house...amenities, such as pools, workshops, sheds and hot tubs...local government...neighborhood...schools...tax rate...proximity to town centers, recreation areas, parks and mass transportation...and proximity to less desirable spots, such as airports, landfills, recycling centers as well as hazardous-waste sites.

The appraiser will factor this information into data on recent sales of similar houses in the area.

Information: To find out about appraisers in your area, contact the National Association of Master Appraisers, 800-229-6262, *www.master appraisers.org*...or the National Association of Real Estate Appraisers, 320-763-7626, *www. iami.org/narea.cfm.*

How to Sell Your Home Faster

Karen Eastman Bigos, real estate broker, Burgdorff ERA Realtors, 545 Millburn Ave., Short Hills, NJ 07078.

If you have your home on the market, here are some invaluable tips that will help you sell more quickly...

• **Walk around the house** with your realtor and a building inspector. Make note of any necessary repairs.

• **Lower your price** if you have not sold your home within 14 days.

• **Stay away from home during showings** and open houses. Before you leave, turn on the lights and open window shades.

• **Ask your listing agent to get feedback** from buyer agents who have already shown your home.

• **Hold an open house on Sunday.** Ask your realtor to send 2,000 postcard invitations with a photo of the house.

• **Make sure your realtor lists your house on common realtor Web sites** and makes a digital tour of the house for the Internet or on a CD-Rom.

• **Offer to pay a portion of the buyer's closing costs.**

• **Consider buyer bonuses,** such as a season ski pass.

More on Selling Your Home Quickly

You may find it easier to sell your house after you purchase a home warranty. This insurance-like service contract covers the cost of repairing or replacing air conditioners, water heaters, plumbing, etc.

Warranties aren't usually needed for newer homes. But buyers may be more willing to purchase an older home if they know they won't have to pay for any unexpected repairs. Most warranties run for one year.

David Schechner, real estate attorney, Schechner & Targan, West Orange, NJ.

When Renting Before Selling

Laurence I. Foster, CPA/PFS, former partner and currently consultant, Eisner LLP, 750 Third Ave., New York City 10017.

There's a potential opportunity—as well as a trap—for those home owners who rent out a home that they have lived in before selling it.

Key: The Tax Code now allows generous "residential" tax treatment for those who sell a home after living in it for only two of the prior five years. This includes a tax exclusion for up to $250,000 of gain ($500,000 on a joint return).

Opportunity: You can claim tax-free residential treatment not only for appreciation in a house's value that occurs while you use it as your home, but also for the appreciation that occurs during up to three years after you convert it to a rental property.

Snag: A loss suffered on a personal residence is nondeductible. So far, no court decision yet applies the new law on this point. In the past, however, the IRS and courts have not allowed losses to be claimed on properties that would qualify as residences.

Result: The same law that gives you a tax break if your house appreciates after you move out, can take away what would otherwise be a capital loss.

You can claim the full loss in value that occurs after converting the house to rental use if the property declines in value after conversion to rental, but before you sell it.

Note: The required two-year-use rule must be two continuous years. You can have interruptions, such as for short vacations—and even rent the property while you are not occupying it—and have that time included in the two years.

How to Find More Time for Your Family

Stephanie Winston, organizing consultant and editor of *Stephanie Winston's Organized Executive,* 1101 King St., Alexandria, VA 22314. She is also author of several books, including *Getting Organized* (Warner).

Here's how to find a little more time in your day, so you can spend it with the ones you love most.

●**Make less is more your motto.** The more stuff we have, the busier we are—using it, maintaining it, cleaning it, storing it. Get rid of anything you don't need anymore—old toys, baby clothes, broken items, etc.

●**Keep what you need at your fingertips.** Do not waste time looking for things. Store items—first-aid kits, batteries, sewing kits, etc.—in easy-to-reach places.

●**Go through children's backpacks daily** so you won't have to run around at the last minute if any announcements require action on your part, such as preparing a costume or a special snack.

Review your kids' homework assignments as soon as they get home from school, to ensure they allot enough time.

When their homework is finished, children should repack their backpacks immediately—rather than wait until the following morning. Leave all their bags—and anything else going with them—next to the door.

●**Organize breakfast at night** to speed morning meal preparation. Set up the coffee maker. Fill glasses with juice—cover with plastic wrap and leave in the refrigerator. Put out cereal, bowls, utensils and napkins.

●**Choose tomorrow's clothes at night**—rather than rushing in the morning.

●**Don't let papers pile up.** Whenever mail or other papers come into your house, apply the *TRAF technique...*

T = Toss if you have no use for it.

R = Refer if it is something for your spouse, friend or colleague.

A = Act on it right away.

F = File it where it belongs.

●**Do chores as a family.** Turn them into a race or a weekend adventure.

Examples: Have your family cook the meals for the week together on Sunday. Or give the kids reward points for finishing their chores.

●**Get some outside help** when you're just swamped. *Inexpensive possibilities...*

●Start a baby-sitting co-op among friends.

●Hire a high school or college student to pick up dry cleaning, go shopping, etc.

17

Your Personal Best

How to Be Happy... Yes, Happy!

When it comes to the pursuit of happiness, many people have it all wrong. They strive for a "perfect" life. If they can't boast of a sizable stock portfolio...a loving mate...and model children, they sink into despair.

The fact is, all of us have the power within us to make ourselves happy even in the face of severe adversity.

UNHAPPINESS VS. DISSATISFACTION

We all have personal goals—to succeed at work or a sport...maintain loving relationships ...or master an art or hobby. If these goals are not met, we're certain to feel dissatisfied.

But we need not become depressed about it.

There is really nothing wrong with dissatisfaction. It spurs us on to improve our lives. The problem occurs when we become *defeated* by our dissatisfaction.

Unfortunately, this happens much too often, largely due to irrational and demanding beliefs.

FAULTY THINKING

Some people expect satisfaction all the time. Instead of thinking, "I would like it to be so," they believe, "It must be so—or life is awful."

Of course, insisting that something must be true doesn't make it true. If you *demand* a certain outcome, you are setting yourself up for misery, anxiety and rage.

Example: A man has a reasonably good job but wants one that offers more freedom, higher pay, better benefits and frequent praise from his boss.

If he maintains an attitude of "I want...," he may say to himself, "It would be nice to have these things, but I don't have them right now." He becomes dissatisfied.

If he demands such conditions, he's going to get angry—at the boss who's denying him...or

---

Albert Ellis, PhD, a renowned psychologist as well as founder of The Albert Ellis Institute in New York City, *www.rebt.org.* He is the author of more than 60 books, including *How to Make Yourself Happy and Remarkably Less Disturbable* (Impact).

at himself. "If I were deserving, I would get what I want," he tells himself. "I am a failure."

Dissatisfaction could motivate him to look for other jobs or new ways to improve his current job.

Anger, however, is likely to damage his morale…or antagonize his boss.

FIRST STEP TO HAPPINESS

Identify the irrational belief that's behind this "must" thinking. Change it to an attitude of "I prefer." Preference has an implicit "but…"

Example: "I'd like to have an intimate partner, but it may take a long time to find such a person. In the meantime, I can be happy with other relationships or even alone." This acknowledges the unpredictable and imperfect nature of our lives.

On the other hand, a demand is nonnegotiable. It leaves you with very little emotional leeway. If you don't get what you want, you become depressed or angry.

Example: "I must have a steady partner. If I don't find him/her, it proves that I am worthless."

This primitive thinking reflects the grandiosity of a child as he struggles to learn his limitations. Adults learn realism but may revert to grandiose thinking during periods of stress.

THE SECOND STEP

Develop a healthy attitude toward any adversity. It's almost impossible to avoid. The trick is to learn to cope with obstacles without derailing your goals.

Important: Be willing to continually revise your goals.

Say that you have decided to play the violin only to discover that you have no aptitude for it. You can insist on playing your violin—and drive yourself crazy because you're not as good as you demand that you be. Or you can switch to the piano or another instrument that comes more naturally to you.

Exception: If you find a particular craft exceedingly difficult to master—but still within your grasp—you may want to persevere until you are proficient in it.

However, many people stick to unrealistic goals rather than look for more suitable alternatives. This is self-defeating.

It's similar to what we learned in Aesop's fable about the fox and the grapes. The fox wants the grapes but cannot reach them. After they prove unattainable, the fox derides them, saying they were probably sour anyway.

I say it's better to accept disappointment about the grapes, grab a banana and move on!

Get People To Do What You Want

David J. Lieberman, PhD, the author of *Get Anyone to Do Anything and Never Feel Powerless Again* (St. Martin's Griffin). Mr. Lieberman lives in Boca Raton, FL.

The actions of other people may seem beyond your control. *In fact, it's often possible to get people to do what you want them to do by using foolproof psychological tactics…*

●**Get anyone to like you.** If you "pair" yourself with pleasurable things other people are experiencing, they will associate you with pleasant feelings. Try talking to someone when he/she is in a good mood—or excited by something. Avoid him when he is clearly having a bad day. *Other strategies…*

●Talk about what you both enjoy doing— and what you have in common.

●Maintain a positive attitude in his presence. No one likes being around a pessimist.

●Tell the person you like him.

●Ask for a small favor. You might think that doing small favors for the person might help get him to like you. This is *not* the case. Strange as it may seem, the right approach is to get the person to do a small favor for *you*. This will encourage him to have warm feelings toward you.

●**Don't make yourself too available.** People want more of what they can't have… and more of what they have to work for.

Try to maintain an element of uncertainty in a relationship, especially if you are trying to rekindle a lost passion. If you remove all doubt from the relationship, the other person may take you for granted.

This is *not* a license to be unkind. Always try to make the person feel good when you are with him.

•Get anyone to say what he is really thinking. Obtaining a truthful opinion from someone can be difficult. You certainly won't drag it out of him by yelling, "You're a liar. What do you *really* think?"

Solution: Pose questions that invite constructive criticism.

Example: You're not sure if a coworker really likes your idea for a new marketing campaign, even though she says she does. Ask, "Do you like the concept?" If she answers, "Sure, it's very original," ask, "What would it take to make you *love* the idea?"

•Get anyone to return your phone call. When we want a call returned, many of us stress the importance or urgency of the matter. This is not very effective, partly because others then expect the call to involve something unpleasant.

The message that will get your call returned quickly is: "I appreciate what you have done. Please give me a call. I would really like to thank you personally."

Why does this work? Because the person knows that your message is without problems. The message exploits the other person's curiosity and his desire for gratification. And because the message is a bit confusing, the person has to call back to find out exactly what you're talking about.

To get a company representative to return your call: Ask the person taking the message whether the company uses pink or white message pads.

No matter which way the person responds, say: "Okay, can you do me a big favor? Draw a smiley face next to the message." You'll be amazed how often people comply. The drawing will make it far more likely that your message is noticed…and your call is returned.

•Get anyone to forgive you for anything. The best way to win forgiveness for what you have done is to take full responsibility for your actions. Don't make excuses. Trying to shift the blame will only exacerbate the situation.

Indicate that you're willing to face the consequences of your actions. Explain how the circumstances that led to the transgression will never arise again.

Whenever it makes sense, couch your explanation in terms of your own fear. This makes you appear vulnerable—and therefore more sympathetic. It also shows you didn't *plan* to betray someone's trust.

Example: "I lied because I feared you would hate me if you knew the truth."

•Get anyone to open up to you. Isn't it frustrating when someone responds vaguely or apathetically to your questions? A coworker says a meeting didn't go well, you ask why and he replies, "It just didn't, all right?"

Often, people respond this way because they do not want to be put in a position in which they have to defend themselves.

Strategy: Pose questions that take the pressure off. Your question to your coworker about the meeting might instead be, "Was there anything you could have said that would have made a difference?"

Other questions to ask in different situations…

• "Okay then, why don't you tell me how you've come to think the way you do?"

• "I know you don't know. But if you were to guess, what do you think it might be?"

• "Can you tell me which portion of this you agree with?"

•Stop jealous behavior. People are most likely to experience jealousy in areas that are connected to their self-worth.

If your partner is jealous of one of your friends, try to figure out the basis for that jealousy—and then actively negate it.

Example: You're a woman with a wealthy male friend—and your boyfriend is jealous. Your boyfriend is wonderful in every way, but he feels bad because he doesn't have much money. This is the source of his jealousy.

To defuse his jealousy, downplay what the other person has that he doesn't. Tell your boyfriend that you feel bad that your friend has to flaunt his money, and that this is just a sign of his feelings of inadequacy. Your boyfriend will feel better about himself.

•Debate effectively. Being skilled in the art of verbal self-defense is an invaluable asset.

The first rule is to never get defensive. The minute you begin to defend yourself against an accusation, you're fighting uphill.

263

The second rule is don't automatically accept your adversary's premise. Go on the offensive. If someone asks you a question that amounts to a cheap shot, ask, "What answer would satisfy you?"

The person will most likely say, "I don't know" or, more likely, respond with something specific. In either case, *you're* the one asking the questions, and the other person is now put on the defensive.

If someone says, "You would be nothing without me," respond with, "Why are you finding fault with everything? Aren't you happy with anything in your life?"

Again, you are forcing the other person to explain himself, putting you in a better position.

Make Failure Your Friend

John C. Maxwell, founder of The Injoy Group, Box 7700, Atlanta 30357, which helps clients maximize their personal and leadership potential, *www.injoy.com*. He is author of 34 books, including the best-selling *The 21 Irrefutable Laws of Leadership* and *The 17 Indisputable Laws of Teamwork* (Thomas Nelson).

What separates the achievers from the also-rans? The ability to accept failure and learn from it. *Failing forward* is the only way to take advantage of new opportunities for success. *My 30 years of training people to be high achievers has shown me that anyone can learn to fail forward...*

●**Don't take all the blame for failure.** No one fails simply because he/she is not "good enough." Fight the urge to assume all of the blame—that is crushing.

Instead: Think through the reasons for the failure, and put your role in proper perspective.

People who overcome failure tend to be those who don't take it personally. They don't see *themselves* as failures. They see themselves as people who have failed.

When working with clients, I always point out that every success we enjoy is accomplished with the help of others. Then I ask, "If we must share credit for our successes with others, why

do we insist on carrying the whole burden of failure on our shoulders?"

Caution: Don't let yourself off the hook *too* easily. Always ask yourself what you might have done to increase the likelihood of success.

●**Take action to reduce your fear.** Once it is clear that you have failed at something, you may be reluctant to act until you can convince yourself that all possibility of failing again has been eliminated.

Of course, it is impossible to remove every possibility of failure—so you wind up in a state of paralysis.

To free yourself to take action, accept the real possibility that you will fail again—but also acknowledge that each failure offers a new chance to learn and move ahead.

●**View failure as something that happened in the past.** Recognize every day as a new day, with new opportunities.

A sign in my office reads, *Yesterday ended last night.* When I come to work after a bad day, I look at the sign just to remind myself. It always makes me feel better.

●**Change yourself, and your world will change.** If you *keep* failing in the same area, it is likely that the problem lies with you—and not with the situation in which you keep finding yourself.

Do you need to improve your skills? Did you pick the right people with whom to work?

Only by understanding your role in the failure—and knowing what you must do differently next time—can you really profit from the failure experience.

If you're unable to answer these questions on your own, seek out help. People who first failed but later succeeded at a similar task are well positioned to spot what you did wrong—and to help you change to minimize your risk of failing again.

Keep in mind: It's not what happens *to* you that makes the difference. It is what happens *in* you.

●**When you succeed, look for bigger challenges.** If you don't fail at least occasionally, you're not stretching yourself. You're avoiding failure by staying in the same safe rut.

Trap: Once you stop challenging yourself, you cease to grow.

When a client claims to be successful in all the things he/she has been doing, I ask, "Are you doing anything new or different?" The answer to this question is almost always "no."

Lesson: Just as you shouldn't let failure grind you down, don't let success lull you into complacency. Don't let a string of successes convince you that you have somehow "arrived." No one ever really "arrives." The best we can hope for is to maintain a state of personal growth.

• **Understand just how small the difference between success and failure really is.** It is human nature to perceive the gap between success and failure as gigantic. When we fail, we often think that we are miles from success—just as we believe that when we succeed, we are miles from failure.

What is the reality? The gap between success and failure is seldom very wide.

Example: A batter who hits .320 might make $5 million a year, while one who hits .220 might get only $500,000. All the .220 hitter must do to increase his salary tenfold is get one more hit for each 10 at bats.

Lesson: To become as successful as you wish, consider the possibility that all you must do is *slightly* increase your ratio of success to failure. If your success ratio is 50% right now, increasing it to 60% would likely make an enormous difference in your life.

Make a concerted effort to learn from each failure, and you will soon find yourself doing more of what you do when you succeed—and considerably less of what you do when you fail.

Simple Strategies to Improve Your Memory

Betty Fielding, a Lafayette, California–based lecturer on the psychology of aging and the author of *The Memory Manual: 10 Simple Things You Can Do to Improve Your Memory After 50* (Quill Driver).

Occasional memory lapses often grow more frequent as we age, making many of us worry about what they portend for the future. But a little thought— combined with modest lifestyle modifications —can prevent most memory lapses.

MEMORY TRACES

Each of our senses leaves a different memory trace of a specific event. So can our thoughts, feelings and actions as we experience an event. Any of these traces can trigger our memory of that event.

The more senses, thoughts, feelings and actions we employ to experience something, the more likely we are to remember it later…

• **Tune in to your senses.** The more conscious you are of what your senses are detecting, the more memory traces you collect.

Example: When introduced to a stranger, *look* at his/her eye color, facial features, etc.…*listen* to the name…*smell* his shaving lotion…and *feel* his handshake.

• **Develop mental images.** Mental images of events are easier to recall than are abstractions.

Example I: If you are given directions to an unfamiliar destination, use them to construct a mental map of the route.

Example II: If you have misplaced a certain object, mentally retrace your actions from the time you last remember holding it.

• **Use words to create additional memory traces.** For instance, to ensure you will be able to find important papers, verbalize your action as you put them away.

• **Increase your focus.** You won't remember it if you didn't pay attention to it in the first place.

Helpful: Make notes of what you need to remember. Ask yourself—"What am I doing now? …Why am I here?…What is next on my list?" Be aware of your feelings so you can consciously respond in a way that helps you keep focused.

• **Organize your learning and your life.** The brain is organized so that fleeting thoughts and unexamined pieces of information never enter your long-term memory. *A vital step in improving your memory is putting your mind in order…*

• Develop a mind-set of curiosity and enthusiasm for research. To prime yourself to remember a lecture, for example, ask yourself—"Who was speaking?…What was his message?…Why does it matter to me?…Where—and when—was the lecture held?…How did the speaker present his material?"

●Utilize your calendar. Keep it in the same place…review your schedule twice daily…enter all family holidays, birthdays and annually recurring commitments before the new year begins… enter all appointments and due dates immediately.

●Organize your surroundings so you can find whatever you need with minimal effort. Have a place for everything, and put it there as soon as you finish using it.

●**Take care of your health.** Always eat a nutritious, balanced diet that follows the guidelines in the USDA food pyramid (*www.nal. usda.gov:8001/py/pmap.htm*).

Particularly important for memory: Adequate amounts of vitamins B-6, B-12 and folic acid, as well as the antioxidant vitamins C and E and beta-carotene.

Also: Have regular medical checkups. Memory problems can be caused by cardiovascular conditions, thyroid dysfunction, diabetes, lung, liver and kidney problems or drug side effects.

●**Exercise.** Healthy people in their 70s who engage in regular physical activity demonstrate better thinking and memory skills than their equally healthy peers who are sedentary.

Exercise expands breathing capacity and increases the supply of oxygen to the brain. It also lowers blood pressure, which may reduce the likelihood of memory problems…and supports brain cell growth.

●**Challenge your mind.** Mental challenges exercise and expand thinking skills and memory capacity. Study a new subject, play bridge and chess, do crosswords, etc.

●**Acknowledge aging-related sensory changes.** Changes in sight or vision can contribute to memory problems.

Example: David N. enrolled in a memory class, saying that he had lost his memory 40 years earlier. But during the class his memory seemed fine. At the end of the course, David confessed, "I have learned that I did not lose my memory 40 years ago. I developed a hearing problem then, and I was too embarrassed to ask people to repeat things. I didn't forget things…I just didn't learn them in the first place."

The central nervous system slows gradually with aging. You will think and act a bit more slowly. So take the time you need to focus on what is important to you, such as a person's name or a creative idea.

Force yourself to pay attention. Watch out for distracting thoughts. Refocus on what you are involved in at the moment.

Lower Stress to Boost Memory

Hormones released under stress interfere with the brain's ability to remember any detailed factual information. Try relaxing yourself to lower levels of stress hormones and improve your short-term memory. If you feel stressed before an occasion that will require sharp memory skills, breathe deeply, go for a walk or drink herbal tea.

Michael Meaney, PhD, professor of psychiatry and neurology, Douglas Hospital Research Center, McGill University, Montreal.

Emotional Alchemy: How the Mind Can Help Heal the Heart

Tara Bennett-Goleman, MA, a psychotherapist based in Williamsburg, MA. She is author of *Emotional Alchemy: How the Mind Can Heal the Heart* (Harmony).

We all have bad habits…and we think we know what they are. They range from minor behaviors, like paying bills late, watching mindless TV, talking and forgetting to listen…to downright unhealthful addictions, like overindulgence in junk foods and smoking.

But the habits that cause the most trouble are often those we overlook. They're *mental* habits —patterns of thinking, feeling and behaving that we developed many years ago. These "schemas" have a profoundly negative effect on our moods and relationships.

It's hard to change habits, as everyone knows, and it doesn't get easier as we grow older. But no one is so set in his/her ways that it's impossible to change.

Scientific research has shown that the brain remains capable of forming new behavior patterns to replace old habits *throughout life.* "The only thing that is permanent about behavior is the belief that it is so," is the way theorist Moshe Feldenkrais put it.

MENTAL PATTERNS

Schemas develop because at one time they were a realistic response to the circumstances of our lives. They helped us cope.

If your parents were so busy working and dealing with their own difficulties that they neglected you, you might have developed the *deprivation* schema. This is a deep-seated belief that your needs will never be met.

This schema runs like a computer program. When an event in your present-day life sets it off —your spouse forgets a gift for your anniversary, for example—you're flooded with thoughts about not getting enough. You're filled with grief or anger...and prone to act on these feelings.

Aside from deprivation, schemas that cause the most trouble...

●**Abandonment.** Early loss makes you sensitive to anything that even hints at your being left alone. An unreturned phone call can trigger pain and grief.

●**Subjugation.** Domination by a parent who insisted that you do everything his way can make "it's your way, not mine" a habitual way of thinking. You find it hard to speak up for what you want—yet become prone to smoldering anger and frustration that periodically explode.

●**Unlovability.** Overly critical or insulting parents leave you feeling deeply flawed...and haunted by fear that anyone who knows you well will see your defects.

Result: Shame, depression or a facade of egotism and arrogance.

●**Mistrust.** This naturally develops in people who went through physical or emotional abuse. Anything hinting at betrayal, even minor slights, arouses suspicion and hostility.

●**Vulnerability.** An unstable early life, or a parent prone to excessive worry, leads to a fear of losing control. Even a minor mishap or uncertainty provokes feelings of dread. Hypochondria or excessive thriftiness can result.

●**Perfectionism.** Parents who never seemed satisfied, no matter what you did—"An A? I was expecting an A+"—can make your own standards too high to meet. You may work harder than you need to, castigate yourself for falling short and neglect leisure and relationships.

●**Entitlement.** People who were spoiled as children may develop the belief that rules don't apply to them. They take advantage of others, with little empathy or concern for them.

TAKING CONTROL OF SCHEMAS

Once the schema is triggered, it takes over. Your mind starts running in well-worn grooves, churning out thoughts which arouse powerful emotions that spur you into action.

Example: Your car makes an unfamiliar *ping* and you wonder what's wrong. If this triggers your "vulnerability" schema, you'll start thinking things like, "My car's about to break down...maybe it will happen when I'm pulling onto the highway ...and there will be a terrible accident." You become flooded with anxiety.

The process is quick, but not instantaneous. There's a gap between a thought and the cascade of feelings that follows. It is within this "magic quarter-second" that you can break the chain. It's the space in which you can stop, reflect, consider the schema that's being activated and decide whether this is how you want to live.

If you realize that a schema makes you prone to feeling vulnerable and anxious, for instance, as soon as you start to think "the car's about to break down," you can direct your thoughts to a more realistic mode. You can think, instead, "If anything's wrong, it's probably not serious."

Instead of falling prey to runaway fears, you can do something constructive, such as have the car checked out at a service station.

LEARNING TO BE MINDFUL

The key to controlling schemas is becoming more aware of your thoughts and feelings as they develop. This process is called mindfulness. *Follow these steps...*

• **Notice when you are having an inappropriate emotional reaction**—one that is more intense than the situation calls for, or does not seem to match the situation (for example, feeling hurt when most people would be angry).

At first, you may not recognize this until minutes, even hours, later. As you practice, you'll catch yourself as the reaction is just beginning.

• **Notice precisely what you are feeling.** Is it just anger? Or a mix that includes hurt, fear or sadness?

• **Notice what you are thinking.** Emotions don't arise out of nowhere. They're triggered by thoughts. It takes practice to catch the thoughts in the background that are deeply involved in the process, like "Nothing works out," "Something terrible will happen" or "They can't treat me like that!"

• **Be aware of your impulses**—the ones you acted on and the ones you didn't. Notice the intention to yell that came before you actually did.

• **Notice how your reaction changes as you become more aware of it.**

Ordinarily, we either act on strong emotions …or try to run away from them. With mindfulness, you simply experience them.

When you let fear, anger or sadness happen—and watch how it waxes and wanes with time—you'll discover that feelings are only feelings. You need not be controlled by them. This is the source of true freedom.

Time to Explore Your Creative Potential

Gene D. Cohen, MD, PhD, director and professor of health-care sciences and professor of psychiatry at the Center on Aging, Health & Humanities, George Washington University, Washington, DC. Dr. Cohen is author of *The Creative Age: Awakening Human Potential in the Second Half of Life* (Quill).

The years after age 50 can be the most creative of your life. Decades of working with people of all ages have proven that to me. Creativity is not restricted to artists.

Simple definition: Creativity is bringing into existence something that is new and valued. It can be a symphony or life-changing invention. But it can also be a recipe, a flower garden or a volunteer activity.

Your creative outlet can be strictly personal, such as painting watercolors that you give to close friends…or it can consist of deeds that will promote the public good, in any of a thousand ways.

Understanding creativity in relation to aging enables mature people to explore their potential and challenges younger people to think positively about the years to come.

WHO IS CREATIVE?

Researchers have looked for common characteristics—such as personality traits or upbringing—in creative people. But they have not found any. As the lead researcher of a 25-year study on creativity and aging in more than 200 senior citizens, I learned that *anyone* can be creative.

The same qualities that fuel artistic creativity in the visionaries whose ideas shape civilizations are found in mature people who pursue new hobbies and activities, jobs, education or community activism.

Traits that encourage creativity—curiosity, perseverance, comfort with experimentation—are not hardwired into our brains. They start in childhood as we build caves out of our bedclothes and can be rediscovered at any age.

Retirement increases our free time and, for many, reduces the pressure to more than make ends meet. That's a powerful combination for nurturing creativity.

Men who had worked very hard can't believe they have so much free time. Women who had devoted their lives to their families—many also working outside the home—can revisit long-postponed interests.

Only in their senior years do many people develop the self-confidence to explore their own creativity.

Creativity requires an acceptance of making mistakes. With maturity, we start to realize that making a mistake won't undo our self-image or others' opinions of us.

Example: The principal agents in the initial Middle East peace agreement were lifelong archenemies. Had they not been in their 60s and 70s, I doubt they would have had the courage to ask, "If not now, when?"

CREATIVITY AND HEALTH

Expressing ourselves in a creative manner can actually improve our health, both mentally and physically...

•**Creativity reinforces essential connections** between the brain cells, including those responsible for memory.

•**Creativity strengthens morale.** It alters the way we respond to problems and sometimes allows us to transcend them. Keeping a fresh perspective makes us emotionally resilient.

•**Challenging the brain can relieve sleep and mood disorders.**

•**Reading, writing and word games increase one's working vocabulary** and help to fend off forgetfulness.

•**Capitalizing on creativity promotes a positive outlook** and a sense of well-being. That boosts the immune system, which fights off disease.

•**Having an active, creative life makes it easier to face adversity**—including the loss of a spouse.

Creativity is a natural, vibrant force throughout our lives—a catalyst for growth, excitement and forging a meaningful legacy.

CREATIVITY IN RELATIONSHIPS

With aging, a longtime intimate partnership can fade. Retirement may bring more togetherness than a couple can handle.

To reenergize, don't let everything ride on the relationship itself in its current state.

Think. What can each of you do outside your relationship—alone or with others? What new activity can each of you do alone or together?

If merely one of those new seeds takes root, it will bring about change. Try doing something together *and* separately.

Example: After a vacation trip, create a scrapbook with photos taken by one person and text written by the other.

CREATIVITY IN BUSINESS

Home computers and their electronic cousins have made it possible for many older people to start their own businesses. Mature people are among the most rapidly growing groups who start small businesses.

You may wish to solicit advice or a loan from the federal Small Business Administration (SBA) (800-827-5722 or *www.sba.gov*). Or, share the experience and wisdom of the Service Corps of Retired Executives (SCORE) (800-634-0245 or *www.score.org*), a resource partner with the SBA. You can even get counseling by E-mail. SCORE also welcomes volunteer advisers.

STUMBLING BLOCKS TO CREATIVITY

•**Negative stereotypes and myths.** *It's too late...You can't teach an old dog new tricks.*

Such canards stifle individual motivation and suppress others' tendency to help.

•**Depression and loneliness.** With help, these can be relieved.

Example: One reason for the eternal popularity of Charles Dickens's *A Christmas Carol* is its moral that it's never too late to climb out of a rut. Even Scrooge could learn to share and celebrate.

YOUR SOCIAL PORTFOLIO

Like a financial portfolio that increases our savings over time, we also have a *social portfolio*—a lifetime investment in relationships and activities as an ongoing resource for creativity. *The portfolio includes four components...*

•**Liquidity.** These are the hobbies, interests and relationships to which you can very easily gain access.

•**Diversification.** Your account should be varied. Depending on the circumstances, some activities and relationships will be better to draw upon than others.

•**Alternative resources.** You can depend on these rainy day resources for self-expression if you suffer physical decline, lose a loved one or if a close friend moves away.

•**Long-term-growth funds.** Purposefully expand a curiosity or passion that can be cultivated through the years.

The social portfolio balances individual and group activities...high-energy and low-energy activities...high-mobility and low-mobility activities. Choose what suits your mental and physical status best.

In choosing the kind of creative energy you wish to tap, decide whether you want to…

- Build on what you have done before or change direction—either somewhat or entirely.

- Join with others in a meaningful—or simply enjoyable—project or activity, possibly doing something public-spirited.

- Find a sense of inner purpose, peace or satisfaction on your own.

For your social portfolio, it's always a bull market. Enter the market now!

A Simple Plan for a More Fulfilling Life

Cheryl Richardson, lifestyle coach in Newburyport, MA, *www.cherylrichardson.com*. She is author of the best-sellers *Life Makeovers* and *Take Time for Your Life* (both from Broadway).

If you really want to change your life, do it incrementally. You increase your chances of success when you commit to completing one small task at a time—such as cleaning a shelf in your closet—instead of trying to organize your entire life in one weekend. Each achievement will build momentum, leading to more successes.

Here is my six-week plan to help improve your life…

WEEK 1: TAKE CONTROL OF YOUR TIME

Before you can make headway on long-term goals, you must address immediate priorities.

Example: You dream of starting a business but are overextended financially. You need to straighten out your financial situation before pursuing this long-term goal.

Most of us let circumstances dictate how we spend our time. Regain control of your time by paying attention to what you say "yes" and "no" to.

This week: **Create a list of your top priorities for the next three months.** Ask yourself, "What needs my attention now? What do I need to let go of?"

Think about all areas of your life—family, friends, work, finances, community, emotional and physical health. It could be anything from mending a neglected relationship to updating your résumé.

Pick out the top five answers from your list, and prioritize. This is the *Absolute Yes* list. Copy this list on to several index cards. Place these cards where you will see them often—on the bathroom mirror, next to the phone, on the car dashboard, etc. They will remind you to say "no" to things that are not on the list.

WEEK 2: ELIMINATE ENERGY DRAINS

Tasks left undone create a distracting buzz in the back of your mind, taking up precious mental energy.

This week: **List 10 things that are draining your energy.**

Examples: Making a phone call you've been putting off…washing your car…reviewing a report for work.

Schedule two hours this week to take care of as many of these energy robbers as possible.

If your list contains more than 10 items, focus on the top 10. Put the rest out of your mind. When you've taken care of the top 10, tackle the next 10. Keep scheduling two hours a week to cross these tasks off your list.

WEEK 3: FOCUS

Any worthwhile goal calls for concentration and discipline. Yet we seem to have lost the skill of focusing on one thing at a time. We spend our days bouncing from one distraction to the next. Sometimes focusing means forgoing opportunities that seem important…or saying "no" to things we would really like to do—for the sake of something we want more.

This week: **Choose one project to which you will devote your concentration and energy.** Schedule at least 30 minutes every day to work on it—uninterrupted—until the project is completed.

At first, your mind may pull you away from your goal. Keep refocusing. This exercise isn't just about finishing your project. It's about training yourself to stay focused.

WEEK 4: DROP ONE BALL

Are you feeling overwhelmed? The only way to recover your balance is to drop a few of the balls you're juggling. The best ones to drop are the unreasonable expectations that you may be putting on yourself.

***This week:* Choose one of these three expectations to challenge…**

- **Pleasing everyone.**
- **Doing everything yourself.**
- **Doing everything perfectly.**

Think about the ways the expectation you select plays out in your life. Commit to handling the situation differently at least once a day.

If you're a people pleaser: Say, "I'll get back to you on that" whenever someone makes a request—instead of automatically saying "yes."

If you do everything: Ask for help at least once a day in order to develop the new habit of accepting support.

If you're a perfectionist: Stop working on a project as soon as it is "good enough," instead of reworking it until it is perfect.

WEEK 5: CLEAR THE CLUTTER

We hold on to piles of paper because we're afraid that we might need them someday. But when we need the information, we often can't find it anyway. And clutter distracts us from the more important concerns. There is no need to be surrounded by paper.

***This week:* Schedule 30 minutes each day to go through an area of clutter,** such as a corner of your desk, a stack of unread newspapers or an overflowing file drawer.

Throw away *more* than feels comfortable. This trains you to be selective about the information that comes into your life, so clutter is less likely to accumulate in the future.

WEEK 6: PAMPER YOURSELF

Most of us drive ourselves hard, with the promise that we will reward ourselves once we have finished everything we need to do. But because there's *always* something more to do, we are likely to keep depriving ourselves.

Ironically, self-care is most important when you are busiest. If you keep pushing without a break, you will wind up sick—a forced "break" you can't enjoy.

Life is much too short to put off being good to yourself.

***This week:* List 10 simple self-indulgences that you would love to do if only you had the time.** Include some that make you feel a little guilty.

Examples: Getting a massage…going to a movie in the middle of the day…staying overnight at a bed-and-breakfast…taking a walk in the park during your lunch hour.

Do one of these this week, then one every week until pampering yourself becomes a regular part of your life.

Surefire Cures for Social Anxiety

Gregory P. Markway, PhD, clinical psychologist at St. Mary's Health Center, and his wife, Barbara G. Markway, PhD, clinical psychologist at Capital Region Medical Center, both in Jefferson City, MO. They are the coauthors of Painfully Shy: How to Overcome Social Anxiety and Reclaim Your Life *(St. Martin's).*

What do Americans fear most? When surveyed about their greatest fear, Americans placed death second. Public speaking was first.

The shakes and cold sweats that many of us feel when we talk in front of a group are just one vivid example of *social anxiety*—an excessive fear of being judged negatively.

People with *severe* social anxiety have few friends…drop out of school…may even be unable to work. Milder forms—which are far more common—take their toll in missed opportunities for advancement, lonely evenings and just plain frustration.

But there's so much you can do to battle social anxiety.

IT'S ONLY NATURAL

Anxiety is the normal response to perceived danger—the body and mind rev up in readiness for fight or flight by producing adrenaline. This is useful. Without adrenaline, we can't perform at our best.

Concern about what others think is natural, too. Humans evolved as a social species. We depend on one another to survive. Fear of negative judgment helps ensure harmony in the "pack."

What inflates these feelings to overwhelming proportions is probably nature *and* nurture. Anxiety runs in families. Certain genes create an overly sensitive "alarm system." If your parents were highly critical or wary of "outsiders" —or if you had some early humiliating experiences—this could have laid the groundwork for social anxiety.

DO YOU HAVE A PROBLEM?

One common consequence of social anxiety is avoidance of situations that cause distress. *Some examples...*

● **You decline party invitations because you're "too busy" or "too tired."** Or you go—possibly fortified with a few drinks beforehand—and spend the evening in a corner.

● **You turn down a promotion because you "don't want the extra work."** But what you really can't face are the presentations and big meetings.

● **Your social life is limited to a few close friends...**you pass up opportunities to meet new and interesting people.

Can you live this way? Of course you can. But wouldn't it be better to take control of your fears and give yourself the power to choose from the full buffet of life's offerings?

ANXIETY ISN'T REALITY

Everyone has an *interior monologue*—a constant stream of thoughts that affects mood and energy. Social anxiety feeds on thoughts that exaggerate danger, foresee dire consequences and attribute negative judgments to others. Thoughts like "This meeting will be a disaster" or "I feel nervous, and it shows" are seeds from which the whole uncomfortable experience— racing heart, cold sweat—grows.

Thinking this way is just a habit. And, like most habits, it can be broken.

Tune in to your thoughts. What are you telling yourself when you feel nervous about entering a room...giving a presentation at a meeting...approaching a salesclerk? Keep a diary to record every situation, thought and level of anxiety you experience.

Anxiety-producing thoughts are generally distortions and exaggerations—"Everyone is staring at me...I always sound like a fool...If I make a mistake, I'll never live it down."

The antidote isn't positive thinking but *realistic* thinking. Examine your anxiety-producing thoughts critically and correct them.

Example: You attend a business lunch with people you don't know. You think, "It will be a disaster...I'll have nothing to say...Everyone will know how anxious I am."

Realistic correction: "Lunch will probably go well...I'm usually articulate and make a nice impression...If things don't go perfectly, it won't be the end of the world. We'll take care of business, and that's what people will remember."

Try relabeling. The symptoms of anxiety and excitement are almost identical. If you feel revved up and think, "I'm getting anxious," it creates a destructive spiral. But if you think of it as "getting excited," you will feel better prepared and capable.

BREATHE AWAY ANXIETY

One of the worst things about anxiety is the feeling that once it starts, it will build uncontrollably. Breathing slowly and deeply from your abdomen will ease anxiety. While lying in bed, rest your hands on your abdomen. Breathe in deeply through your nose to a count of four. Let your abdomen rise up as you inhale. Your chest should remain still. As you breathe out— to a count of four—your abdomen should flatten. Slow your breathing down to eight breaths per minute.

After you become accustomed to this kind of breathing, practice it while sitting, standing and eventually in the course of your everyday activities. Soon it will feel easy and natural.

Then whenever you start feeling anxious, be very aware of your breathing. If it is shallow and rapid, consciously switch to the slower abdominal breathing.

SHIFT YOUR FOCUS

Anxiety will turn your attention inward. You notice your heart pounding...worry that your hands are shaking...grade your performance as you give it—almost always negatively. This is certain to increase your anxiety.

Instead: Focus your attention on the task itself, whether it's emphasizing key points in a presentation or pouring wine at a party. If you're talking to someone, attend closely to what he/she is saying. Think about how he might be feeling rather than what to say next.

If anxiety continues to build, focus on neutral factors…the color and texture of the carpet…the feel of the papers you hold in your hand. Such a shift in focus will interrupt the anxiety cycle and let you attend to the business at hand.

Note: For extreme anxiety, certain drugs can be helpful. If you are anxious in very specific situations—for example, just when giving a speech—beta-blockers, such as propranolol (Inderal), can be helpful. If the anxiety is across many situations and is disabling to a significant degree, then selective serotonin reuptake inhibitor (SSRI) antidepressants, such as paroxetine (Paxil) may be recommended. Talk to your doctor.

Why We Lie and How to Transform Our Lives

Brad Blanton, PhD, CEO of Radical Honesty Enterprises, which leads workshops on honesty, 646 Shuler Ln., Stanley, VA 22851, *www.radicalhonesty.com*. He is author of *Practicing Radical Honesty* (Sparrowhawk), and coauthor, with Neal Donald Walsch, of *Honest to God,* a series of audio- and videotapes.

Most people lie—a lot. Not by telling whoppers, not by lying outright—but by withholding the truth.

I believe that dishonesty is dangerous to physical health, psychological well-being and personal relationships. Withholding the truth from spouses, friends, lovers, coworkers and bosses is a leading contributor to psychological problems and many physical illnesses.

Not fully telling what we think, how we feel and what we do keeps us locked inside self-built jails. To break out, we need to start telling the truth to the people around us. We will all be much healthier for it.

FEAR OF HONESTY

Few of us voice our true thoughts and feelings because we fear that we will hurt another person's feelings. We are afraid of offending someone we care about…or we assume that the other person will think less of us and we won't be able to keep up the image we work so hard to project.

This problem is systemic in our culture today because we put such a high premium on diplomacy and getting along with others without rocking the boat.

Results: A dishonest self-portrait…and a condescending attitude toward other people.

It's actually more disrespectful to treat others in a less-than-honest way than to speak our minds. Secrets, phoniness and half-truths alienate people from one another. We don't really talk, but just float past one another without making genuine human contact.

WHEN WE LIE

In most marriages, spouses are not fully honest with each other. That's one reason why the divorce rate in this country is more than 50%. When we fail to express our needs to a spouse, our resentment builds. We seethe in silence.

Withholding thoughts and feelings is a way of manipulating and controlling others. It wears us out to keep up an image that is based on pretending. Real intimacy is not possible without complete truthfulness.

MOVE TO TRUTH

A simple resolution to tell the truth sounds great, but it is too broad. Begin with a three-week plan.

Start by sitting down with an important person in your life. Tell him/her that you haven't been completely honest. Perhaps you're feeling angry, resentful or guilty about something that has been unexpressed for a while.

Maybe you haven't been telling big lies. But you also haven't been telling the whole truth, so you would like to begin by making a commitment to be completely honest with each other for the next three weeks. Ask the other person to really listen to you and to hold his response until you have finished. Then you will listen to whatever he has to say.

Important: Expect that both of you will say things that upset each other. You'll get mad and feel hurt. Agree to stay with the other person until the end of the discussion.

BASIC RULES

•**Talk face to face.** It's better than communicating by phone or E-mail or leaving messages on an answering machine.

●**Begin with how you feel.** "I resent you for …I get upset every time…" rather than accusations, "You always…"

●**Speak in the present tense.**

●**Focus in on the exact details of what occurred…**what you thought and felt…and what was said. Avoid making general descriptions of behavior or sweeping judgments and characterizations.

●**Focus on what happened**—instead of what *didn't* happen.

●**Enlist other people.** If you are unable to raise the issue or the other person doesn't want to discuss it, ask a third party to help mediate the conversation.

I have worked with countless couples who were willing to take the risk of facing and speaking the truth. About 75% of them stay with the relationship. After breaking the long habit of withholding the truth, they discover better love, better sex, more laughter.

TRUTH AT WORK

The same improvement can occur by bringing truthfulness to workplace relationships.

Example: When an employee's frustration has been building silently toward an overbearing, demanding boss.

In 90% of my clients, if the employee asks to speak to the boss privately and says, "I resent you for…" and discusses specific issues in detail, that employee is likely to get greater responsibility, a raise and perhaps a promotion.

Why? Because truthfulness fosters respect. Both boss and employee may change their perspectives or opinions of the other once they speak honestly and openly.

Truthfulness makes all personal relationships more alive.

EXCEPTIONS TO THE RULE

Though radical honesty is particularly important with people we know, there are two exceptions to blunt, no-holds-barred honesty…

●**When ethics or morality justifies lying.** This distinction is between people you know and corrupt institutional representatives.

Example: If you were hiding Anne Frank and her family in your attic and the Nazis came to your door, of course you should lie.

●**When talking with children.** Parents must be honest, yet simple, in the ways they express the truth to children…

●Avoid extreme harshness, "You're a little brat for treating your brother like that…"

●Be specific…and begin your statement with how you feel rather than with an attack on the child's personality or character.

●Don't soft-pedal the truth to the point of distorting it. For example, don't say, "I wish you wouldn't hurt your brother" when you really mean, "Stop hitting him right now!"

We can learn so much from children. They speak very directly and honestly, and they are loved for their truthfulness.

Fear Is All That Stands Between You and Success

Azriela Jaffe, syndicated business columnist in Yardley, PA, and consultant on small business relationships. She is the author of eight books, including *Starting from No* (Upstart) and *Create Your Own Luck* (Adams).

Fear is one of the biggest—and sneakiest —obstacles to reaching our goals. We may *think* we're stalled because of other people's objections, insufficient resources or circumstances outside our control. But it is often fear that keeps us from seeing a way around barriers—causing us to abandon our dreams.

We can't eliminate fear. But we can manage it—and move past it.

FEAR OF FAILURE

You believe that if you don't succeed, disaster will result. You think catastrophically and expect the worst.

Examples: "I'll let down my family…I'll lose the house…I'll be humiliated."

People who fear failure must learn the difference between *devastation* and *disappointment.* Few outcomes are devastating—that is an appropriate response only when life or health is at stake.

Strategy I: Envision the terrible consequences you fear. Then analyze the situation rationally. How likely is it that your worst fear will materialize? Now forcefully challenge your fears. Talk to yourself—out loud, if necessary.

Example: "I've handled setbacks before. I can rise to the occasion."

This won't feel natural—*but do it anyway.* Like any skill, controlling catastrophic thinking takes practice.

Strategy II: Make up a list of everything in your life that did not turn out as you planned—but ultimately worked out for the best.

Example: "I didn't get the promotion I wanted—which made me quit my job and start my own business."

FEAR OF SUCCESS

Sometimes we are stopped by the fear of what will happen if we do get what we want. That's why some people tend to make mistakes when they are close to accomplishing a goal.

This fear is often based on preconceptions formed in childhood—from our parents' beliefs …or what we observed in the adults around us.

Example: "Successful people are self-centered and ruthless. If I do something well, people will expect more of me—and I will be forced to work even harder."

Strategy: When you are stuck, ask yourself what you stand to gain by not succeeding. More free time? Less responsibility? Identify the assumptions that underlie your thinking. Are they valid?

Example: A manager routinely avoided taking on challenges. As a result, he was regularly passed over for promotions. When he was a child, the manager's father, a salesman, was on the road for long periods. The son was afraid that being too successful would make him an absent father to his own children. Once he acknowledged that assumption, he sought new responsibilities that would bring him success, yet not require him to spend long periods of time away from his family.

FEAR OF BEING IMPERFECT

A perfectionist may avoid pursuing an opportunity if he/she isn't sure he will excel at it—whether it's developing a new skill, going after a big client or just starting a conversation with a stranger.

Perfectionists lose out on learning and growing from mistakes. They also waste time on the details because they're afraid to delegate—they don't trust anyone else to do the job right. If you spend a great deal of time planning for every contingency rather than taking action, you may be paralyzed by perfectionism.

Strategy I: Delegate a minor task, and keep quiet if it's done adequately, but not brilliantly. Practicing nonperfectionism on other people can help you become more tolerant of yourself.

Strategy II: Try a hobby you might like—but think you won't do well at. Take a jewelry-making class if you're all thumbs…or a comedy workshop if you have trouble thinking on your feet. Your confidence—and ability to take risks—will grow as you learn to survive looking silly.

FEAR OF DISAPPROVAL

If you feel you *must* be liked by everyone, you will waste energy trying to satisfy people who are insignificant in your life. Or you may postpone making overtures to the people who could help you.

Strategy I: Put together a support team of friends and family members that you can rely on to build you up when you're down. Turn to them when you feel—or anticipate being—rejected. They can remind you of what you're doing right.

Key: Create this team *before* you need it. Start by giving of yourself to others so that you have a network when you need it.

Strategy II: Keep an "ego file." Save letters and E-mails in which people have complimented or thanked you. When you need reassurance, read through the file.

FEAR OF CHANGE

Even when we really want things to be different, change can make us feel uncomfortable and vulnerable.

Strategy: Build as much familiarity as possible into any new situation. Identify daily routines that make you feel anchored and content—from walking the dog to reading the paper over your morning coffee. Choose at least three of these anchors, and resolve to continue doing them every day, no matter what else happens.

Example: It is difficult to make my sales calls, so I start each morning by reading a prayer book and having my favorite coffee. Then I am prepared to make calls.

MORE FEAR-BUSTING STRATEGIES

●**Take a leap of faith.** People often talk themselves out of what they want because they are unsure of the outcome.

Example: I'd like to move to the Southwest, but I'm not sure how to find a job.

Doing research is smart, but it can take you only so far. You may have to take more concrete action to find out what the next steps are. Don't be afraid to learn as you go.

●**Make what-ifs positive rather than negative.** We tend to focus on the unknowns that frighten us. But there are always positive possibilities, too.

Example: When I became pregnant with my third child, I was overwhelmed—what if the baby wasn't healthy...what if I couldn't handle three children...what if we couldn't manage financially? A friend asked, "What if this child becomes president? Discovers a cure for cancer? Brings you and your husband joy you can't even imagine?"

●**Keep your pipeline full.** Continually build your network of contacts. Be generous with time and expertise. Building and nourishing contacts creates a safety net for when you are in need.

Stop Bad Habits Fast

James Claiborn, PhD, a clinical psychologist in private practice in Manchester, NH. He is the author of *The Habit Change Workbook: How to Break Bad Habits and Form Good Ones* (New Harbinger).

Emotions can trigger overeating, gambling —even fidgeting and nail biting. With the right approach, you can break bad habits before they spiral out of control.

Habits are created by conditioning. When an action is rewarded—the sensory pleasure of sweets, for example, or the excitement of a winning bet—you're more likely to repeat it. Often, the reward is small and subtle. Many habits only momentarily reduce tension, alleviate boredom or dispel discomfort.

The first step toward breaking a bad habit is keeping a daily record of what you're doing.

What to do: Write down the exact sequence of events that precedes the habit you're trying to break.

Example: Instead of "I pick at my skin," you might write down "I notice an uneven spot and rub at it, tearing away tiny pieces of skin till it seems smoother."

In your log, record additional details linked to the undesired habit. Where are you? What are you doing? How do you feel when the urge strikes to fidget or buy a lottery ticket—bored, nervous, irritated? What thoughts are going through your head?

Record the emotions you have while you're performing the habit you wish to quit and how you feel afterward. Are you relieved? Angry with yourself? Do you feel depressed?

Once you start looking at a habit objectively, the experience seems much more manageable. Just paying such close attention to a habit often loosens its grip.

CHANGE YOUR THINKING

If you're aware of the thinking patterns that promote an undesired habit, you can start to change them.

In particular, watch out for...

●**Permission-giving thoughts.** These pass through your mind so swiftly they're hard to catch, but they actually activate the habit.

Examples: "I've had a very hard day and deserve a treat...just a little candy bar won't hurt my diet, and I'll eat less for dinner."

Once you have identified permission-giving thoughts, then question them. "Do they stand up logically? Does evidence support them, or are they rationalizations?"

●**"Should" statements.** After performing an undesired habit, your thoughts are likely to be self-critical. "I should be able to control my nail biting. I'm so weak...I'll never be able to change this habit."

Trouble is, the act of silently berating yourself will create the very stress and guilt that prompts you to engage in the undesired habit again and again.

Instead of being hard on yourself for engaging in an undesired habit, substitute more realistic appraisals. "I shouldn't gamble" becomes "I'd be better off if I didn't gamble."

USE A SUBSTITUTE RESPONSE

If you give up a habit, it must be *replaced* with something else. To do this, find a substitute response.

Examples: Have carrot sticks handy for when you're tempted to reach for a cookie. Go for a walk instead of switching on the TV.

PREVENT RELAPSES

Lapses—occasional slipups where you once more do the habit you've stopped—are common. The question is how to keep them from turning into a *relapse*, a return to the pattern of performing the habit regularly.

Your thinking is key. "I've failed. I might as well stop trying." Such statements reflect black-and-white thinking. Either you've absolutely kicked the habit—or you've absolutely failed. The distress, guilt and self-disgust that follow a lapse trigger a return to the habit.

Better: Be realistic. Does one lapse cancel out *all* your progress? Can you predict that you're doomed to failure? Of course not.

Best: Learn from each lapse...pay attention to the situation, the thoughts and the emotions that led to it. Plan strategies, such as substitute responses and relaxation techniques like deep breathing, which you can use to prevent any further lapses.

Emotional Healing

John W. James, founder of the Grief Recovery Institute in Sherman Oaks, CA, *www.grief-recovery.com*. He is the coauthor of *The Grief Recovery Handbook—The Action Program for Moving Beyond Death, Divorce and Other Losses* (HarperCollins).

The statement "Time heals all wounds" may be well-intentioned, but it does little to help a person who is grieving.

Time alone doesn't heal—it's what you do with the time that helps resolve the pain.

Everyone experiences loss from time to time —whether it's divorce, the end of a relationship or the death of a loved one. Although grief is a natural response to such events, we often deny the strong feelings.

Problem: Unresolved grief can result in depression and low energy levels. It can also weaken the immune system, which can lead to hypertension, ulcers, the flu and other conditions.

Good news: By identifying and acknowledging the emotions associated with grief, you can learn to live with loss—rather than be consumed by it.

Here's how to help yourself—or a loved one —cope effectively...

HOW TO HELP OTHERS

After several days of sadness and emotional shock, the bereaved person inevitably begins to review his/her emotional relationship with the loved one. This is true with all losses, including divorce, job loss, the death of a loved one or even a beloved pet.

Relatives or friends of the griever can facilitate this process by listening in a nonjudgmental way and encouraging the person to talk about his feelings. *Here are several topics that a bereaved person needs to talk about...*

●**Circumstances leading up to the loss.** Grieving people have a strong need to explain exactly "what happened" in a safe setting, without having their reactions judged or being confronted with "insights" from the listener.

●**How the bereaved person found out about the loss.** Did he hear about it over the telephone? In person? Some other way? It's important to talk about how this news was relayed—and the emotions that accompanied it. This will help reduce the emotional tension attached to the bad news.

●**Stories about the loved one.** Hearing fond remembrances from other people helps put the relationship with the loved one into a much broader emotional context.

Even in the case of divorce, truthful memories are helpful. No one gets married anticipating a divorce.

HOW TO HELP YOURSELF

As the reality of loss sinks in, a grieving person also begins to think of things in the relationship that he might have done differently. *All* unresolved grief stems from these regrets. Following a loss, grievers wish they could turn back the clock and resolve these emotional issues. My research has shown that quite convincingly.

The following actions can be taken alone—or with the help of a partner who agrees to keep your conversations private...

●**Evaluate the relationship realistically.** There is a tendency to enshrine someone who dies. Your loved one might have been a good person, but that does not mean he was perfect. In the case of a less-than-loved one or in a divorce, grievers may try to demonize the person.

An accurate memory of someone is always stronger and will be more cherished than a fantasy. Unless you remember your loved one as he truly was, it becomes impossible to complete your emotional relationship. Completion means you will be able to remember the relationship as it was without feeling devastating pain.

●**Create a time line of your relationship.** On a piece of paper, draw one horizontal line, representing the time you and your loved one spent together. The left end of the line is the beginning of your relationship.

Along this line, write significant junctures in your relationship. Record whatever comes to mind, along with the approximate date. If a corresponding event seems positive, write it above the line. List negative events below the line.

The time line will help you discover all the things that are unfinished. While this may be difficult, it is essential to returning to a life that will have meaning and purpose.

●**Categorize your memories.** After you finish your time line, make a list of anything you wish you had done or said at these junctures. *Divide them into...*

●Amends (things you feel a need to apologize for).

●Forgiveness (things you need to forgive the other person for).

●Other emotional statements ("I love you" or "I appreciate the time you spent with me." Or in the case of a less-than-loved one, "I hated the way you treated me.").

●**Write a letter.** Now that you have identified these undelivered messages, write a two-page letter to your loved one. It's best done alone, in a single one-hour session. *Example...*

"Dear Dad, I have been reviewing our relationship, and I have discovered some things that I want to tell you...

Dad, I apologize for... (Repeat this phrase for each undelivered amends on your list.)

Dad, I forgive you for... (Repeat this phrase for each item in your forgiveness category.)

Dad, I want you to know..." (Use this phrase with each emotional statement on your list.)

When you're finished, be sure to conclude the letter with the word "good-bye" and the name of your loved one. *Example...*

"I love you and I miss you. Good-bye, Dad."

For best results, the letter must be read aloud to another person. In the case of divorce or estranged relationships, the letter must never be heard or read by the other person.

Useful Web Sites

Hobbies/Sports

☐ Barbeque Time
www.barbecuen.com

Recipes, tips on grilling, facts about grills and answers to all of your grilling questions.

☐ Better Biking
www.bikeleague.org

The League of American Bicyclists has useful information for the recreational cyclist.

☐ Classical Music
www.classicalarchives.com

Thousands of classical-music selections, plus downloadable sheet music.

☐ Golf Enthusiast
www.pga.com

The official Web site of the PGA of America. Find out about tournaments, buy tickets, learn how to improve your game and more.

☐ Kids' Crafts
http://family.go.com/crafts

Get your children or grandchildren involved in crafts. Everything from sewing to building and modeling.

☐ Kitchen Gardening
http://chefsgarden.com

Order herbs and vegetable plants to create your own organic kitchen garden. Also includes growing tips, recipes and more.

☐ Garden Know-How
www.gardenguides.com

Free electronic newsletters on a wide variety of gardening topics.

☐ Plants by Mail
http://pbmfaq.dvol.com/list

A directory listing almost every plant/garden catalog in the world, along with contact information.

Home

☐ China Replacements
www.replacements.com

More than 175,000 china patterns—some more than 100 years old—as well as hundreds of crystal and silver patterns are offered for sale.

☐ Fix It Yourself
www.thisoldhouse.com/toh

A comprehensive on-line resource for home-improvement articles covering kitchen, bath, yard and garden.

☐ Keep Your Home Healthy
www.uwex.edu/ces/flp/house

Learn how to fix unhealthy conditions in your home, such as mold, mildew, poor ventilation, radon in the soil and more. Click on "About the House," then "Home Health Hazards."

☐ Keeping Clean
www.queenofclean.com

If you have a tough cleaning problem, you'll find the solution at The Queen of Clean. Covers carpet-stain removal, rust removal and a whole lot more.

☐ Spring Cleaning
www.cleaning.com/instructions.php4

Tells you how to clean just about anything—aquariums, boat hulls, bathtubs, birdcages, computer equipment, leather furniture and more.

Just for Fun

☐ Comedy Zone
www.comedy-zone.net

A great site for jokes, trivia, cartoons, games and humorous quotes.

☐ Concerts, Musicians and Tickets
www.pollstar.com

See who's touring—when and where. Also includes music news and ticket-sales information.

□ Contests Galore
http://contests.about.com

Chock-full of contests, sweepstakes, promotions and other assorted ways to win money.

Learning

□ America's Memories
http://memory.loc.gov

This Library of Congress site has primary source materials relating to the history and culture of the US—more than seven million items.

□ Black History Month
www.noblenet.org/year//tty2bla.htm

Provides links to Web sites covering Black History Month. You will learn about everyone from Harriet Tubman to Maya Angelou and other greats.

□ Follow the Stars
http://learnwhatsup.com/astro

Includes maps and information about planets, stars, moon phases, comets and meteors.

□ Learn the Lingo
www.ilovelanguages.com

A directory of more than 2,000 language-related Web sites, with free lessons, translations and more.

Travel

□ Festival Finder
www.festivals.com/~finder

Just type in when and where you will be traveling, to find all festivals going on at that time.

□ Garden Conservancy
www.gardenconservancy.org

Check out the beautiful gardens across the US and Canada that are maintained with the help of the Garden Conservancy.

□ Air Security International
www.airsecurity.com

Find out about travel safety and get daily updates of potential trouble spots.

□ Outdoor Recreation Deals
www.gorptravel.com

Offers domestic and worldwide packages for families, singles and people age 50 and over, as well as weekend getaways for biking, golf and more.

□ Half-Price Theater Tickets
Atlanta: *www.atlantatheaters.org*
Austin: *www.austix.com*
Chicago: *www.hottix.org*
London: *http://home.clara.net/rap/half*
New York: *http://timessquare.nyc tourist.com/broadway_tkts.asp*
San Francisco (and Bay Area): *www.theatrebayarea.org*
Washington, DC: *www.cultural-alliance.org/tickets*

Save a bundle by visiting these sites for half-price theater tickets.

□ History Travel
www.cr.nps.gov/nr/travel

The National Register of Historic Places offers trip itineraries for historic places across the US. Each itinerary provides descriptions of historic sites, the hours of operation, phone numbers, interactive maps and photos.

□ Theme Parks
www.themeparkinsider.com

Gives you news and reviews on many of America's theme parks, as well as information on discounts.

□ Travel Planner
www.123world.com/tourism

Here you'll find links to official tourism Web sites for dozens of cities, states and countries.

18

Business and Career Savvy

Bootstrapping: How to Start a Business for $1,000 or Less

Bootstrapping involves starting a business with whatever money you can scrape together. Hewlett-Packard, United Parcel Service and Walt Disney all began as bootstrap ventures that grew into global giants.

You may not have your sights set that high. But for $1,000 or less, you can bootstrap your own successful business.

The economic slowdown might be reason enough to postpone launching a more ambitious business. But bootstrap operations typically serve a niche. And a niche business, if it delivers the right product or service at the right price, can thrive in any economic climate.

How to bootstrap a business…

●**Stick to what you know best.** The first impulse of many who want to start their own business is to buy an existing business or become a franchisee. Either approach will cost many thousands of dollars and most likely put you into a field where you have no experience. Odds are great that you'll lose your investment.

Best strategy: Carve out a niche in the industry where you have the most experience. Think through products and/or services that would benefit someone in your industry, but that aren't available at a reasonable price.

Examples: If you're in sales, sell to businesses too small to warrant the attention of the full-time sales staff of larger businesses. If you're in marketing, serve your old employer and others in your industry on an outsource basis. With your low overhead, you can profit where bigger ventures could not.

●**Keep costs under control.** Start with as little of your own capital as possible and with no borrowed money. Gambling your time on

Barbara Weltman, Esq., practices in Millwood, NY, *www.bwideas.com*. She is author of many books, including *J.K. Lasser's New Rules for Small Business Taxes* (Wiley) and *Bottom Line's Very Shrewd Money Book* (Bottom Line Books).

the business is one thing, but gambling your retirement savings is something else.

I'm assuming you'll run the business from your home and that you already own a computer. *If so, expect to face these expenses...*

●**Raw materials.** If you're launching a service business, you will require only a second phone line and office supplies. If launching a product-based business, you'll need to invest in materials. Keep initial purchases to a minimum—letting inventory build up only as sales build up.

●**Professional fees.** Whoever does your taxes can handle what additional work the business generates at very little or no added expense. You probably won't need an accountant until the business is much bigger.

Whether you need a lawyer will depend on the form your business takes. You can launch a sole proprietorship without legal help. The main drawback to a sole proprietorship is that your personal assets are exposed to claims against the business.

You can shield personal assets by incorporating or forming a limited liability company. Setup will cost $300 to $600 in legal fees. But you can do it yourself for less (for instance at *www.bizfilings.com*).

●**Start-up costs.** Whatever your business, keep start-up costs to $1,000 or less. Finance growth from business profits. That's what bootstrapping is all about.

●**Set out to make profits.** Some people form their own business simply to fill up their days—especially if they're retired. You can find cheaper ways of killing time than starting up a business. Start the business only if careful analysis tells you it has the potential of making money for you.

The time line: Don't anticipate making money immediately. You'll have start-up costs and a learning curve to get past. It will take time to make yourself known to customers.

If you can't see yourself turning a profit within two years, don't start the business. If the business is not making money within two years, think about folding it.

The more your bootstrap business relies on the skills you developed during your life as an employee, the more likely you are to make money. If you spent many years in public relations, for instance, your best chance for profits is by drawing on your contacts in public relations.

●**Understand the effort involved in running a business.** When you're running your own business, you must handle *everything*—from sales and marketing to accounting and collections. I find that most people are unprepared for the time running a new business takes and the diversity of responsibilities they must take on.

Example: One couple thought their hobby of collecting antiques would make it simple to launch a business selling antiques on-line. They learned the hard way how much time it takes to photograph each item, write the description, post it to the auction site, pack and ship the item and follow up to get paid for the sale.

Don't assume you can start a new business as a hobby, to be worked at part-time and half-heartedly. To make your venture work, you need the same commitment and passion any entrepreneur brings to a start-up.

●**Get your business noticed.** The cheapest way is by word of mouth. If you are in the same field as you were during your years as an employee, hit your Rolodex and let people know you're out there.

Do you need a Web site? A Web site can put a small local venture on equal footing with a global giant. But creating and maintaining a Web site takes time and money. Most start-ups *don't* need one.

●**Avoid the pitfalls that sink new businesses.** The biggest problem for most start-ups is not having a clear focus on what the business will do and what the founder will get out of it.

Every business requires a business plan—even if the business is a bootstrap operation that will never grow very large.

The plan should describe the business in detail, how much it will cost to get started and where you expect the business to be in one, three and five years.

Draw up a budget for what it will cost you to get going and how much more it will cost you each month until you become profitable.

For help in crafting a business plan, turn to the Small Business Administration *(www.sba.gov)*. You'll find a wealth of information about starting businesses. For most bootstrap businesses, the SBA site will provide all the start-up help you need—at no cost.

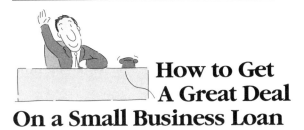

How to Get A Great Deal On a Small Business Loan

Chris Lehnes, vice president of business development, CIT Small Business Lending, a unit of The CIT Group, 650 CIT Dr., Livingston, NJ 07039.

For most business owners, the response to an economic slowdown is to cut their spending and shelve growth plans until hard times pass.

This "hunkering down" strategy works well for businesses in hard-hit industries. But for most other companies, it is not the best move.

Better: Look at the slowdown as an opportunity to borrow your way to a stronger business. *Advantages of borrowing during a slowdown…*

•**Low interest rates let you take out a new loan or refinance old debt** at a lower rate or with a longer repayment term, so that monthly payments are reduced.

•**Commercial real estate**—or rival businesses you want to acquire—is often available at bargain prices.

•**With business running at a less hectic pace,** you may have more time to do some strategic thinking—where you want your company to go and how you can put the resources you have to the most productive use.

Example: You have a product line that has been exceptionally successful. Now that the slowdown has given you some breathing room, you can think about expanding that product line—to be prepared when business picks up again.

WHERE TO BORROW

Interest rates are down at banks and non-bank lenders alike. If you plan to borrow, shop aggressively—not just for the lowest rate but also for the loan structure that works best for your business.

Some of the best deals for small businesses today come through the Small Business Administration (SBA).

Interest rates on SBA loans are capped at the prime rate plus 2¾%—a better rate than a typical small business could find elsewhere. *Additional advantages…*

•**SBA loans carry a government guarantee.** In most cases, the loan can be made based on the strength of the borrower's cash flow rather than relying solely on collateral. Because of this guarantee, small businesses that might not qualify for conventional loans often qualify for SBA loans.

•**SBA lending allows for longer payback periods** than you could get from a bank or other lenders. SBA rules permit working capital to be financed over seven years…equipment over 10 years…and real estate over 25 years. You can get a single SBA loan that covers working capital, equipment and real estate, with a repayment term that is based on all the uses for the money.

Example: A South Carolina woman wanted to expand her day care business. She needed a lender who could provide comprehensive financing that included the money for real estate purchase and equipment acquisition as well as working capital. We structured a single SBA loan, covering all her financial needs, with a term of about 20 years.

MAKING THE GRADE

Few small businesses are aware of SBA loan programs. And—those that *are* aware often have serious misconceptions about the loans.

The SBA was once the last-resort lender for small businesses. In fact, the old rule was that you had to have been turned down by a bank before the SBA would even begin to consider your loan application.

That's not true today. An SBA loan is a very competitive financial product that has many advantages over traditional bank financing in terms of the repayment period and structuring.

Specifics: SBA loans can be for as little as $50,000 and for as much as $2 million. The average loan is $400,000.

To qualify for an SBA loan, a retail business needs to have no more than $5 million a year in revenues.

The cutoff for a wholesale business is a maximum of 100 employees, while the cutoff for a manufacturing business is a maximum of 500 employees.

WHAT BANKS DO BEST

The typical small business in search of capital turns to its bank first. Banks are fine for checking accounts, lines of credit and merchant services. But while any bank can issue SBA loans, few process enough of them to have the necessary expertise.

Banks that do make SBA loans sometimes will cut back when the economy turns sour—which is just when small businesses can put the money to most effective use.

If you're in the market for a loan, and your own bank tells you to try the SBA, consult the SBA Web site at *www.sba.gov* to find names of "preferred" lenders in your area. These lenders have chosen to make SBA lending a major part of their business. They are especially efficient in processing loan applications.

Option: Apply for an SBA loan through one of the 14 SBA-licensed nonbank lenders. These lenders have entire divisions devoted exclusively to processing SBA loan applications. They tend to be more focused on lending than conventional banks, whose lending operations often get pushed down the priority list by the high volume of day-to-day banking services.

Helpful: Nonbank SBA lenders—which include Business Lenders, CIT Small Business Lending, GE Capital and others—will often partner with local banks to provide SBA loans to their customers.

At CIT, we meet with the local bank and explain, "You do the deposits, lines of credit, checking and merchant services. These are things we can't do. What we can do well is make SBA loans."

That allows the bank to take advantage of our experience and expertise to offer SBA loans to its customers. Similarly, when a business owner comes to us and wants a $25,000 line of credit, we refer him/her to our local partner bank.

FINDING A LENDER

Contact the SBA office for your district. You'll find it listed in the government section of your phone book. Or go to the SBA Web site. You'll find lists of district offices and SBA lenders in your area.

Before you search for a lender: Be prepared to demonstrate your creditworthiness. SBA loan officers will want to see business and personal tax returns for the past three years, plus financial statements through the latest quarter.

If you are borrowing to buy a business, lenders will want to see the business's tax returns and financial statements.

They may not ask to see your business plan if you're borrowing just to buy real estate for the business. But they usually will want to see a business plan if you plan to expand or to make an acquisition—so they know you've thought everything through.

How to Get Top-Quality Legal Advice at Bargain Rates

John Toothman, Esq., president of The Devil's Advocate, a legal consulting firm at 300 N. Lee St., Suite 450, Alexandria, VA 22314, *www.devilsadvocate.com*.

Businesses today face a dizzyingly complex maze of laws, litigation and regulation. But few have the in-house legal talent to prevent charges of wrongdoing—or defend against them.

Result: Businesses that have not planned ahead can pile up huge fees for legal advice that can be downright scary.

Better: Set up your legal management strategy *before* your business is sued or charged with a regulatory violation. Doing so requires knowing where you are most vulnerable to legal action and knowing whom to turn to if trouble does strike.

With a plan like this in place, you are prepared to get the best advice for your money.

WHERE TO START

Hiring an in-house attorney will only make sense if you're spending $1 million or more a year on legal fees. Even then, no single attorney is expert in all legal specialties. You would still have to rely on outsiders for some needs.

The in-house attorney for a high-tech company might know something about patents and deal making, for example, but could be completely clueless about defending against an age-discrimination suit.

Strategy: You probably already have a local attorney who helped you set up the business and provides occasional tax advice as well as a little advice on how to comply with local laws. That's the person to go to first if a legal problem arises. He/she can handle the first steps in a legal challenge and help you find the specialized service that will carry you the rest of the way.

If you don't have such a "utility" lawyer, shop for one among local attorneys who have done work for businesses similar to yours.

IDENTIFY YOUR EXPOSURE

The best strategy by far for keeping down legal bills is not getting sued. And—the best way to do that is to protect yourself where you are most vulnerable.

The most treacherous legal area for businesses today is workplace discrimination—age, disability, race, sex—and sexual harassment.

Each law governing discrimination in the workplace has its own threshold for applicability. Some apply only to businesses with more than 15 employees. Others kick in only when the business has 20 employees.

But since these thresholds are based on a moving average of how many employees you had in the last calendar year, whether you are subject to any of them could depend on what week it is.

Caution: Even if you are immune from federal law because your company is too small, state law can come into play.

Have your utility attorney refer you to local lawyers who specialize in each of the major workplace litigation areas.

Look *now* for attorneys who specialize in discrimination cases in your jurisdiction and who are active enough to keep current on all developments. Then—get briefed on the law as it applies to your business.

IF YOU ARE SUED

As soon as your attorney is fully briefed on the case against you, ask him: "How much will this cost me a month? How much will this cost me altogether? Can we work out a budget that keeps the costs down?"

Beware: A firm that refuses to lay out a budget for you either doesn't know what it is doing or has a history of piling up huge bills for other clients. Either way, that's not a firm you want working for you.

Once you have agreed to the budget, don't just assume it will be continuously met.

Monitor fees each month. If a bill is higher than you expected, phone the lawyer immediately to ask for an explanation.

If you don't complain, the lawyer will assume you can live with the bill...and the high charges will most likely continue.

SEEK A SETTLEMENT

The longer a case runs, the higher your legal fees. In numerous business litigation cases, it makes financial sense to settle quickly.

If there is no convincing reason for a failure to settle the case in a timely manner, request a face-to-face meeting with the other party.

There's no restriction on the two sides meeting in a negotiating session outside the courtroom. See if you can resolve the matter without further costly litigation.

Alternative: If the case is dragging on much too long and your attorney's explanation for the delay does not satisfy you, consider consulting another attorney.

Brief the second attorney on the highlights of the case with the basic documents and perhaps a letter from your original attorney advising a particular course of action. That should be enough for him to say, "This looks about right," or, "Hey, this just doesn't seem right."

The cost of obtaining a second opinion could be more than made up by resolving a case that otherwise could have accumulated huge legal fees or even wrecked your business.

Get Paid Faster

To ensure prompt payment from a new customer or client, find out what the client's payment procedure is. Don't expect payment in one week if the client normally pays every 30 days. Call clients a week before their payments are due, and fax a duplicate invoice at that time. This lets them know you expect prompt payment—but you will not come across as pushy. If you do not receive a check promptly, follow up with another polite phone call.

Terri Lonier, president, Working Solo, Inc., corporate strategists for companies targeting the small office/home office (SOHO) market, 126 Climbing Ridge Rd., New Paltz, NY 12561.

Domain Name Danger

Registering a Web site name does not necessarily mean your business has the right to use it. Site registrars do *not* check whether the name violates another company's trademark rights.

Example: If the domain name *mcdonalds. com* were available, a registrar would register it for the applicant. But actually *using* the name would almost certainly result in litigation based on trademark infringement.

Chanley Howell, Esq., Foley & Lardner, The Greenleaf Building, 200 Laura St., Jacksonville, FL 32202.

Little Things Mean a Lot...Successful Direct Marketing

Lois K. Geller, president of Mason & Geller Direct Marketing at 261 Madison Ave., 18th Fl., New York City 10016. She is author of Response: The Complete Guide to Profitable Direct Marketing for Entrepreneurs, Small Companies and Giant Corporations *(Free Press).*

Direct marketing is the best way to form relationships with large groups of customers and generate an immediate buying response.

MASTERING THE MAIL

While direct marketing encompasses telephone selling, TV, radio, magazine space, E-mail and other variations, traditional mail—even at higher rates—is still by far the most effective tool for direct marketers. *Here are some tricks of the trade of successful direct marketers...*

●**Make a big deal out of being a small company.** There's most likely a story behind what makes your company unique and how you came to sell the products or services you do. Tell it. In printed ad copy and direct-mail letters, this story—told by you—will help you establish long-term relationships, not just make sales.

Example: Paint a clear, memorable portrait of your company, as was done for a pecan farmer client. We sent corporate prospects a folksy mailing, very much in keeping with our client's "retired businessman turned pecan farmer" personality. The mailing talked about how he followed his dream and learned the hard way about raising pecans. We offered prospective customers a sample pack of pecans for $10. The orders came rolling in.

●**Get the most from your own mailing list.** Large companies pay thousands to update their databases, often because their original customer lists lacked enough detail.

Being small, you can create a database of names, addresses and buying habits by interviewing customers. Keep this list up-to-date from the start, and you'll have something to build on and grow.

For additional names and addresses, rent lists of national businesses whose target customers most closely match yours.

Example: A company that sells outdoor sports clothing might rent a list from a company that sells fishing and hunting apparel.

●**Don't cut corners on the offer.** Small companies that feel they can't afford to give away something truly valuable as part of a direct-marketing offer aren't considering how much it costs to get a customer the conventional way.

It takes a salesperson's salary…time away from the business…expensive meals that you have to pay for and schmooze over…etc.—to woo new customers if you are not using a direct-marketing campaign.

But if you make your direct-mail offer believable, unique and interactive—and include a guarantee that gives customers some recourse if dissatisfied—customers will come to you.

●**Test two offers instead of "mass-mailing" one.** To improve your chances of success with an offer, split your mailing in two. Send one kind of offer to the first group and another kind to the second. When testing the offer, be sure to leave all other features of the campaign the same. If you change more than one element, you won't know what buyers are responding to.

Example: A restaurant owner mailing out 1,000 direct-mail pieces sends 500 potential customers a letter describing his food, listing sample menu items and offering them a free dessert if they come in bearing the letter. The second group of 500 prospects gets the same letter. However, they are offered a complimentary glass of wine if they bring the letter in when they come.

Important: Keep accurate records while testing offers. Then look at your records and determine which offer drew the most customers. Repeat the successful offer with a new, larger list of targeted prospects.

Better Banner Ads

Banner ads have two failings—many site visitors ignore them…and those who do click on them are taken away from the site. Leading Web advertisers are now experimenting with advertising windows that "reside" within Web pages, with the page content wrapped around

them. Clicking on the window displays an animated message within the window.

Advantages: Visitors are not taken away from the site, and advertisers pay more for window ads than they do for banner ads.

Dana Blankenhorn, writer and Internet consultant at a-clue.com, 215 Winter Ave., Atlanta 30317.

To Deduct S Corporation Losses… Build Up Your Basis

Kevin Anderson, CPA, partner, and Laura Howell-Smith, senior manager, Deloitte & Touche LLP, 555 12 St. NW, Washington, DC 20004.

Companies that choose to elect S corporation status benefit from several significant tax advantages…

●**No corporate income tax** (though there are a few exceptions for S corporations that converted from C corporations).

●**Limited exposure to charges by the IRS** that the owners' compensation is unreasonable.

●**No tax on excess accumulations of profits** or personal holding company income.

Moreover, corporate losses as well as corporate income flow through to S corporation shareholders' personal income tax returns—where they can be of great use.

CASE STUDY

John Smith is the 100% shareholder of Superior Inc., an S corporation. Superior reports a $50,000 loss in tax year 2003, which is passed through to John.

John can deduct the loss on his personal income tax return to reduce his tax bill.

Catch: For John to deduct the full $50,000 loss in 2003, his basis in Superior stock and the company's indebtedness to him, if any, must be at least $50,000.

If John's basis in this organization is only $30,000, he can only take a $30,000 loss on his 2003 personal income tax return. The other $20,000 is considered a "suspended loss."

Suspended losses can be carried forward to future years and deducted when John has sufficient basis in stock or indebtedness.

For the purpose of deducting losses, the question is how can John beef up his basis in his S corporation. *John can…*

●**Give property to the company.** John's stock basis may be increased by either the value or basis of contributed property, depending upon whether the contribution is taxable or tax free…

●If the contribution is taxable (that is, John pays tax on his gain), his stock basis is increased by the net value of any property that John contributes to the company.

●If it is tax free, the stock basis will be increased by the basis of the contributed property in Superior Inc.

●**Lend the company money.** The face value of the loans John makes to his company is included in his basis.

Various types of adjustments can increase or decrease basis. Generally, basis is increased by income and decreased by distributions, losses and deductions.

INDEBTEDNESS BASIS

In the above scenario, John may simply wait to deduct his $20,000 of suspended losses. He might use them to offset future profits.

But if John wants to deduct all the losses right away, he can lend $20,000 to the company. That will give him sufficient basis for a full $50,000 write-off.

The Tax Code is *very* specific as to how such loans should be handled.

The wrong way: If Superior borrows the $20,000 from a third party, John's basis won't be increased. The same is true even if John guarantees the loan so that he's fully at risk (except to the extent John actually makes loan payments).

Even if John buys a $20,000 interest in a loan from a third party, he won't get an increase in his basis in Superior if the participation interest is, in substance, a guarantee of the corporation's indebtedness.

The right way: John must make the loan directly to Superior. That's how the S corporation shareholders get basis via debt.

If John doesn't have $20,000 to lend, he can personally borrow $20,000 from a bank. If necessary, John may use his stock to secure the loan.

Then John can lend that same $20,000 to Superior. This back-to-back loan arrangement increases his basis in the company by $20,000, even though it's just a matter of form.

Alternative: John can increase his indebtedness basis if he can get the bank to exchange the notes, so that John substitutes his note for the corporation's note.

DOUBLE TROUBLE

Many business owners have two or more separate S corporations.

Example: In addition to Superior, an S corporation that's losing money, suppose John Smith also owns 100% of Stalwart Inc., a profitable S corporation.

Trap: Rather than deal with a third-party lender, John may prefer to have cash-rich Stalwart lend money to Superior. Such a transaction won't give John additional basis in Superior.

Strategy: Instead, John can take a cash distribution from Stalwart. If already taxed profits are withdrawn, no income tax will be triggered.

Then John can use that cash to make a personal loan to Superior, increasing his basis and permitting an immediate deduction.

DANGER IN SLOPPINESS

For a loan to provide basis in your S corporation, it must be a bona fide loan…

●**The loan should be in writing,** with a reasonable interest rate and acceptable security.

●**Repayment terms should be set,** along with provisions that will be followed in case of default.

●**The transaction should look like a loan** between unrelated parties.

Safe harbor: The Tax Code provides basis for "straight debt." This is a genuine loan that looks and feels like a loan and is not treated as a second class of stock that might disqualify the corporation from S status.

Trap: Loans that are convertible to common stock *won't* qualify for this safe harbor. Neither will loans with repayment contingent on certain future events. Such loans might create a second class of stock, and S corps may have only one class.

Good news: Treating such loans as equity will provide the owner with basis.

Bad news: You'll blow your S corporation election and lose all the expected tax benefits, including the ability to deduct corporate losses.

USE THEM OR LOSE THEM

S corporation losses you can't deduct immediately can be carried forward to future years, as mentioned. *But there are exceptions...*

• **You convert your S corporation to a C corporation.** After such a conversion, you generally have one year to increase your basis and deduct the suspended losses. After that, they can't be used.

• **You sell the company.** Suspended S corporation losses disappear after sale of shares.

Should you make a loan to an S corporation before selling the stock to free up suspended losses that would otherwise be unused? You would normally expect the loan to be repaid at some time, and the disposition of the company would seem like an appropriate time to expect repayment.

Trap: If you make a $20,000 loan to the S corporation to free up the same amount of losses, the loan repayment may be taxable.

It would likely be ordinary income. That's because the repayment of the loan is not a sale or exchange of the type that could give capital gains treatment.

Even if the sale-or-exchange problem is resolved, the gain may still be short term. If a capital contribution is made, however, long-term capital gains treatment can be preserved.

CANCELLATION OF DEBT

There might be another way to increase your basis in your S corporation. This tactic may be available if the company becomes insolvent.

Example: John Smith's basis in Superior is $50,000. Over the years, he has written off $50,000 worth of losses. Superior becomes insolvent, and creditors agree to write off $500,000 in debt. Under the Tax Code, Superior would pick up $500,000 worth of cancellation of debt (COD) income.

Technically, this income passes to John, the sole shareholder. His basis in Superior increases by

$500,000, allowing him to use up to $500,000 worth of suspended and current losses.

Key: Superior won't recognize COD income because it's insolvent. Can John really have his cake and eat it, too? Not anymore. While the US Supreme Court had allowed John to increase the basis of his S corporation stock by the COD income, a new law in 2002 prevents this basis increase.

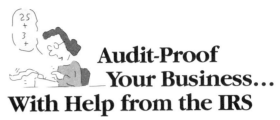

Audit-Proof Your Business... With Help from the IRS

Sidney Kess, attorney and CPA, 10 Rockefeller Plaza, Suite 909, New York City 10020. Mr. Kess is coauthor/consulting editor of *Financial and Estate Planning* and coauthor of *1040 Preparation, 2003 Edition* (both from CCH).

You can audit-proof your business's tax return—and the IRS will help you do it. The IRS is now revealing to the public valuable information about their audit targets and techniques—including "audit technique guides" and training materials that its agents use, and the *Internal Revenue Manual* that directs their operating procedures.

Moreover, many businesses can avoid being audited on key issues by reaching advance agreement with the IRS on how the issues will be handled.

VALUABLE BLUEPRINTS

• **Audit guides.** To make its audits more effective, the IRS has organized teams of analysts who study particular industries. These teams identify key tax issues for each kind of business...and how tax underreporting is most likely to occur within it.

Each team writes up its findings in an audit technique guide. The guide gives IRS auditors detailed instructions about what to look for on the tax return when auditing that kind of business—and how to verify what is reported on it.

Example: The audit technique guide for self-service laundries tells how to verify the business's reported income by examining its water bill.

Opportunity: A company that obtains the guide for its kind of business obtains the blueprint to a future tax audit *before* it occurs…and can use the guide not only to improve overall tax planning, but also to eliminate audit targets from its tax return before they ever exist.

More than 50 audit guides have been put out by the IRS for businesses ranging from architects to veterinarians, and more are being released as they are completed.

The guide may help the company…

• Learn the items on its tax return that need special care.

• Improve their record keeping and documentation procedures to assure that deductions aren't being overlooked.

• Identify gray areas on the return where the company may have legitimate differences of opinion with the IRS—and for which the company should obtain expert advice.

• Correct mistakes made in past tax reporting—and perhaps file amended tax returns to correct past errors or claim tax refunds.

These audit guides are available to the public at *www.irs.gov.* Click on FOIA (Freedom of Information Act) and then on "Additional IRS Products Available Online."

• **Independent contractor training materials.** The single biggest audit issue facing businesses today is the treatment of *independent contractors.*

While businesses make greater use of contractors, the IRS suspects many do so to avoid paying employment taxes.

Trap: Companies that don't follow the detailed tax rules regarding independent contractors risk having the IRS recategorize these workers as employees and impose a big tax bill for back employment taxes.

Congress recently revised the classification rules for determining whether workers are contractors or employees. The IRS has revised its own rules for contractors as well.

As a result of these changes, the IRS has set up a training program to explain the new rules to auditors who conduct worker classification examinations of businesses.

Opportunity: The full 160-page manual of training materials used in this program is available to businesses as well.

Training Materials for IRS Examiners on Worker Classification is available free on the IRS Web site, *www.irs.gov,* by entering the title in the first search box.

Again, this package provides the blueprint of a possible future worker classification audit. A company that obtains the package can use it to ensure compliance with the rules and head off an audit before it arises.

HOW TO AVOID AN AUDIT

• **Tip-reporting agreements.** The IRS is now trying to increase tax compliance while reducing the cost of audit disputes by reaching voluntary advance agreements with businesses. In these agreements, the IRS promises not to audit a business on an issue in exchange for the business's agreement to handle the issue a certain way. Among businesses where tips are involved, the IRS is trying to negotiate tip-reporting agreements.

Risk: Employers whose employees earn tips can incur heavy tax penalties for underpaying the employer half of employment taxes if an audit reveals that employees have failed to report tip income.

The IRS has released a series of voluntary model agreements that enable employers to eliminate this risk by educating employees about tip reporting…and taking steps to facilitate tip reporting.

In exchange, the IRS agrees not to conduct a tip-reporting audit.

The IRS now has published model agreements for the food and beverage, cosmetology and barber, and gaming industries, and all other industries with tipped employees.

In addition, it has published an *IRS Tip Coordinator Listing* that provides phone numbers that companies can use to contact IRS tip program coordinators in every IRS District.

The model agreements and coordinator listings are available by entering "IRS Tip Coordinator Listing" in the first search box at *www.irs.gov.*

• **Private rulings.** A company can eliminate audit risk on a critical issue by asking the IRS for a *private letter ruling* on the issue in advance.

How it works: The company explains its proposed transaction to the IRS even before it occurs, and tells the IRS the ruling it seeks regarding the tax treatment of the transaction.

If the IRS rules favorably, the company will obtain its desired treatment and is protected from future audit risk on the issue. This is true even if other taxpayers in the same situation are given different treatment by the IRS.

There is little risk of obtaining an unfavorable private ruling. If the IRS has a problem with the ruling request, it will call to discuss the matter. The company can then modify the proposed transaction and ruling request to meet the IRS objection...or can simply withdraw the ruling request.

Result: Even a ruling request that has been rejected can alert the company to a problem with a proposed transaction. This can prevent a costly mistake.

A request for a private ruling should be prepared for the company by a tax professional.

Helpful: Details on how to request a private ruling are provided in IRS Revenue Procedure 2002-2; IRB 2002-1,1. This is available in *Internal Revenue Bulletin 2002-1* on the IRS Web site at *www.irs.gov/ind_info/bullet.html.*

THE IRS'S BIBLE

It can be helpful to know the operational procedures the IRS follows.

These procedures are laid out in the *Internal Revenue Manual,* the "bible" of IRS personnel. It covers every area of IRS operations—account processing, audits, appeals, collections, criminal investigation, customer service—even how the IRS rewards informants.

The manual contains the internal policies, procedures, instructions, guidelines and delegations of authority that direct the IRS's operation and administration.

If the company wants to learn how IRS agents do their jobs, how the IRS is administering its case or what to expect next, this can be a valuable resource.

The *Internal Revenue Manual* is on the IRS Web site. Click on FOIA and then "Additional IRS Products Available Online."

Even more help: The various sections of the IRS Web site contain a great deal of useful information that can help businesses reduce audit risk. Take time to explore them.

In particular, the new "Small Business/Self-Employed" section specializes in information for such businesses. Find it at *www.irs.gov* under "Businesses."

Dangers for Company Retirement Plans And Ways to Avoid Trouble

Seymour Goldberg, Esq., CPA, senior partner, Goldberg & Goldberg, PC, One Huntington Quadrangle, Melville, NY 11737, *www.goldbergira.com.* One of the nation's leading authorities on IRA distributions, Mr. Goldberg is author of *The New IRA Distribution Rules* (IRG).

Hundreds of thousands of business owners should have received notices saying they must amend their tax-favored qualified retirement plans to comply with the recent tax law changes.

Trap: While doing so, many will discover that their plans were never properly amended for past law changes—exposing them to penalties that could be extremely costly.

A lucky break: The IRS has issued new rules to let employers report and correct existing plan defects voluntarily, at much less cost than if the IRS discovers them on audit. But you must be prepared to do the necessary paperwork.

Helpful: Ask your retirement plan expert to conduct an audit of the plan's paperwork and its operational practices.

PREPARE NOW

Most small businesses that have qualified retirement plans in place utilize "prototype" plans set up by banks, insurers, brokers, mutual fund companies and other financial institutions.

These "off-the-shelf" plans spare small firms the cost and effort of designing their own plans from scratch.

Now, the IRS is requiring all prototype plans to be amended to comply with numerous law changes. The date by which amendments are required depends on the type of plan and the law change involved.

The financial companies that maintain such prototype plans are amending their plans now and will then mail amendment documents to their clients.

COSTLY TRAPS

Industry experts say that up to 30% of all small business plans may not be in compliance with pre-1995 law changes—due to their failure to file earlier required amendments.

Many small businesses lack the pension departments and in-house experts needed to keep current, so they frequently fail to comply with technical rules—even if by accident. *Common examples...*

● **Eligibility rules** aren't properly followed.

● **Plan terms** discriminate in favor of highly compensated employees.

● **Plan contributions** are misallocated.

● **Years of service** are improperly counted.

● **Benefits** are not calculated correctly or they are paid early or late.

DEFENSIVE MEASURES

To avoid steep penalties or plan disqualification, look for such errors yourself and correct them voluntarily—before the IRS has a chance to spot them.

The IRS's newly revised pension correction program is called the Employee Plans Compliance Resolution System (EPCRS). *It has three main components...*

● **Self-correction program (SCP).** Using this program, an employer can correct operational mistakes without reporting them to the IRS or paying penalty. *The SCP can be used to correct...*

● *Insignificant* operational errors that affect only a small percentage of employees or total plan funds.

● *Significant* operational errors that result from "good faith" misapplication of the complex retirement plan rules. *Examples...*

☐ Eligible employees were excluded from plan participation.

☐ Top-paid employees received excess contributions in violation of nondiscrimination rules.

Solution: Take corrective action to make all affected employees "whole" by putting them in the position they would be in if the error had not occurred.

Generally, errors must be corrected using the SCP within two years after they occur. You must keep full records of the errors and corrective actions taken and have them available for later examination.

● **Voluntary correction program (VCP).** The VCP is used to correct more serious plan errors with IRS approval. *These include...*

● "Qualification failures" that result from plan document errors—such as failing to file required amendments to comply with past law changes, and...

● Operational errors so serious that the IRS might not consider them to have been made in good faith.

Example: Company owners taking improper loans from the plan or making improper use of plan assets.

Key: Using the VCP, the company proposes its own "cure" for the error and submits it to the IRS for approval.

If the IRS approves, the problem is resolved. If not, the employer can attempt to negotiate an acceptable remedy with the IRS.

Option to consider: Make an anonymous "John Doe" VCP application to try to resolve a problem if you fear repercussions if you can't reach an agreement with the IRS.

Employers who use the VCP must pay the IRS a correction fee. "Presumptive" fees will range from $2,000 for plans with 10 or fewer participants to $35,000 for plans with more than 1,000 participants.

● **Audit closing agreement program (Audit CAP).** Plan problems that are first discovered by an IRS auditor, rather than voluntarily reported and resolved by an employer, are handled here.

Under the Audit CAP, you must obtain IRS approval for your plan correction and pay a "sanction" that generally will be much larger than the fee that would have been imposed under the VCP.

If you fail to negotiate a remedy that is acceptable to the IRS, the retirement plan may face harsh penalties—plan disqualification with taxation of plan earnings, retroactive loss of deductions for contributions to the plan and the loss of tax-favored benefits for employees.

Boosting Productivity

Show respect for employees' time, and you will improve their productivity…

●**Give specific durations for meetings.** Insist that attendees adhere to them, and consult employees before extending a meeting.

●**If an employee asks a question you do not know the answer to,** promise a response within 24 hours—and follow through.

●**Create a committee to look into time-wasting reports,** meetings and processes, and eliminate as many as possible.

●**If employees must stay late for an important project,** thank them as well as their families with a voucher for a dinner or movie.

John Cowan, editor, *Positive Leadership*, 316 N. Michigan Ave., Chicago 60601.

Better Conflict Resolution

When dealing with a personality clash in the office, act like a diplomat—not a law officer. Criticize behavior, not people—and only in private. It never helps to get personal. Workers who are criticized in public often feel compelled to justify their behavior to save face, rather than take corrective action. Explain the consequences of the improper behavior so the parties realize why it is improper. Explain what the disciplinary consequences will be if the improper behavior is repeated.

Karl Walinskas, communication consultant for The Speaking Connection, 9 Downing Dr., Dallas, PA 18612, *www.speakingconnection.com.*

Praise Workers Behind Their Backs

Complimenting an individual when he/she is not there allows praise to reach that person through the grapevine. Some employees feel this is the most valued praise. It will spread throughout the company—and he is unlikely to think that the praise is anything but genuine.

Bob Nelson, PhD, Nelson Motivation Inc., 12245 World Trade Dr., Suite C, San Diego 92128, and author of *1,001 Ways to Take Initiative at Work* (Workman).

Shrewder Hiring

Marjorie Brody, president, Brody Communications Ltd., a company that trains organizations and individuals in effective communication, 815 Greenwood Ave., Suite 8, Jenkintown, PA 19046, *www.brodycommunications.com.*

Eighty percent of job applications contain inaccurate information. *Here is how you can avoid being misled…*

●**Use a job application that serves as a legal document.** Have an attorney add in a section at the bottom of the application form where the applicant affirms that the information provided is accurate…and gives the company permission to conduct a background check. The wording should also state the consequences of providing false information.

●**Go beyond checking references.** Verify the accuracy of all diploma listings, driving records, records of convictions, credit history, Social Security number and similar items.

●**Get help.** If you can't perform background checks yourself, you can hire professionals to do them. Costs can range from $30 to $150 per person. Contact your local chamber of commerce or industry association for referrals.

Home-Office Deductions: New Opportunities

Thomas P. Ochsenschlager, Esq., CPA, partner, Grant Thornton LLP, 1900 M St. NW, Washington, DC 20036.

Claiming home-office deductions can pay off up front. Thanks to a law change and a new court decision, your chances of having these deductions upheld have just increased—even if you live in an apartment.

However, deducting home-office expenses can wind up costing you money when you sell your home. So proceed cautiously before taking this write-off.

GROUND RULES

To qualify for home-office deductions, you must have a space in your home that you use regularly and exclusively for business. You cannot use the space for anything else. Just keeping a TV set in the office may enable the IRS to assert that the space is used for other purposes.

A deductible home office may be a room or a portion of a room. But, not everyone with a work space at home qualifies for a deduction. *You must meet at least one of these other tests...*

●**Your home office is a principal place of business.**

●**You use it to meet regularly** with customers, clients or patients.

●**You use a separate structure as your office,** such as a detached, converted garage.

For employees: While home-office deductions are mostly taken by self-employed taxpayers, employees can deduct them if they meet one of the aforementioned tests. In addition, they must be required to work at home as a condition of their employment.

PLACE OF BUSINESS

In prior years, the "principal place of business" test was difficult for salespeople, contractors and consultants to pass. But a law that took effect in 1999 makes it much easier.

Under this law, your home office is your principal place of business if...

●**You use the space for administrative and management activities,** and...

●**There is no other location** for you to do these activities.

Impact: This law helps people who don't actually work at home to claim home-office deductions. Just make sure you set aside a room, or a portion of a room, that you use only for business-related paperwork.

Renters can take home-office deductions, too. In fact, a violinist living in Los Angeles recently won a court battle with the IRS and was able to deduct 40% of her family's apartment rent.

The violinist argued that nothing else but violin practice took place in the apartment's living room (40% of the apartment's total space). The single piece of furniture in this room was used to store all of her sheet music. Even the violinist's young daughter was not allowed to play there.

CRUNCHING THE NUMBERS

If you qualify for home-office deductions, the first step is to calculate the office portion of your home. *Two methods...*

●**Room method.** If one of your home's eight rooms is your office, and those rooms are of similar size, the home-office portion is 12.5%.

●**Area method.** If your home has 2,500 square feet and a home office is 250 square feet, the home-office portion is 10%.

Once you have determined this percentage, you can deduct that portion of your costs for utilities, security monitoring, homeowner's insurance, etc.

For renters: With a 10% home office, you can deduct 10% of your rent.

Depreciation: Homeowners (including condo and co-op owners) can take depreciation deductions calculated as follows...

●From your basis in your home (basis equals purchase price plus capital improvements), deduct the amount allocated to land.

●From the remainder, calculate the depreciation deduction.

Example: If your basis in your home is $250,000, with a $50,000 allocation to land, your investment in the house itself is $200,000. Say your home office is 10% of your house. Thus, you'd have a $20,000 basis in your home office to depreciate—10% of $200,000.

Assuming you start using a home office after May 12, 1993, you'd take depreciation over 39 years, so each year's depreciation would be around 2.5%. (Older home offices were depreciated more rapidly.) In the above example, with $20,000 of basis to depreciate and a 39-year schedule, your annual write-off would be around $500.

Car expenses: Yet another tax break may be available if you qualify for a home-office deduction—you may be able to write off your car expenses going to and from home to a business location.

FILING THE FORMS

If you are self-employed, reporting business income on Schedule C of Form 1040, you claim home-office deductions on IRS Form 8829.

Sideline businesses: You can claim a home office for a home-based sideline business. But, the current year's deduction can't exceed the net income from that business.

For employees: Expenses for the business use of your home are claimed on Schedule A of Form 1040 as miscellaneous itemized deductions. All of your miscellaneous expenses are added up and the amount that exceeds 2% of your adjusted gross income is deductible.

NEW OPPORTUNITY

On Christmas eve 2002 Uncle Sam gave home-based businesses a tax break by issuing new regulations stating that the home sale exclusion need *not* be allocated when a home is sold. This rule applies when the business use (home office) occurs within the same dwelling unit used for residential purposes. In the past, tax experts speculated that the portion of the home used for a home office did not qualify for the exclusion.

Note: Despite new regulations, any depreciation claimed for a home office after May 6, 1997, must be picked up as capital gains—taxed at a 25% rate for those in tax brackets of at least this rate—when the home is sold (the exclusion cannot offset this income).

Example: A taxpayer bought a home in 1998 for $200,000, using one bedroom as a home office for her consulting business. She sells the home in 2005 for $300,000, realizing a $100,000 gain. Assuming she claimed depreciation on the home office of $2,000 in the years 1998 to 2005, she can exclude $98,000 of her gain—the $2,000 depreciation is reported as capital gains taxed at 25% (if she is in a 25% or higher tax bracket in 2005). In effect, use of the home office generated $2,000 in depreciation deductions which she recaptured in the year of sale.

Home-Office Deduction Alert

Be able to prove how you use your home office. The burden of proof is on *you* to show that you use a home office exclusively for work. This can be troublesome if you are audited two or three years after you last used the office—maybe when you no longer even own the home.

Recent case: A taxpayer presented pictures to the Tax Court of his bedroom, which he said he used as an office. But the judge said while the picture showed a sofa, dresser and tea stand, "there was no indication of any desk, filing cabinets or office equipment." So the deduction was disallowed.

To be safe: Take pictures of your office that show how it is used for work, in case you need them later.

Jack C.C. Huang, TC Summary Opinion 2002-93

Tax Deductions For Job Hunting

If you have lost a job—or even if you are still working—you may be able to deduct the cost of looking for a new job. Job-hunting costs are a deductible employee business expense when you look for a new job in your line of work, without changing careers.

Deductible: Employment agency costs, counseling fees, résumé preparation, phone calls, travel and lodging undertaken looking for work, 50% of meal costs and related expenses.

Requirements: You must itemize deductions on your return. The job-hunting costs are included among your "miscellaneous expenses," the total of which is deductible to the extent that it exceeds 2% of adjusted gross income.

Jim Southward, president, California Society of Enrolled Agents, San Carlos, CA.

Interview Questions Every Job Hunter Should Ask

Richard Fein, director of undergraduate placement services, Isenberg School of Management, University of Massachusetts at Amherst. He is author of seven books, including 101 Dynamite Questions to Ask at Your Job Interview and 101 Hiring Mistakes Employers Make…and How to Avoid Them (Impact).

Job interviews invariably include an invitation for questions from the interviewee. Employers evaluate those questions very carefully to help determine if a candidate is a good fit for a position. *Four areas that job candidates should ask about…*

THE JOB

Ask about specifics. Show that you are sincere in trying to determine what it takes to succeed in the company.

Some examples…

●**What skills or personality qualities** are you looking for?

●**What qualities did people have** who did well in the job?

●**What are the most important aspects to focus on** in order to achieve your objectives?

THE COMPANY

Ask a question for which an answer can't be found on the company's Web site or in its annual report. Show that you are thinking about the same things that people already employed by the company think about. Be sure to mention your own research.

Example: "A recent *Wall Street Journal* article suggested that companies in this industry should be more concerned with profit margin than market share. What are this company's priorities? Have they changed recently? Do you expect them to shift in the future?"

THE INDUSTRY

Show that you are looking at the big picture. Ask about the industry as a whole, rather than focusing solely on the company.

Good subjects: International treaties on trade…mergers and acquisitions…the impact of interest rates…whatever relevant issues are in the news at the time of your interview.

Example: If two big firms in this industry have just merged, you might ask, "Do you foresee a trend toward consolidation in the industry? How would that affect this company?"

EXTERNAL EVENTS

You might ask about any of a wide range of topics—fluctuating foreign currency exchange rates, changes in consumer tastes, innovations in technology, etc.

Example: For a chemical manufacturer, you might ask, "Your biggest client in recent years has been China. Is your business at risk as a result of the political tensions between China and the US?"

The idea is not to stump the interviewer, but to show that you are thinking big.

Prepare notes in advance, and bring them with you. You might even ask if it is okay to refer to them—that demonstrates you really did your homework.

Negotiating Job Perks

Everything is negotiable when applying for a job. But never give up anything without getting something in return.

Example: Agree to take a lower salary in exchange for benefits, such as telecommuting.

Also: It may be to your advantage to negotiate via E-mail. This creates a record of discussions and gives you time to think before you respond.

Brian Krueger, Webmaster and content provider for *www.collegegrad.com,* a career Web site for recent college graduates.

Hard Work Isn't Enough— How to Succeed Today

Al Ries, chairman, Ries & Ries, a marketing strategy firm in Roswell, GA. He and Jack Trout pioneered the marketing concept of positioning. They are the authors of *Positioning: The Battle for Your Mind* (McGraw-Hill).

You're applying for a new job or shooting for a promotion. Or maybe you are simply concerned about holding on to your current job in a shaky economy.

Four helpful strategies...

1. Focus on the person you are trying to impress. Most people think hard work is the key to success. That is rarely enough. Unless you stand out in your employer's mind, you are just one of many competent workers.

Figure out what the employer is looking for. What is he/she likely to notice? How do you distinguish yourself from others? *Here's what to do...*

•Research the company on the Internet. Pay particular attention to new products and strategies, which are often outlined in press releases posted on the company's Web site.

•Check the industry press for information.

•Ask about new hires—education, previous jobs, special skills, etc. Or use the Internet and industry resources mentioned above to get information.

•Ask people who work for the company or a competitor about its products and strategies.

Obviously, all this is important if you are applying for a new job at an unfamiliar firm, but it is also very useful if you are already an employee. You may not be up to date on all of management's decisions.

2. Emphasize your specialness. Do you have something the employer wants? Play it up. Or highlight something he might not have thought of and isn't obviously looking for.

If you have a legal background, for instance, but the job description doesn't call for one, point out how legal skills could give you an edge. It may be your powers of persuasion, analytical skills or negotiating savvy.

If something that sets you apart might be considered a liability, put a positive spin on it. If you are older, for instance, you might tout an extensive network of contacts. If you are shooting for a medical-writing slot but haven't done much medical writing, demonstrate that you are skilled at explaining complex issues. The more clearly you define yourself, the better the impression you make.

3. Market your successes. Select an accomplishment and play it up. Say you sold television advertising time to a client who had not advertised before. You don't just sell advertising —you identify advertising opportunities that others overlook.

Or give yourself a *label* to help others zero in on your strengths.

Example: You turned a money-losing division of your company into a money maker. If you look for a new position in your company—or outside—you can label yourself a *turnaround artist.*

4. Hook up with a winner. Even a mediocre jockey can win a race if he rides a good horse. The same is true for career climbers.

If your organization isn't a winner, you are probably not going to go very far no matter how good you are. Get on board with a winning company—and a boss who is on the fast track. If your boss goes places, you will probably go along.

Signs of a winning company: Introduces products one step ahead of its competition... receives favorable press...has stock that performs well...attracts top candidates when jobs open up.

Signs of a boss on the fast track: Handles assignments central to the company's bottom line...tackles problems of concern to senior management...is invited and contributes to important meetings.

How do you switch bosses if yours is a loser? *Very carefully.* Loyalty is prized—naked ambition is not.

Explain to your current boss that you want to change departments so you can broaden your experience. The key is to make it look like a learning experience for you—a way to make yourself more versatile and productive—rather than a way to ditch your boss.

Whatever you do, don't spread gossip or bad-mouth your boss or employer. Negative talk—and its source—has a way of getting back to the boss.

Avoid Telephone Turnoffs

Susan Berkley, CEO of The Great Voice Company in Englewood Cliffs, NJ, *www.greatvoice.com.* Her voice is featured on television and radio ads. She is the author of *Speak to Influence: How to Unlock the Hidden Power of Your Voice* (Campbell Hall).

Making a good impression on the telephone is crucial in a tight job market. *Common mistakes...*

1. Poor body language. Callers can't see you, so what's the harm in putting up your feet while you talk? Plenty, if you're trying to sound professional.

- Sit up straight or—better yet—stand. You will sound more alert.

- Use hand gestures. They make your voice more natural and alive.

- Do not cradle the phone between your ear and shoulder. Use a headset. *Plantronics's* hands-free adapter kits start at $32.95.* 800-544-4660...*www.plantronics.com.*

2. Not smiling. A smile can be conveyed in your voice.

- Put a photo of a loved one by the phone. Look at the photo as you talk. This promotes a positive frame of mind—a simple trick used by radio broadcasters.

- If you are distracted or in a bad mood, don't answer on the first ring...or let voice mail pick up.

- Avoid abrupt responses. If you are taking a message, don't say, "Who's calling?" or "She's in a meeting." Try, "May I tell him who is calling, please?" or "She's not available. Is there something I can help you with?"

3. Overuse of speakerphone. *The only times it is acceptable...*

- When more than one person needs to hear the caller.

- When you need your hands free—for example, to follow instructions from a computer help desk.

- While on hold. When the caller is back, switch off the speakerphone.

4. Filler words. Lots of "ums" or "you knows" are annoying.

To break the habit: When you are about to use a filler word, pause instead. The pause will not seem odd unless it lasts more than four seconds. Within three weeks, you should be cured.

*Price subject to change

19

Education Smarts

Secrets of Getting into A Top College

What is really going on behind the closed doors of the admissions committees at the elite universities? And does it really matter which college your child ends up attending?

Rachel Toor, a former admissions officer at Duke University answers these questions and more below...

•What general advice do you have for parents? Encourage your children to think about a variety of schools. It's a mistake to believe that only a handful of elite colleges— such as Harvard, Princeton and Yale—will make your child successful.

•But you've got to admit that going to a top school like Yale—as you did—certainly helps. I honestly don't know. A study reported in *The Chronicle of Higher Education* compared average salaries of students 20 years

after they enrolled in college. It turned out that the graduates of less selective colleges earned slightly more—$77,000—than the Ivy grads, who earned an average of $76,800.

•How many applicants do top colleges accept? At Duke, we would get about 14,000 applications for an entering class of 1,600 students. Last year, Harvard received approximately 19,000 applications for 1,650 openings.

Plenty of great schools have fewer applicants—for example, the University of Chicago, one of the best schools in the country. Many schools accept a common application, which the student fills in and sends to several institutions. But the University of Chicago's application is so specific and quirky that applicants have to really want to go there to bother filling it out.

•What do you suggest parents with young children do now to give their kids an edge? Encourage your kids to follow their

Rachel Toor, an admissions officer at Duke University from 1997 to 2000. She is author of *Admissions Confidential: An Insider's Account of the Elite College Selection Process* (St. Martin's). She lives in Durham, NC.

passions. To an admissions officer, nothing is worse than talking to a jaded, busy teenager who isn't excited about anything. The most compelling applicants are those who demonstrate genuine zeal for something.

● **But don't colleges look for well-rounded candidates?** Yes and no. So many kids have been told that they have to play sports, participate in student government and do community service that they all do these things. It's hard to make distinctions among applicants.

When I was visiting high schools as a Duke admissions officer, I would explain that we looked for "well-lopsided" kids as well as well-rounded. If all you do is music but you're passionate about it—fine. Every "good" school is trying to create a balanced class that consists of both well-rounded people *and* people who are more focused.

● **How important is the Scholastic Aptitude Test (SAT)?** At Duke, we would say that your SAT score didn't matter much. It was only one of six areas we would use to evaluate candidates. But truly, if you didn't get at least a 1480, you probably weren't going to get in.

My concern about the SAT is that it is a coachable test. Kids who take SAT-preparation courses score higher. I think Richard Atkinson, the president of the University of California system, is on the right track, putting less emphasis on the SAT I and more on the SAT II—what used to be called "achievement tests." It is much harder to coach kids for these. They have to learn the subject matter, not just test-taking strategies.

● **Do the elite colleges draw mostly from top private schools?** Kids from elite private schools—and public schools in affluent areas—do have an advantage. Top colleges select students who have taken the most rigorous programs available at the most competitive high schools. Also, kids from these schools usually have counselors who know them well—and who can tell an admissions officer insightful things about them. Many counselors in big public high schools must write their recommendations without much personal knowledge.

● **What else matters in the application process?** To be honest, it matters a lot which

desk your child's application lands on. We all work hard to be objective, but we are all ordinary people with our own biases. If you were a feminist runner who wrote well, you were my kind of applicant. A colleague of mine favored Eagle Scouts. Sometimes this subjectivity works in the student's favor...sometimes it doesn't.

● **Do gimmicks work in helping an application stand out?** No, they don't. But people keep trying them anyway. One kid sent us an old Duke hat. Pinned to it was a note that read, "I'll pick this up when I get to campus." Our reaction was, "We don't think so!"

Bribery won't work either. I was once offered a trip to a cattle ranch in Costa Rica.

● **Are independent college counselors worth the cost?** Anyone can call himself/herself an independent college counselor. You have to dig to find out what kind of expertise the person has—and no one can guarantee any results. A consultant who tells you he can get your child into his dream school is either naive or lying.

That said, an unbiased outsider with some knowledge of the admissions process can be very helpful. Applicants have to think hard about who they are and present that in a compelling package to an admissions committee. Parents are sometimes not in the best position to help their children do this. A knowledgeable person can also help the student come up with a reasonable list of schools.

The most important thing to keep in mind, however, is that there are quite a few excellent colleges and universities in this country, and there is also a lot of financial aid available. It is just a matter of parents working with their children to find schools that are good matches.

How Kids Can Ace Standardized Tests

Adam Robinson, cofounder of the Princeton Review, a test-preparation company. He is founder of RocketReview, which helps students improve academic performance, New York City, *www.rocketreview.com*.

Essay questions make up one-third of the score on the SAT II Writing Subject Test...roughly one-half the score on most of the Advanced-Placement (AP) tests...and one-third of the score on GREs (the admission test used for most graduate schools).

To maximize essay scores...

● **Spend the first 5% to 10% of the essay time jotting down key ideas and outlines.** This enables students to brainstorm ideas and structure their answers. Students who start writing immediately produce unorganized essays and quickly run out of steam.

● **After the rough outline, write fast and a lot.** Harried graders equate quantity with quality. They have little time to assess each essay, so nuances are rarely considered. A long good essay will probably receive a better score than a short excellent one. A student with compact handwriting should write larger or leave a bit more space between words.

So long as the essay is legible, graders are not influenced by a student's choice of script or print.

Since length is important, don't waste time proofreading, polishing sentences or agonizing over words. Graders recognize students are writing under pressure—they even tend to overlook spelling errors.

● **Indent paragraphs clearly.** Paragraphing conveys at least the appearance of organization, as does the judicious use of transitional phrases, such as "first"..."on the other hand" ...and "in conclusion." One study showed that essays with indented paragraphs received an average score of B+, while those without received an average of B.

● **Use big words.** Graders will assume that a sophisticated vocabulary, which is easy to spot, reflects sophisticated thinking.

● **If the question concerns a specific topic, include as many buzzwords** as is possible. Essay graders often use scoring rubrics, which literally include a checklist of terms that must be used for an essay to receive full credit.

Example: If the question is about McCarthyism, it's important to get in key phrases, such as *Red Scare* and *Senate Hearings*—even if such terms seem obvious.

● **Even when answering general questions, use examples** that show how much has been learned in school. Essay questions often give students the option of citing personal experience as well as academic examples.

Example: One SAT II Writing question might read, "Should all people be treated equally? Discuss with examples from history, literature or personal experience."

Although the question may invite the use of personal experience, essays that use academic examples receive better scores than do those that include a student's experience. Even if the essay question requires the discussion of personal experience, historical, literary or other academic name-dropping is still advisable.

Important: For general questions, students should take advantage of subjects or topics they know well as sources of supporting examples. If a student has just finished reading *Huckleberry Finn* or *Macbeth* or studying the American Civil War, there will be a way to work in illustrative examples from any of these sources—no matter what the question asks.

● **Start and end well.** Graders of standardized tests spend the bulk of what little time they have reading the essay's opening and closing paragraphs—and only skim the rest.

If time is running out, the student should mention that time is short and list the remaining points in outline form. Graders understand that intelligent students will have a lot to say and might not have time to cover everything in depth.

● **Practice writing timed essays.** Writing essays under time pressure is different from writing papers at home, and it is a skill that can be mastered.

My Web site, *www.rocketreview.com*, offers students free, instantaneous feedback—with predicted scores—on essays for the SAT II Writing Subject and the AP Literature Tests, with more tests to be added.

What College-Bound Grads Should Know

Adele Scheele, PhD, director of The Career Center at California State University in Northridge, *www.career inspired.com*. She is author of *Jumpstart Your Career in College* (Kaplan).

For many high school graduates, the transition to college can be very difficult. *Adele Scheele offers some helpful advice below...*

•**Focus on big goals.** In high school, it's possible to get by without doing a lot of work. In college, kids will start to see a huge divide between students who take schoolwork seriously and those who coast. It's common for new college students to crash academically in the first semester. It can be hard to recover.

Encourage your children to study independently...to learn how to do their research on the Internet...to ask professors and other students for help.

•**Join a study group—or start one.** It may not be the best way to study, but it's a good way to make friends. If professors don't announce that study groups are forming, kids should ask around. Chances are, some students are already meeting in the library or a nearby coffee shop.

•**Look for professional guidance.** Your child should talk to a career counselor no later than junior year of high school. He/she can help your child find internships...part-time jobs...or volunteer work in his chosen field.

"Safety Schools" Update

The list of colleges at which students can be reasonably sure of acceptance has changed significantly in recent years.

Example: The University of Southern California now accepts only 33% of applicants—down from 71% a decade ago.

Among the safest schools today: Xavier University in Cincinnati admits 88% of applicants...Southern Methodist University in Dallas, 82%...University of Vermont in Burlington, 80% ...University of Denver, 78%...Gustavus Adolphus College in St. Peter, Minnesota, 77%... Goucher College in Baltimore, 76%.

Comparative analysis by *The Wall Street Journal.*

All About 529 Plans: Hottest New Way to Save for College

Raymond D. Loewe, CLU, ChFC, president of College Money, a college counseling firm, 112-B Centre Blvd., Marlton, NJ 08053, *www.collegemoney.com.*

By now, almost everyone has heard of qualified state tuition programs—called 529 plans after the Internal Revenue Code section that governs them. These plans —introduced in 1997—help parents and grandparents build a college war chest in a tax-advantaged way. *Main tax benefits...*

•**There's no current tax on the earnings** of plan contributions.

•**Any withdrawals used to pay higher-education expenses** are now tax free.

•**Contributors can, within limits,** reduce the size of their taxable estates without paying gift tax.

Section 529 plans do not work out for every family. And since plans vary from state to state, it can be hard to decide which plan to use.

IS A 529 PLAN RIGHT FOR YOU?

Parents and grandparents can contribute to a 529 plan without regard to their income level.

Three factors to consider in deciding whether to set up a plan...

•Financial aid. If you expect a child to need financial aid, a 529 plan probably is inappropriate. Funds in the plan are treated as the contributor's assets, which affects aid if the contributor is the parent.

The income portion of any distribution that is made is characterized as student income. Under the federal financial aid formula, 50% of student income is considered available to pay for college—reducing or preventing eligibility for federal loans and grants.

Your eligibility status for college-sponsored scholarships and loan programs can also be adversely affected.

The funds usually do *not* count against the child for purposes of state financial aid. But such aid comprises only a small part of a student's total financial aid package. The bulk of the package will come from federal financial aid and private endowments.

•Taxes. The tax incentives of 529 plans can be quite attractive—once it's determined that a child won't need financial aid. Contributions are not deductible for federal income tax purposes, but states may offer tax write-offs.

Examples: New York offers a deduction of up to $5,000 per taxpayer ($10,000 for a couple). Virginia offers a deduction of up to $2,000 per year.

•Control. Once you select a plan, you give up control over all the investment decisions. The plan's custodian makes these decisions on the basis of the age of the child, state asset-allocation formulas and other factors. If you think you can outperform professional fund managers, *don't* save through a 529 plan.

WHICH PLAN SHOULD YOU SELECT?

All 50 states now offer 529 savings plans. To view the provisions of each state's plan, go to the Web site *www.savingforcollege.com.*

You don't have to use the plan of the state in which you—or the child—live. You can pick any state's plan. *To help you choose...*

•Compare the tax benefits of various state plans. Some plans offer benefits to residents—a deduction or a tax credit. Check with your state. If there is a state income tax benefit, you'll probably want to opt for your state's plan—unless other considerations (discussed below) counterbalance this benefit.

Caution: Find out if there are any consequences if you move from the state and want to take your money with you. Virginia, for example, requires you to repay whatever tax deduction you got on the contribution.

•Evaluate money managers. Many professional money managers now handle investments in state 529 plans...

•*Alliance*—Rhode Island.

•*Fidelity*—Delaware, Massachusetts and New Hampshire.

•*Merrill Lynch*—Maine.

•*Putnam*—Ohio.

•*Salomon Smith Barney*—Colorado and Illinois.

•*TIAA-CREF*—California, Connecticut, Georgia, Idaho, Kentucky, Michigan, Minnesota, Mississippi, Missouri, New York, Oklahoma, Tennessee and Vermont.

•*Vanguard*—Iowa.

These managers' track records can be checked. But the other states rely on managers for whom there is no readily available track record. For example, New Jersey's 529 plan is managed by the state's retirement fund money managers.

In deciding which plan you should use, ask yourself whether you have confidence in its style and performance.

Caution: Even the best managers can lose money in any particular year. Under the New York plan, for example, fund assets for younger beneficiaries declined in the past couple of years.

•Review asset-allocation formulas. Some plans specify how much of a beneficiary's fund will be invested in fixed-income investments and how much in equities—depending upon the child's age.

Given the ever-rising cost of college—tuition costs are increasing at *twice* the normal rate of inflation—it generally does not pay to be too conservative. You want to select a state that has a plan with a more aggressive asset allocation. If the child is very young, you probably don't want to use a plan that limits investments to conservative, fixed-income investments.

States are still tinkering with their plans and may change asset allocations in the future.

● **Learn the cost of getting out.** What happens if you're unhappy with a plan's performance and want to switch to another plan? Determine the penalties of getting out.

New York, for example, has a three-year waiting period before withdrawals are permitted.

To get around this, consider leaving existing funds where they are and start making new contributions to another state's plan.

● **Check for quirks in a state's plan.** As a rule, if a parent dies, the control over 529 plan funds can be passed on to another adult who is named by the parent as contingent owner.

But in Tennessee, when a custodian dies, the child automatically becomes the owner (unless the custodian has named a successor custodian). He/she can use the funds in any way he wants (subject to tax and penalties if the money is not used for higher education).

OTHER FACTORS TO CONSIDER

Since 529 plans are relatively new, there are many unsettled issues...

● **Medicaid eligibility.** Grandparents who expect Medicaid to pay their nursing home costs should check to see whether 529 funds are treated as an asset for purposes of determining Medicaid eligibility.

Generally, since the contributor remains the owner of the funds and can withdraw them for his own use (subject to tax and penalties), the funds can be considered an available asset for Medicaid purposes—but the law is not fully settled.

● **Creditor protection.** Are the funds in the plan protected from the claims of the owner's creditors? The answer varies from state to state. Where there is clear asset protection, wealthy professionals who fear lawsuits can shelter funds in the plan for the benefit of their children.

Education Expense Loopholes

Edward Mendlowitz, CPA, partner in the accounting firm of Mendlowitz Weitsen, LLP, CPAs, Two Pennsylvania Plaza, Suite 1500, New York City 10121.

To ease the burden of college costs, new incentives were enacted in the *Tax Relief Act of 2001. Here are the main changes, along with other tax-wise ways to cut your education costs...*

Loophole: **Accumulate tax-free tuition money.** You can do this with a Section 529 savings plan or "qualified state tuition program" (QSTP)—they're one and the same. These state-sponsored investment programs give families tax breaks as they save for college expenses.

Money withdrawn from 529 accounts to pay tuition and related expenses is now *tax free*.

How they work: Contributions to the plans are considered gifts, and qualify for the $11,000 annual gift tax exclusion that's in effect for 2003. You can elect to treat a $55,000 contribution to a single beneficiary in one year ($110,000 when spouses "split" gifts) as having been made in equal payments over five years. That way, the entire contribution is gift tax free, even though it exceeds the $11,000 annual limit.

Other benefits of 529 plans: When you give money to the plan, you remove income and the future appreciation from your taxable estate. You can set up these plans for any number of children, grandchildren or other beneficiaries whether family members or not. Go to your state's Web site to learn how to set up a 529 plan, or visit *www.collegesavings.com*.

Loophole: **Take a tax deduction for education expenses.** Taxpayers with incomes under $130,000 (joint) or $65,000 (single) can now claim a $3,000 above-the-line deduction for the costs of higher education. The deduction rises to $4,000 in 2004.

Loophole: **Minimize your adjusted gross income (AGI) to avoid phaseouts of certain education tax benefits.** *You can do this, for* *one year at least, by accelerating expenses into the current year and deferring income into the next year...*

•Qualified education loans. Interest of up to $2,500 on qualified education loans is fully deductible until AGI reaches $100,000 on joint tax returns. (A qualified loan is one where the proceeds are used only for qualified higher education expenses.) The interest deduction begins phasing out and then disappears when AGI exceeds $130,000. The phaseout starts at $50,000 on individual returns, and the deduction disappears when AGI exceeds $65,000.

•Education credits. The Hope credit of $1,500 and the lifetime learning credit of $1,000 ($2,000 in 2003) phase out between an AGI of $82,000 and $102,000 on a joint return ($83,000 and $103,000 in 2003) and $41,000 and $51,000 for singles in 2002 and 2003.

Loophole: **Offset child-care expenses with child-care credits.** Generally, couples do not qualify for child- and dependent-care credits if only one spouse works.

Exception: If one spouse is a full-time student and the other works, the couple may qualify. The tax law assumes that the nonworking spouse had income ($200 a month if there is one child, $400 a month if there are two or more children) and calculates the credit accordingly.

For married taxpayers, expenses that qualify for the child-care credits are limited to the lower-earning spouse's income. That would normally be the income of the parent in school, with income calculated according to the figures above. The credit is a percentage of the income.

Loophole: **Take full advantage of the employer educational assistance plans.** When companies offer these plans, the first $5,250 of educational expenses paid by your employer is tax free. Tuition, fees, books and supplies are all eligible expenses. The plan must be in writing and must be equally available to all employees.

Courses you take need not be job related to qualify for this tax break, so you could use the plan to help pay for a college or even a graduate degree.

Loophole: **Don't pay tax on employer-reimbursed education expenses.** When your employer reimburses you for education costs, you do not have to include the reimbursement on your tax return—as long as you account to your employer for the expenses. That is, you must submit bills and receipts.

Loophole: **Deduct job-related education expenses.** Anyone can deduct job-related education expenses for courses taken to maintain or improve the skills required in his/her present line of work. Courses that train you for a new trade or business are not deductible.

Deductible items include tuition, books, supplies and the cost of getting from your job to school. When you qualify, education expenses are treated as "miscellaneous itemized" expenses, and they are deducted to the extent they exceed 2% of your AGI.

Loophole: **Buy off-campus housing for your child.** One way to cut your cash outlays for college living expenses is to buy a house or an apartment near the campus for your child to live in. The tax deductions the property generates will subsidize the expense.

If the property is your second residence, mortgage interest is fully deductible, as are real estate taxes.

If you rent out part of the home, it will qualify as a rental property. Your tax deductions, including the depreciation, may exceed your rental income from the property, producing a loss. Up to $25,000 of these rental losses are deductible each year against your salary and other income, as long as your AGI doesn't exceed $150,000.

How to Qualify for More College Aid

It's best to take capital gains before January of your child's high school junior year.

Reason: When determining aid amounts, colleges count income more heavily than assets—so take gains before the tax year that will be considered for aid eligibility.

Example: If a child is going to college in the fall of 2005, aid will be based on your 2004 tax returns—so take profits in 2003.

If you are self-employed: Accelerate income before January of your child's junior year …and defer expenses until after that date.

Kalman Chany, president, Campus Consultants Inc., financial aid advisory service for families, 1202 Lexington Ave., Suite 327, New York City 10028.

College Financing Strategy

Monthly Payment Plans (MPPs) are a way to finance college interest fee. Most colleges and universities—and many prep schools—allow you to spread out payments so you can borrow less or avoid taking out student loans. If your school does not have an MPP, you can pay an average annual enrollment fee of $55 and make monthly payments to an educational service company. The company then will pay the school on the usual twice-yearly schedule. Your school's bursar or financial-aid officer can help you make this arrangement.

Maureen McCarthy Mello, senior vice president for marketing and corporate communications at Academic Management Services, a provider of MPPs and loans, Swansea, MA.

Smart Investing For College

Change your asset allocation for college savings as children get older. Until your child reaches age 13, consider putting 100% of college savings in stocks. Conservative investors may want to keep up to 40% in bonds—but at least 60% should be in stocks. For children ages 14 to 17, savings should be 25% to 50% in stocks and 50% to 75% in bonds—again, more conservative investors will want higher fixed-income percentages. Once a child turns 18 and throughout his/her years in college, investments

should be 100% fixed income. Be sure to use money market funds, certificates of deposit and short-term bond funds.

Sue Stevens, CFA, CPA, director of financial planning, Morningstar Associates, Chicago.

Don't Put College Savings In a Child's Name

The standard college financial-aid formula requires children to use 35% of their own assets to pay for college costs before receiving any aid. Parents are expected to contribute only up to 5.6% of their assets. Grandparents aren't required to contribute anything.

Trap: Placing funds in a child's name to help pay for college may result in the child losing financial aid and the family paying more for the child's tuition.

Better: Keep college savings in your own name, then pay some college costs after the child receives tuition assistance.

Barbara Weltman, Esq., practices in Millwood, NY, *www.bwideas.com.*

Better Adult Education

To get the most benefit from your adult education course…

●**Talk to an admissions or academic representative** of the school before applying to be sure you understand the curriculum.

●**Talk to the people closest to you** before you go back to school, so they understand that your schedule will be hectic for a while.

●**Strongly consider taking courses in technology.** It is essential for any job that you might consider, including part-time or volunteer work.

Doug Houston, director, master of business administration programs, University of Kansas, Lawrence.

20

Safe and Sound

Bioterrorism Self-Defense

The threat of biological and chemical warfare continues to worry and frighten many Americans. Some people have even taken matters into their own hands by purchasing antibiotics and/or gas masks.

How serious is the risk? Will any of these measures really protect us? *Chemical and biological weapons expert Jonathan B. Tucker, PhD, answers these questions and more...*

•What are the health risks of a bioterrorist attack? As everyone knows, a number of cases of anthrax exposure and infection have already occurred.

Inhalation anthrax occurs if enough spores of the bacterium *Bacillus anthracis* are inhaled. It's not contagious. Flulike symptoms typically start within one to seven days of exposure. Inhalation anthrax should be treated *before* symptoms begin with an antibiotic, such as

ciprofloxacin (Cipro), *penicillin, tetracycline* or *doxycycline.* Once symptoms develop, the condition is fatal in more than 80% of cases.

Skin (cutaneous) anthrax infection results when the bacterium enters cuts or abrasions in the skin. Although fatal in up to 20% of cases if left untreated, cutaneous anthrax generally responds well to antibiotics.

The other agents most likely to be used cause three illnesses.

The first is botulism. This disease is a type of poisoning caused by a toxin produced by the bacterium *Clostridium botulinum.* About 50% of victims die unless treated with an antitoxin.

The second is pneumonic plague. Caused by the bacterium *Yersinia pestis,* the disease causes flulike symptoms and is highly contagious. It's deadly in more than 50% of cases

Jonathan B. Tucker, PhD, director of the Chemical & Biological Weapons Nonproliferation Program at the Monterey Institute of International Studies in Washington, DC. He is the author of *Scourge: The Once and Future Threat of Smallpox* (Atlantic Monthly Press) and *Toxic Terror: Assessing Terrorist Use of Chemical and Biological Weapons* (MIT Press).

unless victims are treated with antibiotics, such as *streptomycin, tetracycline* or *gentamicin*.

The third is smallpox. Caused by the *variola* virus, this disease, which was eradicated worldwide in 1979, is marked by fever and a rash that first looks like chicken pox and later turns into pus-filled lesions. It's highly contagious if one comes in close proximity to someone with symptoms, which develop about two weeks after exposure to this virus. Around 30% of patients die unless they are vaccinated within three to five days after exposure. No drug treatment is available.

● **Is the US government prepared to cope with these types of attacks?** There are adequate stocks of antibiotics to treat anthrax and plague and antitoxin to treat botulism.

The Centers for Disease Control and Prevention (CDC) is procuring more smallpox vaccine to supplement the 15.4 million doses that are currently available. Fifty-four million additional doses should be available in 2003. In addition, government officials have said they are negotiating to buy 300 million doses of the vaccine— enough for every American.

Still, large gaps exist in the public and private health-care systems, which are the first line of defense against a bioterrorist attack. Doctors and nurses must be trained in how to recognize symptoms and how to treat them. City, county and state health departments need more staff and resources. Diagnostic laboratories also need to be outfitted with the technology to identify infections like anthrax in time to treat them.

● **What can individuals do to protect themselves?** If you develop an unusual illness or skin rash, notify your physician and local health department at once.

It's also a good idea to ask your doctor to take continuing education classes about the symptoms and treatment of anthrax, smallpox and other infections.

To educate physicians, *The Journal of the American Medical Association* (JAMA) recently began publishing a series of review articles on bioterrorism agents. For more information, go to the JAMA Web site at *http://jama.ama-assn.org*.

● **Law-enforcement agencies have urged Americans to be alert. What exactly does this mean?** It is important for individuals to report any suspicious behavior to the authorities. This means calling 911 if you see someone leaving any package unattended or spraying something in a subway, a crowded shopping mall or near the air-intake system of a building.

● **The antibiotic Cipro is FDA-approved for use as an anthrax antidote. Should I ask my doctor for a prescription just in case?** Individuals should *not* stockpile antibiotics. Self-administering these drugs in the absence of anthrax exposure can cause harmful side effects.

Overuse of antibiotics increases the resistance of pathogenic bacteria to these lifesaving drugs, making them less effective when they are really needed.

● **If a person understands the importance of not taking an antibiotic, such as Cipro, unnecessarily, what's wrong with getting the drug?** If thousands of people stock up on Cipro, they could deplete the national supply that would be needed in an actual emergency.

In the event an outbreak of anthrax occurs, the federal government will distribute Cipro to the affected population within 12 hours. That's what happened in the previous cases involving anthrax exposure.

● **Will a gas mask protect me in case of an attack?** Probably not. A poison gas, such as sarin, or a biological agent, such as the bacterium that causes anthrax, is generally odorless and colorless—and it's unlikely that you would have warning that it had been released. That means to *really* protect yourself you'd have to wear the mask all the time, which is impractical.

● **What about vaccines for anthrax and/or smallpox?** These vaccines are currently in very limited supply and are only available to military personnel, who are at far greater risk than civilians. What's more, there is concern over possible complications of these vaccines.

Back in the 1960s, the smallpox vaccine caused serious complications, such as brain damage and even death, in roughly one of every million people vaccinated.

It would make sense to begin vaccinating the US population as a preventive only if the threat of a terrorist attack with smallpox were so high that it outweighed the risk of complications from the vaccine. Currently, that is not the case. But government officials are increasing supplies of the vaccine in case the situation changes.

If a smallpox outbreak ever occurs, the federal government will provide smallpox vaccine to individuals exposed to the disease or at immediate risk.

Fortunately, the smallpox vaccine works extremely fast, producing full immunity within 10 days. It is even effective at preventing the disease or rendering it less severe when administered up to three to five days after infection.

Amazing Advances In the Fight Against Terrorism

Daniel Burstein, managing partner, Millennium Technology Ventures Advisors, 350 Park Ave., New York City 10022. He manages a $160 million venture capital fund that invests in leading-edge technology.

The war on terrorism has so accelerated the development of new antiterrorist technologies that we are starting to see some major breakthroughs.

These advances will at first be applied to defense and security, but most will eventually offer substantial benefits to consumers and commercial users as well. They will also provoke debates about privacy, personal freedom and bioethics.

COMING SOON

•**Advanced identification systems.** Identifying people using fingerprints is slow and not terribly accurate. Scans of the retina and underlying facial features are more precise.

Low-grade applications of these technologies are already in use in high-security government installations. More advanced systems will be in commercial use soon at airports, banks, etc.

Eventual applications: You will no longer have to enter in your personal identification number at your bank ATM. The computer will instantly recognize you. You will gain access to the Internet through an image-recognition system rather than by using a password.

•**Remote video monitoring of airplane cockpits.** The ability to see inside the cockpits of the planes hijacked on September 11 would have quickly shown authorities what was happening. Miniature video cameras are already on the market, but are easy to detect and disable—plus the images are of poor quality. Soon there will be hidden systems in place to transmit high-quality video images to a monitoring facility.

Rudimentary video monitoring is also currently available for consumer use, particularly for working parents who want to check on their children at home or in day care. We will see quantum leaps in quality and ease of use of these systems in the months ahead.

ONE TO FOUR YEARS

•**Improved access technology.** Current metal detectors are inadequate. People must pass through one at a time. At each alarm, the line must stop while the individual who set off the alarm is searched. The work is so tedious that screeners miss security breaches.

One answer is an enveloping full-body scan that will not require people to pass, one by one, through a choke point. Scanning will be instantaneous, and more than one person will be able to pass through the scanner at a time. Weapons or other devices that breach security rules will be visible instantly with no physical search. Early versions of this were used at Ground Zero in New York City to help find bodies buried under the rubble.

•**Large-panel radiography scans.** Just as people have to be screened one by one, items have to be scanned individually by security personnel. Large-panel radiography systems would scan an entire truck or cargo bay at one time. Bombs or weapons would be visible instantly. Large-panel scanning devices should be ready for widespread use by border patrols, harbormasters, customs authorities and airport authorities in less than two years.

Eventual applications: These instruments could scan just about anything. For example, they would allow building contractors to see underground before they start digging, eliminating the possibility of cutting into gas and water mains, telephone lines and power cables.

●**Wireless lie detector.** Scientists have just developed a camera-like device that can assess heat patterns and muscle movements around the eyes when a subject is answering a question—and indicate, with 75% accuracy, whether the person is lying. That's about the same accuracy as a lie detector test but without electrodes, and no consent is needed from the subject.

Within two years, this technology could be a backup tool for check-in attendants when they ask travelers if they have dangerous items in their luggage, etc. One can imagine many uses for this type of technology in business and consumer life.

●**New initiatives in artificial intelligence.** Big breakthroughs are coming in pattern recognition and in data mining. It will be possible, for example, to monitor thousands of cell phones, looking for keywords and patterns.

Some of this technology, still in its infancy, is being used by the intelligence community. Advanced systems to monitor phone calls and other voice systems will be ready in three years …and systems to monitor Internet usage will be available soon.

We will see artificial intelligence programs that ferret out illegal activity by rapidly sorting and correlating information from all the airline-reservation databases, financial markets, phone logs and E-mail.

FIVE TO 10 YEARS

●**Biotechnology that can defeat bioterrorism.** Biotechnology was on a roll even before September 11. Now even more money is going toward developing "counterspores" and "countermicrobes." A counterspore administered to someone exposed to anthrax, for example, would instantly render the anthrax spore harmless without further medical treatment.

Laboratory work may take five years. But regulatory approval could delay time to market by a year or two beyond that.

Skills gained in combating bioterrorist threats will translate into products and techniques able to fight many deadly illnesses—ranging from immune system disorders, such as AIDS, to Ebola, smallpox and some cancers.

Be on the Watch…

Suspicious activity to watch out for…people you don't recognize sitting for long periods in a car in your neighborhood and strangers loitering around your office building taking notes, making sketches or asking questions. Someone with a bulge under his/her coat—particularly in large crowds, on subways, etc.—which could indicate weapons possession.

Important: Report suspicious activity to the police. Describe the people—height, weight, age, hair and clothing color and bags they carried. If possible, take the car's license plate number.

And: Do not open, shake or move packages or open large envelopes if you're not familiar with the sender.

Tanya DeGenova, former FBI agent, now president of TSD Security Consulting Group Inc., Boston, *www.tsdcon sulting.com.*

Safer Parking

To stay safe when parking your car in a lot or in a garage…

●**Park in well-lit, open areas.** Choose places well away from doorways, shrubs and other places that could hide a criminal.

●**In garages, park close to the exit.**

●**Always leave your car doors locked,** windows all the way closed and the antitheft device activated.

●**Have your keys ready** well before you get to your car.

●**Check the backseat**—even if you are sure you left the car locked.

●**If you feel uncomfortable,** ask a security guard or store employee to escort you to your car.

Sebastian Giordano, CEO, Top Driver, a driver- and vehicle-safety instruction company with offices around the country, *www.topdriver.com.*

The Invisible Man Tells How to Burglar-Proof Your Home

J.J. "Jack" Luna, who spent 11 years eluding capture by the police as a secret humanitarian operative in Franco's Spain. He now works as an international security consultant. *www.howtobeinvisible.com.* He is author of *How to Be Invisible: A Step-by-Step Guide to Protecting Your Assets, Your Identity and Your Life* (St. Martin's).

Fears of terrorism have renewed Americans' interest in many kinds of security issues. *One vital area:* Home security.

Here's how to make your home less vulnerable to burglary without investing in a high-end security system...

SECURE YOUR HOME'S EXTERIOR

●**Trim hedges and shrubs.** There should be a clear view of your home from the road and neighbors' homes. Be particularly wary of plants that might provide cover to someone in front of your windows or at your front door.

●**Install motion-sensitive lights** in the front and at the rear of your home.

●**Burglar-proof sliding glass doors,** a common entry point. Place a rod in the track so the door cannot be forced open. Install a shim—about ⅜-inch thick—in the track above the door. A shim prevents a sliding door from being moved up and down. Without one, it is possible to lift the door out of its track. The shim must be installed in such a way that it doesn't interfere with the sliding of the door.

Note: Burglars rarely smash through glass doors. It makes too much noise.

●**Secure exterior doors.** Replace hollow wood doors with solid-wood or metal doors. Install reinforced hinges, ideally four per door, attached with 1½- to two-inch screws. Make sure all deadbolts are long-throw deadbolts—which project a full inch into the door frame. Without these modifications, a burglar could kick in your door.

●**Place blinking red LED lights in one or more windows.** Sold at Radio Shack for a few dollars, these create the impression that the house has a high-tech security system. Just the threat of such a security system may be as effective a deterrent as the security system itself.

SECURE YOUR HOME'S INTERIOR

●**The rules that apply to your home's exterior doors**—solid doors, strong hinges and long-throw deadbolts—also apply to...

●The door into the house from the garage.

●The door to the master bedroom.

●The door into any first-floor bedroom.

Lock all of these doors before you leave the house.

These interior-door security measures won't stop a determined burglar, but they might frustrate an amateur or make the burglar leave out of concern that his/her entry was noted. And if a member of your family is home at the time of the break-in, these doors provide crucial minutes to call for help.

●**Consider setting up a *safe* room.** If I were out of town and my wife woke to a suspicious sound, the first thing she would do is lock the deadbolt on the bedroom door. Then she would grab the cell phone and head into our bedroom closet. We've replaced the hollow closet door with a solid door that has a deadbolt. Keep pillows and warm blankets in the safe room.

A cell phone is more trustworthy than a land line in these situations. Burglars often take a downstairs phone off the hook or cut phone lines when they enter a home.

For those with children: Install a locking solid door in the hallway before the bedrooms.

●**If you're building a new house, consider including a secret room**—perhaps off the master bedroom. Virtually any experienced builder will have installed them before. A secret room is connected to the rest of the house by a door that looks just like a bookcase or a mirror. Such rooms are great places to store valuables when you're headed out of town—or to hide yourself during a break-in. They are usually the size of a walk-in closet.

If you don't have a secret room: Hide valuables in a child's room. Burglars are less likely to search a child's room carefully than other places in a home.

● **Get a dog with a big bark.** If you like animals, by all means get a dog that makes its presence known to visitors. Dogs are wonderful deterrents. But they're also a lot of work—don't decide to get one unless you're ready for the responsibility.

● **If you want a gun, make it a shotgun.** The risks and hassles of gun ownership usually outweigh guns' value as personal security devices—particularly for families with children. But if you decide to keep a weapon in the home and you're not a firearms expert, choose a shotgun.

At close range, even a nervous and inexperienced gun owner should have little trouble disabling his target. And because of the shotgun's barrel length, it is less likely that you will accidentally shoot yourself.

DON'T BECOME A TARGET

● **Never give out your home address to strangers.** Your address must not be connected to your name in any directory, database or mailing list. Once a criminal can connect your name or face to a specific address, he can figure out when you're away—or when you'll be home if he has something worse than burglary in mind.

Helpful: When filling out forms or documents, consider using a post office box, a commercial mail-receiving company—such as Mail Boxes, Etc.—or an office address. Don't put your address on luggage tags. The fact that you're carrying luggage in the airport shows thieves that your home might be unoccupied for a few days.

● **Lower your profile.** If you look like the most affluent person in your neighborhood, your house is most likely to be targeted.

Example: If you drive a Jaguar in a town full of Hondas, don't leave your car parked out in the driveway.

● **Avoid tip-offs that you are out of town...**

●Mail, newspapers and packages should never be delivered while you're away.

●Ask a neighbor to pick up any flyers or other items left at your door or in your mailbox.

●If there is a chance of snow, arrange for your driveway to be plowed and walks shoveled.

● **Use timers to control lights.** Use several throughout the house. Set them so lights turn on and off at natural intervals—an entire house switching off all at once looks unnatural.

Complex computerized systems are available to simulate activity in the home. But they can be confusing to program.

● **Leave a radio on and tuned to a talk station.** Any burglar coming close to the house might be scared off by the sound of voices.

More from J.J. "Jack" Luna...

How to Protect Your Identity, Your Assets and Your Life

Keeping personal information private will help protect you from frivolous lawsuits ...identity theft...and unwanted sales calls. It could even derail a stalker or someone else looking to do you physical harm.

How far you should go to protect your privacy is a personal decision. *But I believe these steps make sense for just about everyone...*

BIRTH DATE

While most people are careful with their Social Security numbers, many of us give out birth dates without a second thought. If someone wants to track you down—a private investigator, a con man, an ex-lover—you have just made it much easier for him/her.

Most people are listed in thousands of databases, compiled from medical records, divisions of motor vehicles, credit agencies, employment records, court records, Internet companies, etc. Not all of these records are secure.

If it is just your name in a database, it doesn't mean much—there are probably many people who share your name. But combine that name with a date of birth, and the pool shrinks by more than 99%—enough for any competent private investigator to find you.

Safer: Do not provide the date of your birth. When you cannot avoid it, consider making some minor alteration to the date that can be called an innocent error if it is picked up later.

Example: Suppose that your birth date is December 4, written 12/4. In most countries other than the US and Canada, this is written as 4 December—or 4/12.

Obviously, if your date of birth is after the 12th, this won't work. Then you might "mistakenly" enter the month and date of a family member. But be honest on government forms, loan applications or anywhere else that it is likely to be checked.

The personal information that is already in databases is there for good. Your only "solution" is to move…get a new phone number …and never again allow your true name to be coupled with your true address, thus leaving only the old information in the databases.

PROVIDING ID

When someone insists that I show identification, I show my *passport*. Unlike a driver's license, it does not provide my home address.

This strategy is particularly useful for women who might be asked for identification at a bar —and then get an unwelcome visitor later.

Exception: When the police ask for a driver's license, that is what you must provide.

TELEPHONE

Anyone who wants privacy should get an unlisted phone number and *caller-ID blocking*. Then people you call can't find out your number, even if they have caller ID. Fees for this service vary by provider—usually a few dollars per month.

Note: Caller-ID blocking does *not* work when you call toll-free or 900 numbers…or when you call many US government offices. Calls to 911 will show your street address and phone number.

If you are serious about not being tracked down, an unlisted phone number is just not enough. Instead, get an unlisted number under a *different* name. Then no one will be able to trace that number to you.

Use a prepaid phone card at a pay phone for calls that require extra security.

Prepaid *cell phones* also are now available. While any cell phone call can be intercepted, prepaid cell phone calls can't be tracked to you…and no one can run up a huge bill on your account.

US MAIL

More than 100,000 residential mailboxes are burglarized every day. Unsecured mailboxes make a tremendous amount of personal information available to anyone who cares to know it. *In addition to your name and address, your mail could provide someone with…*

- **Signed checks that can be easily altered.** A $20 check could become $2,000.

- **Account numbers** from bank, credit card and investment statements.

- **Preapproved credit card solicitations.**

- **Social Security and other personal information** from government forms.

- **A profile of your interests** and shopping habits.

To keep your mail private…

- **Outgoing mail.** Use *indoor* mailboxes located at the post office or other public areas.

- **Incoming mail.** Consider using a commercial mail-receiving agency, such as Mail Boxes Etc. (888-346-3623…*www.mbe.com*) or PostNet (800-841-7171…*www.postnet.net*).

Post office boxes are yet another alternative, although they cannot be used for deliveries by private shipping companies.

These are imperfect solutions because all these services require identification to open a mailbox. Many people have arranged to receive mail through their real estate agents, accountants, lawyers or other advisers.

E-MAIL

E-mail sent via your work computer is not protected by personal privacy laws—so your employer can "spy" on you.

To keep your E-mail private: Consider sending messages via an "anonymizer" Web site, such as *www.lokmail.com*. This free service encrypts messages to assure that only the intended recipients can read them. The encryption works only if the sender and the receiver both use LokMail addresses.

BANKS

If someone is thinking of suing you, the first thing he/she will do is ask a lawyer if he has a case. The first thing the lawyer will do is call a private investigator to find out if you have the money to make it worth his while.

A private investigator will subpoena the records of all the banks in your town—and perhaps the surrounding towns—looking for accounts. Most banks insist they would not provide such records, but a good investigator can get the information.

Self-defense: Move all but a small amount of cash to a bank outside your immediate region —at least in another state—or a national investment company, such as Fidelity (800-343-3548) or Merrill Lynch (800-637-7455). An attorney will then be less likely to find your assets.

Bonus: US Treasury money market accounts at investment firms offer better returns than bank accounts, with low risk and similar services— including checking.

GARBAGE/RECYCLING

It is perfectly legal for anyone to snoop through your garbage or recycling stack once you put it at the curb. A paper shredder is an inexpensive way to deter invasion of your privacy for any personal or financial documents.

A standard shredder ($25 to $55) is enough for most people. If you have serious privacy concerns, a cross-cut shredder (about $100) leaves documents so diced that they can never be put back together.

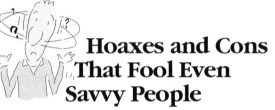

Hoaxes and Cons That Fool Even Savvy People

Chuck Whitlock, an investigative reporter located in Washougal, WA, *www.chuckwhitlock.com.* He is author of many books on white-collar crime, including *Mediscams* (Renaissance), and his reports have been featured on television shows such as *Hard Copy* and *The Oprah Winfrey Show.*

Con artists don't just prey on the ignorant. Even successful, sophisticated people are victims of scams.

Why? Successful people consider themselves smart enough to recognize a good deal…they are too busy to check details…and they are driven to move forward and take chances. Most of all, they make juicy targets because they have the most money to steal.

Some cons that prey specifically on successful people…

TAX-AVOIDANCE SCAM

Someone you trust—a financial planner, a close friend or a relative—comes to you with a proposition. Put up $25,000, and you can easily double your money in a month. *Sound too good to be true?* This trusted person already tried it, and it worked like a charm.

But this person explains that it's not exactly legal. No one will get hurt, but the government will lose out on taxes.

Example: You are told your money will be used to buy high-end automobiles in a foreign country and bring them into the US without paying import duties. Because the dealings are under the table, your profits will not be reported to the IRS.

How the con works: Your trusted relative probably *did* double his/her money in a month. The con artist predicted the friend would invest again during the next month and bring in others with him.

This time, the con artist reports that there are some problems. Perhaps the shipment was stopped at the border and everyone has to chip in another $10,000 for taxes and penalties. Next, he says the truck driver needs an expensive lawyer or he is going to name names— including yours.

Eventually, you are told there is good news and bad news. The money you invested is gone, but the truck driver isn't talking, so you have no IRS worries. You might walk away relieved despite your financial loss. You won't go to the police even if you suspect you were duped because you knew you were breaking the law.

Variations on this con use all sorts of illegal activities—from insurance scams to fencing stolen goods to counterfeiting or scalping tickets to sports or entertainment events. One common version is aimed at children of affluent people when they go away to college. The students are told they can make a fortune quickly by fronting money for a campus drug dealer.

Self-defense: Be wary whenever anyone— including a friend—offers an opportunity that bends the law even slightly. Such investments are never worth the risk.

BANK GUARD SCAM

You go to use your bank's automated teller machine during nonbusiness hours and find an out-of-order sign on the machine. A uniformed "bank guard" with a clipboard and cash box says he can handle your transaction.

How the con works: Successful people are accustomed to the convenience of 24-hour banking, and they are ready to trust people in uniform. The con takes place in the evening, when victims are tired and anxious to get home. Some victims are depositing their company's money, not their own.

Don't think it would work? I simulated this con once for a television program. Among my 25 victims were a congressman, a police officer and a man responsible for the receipts of 18 pharmacies—totaling $118,000. Only one woman was suspicious, and I managed to talk her into leaving her money with me as well.

Even if you do not deposit any money, in exchange for your withdrawal you would be asked for your name, account number, personal identification number, Social Security number, address and mother's maiden name. Provide this information, and the con man can clean you out.

MEDICAL QUACKERY SCAMS

People who have a deadly disease that is either incurable or not easily helped by mainstream medicine may fall prey to medical scams touting miracle cures.

Example: You are told you have an inoperable cancer. On the Internet, you learn about a controversial procedure involving an intravenous drip of crushed apricot seeds, often referred to as *laetrile*. It is not accepted in the US, but doctors in Mexico have achieved remission in many patients. Desperate, you seek this out. These people have found a con so attractive that their victims come right to their door.

Why the con works: The victim is vulnerable due to emotional distress. Based on my research, approximately 17% of all cancer cases go into remission *without* getting treatment, although many later recur. The apricot seeds have no proven positive effect. Nor does the solution similar to toilet-bowl cleaner that one quack labeled as *Immunostim* and, until very recently, injected into cancer patients' veins.

These con artists count on the fact that their "success stories" will sing their praises—while their failures may not be around to complain.

BUSINESS SCAMS

Any business in which the owner does not directly oversee every transaction is a target for con artists.

Example: An employee might get into your payroll files and arrange for checks to be cut twice a month to nonexistent employees. Or issue payments to a nonexistent supplier for hard-to-confirm services, like consulting or cleaning, that were never provided.

Self-defense: Your firm is less of a target if certain safeguards are in place...

• **Immediately discontinue computer passwords** of ex-employees.

• **Institute cross-training procedures.** Require each employee to make a procedure manual for his/her job. Everyone in your company should make at least one colleague familiar with his accounts and files. This makes it less likely that any employee will think he can get away with something.

• **Check the books carefully** when someone in payroll or accounting declines to take a vacation. Embezzlers may be hesitant to let someone else look at their books.

• **Institute firewalls** around your computer system. Use codes with both numerals and letters to protect against cyber-criminals outside your firm. Do not let employees use names or birth dates as codes.

No security system is foolproof, but you can make it harder for the high-tech criminals. The right computer security program depends on your system and the sensitivity of your data. I prefer to use a program from McAfee Software (*www.mcafee.com*).

• **Create written procedures for purchasing,** expense reimbursement and payroll functions. These should include supervision by more than one employee.

More from Chuck Whitlock...

ATM Protection

A new ATM scam provides crooks with your card and personal identification number (PIN). The scammer puts a thin wire loop into an ATM, then stands nearby. When the victim puts his/her card in the slot, it doesn't come out. The scammer says the same thing happened to him once and offers to help. He has the victim enter his PIN and watches over the victim's shoulder. Entering the code does nothing. After the victim leaves, the scammer pulls out the loop, retrieves the ATM card and uses the PIN to withdraw money.

Self-defense: If your card gets stuck in an ATM, phone the bank immediately…and change your PIN.

How Safe Is Your Safe-Deposit Box?

Thieves may be able to gain access to your safe-deposit box even though it is locked up in a concrete or steel vault equipped with sophisticated security devices and strict access procedures. FDIC insurance does not cover the contents of the box.

Protection: Some homeowner's or tenant's insurance policies cover theft up to a certain dollar amount. You can purchase additional insurance protection—speak with your insurance agent.

Other good strategies: Keep a list of the box's contents…make copies of important documents…and take photos of items in the box. These steps increase the chance of recovery. Cash, savings bonds and stock certificates should be stored at home in a fireproof safe, with copies of documents in the safe-deposit box.

Edward Mrkvicka, Jr., president of Reliance Enterprises Inc., a financial consulting company, 2115 O'Connell Rd., Marengo, IL 60152, and author of *Your Bank Is Ripping You Off* (St. Martin's).

Disaster-Proof Your Important Papers

Barbara Hemphill, organizing consultant in Raleigh, NC, *www.thepapertiger.com*. She is author of *Taming the Paper Tiger at Home* (Kiplinger).

In case you have to evacuate your home in an emergency, keep copies of vital papers in a portable container.

Keep originals of difficult-to-replace documents, such as birth certificates and titles, in a safe-deposit box that is in more than one person's name.

While information regarding any of your bank accounts, insurance policies and investments can be reproduced from account numbers, having immediate access to hard copy may be helpful.

Most important: Maintain a list of all the documents and where they are located. Make sure that family members and those who need access to the documents know where to find the master list.

VITAL RECORDS

- **Birth certificates and adoption records**
- **Marriage certificates and divorce decrees**
- **Driver's licenses**
- **Passports/visas/green cards**
- **Social Security cards**
- **Property titles, deeds and registrations**
- **Wills and trust documents**
- **Mortgage and loan information**
- **Insurance policies**
- **Bank account records**
- **Investment records**
- **Credit card statements**

Contact numbers to carry in your wallet: Doctor…employer…kids' schools…banks…insurance agents…clergy…relatives, friends, neighbors…utility and alarm companies.

Check Fraud Is On the Rise

A new law shifts the burden to the *customer* if the bank can prove any negligence, such as leaving your checkbook somewhere.

Self-defense: Keep blank checks secure… be precise when writing out a check…reconcile your bank statement—you're off the hook if you catch fraud within 30 days of its mail date.

Frank Abagnale, president of Abagnale & Associates, a secure-document consulting firm, Washington, DC, *www. abagnale.com.*

More from Frank Abagnale…

Check Fraud Self-Defense

It takes just eight seconds for an experienced forger to memorize the name, address and bank-account number printed on your check.

Self-defense: Be careful when writing out a check in case someone is watching over your shoulder or standing close to you. When ordering checks, do not have your driver's license number printed on them.

Beware of New Social Security Scam

Don't be fooled into providing personal information if you receive a flyer promising additional Social Security payments.

More than 25,000 people were recently duped by two anonymous flyers that falsely promised them money from the government if they mailed their name, address, phone number, date of birth and Social Security number to a post office box.

One flyer promised higher Social Security benefits to "notch babies" born between 1917 and 1926. The other promised a $5,000 payment under the fictitious *Slave Reparations Act.*

If you suspect fraud: Contact the Social Security Administration fraud hot line at 800-269-0271.

James G. Huse, Jr., Inspector General, Social Security Administration, Baltimore.

Self-Defense Against Charitable Giving Scams

Not all solicitations for donations are legitimate. *Here is how to protect yourself against fraudulent charities…*

●**Check a charity's name and record with the Better Business Bureau** (703-276-0100… *www.give.org*)—some of the phony groups use names similar to those of legitimate charities.

●**Be skeptical of vague emotional appeals** —focus on charities that say specifically what they do with donations.

●**Some groups soliciting funds are political or lobbying groups**—they may be legitimate, but donations are not tax-deductible.

●**Never give out a credit card number** when solicited by phone.

●**Do not donate cash**—make your check or money order out to the specific charity, not to an individual.

Bennett Weiner, chief operating officer, BBB Wise Giving Alliance, Arlington, VA.

Tricky Telemarketing

Beware of a telemarketing scams that offers free merchandise. People who respond to these calls get a shipping and handling fee of $6.95 or more…*plus* a previously unmentioned bill for membership in a shopping club.

Self-defense: Decline the goods—and don't give anyone credit card information.

If you have fallen for this scam: Dispute the charge through your credit card issuer.

Holly Anderson, director of communications, National Consumers' League's National Fraud and Information Center, Washington, DC, *www.fraud.org.*

How to Find Out What Uncle Sam Knows About You

Charles N. Davis, PhD, executive director, Freedom of Information Center, an FOIA reference and research library at the University of Missouri School of Journalism, Columbia, where he is also an assistant professor of journalism.

Sooner or later, the average citizen will probably face some type of government action that he/she opposes.

Perhaps the Internal Revenue Service (IRS) will claim that you owe back taxes. Or you'll hear that a road is to be built right behind your house. You'll want to fight back, but you need more information.

Or maybe you're just curious to find out what kind of information the government has about you.

Maybe you protested the Vietnam War...or you often travel on business to the Middle East, and you wonder if the Federal Bureau of Investigation (FBI) or the Central Intelligence Agency (CIA) has a file on you.

Maybe you've even tried to get the information, but government officials told you it wasn't available. *Don't believe them.*

KNOW YOUR RIGHTS

The 1966 *Freedom of Information Act* (FOIA) allows US citizens access to government data. This law states that Americans have a right to most unclassified government information collected about organizations, businesses, the US government or foreign governments.

The 1974 *Privacy Act*, essentially an amendment to the FOIA, says that every American citizen has the right to obtain any unclassified information that the government has about him.

In 1996, this act was updated to permit filing information requests electronically and to require agencies to post data on public Web sites. For this reason, vast amounts of government material have become accessible from any computer.

HOW TO DIG UP DATA

With the mountains of data available, how do you find the information you need?

Start by going to the Web site *http://foi.missouri.edu*, which I oversee for the University of Missouri School of Journalism. This free site offers a complete list of federal agencies with addresses, phone numbers, Web sites and E-mail addresses.

The site also provides sample letters and fill-in-the-blank forms to request specific information about yourself.

Want a little dirt on that creepy neighbor or annoying coworker? Forget about it. Privacy exemptions essentially prohibit the release of information about other individuals.

In your request, clearly describe the records or information you're seeking. If you're vague, the agency will ask for clarification. This will slow the process.

The time it takes to fulfill a request varies from weeks to years. It all depends on what you're requesting and from which agency. If an agency has not responded to you within two months, contact it again.

If you find that the information about you is not accurate, contact the *Records Custodian* at the agency in question to request that your file be corrected.

FEDERAL AGENCIES

Here are the agencies that are contacted most often and examples of the kinds of information they can provide...

● **Centers for Disease Control and Prevention (CDC).** The CDC is a vast repository of data on diseases, including bioterrorist threats, such as anthrax and smallpox.

CDC, 1600 Clifton Rd., Atlanta 30333. 800-311-3435... *www.cdc.gov.*

● **CIA.** The CIA gathers intelligence about suspicious overseas activities of individuals, groups and businesses. If you conduct business overseas, the CIA may have a file on you. This is especially likely if large amounts of money are wired to your business.

Although the CIA will try to withhold as much information as possible, you may be able to learn if any allegations have been made about you and by whom.

CIA, FOIA and Privacy Coordinator, Washington, DC 20505. 703-482-0623... *www.cia.gov.*

●**Environmental Protection Agency (EPA).** The EPA gathers information about environmental hazards. You can find out if any dangerous chemicals are stored in your area or if a company has any EPA enforcement proceedings pending against it.

EPA, Associate Director, FOIA Operations, 1200 Pennsylvania Ave. NW, Washington, DC 20460. Go to *www.epa.gov,* and then click on "Where You Live."

●**FBI.** This agency collects information about people, organizations and other entities that are of interest to federal law enforcement. Say, for example, you protested the World Trade Organization talks. The FBI may have a file on you that includes reports from law-enforcement officials and/or local informants.

Or perhaps you're a business owner and an employee was investigated for money laundering. If so, your good name may have been hurt by this association.

FBI, FOIA/PA Section, FBI Headquarters, 935 Pennsylvania Ave. NW, Rm. 7972, Washington, DC 20535. 202-324-3000...*www.fbi.gov.*

●**Immigration and Naturalization Service (INS).** The INS collects information about US immigrants. If you emigrated to the US, check your INS file, especially if you experienced unwarranted delays when applying for US citizenship. It may contain erroneous information from your home country, perhaps connecting you with a crime.

INS, 425 I St. NW, Rm. 3260, Washington, DC 20536. 800-375-5283...*www.ins.usdoj.gov.*

●**IRS.** The IRS gathers data on the income and tax status of people and businesses. If you have ever challenged an IRS action, such as a fine, you can check your file to see if the information is accurate.

IRS, Director, Freedom of Information, Office of Disclosure, 1111 Constitution Ave. NW, Washington, DC 20224. 202-622-6250...*www.irs.gov.*

●**Nuclear Regulatory Commission (NRC).** It supplies information about nuclear security procedures. This is very valuable to citizens concerned about nuclear safety, especially if they live near a nuclear power plant.

NRC, FOIA/PA Officer, Washington, DC 20555. 800-368-5642...*www.nrc.gov.*

●**State Department.** This agency gathers information useful for conducting foreign policy. Americans who travel overseas several times a year...live abroad...or are involved in any diplomatic activity, such as working for the United Nations, may want to look at their State Department files.

Director, Office of IRM Programs and Services, SA-2, Re: FOIA Request, 2201 C St., Rm. 4428, Washington, DC 20520. 202-647-7022...*www.state.gov.*

FOR STATE AND LOCAL RECORDS

Every state has its own version of the FOIA that spells out which state and local records are open to the public. Contact your state attorney general for details.

Cell Phone Warning

Your cell phone records can be used to harm you. Thieves may obtain copies of your bill from the phone company and sell them on Web sites. Buyers can use them to track whom you call...get details of your lifestyle...even steal your identity.

Self-defense: Tell your cell phone company not to release your phone records to anyone unless the individual provides a predetermined password.

If you suspect trouble: Contact the Federal Trade Commission (877-382-4357, *www.ftc.gov*) and your state attorney general.

Larry Ponemon, CEO, The Privacy Council, Richardson, TX, which advises Fortune 500 corporations on handling personal data.

Keep Your Medical Records Out of the Wrong Hands

John Featherman, personal privacy consultant and president, Featherman.com, Dayton.

Medical privacy can be even more worrisome than financial privacy. Breaches of confidentiality may be embarrassing—or worse, if information is misused by employers, insurers or government agencies. *Recent real-life situations...*

●**An Atlanta truck driver** was fired after his health insurer told his employer that he had sought help for a drinking problem.

●**The manufacturer of Prozac** sent out an E-mail to more than 600 Prozac users that contained the names and E-mail addresses of all the recipients.

●**A Florida public health worker** gave several newspapers the names of 4,000 HIV-positive individuals.

SELF-DEFENSE STRATEGIES

●**Limit the amount of information given out about you.** Insurers need your medical records to pay claims. If there is information that you do not want released to *anyone*, tell your physician.

However: If your doctor does not report your condition, insurance may not reimburse him/her, so you may have to pay for treatment.

●**Do not sign the customary blanket waiver.** Change it so that the release of information is limited to the specific date, doctor and condition.

●**Ask to see a copy of your file before it is sent out to a third party.**

True story: A woman with an on-the-job wrist injury authorized her insurer to send information about the injury to her employer. When she reviewed her file at work, she found it contained her entire medical history—including fertility problems.

●**Be cautious when filling out questionnaires** in doctors' offices and on Web sites.

●**Ask about retailers' privacy policies** before having prescriptions filled.

●**Do not participate in public health screenings**—unless you know the results will be kept confidential.

More from John Featherman...

Identity Theft Update

Consumers will now have less time to take action against credit bureaus in cases of identity theft. A recent Supreme Court ruling struck down a prior decision that the two-year clock begins ticking when the wrongdoing is *discovered.* Instead, consumers now have two years from when the theft occurred.

Self-defense: Check out your credit report twice a year at one of the three major bureaus—Equifax (800-685-1111), Experian (888-397-3742) and TransUnion (800-888-4213).

Cost: About $9. In some instances, it is free. Consider using a credit-monitoring service, such as Credit Insight (*www.privista.com,* $49.95/yr.) or Privacy Guard (*www.privacyguard.com,* $69.99 to $119.99/yr.).

Also from John Featherman...

Beware of E-Mail Pitfalls

Security glitches are much more likely with instant messaging, which lets users have real-time conversations on-line, than with regular E-mail because the technology is so much newer. Never instant-message sensitive business information or personal data (Social Security numbers, passwords, etc.). Identity thieves, pedophiles and other troublemakers seek this information.

Other precautions—for home and work...

●**Don't share your password.** A classmate found out the password of a colleague's daughter and then used it to send embarrassing messages to everyone on her "buddy list."

●**Scan all messages** for viruses.

●**If you receive a message that seems out of character** for the sender, phone the person to verify the source.

●**Don't choose an obvious password**—the name of a family member, your birth date, etc.—and change your password every three months. Cyber-burglars can steal passwords via key-stroking software.

●**Don't save your password in someone else's computer.**

●**Block people who are not on your or your child's buddy list.** Strangers can pick up screen names in chat rooms.

In regular E-mail, most errors are easily prevented by reviewing the message before you send it. *Biggest blunders...*

●**Replying to all recipients** instead of only the sender.

●**E-mailing your comments back to the sender** when you meant to forward them to someone else.

To ensure accuracy, send important messages to yourself to read first.

Another E-Mail Trap

Phillip M. Harter, MD, assistant professor of surgery at Stanford University School of Medicine, Palo Alto, CA. His experience was reported in Fast Company, *375 Lexington Ave., New York City 10017.*

Phillip M. Harter, MD, received an E-mail message containing interesting statistics about the world population. He thought some of his friends would like to see it, so he forwarded it to them—with his E-mail software automatically attaching his name as well as the Stanford University School of Medicine address to the message.

Soon he began receiving calls and messages from media companies, government agencies and people around the world asking him about his data.

The World Health Organization called. A full-page story was dedicated to him in a Latvian newspaper. And the E-mailed message was incorporated into the curriculum of a population course at another major university.

All the while, Professor Harter had no idea about the real source of "his" data, or whether it was true.

He finally resorted to setting his voice mail message to tell everyone who called him that he didn't write that message. But he still answered incoming E-mail inquiries individually.

Lesson: Whenever you compose E-mail, realize that it can be distributed and published around the world...literally.

If you write a message that you want only one recipient to see, make sure that he/she will not permit it to be transmitted beyond his own E-mail box.

Never put your name on anything you don't want associated with you, even if someone else wrote it.

Web Site Security

Look for a padlock symbol at the bottom of the site's home page before doing any transaction or providing any personal information. This symbol indicates the site is well-protected against hackers. Tell children never to give out family information while on-line—some sites promise kids prizes if they answer questions about family income, autos or education. Be especially wary at contest and sweepstakes sites and ones offering anything for free. Check a site's privacy policy—and avoid those with hard-to-find or difficult-to-understand policies.

Daniel S. Janal, Internet marketing consultant, Shorewood, MN, and author of Risky Business: Protect Your Business from Being Stalked, Conned, or Blackmailed on the Web *(Wiley).*

Protect Your Home From Disasters

*Cynthia Ramsay Taylor, spokesperson, Federal Emergency Management Agency, Washington, DC. 800-462-9029...*www.fema.gov.

Here is some practical advice on how to protect your home from the following natural disasters...

●**Wildfire.** Create a 30-foot defensible zone around your house...prune the branches near your home to no more than eight- to 10-feet high...remove dead needles, limbs and debris from roof and gutters.

●**Hurricanes.** Install storm shutters...reinforce roof with bracing and hurricane straps ...bring lawn furniture inside when a watch or warning is issued.

●**Earthquake.** Secure bookcases, furniture and appliances with bolts...and large, fragile or heavy items to lower shelves...buy earthquake insurance.

●**Flood.** Elevate the main breaker or fuse box and any heating, ventilation or cooling equipment...purchase flood insurance...keep insurance policies, important documents and other valuables in a safe-deposit box...install check valves in sewer traps to avoid backflow.

smoke alarms. Test them monthly, and replace batteries annually. Buy new smoke alarms to replace those that are more than 10 years old.

Julie Reynolds, assistant vice president, National Fire Protection Association, Quincy, MA.

Best Smoke-Alarm Protection

Place working smoke alarms on *each* floor as well as inside bedrooms. Consider installing a dual-sensor alarm—or a photoelectric *and* an ionization alarm. (Photoelectric alarms respond slightly faster to smoldering fires...ionization alarms, slightly faster to flames.) Place alarms on the ceiling, at least four inches from any wall—or high on the wall and at least four inches below the ceiling. Do not put smoke alarms in corners...or areas near windows, outside doors and vents. Air currents may move the smoke away from the alarm. Don't paint

Childproof Your TV

Toppling TVs and furniture send 8,000 to 10,000 victims a year to hospital emergency rooms...and many more kids are less seriously injured.

Self-defense: Place the TV on lower furniture and as far back as possible. Use braces or anchors to secure furniture to the wall. Do not put a TV on furniture that is designed for other purposes, such as a dresser. Do not let children climb on or play near TV sets.

Ken Giles, spokesperson for the Consumer Product Safety Commission, Washington, DC.

21

Very, Very Personal

Never Go to Bed Mad and Other Marriage Myths

Many marriages fail because people base their attitudes and behavior on widely held beliefs that simply are not true. One of the most destructive is the belief that if you desire someone else, something must be wrong with your relationship.

Example: You fantasize about a coworker, then worry that you're "betraying" your spouse. Or you see your spouse eyeing someone and question his/her fidelity.

Human beings have their heads turned by others. That is just the way it is, it is not a sign of infidelity.

Of course, there is a big difference between desire and action. Fantasy is harmless and can be better than reality.

Other myths to watch out for…

Myth: **You should be best friends with your spouse.**

Women, in particular, frequently want their husbands to be their best friends. They want them to reveal everything…share their deepest feelings…chat for hours about relationships. Men are rarely like that—so their wives become disappointed.

Reality: You look for different characteristics in a spouse than you do in a friend. A best friend might think the same way you do and enjoy the same things. But when you evaluate a potential spouse, odds are that you consider sexual attraction…parenting potential…financial solvency, etc.

You can have a great marriage and not be best friends. Couples can have fun and enjoy their time together without seeing the world in exactly the same way.

Myth: **You should never go to bed mad.**

Pepper Schwartz, PhD, professor of sociology at the University of Washington, Seattle. A renowned authority on sexuality, she is a board member of the Sexuality Information Council of the United States and past president of the Society for the Scientific Study of Sexuality. She is author of a dozen books, including *Everything You Know About Love and Sex Is Wrong* (Putnam).

Simmering anger invariably comes to a boil …and every couple is happier when they "let off steam." Right? Wrong.

Nothing gets solved when people are enraged. In fact, expressing anger produces even more anger from the surge of adrenaline and other stress hormones.

It's better to go to bed mad than to say or do something you'll regret later…

● **Tell your spouse, "I can't handle this right now."**

● **Agree on a convenient time to discuss your disagreements.**

● **Once you are calm, slip some praise and compliments into the discussion.**

Example: If you are upset about a purchase your partner made, remember to mention that, most of the time, you agree with and respect his money management.

One researcher found that it takes about five positive comments to undo the anger-causing impact of one negative remark.

Myth: **You should always be 100% honest.**

People get angry when I say that it is not always good to be honest with your partner and share the intimate details of your life. Should a man tell his wife he kissed a neighbor three years ago? Should a woman tell her husband that she has a harmless crush on a coworker?

Don't use your partner as your confessional. Think twice before you tell something that will forever cause your partner to doubt your word or be jealous of your relationships with friends.

Myth: **Sex that is not satisfying in the beginning can always be fixed.**

Great sex will not necessarily keep a couple together. But bad sex leads to frustration, alienation and/or anger. If sex is unsatisfactory early on, don't assume things will get better. Some problems—impotence, painful intercourse and premature ejaculation—may be solved. *Others are unlikely to change…*

● **Differences in desire.** If one of the partners rarely wants sex and the other wants it a lot, the relationship will suffer.

● **Incompatible sexual tastes.** If one partner has "kinky" desires and the other doesn't, tension is inevitable.

Most partners can learn to satisfy each other, but only if their sexual desires are similar.

Myth: **No marriage can survive infidelity.**

Few experiences are more painful than discovering your partner has been unfaithful. But an affair is not necessarily a sign that your marriage is over.

There are many reasons why a spouse may have an affair—the need to feel attractive to others…loneliness when a partner is away… giving in to an opportunity, etc. But these say little about the quality of a marriage or the strength of the unfaithful spouse's commitment.

If you've been betrayed, ask yourself what is most important to you. If it's sexual loyalty, then the affair can mean the end of the marriage. But if you value your partner and the other good things in your marriage, it's worth making the effort to work through the crisis.

If you are the offender, knowing there is a chance for forgiveness might mean the difference between choosing to stay or leave. Often, the discovery of an affair provides the impetus to seek counseling to strengthen a marriage.

How to Make Sex Exciting… Again

Dagmar O'Connor, PhD, a sex therapist in private practice in New York City. She is the author of the book/video packet *How to Make Love to the Same Person for the Rest of Your Life—and Still Love It* (Dagmedia, 800-520-5200).

Passion is a powerful force in the beginning stages of most intimate relationships. Unfortunately, our hectic work schedules, child-care responsibilities—even Web surfing— can prevent couples from really nurturing their sexual relationship.

Good news: You *can* restore the sexual excitement of your relationship. The key is to make time for sensual contact. Remember, arousal is just as important as orgasm.

In my 30 years as a therapist, I have found that the best way to become a passionate lover is to stop blaming your partner…and to start identifying—and communicating—your own needs in a constructive way. *Here's how...*

●**Express your emotions and clear up any resentment.** Sexual feelings are intimately linked to emotional expression. Many of us were raised to repress basic emotions—particularly anger or sadness. This can inhibit sexual response.

People who have sexual difficulties often grew up in families with parents who never raised their voices. Those who don't argue usually consider anger "unacceptable."

If you have difficulty expressing anger constructively, practice venting this emotion on your own. When driving alone in the car or showering, yell as loud as you can. After the initial embarrassment subsides, you may feel great. But you may feel sad later on. Anger often masks hurt or sadness.

●**Tell your partner *exactly* what you want—and need.** Many people are much better at expressing disappointment and anger than they are at communicating their desires.

Practice asserting your needs in all areas of your life. Being "nice" all the time prevents you from knowing what you are actually feeling.

Self-defense: If you typically say "yes" to all requests, try saying "no" 10 times each week. Also practice making requests of others. Learn to be more "selfish."

●**Become comfortable with your body.** If you are very self-conscious about your physical appearance, you won't get much pleasure out of sex.

Helpful: Relax in a bath a few times each week. Use the opportunity to look at and touch your body in a nonsexual way.

Stand nude in front of the mirror for a few minutes each day. Don't criticize your body. See it as an artist would. Appreciate what you have —don't dwell on your perceived imperfections.

When privacy permits: Lounge around in the nude with your partner. If you feel like it, touch each other in nonsexual ways. Once you've established this sort of physical intimacy, taking the next step to sex becomes much easier.

●**Put yourself in a sensual mood.** Fantasy is one of the best ways to do this.

Helpful: For women who feel inhibited about being sexy, consider going into a store to try on provocative dresses or lingerie. You do not have to buy this stuff—just see yourself in a different way.

Share your sexual fantasies with your partner. It's not necessary to act out these fantasies— though you may choose to. Your goal is to simply create your own sexy movies in your head.

●**Concentrate on *your* sexual pleasure.** Sex is not only an expression of love. It's also an opportunity to experience pleasure. Good lovemaking involves two partners "using" each other for their own pleasure.

Don't expect your partner to take care of everything. And don't be afraid to tell your partner exactly what you like and want from sex. You'll both benefit if each of you is willing to behave a bit selfishly.

●**Develop a nonverbal language with your partner.** Showing is inherently less critical than telling. Make a pact to communicate in a nonverbal way—by moving your partner's hand, for instance—if you find something unpleasant or pleasant during sex.

Helpful: Set aside 45 minutes to let your partner explore your body. Then reverse roles for 45 minutes.

●**Touch each other often when not in bed** to create a sense of closeness all the time.

●**Take turns initiating sex.** When to have sex is a big issue for most couples. One person might prefer it in the morning...the other at night.

If you started things last time, your partner should initiate the next sexual encounter.

Important: For this to work, the noninitiating partner should not say no.

●**Schedule a weekly "date" with your partner.** Set aside one night a week to be intimate. Do whatever you want—sensual touching, talking together or just reading the paper.

If you have children: Hire a baby-sitter to take the kids out while the two of you stay at home. Take the phone off the hook and spend a few hours in bed.

To nurture your sex life at home, make your bedroom a place for rest and sensuality. Lock the bedroom door, banish the television from the room and avoid arguing or discussing problems while in bed—it should be a place for rest and pleasure.

10 Foods That Boost Sex Drive

Foods rich in vitamin E, magnesium, niacin, potassium, zinc and the amino acid L-arginine all increase libido, boost sexual stamina and improve performance.

Top 10 "sexiest" foods…

1. Celery

2. Asparagus and artichokes

3. Avocados

4. Onions and tomatoes

5. Almonds

6. Pumpkin and sunflower seeds

7. Romaine lettuce

8. Whole-grain breads

9. Fruits and nuts

10. Chilies, herbs and spices, such as mustard, fennel, saffron and vanilla

Barnet Meltzer, MD, a physician in private practice in Del Mar, CA, and the author of *Food Swings* (Marlowe and Company).

Exercise Makes Men Sexier

A recent British study compared men aged 55 to 65 who led a sedentary lifestyle with men of the same age who were members of running clubs and participated in regular vigorous exercise.

Finding: Among the exercisers, levels of testosterone (which fuels sex drive) averaged 25% higher, and the level of growth hormone (which maintains muscle and bone) averaged four times as high.

Note: Levels of both testosterone and growth hormone normally decline after age 40. Stopping or reversing this decline is one way that exercise can help people stay young.

Pat Kendall-Taylor, MD, professor of endocrinology at University of Newcastle upon Tyne Medical School, William Leech Bldg., Framlington Pl., Newcastle upon Tyne NE2 4HH, England.

Curb Blood Pressure Without Curtailing Sex

One side effect of hypertension medication is sexual dysfunction. But among hypertensive men who took the blood pressure medication *losartan* (Cozaar) for 12 weeks, sexual satisfaction jumped from 7% to 58%. Those who reported having sex at least once a week increased from 40% to 62%.

If you suffer sexual side effects from hypertension medication: Ask your doctor about switching to losartan.

Carlos Ferrario, MD, professor and director, Hypertension and Vascular Disease Center, Wake Forest University School of Medicine, Winston-Salem, NC.

Unexpected Ways To Be Romantic

Gregory Godek, best-selling author of *1,001 Ways to Be Romantic* (Casablanca Press). He is a La Jolla, California–based publishing/marketing consultant who gives romance seminars in his spare time.

If you're looking for some easy ways to put more romance into your relationship, try out some of these ideas…

●**Unplug the TV and leave a note** on the screen saying, "I'll turn you on instead."

●**Write a love note to your partner,** and insert it in the book he/she is reading.

●**Don't just walk into the house tonight as usual.** Pause on the porch, ring the doorbell and greet your partner with one red rose and a bottle of champagne.

• **Always give gifts that are gift wrapped** with quality wrapping paper and fancy bows.

• **Accompany your partner to appointments with the physician.** If it's a routine checkup, you can have a quick coffee date... and if there is a serious problem, you can provide emotional support.

• **Say to your partner, "Let's plan a special outing.** You choose the time and place, and I'll be there—regardless of my previous plans."

• **Leave notes on household products.** *Example:* Joy dishwashing liquid—"Every day with you is a joy."

• **Get up earlier on a weekday** and take your partner out for breakfast.

• **Videotape a big athletic event,** then take your spouse out for dinner during the game.

• **Buy a lottery ticket and give it to your mate with a note attached,** "I hit the jackpot when I married you!"

• **Mail a romantic greeting card to your partner at work.**

Getting Help for Embarrassing Medical Problems

Margaret Stearn, MD, a physician who practices general medicine in Oxford, England, with a special interest in diabetes and urologic medicine. Dr. Stearn is a Fellow of the Royal College of Physicians and the author of *Embarrassing Medical Problems: Everything You Always Wanted to Know But Were Afraid to Ask Your Doctor* (Hatherleigh Press).

If you suffer from a backache or dizziness, it's easy to tell your doctor. But what about those nagging symptoms that you are too embarrassed to discuss?

Unfortunately, many patients deprive themselves of effective treatment and, in some cases, endanger their long-term health by failing to disclose certain medical problems. *How to get some help...*

BAD BREATH

Saliva production diminishes during sleep, allowing food debris to stagnate in the mouth. Bacteria break down these residues, producing an unpleasant smell. That's why almost everyone has bad breath (halitosis) upon waking. It usually disappears after you brush your teeth.

To determine if you have bad breath: Lick the inside of your wrist, wait four seconds, then smell.

Persistent halitosis is generally caused by gum disease (gingivitis). If your gums bleed when you brush your teeth, you most likely have gum disease and, as a result, bad breath. *What to do...*

• **See your dentist** for a checkup and thorough cleaning.

• **Brush your teeth at least twice daily.** *Best method:* Clean teeth two at a time for six seconds, moving the brush in a small circular motion while angling it toward the gum.

Or consider buying a battery-powered toothbrush, which often controls gum disease better than manual brushing. *Cost:* $20 to $120.

• **Clean the back of your tongue,** where bacteria accumulate. Use your toothbrush or a tongue scraper.

• **Use an antibacterial mouthwash,** such as Biotene Antibacterial, Cepacol Antiseptic or Listerine Antiseptic.

• **Floss nightly**—especially the molars.

If halitosis persists: See your doctor.

EXCESSIVE PERSPIRATION

Perspiration itself is not smelly, but it is a breeding ground for bacteria that will quickly break down into malodorous fatty acids.

Excessive perspiration (hyperhidrosis) could affect armpits, feet or palms. *What to do...*

• **Armpits.** Women and men should shave their armpits to reduce bacterial buildup.

Also switch to an antiperspirant with an active ingredient different from what you're currently using.

• **Feet.** Wear clean, loose-fitting socks made from wool or cotton and at least 30% man-made fiber, such as nylon or polyester. Wash socks in hot water to kill bacteria.

Avoid shoes made from synthetic materials. They trap moisture, which allows bacteria to multiply. This is also true for sneakers, so don't wear them for more than four hours a day.

Bathe your feet daily in warm water that contains about 10 drops of tea-tree oil per pint of water. It has antibacterial properties. Use a pumice stone to remove hardened, dead skin from your heels and soles.

●**Palms.** Rub palms every few hours with an astringent oil, such as cypress or geranium. These essential oils, available at health food stores, can be added to almond oil or a lotion.

If self-treatment doesn't help: Discuss with your doctor. He/she may prescribe a 20% *aluminum chloride* solution or an anticholinergic drug, such as *propantheline* (Pro-Banthine), to reduce the perspiration.

Botulinum toxin (Botox) injections are also a new treatment option for severe hyperhidrosis.

As a last resort, surgical division of the sympathetic nerves that cause sweating is almost 100% effective for feet and palms and about 40% effective for armpits.

FEMININE ITCHING

Itching of the vulva (vulval pruritis) is usually caused by a vaginal yeast infection. *What to do...*

●**Try an over-the-counter cream,** such as *butoconazole* (Gyne-Lotrimin) or *miconazole* (Monistat 3). If this doesn't help within a few days, your doctor may recommend a prescription medication, such as *fluconazole* (Diflucan).

Other possible causes include eczema, psoriasis or an allergy.

To relieve the itch: Soak in warm water that contains two handfuls of Epsom salts or ordinary kitchen salt...or dip a washcloth into a salt-water solution and apply to the affected area.

●**Wash only with unscented cleansers,** such as Dove Unscented Beauty Bar or Neutrogena Transparent Dry Skin Formula Fragrance Free. When shampooing your hair, don't let the foam touch your vulva.

●**Don't use feminine deodorants** or apply deodorant or perfume to sanitary pads...wash underwear with an enzyme-free, perfume-free detergent for sensitive skin...don't use fabric softener...and don't swim in chlorinated water.

FLATULENCE

It's normal to have some gas. Air swallowed during eating typically collects in the stomach and is passed via belching.

Bacteria also cause certain foods, especially beans, to break down into hydrogen, methane and carbon dioxide.

Most people experience gas (flatulence) more than 10 times a day. *What to do...*

●**Avoid eating large quantities of gas-causing foods at one time.** These include beans, peas, broccoli, cauliflower, artichokes, cabbage, raisins, prunes and apples. They contain hard-to-digest carbohydrates that ferment in the bowels.

Foods that don't cause flatulence: Potatoes, rice, corn and wheat.

●**Avoid carbonated beverages** as well as hot drinks.

●**Take your time while eating.** Don't rush when you eat...put your fork down between bites...and be sure to chew food thoroughly.

●**Don't chew gum.**

Over-the-counter antiflatulence aids—such as Beano, charcoal tablets, Gas-X or Phazyme —can also relieve flatulence.

JOCK ITCH

Jock itch (tinea cruris) causes an itchy, red rash in the groin area. The rash is triggered by the same fungus that causes athlete's foot. In fact, it's often "caught" from your own feet. *What to do...*

●**Try an over-the-counter antifungal ointment,** such as *tolnaftate* (Tinactin). If this does not help, consult your doctor.

●**Wear loose, 100% cotton underwear.**

●**Wash with unscented soap,** and dry the groin area carefully after bathing.

●**Wash underwear with an enzyme-free,** perfume-free detergent.

Natural Relief for Crohn's Disease and IBS

Peppermint oil relieves the painful cramping brought on by Crohn's disease and irritable bowel syndrome (IBS).

Helpful: Place one drop of the oil in a cup of warm water, add some sugar, if desired, and drink the mixture 15 to 30 minutes before eating—or when symptoms begin.

Warning: Don't take peppermint oil straight, and stop taking the mixture if it causes heartburn. Peppermint oil can be purchased at most health food stores.

Tim Koch, MD, chief, section of gastroenterology, West Virginia University School of Medicine, Morgantown.

Get This Test if You Have IBS

Irritable bowel syndrome (IBS) may be triggered by too much bacteria located in the small intestine. In a recent finding, among IBS sufferers who took a breath test to detect excessive bacteria levels, 78% tested positive.

Good news: After a 10-day course of an antibiotic, 25 of 47 patients had no signs of bacteria overgrowth. Half of patients whose bacteria levels were reduced had no symptoms of IBS. The other half reported less severe symptoms.

Important: Not all IBS cases are caused by excessive bacteria, so patients should be tested before considering antibiotic therapy.

If you have IBS, ask your doctor about the lactulose hydrogen breath test.

Mark Pimentel, MD, assistant director of the GI Motility Program, Cedars-Sinai Medical Center, Los Angeles.

Nature's Rx for Women's Health Problems

Jamison Starbuck, ND, a naturopathic physician in family practice and a lecturer at the University of Montana, both in Missoula. She is past president of the American Association of Naturopathic Physicians and a contributing editor to *The Alternative Advisor: The Complete Guide to Natural Therapies and Alternative Treatments* (Time Life).

Women often resort to quick drugstore fixes when they experience "female complaints." I advise women to consider their alternatives. Many women's health problems respond to gentle, natural medicines …and to lifestyle changes that improve your overall health. *My recommendations…*

•**Bacterial vaginosis (BV)** causes a gray-white discharge, mild burning and vaginal itching. Gynecologists often prescribe antibiotics to treat this condition.

But antibiotics can create problems. Like the digestive tract, the vagina is filled with bacteria that keep mucous membranes in good health. Antibiotics disrupt the vaginal "ecosystem" by eliminating not only the offending bacteria, but also the beneficial ones, like *lactobacillus.*

This can bring on another type of vaginal infection—*candida vaginitis.* Also known as yeast infection, this causes vaginal itching and burning and a thick, white discharge. For this condition, doctors typically prescribe antifungals—again upsetting the vaginal ecosystem and increasing the likelihood of BV. Many women get stuck in this cycle. *I tell my patients with these conditions to…*

•Avoid refined foods, sweets and alcohol. Each can weaken the immune system. Stick to these restrictions for at least one month after the infection clears up.

•Use capsules to encourage growth of beneficial bacteria. During the acute infection, insert one capsule of Oregon grape root (*Berberis aquifolium*) powder into the vagina each evening. Each morning, insert one lactobacillus acidophilus capsule. The capsules are available at most health food stores.

•Abstain from sex during treatment. It can irritate vaginal tissue.

An infection that's acute should clear up in one week. For stubborn cases, repeat the capsule protocol on alternating weeks for a total of four treatments.

●**Urinary tract infections (UTIs)** often occur when bacteria migrate from the vagina through the urethra into the bladder. Sexual intercourse, vaginal infection and chronic vaginal dryness increase your risk.

If you suffer from recurrent UTIs, see your family doctor for antibiotic treatment for the acute infection. *Then follow these steps to prevent relapse...*

●Drink 64 ounces of water daily to rid your bladder of pesky bacteria.

●Take an acidophilus/bifidis supplement that contains three billion of these live organisms every night at bedtime.

●Drink 12 ounces of unsweetened cranberry juice each day. It acidifies your urine, preventing bacteria from adhering to the bladder wall. If you don't like cranberry juice—or don't want the extra calories—take a daily capsule containing 900 mg of cranberry extract.

●**Fibrocystic breasts and PMS** can both be caused by poor dietary habits. If you have fibrocystic breasts, avoid caffeine and sugar ...and cut back on fat and refined food. Eat more whole grains, beans, peas, fruits and veggies. Take 50 mg of vitamin B-6, 400 international units (IU) of vitamin E and 3,000 mg of flaxseed oil or 1,500 mg evening primrose oil daily to reduce inflammation.

Low progesterone levels may contribute to PMS. For this condition, follow the fibrocystic breast protocol and try chaste tree berry (*Vitex agnus-castus*) to boost production of the hormone progesterone. Two weeks before your menstrual period starts, take 60 drops of Vitex tincture daily. Discontinue for two weeks following menstruation, then repeat.

Note: Pregnant women should check with their doctors before taking any herb.

Breast Cancer: What Every Woman Must Know *Now*

Rowan T. Chlebowski, MD, PhD, professor of medicine, University of California at Los Angeles School of Medicine, and chief of the division of oncology and hematology at the Harbor-UCLA Medical Center in Torrance, CA.

Until just recently, early detection through mammography and breast physical exam were the only ways to reduce the threat of breast cancer.

What's the latest: Researchers have now identified preventive therapies for those at high risk for breast cancer—due to family history and other risk factors.* The preventive strategies include drug therapy or, for a small group of women at greatly increased risk, a surgical alternative, such as removal of both breasts (prophylactic bilateral mastectomy).

Although men can develop breast cancer, the following therapies are generally not used for them because their risk for the disease is only 1% of a woman's.

DRUG THERAPY

The prescription anticancer agent *tamoxifen* (Nolvadex) has been used to treat breast cancer for nearly 30 years. Only recently have researchers discovered that the drug also reduces *risk* for the disease.

Studies indicate that the hormone estrogen plays a significant role in breast cancer. Tamoxifen is believed to reduce the risk for breast cancer by partially blocking the effects of estrogen on breast tissue.

In a new finding: Early-stage breast cancer patients who were treated with tamoxifen for five years following breast surgery were 47% less likely than women not given the drug to have a recurrence of the disease.

In another study, the researchers evaluated whether women at increased risk benefited from 20 mg of tamoxifen daily. Among 13,388 women, tamoxifen reduced the incidence of

*For more information on breast cancer risk assessment, visit the National Cancer Institute Web site at *www.cancer.gov/cancer_information/*.

breast cancer by nearly 50% during a four-year period.

Caution: Before considering the use of tamoxifen, the risk of potential side effects, such as blood clots in the legs and lungs, must be weighed against the drug's benefits.

The symptoms of estrogen deficiency, such as hot flashes, increase in up to 20% of women who take the drug. In rare cases, tamoxifen has been linked to uterine cancer. Postmenopausal women, especially those who are obese or have previously taken estrogen, are at higher risk of uterine cancer.

Another promising drug is *raloxifene* (Evista). Currently used in the prevention and treatment of osteoporosis in postmenopausal women, raloxifene—like tamoxifen—partially blocks the effects of estrogen.

Although raloxifene is not used in the treatment of breast cancer, its effect on risk for the disease has recently been monitored in trials involving thousands of women.

In one study, women who took the drug for 40 months experienced a 65% reduction in breast cancer risk.

Because raloxifene is a relatively new drug, the long-term side effects are still unknown. However, it is expected to confer a lower risk for uterine cancer than does tamoxifen.

MASTECTOMY

Prophylactic mastectomy is an option for women at very high risk for the disease.

In a 1999 study at the Mayo Clinic, bilateral mastectomy reduced the risk for the disease or recurrence by 90%.

Dutch scientists completed research earlier this year that presents even stronger evidence that prophylactic mastectomy saves lives. In the study, researchers identified 139 women who tested positive for BRCA1 and BRCA2 gene mutations. Both are linked to increased breast cancer risk. Of 76 women who opted for prophylactic mastectomy, none had developed breast cancer within three years.

Of the remaining women who chose to undergo annual mammograms or magnetic resonance imaging (MRI) scans, regular doctors' visits and monthly self-exams, eight developed breast cancer. One woman died.

Although mastectomy can be emotionally painful, most women who have undergone the procedure have stated in interviews that they do not regret having it done. Still, up to 20% report some dissatisfaction.

Women who decide on prophylactic mastectomy may want to consider counseling to help cope with the emotional aspects of that decision. Ask your doctor for a referral.

EARLY DETECTION

Despite the new preventive strategies, early detection and prompt treatment are still vital.

The American Cancer Society (ACS) recommends that all women perform a monthly self-exam and have their breasts examined by a physician at least once every three years up to age 40 and yearly thereafter.

The ACS also recommends that women age 40 and older receive annual mammograms.

But mammography is not foolproof. One in five breast cancers is not detected by radiologists. To improve the accuracy, schedule your mammogram at a facility that offers a second reading by a different radiologist or uses Image-Checker, a computer-assisted detection system. It increases detection rates by 20%. About 200 units are in use worldwide.

To locate a radiologist in your area who uses ImageChecker, contact the manufacturer, R2 Technology, 866-243-2533 or *www.r2tech.com.*

Women can also lower their breast cancer risk by eating more fruits and vegetables… reducing fat intake…limiting alcohol intake to no more than one drink a day…and exercising for one-half hour at least three times a week.

More on Breast Cancer Protection

Marisa Weiss, MD, a Philadelphia-based oncologist and founder of the nonprofit information resource *www.breast cancer.org.*

If you've been following the recent debate over breast cancer screening, it's easy to get confused by all the conflicting information.

What's the truth? *Women should take advantage of all the tools that are now available…*

●**Mammography.** Danish researchers have recently raised questions about the number of lives saved by mammography. Yet the American Cancer Society continues to recommend annual mammograms for women over age 40. To help ensure a reliable reading, request that your mammogram be evaluated by two radiologists.

●**Self-exams and clinical exams.** Up to 25% of breast tumors *don't* show up on mammograms, but they may be detected by a physical exam of the breast.

Even though women know they should perform monthly self-exams, few are careful to examine the entire breast area. This extends from the collarbone to the bottom of the breast and from the middle of the chest to the armpit. See your doctor if you discover a lump or an indentation or if you notice any nipple discharge or crusting.

For detailed instructions on breast self-exams, contact the American Cancer Society, 800-227-2345, *www.cancer.org.* Also be sure your physician examines your breasts at least once a year.

Estrogen Trap

Estrogen replacement therapy (ERT) may contribute to asthma.

Recent finding: Menopausal women on ERT have an 80% higher chance of developing asthma than women not taking hormones.

Theory: Estrogen affects cells involved in the body's allergic or inflammatory response.

Important: Women considering estrogen therapy should discuss these findings with their physicians. Asthma risk must be weighed against the potential benefits of ERT in treating menopausal symptoms and preserving bone strength.

Graham Barr, MD, fellow at Channing Laboratory, Brigham and Women's Hospital, Boston.

Fighting Hot Flashes in Women…and Men

Hot flashes in menopausal women—and in men being treated for prostate cancer with hormone therapy—can be effectively quenched with antidepressants.

In one recent study, menopausal breast cancer patients who took about half the standard dose of *venlafaxine* (Effexor) had a 61% reduction in hot flashes.

Preliminary results suggest a similar effect with other antidepressants, such as *fluoxetine* (Prozac) and *paroxetine* (Paxil).

That's great news because breast cancer chemotherapy often triggers early menopause, bringing on hot flashes as well as night sweats, disrupted sleep and mood swings.

Hormone treatments for menopausal women help—but may stimulate tumor growth. So antidepressants are a safer option.

Charles L. Loprinzi, MD, professor and chair of medical oncology, Mayo Clinic, Rochester, MN. His study was presented at a meeting of the American Society of Clinical Oncology.

Coffee Raises Urinary-Tract Cancer Risk

Previous research linked coffee to urinary-tract cancer, but some experts have criticized those studies for not also taking smoking into account.

Recent finding: An analysis of 37 clinical studies reaffirms that coffee increases risk for urinary-tract cancer, even after adjustment for smoking. Coffee drinkers experienced a 20% increased risk for urinary-tract cancer, compared with non-coffee drinkers.

For tea drinkers: Your beverage of choice appears not to increase cancer risk.

Maurice Zeegers, PhD, assistant professor of epidemiology, Maastricht University, Maastricht, the Netherlands.

Male Menopause? Yes, There Really Is Such a Thing

Jed Diamond, LCSW, psychotherapist, educator and trainer on men's health issues, Willets, CA. Mr. Diamond is cofounder of the Androc Men's Health Center, San Rafael, CA, and director of MenAlive, a program designed to help men live healthier and happier lives, *www.menalive.com*. He is author of *Male Menopause* (Sourcebooks).

Just like menopause in women, male menopause involves changes in hormone levels and other physical characteristics. It affects a man's psychology and sexuality.

In women, menopause will come on fairly rapidly, around age 45 or 50. It's clearly linked to the cessation of ovulation.

The same changes happen more gradually and are less obvious in men. Since men retain the capacity to reproduce as they get older, the medical community has tended to gloss over these age-related changes.

Men's health expert Jed Diamond answers some questions…

●**What are the signs of male menopause?** The most common signs are anger and irritability, erectile dysfunction or reduced libido, as well as fatigue.

These changes usually begin between age 40 and 55, though they can start as early as age 35 or as late as age 65.

There is a decline in testosterone levels as well. The decline is usually gradual, but it can be very rapid.

Since testosterone levels vary greatly among men, it is important for men to know their testosterone levels at various times in their lives.

As a result of this decline, erections take longer to occur and are not quite as firm as they once were. Often, it takes more physical stimulation to become aroused. The urge to ejaculate is not as insistent as it once was, and the force of ejaculation is weaker.

There are also age-related declines in frequency of orgasm and sexual thoughts.

●**What about nonsexual changes?** Men also experience a decline in lean muscle mass and a tendency to put on weight. Aches and pains become more pervasive. Some men complain of anxiety or insomnia.

Full-blown depression often occurs during male menopause, although feelings of anger and frustration are more common.

Men report that "everything seems to bother them," while their wives complain that their husbands "used to be loving and gentle, but now there's no pleasing them."

●**What's the best way to respond to these changes?** Men—and their partners—must be aware of what is happening, not only hormonally and physically, but psychologically and spiritually.

Many of the changes associated with male menopause are actually preparation for moving from "first adulthood" to "second adulthood," or "super-adulthood." If men embrace the passage, they'll find this next phase brings more power and passion than any other time of life.

In the second half of life, men shift from a focus on career to a focus on their "calling." They want to do something that they enjoy, but that also helps their community and the world. This may mean a modification of their previous career, or it may involve something totally different.

●**Are any supplements or medications recommended for male menopause?** Yes. If you are having problems, ask your doctor about getting a testosterone blood or saliva test. If your level is low, consider testosterone replacement therapy (TRT). Testosterone is now available as a shot, patch or gel. Each has benefits and drawbacks. Testosterone is also sold in pill form, but the only type now available in the US reportedly has been shown to cause liver problems.

TRT helps men lose fat and gain muscle, and increases their sex drive. If erectile dysfunction becomes a chronic problem, ask your doctor about Viagra…or try a natural alternative like *L-arginine* or *gingko biloba*.

In addition, I recommend that men have *all* of their hormone levels checked—DHEA, pregnenolone, thyroid, melatonin, human growth hormone and even estrogen levels—as well as levels of all vitamins and minerals.

Even if no deficiencies are found, take the daily antioxidant formula developed by Dr.

Andrew Weil, author of *Eating Well for Optimum Health*—mixed carotenoids including lycopene (25,000 IU), natural vitamin E (800 IU), selenium (200 mcg), vitamin C (200 mg) and coenzyme Q-10 (60 mg).

● **Are there any other tests you advise?** Men over age 40 should get an annual prostate-specific antigen test to check for prostate cancer. This test is essential if you're considering TRT—because if you have prostate cancer, testosterone supplements will fuel its growth.

Since irritability and/or insomnia are often the signs of depression in men, consider getting checked for depression and perhaps taking an antidepressant if you have these symptoms.

● **Any other advice?** Eat a low-fat diet and get plenty of exercise. I recommend a mix of aerobic exercise, strength training (to maintain muscle mass) and stretching (to keep your joints and back flexible).

Eating Fish Reduces Prostate Cancer Risk

In one of the first long-term studies of fish consumption and prostate cancer, men who ate little or no fish had up to three times the risk for prostate cancer as did men who ate moderate to high amounts of fish. Essential fatty acids in fish seem to inhibit growth of prostate cancer cells. To achieve this benefit, eat two to three servings of salmon, mackerel, herring or other fatty fish per week.

Paul Terry, PhD, MPH, department of epidemiology and social medicine, Albert Einstein College of Medicine, Bronx, NY.

Viagra Trap

Male potency seems to wane in long-term users of *sildenafil* (Viagra). In one recent study, 74% of Viagra users were able to maintain an erection after they took initial doses of 25 mg to 100 mg. But within one to 18 months, the effects began to wear off. After taking the drug for two years, 20% of the men had to increase their dose by 50 mg to achieve the same results. If you take Viagra, ask your doctor about increasing the dose if the drug has become ineffective.

Rizk El-Galley, MD, assistant professor of surgery, division of urology, University of Alabama, Birmingham.

Men Need Folic Acid, Too

Low folic acid levels in men are associated with low sperm count. A recent study has led investigators to hypothesize that low folic acid could also damage the DNA that sperm carry—which could lead to chromosomal damage in a fetus.

Self-defense: Eat plenty of folate-rich fruits and vegetables and fortified grain products.

Lynn Wallock, PhD, nutritionist, assistant research scientist, Children's Hospital Oakland Research Institute, and leader of the study for University of California at Berkeley and US Department of Agriculture.

Useful Web Sites

Business

☐ Free Advice
www.pueblo.gsa.gov

Low-cost or free brochures from the federal government on starting a small business. Includes information on scams, copyrights and business credit for women, minorities and small businesses. Simply click on "Small Business."

☐ Legal Forms
www.findforms.com

Thousands of free legal forms—power of attorney, sample contracts, US court forms, etc.

Employment

☐ For the Disabled
www.jan.wvu.edu

A free consulting service providing information on job accommodations and the employment of people who have disabilities.

☐ Interview Help
www.joblink-usa.com

If you are looking for a job but don't interview well, this site can help you. Learn how to get an interview and prepare for it and what types of questions the interviewer might ask. Just click on "Interview Tips."

☐ Job Listings
www.careerbuilder.com

More than 400,000 updated job listings across the nation, as well as access to job seekers. Similar sites include *www.hotjobs.com*, *www.monster.com* and *www. employmentoffice.net*.

☐ Planning a Career
www.mapping-your-future.org/ planning

Advice on how to choose a career. Useful hints on job hunting, résumé writing and interviewing.

☐ Resources
www.rileyguide.com

A directory of employment and career resources, with instruction on how job seekers can use the Internet to their best advantage.

Education

☐ College Board
www.collegeboard.com

Information on taking the PSAT and SAT tests, finding the right school, financing college and more.

☐ Federal Aid for College Students
www.fafsa.ed.gov

Sponsored by the US Department of Education, this site provides a free application for federal aid, deadlines and other valuable information.

☐ Homework Helpers
www.homeworkspot.com

A mega-directory with encyclopedias, libraries, museum links, advice from experts and much more.

☐ Saving for College
www.savingforcollege.com

Compare state 529 plans, check the plans' investment results, keep up with recent federal and state developments, read articles about 529s and much more.

☐ Text Translations
www.world.altavista.com

Translates Web pages written in foreign languages. Enter the page's Web address and the site is translated into your preferred language.

Relationships

☐ Children's Bill of Rights
www.aaml.org/billrts.htm

Here are some things parents shouldn't forget when the family is in the midst of a breakup.

□ Divorce Manual
www.aaml.org/manual.htm

This on-line booklet from the American Academy of Matrimonial Lawyers educates you on the legal process of divorce.

□ Family Funeral
www.funerals.org

Find out everything you need to do after a death in your family.

□ For Romance
www.getromantic.com

Hundreds of ideas on how to spice up your relationship. Includes romance tips, a kissing guide, dating advice and much more.

□ Good Manners
www.emilypost.com

Advice on everything from business etiquette to raising polite children.

□ Grandparenting
www.igrandparents.com

Provides a wealth of information, ideas, advice and support aimed at enhancing the grandparent/grandchild relationship.

□ Parenting Help
www.parenthoodweb.com

Parenting topics including pregnancy, birthday planning, bargains and shopping, recalls and more. Also posts a calendar of family-oriented events in various cities across the country.

Personal Organization

□ Family Files
www.familyfiles.com

A simple, safe way to store and maintain your vital information on-line.

□ Kitchen Organization
www.123sortit.com/RO/kitchen.html

Written in a recipe format, this kitchen organization site is fun, helpful and easy to follow.

□ Planning Your Move
www.homefair.com/homefair/wizard

An interactive tool to help people plan better moves. Creates a moving timeline, calculates costs of moving and renting versus buying, and even helps you find a home or apartment.

Volunteering

□ Big Brothers Big Sisters of America
www.bbbsa.org

Sets up mentoring relationships between adult volunteers and children primarily from single-parent families throughout the US.

□ Volunteer Opportunities Around the World
www.globalvolunteers.org

This nonprofit organization sends teams of volunteers to live and work with local people in the US and around the world on human and economic development projects identified by the communities themselves as important to their long-term development.

□ Locks of Love
www.locksoflove.org

Donate your hair and help these young children suffering from long-term medical problems feel better about themselves.

□ Meals on Wheels
www.givemeals.com

Has organizations everywhere that provide nutritious meals to people who are homebound and/or disabled or would otherwise be unable to maintain their dietary needs. Find out how you can help at this Web site.

□ Volunteer Match
www.volunteermatch.org

This site posts thousands of opportunities at nonprofit and tax-exempt groups in hundreds of cities across the country.

Index